T5-CRC-617

A HISTORY OF THE AMERICAN PEACE MOVEMENT FROM COLONIAL TIMES TO THE PRESENT

A History of the American Peace Movement from Colonial Times to the Present

Charles F. Howlett
and
Robbie Lieberman

With a Foreword by
Harriet Hyman Alonso

The Edwin Mellen Press
Lewiston•Queenston•Lampeter

Library of Congress Cataloging-in-Publication Data

Howlett, Charles F.

A history of the American peace movement : from colonial times to the present / Charles F. Howlett and Robbie Lieberman ; with a foreword by Harriet Hyman Alonso.

p. cm.

Includes bibliographical references and index.

ISBN-13: 978-0-7734-5092-9

ISBN-10: 0-7734-5092-0

1. Peace movements--United States--History. I. Lieberman, Robbie, 1954- II. Title.

JZ5584.U55H69 2008

303.6'6--dc22

2008020608

hors série.

A CIP catalog record for this book is available from the British Library.

Front cover: July 12, 1935, Massachusetts.
Miscellaneous Events, Demonstrations, 1938-1950, Photograph Collection, Swarthmore College Peace Collection

The Edwin Mellen Press
Box 450
Lewiston, New York
USA 14092-0450

The Edwin Mellen Press
Box 67
Queenston, Ontario
CANADA L0S 1L0

The Edwin Mellen Press, Ltd.
Lampeter, Ceredigion, Wales
UNITED KINGDOM SA48 8LT

Printed in the United States of America

To

Charles Howlett's grandchildren Amy Marie and Jack, and all of Robbie Liberman's students, past and present, who have expressed interest in the struggle for peace and justice

TABLE OF CONTENTS

EDITORIAL NOTE

Given the magnitude and scope of this work the authors have made every attempt to be as inclusive and accurate as possible. There are, however, a few points we wish to alert readers about before beginning this survey. First, terminology can always be problematic when set in historical context. The capitalization of the term Conscientious Objector was done purposely to highlight courage as opposed to cowardice. It takes a great deal of fortitude to stand one's ground in the face of tremendous public and governmental pressure to conform. While the word pacifist is used early on in this survey it is important to note that it did not become part of the English vocabulary until the time of World War I. As noted in our End Notes it was first popularized by the French in the 1890s. Non-resistance is also another term that is widely used and not introduced until the antebellum period with the rise of the New England Non-Resistance Society. Yet the Religious Society of Friends, more commonly known as "Quakers" or "Friends," practiced non-resistance: the belief that force or violence should not be used to oppose arbitrary authority, however unjust it might be. The practice of non-resistance also characterizes Conscientious Objectors, religious or otherwise.

While terminology presents problems of its own it is also important for students of history to understand the complexity of relationships between early Native American tribes as discussed in the beginning of this book. The Lenape was not an entirely independent tribe when it came to relations with other indigenous tribes other than their own. The Lenape can be considered a client state of the Iroquois Nation. The Iroquois was a much more powerful nation. As the Curator and Swarthmore College Peace Collection historian Wendy Chmielewski pointed out to the writers, there existed a gendered component to the Iroquois' relations to the Lenape. A more accurate and understandable description of this relationship is one in which the Six Nations was considered the husband who protected them from other tribes who were not part of the Confederacy in exchange for their compliance with the Iroquois system.

Third, scholars should be encouraged to do more research on untapped resources involving the role of women in the years before the American Civil War. Women contributed to the cause of peace in the young republic in two distinct ways which were not always aligned with abolitionism or women's rights. In the area of literature, for example, women were quite effective in evoking the strains of war, violence, and intolerance. Sarah Hale editor of Godey's Lady's Book, was a crusader for peace and her poem "The Three Sceptres: A Vision," boldly and provocatively linked women with peace ideals. Lydia Sigourney published a well-received peace poem "The War Spirit," appearing in the American Peace Society's magazine, The Calumet. One of the most noted poets of this period was Elizabeth Chandler. Her 1831 poem "Brandywine," was one of the first pieces of literature criticizing the Revolutionary War's military virtues and was soon followed by "Looking at Soldiers." Women also attempted to form their own separate societies. As early as 1818, for example, a Female Charitable Society had been distributing peace tracts. In 1821, reports had circulated that outside Cincinnati women had formed a "Female Peace Society, and in 1823, near Wilton, New Hampshire, a women's peace group had been created. In all likelihood, many of these groups were female auxiliaries of state peace societies. With the reform movement of the 1830s that included temperance, abolitionism, and woman's rights, seven peace societies emerged composed solely of women. Among these groups were the following: Essex County Olive Branch Circle, the Bowdoin Street Ladies' Peace Society (renamed the Boston Ladies Peace Society), the Philadelphia Ladies' Peace Society, the Lynn Female Peace Society in Massachusetts, and three small groups in Hallowell, Maine, Newark, New Jersey, and Brighton, Massachusetts. In these groups women met daily and discussed and distributed peace tracts as well as raised money for the newly-organized male-dominated peace movement.

For the record it is important to note that women sought to form their own societies even though they remained an appendage to the largely male-led organized peace movement that developed in nineteenth century America. After the Civil War, women would play a greater role in the peace movement. But their efforts during the antebellum period in terms of writing and organizing on their own should be explored more thoroughly by scholars interested in pre-Civil War American peace history.*

As a guide to this survey we have also included in the front matter three important items: a glossary of certain peace terms, a list of peace and justice organizations with abbreviations for most, and a list of peace leaders in American history. We hope these supplementary materials will enable readers to follow more carefully the narrative and identify important events, groups, and personalities as they appear in this story.

* Refer to Wendy E. Chmielewski, "'Binding Themselves the Closer to Their Own Peculiar Duties': Gender and Women's Work for Peace, 1818-1860," Peace & Change 20 (October 1995): 466-490, and "'Mid the Din a Dove Appeared': Women's Work in the Nineteenth-Century Peace Movement," Over Here: A European Journal of American Culture 17 (Winter 1997), passim.

GLOSSARY OF PEACE TERMINOLOGY

INTERNATIONALIST. Any person who accepts nations as a unit and advocates or works for cooperation within the interstate system. The cooperation may be either political or nonpolitical and may involve governmental and/or nongovernmental agencies. An acknowledgement of each nation's sovereignty and the nation-state system is implicit in internationalist beliefs and actions. Politically inclined internationalists seek to mitigate conflict within the nation-stte system, with their strategies and objectives more important historically then their desire for peace.

MILITARISM. The supremacy of or the placing of high priority on military force and military values in the resolution of international or dometic conflicts and in the safeguarding of national well-being. Generally viewed by pacifists as a threat or danger to democracy.

PACIFISM. A term which was first coined by the French at the end of the nineteenth century to describe either the absolute renunciation of war or the refusal to participate in or the opposition in principle to a specific war or governmental programs on religious, philosophical, humanitarian, or social-justice grounds. The values held in advocating peace as more desirable than war are significantly more important than motives, and the behavior should be predictably consistent.

PACIFIST. One who subscribes to or demonstrates the tenets of pacifism.

PEACE. The absence of war; a condition marked by tranquility and governed order within the international community.

PEACE ACTIVIST. An individual with clearly stated goals involved in anti-war potest through group action or public activity directed toward policy change. It is generally related to the period since 1960.

PEACE ADVOCATE. Anyone who actively promotes ideas and publicly manifests a concern for eliminating, avoiding, or minimizing the unilateral use of force by nation-states, usually by suggesting alternative proposals that would modify national policy or behavior. Leadership is implied.

PEACE MOVEMENT. A loose assemblage of groups and individuals, often with dissimilar programs but in accord on seeking to reduce conflict or end war through achieving some change in foreign policy.

PEACE WORKER. Anyone who contributes time and energy in supporting programs, societies, or agencies seeking to modify organized violence between states or opposing military systems. Such a person need not manifest special convictions or be instrumental in the development of ideas or programs.

SANCTIONS. Derived from the Latin *sanctio* or *sancire*, the term originally implied consecration or obligation. The latter meaning has prevailed with commitment by pacifists to awaken public opinion by applying moral pressures against wrongdoers. Other observers advocate economic or military action to uphold agreements or treaties or to curb aggressors.

SOCIAL JUSTICE. Concerted and sustained efforts by activists to transform society through political and economic actions. The expressed goal is to achieve a permanent state of egalitarianism through non-violent means.

TRANSNATIONALISM. A belief in or a commitment to values and communities of interest that transcend the nation-state system and that are entirely political or nonpolitical.

WAR. Any conflict in which organized military force is employed. Insurrections and armed rebellions may or may not be included, depending upon their nature.

LIST OF PEACE AND JUSTICE ORGANIZATIONS AND GROUPS

A Quaker Action Group (AQAG)

Abalone Alliance

American Against Escalation in Iraq (AAEI)

Americans Against War with Iraq (AAWWI)

American Anti-Slavery Society

American Civil Liberties Union (ACLU)

American Friends Service Committee (AFSC)

American Peace League (APL)

American League Against War and Fascist (ALWF)

American Peace Mobilization (APM)

American Peace Society (APS)

American School Peace League (ASPL)

American Society of International Law (ASIL)

American Student Union (ASU)

American Union Against Militarism (AUAM)

American Youth Congress (AYC)

Another Mother for Peace

ANSWER

Anti-Enlistment League

Anti-Imperialist League

Atlantic Life Community

Catholic Peace Fellowship

Catholic Worker Movement

Carnegie Endowment for International Peace (CEIP)

Church Peace Union (CPU)

Civilian Public Service Camps (CPS)

Clams for Direct Action at Seabrook (CDAS)

Clergy and Laity Concerned About Vietnam (CAL-CAV)

CODEPINK for Peace

Committee in Solidarity with the People of El Salvador (CISPES)

Committee for Non-Violent Action (CNVA)

Committee for a Sane Nuclear Policy (SANE)

Committee on Militarism in Education (CME)

Communist Party (CP)

Community for Creative Nonviolence (CCNV)

Congress of Racial Equality (CORE)

Copperheads

Educators for Social Responsibility (ESR)

Emergency Peace Federation (EPF)

Federation of Atomic Scientists (FAS)

Fellowship of Reconciliation (FOR)

Grandmothers against the War

Hopedale Community

Industrial Workers of the World (IWW)

Intercollegiate Peace Association

International Law Association (ILA)

Interorganizational Council on Disarmament (ICD)

Iraq Veterans against the War (IVAW)

Jeannette Rankin Brigade

Jewish Peace Fellowship

Keep America Out of War Congress (KAOWC)

Knights of Labor

League of Nations Association (LNA)

League of Universal Brotherhood (LUB)

League to Enforce Peace (LEP)

Livermore Action Group (LAG)

Massachusetts Peace Society (MPS)

Mennonites

Mobe (National Mobilization to End the War in Vietnam)

Modern Times

Moratorium

Movement for a New Society (MNS)

MoveOn.org

National Arbitration League (NAL)

National Association for the Advancement of Colored People (NAACP)

National Association of Cosmopolitan Clubs

National Coordinating Committee to End the War in Vietnam (NCCCEWV)

National Council for Prevention of War (NCPW)

National Committee on the Cause and Cure of War (NCCW)

National Peace Federation (NPF)

National Woman's Suffrage Association (NWSA)

National Youth and Student Peace Coalition

New England Non-Resistance Society

New York Peace Society (NYPS)

Nuclear Weapons Freeze Campaign (NWFC)

Oneida Community

Outlawry of War Crusade

Peace Action (Formerly Committee for a SANE Nuclear Policy)

Peaceful Tomorrows

Peace History Society (PHS)

People's Council for Democracy and Peace

Physicians for Social Responsibility (PSR)

Plowshares Movement

Sanctuary Movement

Socialist Party (SP)

Society of Friends

Solidarity Movement

Southern Christian Leadership Conference (SCLC)

Student League for Industrial Democracy (SLID)

Student Nonviolent Coordinating Committee (SNCC)

Student Peace Union (SPU)

Students for a Democratic Society (SDS)

Turn Toward Peace (TTP)

United Farm Workers (UFW)

United World Federalists (UWF)

Universal Peace Union (UPU)

Veterans for Peace

Veterans of Future Wars

Vietnam Veterans Against the War (VVAW)

War Resisters League (WRL)

War Tax Resistance Movement

WHY WAR?

Witness for Peace (WFP)

Woman's Christian Temperance Union (WCTU)

Women's International League for Peace and Freedom (WILPF)

Women's National Council (WNC)

Woman's National Loyalty League (NLL)

Woman's Peace Party (WPP)

Women's Peace Union (WPU)

Women's Pentagon Action

Women Strike for Peace (WSP)

Workers' Education Movement

World Alliance for International Fellowship

World Can't Wait

World Peace Foundation (WPF)

SOME NOTED PEACE MAKERS IN AMERICAN HISTORY

Seventeenth Century

William Penn	Englishman who established Quaker colony in the New World based on peace and friendship

Eighteenth Century

Anthony Benezet	Advanced Quakers pacifism through literal interpretation of Christianity
Benjamin Rush	Surgeon General of Continental Army and author Of "A Plan for a Peace-Office in the United States"
John Woolman	Famous Quaker pacifist and abolitionist; his journal remains a classic in the annals of pacifist thought

Nineteenth Century

Elihu Burritt	Founder of the League of Universal Brotherhood
David Low Dodge	Founded New York Peace Society in 1815

William Lloyd Garrison	Famous abolitionist and founder of New England Non-Resistance Society
Sarah and Angelina Grimke	Quakers and female leaders in the Abolitionist Movement
William Ladd	Helped create the American Peace Society (1828); Harvard graduate and sea captain
Alfred Love	Founder of the Universal Peace Union
Lucretia Mott	Linked peace with women's rights
Charles Sumner	Delivered noted oration "True Grandeur of Nations" and U.S. Senator opposed to Mexican War
Noah Worcester	Established Massachusetts Peace Society
Twentieth Century	
Jane Addams	First noted woman pacifist who helped found the Woman's International League for Peace and Freedom; shared the Nobel Peace Prize in 1931
Devere Allen	Author and editor of Fellowship of Reconciliation's The World Tomorrow and later published his own international newspaper, No Frontier News
Fannie F. Andrews	Organizer of the American Peace School League

Emily Greene Balch	Leader with Jane Addams in the Women's International League for Peace and Freedom; Awarded Nobel Peace Prize in 1946
Roger N. Baldwin	Founder of National Civil Liberties Union during World War I, later the American Civil Liberties Union (ACLU)
Daniel and Philip Berrigan	Catholic priests opposed to the Vietnam War and later leaders in Peacemakers
William Jennings Bryan	Tolstoyan pacifist, anti-imperialist, former secretary of state in the Wilson administration; noted populist and presidential candidate who gave the famous "Cross of Gold" speech in 1896
Nicholas M. Butler	President of Columbia University; president of Lake Mohonk Arbitration Conferences and later president of the Carnegie Endowment for International Peace
Andrew Carnegie	Steel magnate and philanthropist who funded the establishment of the Carnegie Endowment for International Peace
Carrie C. Catt	Established Woman's Peace Party (1915) and National Committee on Cause and Cure of War (1924)
William Sloane Coffin	Social justice minister, Yale University chaplain, and former pastor of Manhattan's Riverside Church

Helen Caldicott	Physician and author of Nuclear Madness, she was a principal figure in Physicians for Social Responsibility
Julien Cornell	Quaker attorney who defended COs during World War II
David Cortright	Activist educator, past director of SANE and president of Fourth Freedom Foundation
Norman Cousins	Internationalist and leader of SANE; social activist and respected intellectual
Ernest H. Crosby	Tolstoyan pacifist and anti-imperialist in the late 1980s and early 1900s
Dorothy Day	Established the Catholic Worker Movement in the 1930s
Eugene Debs	Leader of Socialist party and WWI opponent
David Dellinger	Conscientious Objector during World War II; radical pacifist opponent of Vietnam War
Barbara Deming	Social justice advocate who wrote influential works regarding peace and equal treatment for women as well as leading civil disobedience protests
Dorothy Detzer	Noted leader in Women's International League for Peace and Freedom

John Dewey	Famous philosopher, supporter of WWI, and later intellectual spokesman for Outlawry of War Crusade
Ralph DiGia	Important figure in the War Resisters League
Clark Eichelberger	Director of League of Nations Association
Albert Einstein	Renowned physicist and member of Committee of Atomic Scientists
Randall Forsberg	Nuclear arms policy analyst, she helped launch the Nuclear Freeze campaign of the early 1980s
Harry Emerson Fosdick	Liberal Protestant peace minister; active in Federal Council of Churches
Raymond B. Fosdick	Liberal internationalist; helped form League of Nations Non-Partisan Association
Edward Ginn	Boston publisher; created World Peace Foundation
Richard Gregg	Author of <u>The Power of Nonviolence</u>
Ernest Gruening	Physician, journalist and U.S. senator who opposed Vietnam War
Alice Hamilton	Physician and member of the 1915 American Delegation to The Hague that led to the creation of WILPF

John Haynes Holmes	Liberal pacifist minister active in Outlawry of War
Hamilton Holt	Editor of Independent; helped form League of Nations Non-Partisan Association
Jessie Wallace Hughan	Founder of American Branch of War Resisters League
Addie Hunton	Early African American leader in WILPF
Homer Jack	Helped organized SANE
David Starr Jordan	President of Stanford University; anti-imperialist; head of World Peace Foundation and figure in WWI's American Union Against Militarism
John Kerry	U.S. Senator and leader in the Vietnam Veterans Against the War
Coretta Scott King	Noted spokesperson for social justice and equal rights for women and minorities, WILPF member
Martin Luther King, Jr.	Most noted leader of the non-violent wing of the civil rights movement; opponent of Vietnam War
Salmon O. Levinson	Chicago attorney who established the Outlawry of War Crusade leading to Pact of Paris (1928)

Frederick Libby	Created National Council for Prevention of War in the 1930s
Staughton Lynd	Former Yale history professor turned lawyer; critic of the Vietnam War
Brad Lyttle	Member of CNVA and leader in peace walks
Peter Maurin	Christian Brother, editor of The Catholic Worker, and leader in Catholic Worker Movement
Charles MacFarland	Minister who aided Lynch in forming Church Peace Union
Bertha McNeil	African American leader in WILPF and supporter of improved relations with Cuba
David McReynolds	Critic of Vietnam War and leader in WRL
Edwin D. Mead	Active in practical peace movement; helped reinvigorate American Peace Society
Lucia Ames Mead	Teacher and member of WILPF and World Peace Foundation
Cord Meyer, Jr.	Leader of post-World War II United World Federalists
Charles Clayton Morrison	Founding editor of Christian Century and author of Outlawry of War

A.J. Muste	Most noted pacifist of the 20th century; executive secretary of FOR and leader in war tax resistance movement
Tracy Mygatt	Leader in American branch of War Resisters League; a moving force within the League
Kirby Page	Leading interwar peace leader who helped organize No Foreign War Crusade in the 1930s
Jim Peck	Member of War Resisters League and leader in the Direction Action movement of the late 1950s
Elihu Root	Legalist who helped form Carnegie Endowment for International Peace; received Nobel Peace Prize in 1913
Bayard Rustin	African American civil rights organizer and pacifist who helped found CORE and FOR member
John Nevin Sayre	Longtime leader and former executive secretary of the FOR and sponsor of the peace mission to Nicaragua in 1927-28
Lawrence Scott	Leader and organizer of Committee for Non-violent Action; proponent for Nuclear Freeze

James T. Shotwell	Liberal internationalist and promoter of legal renunciation of war; president of Carnegie Endowment for International Peace
Albert and Alfred Smiley	Quaker brothers who established Lake Mohonk Arbitration Conferences
Benjamin Spock	Famous pediatrician and critic of Vietnam War
John M. Swomley, Jr.	Pacifist leader in FOR involved in civil rights
Norman Thomas	Leader of Socialist party, organized Keep America Out of War Congress in the late 1930s and Turn Toward Peace in 1961, ran for US president on numerous occasions
Benjamin F. Trueblood	Quaker cosmopolitan peace leader and the one of the American Peace Society's most active recruiters; also supported AUAM
Oswald G. Villard	Editor of the Nation; supported AUAM
George & Lillian Willoughby	Quaker activists and leaders in the CNVA
Frances Witherspoon	Mygatt's life partner and noted WRL figure
Howard Zinn	Political Science professor and author of popular history text devoted to the underrepresented

FOREWORD

In "Imagine," former Beatle and rock-star John Lennon asks us to picture a world of peace and social justice, a time and place where all people unite in the commitment to equality, respect, and compassion. In this introduction and scholarly resource to the history of peace and social justice in the United States, authors Charles Howlett and Robbie Lieberman take us on a journey into that world where theorists, activists, and historians live and work in the belief that John Lennon's imaginary world can become a reality. This book is not so much about dreamers as it is about doers, those people who put their lives and careers on the line in efforts to eliminate violence and intolerance in areas from international politics to domestic concerns. Their tale takes us from early Native American tribal politics to the global strife of the twenty-first century. Throughout, they ask us to suspend current cynicism in order to remain open to possible alternatives to violent governmental politics and to perhaps adapt some of the non-violent strategies and tactics which history has proven to be effective in our struggle to make our nation and the world a place of peace and justice.

Howlett and Lieberman lay out five themes in their voyage through peace history. First, they stress that they are committed to presenting the possibility of creating a better America by illustrating how individuals and organizations have worked toward those ends. This greater United States would be a place where peace and justice prevail—not just a land of no war, but one whose people benefit from the wealth garnered through our capitalist system. Justice means that all inhabitants would have homes, jobs, health care, free education, and equal opportunity, and that racism and sexism would be a thing of the past. This might sound idealistic to the average reader, but the authors sent us with numerous examples of this vision. They trace, for example, the efforts of non-violent abolitionist societies that ran the underground railroad, thereby leading hundreds of enslaved people to freedom and, hence, to productive lives where they became valuable contributors to their communities. They speak of women's rights organizations which struggled to ensure that domestic and institutional violence against women would become obsolete and who, over the years, have been successful in improving the lot of millions of women from all races and economic classes. They also talk about civil rights organizations which gained legislation for equality under the law for African Americans and, indeed, for all disenfranchised people in the land. And they speak of labor union activists who have helped garner workers' rights throughout our nation's history, putting an end to such horrors as child labor and sweatshop working conditions.

Second, Howlett and Lieberman stress that connecting individual conscience and individual rights in a democracy has always been a key component of peace work. They illustrate how organizations such as the War Resisters League and the Fellowship of Reconciliation have worked to protect the desires of conscientious objectors not to be sent to war to kill other humans. They demonstrate how women in the suffrage movement held strong to non-violent methods of demonstrating in order to gain the right to vote for all women in the society. Leading figures in the peace movement such as the colonial era Quaker John Woolman worked for support of the poor, for Native American rights, and an end to slavery. William Lloyd Garrison lived in relative poverty in order to put out his weekly newspaper, *The Liberator*, from 1831 to 1865 to work for the abolition of slavery. Jane Addams devoted her life to the settlement Hull-House which took its initial program of helping poor immigrants to adapt to U.S. life to the streets with efforts that led to the first sanitation department in Chicago and the institution of fair treatment for juvenile delinquents. In more modern times, we can see individual conscience directing activists to take stands on environmental issues such as global warming and nuclear waste management or against wars all over the world, but currently especially in Iraq and Afghanistan. Whether movement participants write letters to editors, march in many local or national demonstrations, or put their bodies on the line by aiding relief organizations, they continue to act in a belief that the world's people have a right to live without fear of harm, poverty, or destitution.

Third, the authors stress the economic destructiveness of war which peace activists pointed out from the earliest days of our republic. It may surprise some readers to know that the first loud and clear protest against war was in 1812 when many people in the U.S., especially those in the Northeast, launched a powerful non-violent attack on lawmakers who had practically crippled the economy of the Atlantic ports by instituting a trade embargo. Or perhaps it might surprise you to know that another, even more influential movement—the anti-nuclear movement—helped to put an end to the terrible toll that the Cold War nuclear arms race placed on the economies of both the United States and the Soviet Union. Wars and the preparation for war may seem lucrative for industries, but the loss of breadwinners and the excess taxation to support wars often create devastating situations for citizens of the nations involved. The peace movement has consistently acted as the conscience to those governments who have lost their sense of humanity in their quest for power and wealth.

Four, the authors talk of the role that peace activists have played in the creation of international laws, world courts, and peace treaties which have saved many lives. The 1910 founding of the World Peace Foundation and the Carnegie Endowment for International Peace (which is still vitally active today) pushed forward efforts to institutionalize peace. The 1928 Kellogg-Briand Pact which over sixty nations signed is another case in point as it was the first time in history that leaders agreed to sit down and negotiate before jumping into a war. Peace activists had lobbied long and hard for the legislation which they fondly called "the law to end all war." Activists also rallied behind the creation of the United Nations, many organizations applying for and receiving NGO status. Their members are a constant presence at UN general assembly meetings and in other areas of work throughout the world.

The Women's International League for Peace and Freedom (WILPF) was one of the first NGOs to be recognized by the UN and remains active to this very day. Their constant pressure has ensured that nations address children's well being and violence against women as well as issues of disarmament and social justice.

Finally, the authors stress how most peace activists see themselves as patriotic Americans who are looking out for the betterment of the nation and for it to live up to its democratic principles. Those people like Eugene V. Debs who spent World War I in prison because of his outspoken antiwar and pro-labor positions or Martin Luther King, Jr. who gave his life for racial equality and non-violence or Dorothy Day who devoted her life to the Catholic Workers Movement to help the poor and working classes exemplify love of country. So does an individual like Cindy Sheehan who began one of the most visible protests against the current war in Iraq after the loss of her son, a member of the U.S. military killed in combat.

Throughout this work, readers will be introduced to numbers of individual peace activists, organizations, and actions throughout the history of the nation. They will also get a flavor of some of the cultural expressions of the movement, including the humor of Mark Twain, the utopian novels of William Dean Howells and Edward Bellamy, the novels of Willa Cather and John Dos Passos, and the music of Pete Seeger and Buffy Sainte-Marie. In the many pages before you will be the brave actions of conscientious objectors, imprisoned war resisters, nuclear pacifists facing up to naval destroyers or missile bases, and the actions of everyday people like you and me.

I hope that after you conclude your reading journey, you will take time to peruse the excellent endnotes and bibliographic essay which Howlett and Lieberman have included. These informative sources point the way to more detailed study in all of the areas these two eminent historians have introduced you to. Also, please take note of their brief description of the work of the Peace History Society. You may just want to join this scholarly activist group whose members take delight in singing folk songs and sharing humorous stories at the same time that they debate and research the serious topics you have just read about. It is in the spirit of the love of humanity that they carry on the work of preserving peace and justice history while making that history themselves.

Harriet Hyman Alonso
Professor of History
CUNY and Graduate Center.

PREFACE

History provides us with some noble and shining examples of individuals who, through conscience and determination, have done exceptionally honorable things. Very often their actions were prompted by a conviction that led them to challenge those in authority. Consider, for example, the courageous stand of Elijah P. Lovejoy. Before the Civil War passions were at fever pitch over the issue of slavery. Abolitionists aroused widespread opposition to their demands that slavery be ended without compensation. Lovejoy, an abolitionist editor who lived in Alton, Illinois, paid the ultimate price. He was murdered trying to prevent a hostile mob from destroying his printing press. In Canterbury, Connecticut, citizens became enraged when Prudence Crandall turned her boarding school into a teacher-training institute for African American females. They polluted her water supply, attempted to burn her house, and constantly harassed her. In 1834, an angry mob even assaulted her. Sojourner Truth, a former slave, was attacked by angry white mobs determined to break up meetings in which she denounced both slavery and the unequal treatment of women in American society. Harriet Tubman, a fugitive slave, returned to the South numerous times. She risked life and limb leading many slaves to freedom by way of the Underground Railroad. Carrie Chapman Catt experienced derision from male counterparts who insisted that her involvement in the struggle for women's rights and the peace movement was improper and unbecoming for a lady. Evan Thomas, a pacifist like his brother, socialist leader Norman Thomas, was beaten and mistreated while imprisoned at Ft. Leavenworth during World War I; he refused to fight on the grounds of Conscientious Objection. Bayard Rustin, a black pacifist experienced the same fate during World War II while serving a term at the federal prison in Danbury, Connecticut. Later, he played a pivotal role by taking part in interracial freedom rides in the South. The noted black intellectual W.E.B. DuBois was the constant target of federal investigations and harassment for his outspoken views on race and American foreign policy. Of course, most Americans, if not all, are familiar with the life and times of Martin Luther King, Jr. Like Lovejoy more than a century earlier, King paid the ultimate price for his convictions in the name of peace and justice.

This work is inspired by Edward Bellamy's popular 1887 utopian novel, "Looking Backward." Troubled by the problems associated with modernization and industrialization, Bellamy envisioned a society in which peace, equality, and justice were the benchmarks. He called for a humane society, a better America. In many ways that is the essence of this work. It is time for readers to understand that peace activists were motivated by a vision to build a better America. Does this mean that these individuals were naïve and backward in their thinking? Certainly not! By "looking forward" they were upholding the ideological principles of the American democratic tradition. Despite the enormous obstacles encountered in the struggle for peace and justice, the vision they hoped to achieve one day in large part is the vision upon which this nation was founded.

The present story is a comprehensive survey of the history of the struggle for peace and social justice in America. It is also a story about conviction and conscience. It begins with an analysis of the Native Americans of the Iroquois Confederacy and the Great Law of Peace and goes on to address the following topics: the pacifist sects from Europe who planted the seeds for a nonviolent way of life, the emergence of Conscientious Objection by Quakers during the American Revolution, the birth and rise of a nonsectarian organized peace movement in the early years of the nineteenth century, the struggle against slavery and support for women's rights, post-Civil War criticisms of cosmopolitan internationalism, support for labor organizing, and the battle against late nineteenth century imperialism. Twentieth century issues include opposition to U.S. involvement in World War I and the support of civil liberties during the war, the emergence of the "modern" movement and its emphasis on social and economic justice between the world wars, the growing importance of direct action after World War II, protesting the horrors of atomic and then nuclear weapons, participation in the civil rights struggles of the Cold War period, massive anti-war demonstrations during the Vietnam War, citizen-activism against the construction of nuclear power plants, the anti-apartheid and anti-interventionist movements of the 1980s, and finally the impact of cyberactivism in the current war in Iraq.

In our historical survey the pioneers for peace and justice in America relied on their conscience and their convictions to guide them. Frequently they were met with derision and vilified for their actions, and at times they were beaten or imprisoned. But in the face of stiff resistance they continued struggling in order to make their nation and the world a better place in which to live.

This is also a scholarly reference work. The ample end notes and the bibliographic essay stand as testimonies to the growing importance of peace research in history. Throughout the narrative we have taken great pains to highlight the events and personalities, as well as travails, in attempts to build a better society. More often than not pioneers of peace have been visionaries whose greatest challenge was entrenched institutions resistant to change. Nonetheless, they plowed ahead with their vision and their conscience intact. The peace pioneers of today are no different than their predecessors. While some of the methods may have changed the end still remains the same: a just society in which people live in harmony.

Paradoxically, while the United States, today, is the only superpower in the world, has the most advanced military technology available, and perhaps the best-trained forces, it is also a country with one of the longest peace traditions in history. Although military engagements have attracted most of the attention in popular works and school texts, one should not forget that the seeds of an organized peace movement began almost two hundred years ago. In fact, as American's pioneer peace historian Merle Curti noted many years ago, the United States may actually be the first nation in history to have established an organized movement for world peace. (The establishment of peace societies in America occurred almost simultaneously with ones in Great Britain.) Yet peace work in America continues to be a largely unknown part of the nation's heritage. It is time to give it its just due.

We are indebted to a number of people for contributions that have been invaluable to us in our efforts to complete this survey. Members of the Peace History Society have been instrumental with their generous support, interest, encouragement, and, most of all, scholarly discoveries enabling us to further the discipline of peace and justice research. There are certain scholars deserving our praise. Among them are the late members Merle Curti, Charles DeBenedetti, and Arthur A. Ekirch. Current and retired scholars who also richly deserve our thanks are Charles Chatfield, Larry Wittner, Bernice Carroll, John W. Chambers II, Geoff Smith, Nigel Young, Mitch Hall, Harriet Alonso, Blanche W. Cook, Jo Ann O. Robinson, E. Timothy Smith, Kathleen Kennedy, Frances Early, David S. Patterson, Christy Jo Snyder, Mike Foley, Barbara Steinson, Mel Small, and Scott Bennett. We also want to acknowledge other scholars who have contributed important new insights to the links between peace and justice, including Marian Mollin, Ian Lekus, David Hostetter, and Joyce Blackwell-Johnson. Each in their own way offered valuable insights and new passageways to our understanding of the field.

We would also like to thank the Director of Edwin Mellen Press, Dr. John Rupnow. A scholar and gentleman himself, John has always been receptive to new ideas and interpretations. A generous grant from the Molloy Scholarship and Research Committee enabled Charles Howlett to undertake an examination of the hundreds of photographs housed at the Swarthmore College Peace Collection. We are most thankful to Dr. Wendy Chmielewski and her outstanding staff for their patience and assistance in this effort. Wendy is a recognized scholar of peace history in her own right.

Charles Howlett would like to thank Dr. Peter Lynch and Barbara Lynch, who carefully read the entire manuscript during its infancy and provided numerous editorial suggestions for improving the book's organization and style. Colleagues Audrey Cohan, Sr. Bernadette Donovan, Maureen Walsh, Kevin Sheehan and Sr.

Anne Christine Janke were also enthusiastic supporters of this project. He would also like to thank Mike Brecciano, Robert Windorf, Erin Geiger, Steve Abt, Jim Stankard, Eric Dunn, Patrick Aiello, Tamara Grosso, Paul Washington, Jessie Stiller, Patrick Hoey, Mary Berblinger, and Jim Perrotta. Given the magnitude of this work, they provided invaluable support in terms of fact-checking and cross-referencing materials. As usual, Chris Collora was his dependable self when it came to the larger task of formatting this book in order to meet the specifications required by the publisher.

Robbie Lieberman would like to thank the Department of History and the Dean's office of the College of Liberal Arts at Southern Illinois University Carbondale for supporting her work as editor of *Peace & Change*, service that helped enrich her view of the field of peace history. She would also like to thank her student, Deidre Hughes, whose work over the years as a student of peace history and an activist has helped make endeavors such as this one especially meaningful.

West Islip, NY
Carbondale, IL

Charles F. Howlett
Robbie Lieberman

“It will be a great day when our schools get all the money they need and the Air Force has to hold a bake sale to buy a bomber.”

– Anonymous

INTRODUCTION

> ....It is of crucial importance that we should understand that for the individual to put himself in Holy Disobedience against the war-making and conscripting State, wherever it or he be located, is not an act of despair or defeatism. Rather, I think we may say that precisely this individual refusal to "go along" is the beginning and the core of any realistic and practical movement against war and for a more peaceful and brotherly world.
>
> A.J. Muste, "Of Holy Disobedience" (1952)

In twentieth-century America perhaps no one was more qualified to speak on behalf of the peace movement than Abraham Johannes Muste. He was the symbol, the preacher, and the prophet who elevated the conscience and actions of proponents for peace. Confronted with the perplexing paradox of a country that cherished survival but chose the terrifying instrument of war – the atomic bomb – to preserve its existence, it was Muste who gathered his flock to make noise in a wilderness of uncertainty and insecurity. The human being, God's child, Muste proclaimed, must understand that humankind is the only "real" thing in the face of machines and mechanized institutions of one's age. Given the harsh reality of the atomic bomb's ability to destroy civilization, Muste encouraged his fellow peace activists to go out into the wilderness and inform their fellow humans that the only kind of morality quite capable of withstanding pressures for war and conformity is that of individual conscience. That was the only way to peace.

Peace has been the one reform sought most vocally by Americans, along with people around the world, but it has also been the most elusive.[1] Students of American history have been exposed to surveys and monographs dominated by discourses on war. Whether describing preparations for war, battles, military leaders, or postwar plans, these books do so in terms of the glory and necessity of war. Consider the vocabulary itself: "antebellum period"; "interwar period"; "Cold War"; "War on Terrorism"; "prewar economy"; "postwar planning"; etc. It is by no means a coincidence that one of the most frequently mentioned nouns in the English language is "war." According to the "Concise Oxford Dictionary," the word "war" ranked as the number 49 most commonly used noun, while "peace" did not even make the top one hundred. Such vocabulary and use of said noun implies that the United States has been in a virtual state of war throughout its existence. The reality is, however, that this emphasis is out of proportion to the actual amount of time Americans have spent fighting in wars. It is proper to ask, "Since the clock hours of peacetime do, in fact, far outweigh those of war, why do historians devote so much of their scholarship and teaching to war and, conversely, so little to peace study?"[2]

Despite their relative absence from history books, peace activism and peace movements have played a vital role in our past. The conflict of priorities throughout U.S. history between seeking the accumulation of wealth and working toward more humane and just relations, for instance, captured the attention of peace activists in the nineteenth and early twentieth centuries. From peace activists like Elihu Burritt and his League of Universal Brotherhood to Muste and the Fellowship of Reconciliation there have been well-intentioned Americans who have been engaged in reforms that have defended the rights of workers and their demands for a just economic order. Bitter labor strife such as the Railroad Strikes of 1877, the Homestead Steel Strike of the early 1890s, the 1919 postwar struggles, and the industrial organizing drives of the 1930s captured the time and attention of peace activists who were willing to challenge the tactics of corporate owners putting profits above economic justice and worker safety. Rarely, if at all, have history books made the connection between the role of peacemakers and the organization of workers in America's past. This study will correct that omission.

Certainly, the brutality and consequences of war have received their fair attention in history books. But in almost every instance such discussions have been undertaken with a patriotic veneer. Little has been done to give credit where credit is due when it comes to the peace movement and its supporters. Equally important, when peace movements or pacifists have been included in textbooks, diplomatic studies, or histories of domestic America, it has often been pejoratively, in order to criticize peacemakers as obstructionists or traitors to the realpolitik patriotism of the national policy known as war. The justification for omitting peace activism has been that without war, or at least the threat of war, pacifism is merely a reactive ideology, with little to offer on its own.

A reactive ideology and unpatriotic could not be farther from the truth. U.S. history is replete with examples of Americans who boldly chose to criticize their nation's foreign policy in the name patriotism. Proponents of peace are the staunchest defenders of American principles, especially the democratic right to criticize a conflicting tradition in American history that justifies and glorifies war and violence in the name of peace. A closer look at the record reveals that despite heavy-handed attempts to crush dissent during wartime, the Society of Friends (Quakers), Eugene Debs and the socialists, Muste, Jane Addams, David Dellinger, William Sloane Coffin, Martin L. King, Jr., and a host of other individuals and organizations have called for a peaceful resolution to violence in the name of democracy. Many went to jail, lost their lives, and had their reputations destroyed all in the name of peace and justice. What has not been properly addressed is that their patriotism was shaped by their vision of a better America for all its peoples.

A better America for all is one of the organizing principles and central themes of this work. The broad notion of peace as not only the absence of war but also the presence of justice defines the history of the movement and participants. Social and economic equality resonates throughout the story of peace activism. Once again, there are numerous examples highlighting this very point. John Woolman and the Quakers spoke out against war, encouraged friendly relations with the original inhabitants of the land, and called for an end to the pernicious institution of slavery. In antebellum America William Lloyd Garrison and the New England Non-Resistance Society, daughters of a South Carolina plantation owner Sarah and Angelina Grimke, and other peacemakers tied their crusade for abolitionism with equal rights for women. After the Civil War Alfred Love and his Universal Peace Union criticized the subjugation and conquest of Native Americans in the west as well as supported the efforts of the Knights of Labor. In the Progressive Era the peace movement's leading lady, Jane Addams, helped establish the settlement house program to assist poor immigrants in their transition to urban-industrial life and participation in civic democracy. During World War I critics of capitalism like Eugene Debs and Emma Goldman argued that wars perpetuate social and economic oppression. The World War I era witnessed the birth of new peace organizations such as the Fellowship of Reconciliation, Women's International League for Peace and Freedom, and the War Resisters League, which along with their proponents Muste, Jane Addams, Norman Thomas, Jessie Wallace Hughan, Kirby Page, Emily Greene Balch, and John Nevin Sayre, led the way in the areas of civil rights, unionization, equal rights for women, and better living conditions in the cities. Peace as justice took on added importance during World War II in defending the rights of Conscientious Objectors, the civil rights struggles of the 1940s to 1960s, the 1960s and 1970s feminist movement, and environmental awareness and anti-nuclear plant campaigns of the 1970s and 1980s.

Connecting conscience with individual rights in a democracy is another important component to this story. Peacemakers and peace activists have always appealed to people's better nature, bringing issues to the surface, asking people to take a stand for what they know or believe is right. Once again, America's past is full of examples of how people of conscience called upon their fellow citizens to live peaceably and respect one another. Long before the first Europeans set foot in the New World a peace tradition had been put into practice by the Native Americans. The Iroquois Confederation had established a "Great Law of Peace." Tired of tribal warfare, the "Great Law" became the founding constitution of the Six Nations Iroquois Confederacy. It defined the functions of the Grand Council and how the native nations could resolve disputes among themselves and establish a lasting peace. By the eighteenth century some American colonists were implementing that tradition in their relations with various Native American tribes. The Quakers, for instance, planted the seeds of non-violence as a way of life and entered into peaceful land treaties with the original inhabitants. In the nineteenth century, as sectarian war resistance gave way to a more organized movement, peacemakers like David Low Dodge, William Ladd, Noah Worcester, and Elihu Burritt wrote persuasive arguments insisting that war was barbarous, economically wasteful, and contrary to the precepts of Christianity.

Matters of conscience were visibly illustrated during World War I, moreover, when individuals such as Evan Thomas were handcuffed to cell bars and starved because their conscience would not allow them to take up arms. Reputations were also tarnished as in the case of Swarthmore College Phi Beta Kappa graduate and Quaker schoolteacher in the New York City School System, Mary Stone McDowell, who lost her job because she chose to remain silent in the classroom rather than proclaim the virtues of patriotism and martial fortitude. The Second World War provided more powerful examples of conscience as in the experience of Stanley Murphy and Louis Taylor. Both were placed naked in "strip cells" and beaten by guards at a federal prison hospital in Springfield, Missouri for having led an 82-day hunger strike at the federal prison in Danbury, Connecticut. The Vietnam War provides further proof with the Catholic priests Daniel and Philip Berrigan, who were imprisoned for their actions at the Selective Service Center in Catonsville, Maryland.

When the Vietnam War ended peace activists were also arousing the country's social conscience with regard to environmental issues. The massive protests against the construction of nuclear power plants witnessed the birth of the Clamshell Alliance. This non-violent protest group awoke the town of Seabrook, New Hampshire. Peace activists from all over the nation came to this quiet New England seashore town and raised the country's consciousness about energy and environmental issues. In one of the most successful acts of non-violent civil disobedience since the Vietnam War, the anti-nuclear plant campaign demonstrated the peace movement's commitment to social change.

What is most obvious, however, is that proponents of peace have always been present in America's past, even if their actions – as individuals or in groups – have not been fully recorded in the history books. One of the most often heard criticisms of peace activists, pacifists, and peace movements is that the body of their thought is too idealistic. Yet in many ways, peace activists have been quite realistic in their assessments of human behavior and the role of nation states. Peacemakers insist that the abolition of war does not necessarily require a profound change in human behavior. Rather, they argue that an informed citizenry is the best way towards changing the sinister aspects of the nation-state system and its social components. They have tried to construct a culture of peace that is built upon more than the absence of war while pointing out the devastating social, economic, and biological effects of war and social injustice.

Peacemakers are also accused of neglecting human nature. But how many students of American history are aware of Harvard philosopher William James' "Moral Equivalent of War," which tackled this issue head on. Granting that the barbarous side of human nature had presented problems in the past, James refused to acknowledge its continuance. Instead, he insisted that there were reasonable alternatives to channeling human aggression. The brilliant student of John Dewey, Randolph Bourne, took to task those intellectuals who supported President Wilson's call to arms in 1917 by pointing out the deleterious effects of war on the human psyche. His essays called upon people of conscience to challenge the very existence of "war as the health of the State." Such critics emphasized the potential of human beings to do what is right, in Bourne's terms, to value reason, beauty, and truth, more than conformity to the demands of war.

The economic destructiveness of war has occupied a major portion of the peace movement's contribution to building a better America. The end of the War of 1812 and later witnessed peacemakers like Worcester, Ladd, and Burritt challenging the forces of war as an industrializing tendency; these views would take on a more anarchistic flavor with Josiah Warren and the utopian experiences of the mid-nineteenth century. After the Civil War peacemakers such as Alfred

Love would rely on economic arguments to not only address the problem of war's brutality but also how the acquisition of wealth in the industrial age has been disproportionately applied. The uneven distribution of wealth was a basic cause of labor strife in the late nineteenth century and would also become a basic factor during the civil rights struggles of mid-twentieth century America. The peace movement would play a major role in bringing this to the attention of the public.

Discussions on international law, the role of courts, arbitration, and peace treaties have also been of major concern to peace proponents and peace groups. Organizations like the World Peace Foundation and the Carnegie Endowment for International Peace took the lead in the early twentieth century in scholarly examinations of the causes of war. Though conservative in their approach and not pacifistic by any stretch of the imagination, they gave the legalist bent to the peace movement a respectable demeanor. At the end of the First World War, moreover, peacemakers and peace organizations were able to build upon the collective arguments put forth by religious and sectarian pacifists as well as non-pacifist legalists and internationalists to build a powerful argument in favor of realistic approaches to end modern warfare and its destructiveness. Today, the fact that nations possess nuclear weapons yet refuse to use them – with the exception of the atomic bombs dropped on Hiroshima and Nagasaki in 1945 – strengthens the realist arguments raised by proponents of peace.

This book encompasses much more than a story about the crusade against war or particular weapons systems. Proponents of peace have been, and always will be, about making America a better society. This line of thinking also challenges disciplinary perspectives in the fields of political science and international relations. These disciplines have always emphasized the shifts in power and the struggle for power among various national states. Since World War II, in particular, the field has been dominated by the "realist" school of international relations. Disavowing the idealism generated by World War I Wilsonians these scholars consider war endemic and part of a natural confluence involving shifts in power associated with the beginning of armed conflict. Thus the study of alliances, international tensions, and military buildups suggest that power politics itself represents a series of steps to war, and that each aspect increased the chances of conflict between equally competing states. While scholars of the "realist" school maintain that wars occur when a rising state challenges the dominant power of the system, none has been able to provide a precise or compelling explanation of war.

Opponents of war have frequently been accused of being unpatriotic as a way of discrediting their views. Throughout our history there have been numerous examples of those who spoke out against the conduct of the nation's foreign policy only to be labeled a traitor by those in power. Can you be critical of the country and patriotic at the same time? One need only examine the record of Massachusetts Senator Charles Sumner whose July 4, 1845 oration, "True Grandeur of Nations," remains one of the most compelling anti-war, anti-expansionist speeches in nineteenth century America. Mark Twain, no less a patriot, questioned America's foreign policy at the end of the nineteenth century in his essay, "To a Person Sitting in the Darkness." Criticism of the war with Spain in 1898 was expressed in a popular novel, Captain Jinks, Hero, by former army major and judge on the International Court, Ernest Howard Crosby. William Jennings Bryan, one of the greatest political orators in American history and three-time Presidential candidate, resigned his position as Secretary of State when it became apparent that Woodrow Wilson would lead the U.S. into war. Jeanette Rankin, the respected Congresswoman from Montana, was the only legislative leader in our history to have voted against both world wars. She did so out of love for her country and not to aid the forces of autocracy and fascism. Vietnam Veterans Against the War along with former World War II army officers such as the Reverend William Sloane Coffin, Yale University Chaplain and later head of Riverside Church in Manhattan, and Father Philip Berrigan, leader in the Catholic Peace Fellowship, opposed the war out of love for their country and not because of their disdain for the military. The current war in Iraq has witnessed former Vietnam Veteran Chuck Hagel, Republican senator from Nebraska, challenging his own party's leadership and conduct in this war. Love for one's country entails taking risks to ensure that democracy does not fall victim to the repression of the exchange of free ideas in the market place or within the arena of political dialogue.

Throughout the American past the peace movement and its members have had their own special history, leadership, organizational base, and tradition of social reform. The movement has been a purposive and collective attempt by numerous and well-intentioned people to change the thinking of individuals and groups and reform societal institutions. One of the more notable contributions to the establishment of a peaceful and just America is the rich diversity of peace activists and thinkers who have been part of the much larger reform movement in our past. How history looks when we don't use war or patriotism as the organizing principle is easier to comprehend when studying the peace movement as part of America's collective heritage.[3]

Proponents of peace as well as their representative organizations have sought the peaceful resolution of conflict through a variety of measures. They have distinguished themselves by contributing their time and energy to organizing to prevent organized violence and minimize its effects.[4] They have argued for a more organic world consciousness, proposing economic and social changes such as the disallowance of trade advantages, international regulation of the world's food supply, international control of the arms industry, and establishment of international health and education programs.[5] Guided by their conscience, moreover, peace proponents insist that peace is the primary basis for ongoing human relationships that preclude resorting to violence.[6] But above all, peacemakers have diligently connected their actions to broader social and political concerns including civil rights, feminism, socialism, and ecological devastation. They have argued that war is an integral part of an unjust social order. They have pointed out that the instruments of political control involve the hidden threat of violence and that these were in the very hands of the classes opposed to change. Thus throughout the course of America's past, peace proponents and their organizations have both formed ideal communities for the larger society to emulate and engaged in reform activities intended to replace those political policies, social institutions, or cultural patterns that have prevented the triumph of lasting peace.[7] Yet the diversity of views and issues encountered within the movements themselves presents challenges to any attempt to describe the actions of peace proponents and their organizations.

For starters, students should consult Charles Chatfield's edited work, Peace Movements in America. Chatfield has argued that each peace effort must be defined with respect to the specific issues and choices that engendered it. Much activity labeled peace work has thus been a reaction to concrete problems facing society as a whole, such racial injustice and imperialism of the late nineteenth century, World War I, the rise of totalitarianism in the 1930's, military intervention in other parts of the world, including the so-called "war on terror," and the ever-present threat of nuclear annihilation. War and social injustice have presented unique challenges to each generation of peace seekers. Peace leaders in every area have differed among themselves in assessing massive social crises. The response of each peace movement has been distinctive with regard to policy issues as well as to the kind of society within which it operated.[8]

Equally important, peace efforts must be understood in light of the political context of their times. Again, Chatfield explains, and this is most critical, that the membership of each organization is bonded by a distinct viewpoint (e.g., pacifism, world court, international government) together with either social characteristics (e.g., Christianity, feminism, socialism, humanism) or functional programs (e.g., lobbying, publicizing issues, protests and rallies, educating). All of these groups enlist or recruit some members who are interested in a variety of issues. In this instance, an anti-war constituency may attract groups with inconsistent interests: opposition to World War I aligned socialists with some moderate liberals; the stance of strict neutrality in the 1930's drew both isolationists and pacifists; condemnation of the Vietnam War linked together New Left radicals, conservative business leaders, and liberal pacifists; the Freeze campaign of the early 1980's drew a wide array of supporters from former Students for a Democratic Society (SDS) radicals to apolitical grandmothers; and the current war in Iraq has seen an alignment of old-line anti-imperialists joining in protest demonstrations with Gulf War and Vietnam War veterans. Significantly, the peace movement, bonded by alternative strategies to global harmony, has been noted for its ability to form coalitions that vie with prowar groups or with the government for public support in the political realm.[9]

As Chatfield carefully explains, peace activists or advocates "shared some values, beliefs, and roles which they consciously forged for themselves; they had others . . . imparted to them through the culture in which they were socialized." In essence, like other social reformers, peace activists are both dissenters from and prisoners of their own political cultures.[10] For example, many male peacemakers fiercely challenged what they saw a unjust wars, but were unable to transcend social norms that kept women from playing more prominent roles in such struggles.

Nevertheless, throughout history, one can ascertain a certain consistency to the lives of peace movements in America where the challenge to war is concerned. Many years ago Lawrence Wittner's Rebels against War provided a useful analogy: in his analysis, the peace effort resembled an onion, with the absolute pacifists in the center and the less committed non-pacifists forming the outside layers. At times of popular enthusiasm for war, the less committed outside layers peel off, leaving the pacifist core. During times of strong aversion to militarism, new layers suddenly appear, and the onion grows in size. Such structural fluidity accounts for both the American peace movement's repeated weakness in times of international tension and for its peculiar resiliency.[11]

Wittner's work was largely inspired by the first chronicler of the peace movement, Merle Curti. In Peace or War: The American Struggle, 1636-1936, Curti wrote, "The history of this crusade," he wrote, "is a stirring one. The struggle could be waged only at the cost of great toil and devotion and sacrifice." The struggle affects all of us and remains part and parcel of a much greater effort for social change. And as Curti reminded us: "The American pageant of peace cannot be understood without taking into account the stage on which it was enacted. What Americans did to limit or uproot the war system was at every point affected by the traditions and ideals of American life which were dominant in varying degrees at different times."[12] The story you are about to read is one describing those who hoped that words would one day become more powerful than munitions.

The present volume contains considerable primary source research. It also relies heavily on the interpretations and insights provided by the pioneers in the field. As a survey it is intended to acquaint students and interested teachers with the origins, development, and maturation of the struggle for peace in America's past. Throughout this survey numerous references will be made to the historians who have researched the field, attribution given to primary sources they and the authors have relied on, and serious attention devoted to the emerging discipline of peace history itself. Each chapter is divided into subtopics for reader convenience and comprehension; most subtopics have ample citations where appropriate. The history of the movement is told through the people and events that have shaped it.

Two final thoughts: first, the historical record seems to indicate that peace movements are a consequence of wars. However, the interesting point to consider in American history is that peace movements have existed even when the nation has not been at war. Why is this so? Perhaps the answer is because the movement has evolved into one that considers peace more than just the absence of war. For this reason the peace movement, at least since the early 1900s, has achieved a sense of relevancy in our lives. It is no longer just about abolishing war. The peace movement has come to encompass the fields of labor organization, civil rights, women's equality, and a livable environment. To secure lasting peace it is imperative that a just and equitable domestic order be established first. For close to one hundred years now the movement's main thrust has been to encourage its followers to challenge the established cultural ways of thinking in order to make peace a more realistic option than war. Simply put: the struggle begins and ends at home.

There is also that age-old question of just how effective peace movements have been in preventing wars. Borrowing a page from Lawrence Wittner, therefore, maybe it is best if we examine how peace movements have limited the expansion and duration of wars as opposed to whether or not they could have been stopped. In this case there are some examples worthy of examination. During the War of 1812 strong opposition to the conflict between Great Britain and the United States was raised by Federalists and merchants from the northeast. The dissent was loud and strong, so much so that the Madison administration called off efforts to invade Canada and ultimately reached a peace agreement in which neither side claimed a clear-cut military victory. The Mexican War of 1846-1848 witnessed some of the most aggressive critiques of expansionism. Orations by William Sumner, tracts by members of the American Peace Society, and anti-expansionist views in New England based upon opposition to slavery, particularly Henry David Thoreau's "Essay on Civil Disobedience," eventually forced James K. Polk to abandon his desire to obtain further territorial concessions from Mexico south of the Rio Grande River. The Spanish-American War of 1898 was over quickly, but it did give birth to the Anti-Imperialist League whose membership consisted of some of the nation's most famous business people and writers like Mark Twain. The League pressured the McKinley and later Theodore Roosevelt administrations to end the fighting in the Philippines. In more recent times, the intensity and magnitude of the Anti-Vietnam War protests were unparalleled in American history up to that time. While it may be true that the American public finally got tired of the fighting in the nation's longest war, it remains clear that the anti-war movement was responsible for putting the pressure on President Nixon to seek a negotiated settlement. Such pressure also led Congress to override President Nixon's veto and pass the War Powers Act in 1973 which imposed a limit on the number of days the President could commit troops to combat without Congressional authorization. In the 1980's, the peace movement mobilized public opinion in support of the Nuclear Freeze Campaign – the bill passed in the House of Representatives. Although the referendum fell short of the necessary two-thirds vote in the Senate, the Reagan administration did undertake further nuclear arms limitation talks leading to a reduction in strategic nuclear weapons. The growing unpopularity of the Iraq War in America has been the result of peace groups using the Internet, among other tools, to stimulate discussion and mobilize public opinion in favor of U.S. troop withdrawal. Although the jury is still out with respect to America's current war, anti-war awareness is at the highest level it has ever been in American history. At present, sixty percent of the American public opposes the war in Iraq. These are the most obvious examples of peace work effectiveness covered in this survey.

So long as we have economic and social injustice at home and wars abroad, the need to remind readers of the importance of peace work will remain of paramount importance. The efforts of peace activists should not be forgotten and their role in American history must never be dismissed or ignored.

CHAPTER ONE

THE ORIGINAL INHABITANTS, RELIGIOUS PACIFISM, AND THE CALL FOR INDEPENDENCE

…I say, Justice is the Means of Peace, betwixt the Government and the People, and One Man and Company and another. It prevents Strife, and at least ends it: for besides Shame or Fear, to contend longer, he or they being under Government are constrained to bound their Desires and Resentment with the Satisfaction the Law gives. Thus Peace is maintained by Justice, which is a Fruit of Government, as Government is from Society, and Society from Consent.

William Penn, "Essay Towards the Present And Future Peace of Europe," 1693.

INTRODUCTION

These words by William Penn ably capture the sentiments and feelings of some of America's earliest pioneers for peace. Seeking to build a just society in the New World, they chose non-violence as their instrument. At first, however, the colonies established in seventeenth and eighteenth century North America developed and matured in an age when few questioned the use of violence. Old World rivalries in the Age of Exploration and taming a frontier wilderness fraught with uncertainty sanctioned a resort to arms. Yet, some Europeans who dared set foot on the North American continent carried with them peace practices and beliefs defining bold new parameters to the Western Peace tradition. That tradition had been born during a period of persecution and oppression.

Yet such tradition was not so easily implemented in the New World. Throughout seventeenth and eighteenth century America prospects for peace and justice were challenged in a variety of ways. Religion, for instance, acted as a double-edge sword. The first Europeans who came to New England relied on God and the bible as dispensers of justice and power when it came to relations with native peoples. More often than not the accumulation of wealth and the acquisition of territory somehow found scriptural justification. The arrival of the Quakers in the middle part of the seventeenth century provided a different religious prescription. Settling in the Delaware Valley, Friends transported their doctrine of non-violence from England, which aided in their peaceful negotiations with Native American neighbors. The emergence of sectarian war resistance in the New World was largely due to Friends practicing what they believed. For them non-violence was an extension of social justice and it would come full circle during the French and Indian War of 1756-1763. Having cultivated peaceful relations with their neighbors, the Lenni Lenape, they could not condone the British Crown's insistence that they take up arms against other Native American tribes and the French to the north and west in the name of imperial protection. For the first time Friends challenged the very nature of civil authority while taking comfort in their Conscientious Objection to war. Though some Quakers supported the call for independence from Great Britain the majority of Friends' Meetings rejected the notion that the use of arms was necessary to secure peace and protect borders. For almost two hundred years after the arrival of the first Europeans to the New World, the establishment of a peace tradition depended primarily on matters of religious beliefs, dealings with civil authority, and, most importantly, interaction between whites and native peoples.

THE ORIGINAL PEACEMAKERS

Long before Europeans came to the New World nature held a special place in the hearts and minds of those who first lived here. The land was marked by a great natural beauty. It was a rich land with a variety of climates, abundant plant and animal life, a rolling carpet of green forests, and hills and mountains where the eye could see blue lakes sprinkled throughout the countryside and winding rivers flowing endlessly down to the sea. There were also grassy fields and meadows suitable for farming, while forests provided an excellent supply of deer meat for nourishment and beaver furs and deer skins for clothing and shelter.

Before the first Europeans "discovered" the New World Native American tribes had inhabited the Americas for many centuries. Some of the tribes adapted their way of life to the heavily watered, densely forested regions of what are now the eastern parts of Canada and the United States. It would be these tribes who first established a tradition of peace in North America.

The Iroquois Confederation, consisting of the Mohawk tribe, the Oneida tribe, Onondaga tribe, Cayuga tribe, and Seneca tribe, decided after years of warring upon one another for food and territory to replace violence with peaceful relations. Living in harmony with the land defined their culture and way of life. But the rampant violence had forced them to abandon their agricultural communities and hilly cornfields and resort to a more primitive existence in the forests.

Faced with this crisis the five Iroquois peoples adopted a "League of Peace," also known as the "Great Law of Peace." The Great Law consisted of three interconnected concepts, which if adhered to, would assure peace among the member nations of the Confederacy. The first concept, righteousness, maintained that the people, clans, chiefs, Clan Mothers and the entire nation must treat each other fairly. Each individual must possess a strong sense of justice and treat people as equals. All people must enjoy equal protection under the Great Law and shape their own personal conduct so as not to build up resentment or hatred toward one another. The second concept, health, encouraged soundness of mind, body, and health; it also meant peace in that a strong mind uses its rational power to foster well-being among peoples and between nations. The third concept, power, means authority, tradition, and stability; it also involves law and custom, backed by force, to make justice prevail. Power also means religion in that the enforcement of justice depends on the will of the Holder of the Heavens and has his blessings. People and nations need just enough power to maintain peace and ensure the well-being of the Confederacy.

The most difficult part of the "Great Law" to comprehend was the meaning of the concept of peace. Peace was not simply the absence of battle. For the Iroquois Confederacy peace represented a state of mind. One heart, one mind, one head, and one body enabled the Confederacy to remain united in the face of conquest and European expansionism. More importantly, the concept of peace was based on the spiritual power of each individual. As one progresses through life's journey, the individual experiences different things, learns more, and connects to other forms of spiritual power; in the process the individual's spirit grows as well. The ultimate power of the "Great Law of Peace" rests in how well the individual person develops his or her sense of self and, in so doing, develops that sense with regard to the welfare of others in the clan, village, nation, and the entire Confederacy.

The "Great Law of Peace" had effectively preserved the unity and harmony among the tribes of the Iroquois Confederacy for hundreds of years. But with the arrival of whites came epidemic diseases, economic dependency, imperial battles, and the annexation of Native American lands. Thus by the time of the French and Indian War this decentralized confederacy had basically become a colonized people.

There were, however, some notable examples of peaceful coexistence between the newly arriving whites and indigenous tribes. In New England, for instance, some Native American tribes chose peace through accommodation rather than extinction. Despite some brutal tactics employed by members of the Plymouth Colony against the original inhabitants, Wampanoag Chief Massasoit, the "war chief," concluded a treaty of friendship with the new and struggling colony as early as 1621; peaceful relations lasted more than a half century. Of course, Massasoit needed an alliance with the Puritans in order to strengthen his rivalry against the Narragansetts. In fact, when the Pequot War of 1637 broke out

– discussed later – Massasoit did not interfere with the colonies of Massachusetts and Connecticut.

Massasoit had succeeded in maintaining peace during the course of his lifetime. But his son, Metacom, derisively called "King Philip" by the English settlers, lacked his father's prestige and diplomatic skills. Facing an ever-growing tide of white settlements, he chose resistance to accommodation and suffered the consequences. "King Philip's War" of 1675, of which more will be said later, led to the destruction of his people. The remaining survivors ultimately formed a dependent class of servants and tenant farmers.

Meanwhile, the Lenni Lenape of the Delaware Valley represented one of the most successful attempts at peace and justice. The tribe's name means "the original people." Perhaps more than their northern counterparts, the Iroquois, the Lenni Lenape highlighted their peace inclinations around 1682-83 when some of their chiefs at the village of Shackemaxon (now part of present-day Philadelphia) met with Quaker leader, William Penn. There both sides agreed to a Great Treaty of Friendship. And while more will be said about this in our discussion of the Quakers, it should be noted that this was the only agreement between the Native Americans and Europeans never to be sworn to or broken. The famous paintings by Benjamin West and Edward Hicks remain iconographic testimonials to this important event.

Equally important, even before Penn's arrival in the New World, the Lenape were long considered respected mediators and peacemakers. In 1676, for instance, Rinowehan, a Lenape chief, with the backing of Governor Edmund Andros of the colony of New York, successfully mediated an impending conflict between the Iroquois and the Susquehannocks. Compared to the conflicts in New England and Virginia, the Native-American-European peace agreement in the Delaware Valley stood as a remarkable achievement. Efforts to avoid warfare with European colonists on the part of various Native American tribes, moreover, would also be reinforced with the appearance of certain religious sects who brought with them religious peace traditions from the Old World.

A EUROPEAN RELIGIOUS PEACE TRADITION COMES TO AMERICA

From 1620 to 1763, religious sectarians dedicated to traditional Christian tenets and suffering from alienation by governing authority settled along the Atlantic seaboard. In these British colonies, the followers of Christ reaffirmed a social commitment to the importance of organized peace. Weakened by the Protestant Reformation a century earlier, the rise of nation-states, and weary of Old World violence marked by religious persecution, resolute members of Protestant Europe's most radical reform sects moved to North America in search of harmony and peace.[1]

The sectarians' determination to live solely by Christ's authority brought them into direct conflict with the power of established churches and the developing nation-states. Yet, even in the face of contention, the radical religious sects managed to survive and carry their convictions with them when migrating to North America. By 1763, with the conclusion of the French and Indian War, nearly 60,000 Anabaptist communitarians and Quakers had established in the New World a dissenting peace tradition based on their devotion to Christ's teachings.

Anabaptists, offspring of the Reformation, were distrustful of all forms of earthly government. Beginning in the 1680's, Mennonites, Moravians, and Dunkers (those sects which made up the Anabaptist community) were entirely German speaking and found their way from Central Europe to Pennsylvania and Virginia where they settled. Bringing with them their doctrine of non-resistance, which they called *Wehrlosigkeit*, a belief dating as far back as 1527, these Disciples of Christ renounced war as well as participation in politics. Isolated from society at large, they took solace in their pacifism and clung steadfastly to their own cultural mores.

It was in Germantown, Pennsylvania, in 1683 to be exact, where the first permanent Anabaptist Mennonite community was established. As pacifists the

Mennonites were the first to publicly protest against the institution of slavery in the New World. Another religious sect with European Anabaptist connections was begun by Alexander Mack in 1703. The Church of the Brethren in America was officially formed in 1723 and by the following decade attracted numerous immigrants from western Germany. Branded as heretics and civil anarchists, these Anabaptist communities contributed to the early reform tradition in America by linking their religious beliefs to public causes, especially peace and abolitionism. In many ways they expanded the definition of peace to incorporate all forms of social justice and equality.

These religious sects were opposed to state violence. Their members of these churches steadfastly refused to pay war taxes, rejected payment for exemption from state militia service, and were unwilling to perform alternative service. These religious pacifists were known as absolutists. In their steadfast adherence to an ethic of love, they could not condone cooperation with civil authority when it came to causing bodily injury. If forced to break the law in such instances, they would rely on civil disobedience in order to defend their beliefs.

Unlike their continental brethren, the Quakers hailed from England and were far more assertive in matters of politics. They did not identify civil authority with state violence, thus making it easier for them to participate in politics. Quakers in the New World believed that civil authority should flow directly from the power of the people's experience of "Inner Light" (direct personal knowledge of the good). What drew them together was their common hatred for war and violence, belief in non-resistance as a way of life, and love for Christ. It would be the Quakers, officially known as the Religious Society of Friends, who would influence most the emerging peace tradition in eighteenth-century America.

The practice of dissent was nothing new to the Quaker way of life; the Quakers were by far the largest number of radical peace dissenters in the New World in the seventeenth and eighteenth centuries. They were prone to criticizing the Anglican Church and its head, the reigning monarch of England. What made their position unique in the American experience was their identification with the practice of non-violence; refusing to bear arms in a new land filled with peril and danger required the courage of one's conviction, and the Quakers had plenty of that. Of course, in the New World, where state religion would not be sanctioned, the Quakers were free to practice what they preached. Colonial peace seekers, particularly the Quakers, defined a sectarian peace vision that remained the foundation of organized peace action in the colonies until the age of commercialism and nascent industrialization transformed the American landscape – one marked by the birth of a new nation. The history of America's earliest peace movement is the history of the Quakers. Yet the Quakers would not be the first religious group to grapple with issues involving peace and war.

THE PURITANS AND SCRIPTURAL AMBIVALENCY

Prior to the arrival of the Quakers the theory and practice of war was first discussed by a group of religious dissenters who settled in New England. Devout followers of John Calvin's teachings, these opponents of the Church of England were the first to question the use of violence as a result of their contact with the Native Americans. While the origins of a colonial peace movement in America can be attributed to the Quakers, the Puritans were the first Europeans to broach the idea of peace in the vast wilderness of North America.

Before the Anabaptists and Quakers set foot in the New World, the intellectual seeds for peace in America were planted first in New England. Religious dissenters in England, who clamored for a purification of the Anglican Church, left the Old World in search of religious toleration. Two groups of Calvinists -- Separatists (Pilgrims) and Non-Separatists (Puritans) -- sailed to America and established distinct settlements in Plymouth and in the back bay of Boston. There they created strong religious communities in which salvation would be marked by knowledge of the bible and public profession of one's faith. A society of visible saints was established, along with a covenant encouraging peaceful relations among neighbors and friends.

The transference of European peace values to the New World thus began with the great Puritan migrations of the 1630's and continued through the Thirty Years' War in Europe later that century. For nearly fifty years, these English followers of John Calvin had been involved in a bitter power struggle to purify the Church of England. They wanted to eliminate all remaining Roman influences. Although the battle had been fought and Catholicism had been defeated in England, little had been done to transform centuries of long-standing religious practices. English monarchs were reluctant to make wholesale changes in matters of religion. They were more determined to maintain their power and did not take kindly to critics of the Anglican Church.

Very early in the 1600's, English King James I summed up his policy regarding religious toleration in the phrase "no bishop, no king." By that, he meant that the enforcement of the bishops' monarchical authority in religion was essential to the maintenance of his own monarchical power. Church and state were now one and the same. James took steps against what he held to be Puritan nonconformity. In 1604, he called a conference of Anglican bishops and leading Puritans at Hampton Court, at which he personally presided and used the full force of his pedantic scholarship against the Puritans; his version of the bible would be the benchmark for Protestant religious teachings in England. The publication of the King James Bible thus placed the full political weight of his power upon those Puritan dissenters challenging his authority as head of the Church of England.

After 1625, Charles I, his son, continued James' oppressive policies against the Puritans. Charles' policies were shaped by the High Church Archbishop of Canterbury, William Laud, who systematically enforced Anglican conformity and deprived even moderate Puritans of their pulpits. Puritans were sometimes brought before the Starr Chamber, long a highly respected administrative court, but now gaining a reputation for high-handedness because it denied the accused the safeguards of the common law. The price for religious freedom was often-times the loss of civil liberties.

During the 1620's and 1630's religious intolerance at home and the Stuart kings' refusal to grant greater political freedoms drove nearly 20,000 Puritan dissidents to the Massachusetts Bay Colony. There they resolved to build a model biblical community, a "city on a hill," which all of Europe could emulate. A few even carried with them the belief that wars and violence jeopardized society's harmonious relationship with God. The Puritan divines, who laid war at the door of man's lusts and who believed that divine law sometimes justified even offensive warfare, held that the justice of a war ought to be, in the words of one of the colony's greatest intellectuals, Cotton Mather, "notoriously Evident and Apparent."[2] Thus, the idea that the justice of a war must be proved exerted a restraining influence on the martial thought and actions of the Puritans. Of course, there would be times when the New World settlers would test that belief in their discourse with the Native Americans, much to the latter's disadvantage.

Perhaps the earliest known opponent of war in America and supporter of justice and equality was Roger Williams, the rebellious Puritan divine who founded the colony of Rhode Island after he was expelled in 1635 from Massachusetts Bay. As the late Harvard professor and authority on Puritanism, Perry Miller, observed, Williams was by no means a saint. He had many rough edges; however, he was brilliant in his own right and certainly filled with righteous indignation relative to matters involving church and state. He was a separatist at heart and found it more comforting preaching among those who had settled in Plymouth. Much to the chagrin of those in charge of the Bay Colony, he had no desire to reform the Anglican Church. While serving as minister to churches in Plymouth and Salem, he publicly denied the right of the civil government to enforce religious tenets and maintained that the colony's land was legally the property of the Native Americans. At a time when English common law determined property rights and Puritan settlers were staking a claim to the land, it is easy to understand why conflict might erupt with the Native Americans. America's first inhabitants did not share European concepts of land ownership and could not fathom how European settlers could erect fences to keep them out.

Paralleling this thinking, it was Williams' attitude toward the Native Americans which made him an opponent of war and defender of equal justice, for he did not acknowledge Puritan ownership of Massachusetts Bay by right of conquest. The men of Massachusetts, because of their theological orientation, required scriptural justification for all their actions. They sanctioned bloody slaughters of the Native Americans on the contrived grounds that the Indians were children of Satan, in whose extermination a solemn God rejoiced.

This religious precept was first tested by the Pilgrims of Plymouth Plantation. In the spring of 1623, despite friendly relations with Wampanoag Chief Massasoit and his tribe, members of the Wessagusset settlement began stealing from other Native Americans. Massachusetts tribal leaders, Wituwaument and Pecksuot, decided to destroy the Pilgrims. When word got out about their plan, the leaders of Plymouth dispatched their military leader, Captain Myles Standish. Short in stature but well-trained in the art of combat, Standish and his men, armed with muskets, arrived at Wessagusset on April 4, 1623. The next day, they met with the Native American leaders and a large contingent of tribesmen inside the settlement's stockade. There, without any warning, Standish and his troops killed five Native Americans, among them Wituwaument and Pecksuot. The rest of the tribesmen were quickly routed and fled. Wituwaument was beheaded and his head taken back to Plymouth where it was put on display at the fort as a warning against future plots.

While the Pilgrims were the first to use force in New England in the name of Christianity, the Non-Separatist Puritans would soon follow suit. In 1635, only five years after the establishment of the Massachusetts Bay Colony, violence erupted between the new settlers and the Native Americans. The most powerful tribe in southern New England, the Pequots, realized that their way of life, and even their future existence, was being threatened by the rapid expansion of white settlements. From 1635 to 1637, the Pequot War took place, a series of intermittent raids by Puritans and Indians on each other's settlements. Finally, in 1637, the Puritans, with superior arms, surrounded a fortified Pequot village and burned it to the ground. Close to four hundred Pequots, mostly women, children, and old men, were burned to death or were shot as they tried to escape; others were hunted down and killed, or sold as slaves. A small number of Pequots survived the war. The result was a growing hatred among the remaining Native American tribes towards the white settlers of New England.

Roger Williams, who had purchased land from the Narraganset Indians to establish the town of Providence, inveighed against the murder of innocents as a gross immorality. He protested vigorously, denouncing the Puritan clergy's "bloody doctrine of persecution for the cause of conscience."[3] He was particularly repulsed when told to forward to Boston the hands of slain Pequots in 1636. Williams insisted that the Native Americans owned North America by virtue of their occupation and that the English must purchase the land if they were to settle it legally. He maintained that the King's grants to the Puritans were invalid; the King could not grant what he did not own. To the dismay of the colony's leaders, Williams was striking at the heart of the Puritans' covenant theology which regarded contracts, including colonial charters, as inviolable.

Residing in the wilderness with the Native Americans after his exile from Massachusetts Bay, Williams learned their language and garnered their complete support. Unlike French philosopher Jean Jacques Rousseau, Williams did not sentimentalize the Native Americans as noble savages. He was wont to insist that as Englishmen "we . . . were ourselves at first wild and savage Britons." In 1654, Williams successfully convinced his fellow colonists that it was far more conducive to use the Bible instead of rifles to win over the hearts and minds of the Native Americans. In avoiding war that year with the Narragansetts, Williams beseeched his fellow Englishmen to "consider how the name of the most holy and Jealous God may be preserved between the clashing of these Two: "The Glorious Conversion of the Indians in New England and the Unnecessary Warrs and cruell Destructin of the Indians in New England." His honest dealings with New England's first inhabitants and abhorrence of bloodshed helped postpone the final battle of extinction until the late 1600's when King Philip's War dealt the final blow.[4]

In striving to establish a Christian social order based on tenets derived from Scripture, North American Puritans proved ambivalent when confronting matters of war and peace. Generally, the Puritan divines wavered between two of Christianity's most durable positions: the just war and the crusade. Most New England clergymen felt comfortable with the just war position despite Williams' own arguments against war. They argued that war was morally justifiable when defensive in nature, authorized by legitimate authority, and carried out as a matter of justice. It proved a convenient rationalization to eliminate or push back those blocking their path to material security while strengthening the growing claim to the state's monopoly of war-making power in the 1600's.

But there were times when the Puritans moved beyond the "just war" position and endorsed military combat, considered a positive good when waged in defense of the True Faith. Literally, Puritans were obedient Christian soldiers. Seeing life as a battle against sin and Satan, Puritans exalted the martial virtues of courage, discipline, honor, and sacrifice as vital to individual saintliness and firm social order. As inert warrior-saints in Christ's army, they looked upon war as the "work of the Lord's revenge," as Connecticut's founder, Thomas Hooker, so casually and bluntly stated.[5]

Although New England Puritans worked diligently to sustain a commonwealth of harmony and peace, they constantly lived in expectation of major violence. Surrounded by the uncertainties of an unfamiliar land, Puritans accepted the resort to arms as a test of their faith; over the seventeenth century, by their win measure they met their test well, successfully eliminating local native resistance in the Pequot War of 1635-37 as well as King Philip's War of 1675-76.

The latter conflict is important to place in context. It was marked by the growing resistance of New England's Native Americans towards the aggressive and expansive land policies of the European settlers; the embers from the Pequot War still simmered in their hearts. In 1675, Metacomet, a Wampanoag chief whom the Puritans called King Philip, entered into an alliance with the Narragansetts and other tribes. When the white settlers continued their practice of establishing settlements on sacred land, Metacomet declared war. At first, Metacomet and his followers successfully outmaneuvered the settlers; they burned or partly destroyed several villages. The tide quickly changed, however, when the Native Americans were soon outnumbered four-to-one and began facing starvation. The end of the war came when a Christian, or "praying" tribesman, murdered Metacomet and scores of his warriors were shipped into slavery in the West Indies.

Of course, at the time, the Puritan divines turned bloodshed into a moral lesson aimed at salvation. Shortly after Philip's war, Increase Mather, father of Cotton, penned his A Brief History of the War with the Indians in New-England (1676). In the second volume of his classic work, The New England Mind, Miller likens Mather's work to "a classical French tragedy with an intelligible theme." What is most telling is that the theme of regeneration filters through Mather's history. The capture of Philip, Mather tells his readers, signified "the turn of Providence towards us in this colony, and against the Enemy in a wonderful manner, from this day forward." Whatever sins his fellow colonists may have committed were absolved by the "wonderful success against the Enemy, which the Lord hath blessed them with, ever since they renewed their Covenant with him." Such renewal of the Covenant had been achieved through the force of arms, not prayer. According to Miller, Mather's analysis of King Philip's War served as a religious awakening, a call to introspection, if you will, one serving the useful purpose of a jeremiad. No wonder Mather cautioned his readers to take notice that "we have good reason to hope that this Day of Trouble is near to an end, if our sins doe not undoe all that hath been wrought for us."[6]

Throughout the seventeenth century Massachusetts Bay's settlers used their religion as a driving force behind conquest. In the process, Puritans found an opportunity to regenerate their souls, their church, and their fortunes. Despite noble intentions, these armor-clad soldiers of Christ, believed that the best way toward individual and social regeneration was by use of sword and musket.[7] Despite the intellectual foundations in support of peace first appearing in New England (best exemplified in the words and deeds of Williams) Puritan ambivalence regarding war and peace was never entirely rectified. It would be the Quakers in the Middle Colonies who would reject this ambivalence.

THE QUAKERS AND NON-VIOLENCE

While the Puritans quelled resistance to their territorial ambitions, England struggled through a bloody revolution and civil war. This battle between the followers of Oliver Cromwell and supporters of the Crown culminated in a limited monarchy, radical republican thought, and religious ferment. Within this ferment of religious awakening in mid-seventeenth century England emerged a group that called itself the First Publishers of Truth. These enthusiasts concluded in the late 1640's that, since Christ revealed Himself in an Inner Light within every person, Christians must help everyone to uncover and live by the spirit dwelling within. Led by the itinerant cobbler George Fox, these religious enthusiasts traveled throughout England in the 1650's, urging listeners to recognize the Christ within them and reject the material wants of the existing social, political, and economic order. Though their enemies called them Quakers – seekers who trembled at the thought of the inner spirit – they called themselves "Friends in Truth," or simply "Friends."

The Quakers were Puritans of the Puritans; they eschewed all worldly show, finding even buttons ostentatious. They found the names of days and months indecently pagan, the polite form "you" in the singular a piece of social hypocrisy, and legal oaths or undertakings, long the bulwark of the jurisprudence system, most impious. Hence, they met for worship on what they called "First Day" rather than the day of the sun god; they addressed another person as "thee" or "thou" in order to promote communal brotherhood; and they took so seriously the Protestant doctrine of the priesthood of the believer that they congregated entirely without a formal ordained ministry. In the Religious Society of Friends, any worshipper who felt the spirit move within him or her might testify in what other sects would call a "sermon." Friends genuinely understood the impossibility of forcing anyone to see the "inner light" or coercing people to accept faith. They would abstain entirely from force, particularly from war, and would go their own way in Christian peace.

By the 1660's, during a wave of persecutions initiated by the restored Stuart monarch, Charles II, the Quakers officially accepted pacifism as part of the "ever-present, ever-teaching Spirit of Christ." In practice, pacifism served to bridge the inward and outward emphases of the Quaker way. Quakers sought a personal peace that was "purely inward, subjective, unilateral, if you like—a search for peace of mind."[8] Itinerant Quaker ministers both lived pacifism for the sake of inner peace and publicly proclaimed it as the working way to Christ's earthly kingdom.

Almost from the start of the sect, Quakers settled in different parts of the New World. Their influence on the American peace movement during the late seventeenth century and throughout the eighteenth century was profound. There were other pacifist sects, of course. John Woolman, a noted American Quaker of the eighteenth century, recorded in his journal the case of a Mennonite who slept in the woods rather than receive hospitality from a slaveholder. But the Quakers were more numerous, and, as Englishmen, they were more in touch with the English majority in the colonies than continental Pietists could hope to be.

The Quakers insisted stubbornly on resisting what Roger Williams called "that body-killing, soule-killing, and State-killing doctrine of not permitting, but persecuting all other consciences and wayes of worship...." It is quite fair to argue that the sectarian peace movement in American history is largely the story of the Quaker testimony to peace. Wherever they took up residence in the New World, they opposed—for reasons of conscience—militia drills, oath taking, jury service, war, and religious taxes. In numerous cases, they spoke out against defense appropriations. One Quaker, Samuel Carpenter, stated candidly—"The King of

England knows the judgment of Quakers in this case...But if we must be forced to do it, I suppose we shall rather choose to suffer than to do it...."[9]

Frequently, their commitment, exemplified by Carpenter's actions, cost them their property. Sometimes, they paid with their lives as in Puritan Massachusetts where some were banished, tortured, and then executed in the late 1650's, because the experimental nature of their Inner Light contradicted the scriptural bases from which the Puritan government drew its authority. Puritan divines did not like Quakers, despite their own ambivalent attitude toward war and peace. During King Philip's War, for instance, the General Court of Plymouth complained to Charles II that the Quakers "took in many of our enemies that were flying before us, thereby making profit of our expense of blood and treasure."[10]

The story was different, however, in other colonies. In Rhode Island, Quakers were granted political autonomy—a result of the Puritan dissenter Roger Williams' commitment to toleration. Meanwhile, in Virginia, they were first persecuted and then tolerated. The same held true in Maryland, but not before the earliest recorded case of persecution for refusing to bear arms occurred in 1658 when a Quaker, Richard Keene, rejected military training and was fined the sum of 61 pounds and 15 shillings. The sheriff collecting the fine drew his sword, hit him on the shoulder and shouted, "You dog. I could find it in my heart to split your brains."[11]

The attempt among Friends to gain a colonial foothold with greater autonomy finally succeeded in 1681, when a well-born Oxford student turned Quaker convert named William Penn settled a family debt with King Charles II. He willingly accepted the proprietorship of a huge tract of land in the lower Delaware Valley, which he called "Penna." With other enthusiasts, Penn hoped to establish there a "holy experiment" in the working Quaker way. His penurious instincts also led to his accepting Charles' offer in the expectation that this proprietorship would line his pockets with gold. Apart from their pacifist ways, Quakers were an industrious and enterprising sort.

Pennsylvania, which Penn preferred to call the "Holy Experiment," became home to many different settlers. The colony's leader invited honest, industrious settlers to come in exchange for religious toleration, representative rule, and, most importantly, cheap land. Apart from the Native Americans, settlers from all over poured in – Quakers from England, Wales, and Ireland; Scotch-Irish Presbyterians; Swiss and German Protestants from the continent; and Catholics and Jews from various European countries. A small number of Africans also settled in the colony before slavery was legally recognized there in 1700 – thus calling into question how "holy" was Penn's experiment.

Developing an intense religiosity anchored by a body of beliefs that were socially conservative, politically radical, and commercially adventuresome, Penn established a model Christian community that operated on a voluntary social consensus and without physical coercion. He conceived of his colony as a profit-making enterprise, but also as a "Holy Experiment" in which Friends could test their visions of "brotherly love." Penn and his brethren viewed both man himself and society as perfectible. Religious strife, they believed, could be ended in a society where all were free to worship as they pleased. Social conflict would be eased by a representative government in which the general citizenry participated. And war could be banished, they thought, by society's refusal to wage it. Thus in support of peace, order, and popular self-determination, Penn drafted in 1682 a constitutional Frame of Government that provided unusually broad representative government and extensive religious toleration. Included in this proposal was a sincere effort to accommodate the natives' needs.

The focal point of Penn's experiment was the colony's relationship to the Native Americans, presenting an alternative to the violence of the past. Penn was infamous in England for his nonconformist views (inspired mainly by radical Whigs like Algernon Sidney), and he wrote of his beliefs about the Native Americans before arriving in the province. The Quaker belief "that God within each man" met a counterpart in the Indians' concept of the "Great Spirit" helped pave the way for future peaceful relations between the Quakers and Native Americans.

In Penn's estimation, war with the Native Americans was out of the question; he believed that justice and reason could settle any dispute. For him, peace was an extension of justice, an extension which should be embraced by all earthly beings. In an "Address to the American Indians," November 1682, Penn stated unequivocally that "We are met on the broad pathway of good faith and good will, so that no advantage is to be taken either side, but all to be openness, brotherhood[,] and love...." His friendship with the Native Americans was not bonded by a chain, "for the rain may rust it, or a tree may fall and break it." Instead, he considered the Native American "as the same flesh and blood with the Christians, and the same as if one man's body were to be divided into two parts." In turn, the Native Americans were impressed with the fact that he insisted on purchase of the land "as being an act to which both parties must actively consent." They felt the final price to be fair enough to remove their claims and, "of great importance to the future of the treaty, did not feel cheated by the usual tricks of bribery or redone maps."[12]

However, purchase was not to be the sole reason for what was to become known as the "Great Treaty"; friendship played a vital part as well. The treaty, signed with the Delaware Indians at Shackamaxon in 1683, was a working reality for nearly seventy years. The famous French political theorist, Voltaire, wrote, "It was the only treaty made by the settlers with the Indians that were never sworn to, and the only one that was never broken." The commonwealth remained non-violent even though "harassing and exterminating" wars were occurring between Native Americans and colonists in nearly all other colonies. In part, the treaty included the following: "(1) that all paths should be open and free to both Christians and Indians; (2) that the doors of the Christians' houses should be open to the Indian and the house of the Indian open to the Christians, and they should make each other welcome as friends; (3) that the Christians should not believe any false rumors or reports of the Indians, nor the Indians believe any such rumors or reports of the Christians, but should first come as brethren to inquire of each other."[13]

Through patience and understanding, not hatred and bloodshed, Quakers and Native Americans carved out a record of peaceable relations that remains a model in the annals of migratory peoples. Nearly 12,000 English Friends flowed across historically Native American land in the last years of the seventeenth century, yet conflict was kept to a minimum and violence was rare. As testimony to its commitment to peaceful relations with its Native American neighbors, the Society of Friends enacted its own guidelines entitled, "Friendly Association for Gaining and Preserving Peace with the Indians by Pacific Measures."

To a considerable extent, Penn and his religious followers deserve a fair amount of credit for this achievement. The Friends' doctrine of non-violence was a natural extension of their belief in social justice as well as respect for Native American rights and culture. Lest one forget, however, Penn and his brethren depended mightily upon a friendly and reciprocal indigenous response.

Although Penn continued to maintain that working peace must be organized and institutionalized in social forms, his "holy experiment" was not entirely successful in this regard. After his death in 1718, the colony of Pennsylvania experienced new difficulties as an influx of Scotch-Irish settlers swept into the colony demanding more of the Native Americans' lands. By the 1740's, Quaker leaders faced strong new demands from the family proprietors, imperial authorities, and non-Quaker colonists for more aggressive action in the back country against the French and Native Americans. At first, they tried to reduce the pressure by declining to vote tax monies specifically for imperial wars, but agreeing to contribute funds in general "for the king's use," and authorizing voluntary enlistment in the militia. Their equivocation bore all the earmarks of a classic dilemma: an attempt to reconcile their sectarian refusal to bear arms with their worldly desire to maintain a legitimate government in the physical defense of its citizens.

The failure to reconcile religious conviction and political reality finally came to a head when the outbreak of the French and Indian War, or Seven Years' War as it was called in Europe, precipitated an irresolvable crisis. Between 1689 and 1748, France and Great Britain engaged in a long and protracted war. The fighting occurred on and off throughout these years. The two nations fought for control of the seas and colonial possessions. North America was only one of several prizes the two combatants hoped to win. The decisive worldwide struggle finally broke out in 1756. The conflict resulted when the British colonies in North America began expanding into the Ohio territory and Great Lakes where they clashed with French settlements.

The French defeat of General Braddock's forces, thereby exposing the province's western frontier to attacks by hostile Native American tribes, presented a dilemma for Quakers living in Virginia and Pennsylvania. The Virginia Assembly immediately instituted more stringent militia regulations. The Act of May 1756 stated that if the quota for the state militia was not met by voluntary enlistment, a ballot would be taken up among single able-bodied men to select every twentieth male for active service. At the Virginia Friends Yearly Meeting in June 1756, a committee was appointed to address what steps would be taken in dealing with the authorities. Previously, seven young members of the Cedar Creek Monthly Meeting had been arrested for failing to comply with the new militia act. A decision among Virginia Friends was reached to collect money for Quaker conscripts to assist them and to press for their release.

For Pennsylvania Friends, the debate within their colony's assembly also reflected just how troubling the issue of conscription, war taxes, and exemption by payment had become. Pressured by imperial authorities and an anti-pacifist Assembly faction headed by Benjamin Franklin, a group of Quaker assemblymen, led by the vociferous Isaac Norris, supported a war tax as compatible with their commitment to peace. Herein was the contentious issue involving matters of civil authority and individual conscience. Their action led to the demise of the Quakers' political unity and policy-making effectiveness. Spurred by dissidents like John Churchman and John Woolman, a faction of Friends attacked the war levy and demanded the withdrawal of all conscientious Quakers from the Assembly. In June 1756, six Quakers therefore quit the Assembly in demonstration of their Christian peace commitment against imperial authority. As one Friend stated—"I found it best for me to refuse paying demands on my estate which went to pay the expenses of war; and although my part might appear at best a drop in the ocean, yet the ocean, I considered, was made up of many drops."[14]

The Philadelphia Yearly Meeting, the strongest coordinating body among Friends in the colonies, reinforced the new pacifist militancy by cautioning its members against holding any public office within the warring state. The Meeting also urged Friends to respect their peace testimony at the risk of state confiscation of their property. In toughening their pacifism, Quakers intended to employ pacifism for the sake of greater social justice. Though standing apart for the first time from provincial politics, Pennsylvania Quakers formed the Friendly Association in 1756 as a neutral mediating agency between warring natives and colonists. This represented the initial step in what became a Quaker tradition of acting as reconcilers between various North American native tribes and European colonists.

JOHN WOOLMAN: AMERICA'S FIRST PEACE AND JUSTICE HERO

While Pennsylvania Quakers intended to employ pacifism for the sake of social justice and mediation, a simple tailor from Mount Holly, New Jersey, actually carried it out. John Woolman was one of a number of Friends who refused to pay taxes levied for the Indian Wars in 1759. Woolman summarized the problem quite compellingly: "To refuse the active payment of a Tax which our society generally paid was exceedingly disagreeable, but to do a thing contrary to my conscience appeared yet more dreadful."[15] Woolman, as did other Friends, found the negative effects of war overwhelming, despicable, and sinful:

"Being thus fully convinced, and feeling an increasing desire to live in the spirit of peace, I have often been sorrowfully affected with thinking on the unquiet spirit in which wars are generally carried on, and with the miseries of many fellow-creatures engaged therein; some suddenly destroyed; some wounded, and after much pain remaining cripples; some deprived of all their outward substance and reduced to want; and some carried into captivity."[16]

Woolman was, by far, one of the wisest and most prescient representatives of Quakerism. He is considered one of America's earliest social reformers, an individual who symbolized the peace movement's true objective: the attainment of justice and equality through non-violence. In his analysis, violence and wars were bred by the spirit of possessiveness and the lust for riches. Appetites for profits are the seeds of war which may quickly ripen. "The rising up of a desire to obtain wealth," he wrote, "is the beginning. This desire being cherished moves to action; and riches thus gotten please self; and while self has a life in them, it desires to have them defended." This identification of wealth-seeking with war and violence and his appeal to conscience caused Woolman to anticipate the Marxist interpretation of war on the one hand and Thoreau's critique of materialism on the other: "Oh! that we who declare against wars...may examine our foundation and motives in holding great estates! May we look upon our treasures...and try whether the seeds of war have any nourishment in these our possessions, or not."[17] He was one of many Quakers who attempted to achieve Christ's peace without violence.

Woolman's concept of peace was based on just social relationships and was a clear example of the Quaker ethos that pervaded the religious Anglo-American peace societies of the early nineteenth century. Its enlightenment ideas helped inspire subsequent social reform movements such as women's rights, temperance, mental health, and the anti-slavery program. Woolman's pacifism expressed a faith in rational and evolutionary progress based on the application of the absence of conflict to social organization. His liberal confidence in the benign power of peace—a view which would be shared by nineteenth-century reformers like Adin Ballou, Josiah Warren, and others—reflected the importance of social justice. Wars, Woolman believed, came about because some people had too much and wanted more, while other persons had not even the decencies of life.

Woolman's pacifism was also tied to an implicit humanitarianism opposed to slavery. In colonial America, Woolman was not the first Friend to condemn the evils of slavery; as early as 1688, the Quakers of Germantown, Pennsylvania, spoke out against it, denouncing the owning and selling of human beings as property. But it was not until the mid-1700s, as the institutionalized system of slavery became embedded in southern culture and rationalized in some quarters of northern thinking, that Quakers such as Woolman took a more aggressive stand. In the 1750's Woolman emerged as a leading crusader on behalf of human rights and social justice. He journeyed through the colonies trying to persuade Quakers to free their slaves and educate them. He kept a careful record of his trips in his now famous journal.

Urging Friends to socialize their faith, Woolman argued for support of the poor, defense of Indians' rights, and an end to slavery. He expressed his feelings in <u>Some Considerations on the Keeping of Negroes</u>. By 1780, thanks in large measure to Woolman's efforts, almost no Friends in the United States held slaves. Woolman's commitment to the concept of a compassionate religion with disinterested service to the lowly was concretely expressed by his life and his writings. He also preached the Christian virtue of a just distribution of man's worldly goods. Woolman was exceptional for the emphasis he put on the social implications of Quakerism. When the philosophers of the European Enlightenment idealized the Pennsylvania Quakers for their humanitarianism, their condemnations of excessive riches and vanity, their pacifism, and their simple morality, they could have pointed to John Woolman as the outstanding model for their convictions. If William Penn was the first authentic peace hero in Anglo-American history, John Woolman must be considered the colonies' first native born peace champion. His Journal is still read and admired today as one of best examples for implementing peace as social justice.

QUAKERS AND THE REVOLUTION: CONSCIENCE VERSUS CIVIL AUTHORITY

The views of Penn and Woolman, in particular, and the Quakers, in general, on behalf of non-violence, were tempered by the appeal to arms in 1776. Even though many Americans disapproved of the idea of war in theory, the majority believed that—when peaceful efforts to address wrongs had obviously failed—a resort to sword and musket was justifiable and necessary. After listening to discussions about the structure of the empire, taxation, representation, and the rights of British subjects, patriots followed leaders like Patrick Henry, Samuel Adams, and Thomas Jefferson who argued "the natural right of man to resist tyrannical authority." The much despised Stamp Act of 1765 and other Parliamentary attempts to raise money from the colonies in order to help defray the costs of the French and Indian War furthered the independence debate. While a majority of colonists did not quibble over paying their fair share of the costs, it was the way in which acts were imposed without consent that ruffled feathers. Thus, the natural right of revolution was now carried out to its logical conclusion.[18]

The process of withdrawal from politics and renewal of the peace testimony, which Woolman and other mid-century Quaker radicals had initiated, was also upheld mainly as a consequence of Friends' experiences during the American Revolution. American Friends, according to peace historian Peter Brock, opposed the war that broke out between colonists and Great Britain in 1775, which created a dilemma for them: "In the first place, as pacifists they could not participate...in the fighting—on either side. But a second, and complicating, factor existed in their war resistance...Quakers...regarded loyalty to the powers that be [government] as a religious duty which they must uphold even at the cost of suffering."[19] A few Tory sympathizers were members of the society, but the overwhelming majority of Quakers strove to uphold a position of non-violence neutrality during the years of conflict. As one of them put it, "It was impossible for a true Quaker to be either a Whig or a Tory, for they implied opposite parties, and both believed in war, but Friends did not."[20]

Conscientious Objection involved many different forms of resistance. When, for the first time, Pennsylvania enacted a compulsory draft in March of 1777, there was no region under the new government's rule where conscription was not enforced. Quakers were unqualified in their opposition to compulsory service and even if they had the money to pay for their exemption, refused to do so. Authorities seized property from resisters who chose not to pay. Fines often exceeded the amount that had been required by statute. A number of draft-age Quaker conscripts were severely punished for their personal resistance, and many draftees were held in jail for days or months.

One of the foremost Quaker opponents of the Anglo-American conflict was Anthony Benezet. Born of French Huguenots, raised in England, and settling in America in 1731, Benezet had opened a school for African Americans in Philadelphia in 1750. He also wrote one of the earliest pacifist treatises in American history. In Thoughts on the Nature of War (1750), he condemned war as "the premeditated and determined destruction of human beings, of creatures originally formed after the image of God." In 1763, when British and colonial forces were preparing to launch an attack against the Native Americans allied with the French in New York, Benezet implored military leaders "from the nobility and humanity of his heart that [they] would condescend to use all moderate measures…to prevent that…cruel effusion of blood…that must fill the breast of so many helpless people should an Indian war be once entered upon." Following Woolman's lead, Benezet held that greed provoked warfare and that it was the duty of all Christians to reconcile their governments to the "divine government, the fundamental law which is love." Preaching and practicing tax refusal, he badgered British and American military officers to reflect upon their actions, and demanded that Christians act in unison against the war menace. At best, Benezet hoped that Thoughts would demonstrate the utter futility of war. At least, he felt that it would "lessen, if not remove, any prejudice which our Friends' refusal to join in any military operation may have occasioned" among other colonists of a more patriotic persuasion.[21]

Gradually, in the wake of human suffering and destruction, Benezet reached two radical conclusions: First, war was "too evil to originate in the will of an all-loving and all-caring God"; and second, it was "too destructive to remain the sole concern of traditional peace sects." Thus moving beyond Quaker meetinghouses, Benezet distributed tracts, leaflets, and notices and urged audiences everywhere to act directly against the war. Throughout the war, he never abandoned the hope that Christian peoples would someday turn swords into plowshares; he never underestimated the magnitude of the cause or the obstacles before it. It was "a fundamental Truth," he maintained with certitude, "that Christ overcame with patient suffering, leaving us an example...that we should follow his steps; ...very few indeed are willing to be as pilgrims and strangers in their passage thro' life."[22]

Observing Benezet's stand, Quakers were precluded from assisting either of the conflicting armies with their labor. For example, farmers who volunteered horses and carts for military employment became liable for disciplinary action by their local meeting. The tax issue continued to cause much soul searching among Friends. During the war, the question—to pay or not to pay?—was debated vigorously. Many Friends refused to pay the war taxes; some advocated a complete tax boycott. Further complications arose when the American authorities imposed an oath of loyalty. Though the government recognized Quakers' long-standing objections to judicial oaths, and were ready to agree to the substitution of a mere affirmation, the Society forbade its members to take the Test.[23] The very practice of Conscientious Objection earmarked the doctrine of Quaker pacifism. It was born in religious practice and carried out in life-affirming ways. The Revolutionary War made Conscientious Objection an effective philosophical instrument later known as passive non-resistance.

Most Quakers respected the sect's traditional injunctions against the bearing of arms or the payment of soldier-substitutes, but their conscientious behavior came at a heavy price. Inflamed local patriots executed two Friends in Pennsylvania. In another instance, Continental Army soldiers tied muskets to the backs of fourteen Quaker "non-combatants" at the Valley Forge encampment in an attempt to force them to bear arms. George Washington, disconcerted by such treatment, later ordered their release and sent them home. One North Carolina Quaker received forty lashes for his refusal to shoulder a musket; numerous draft-age Friends were arrested, abused physically, and jailed throughout the rebel colonies for refusing to serve in the Continental Army.

The Revolutionary authorities also reacted quickly to the Quaker position of non-resistance. Conscientious Objectors were imprisoned, sometimes for as long as two years. Active opponents of the war were, on occasion, roughly handled. In 1777, a group of wealthy Friends, falsely accused of treason, were deported to Virginia. Members of the Society suffered most heavily as a result of the financial penalties for resistance to wartime decrees. According to Brock, their goods "were distrained and their property requisitioned to the value of over one hundred thousand pounds. This seemed to confirm Woolman's message: worldly possessions and Quaker peaceableness had now proved incompatible in fact as well as in theory."[24]

Quaker pacifism did not sit well with British soldiers either. Their neutral position in the conflict was no solace to British authorities, who considered them disloyal to the Crown. Thomas Lamborn, a Quaker farmer from Chester County, Pennsylvania, saw his farm plundered by British troops when they were in the area. According to the <u>Friends Meeting at New Garden</u>: "They took everything available; almost everything that could be carried or driven away, beating the wheat battens against the posts in the barn to get the grain out, then throwing back the balance into the mow, saying 'there, Lamborn may have that.' At another time he was plowing in the field, when some officers of the [British] army detached the horses from the plow and unceremoniously appropriated them to the use of the army."[25] Lamborn suffered the loss of his farm, which had to be sold by the sheriff at a low price. Happily, it was bought by a non-Quaker who returned it to Lamborn after paying off the debts.

The continuing tension between peace-making Quakers and war-making authorities moved Friends to withdraw further from public politics and into a deeper self-contained society. The growing Quaker emphasis on group discipline and self-purification ultimately led to a less active political stance on the part of the Friends. By the conclusion of the American Revolution, as Charles DeBenedetti points out, the core of peace reform centered in what came to be called the Historic Peace Churches—those Pennsylvania Anabaptist remnants (Mennonites and Church of the Brethren) and the 50,000 Quakers who were scattered in nearly eight meetinghouses throughout the colonies. Consequently, Quaker influence upon peace thought among the general populace became less active and more restricted.

The Quaker experience in a major war and the principle of Conscientious Objection received its first true test during America's struggle for independence. This challenge to the war- making powers of government would become part of the tradition of democratic dissent throughout the nation's history. With respect to military service, the Society of Friends was the first major group in American history requiring its members not only to refuse to take up arms but also to deny payment of a fine for failure to appear at muster. Friends were insistent in their conviction that no person should have to pay for doing what one considered to be right. The "sufferings" attached to refusal to serve—excessive fees attached to property taxes or imprisonment if a man did not own land—were considered a small price to pay for upholding a clear conscience.

Although Quaker peace activism no longer would command center stage, the American Revolution itself—if viewed as a revolt against old-fashioned imperialism based on the supremacy of the commercial class—promoted the ideals of peace and justice. The troubles of mid-seventeenth century England had bred antimilitarism into colonial bones; the observed behavior of contemporary

European professional armies and English imperial garrisons served to strengthen the feeling. In 1776, for example, Thomas Jefferson articulated a long-held belief that the establishment of a standing army and the King's attempt "to render the Military independent of a superior to the Civil Power" were high among those royal "injuries and usurpations, all having in direct object the establishment of an absolute Tyranny over these States." The colonists had fought a war to rid themselves of the specter of permanent armies.[26]

The necessity of fighting a long war for independence seemed to increase, rather than diminish, American opposition to military power and influence. A significant legacy of the war was suspicion and antipathy between civilian and military, the subject of a very thorough study by the late historian Arthur A. Ekirch, Jr. In The Civilian and the Military, he points out that new state constitutions customarily asserted, along with the right of a people to bear arms in their own defense, the danger of standing armies in time of peace, the superiority of the civil over the military authority, the right to freedom from troops being quartered in private dwellings, and prohibitions against military appropriations for longer than one or two years. When the Articles of Confederation proved ineffective in uniting the thirteen independent states, it was replaced by a Constitution that embodied the antimilitaristic scruples of the common people.

The Constitution sought to limit possible military dominion by enforcing a separation of powers on all questions of peace and war. Only the Legislative Branch – the Congress – would have the power to declare war. Troops were not to be quartered with citizens in time of peace, and the civilian arm of the government was to control the army. The president was to be its commander-in-chief, and Congress was to renew its appropriations each session. Thus, among the principles of 1776 was the reaffirmation of the Anglo-American tradition that military rule was at odds with the ideals of a democratic society. Individual freedom, representative government, and limits on the powers of the national state or executive were all accepted as principles that would be endangered if the military authority should take command or precedence in civil affairs. These very principles had been codified in the first ten amendments to the Constitution, the Bill of Rights.

DR. BENJAMIN RUSH'S VISION FOR PEACE

With the adoption of the Constitution, plans to promote peace were given a wider audience in the early 1790's. One of the most captivating proposals put forth was by Benjamin Rush, the Philadelphia Quaker physician and former Continental Army Surgeon-General. Rush, one of the signers of the Declaration of Independence, was a fascinating figure who blended evangelical Christianity with a scientific intelligence that placed him in the company of Benjamin Franklin and Thomas Jefferson. After completing his medical training at the University of Edinburgh, he became one of the best known doctors in America. He was an enthusiastic reformer who championed the causes of public education, women's rights, temperance, abolitionism, and, most especially, world peace. He was particularly outspoken on the need for an inclusive, democratic intellectual life. "The business of education," observed this distinguished physician, "has acquired a new complexion by the independence of our country. The form of government we have assumed has created a new class of duties to every American."[27] He was also a humanitarian who took the idea of peace seriously as part of one's civic responsibility.

Writing in 1793, Rush embodied Quaker ideals by urging the formulation of a national peace office under the direction of a man who was a "genuine republican and sincere Christian, for the principles of republicanism and Christianity are no less friendly to universal and perpetual peace, than they are to universal liberty." It represented the first such proposal in United States history. Aiming to substitute a culture of peace for the glamour of war—a problem perplexing peace advocates even to this day—Rush believed the peace office should establish throughout the country free schools that would promulgate pacific Christian principles, work to eliminate all capital punishment laws, and seek the elimination of military parades, titles, and uniforms.[28]

In Rush's estimation, all militia laws should be repealed because they generated idleness and vice, thus producing the wars they were said to prevent. Military titles fed vanity and created ideas in the mind that lessened the true folly and misery of war. In the lobby of his proposed office, Rush suggested that painted representations of all the military instruments of death be displayed, along with a plethora of art examples depicting human skulls, broken bones, unburied and putrefying dead bodies, hospitals overcrowded with wounded soldiers, villages on fire, rivers dyed with blood, and vast plains without trees or fences in the backdrop of the ruins of deserted farm houses. Above these graphic scenes Rush suggested that the following words, "NATIONAL GLORY," be inscribed in red characters to represent human blood.

QUASI—WAR WITH FRANCE AND DR. GEORGE LOGAN

Rush's was a noble and enduring vision, but one that was surely ahead of its time. While Rush was formulating his plan for a peace office, the 1790's were anything but tranquil for the new nation. A strong spirit of nationalism arose marked by the glorification of the Revolutionary War, open conflict between Native Americans and settlers pushing their way endlessly into the Northwest, and French Revolutionary tensions in Europe. It was actually the deteriorating situation in U.S. diplomatic relations with both France and Great Britain that caused the greatest alarm among the supporters of peace. During the so-called Quasi-War Crisis, President John Adams, out of dedication to peace, carefully and consciously resisted a widespread belligerent public temperament by dispatching a minister plenipotentiary to France. Yet Adams' actions had been preceded by the individual efforts of one Pennsylvania Quaker, Dr. George Logan. It stood as the last visible peacemaking effort in eighteenth century America.

Logan, who had been born into a wealthy, strict Quaker family, did not become a prominent peace proponent until the age of forty-five. His early education took place in England, and despite his own interest in medicine, he was forced to return to Philadelphia where he entered the family business. While serving an apprenticeship in the counting house, he read medical books and, in 1779, graduated with a medical degree from the University of Edinburgh. Although a Quaker, Logan did not object to the notion of "defensive war." He joined the Pennsylvania militia and, in 1791, was separated from the Society of Friends. Feeling ostracized and personally motivated by his conflict with Friends, he undertook his own one-man crusade for peace in the late 1790's.

A self-appointed envoy, Republican gentleman, and friend of France, Logan set out for Paris in June 1798. Despite the bewildering domestic forces opposed to peace—patriotic resentment at foreign plundering of U.S. commerce, the political rivalry of Federalists and Anti-federalists, both of whom stood to gain by war for different political reasons, and the economic interests of land-hungry Westerners whom hostilities might profit—Logan, after raising money by selling some of his land and armed with a note of introduction from Jefferson, visited numerous French officials and discussed the situation with French Minister Talleyrand. Before he left, France agreed to reduce its attacks on American ships, free some captured American seamen, and welcome an official U.S. envoy.

Despite the success of his mission, Logan was greeted with official contempt upon his return. Federalist newspapers denounced the peacemaker as a wily intriguer, ready to sacrifice the honor of his country to advance the pro-French party of Jefferson. On January 30, 1799, the Federalist majority in Congress passed the Logan Act, making it illegal for a private citizen to conduct diplomatic negotiations without prior authorization from the American government. (Interestingly, this law, still in force, has never been paralleled by one making it a crime for a private citizen to do what he can by propaganda or by selling munitions to stir up war with a foreign state). But Logan's initiative encouraged President Adams to persist in seeking a peaceful resolution of the crisis, and war between the United States and France, much to the disappointment of leading Federalists, was successfully averted.

CONCLUSION

Attempts to foster an ideology of peaceful coexistence began with the first inhabitants and culminated with the sectarian war resisters during the Revolutionary Period. Yet even though an antimilitarist bias had spread through the populace, the political leaders of the New Nation immediately pleaded for a small regular army and the strengthening of coastal defenses. Consequently, the door became permanently shut on a national peace office while the windows of Congress remained open to allow the passage of America's first defense bill, the Uniform Militia Act of 1792.[29]

Still, the contributions colonial Quakers and other pioneers made on behalf of peace were important. No other government would permit so many men of religious conscience to avoid military service. No other country would erect so many constraints against a peacetime standing army, though one would be established. And no other people defined their national identity so firmly with the mission of redeeming the world for peace.

Colonial peace activism claimed some remarkable leaders in Roger Williams, William Penn, John Woolman, Anthony Benezet, Benjamin Rush, and George Logan. They helped shape the rise of the sectarian peace movement in America. Even though Quakers were instrumental in seeking to achieve Christ's peace without violence, the Society of Friends emerged from the years of the war a rather different body from the one it had been on the eve of the Revolution. By the end of the eighteenth century, the radical spirit which had regenerated the Quaker witness to peace as a strictly sectarian endeavor was forever laid to rest. In its place would be a humanitarian search for peace dependent upon private volunteer societies without religious affiliation. The new peace movement that developed, though keeping alive the sectarian peace vision, would be characterized by nonsectarian interests showing universal concern for human beings as Christian creatures. It would continue to address issues of social justice as well as peace, becoming more diverse in the process.

More importantly, the new movement would be characterized by its diversity. The emergence of female activists would highlight the changing stature of the movement. One cannot but help wonder how the sectarian peace movement would have progressed if women had played a role in it.[30] Throughout the Colonial and Revolutionary Periods women were noticeably absent in the struggle for peace and justice. All that would begin to change in the years after the War of 1812.

CHAPTER TWO

THE PEACE REFORM IN ANTEBELLUM AMERICA

> ....Whenever allusion is made to that distinction which American prejudice has made between those who wear a darker skin then we do, I feel ashamed for my Country, ashamed for the Church, but the time is coming when such 'respect for persons' will no more be known in our land, and the children of the Lord will think no more of a difference in the color of the skin than that of the hair or eyes.
>
> Angelina Grimke to Sarah Douglass, April 3, 1837

INTRODUCTION

While preparing for an upcoming convention of antislavery women Angelina Grimke and her sister, Sarah, urged their African American female friends to attend the Anti-Slavery meeting in New York City in 1837. Angelina and Sarah were born to a wealthy aristocratic slaveholding family in the early 1790s. Eventually rejecting slavery and their Episcopal upbringing, they found in Quakerism a means through which they could express their peace and justice activism. The Grimke sisters spoke out against slavery in cities from New York and the north under the auspices of the American Anti-Slavery Society. In the process, they encountered intense hostility and criticism. But they persisted at their own expense. Despite the harsh truth that racial prejudice would be difficult to bear, Angelina still encouraged her African American female companions to attend the convention and help draft documents pertaining to their race. Yet Angelina's letter to Sarah Douglass of Philadelphia represented more than a call to end slavery; it was an extension of her own nonviolent beliefs that peace was closely tied to the struggle for social justice and women's rights.

The search for peace and justice found new avenues of expression as the nation began to mature in the early years of a new century. In spite of the establishment of a new constitutional republic with imperial ambitions, a more organized peace movement, largely characterized by Christian principles, emerged. Breaking the bonds of its earlier heritage of sectarianism the early nineteenth century peace movement was inspired by a host of other humanitarian crusades. Despite the conservatism of many peace societies to join other social reforms the movement found useful allies in women's rights, the abolitionist cause, the organization of factory workers, and utopian communities. It would decidedly broaden its focus on such matters as social justice, not just abolishing war or refusal to fight. But before it could organize itself into a coordinated movement it had to wait until the second war with Great Britain was concluded.

OPPOSITION TO THE WAR OF 1812

No sooner had President Jefferson entered his second term in office when Anglo-American relations took a turn for the worse.[1] The young nation soon faced an agricultural depression, which along with Napoleon's military success in Europe, led to differences between Washington and London. These differences became magnified over issues such as British aid to Native American tribes in the northwest and American exchange of goods with France.

The darkening diplomatic climate sparked anxious policy debate at home. Northeastern merchants, particularly in New England, were extremely concerned about revenues. They were explicit in their warnings that a war with the powerful British navy would destroy American commercial prosperity. Federalist politicians complained that the Republicans' anti-British policies catered to Napoleon's imperial ambitions and threatened the American republic's independence and stability. New England clergymen, swayed as much by commercial pressures as by theological beliefs, criticized Washington's recognition of the Napoleonic regime. Despite these protests, domestic critics had little effect upon Republican policymakers. Yet, they did succeed in laying the basis for the formation of a full-scale anti-war movement that appeared in June 1812, when the United States declared war on Britain over the impressments of American sailors and began making preparations for the invasion of Canada.

Opposition to the war at home was as vitriolic and widespread as any movement in the new nation's brief history. Indeed, the noted historian Samuel Eliot Morison argued that the War of 1812 was "the most unpopular war that this country has ever waged, not even excepting the Vietnam conflict."[2] Although support for the war came mostly from the South and West, that support quickly dissipated as anti-war advocates, mainly from New England, began to enlist numerous followers throughout the nation.

Thirty-four anti-war Federalists, for instance, incensed for being outvoted in the House of Representatives, circulated a widely-read protest. Spurred on by the indomitable and vigorously acerbic Josiah Quincy, a New Englander with deep Puritan roots of self-righteousness and self-indignation, presented their own reply to President James Madison's call for war against Great Britain. For these representatives, war was an immoral choice. Many Americans agreed, doubting the justification of another war with England. Commercial New Englanders, fearing trade would be ruined, strongly opposed a younger generation of politicians clamoring for national self-assertion. Others, more reform-minded and influenced by a surge of humanitarianism and equalitarianism, feared that war would encourage expansionists to ignore moral crusades against slavery and the conquest of Native Americans.

To members of the peace Churches, the war brought confrontation with militia statutes, though most states provided for commutation by monetary payment. When some Quakers refused to pay commutation fees or fines, their property was seized and those who had no property were sometimes jailed. In this regard little had changed since the Revolutionary War.

Pressed by the war, Quakers, in particular, developed a keener sense of personal responsibility for society's violence. In his important survey, The Peace

Reform in American History, Charles DeBenedetti recounts the tale of a free black Quaker farmer from New Jersey. This notable individual, who subsisted from the produce he sold to workers at a nearby iron factory, stopped his trade when he found out that the shop was casting cannon for war service. This simple act of "heroism" reflected the deepening integration of personal witness and social commitment characterizing the Society of Friends' activities throughout the nineteenth century.

At the same time, as Quakers clung to their peace witness in the face of varying wartime pressures, mainstream American churches disagreed about the righteousness of America's "second War of Independence." While Baptists and Presbyterians supported Madison's war with Britain, Congregationalists condemned the war as an attack on Protestant England on behalf of "Napoleonic satanism," and millennialists on all sides "argued whether the crisis signaled divine punishment or a positive challenge for spiritual renewal." Aggravating internal division over the war, the churches' controversy encouraged American peace negotiators at Ghent to seek as quickly as possible an acceptable and diplomatically permissible solution to ending the hostilities.[3]

Widespread political opposition also proved troublesome to the first-term Madison administration. Massachusetts and other northeastern states opposed the expansionist policies of the War Hawks (those from the south and west favoring more land for farming and plantations), and refused to heed the administration's call for troops. The War Department got only a fifth of the fifty thousand man army authorized. The anti-militarist flesh on the nation's bones remained firm. Federalist-controlled banking houses rejected the government's plea for loans; merchants ignored wartime trade restrictions. When the possibility of military conscription was discussed in Congress, Daniel Webster attacked the proposal in an historic speech on the House floor. "The nation is not yet in a temper to submit to conscription," said Webster defiantly. "The people have too fresh and strong a feeling of the blessings of civil liberty to be willing thus to surrender to it."[4]

The New England anti-war Federalists, clutching firmly and vainly to their last political straw, convened the Hartford Convention. Delegates from Massachusetts, Connecticut, and Rhode Island met from December 15, 1814, to January 5, 1815, in the city of Hartford, Connecticut, and proposed several constitutional amendments to limit the war-making power of the federal government. The convention heard proposals for seizing customs houses, impounding federal revenues, declaring neutrality, nullifying conscription, prohibiting new western states from outvoting charter members of the Union, and stopping Jeffersonian–type embargoes. There was even talk of open secession should the conflict continue.

Clearly, sectional and partisan politics played a major role in opposition to the war. New England Federalists feared that western expansion would weaken the political influence of the eastern seaboard. They believed the war would invite the British navy to destroy their maritime commerce and invade their coastal towns. Three days after the declaration of war, former President John Adams sarcastically—in keeping with his disposition—proclaimed: "The danger of our government is that the General will be a man of more popularity than the President, and the army possesses more power than the Congress."[5]

The strongest and most visible opposition to the war took place in New England, of course, where governors refused to call out the state militia. Massachusetts was the most virulent in terms of anti-war sentiment. There the legislature called for establishing a peace party. In July 1812, delegates from 53 towns attended a convention in Northampton. They signed a petition declaring the war to be "neither just, necessary, nor expedient," and urged Madison to reach a quick settlement. In November 1814, Governor Caleb Strong even sponsored a secret mission to make peace with the British. He dispatched Thomas Adams to Halifax to meet with General Sir John S. Sherbrooke in order to ascertain the British government's position should a conflict occur between Governor Strong and President Madison.[6]

Though their opposition was not as pronounced as their New England neighbors, New York Federalists also tried to pressure the Madison administration into a peace settlement. After war was declared, a Federalist majority took control of the state assembly. Federalists established a Committee of Correspondence in an effort to coordinate activists in New York and other states. Federal militia in the upper Hudson Valley refused to participate in raids into Canada and would not cross the Niagara River in October during the Battle of Queenston. In the winter of 1812-1813, large numbers of militiamen deserted their units and returned to their farms. When Governor Daniel D. Tompkins called up 5,000 men for the 1813 campaign, only 1,500 reported. Rensselear County, on the other side of the Hudson River from the state capital of Albany, also resisted the draft, leaving several companies without any men.

The city of Baltimore, Maryland, was the scene of riots in June and July of 1812 that resulted in one death and considerable destruction. Alexander Hanson, the 26-year-old editor and co-owner of the Federal Republican, a paper serving the mercantile interests, denounced the war declaration and stated his publication's intention of continuing its criticisms. On Monday evening, June 22nd, a mob led by a French apothecary demolished the newspaper's offices. The mob then marched to the wharves, where it torched some ships and damaged adjacent property owned by Federalist merchants. The newspaper continued publishing its objections to the war from outside the city. On June 27th, after the offices were re-opened, an anti-Federalist mob began throwing stones. When the mob forced open the front door, General Henry "Lighthorse Harry" Lee, a defender of the press, and his men opened fire, wounding several mob leaders and killing another. City magistrates promptly called out two companies of militia under Brigadier General John Stricker and ordered him to restore order. The next day General Stricker reached a truce with the defenders, some of whom were seriously injured. The authorities guaranteed the Federalists safe conduct to the county jail, where all would answer to charges of murder. They were also promised military protection while in custody.

On the mile march to the jail, the newspaper's defenders were pelted with cobblestones before the frenzied mob returned to destroy, once more, Hanson's offices. That night, the mob gathered outside the jail and began intimidating the guard at the gate. The guard, fearing for his safety, allowed the mob to enter the jail. The scared prisoners elected to try their luck with flight. Many were waylaid to face an ugly, extended beating marked by hideous torture. Lee was crippled for the rest of his life. Revolutionary War General James Lingan, a 70-year-old defender, died at the hands of his assailants, who were deaf to his pleas for mercy. Hanson's injuries were so dire that he would die in 1819 at only 33 years of age. Prominent Maryland Republicans blamed the publishers of the Federal Republican, condemning the paper as treasonable, while the city of Baltimore produced its own report whitewashing the affair with scores of euphemisms and exculpating authorities of any neglect or wrongdoing.

Nothing, however, came close to matching the opposition movement promoted by John Lowell and the Essex Junto. The Junto consisted of members from prominent families in Essex County, Massachusetts, including political leaders like Lowell, Harrison Gray Otis, Judge Isaac Parker, and Senator Timothy Parker. Lowell's proposal called for the original thirteen states to draft a new federal constitution to protect New England's maritime and commercial interests. Lowell actually was sponsoring a secessionist plan aimed at kicking the West out of the Union. As preposterous as the idea appeared, it gained support from the likes of Senator Pickering, Gouverneur Morris of New York, and Charles Carroll of Maryland. The most respected of Boston's Federalist newspapers endorsed the idea and called for New England states to meet in Hartford, Connecticut, to discuss it.

However, two factors tended to obscure the widespread opposition and even discredit some of it politically. First, although the outstanding differences remained unresolved, a peace settlement was negotiated in 1815. Second, the military victory at New Orleans – actually fought after the treaty was signed – fostered tremendous national pride and secured a permanent place in the history books for Andrew Jackson.[7] Nevertheless, anti-war feelings did play an instrumental role in fostering a religious radical condemnation of war as un-Christian, economically wasteful, and barbaric. Such feelings actually left an important legacy. Opposition to the war did not spark a genuine peace movement; however, it did provide an avenue of expression questioning just how far some parts of the country would go in protesting a government's decision to go to war. If there was one concrete piece of evidence of the anti-war opposition's success, it was in stifling attempts to annex parts of Canada.

Although nationalist pride fueled the fires of patriotism, Americans after 1815 still felt a certain responsibility for promoting the idea of peace. Steeped in evangelical Protestantism and Enlightenment rationalism, nationalists felt predestined to lead the world toward a "republican millennium" of peace and prosperity. In their resolve to advance as one, Americans held a common vision of their country spreading the ideals of free trade, antimilitarism, social justice, and self-governing republicanism as part of a new global mission. The nation's second war with Britain in fewer than thirty-six years reinforced this vision while helping produce the first organized peace movement in American history.

THE ORGANIZED PEACE MOVEMENT BEGINS

The American peace movement that developed after the War of 1812 was a generally organized, non-sectarian form of war resistance. It represented the first great growth period in the movement. Bolstered by the spreading spirit of evangelical Christianity and romantic faith in human perfectibility, the first major peace societies gathered for the purpose of publicizing the benefits of peace. The early peace societies established periodicals and published tracts designed to convince mankind that war was unchristian, wasteful of life and treasure, and an ineffective method of solving disputes between nations. The criticisms of war that had been made earlier in history by Desiderius Erasmus, Hugo Grotius, Immanuel Kant, Jean Jacques Rousseau, and Anne Robert Jacques Turgot were made available in popular form. In addition to the religious, humanitarian, and economic attack on war, the peace societies tried to popularize proposals for the prevention of war. Such writers as Pierre Du Bois, William Penn and the Abbe de Saint-Pierre had advocated permanent arbitration tribunals and federation of nations, and the Holy Alliance of Alexander I seemed to be an indication that these ideas might be workable. American friends of peace like Noah Worcester, William Ladd, and William Jay contributed to refinement of the traditional schemes for world organization in the struggle against war. Thus, through the creation of private volunteer societies, peace making gained force as an essential humanitarian calling in the new century's approach to the elimination of war. Typically, peace workers of this era were romantic reformers. According to Charles DeBenedetti, they were "individualistic yet organized; rationalistic yet sentimental; personally conservative yet socially radical; humanly optimistic yet scripturally literalist."[8]

The leaders of the newly emerging peace societies were inspired not only by a religious conviction that war was un-Christian but also a wave of humanitarianism that quickly and forcefully expressed itself in a variety of reform movements. The peace societies organized prior to the Civil War shared a common belief with those that followed – namely, that all forms of human suffering should be redressed. Reform societies formed to promote temperance (the early-day prohibition movement), elimination of capital punishment, abolition of slavery, care for the mentally ill, and women's suffrage were indicative of the mentality sweeping the nation before the Civil War disrupted their goals. Common among them was the conviction that social ills had to be combated and that suffrage, no less than citizenship, belonged to every man and woman regardless of race or nationality. Measures taken by reformers included agitation, enlightenment, and democratic pressure via conventions and societies.[9]

The connection between democracy and reform movements, particularly the search for peace, derived from the eighteenth century Enlightenment and Christianity. Peace reformers drew confidence from their belief in the progress and perfectibility of humankind and one's importance as an individual possessing a soul and entitlement to certain natural rights. Enlightened humanitarianism and Christian charity, elements of social improvement, became the ideological lynchpins of peace and social justice. The powerful effects of religious radicalism and pacifism on abolitionism and the woman's rights movement were noticeable.

Significantly, the early leaders of the nonsectarian peace movement were notable citizens. They were not rag-tag, destitute workers searching for peace as a way to end industrial oppression. Rather, they were preachers, lawyers, merchants, and public servants. Personally conservative in both taste and politics, most were "Congregationalist and Unitarian gentlemen accustomed to social deference and committed to moral improvement through gradual enlightenment."[10] The non-sectarian peace leaders were well-educated members of a northeastern urban middle class; their anti-war arguments made much of the fact that peace promoted trade and prosperity; that wholesale bloodshed was ruinous to property, let alone the frailties of the human anatomy; that it involved all kinds of financial deficits such as inflation, public debt and excessive taxes; that, in short, it was economically wasteful. Yet , as Merle Curti explained, the "middle-class prejudices and practicality of the founders and supporters blinded them to many of the economic causes of war, which they seldom appreciated even in broader outline."[11] On record, their proposals for eliminating war said nothing of competition for markets and raw materials, trade rivalry, struggle for empire, and only minimally addressed the vested interests of the war system. The emphasis was put on persuasion, appealing to the reason and sentiment of mankind. Theirs was the voice of the eighteenth-century enlightenment, not the demands that would later mark twentieth-century protest.[12]

Although the peace societies were dominated by white males, women did play an active role in the peace movement, and in the struggles for equality and justice. During the Revolutionary period a few voices alluded to women's rights. But in the conservative reaction which followed the enactment of a Constitution that only protected white male property owners twenty-one years of age or older, women were quickly relegated to domesticity. Only the Quakers were willing to admit women on equal terms, but only to religious fellowship.

By the period of Jacksonian democracy, however, women who had endured the hardships of frontier life were gradually making their way into employment in the new industrial era. Many women found jobs in the textile factories of New England. With more and more women working outside the home, they started demanding rights commensurate with their increasing economic importance. The emerging struggle for women's rights found appropriate avenues of expression in matters of non-violence and abolitionism. As will be discussed shortly, the southern sisters who converted to Quakerism, Sarah and Angelina Grimke, serve as excellent examples of women willing to blend non-violence with the crusade for equality in both racial and gender spheres of influence. What stands out among reformers like these was a strong belief in equality for all people; it undergirded all their reform efforts including that of peace.

After the War of 1812 the peace movement grew to prominence largely as a result of the endeavors of peace leaders such as Noah Worcester, David Low Dodge, William Lloyd Garrison, the Grimkes, Lucretia Mott, Lydia Child, and William Ladd. These builders of the early nineteenth century peace movement were heroes just as truly as any leading military specialists in the art of death and destruction.

The peace movement as an organized effort gained considerable momentum through the initial efforts of Noah Worcester. A man of strong religious conviction, Worcester served as a fife-major in the Continental Army and was a veteran of Bunker Hill. Settling in the Brighton area of Boston shortly after studying for the ministry, he was deeply affected by the Federalist anti-war sentiment during the War of 1812.[13] In 1814, at the conclusion of the war, he anonymously published his manifesto, A Solemn Review of the Custom War, in which he proclaimed that "there is nothing in the nature of mankind, which renders war necessary and unavoidable – nothing which inclines them to it which may not be overcome by the power of education...."[14] Accordingly, he recommended the establishment of peace societies "in every nation of Christendom" whose purpose would be that of "diffusing light, and the spirit of peace in every direction" and of "exciting a just abhorrence of war in breast."[15] These educational efforts were to be carried out through newspapers, tracts and periodical works, through churches and religious observances, and through educational institutions. He did not bring up the issue of either defensive war or Conscientious Objection, aiming instead at influencing as many readers as possible. Considered a "peace classic" by historians, Solemn Review insisted that war was incompatible with the Christian religion and the result of "collective delusion."

Putting his ideas into action, Worcester helped found the Massachusetts Peace Society (MPS) in 1815, began publishing a quarterly journal, Friend of Peace (1815-1827), and was soon producing numerous peace tracts, including some designed especially for children.[16] Between 1817 and 1820, the Massachusetts Peace Society even went so far as to conduct statistical studies on the causes and effects of wars in order to strengthen their arguments with empirical evidence and disseminate the results. Worcester was the heart and soul of the Society. At its pinnacle, the Society had close to a thousand members, mainly Congregational clergymen, merchants, bankers, lawyers, and teachers.[17]

As the Society's secretary, Worcester oversaw the distribution of some 155,000 tracts, addresses, reports, and sermons. Criticizing war as a public institution, the Society urged the need for peace education to eradicate social ills like privateering and dueling, extermination of Native Americans, and national prejudices. Worcester published numerous tracts in support of the right of Conscientious Objection to military service. Boston was the center of the Society's activities, though other branches were established throughout New England. The Society also maintained contacts with peace activists in other states as well as Canada. There is some indication that Worcester adopted a pacifist position in later life. But his primary goal was to encourage people of different opinions to join the peace movement, thus he refused to criticize those Christians who supported war for whatever reasons they might have had.

While Worcester was establishing his peace society in New England, David Low Dodge, the well-to-do New York City merchant "who tucked peace tracts into the boxes of goods sent out from his storerooms," created the New York Peace Society (NYPS) in 1815.[18] Dodge's interest in peace had been prompted by two life-altering events. First, his two half-brothers had been killed while fighting for the cause of independence. His father and mother, strict Calvinists, instilled strong religious values promoting respect for human life. Second, in 1805, while carrying a large sum of money, he shot and nearly killed an innkeeper who had mistakenly wandered into his room late at night.

In 1809, having survived an attack of spotted fever a year earlier, Dodge anonymously published a biblical injunction condemning personal self-defense and defensive war. Entitled, The Mediator's Kingdom Not of this World, the first edition of 1,000 copies sold out quickly. After its publication, Dodge began gathering a small circle of like-minded peace reformers. Early in 1812, Dodge and his followers discussed organizing a group to enlist the evangelical churches in waging a campaign against war. The outbreak of war with England later that year postponed the budding adventure.

Nevertheless, that same year Dodge wrote his most famous peace work, War Inconsistent with the Religion of Jesus Christ. But publication was delayed until the conclusion of the War of 1812. It was one of the most effective statements of Christian pacifism published in the first part of the nineteenth century.

Believing that war was a barbarous anachronism which destroyed good order, subverted human liberty, and inhibited Christ's global victory, Dodge also argued in this tract that war ensnared people in vice, intemperance, and Sabbath-breaking, and that God intended to end war through men: "I will drop a word of advice...that whatever indulgence you may grant your grand-children, I entreat you not to give them military toys, not take them to visit military reviews; for not anything takes so strong hold of young and tender minds as martial music, and the gaudy trappings of military service." He implored peace loving parents to caution their children about the trappings of martial spirit because "When they have accidentally caught the sounds of music, and seen the brilliant parade of troops, then explain to them the nature and fruits of war, and that the parades were designed to foster the spirit and teach the art of war....[19]

On August 16, 1815, Dodge organized the New York Peace Society and became its first president. The Society numbered between thirty and forty, and, like Worcester's group, consisted of members who were respectable and bourgeois. The Society's objection to offensive and defensive war limited its appeal, yet distinguished its brand of non-resistance from other peace societies established at this time.

Even though Worcester and Dodge agreed that war was barbarous and contrary to Christ's teachings, they differed in their strategies for achieving peace. One of the many contributions historians of the antebellum peace movement have made is their analysis of how the first organized endeavor against war attempted to grapple with the issue of radical non-resistance. Dodge condemned it as contrary to Christ's teachings while Worcester chose to ignore it for fear of stunting the popular appeal of the movement. The differences between Worcester and Dodge clearly illustrate just how difficult the problem had become for pacifists and non-pacifists in the peace movement.

Interestingly, Worcester moved from his previously-held religious arguments to secular ones. Avoiding the sticky issues of defensive war, Worcester urged Christians to unite and renounce "the heathenish and savage custom" of war, support benevolent rulers, and cultivate "a mild and pacific temper among every class of citizens."[20] Dodge, on the other hand, argued from secular premises to a radical Christian peace position. Christians must remember, Dodge proclaimed that "their kingdom was not of this world... [and] the mainspring of all warlike powers, and when he is bound wars will cease...." Christians must, therefore, work unceasingly to bind Satan and war "until God in his providence, raises up some to bear open testimony against it; and as it becomes a subject of controversy, one after another gains light, and truth is at length disclosed and established."[21]

Although differences would grow sharper between Worcester and Dodge concerning the problem of defensive war both the New York Peace Society and the Massachusetts Peace Society worked to distribute peace literature and encouraged the formation of local and state peace societies. With their assistance, nearly fifty societies appeared in the immediate postwar period, stretching from Maine to Philadelphia to Ohio. Naturally, these societies were also dominated by businessmen, educators and clergymen.

Division over the issue of defensive war was magnified in the early 1820's as the working peace movement began losing strength. Poorly organized and under-funded, the country's new peace societies lost their direction and purpose. Even though anti-militarist sentiment flared throughout the northeast due to worker opposition to compulsory military drills (the earliest inklings of worker organization, especially in the textile mills of New England), no mechanism was built to translate this resentment into a program of positive peace action.[22]

But just when it appeared as if the peace movement would die an early death, it received a breath of life; it gained strength as a result of the philanthropic concerns of a former Harvard student, retired sea captain, and prosperous Maine farmer named William Ladd. Ladd spent most of his years at sea between his graduation from Harvard in 1797 and 1814, when he purchased a farm near Minot, Maine. His interest in peace as an organized endeavor began in 1817 after he read Worcester's <u>A Solemn Review</u>. Yet even his conversion was gradual, not immediate. It would not be until 1824 that Ladd joined the Massachusetts Peace Society, where he quickly rose through the ranks and helped organize six new branches. Two years later, he established the Maine Peace Society.

A popular speaker and tireless campaigner, Ladd continued to lecture, organize, write, and work long after he became an invalid. In fact, on his last lecture tour in 1841, he was forced to deliver his message sitting on stools in church pulpits because his legs were so badly ulcerated. Extremely optimistic, Ladd urged peace seekers to work initially for the conversion of public opinion, "for the continuance of war rests entirely on that. He urged citizens to "make the most of your suffrage in favor of peace," asking, "Can you support a man for office who is for settling every trivial difference with a foreign nation by the sword, regardless of the misery he brings on his own country, and the danger to which he exposes your property, liberty, morals and eternal salvation?"[23] In numerous articles, Ladd proffered his opinion that the desire for territory and blind devotion to military glory were contributing causes for war. He believed that one of the primary goals of peace societies should be persuading civilized, Christian governments to establish institutions for the peaceable resolution of international disputes.

FIRST NATIONAL ORGANIZATION: THE AMERICAN PEACE SOCIETY

Ladd, convinced that the country's shrinking peace movement needed to become national in scope and more efficient in operational matters, journeyed from Maine to Ohio preaching the necessity of a central peace organization. Encouraged by the response to his tour, Ladd thus joined other peace leaders in May 1828 and presided at Dodge's New York City home over the formation of the American Peace Society (APS). It was the first secular peace organization in American history with a national focus.

The American Peace Society affiliated itself with state and local societies—including the New York Peace Society and the Massachusetts Peace Society—and welcomed into its membership anyone wanting to abolish the custom of war. The Society promoted such sophisticated measures as negotiation and arbitration. Ladd envisioned the eventual settlement of all disputes by a "Congress of Christian Nations, whose decrees shall be enforced by public opinion as it now is, but by public opinion when it shall be enlightened by the rays of the gospel of peace."[24] Although Ladd was ambivalent at first on the matter of whether or not all wars were contrary to Christianity, he eventually accepted the principle that all followers of Christ should reject as morally wrong both offensive and defensive war.

Unfortunately for Ladd this did not sit well with some of his most ardent supporters. Take, for instance, the case of the Reverend William Allen, president of Bowdoin College and author of the monumental work American Biographical Dictionary published in 1809. Allen was an enthusiastic supporter of the peace crusade. Shortly after the creation of APS Allen became one of its most important publicists and contributors. Allen maintained that war remained at best a cruel expediency and a valueless hoax impeding the goal of universal peace. Yet he insisted that defensive war was justified when fighting, for example, pirates or murderous barbarians invading one's native soil. Men of the gospel would be foolish to condemn defensive war. In 1833 he devoted his Phi Beta Kappa address at Bowdoin to international peace with justifications for defense of one's person and property. But when Ladd and APS waffled on the issue and later condemned both offensive and defensive warfare as contrary to the spirit of the Christian gospel, Allen renounced his life membership in the organization and began publicly attacking the society's revised constitution.

But like Worcester, Ladd resisted any attempts to limit Society membership to only those Christians who subscribed to his own personal beliefs. It was a difficult balancing act given Allen's criticisms and those who still subscribed to the defensive war proposition. The American Peace Society included individuals with very different peace perspectives. For the more radical non-resisters in the Society, the inclusion of so many members with divergent views made its programs equivocal and difficult to follow.

During its first years, the American Peace Society operated as a traditional agency of organized good will. Combining a firm Christian commitment with a rational faith in the ability to resolve any and all international disputes, the Society distributed tracts, sponsored speakers, and encouraged local volunteers to help advance the cause of peace. Mostly at his own expense, Ladd served as the Society's main traveling representative. After 1835, he was assisted by the Congregationalist minister George C. Beckwith, who agreed to work for a salary of $2 per day as well as expenses. With their leadership, in 1840 the Society attempted to generate interest in the peace cause by offering a $1000 award for the best essay on the idea of a Congress of Nations. Ladd published the five best essays submitted. This proposal was mainly an outgrowth of Ladd's own "Essay on a Congress of Nations," which suggested the creation of a two-tiered system of international justice based on Christian principles of morality and an international court "of the most able civilians in the world" to adjudicate all international disputes.[25] The Society also went to great lengths to capture church support for its ideals. Society leaders urged numerous denominational organizations and individual ministers to pray for peace and encourage support for a Congress of Nations.

ABOLITIONISM AND THE NEW ENGLAND NON-RESISTANCE SOCIETY

While the peace movement continued to grow in terms of respect, the slavery issue came to dominate American politics. During America's "age of reform," the peace and abolitionist movements were never very far apart. This was a period in which the idea of peace was applied to the goal of social justice. In 1829, David Walker, a free Boston black, issued a powerful tract, The Appeal to Reason, in which he lamented the idea of gradual emancipation and African colonization. His essay was a powerful call for bold and vigorous action by African Americans. Whether free or slave, blacks must strike for their freedom by any means necessary. If a racial war is to be prevented, Walker wrote, then white America had to recognize immediately the rights and humanity of all African Americans. Many in the North, including white anti-slavery forces, condemned Walker's Appeal as dangerous and too inflammatory.

Slaveowners' fears were realized two years later when some twenty slaves, led by Nat Turner, revolted against their master in Virginia's Southampton County. Nearly sixty whites died, leaving the South in a virtual state of panic (though twice as many African Americans were killed in response). The Virginia legislature suspended debate on the gradual emancipation of its slaves. The following year, the South Carolina legislature nullified a federal tariff law – calling it the Tariff of Abominations – calling it was injurious to the state's slave economy. Asserting the doctrine of states rights, South Carolinians stood behind one of their revered political leaders, John C. Calhoun, and his own defiance of federal authority. The legislature's action, mixed with the possible threat of secession, led to a serious constitutional confrontation with the Andrew Jackson administration. The adoption of the Force Bill – which enabled the government to collect the tariff – resulted in an uneasy and tenuous agreement. Though a temporary peace had been achieved, many northerners now began calling for the complete abolition of slavery.

The cry to abolish slavery was heard throughout reform circles after 1830. Elijah Lovejoy, an abolitionist editor from Illinois, published numerous editorials calling for an end to slavery. Even in the North, there was violent disagreement. An angry mob killed Lovejoy when he tried to prevent the destruction of his printing press. This instance inspired non-violent opponents of slavery to search for ways to prevent further violence. Peace workers were also anxious to prevent a possible war between the slaveholding South and the industrial North. The peace and abolitionist crusades had much in common, with roots extending from Quaker sensibilities to an enlightened New England conscience. Both drew deep inspiration from the romantic idealism of the 1820's, issuing forth from the religious revivalism of Horace Bushnell, Lyman Beecher, Charles Grandison Finney, and other itinerant Great Awakeners.

The link between organized peace making and abolitionism became reality in the early 1830's as the two reforms advanced with a common feeling of immediacy, determination, and likeminded crusaders. After 1830, the abolitionist movement spread with exceptional fervor throughout the villages of New England and the rural Northwest. The movement was composed of a spirit of religious perfectionism, a receptive upper-class female audience, and energizing powerful orators. In western New York, Arthur Tappan gave voice to the cause, while Theodore Weld carried the banner in the Ohio Valley. The northeast witnessed the persuasive efforts of Sarah and Angelina Grimke. In New England, William Lloyd Garrison led the way, prompted in part by the runaway slave, Frederick Douglass.

African-American abolitionists like Douglass worked hand-in-hand with the predominantly while anti-slavery societies. Black and white abolitionists undertook a number of novel and bold non-violent actions. Apart from employing the technique of the boycott, direct action methods such as sit-ins, eat-ins, and walk-alongs were also carried out. African Americans sat in white sections of railroad cars, sat at tables reserved for whites, and even attempted to integrate steamboats along the Ohio and Mississippi Rivers. Walk-alongs saw whites and African Americans marching down streets arm in arm before entering a place to eat. Much like the resistance to such actions in the South during the heyday of the modern civil rights movement, these protesters were often met with violent attacks. Resisting reprisal, these nonresistants followed the lead of Douglass, who at the time was a leading proponent of non-resistance.

In 1841, Douglass joined the New England Non-Resistance Society. An escaped runaway slave from Maryland, Douglass learned to read and write on his own. Articulate and passionate about his cause, Douglass traveled throughout the North providing personal accounts of the horrors of slavery. He was an excellent orator and skilled storyteller. His own recollections, Narrative of the Life of Frederick Douglass, An American Slave, published in 1845, represent one of the most compelling eyewitness stories of an individual determined to be free. In 1846, Douglass spoke out against the call for war as a means of emancipation. His arguments were sincere and compelling, insisting that "Were I asked the question whether I would have my emancipation by the shedding of one single drop of blood, my answer would be in the negative." He held to this position in 1849, moreover, while affirming the right of slaves to revolt, noting that the "only well grounded hope of the slave for emancipation is the operation of moral force." Douglass' views were also supported by the respected female African American abolitionist, Sojourner Truth. In her opinion, emancipation would only come about by a change of heart in white America that would guarantee lasting freedom.[26]

More than anyone, however, William Lloyd Garrison typified the pacifist as abolitionist, and he changed the latter movement in significant ways, rejecting gradualism and the idea that slaveholders should be compensated for their losses. He also represented the peace movement's sectionalism, which narrowed, along with the rest of romantic Protestant reformism, as a result of the slavery issue. An abandoned son of an itinerant Baptist preacher from Massachusetts, this unschooled radical pacifist entered the abolitionist movement in January 1831, by distributing the first issue of <u>The Liberator</u>. "I am in earnest—I will not equivocate—I will not excuse—I will not retreat a single inch—and I <u>will be heard</u>," he proclaimed.[27] Garrison's social radicalism and pacifism merged as one conviction. In 1835, he argued that the non-resistant reformer must return good for evil and "forgive every injury and insult, without attempting by physical force or penal enactments, to punish the transgressor."[28]

Garrison's zealous stand on abolitionism and non-resistance eventually led him into open confrontation with the American Peace Society. The nonresistants, led by Garrison, attacked the Society for not rejecting all forms of social injustice. They felt that the parent organization was not aggressive enough in working against war. With Adin Ballou and Henry C. Wright at his side, Garrison staged a walkout at the Society's 1838 September convention in Boston. What resulted was the creation of a tiny organization – the New England Non-Resistance Society.[29]

The New England Non-Resistance Society issued a Declaration of Sentiments resolving "to carry forward the work of peaceful, universal reformation" through "THE FOOLISHNESS OF PREACHING" and the "Spiritual regeneration" of corrupt human institutions. Society members willingly pledged to oppose all military undertakings (preparations for war, office, monuments, and dress) and "to live peace with a universal sense of human equality." In a bold proclamation the Declaration further declared:

> We register our testimony, not only against all wars, whether offensive or defensive, but all preparations every naval ship, arsenal, every fortification; against the militia system and a standing army against all military chieftains and soldiers; against all monuments commemorative of victory over a foreign foe, all trophies won in battle, all celebrations in honor of military or naval exploits; against all appropriations for the defense of a nation by force and arms; on the part of any legislative body; against every edict of government requiring of its subjects military service. Hence, we deem it unlawful to bear arms, or to hold military office.[30]

In the meantime, the formation of the New England Non-Resistance Society provoked a short-lived but bitter argument within reform circles over the implications of non-resistant anarchism. Historians of the antebellum peace movement have highlighted the torment strict pacifists faced in limiting their non-resistance by allowing the government broader powers necessary for carrying out its police functions. Thus moderate abolitionists like Theodore Weld complained that the non-resistant attack upon government smacked of anarchy, while Garrison tried to explain that revolutionary non-resistance stood not for anarchy but for Christian anarchism—the government of God. The controversy was complicated further by the interest that some reformers showed in model communitarian experiments, such as those created by John Humphrey Noyes and Adin Ballou, which sought to create alternative models of peaceable living.

PACIFIST PERFECTIONISTS SEEKING ALTERNATIVE MEANS OF SOCIAL JUSTICE

Along with crusades for world peace and abolitionism, the search for models of peaceable living was also part of the Utopian Socialist thinking of this era. Determined to change the existing social and economic order in the name of justice and equality, utopians developed alternative ways of living in response to the young nation's industrialization. Control of industry by a small minority prevented the masses from realizing the democratic possibilities inherent in technological development. Followers of Robert Owen and Charles Fourier, as well as spokesmen for the industrial classes, stressed the necessity of equal rights in politics, peaceful resolution of labor issues, and, of course, economic justice.

Influenced by religious radicalism that eschewed the conventional emphasis on Christian charity and humanitarianism, various communitarian societies emerged that were distinguished by a socialist insistence on a total revolutionary change in society. The Oneida Community, for instance, led by Noyes, was characterized by its rejection of traditional marriage, private property, and war. Noyes and his followers were basically Christian Perfectionists, practicing what they called Bible Communism as their model for the perfect society. "Our business," wrote Noyes, "is to be coworkers with God in ushering in the last period of man's education—the second Reformation—the victory and reign of spiritual wisdom and power."[31]

The Oneida perfectionists succeeded in establishing one of the most prosperous Christian-Utopian communist experiments in nineteenth-century America. Although the storm of controversy surrounding the "complex marriage" tenet ultimately led to its downfall in the late 1870's, there was much more to Noyes' experiment. The Oneida Community, founded officially in 1848 near Syracuse, New York, bridged the gap between the pure Christian communism of religious sects like the Shakers of Watervliet, New York, (near the city of Troy) and the secular utopianism of experimental groups such as Brook Farm, which based their views on the writings of Frenchman Charles Fourier.

In fact, Noyes, who originally came from Vermont, was a graduate of Dartmouth College and later studied theology and law at Andover Theological Seminary and Yale. Noyes and his followers adopted communism as a result of the writings of Fourier. Although the Oneida Perfectionists did not subscribe to

Karl Marx's version of Communism, their community was designed as a countermeasure to the economic wastefulness of modern industrialization. Only through religious communal living, they believed, would it be possible for the individual to realize his or her ultimate destiny. Of all the utopian communal undertakings of this period, the Oneida Community proved to be the most economically self-sufficient. Before its demise in 1879, a result of local community opposition to the Complex Marriage System, members of the Oneida Community owned more than 300 acres of arable land and conducted a thriving business in the manufacture of items such as animal traps and the dying of silk thread. Most members of this community were skilled mechanics and farmers. Their general cultural standards, based on peace and economic equality, were far in advance of the average American of their day.

Another Christian socialist alternative was the Hopedale Community, founded by Adin Ballou. Born in Rhode Island in 1803, Ballou, according to his Autobiography, was greatly influenced by spiritual forces in his youth. His lifelong commitment to Christian principles began when he was nineteen and had a vision in his sleep of a deceased brother. In this dream his brother commanded him to preach the gospel of Christ to his fellow Americans lest he suffer the "blood of their souls" for his sin of omission. Entering the Christian ministry, Ballou remained faithful to his pledge, and when the issue of chattel slavery divided the nation, his voice was one of the most bitter in condemnation of that institution.

Ballou was the first social reformer to suggest that one could formulate a process of principled pacifism not founded upon religious considerations. For him there were basically three kinds of pacifism. The first, philosophical pacifism, maintained that violence is irrational. The second, Christian pacifism, the type that the Peace Churches and first organized peace societies proclaimed, was based on the willingness to follow the example of Jesus Christ. The third, sentimental pacifism, was premised on humanitarian principles and acceptance of the idea of human perfectibility.

With respect to the peace movement, Ballou's ideas were a curious blend of the religious Universalist backing for radical individualism and social reform and an evangelical penchant for promoting peace and non-resistance through alternative measures. Shunning conservative Christian thinking for individual moral reformation, Ballou added his own socialist twist to the conventional dictates of organized religion.

In establishing his Christian Socialist experiment, Ballou emphasized that non-resistance could spring from secular roots because of the failures of conservative Christianity to remake society. Traditional religion, Ballou insisted, was focused more on saving souls and maintaining church attendance. Failure to examine the root causes of societal ills was responsible for the abandonment of faith. The adoption of non-resistance as a plausible measure when dealing with labor strife, abolitionism, and women's rights defined Hopedale's communitarian philosophy.

The anarchistic basis of Hopedale certainly wavered between an individualistic vision of a good society and a communitarian outlook on how righteous people should conduct their relations with one another. But what really stood out with Ballou's experiment was the nature of his understanding of anarchism. The ultimate goal of Ballou's community and that of all anarchists, including those writings that would characterize the industrial conflicts in post-bellum America, was the creation of a society that would conduct itself non-violently and without the need of an aggressive and oppressive state. Such a vision connected prewar and post-Civil War peace pioneers and would remain a vital link in the non-violent principles espoused both in the nineteenth and twentieth centuries.

In 1841, Ballou and a handful of like-minded nonconformists in Massachusetts withdrew from the world to establish Hopedale, one of the "most intentionally anarchistic communities ever organized in America." The fundamental constitution by which Hopedale was governed was the "Standard of Practical Christianity" drafted at a conference held at Mendon, Massachusetts, two years previously. Calling themselves "Restorationists," and mindful of their Anglo-Saxon heritage, they proclaimed their religion to be one of love and their primary social objective the "restoration of man, especially the most fallen friendless." The anarchistic sentiments of the group were plainly evident in their declaration that they would not, under any circumstances, be bound by the will of man acting through government, but only by the will of God as they interpreted it. Prospective members were, before being admitted to the community, to assent to a declaration that read in part: "I hold myself bound never…to kill, assault, beat, torture, enslave, rob, oppress, persecute, defraud, corrupt, slander, revile, injure, envy, or hate any human being, even my worst enemy; ... never to serve in the army, navy, or military of any nation...; or ask governmental interposition, in any case involving a final authorized report to physical violence..."[32]

While they declared themselves willing to pay taxes and otherwise passively obey the edicts of positive law, they reserved the right to engage in civil disobedience when the "pronouncements of government were clearly out of line with the imperatives of natural right." A considerable amount of this non-violent philosophy was popularized by Ballou in his essay, Christian Non-Resistance (1846); in this work Ballou proposed what he liked to call his Law of Reciprocation. This "law" claimed that "absorbing injury and responding with a benevolent insistence upon justice perfects human society," while resorting to injuring another will only result in further injury.[33] Ballou's commitment to change would also be emulated by a number of female reformers who linked their peacemaking efforts to the causes of humanitarianism, abolitionism and women's rights.

DOROTHEA DIX AND THE HUMANITARIAN IMPULSE

While utopian reformers made their own implied criticisms of the current state of affairs in an emerging industrialized society through building alternative communities, other courageous female advocates began carrying out their own individual campaign for fair treatment of the less fortunate. For some antebellum reformers the notion of peace extended to how society treated those incapable of handling their own personal affairs. They often acted as the conscience of society. Take the case of Dorothea Dix. This courageous New Englander had to overcome entrenched male institutional resistance when it came to the treatment of the mentally ill. Her personal efforts made her one of the most influential figures in the history of humanitarian reform.

Inspired by contemporary reformers such as William Lloyd Garrison and Susan B. Anthony, Dix found her own special calling when dealing with the horrible conditions surrounding those who were classified as insane. In 1840, a majority of those diagnosed as insane were confined to private care, isolated in locked rooms, cages, outhouses, jail cells and even poorhouses. Like centuries past they continued to be considered society's outcasts, largely neglected and poorly treated. In 1841, at the urging of a young theological student, Dix was asked to teach a Sunday school class in the women's department of the House of Correction in East Cambridge, Massachusetts. She was appalled to find insane females housed with prisoners in a dark, dank, cold room. Aroused at witnessing such deplorable conditions she contacted Charles Sumner, whose later oration on "The Law of Human Progress" represented the most significant treatment of the subject of any contemporary at that time in the U.S., and Samuel Gridley Howe and requested that they investigate her allegations. When Sumner and Howe supported her findings Dix immediately began writing articles demanding better treatment for the mentally ill. She then undertook her own two-year investigation of all the jails and almshouses in the state. In 1843 she presented her findings to the Massachusetts state legislature. Receiving support from Sumner, Howe, and Horace Mann, the legislature appropriated additional funds to build a new extension to the Worcester hospital for the insane.

Bolstered by this legislative victory Dix then began a nationwide campaign for state-supported hospitals for the insane. Between 1844 and 1854, Dix traveled thousands of miles – some estimates say close to 60,000 – visiting well over 9,000 "insane, epileptic, and idiotic" persons in prisons, almshouses, jails, and hospitals. Gathering thousands of documents and testimonials Dix launched a one-woman crusade against the mistreatment of those considered mentally deranged. In 1848, aware that land grants were awarded by the federal government for educational purposes, Dix asked the U.S. Congress to support her proposal for establishing national hospitals for the mentally challenged. In 1850 her bill finally passed the Senate but was defeated in the House. Finally, in 1854, both houses supported the bill. President Franklin K. Pierce, however, vetoed it on the grounds that the federal government could not assume the responsibility of helping the less fortunate and that making land grants of this nature was unconstitutional.

Stung by this defeat Dix took time off and traveled to Europe. When the nation became embroiled in a bitter civil war over slavery Dix served as superintendent of women nurses for the Union Army. After the war she once more started up her crusade for the mentally ill until age and physical ailments forced her into retirement. Despite the restricted status of women at this time, Dix's commitment to social and humanitarian justice ultimately bore fruit. When she began her individual campaign in the 1840s there were only thirteen asylums or hospitals for the insane in the United States. Some forty years later, shortly before her death in 1887, the nation had close to 140 private and public asylums for the insane; of the public ones Dix had a direct hand in the establishment of thirty-two. This brave woman single-handedly aroused public opinion thus forcing the government to provide institutional care and treatment for the mentally challenged. Her own effort served as an inspiration to other female reformers, especially those in the abolitionist and women's rights movements.

FEMALE ABOLITIONISTS AND WOMEN'S EQUALITY

Activities of female reformers illustrated the belief in promoting peace and social justice as part of the idea of progress that was prevalent in ante-bellum

America. First and foremost are the Grimke sisters. Sarah and Angelina were early advocates of abolitionism and women's rights. Experiencing firsthand the evils of slavery on their family's plantation as well as societal discrimination against women, they traveled throughout the northeast lecturing on these twin abuses. In the process they linked their abolitionist work to equality for women. Their efforts were bold and gutsy. As Kathryn Kish Sklar points out in Women's Rights Emerges within the Antislavery Movement, 1830-1870, their participation in the most radical form of antislavery protest set in motion their own innovations on behalf of women's rights. By breaking down longstanding prejudices prohibiting women from speaking in public the Grimke sisters ultimately transformed the definition of acceptable behavior for women's role in the public sphere.

Sarah, the older of the two female reformers, joined a Quaker meeting after taking her father to Philadelphia for medical treatment during the War of 1812. Some years later Angelina converted to the Quaker faith and both remained in the north after 1829. In 1835, Angelina wrote a letter to The Liberator which its editor, William Lloyd Garrison, published without her knowledge. Immediately, the Society of Friends, which had disavowed political activism since the time of the Revolutionary War, demanded that the sisters either become members in good standing or forsake their religious community for the abolitionist cause. They decided to work actively in opposing slavery. During the 1830s the sisters were traveling and lecturing throughout the northeast calling for an end to the system of slavery. At first, they spoke in private homes to members of the abolitionist movement and then broadened their appeal to public audiences about their personal experiences and knowledge of the plantation system. Drawing intense criticisms from the Quaker community and male reformers who felt it improper for women to take to the public platform, the Grimke sisters then began drawing parallels between their own oppression as women and that of the system of slavery. They were among the first women to speak publicly on behalf of abolitionism and women's rights. Noting that women were oppressed and without power, they argued that it was impossible for females to address the wrongs of society unless they took power into their own hands.

Searching for a more meaningful religious faith than their mother's Episcopalianism and touched by the powerful forces of evangelical Protestantism – the Second Great Awakening – the sisters underwent a religious conversion marked by a feeling of guilt over their privileged life. Sarah was the first to embrace Quakerism and with it a plain style of dress, orderly habits, and condemnation of slavery as ungodly. Angelina's conversion to the Inner Light was more prolonged as she struggled for some time between Sarah's Quakerism and her affinity for Presbyterianism where she had organized daily prayer meetings attended by Baptists, Methodists, and Congregationalists. Eventually, Sarah's Quakerism prevailed when Angelina stuffed a cushion with the laces, veils, and trimmings of her fine dresses.

Promoting the theme of reconciliation and social justice, Angelina wrote a tract in 1836 entitled, "Appeal to the Christian Women of the South." She claimed that "men and women were CREATED EQUAL" and that "whatever is **right** for man to do, is **right** for women...." Challenging clergymen who quoted the Bible to justify female inferiority and servility, she wrote a friend in 1837 that "I ask no favors for my sex. I surrender not our claim to equality. All that I ask of our brethren is, that they will take their feet off our necks, and permit us to stand upright on that ground which God designed us to occupy."[34] Her letters became the primer for crusaders for women's rights including Lucretia Mott and Elizabeth Cady Stanton.

Stoic in tone yet powerful in persuasion, she called upon white southern women to join the abolitionist movement for the sake of womanhood and the emancipation of slaves. Her argument rested on the belief that slavery was detrimental to white womanhood because it destroyed the sacred institution of marriage when white plantation owners sired their slaves' children. Such comments created a firestorm, but the embers of their views remained hot with conviction. Sarah followed this line of reasoning by publishing her own commentary, "Epistle to the clergy of the Southern States" the same year. A year later Angelina expanded her 1836 tract with the title, "Appeal to the Women of the Nominally Free States."

By 1837 the sisters were in full swing. They went on a tour of Congregationalist churches in the northeast. Not only did they denounce the practice of slavery they also condemned racial prejudice. Their arguments were advanced as well as controversial. The particular view that white women had a natural affinity with black female slaves elicited attacks from radical abolitionists, including Catherine Beecher. Responding to Beecher's criticisms, Angelina published "Letters to Catherine Beecher" in which she defended her and Sarah's right to speak publicly for the abolitionist cause. Most notably, after being denounced by Congregationalist ministers for their radical views on slavery and women's rights, Sarah wrote a series of letters published as "Letters on the Equality of Sexes." In this tract she vigorously defended a woman's right to speak on the public platform. The Grimke sisters received so much attention because of the attacks on their views that by 1838 thousands of people came to hear their lecture series in Boston.

The women's rights movement, moreover, grew out of this ferment of reform as female abolitionists asserted their right to be heard in public. Eight years after the furor that was caused by the refusal of the World's Anti-Slavery Convention in London to seat female delegates the first national women's rights convention, held in Seneca Falls, New York (1848), issued its own Declaration of Independence, which began, "All men *and women* are created equal…." It went on to list demands for political, social, and economic quality with men. In 1851, following the Declaration of Sentiments, an aged African-American woman, born a slave in New York, rose to her feet and loudly protested the discrimination against her race and her sex. In "Aren't I a Women," Sojourner Truth boldly proclaimed to her male counterparts that "You need not be afraid to give us our rights for fear we will take too much….Well, if women upset the world, do give her a chance to set it right side up again….Man, where is your part? But the women are coming up blessed by God and a few of the men are coming up with them. But man is in a tight place, the poor slave is on him, woman is coming on him, he is surely between a hawk and a buzzard."[35] Perhaps more than any other female in antebellum America Truth withstood the triple impediment of being black among white reformers, being an abolitionist in a country that permitted slavery, and being female in a reform movement run by men. Like the Grimke sisters she was not intimidated by shouting and jeering mobs. This tall and slender reformer spoke her mind. In numerous speeches, and later in her emancipationist actions, Sjourner Truth equated the liberation of slaves with the rights of women to have their own place in the public sphere. Until the Civil War broke out, Truth had hoped for a peaceful resolution to the issue of emancipation.

A number of other women's rights proponents allied themselves with the peace and abolitionist movements. One, Lucretia Coffin Mott, a New England Quaker, was one of the original writers of the Declaration of Sentiments at Seneca Falls. Mott dedicated her life to the abolitionist, women's rights, and peace crusades. In 1833, while serving as a Quaker minister, she attended the founding convention of the American Anti-Slavery Society. Not allowed to join because of her gender, Mott established her own Philadelphia Female anti-Slavery Society in 1839. A year later she then joined the New England Non-Resistance Society.

Mott's non-resistance philosophy rested on the position that no person should support a government that resorted to coercion and the use of arms. One of her noblest attempts as peacemaker was mediating disputes between the various factions within the abolitionist and women's rights movements. Though disappointed at the Garrisonians' degree of stridency, Mott integrated her Quaker peace testimony into her fight for the rights of women and end slavery as necessary measures for advancing democratic justice.

Mott's convictions were shared by one of the nation's most celebrated female abolitionists and peace proponents, the Boston writer Lydia Maria Frances Child. Child's belief in peace and non-resistance was reflected in her many writings on those subjects. She argued that mutual understanding, not the use of violence, would ultimately triumph over all forms of injustice. Her 1833 book, An Appeal in Favor of that Class of Americans Called Africans, enabled her to achieve national prominence as a leader of the abolitionist movement and subsequent election to the executive board of the American Anti-Slavery Society and editorship of the National Anti-Slave Standard.

For Child, like other radical peace activists, abolition, women's rights, and peace were inextricably connected. Equality for all people and peaceful cooperation were essential instruments for human advancement. Despite threats of death and derision because of her gender and support for abolitionism, Child never backed down. Her feminism was emboldened by these philistine acts of intolerance, especially on the part of male reformers. Most importantly, her pacifism was strengthened by meeting her enemies' violence with petitions and prayers instead of bullets. But even her example proved futile when it came to the divisiveness the anti-slavery movement encountered by the decade of the 1840s.

SPLIT WITHIN THE ANTI-SLAVERY MOVEMENT

Neither the New England Non-Resistance Society, the communal experiments of Noyes, Ballou, and others, nor the female abolitionists had a lasting effect on the inner workings of the organized peace movement. Shortly after 1840, the New England Non-Resistance Society, "isolated in its purity," shrank into a Boston-area fellowship. Similarly, the larger appeal of revolutionary non-resistance faded in importance. Proponents drifted in different directions, attempting to rejuvenate their zeal and enthusiasm for such endeavors. Non-resistance grew appreciably weaker in the early 1840's as abolitionists argued over the role of women in the movement and over the development of a successful political strategy.

The American Anti-Slavery Society, which had strong ties to the peace movement became split by ideological differences among its members. Garrison alienated more moderate members when he insisted on the right of women to hold leading positions in the Society and to address publicly mixed audiences. In 1838, he held his ground when an angry mob tried to break up a meeting in Philadelphia at which Angelina Grimke and other females spoke. The mob burned the hall the next day, and Garrison's abolitionist foes kept insisting that the struggle for women's rights remain separate from the anti-slavery crusade. Garrison also antagonized members of the Society in other ways. Denouncing the churches and the federal government for compromising with slavery, he argued that all anti-slavery people should refuse to vote or hold public office. To him, the U.S. Constitution protected slavery.

The conflict also brought to light the importance of peace as a women's issue. As noted previously, female Garrisonians found important ways to connect the violent nature of the master/slave and male/female relationships and argue for peace and social justice. Quaker poet Elizabeth Chandler, Sarah and Angelina Grimke, Lydia Maria Child, and Lucretia Mott popularized the view within female anti-slavery societies that non-violent action was an appropriate response to institutionalized violence like slavery. While they fought to enter the public sphere, female abolitionists recognized that women had a special role to play as the gentle, nurturing, moral guardians of humankind. Male-dominated anti-slavery societies refused to hear their voices, yet female abolitionists presented themselves as the natural advocates of equality, peace, and non-violence.

It is quite clear that the early history of the peace movement was dominated by white males, yet the female Garrisonians were instrumental in promoting peace in their own right. The Massachusetts female peace society the Essex County Olive Branch Circle, for instance, was founded in the 1830s and its members wrote short peace stories, mostly for children that later appeared in an edited volume entitled, Sister Voices for the Field, Factory, and Fire-Side. One can only speculate as to how successful the peace and abolitionists movements might have been had women not been forced into subordinate positions.

Eventually, faced with such controversies, Garrison declined to push the reforms of abolitionism and radical pacifism in working combination. The

American Anti-Slavery Society split apart. Garrison controlled the remnants of the original organization, while a new society began promoting a more moderate agenda.

INTERNATIONALISM AND WORKERS: A JUDGE AND A "LEARNED BLACKSMITH"

The "ultra" nonresistant quarrel of the 1830's and early 1840's presented problems for the organized peace movement. Yet it did not disrupt the efforts of the American Peace Society to proclaim the importance of reconciliation and harmony. During the early 1840's, the Society began to operate openly as a modern volunteer society; it informed, organized, and concentrated citizen pressure on behalf of the peaceful resolution of complex problems. In circulating petitions and urging arbitration, the Society stressed the necessity of global harmony.

Global harmony was the focal point of Judge William Jay of Westchester County, New York. Elected Vice President of the American Peace Society in 1844 and later its president from 1848 until his death in 1858, Jay contributed both with pen and purse to the cause of internationalism. Son of one of the nation's founders, noted diplomat John Jay, William made his greatest contribution to world peace in 1842 with the publication of War and Peace. Focusing on the role of law in an international context Jay discussed the positive attributes of international arbitration. According to British abolitionist and peace advocate Joseph Sturge, Jay's proposal was the first of its type. Noting that both the slave trade and liquor traffic had been eliminated because of public opinion and the creation of reform agencies, Jay maintained that the evil of war might also be eliminated through similar means. Though not denying the right to personal and national self-defense, Jay proposed that the United States establish a new precedent in international relations by writing a clause into treaties with foreign nations. Essentially, it would be a declaration that, if negotiations broke down, the dispute would be submitted to a special convention. One or more friendly powers would serve as arbitrator, and the two disputing powers would then agree to abide by the decision of the convention. Since arbitration had worked in the past to resolve international disputes, it was not beyond the realm of possibility to include it in future alliances and treaties. Jay was confident it would receive great public support.[36]

Jay and the Society's interest in world peace attracted the likes of Elihu Burritt, who joined the American Peace Society in 1843. Throughout the 1840's and 1850's, he symbolized the Society's idealism, while enthusiastically enacting the spirit of internationalism. Burritt was nineteenth century America's most important peace ambassador.

Born in New Britain, Connecticut, in 1810, son of an eccentric shoemaker and farmer, Burritt was both brilliant and precocious. Referred to by Merle Curti as the "learned blacksmith," the self-educated, radical pacifist had mastered more than thirty languages—a true commitment to his international sentiments. He anticipated many of the most effective modern propaganda techniques. From temperance circles, he adopted the idea of a pledge of a complete abstinence from every possible form of war. Burritt also helped organize women's peace societies such as the Olive Leaf Circles where they raised thousands of dollars for international peace work. Additionally, he spent time urging the working class to overthrow the yoke of war's burden, despite "the romance of chivalry, and many martial songs of military glory...." Conscious of war's brutalizing effects, he called upon the "workingmen of Christendom" to put an end to "such pretentious valuations upon their earthly possibilities as to believe they are worth more for producing food for man and beast, than for feeding with their own flesh and blood the hungry maws of mortar and <u>mitrailleuses</u> on fields of human slaughter."[37]

Burritt was one of America's first reformers to link the role of labor with efforts to end war. His line of reasoning was to demonstrate that economic injustice at home was one of the basic causes leading to war. Representatives of the working-class pointed out that the elite composition of peace societies rendered them ill-equipped when it came to recognizing the economic causes of war.

Burritt concluded that worker injustices were symptoms of oppression and conflict due to the industrial system. The reformers' tendency of this period encouraged the government to abolish monopoly and privilege. Labor spokesmen denounced the autocratic discipline of the machine system – symbolized by the Lowell Factory System in Massachusetts – and the loss of individuality that was part and parcel of factory toil and urban life. If industrialism threatened American workers with regimentation, slums, and degradation, moreover, it was even more alarming to witness business owners, the courts, and even state militias resisting worker attempts to organize – all under the ruse of law and order.

Burritt and other peace reformers were upset at officials crushing worker dissent in the name of Americanism and patriotism. Yet it was the worker who was called upon to bear arms for his country. Therein lies the irony. Efforts to prevent workers from earning a decent living and achieving safer working conditions was being accomplished by using military units. In fact, anti-militarist sentiment appeared as early as the 1820s when workingmen's organizations began considering the militia system a discriminatory economic burden. While the men of the wealthy classes were able to escape service by paying fines, the poor male worker lost both time and money in having to attend drills or muster. It was this insult to injury that prompted the "Learned Blacksmith" to reach out to the working classes of America.

Though never sure where the next dollar would come from, Burritt founded a weekly newspaper, the Christian Citizen, at Worcester, Massachusetts, in 1844. This admirable international pacifist publication dragged him deeply into debt before he was forced to abandon it in 1851. During the Oregon crisis between Britain and the United States in the mid 1840's, Burritt, while editing the APS' Advocate of Peace and Universal Brotherhood, besieged Congress with peace propaganda. He cooperated with Friends and other peace activists in England in an exchange of "Friendly Addresses" between British and American cities, merchants, ministers and laborers, and women.[38] Burritt himself carried two "Friendly Addresses"—with impressive lists of signatures—one from Edinburgh, Scotland and another from women of Exeter, England to Washington, where Senator John C. Calhoun and other senators applauded this "popular handshaking" across the Atlantic.[39]

THE PLIGHT OF NATIVE AMERICANS

While Burritt was encouraging the working-class to carry the banner of internationalism other peace activists looked with dismay at the treatment of Native Americans. Between the close of the War of 1812 to the outbreak of the Civil War the ever-expanding frontier and abundant material resources of the young nation provided for a rapidly growing population. Feeling the effects of white settlement and a patriotic confidence in the future of America's progress were the land's first inhabitants. During the 1830s and 1840s, continuing a process which began much earlier, many Americans endorsed the claim that the Native Americans were doomed to extinction by the inevitable laws of progress. Justifying the removal of Indians from their land were individuals like Lewis Cass, Governor of the Michigan Territory, South Carolina statesman and diplomat Joel R. Poinsett, who elaborated his views in Inquiry into the Received Opinions of Philosophers and Historians on the Natural Progress of the Human Race from Barbarism to Civilization (1834), and President Andrew Jackson, who defended the removal of the Cherokee Tribe as an inevitable step in progress during his Second Annual Message to Congress.

The process of conquest and removal had been underway prior to Jackson's decree. Shortly before the outbreak of the War of 1812, Governor William Henry Harrison of the recently organized Indiana Territory met with Shawnee Chief Tecumseh in order to broker a peace agreement. Since the British and Native Americans were allied in the Ohio Valley, pressure mounted on Harrison to prevent a confrontation. Tecumseh reiterated to Harrison the Native

American philosophy of land ownership. Harrison, not satisfied, then managed to bypass Tecumseh and secure the cession of three million acres of Indian land to the United States. When Tecumseh mobilized a number of Indian tribes to save their lands, Harrison decided to attack Tecumseh's village, Prophetown, on the mouth of the Tippecanoe River in late 1811. Tecumseh and most of his warriors were not in the village when Harrison attacked, and Prophetown fell after two days of battle. Harrison, despite suffering more losses, burned the buildings, destroyed all the food and possessions, and immediately declared victory.

Tecumseh's dream of a united Indian confederacy died with him in battle in 1812. After the close of the War of 1812, the Native Americans of the Old Northwest Territory found themselves removed from the territories of Michigan, Ohio, and Indiana. The process of removal then continued as American statesmen, unsympathetic to Native American culture, began engineering their relocation under the guise of beneficent guardianship and paternalistic friendship.

The classic case in point was the removal of the Cherokees, who were peaceful farmers, from Georgia in the early 1830s. In 1829, despite being peaceful farmers, the state of Georgia appropriated all Indian land within its borders, declared all Cherokee laws null and void, disallowed them from testifying in court against state citizens, and distributed their lands to white settlers in a lottery system. With the passage of the Cherokee Removal Act in May 1830, tribal chiefs appealed to the Jackson Administration. But it was in vain. Even after Chief Justice John Marshall partially reversed himself in the case of Rev. Samuel A. Worcester v. the State of Georgia (1832), President Jackson dismissed the ruling and condoned Georgia's appropriation of seven million acres of land. After the Cherokee refused to move for three years, General Winfield Scott led a 7,000 man force and removed some 1,700 Cherokees in the middle of winter without prior warning. The path they were forced to tred, known as the "Trail of Tears," went to Arkansas and then to Oklahoma. Along this terrible journey nearly 100 Native Americans, including many women and children, died each day from the cold, hunger, and disease that ravaged them during their forcible removal. Some four thousand died.

The actions of the Jackson Administration were met with criticism by peace groups, especially the American Peace Society. Members such as Ladd and George Beckwith questioned the justification for such removal and the way in which it was carried out. In their opinion, the Cherokee were peaceful," civilized" people who had even written their own constitution modeled after that of the federal government's. New England peace poet Lydia Sigourney helped promote one of the first national women's petition campaigns against the removal. The Quakers, moreover, condemned the use of military troops to force the Cherokee from their homeland. In addition, the American Board of Commissioners for Foreign Missions waged its own campaign. Rallying hundred of church groups, the American Board submitted to Congress hundreds of memorials harshly criticizing the removal policy as a violation of Native American rights. Expressing the pacifist view of peace as justice was Jeremiah Evarts, the Board's secretary, who in a series of interesting essays written under the name of William Penn, argued that the original treaties guaranteeing the Native Americans land rights must be upheld. A strong belief in equality underscored his message.

But the belief in inevitable "progress" and opportunity was too much for white settlers to ignore. By the 1840s "winning the West" was inextricably tied to the ideological virtue of "Manifest Destiny," the idea that the U.S. had a god-given right to expand its borders from the Atlantic to the Pacific Ocean. A war with Mexico gave added currency to those who believed in the righteousness of territorial expansionism.

OPPOSITION TO WAR WITH MEXICO

While Burritt's overseas peace overtures brought greater attention to the American Peace Society's efforts, the Society received an additional boost in 1845 when the brilliant Boston lawyer and later United States senator, Charles

Sumner, criticized America's growing imperialistic designs. The turning point of Sumner's career was his Fourth of July oration, in which he examined and condemned the whole war system as a pitifully insufficient method of determining justice. While uniformed military guests seated in the front row listened in horror, Sumner castigated the false prejudice of national honor: "Our minds, nursed by the literature of antiquity, have imbibed the narrow sentiment of heathen patriotism. Exclusive love for the land of birth was part of the religion of Greece and Rome. It is an indication of the lowness of their moral nature, that this sentiment was so material as well as exclusive in its character." He cogently argued for the substitutes recommended by friends of peace: "The various modes, proposed for the determination of international disputes, are Negotiation, Mediation, Arbitration, and a Congress of Nations—all of them practicable and calculated to secure peaceful justice." For Sumner, "The True Grandeur of humanity is in moral elevation sustained, enlightened and decorated by the intellect of man. The surest tokens of this Grandeur, in a State, are that Christian Beneficence, which diffuses the greatest happiness among the greatest number, and that passionless, God-like Justice, which controls the relations of the State to other States, and to all the people committed to its charge." This speech marked the beginning of Sumner's influential role in the peace movement.[40]

Although Sumner's July 4th oration set off a groundswell of enthusiasm among peace disciples, it was scarcely enough to contain the ambitions of President James K. Polk and the promoters of America's "Manifest Destiny," who equated expansion with progress. After finally reaching a settlement with Britain over the Oregon boundary, the President, in early 1846, turned his attention to Mexican-American relations – with the aim of making the Rio Grande the Southern border of the U.S. – and to U.S. aspirations for California. In May, open warfare broke out between the United States and Mexico.

According to historian Frederick Merk, the Mexican War was the first time that a president informed Congress of the existence of a war before a declaration of war had been made by Congress.[41] Ultimately, with administration stampede tactics, a war bill passed overwhelmingly, 174 to 14. The negative votes were nearly all from New England, with a few from the West.[42]

Almost as quickly as war broke out, anti-war opposition surfaced in different parts of the country. It was most vociferous, however, in the northeast where American Peace Society president, William Jay, publicly condemned Polk and his supporters' imperial designs. In his Review of the Mexican War, Jay claimed that Polk's proclamation of war against Mexico was nothing more than an extension of American aggression against Mexico that had begun as early as 1819. He was convinced, as many Society members were, that the territory in dispute was Mexican, and that American blood was shed on Mexican, not American territory. When Polk sought to counter these charges by pointing to unsatisfied claims of American citizens against Mexico stemming from losses incurred during periods of unrest in Mexico, Jay belittled them as "insignificant and unworthy of bloodshed." Personally, Jay believed that the real object of the war was the conquest of more territory for the extension of slavery. He was thus typical of the overwhelming majority of abolitionists who strongly opposed the war because they saw it to be a plot to obtain more land for slaveholders.

Most noticeable were the voices of protest that echoed throughout the New England countryside. Politically, in many ways, the Whig Party's dissent paralleled the Federalist dissent during the War of 1812. First, in both instances, New England was the stronghold of dissent, although opposition spread more widely from 1846-1848. Second, the grievances of New England included the administration's policies of westward territorial expansion – which implied "a permanent diminution of New England's political power." In the Mexican War, of course, westward territorial expansion was immediately at issue. Third, fear of "a reduction in New England's power sprang not only from direct political interests," but from distaste for the whole southern and western economic and cultural system – seen by dissidents as represented in Washington and the administration's war. Last, in both instances, opposition to the war was reinforced by the "self-conscious Christianity of New England tradition." New England dissent from the

War of 1812 had led to the founding of peace societies, which later helped mobilize opposition to the Mexican War.[43]

The mobilization of this Christian anti-war tradition in its New England centers, when New England also happened to be experiencing its first great literary renaissance, gave an unprecedented literary aspect to dissent against the Mexican War. Noted intellectuals, such as Ralph Waldo Emerson, Theodore Parker, Henry David Thoreau, and Henry Wadsworth Longfellow, spoke out against militarism in general and the war, in particular. Many of these thinkers were connected to an intellectual movement known as Transcendentalism. Transcendentalism was a philosophy grounded in moral and individual progress and directed many of its criticisms at the emerging industrialization of the northeast.

Emerson, the sage of New England Transcendentalists, was so disgusted with the war that he predicted the United States would absorb Mexico "as the man swallows the arsenic, which brings him down in turn." But he was too engrossed in his own solitary intellectual pursuits to actively enter the anti-war ranks, despite his own proclamation that "If peace is to be maintained, it must be by brave men... [who will] carry their life in their own hands... and will not seek another man's life." Not so the Unitarian minister and Transcendentalist Theodore Parker, who was drawn into the inner circles of the peace movement by the Texas-Mexican issue. Alarmed by the nation's "lust" for more land, he wrote in evangelical tones: "We can refuse to take part in it; we can encourage others to do the same.... Men will call us traitors; what then? That hurt nobody in '76. We are a Rebellious nation; our whole history is treason; our blood was attained before we were born....Though all the governors of the world bid us commit treason against man, and set the example, let us never submit. Let God only be a master to control our conscience." Emerson and Parker's opposition to the Mexican War was mild compared with that of Henry David Thoreau. Relying on Emerson's "Brahmin insights" and Parker's emotional appeal, Thoreau produced one of the most thought-provoking criticisms of war in general and one of the most important statements in the history of non-violence.[44]

Thoreau rejected the war by defiantly refusing to pay the tax levied to support it. To demonstrate his protest, he spent one night in the Concord jail. From that brief incarceration was born his famous essay "Civil Disobedience," which profoundly influenced pacifist thinkers such as Leo Tolstoy, Mohandas Gandhi, and Martin Luther King, Jr. His essay is an impassioned plea for moral commitment in the face of injustice and a justification for opposing the state when law and conscience conflict. "There will never be a really free and enlightened State," he asserted firmly, "until the State comes to recognize the individual as a higher independent power, from which all its own power and authority are derived, and treats him accordingly." Those who blindly serve the state and are "commonly esteemed good citizens" are, in reality, nothing more than mere animals or machines. Their minds are empty vacuums operating intellectual wastelands with absolutely no sense of individual integrity. "The mass of men serve the state thus, not as men mainly, but as machines, with their bodies," he noted. ".... In most cases, there is no free exercise whatever of the judgment or the moral sense; but they put themselves on a level with wood and earth and stones.... Such command no more respect than men of straw or a lump of dirt. They have the same sort of worth only as horses and dogs." As for the punishment which might befall those who followed Thoreau's challenge not to cooperate with injustice, the transcendentalist argued that: "Under a government which imprisons any unjustly, the true place for a just man is also a prison."[45]

Thoreau's anti-war sentiments were endorsed by the noted poet Henry Wadsworth Longfellow. After visiting Springfield, Massachusetts, where the "row of guns on the wall of the arsenal suggested the organ pipes of death," Longfellow responded with the poem "The Arsenal at Springfield." The first two and last four stanzas capture Longfellow's pro-peace feelings in true poetic fashion.

This is the Arsenal. From floor to ceiling,

Like a huge organ, rise the burnished arms;
But form their silent pipes no anthem pealing
  Startles the villagers with strange alarms.
Ah! What a sound will rise, how wild and dreary,
  When the death-angel touches those swift keys!
What a loud lament and dismal Miserere
  Will mingle with their awful symphonies! ...
Were half the power that fills the world with terror,
  Were half the wealth bestowed on camps and courts,
Given to redeem the human mind from error,
  There were no need of arsenals or forts:
The warrior's name would be a name abhorred!
  And every nation that should lift again
Its hand against a brother, on its forehead
  Would forevermore the curse of Cain!
Down the dark future, through long generations,
  The echoing sounds grow fainter and then cease;
And like a bell, with solemn, sweet vibrations,
  I hear once more the voice of Christ say, "Peace!"
Peace! And no longer from its brazen portals
  The blast of War's great organ shakes the skies!
But beautiful as songs of the immortals,
  The holy melodies of love arise.[46]

In addition to literary verses, the 1846-1848 conflict was accompanied by loud voices of protest and dissent from politicians. New England Whigs in Congress, led by former President John Quincy Adams, denounced the war as nothing more than a move to expand slavery. The protest by the "Conscience Whigs," as some called this group, was part of the vigorous New England abolitionist movement. Anti-slavery Whigs attempted to stem the westward tide of slavery with the Wilmot Proviso, a rider to an appropriations bill, which called for slavery to be outlawed in newly-acquired territory. The bill was voted on numerous times, only to pass in the House and fail in the Senate.[47]

Several legislators were concerned over the legality of the war, and raised serious questions about the war-making powers of the President. Many wondered if Democratic President Polk had war on his mind during his campaign, and if, through his orders to General Zachary Taylor, he had provoked the Mexicans into the incident he used to justify his war declaration. In Congress anti-expansionists passed a resolution, 85-81, "declaring that the war with Mexico was unnecessarily and unconstitutionally commenced by the President."[48]

Though much denounced in the North, the war with Mexico was also not popular with all groups in the South. To many Southern leaders, the war seemed certain to result in "demands for higher tariffs to pay the costs of an army and an increasing horde of federal officeholders." Alexander H. Stephens of Georgia, a leader of the Southern Whigs, vied with his Northern colleagues in Congress in his denunciation of the war. Robert Toombs, another Georgia Representative, criticized Polk's attempts to stifle all opposition. Toombs also opposed any increase of the regular army and, as early as January 1847, called for a peace offer to Mexico. In South Carolina, the Charleston Mercury, former Vice President John. C. Calhoun's mouthpiece, was hostile to the war. Calhoun, himself, was unsparing in his criticisms. Speaking on his resolution—which affirmed that the war with Mexico should not be one of conquest—he called for a purely defensive war. The alternative of aggressive war would result, he feared, in an army greatly increased in size and cost. He concluded that the Mexican conflict had cast doubt upon the United States' reputation for justice, moderation and wisdom. Calhoun also maintained that the increasing powers the conflict gave to the government violated traditional American rights and liberties.

Anti-war sentiment reached its peak in late 1847. Mounting public impatience with the war created a political climate that frustrated Polk's attempt to conquer all of Mexico and forced him to settle for less territory. Clearly, this is one of the first examples in American history where the organized peace movement proved effective in bringing an end to hostilities. The American Peace Society had a direct effect on Federal enlistments in New England; its journal, Advocate of Peace, edited by George Beckwith, published numerous articles criticizing the Polk administration as did the Pennsylvania Freeman edited by abolitionist and peace activist Mary Grew. The efforts of anti-war critics and pacifists were instrumental in forcing a peace settlement with Mexico. The war finally ended in 1848, but the controversy lingered over matters involving slavery and territorial expansion. While peace crusaders helped contain the violence and prevented further bloodshed, domestic political passions and sectional animosity were on the rise as anti-war abolitionists persuaded many northerners that the southern slave states were disrupting the national mission of freedom for all.

THE LEAGUE OF UNIVERSAL BROTHERHOOD

While opponents of war attacked U.S. imperial designs, the energetic Burritt continued his personal quest for peace and justice. In the late 1840's, he undertook a number of actions designed to promote international understanding. Criticizing the American Peace Society for its elitist approach to peace making—and converting key opinion makers—Burritt showed his preference for carrying the peace message to the masses. In the autumn of 1846, having established close ties with British Friends, he founded the largest and most uncompromising nonsectarian pacifist organization yet known among Western peace seekers: the League of Universal Brotherhood. By 1850, this "world peace society" had seventy thousand British and American signatures to its pledge of complete disavowal of war. It was the League that sponsored the "Friendly Address" movement, noted earlier, an exercise in "people diplomacy" by which different cities were paired (Boston, Massachusetts and Manchester, England) and citizens by the thousands exchanged expressions of goodwill. Burritt also induced the League to sponsor "The Olive Leaf Mission," through which peace propaganda was inserted in forty continental newspapers. Between 1850 and 1856, he estimated that the Olive Leaves reached one million readers monthly.[49]

Perhaps Burritt's greatest effort was the organization of the Brussels Peace Congress in 1848, which inaugurated a series of meetings held in the following years at Paris, Frankfurt, London, Manchester, and Edinburgh. To bring the American peace movement into this truly international peace organization, Burritt, in 1850, organized eighteen state peace conventions which resulted in forty Americans attending the Frankfurt Congress that year. These peace congresses won increasing attention from the European and British press, while in the U.S. the American Peace Society's leaders praised them as signs of true international cooperation against war. At each Congress, Burritt ably argued for such a world peace organization and Court of Nations as William Ladd had done on many occasions.[50]

Finally, Burritt proposed the creation of an international workingman's parliament as a means of achieving peace, and he laid plans for an "organized strike of the workingmen of Christendom against war" in the event of failure to establish a congress of nations and bring to fruition some form of complete disarmament.[51] Burritt devoted time to a related scheme of cheap international postage as an inexpensive means of maintaining transoceanic goodwill, as well as developing plans to prevent a civil war on American soil by urging that slaveowners be compensated with additional land for emancipating their slaves.

Burritt's ability to express his views in internationalist terms was an inspiration to all peace seekers. His views were intelligent and far sighted, but by the 1850's his reasonableness and prescience no longer proved suitable as a model for peace reformers. The American peace movement diminished in importance as heated national politics overflowed with unparalleled bitter sectional animosities, silencing the voices of pacification and moderation. In 1860 the American Peace Society, long considered the country's major nonsectarian peace organization, failed to hold its annual business meeting for lack of a quorum.[52]

CRITICISMS OF THE CIVIL WAR

The events of the 1850's – "Bloody Kansas," the Dred Scott Decision, and John Brown's raid on the federal arsenal at Harper's Ferry, Virginia, (an attempt to spark a massive slave insurrection) – indicated that the slavery issue would likely be decided by force of arms rather than reason and calm. In particular, the harsh Fugitive Slave Law (part of the 1850 Compromise), "Bleeding Kansas," and the Dred Scott Decision convinced many peace seekers to accept the need for violent means to abolish slavery. Some decided that promoting peace in a slave republic was unacceptable when matched against the growing opportunity to eliminate slavery. The conflict between violence and social justice placed many peace proponents in a precarious position, and for many he desire to abolish slavery outweighed their acceptance of nonviolence. Peacemakers who shifted positions, accepting war as the lesser of two evils, included Frederick Douglass, Lydia Child, Lucretia Mott (she remained very ambivalent), and leaders of the American Peace Society. Second, Garrisonian non-resistants, in particular, personalized their acceptance of violence so long as it worked towards God's liberating purposes. Non-resistants in the 1850's no longer looked for self-purifying individual perfection. They were more than willing to stand behind a righteous God who would pass judgment upon a sinful people and advance the cause of peace through national suffering. In fact, the American Peace Society publicly acknowledged the right of the Union government to enforce laws and maintain internal order through loyal allegiance. The Civil War presented nineteenth century peace activists with their most daunting challenge to date: deciding between accepting violence to free the slaves and religious obedience to Christ's teachings through non-violence. It proved extremely disconcerting trying to temper an ethic of love with an acceptance of coercion.

When war finally did break out between the North and the South in April 1861, not all Americans were willing to accept the fighting as willingly as Garrisonian non-resistants. Anarchists, for example, aspired to a society that would function non-violently without need of the aggressive state. Josiah Warren, a peace advocate and pioneer American anarchist, blasted the war as barbarous in True Civilization, an Immediate Necessity (1863). As early as 1833, Warren, a social reformer, inventor, musician, and America's first true philosophical anarchist, expressed his own thoughts on peace in a journal he published himself, Peaceful Revolutionist, which generated four issues espousing the creation of an orderly, just community erected through non-violence. Disillusioned by his own personal experience as a willing participant at Robert Owen's utopian community at New Harmony, Indiana, Warren began preaching the twin themes of individual liberty and non-violence – the centerpieces of his future political and social commentary.

Warren blamed war largely on the greed of speculators and tariff supporters, the ambitions of profiteers. At the time the war broke out, Warren was living in a utopian colony, Modern Times, some forty miles east of New York City, on Long Island. To his utter consternation, some members of the community demonstrated their patriotic feeling with a brass band, and ten even volunteered for the Union cause. This "eccentric arch-individualist" made a strong plea for a fundamental reorganization of society without "violence, force, or compulsion either for the perpetuation of the union, the protection of private property, or the enforcement of the laws." He wrote that "Nothing but the clamor of war and the fear of prisons and violent deaths smother, for the moment, the low moan from desolated hearths and broken hearts from the depths of hell we are in."[53]

The more radical labor unionists, those most influenced by revolutionary developments abroad, also agreed with Warren's indictment of war. Under the leadership of the incorruptible William H. Sylvis, future head of the National Labor Union, and his Committee of Thirty-four, they vigorously opposed the resort to arms. Sylvis and his committee looked upon the conflict as a quarrel between two sets of masters, the workers having nothing to do with it. In short, they adopted the classic social revolutionary attitude toward all "capitalistic wars." Sylvis' group demanded that if men were to be conscripted, so should capital. Calling upon the workers of both North and South to prevent further bloodshed by every means within their power, Sylvis' Committee of Thirty-four organized huge mass protest meetings from Boston to Louisville, Kentucky. It represented the first time in American history that workers exchanged their patriotic suits for anti-war coveralls.

Politicians also spoke out against the war. Representative Clement L. Vallandingham of Ohio declared openly that the people should sabotage this "wicked, cruel, and unnecessary war." As head of the Peace Democrats or Copperheads, so designated by Union sympathizers who named them after the poisonous snake, Vallandingham, working in conjunction with secret societies such as the Knights of the Golden Circle, plotted against what he considered a war for the fattening of "Eastern capitalists." Generally described as seditious in both North and South, the Copperheads advocated a union restored by negotiation rather than war. They denounced military arrests, conscription, and even emancipation, along with other war measures. Other leaders of this group included Alexander Long of Cincinnati, Fernando Wood of New York, L.B. Milligan of Indiana, and B.G. Harris of Maryland.

The Copperheads argued that the war's costs in lives, money, and restrictions on personal liberty were too great to be sanctioned. What motivated their opposition to this war was a belief that the Union government had been prompted to wage war in order to fatten the wallets of the industrialists. The North's economy had rapidly industrialized since the early 1820s and huge profits could be made in terms of supplying war material to the Union troops. Sympathetic to the Democratic Party, the Copperheads were suspicious of any Republican justification for war. They also argued that the South could not be defeated and that the war was useless. They insisted that even if the North prevailed in preserving the Union and freeing the slaves, a Union based on compulsion was a refutation of the basic principles of democracy as codified in the Constitution.

Though simplistic in their arguments and not "overly repugnant to the use of force either to end conscription or to repulse Confederate military excursions into border states," the Copperheads represented a small band of opponents of war who wished to stop the carnage by "undermining the morale of soldiers and encouraging desertion."[54] During the war, they helped Confederate prisoners escape and smuggled war materials into the Confederacy, demonstrating that they were certainly not beneath acts of espionage. Vallandingham, who had been a member of Congress, was finally arrested in 1863 and convicted of opposing the Union's war effort. Lincoln, trying not to make a martyr of him, decided to banish him to the Confederacy, but Vallandingham promptly headed north to Canada instead.

DRAFT OPPOSITION

In the North, anti-war Democrats severely criticized the Lincoln administration's handling of the war and called for a negotiated settlement. Part of the political opposition was openly racist, charging that the enslaved blacks had caused the conflict. When the Union introduced a draft in 1863, anti-draft riots broke out in many places. The most serious were in New York City, where rioters fought federal troops for three days. There, mobs of whites burned an orphan asylum for black children, and demolished shops and houses of white abolitionists along with those of African-Americans. Rioters destroyed many buildings and estimates of deaths ranged as high as a thousand or more.

The Conscription Act of 1863 sparked violent opposition especially from recent Irish immigrants. The newly-arrived Irish, having suffered at the hands of the British Crown in their native land and seeking better economic opportunities in the new, did not want to be forced to fight a war that was likely to increase the number of free blacks, with whom they competed for unskilled jobs. African-American male workers, unable to get jobs because of their race, at times broke strikes by Irish dock workers and other laborers. This fact, coupled with uncertain military successes early on, had led to a growing dissatisfaction among draft-age men. North and South had laws permitting drafted men to buy exemption from military service, but most workers could not afford to pay the $300 to the government for this purpose, making the war for all practical purposes "a rich man's war and a poor man's fight."

Not comforting to the Administration's ear was a fife and drum song entitled "Grafted into the Army," which clearly showed a shift in attitude from exuberant support to disillusionment with war. The song tells how an uneducated northern mother grieves for her son who has been "grafted" into the army:

> Our poor Jimmy has gone for to live in a tent.
> They have grafted him into the army.
> He finally puckered up courage and went,
> When they grafted him into the army.
> I told them the child was too young, alas!
> At the captain's forequarters, they said he would pass,
> They'd train him well in the infantry class,
> So they grafted him into the army.
> Oh Jimmy farewell! Your brothers fell away down in alabamy.
> I thought they would spare, a lone widder's heir,
> But they grafted him into the army.[55]

This parody of a popular song of Civil War America dramatizes the massive intrusion of the federal government into the personal lives of virtually all Northern families between July 1863 and April 1865. Economic and ethnic considerations played a role in opposition to the draft. During that period, four national drafts were held. But of the 776,829 men called, only 46,347 actually served. More than one-fifth of all individuals called to serve—161,244 men—refused to report to their draft boards. Throughout the North, more men chose illegal evasion of the draft than the combined total of individuals who paid commutation fees or obtained substitutes and more opted against participating in the draft system than were able to avoid service because of some physical disability. While internal opposition also plagued the Confederate war effort,

Northern draft resistance was far more widespread and disconcerting to the Republican administration than its counterpart was to the Jefferson Davis regime.

The high rate of illegal draft evasion was in part caused by the technological transformation of northern agriculture and industry in the first half of the nineteenth century. Northern society, with its obvious social divisions often defined by class and ethnicity, contained the potential for internal disruption, dislocation, and violence. Certain groups, including the Irish, perceived by others as alien cultures residing in America and seemingly part of that permanent lower class too poor to opt for legal methods of avoiding military service, used illegal draft evasion to express resistance to modern economic, social, and political development. Republican leaders showed obvious disdain for a permanent underclass incessantly toiling for wages and incapable of economic independence because of an inability to conform to the values and virtues requisite for success in a modernizing society. Conscription legislation—with its reminders of European horrors and protective qualities for propertied classes—appeared particularly threatening to working-class people, heavily comprised of new citizens still reluctant to cast off European traditions. As we will see, by the time of World War I, labor critics of the capitalist system had crafted some compelling socialist anti-war critiques aimed directly at conscription laws.

CONSCIENTIOUS OBJECTORS

If draft resistance based on economics explains the high percentage of northern illegal evasion, religious opposition showed no geographical preference. The Historic Peace Churches officially refused to condone military service, though some Quaker men joined the Union army.[56] Both the Union and Confederacy provided limited exemption from military service for religious objectors from traditionally pacifist sects, but these concessions were considered insufficient by most objectors. In the North, some were jailed for refusing to serve or to obey military orders when forcibly inducted into the army. They had to endure various tribulations before being released as a result of Friends' urgent appeal on their behalf to President Lincoln and Secretary of War William Stanton, both of whom proved sympathetic. Unfortunately, Cyrus Pringle, a Vermont Quaker, apparently did not have the ear of the President and Secretary of War; he was tortured by being spread-eagled on the ground for several hours in the hot sun.

In the South, as a result of lobbying by Quakers, Mennonites and Brethren, the government eventually agreed to exempt religious objectors on the condition that they pay $500 for this privilege. A small number refused to take this way out and, after induction into the army, suffered hardships, including the application of torture that was more brutal than that meted out to northern COs. The case of eighteen-year-old apprentice potter, Tilghman Vestal, is instructive. Conscripted and assigned to the 14th Tennessee regiment, he was ordered to the Orange County House, Virginia, for refusing to drill with musket. There one officer knocked him down and numerous soldiers pierced him with bayonets more than eighteen times for his refusal to bear arms. He was then sent to Salisbury prison where he was forced to sleep in his own vermin. Confederacy manpower needs, combined with local suspicion of the Quakers' longstanding opposition to slavery, imposed greater hardships on COs living in the South.

Still, numerous Quakers refused to pay war taxes (a consistent historic pattern to their war resistance) and both the Union and Confederate governments seized property in lieu of payment.[57] However, there were also acts of kindness, particularly in the North where politically-connected Friends had access to Union officials. By February 1864, for instance, the Lincoln administration permitted religious pacifists to do hospital work as an acceptable alternative to bearing arms. The view of providing humanitarian relief thus led to the first alternative service legislation in American history. It would become a historical principle later applied to America's twentieth century world wars.

One of the more notable peace efforts by Historic Peace Churches was undertaken by the Mennonites. Though not as radical as the Quaker position on refusal to pay war taxes, the Mennonites offered some noteworthy comments regarding their ideological opposition to the draft and war in general. The following stories have been given full treatment in Brock's Pacifism in the United States.

One Northerner who was most concerned about re-invigorating the Mennonite peace testimony was the publisher and editor John F. Funk. In a sixteen-page pamphlet entitled Warfare, Its Evils, Our Duty, Funk discussed the Mennonite doctrine on war while explaining the grounds for taking the conscientious objector stand. It was the first American Mennonite publication devoted solely to the issue of war. In it, Funk contrasted the hatred and destruction rising out of war with the loving spirit of Jesus, and argued that the two were totally irreconcilable. He expressed forcefully his "sense of disappointment at the destruction in his country, which had been so recently the home of peace and law." He encouraged the uncertain and undecided to remain steadfast in their reluctance to kill their fellow human beings.[58]

Inspired by Funk's plea, a Mennonite minister from Ohio, John M. Brenneman, penned his own thesis against war. Christianity and War, a sixty-four page tract, was written as an exposition of Mennonite pacifism for the general Christian reader. The tract was poorly written and badly organized. Despite Brenneman's poor penmanship, he successfully reasserted the traditional Mennonite insistence on discipleship. His primary argument was that the "example of Christ and the apostles must be followed even at the cost of life itself." To follow the word and spirit of the gospels, with their many injunctions to return good for evil, was to enter into "a way of life which precludes the bearing of arms, no matter how seemingly righteous the cause."[59]

The draft issue, which prompted Funk and Brenneman's response, also aroused the non-resistant spirit of Daniel Musser. His influential tract, Non-Resistance Asserted, later earned him praise from Leo Tolstoy. In Musser's view, the truth of non-resistance must be "comprehended in light of an impartial reading of the gospels." The essence of this teaching is the gospel of love. There were well meaning people on both sides, and it was extremely difficult "to determine where right and wrong lay in the dispute which led to hostilities." Of course, for those who truly believed that the cause of non-resistance embodied the gospel message, there was no dilemma. Musser's nonconformity is clearly spelled out in his discussion of the relationship between non-resistance and civil government. Borrowing a page from Thoreau, Musser maintained that the refusal to participate in war—a total renunciation of the issue of violence—is only "admissible in one who has also renounced a world in which violence is an essential element."[60]

Northern Mennonites, with ideas coalesced by the draft, publicized their view of Christian non-resistance. Those below the Mason-Dixon Line, though smaller in number and not as vocal because of a less tolerant government, also upheld the spirit of non-resistance. Although southern Mennonites suffered greater abuses because of their pacifist beliefs and produced fewer ardent spokesmen, one self-educated preacher refused to be silenced; his name was John Kline.

This Virginia minister did not write any great tract comparable to his northern counterparts, but his letters to public and military officials, including his sermons, speak for themselves. Kline was an activist, who proved remarkably successful in keeping his Virginia followers in line with his anti-slavery and anti-secessionist views during the Civil War. For Kline, the word patriotism implied a broader view—the entire human family; in its narrower sense, "a love of one's country makes its possessors ready and willing to take up arms in its defense." He believed this philistine definition should be expunged from every national vocabulary. Christian principles, constitutional precedent, and "shrewd diplomatic appeal to the Confederacy to respect exemption for Conscientious Objectors" can be found in a revealing letter Kline wrote to Confederate Colonel Lewis on behalf of the men who had been "forced into the ranks despite their opposition to military service." The letter, in part, stated the following: "The privilege usually granted Christian people to pay a fine has been overruled and set aside, and they are compelled to take up weapons of carnal warfare....This is without precedent in a land of Christian liberty....None that have the spirit of Washington or Jefferson in their hearts would desire to compel their fellow countrymen to take up arms against their conscience, and to force them to kill their fellow man... a great breach of the constitution has been enforced, restrained and molested because of our religious belief and opinion." Kline's appeal was eventually honored by the Confederate government, and his activities confirmed the southern Mennonite position of "preserving the testament of their forefathers."[61]

NORTHERN FEMALE PEACE ACTIVISTS

Although the issue of male Conscientious Objection dominated the Historic Peace Churches' ideology, the developing women's rights movement was an important part of anti-war expression. Some female pacifists chose relief work and assisted freed slaves, while others decided to express their anger at the human carnage. Despite their own support for the Union cause, for example, Child and Mott were overcome by the war's brutality. It only strengthened their previous conviction that resistance, rather than the force of arms, was the correct course to follow in making American a better nation. In 1863, two of America's most famous woman's rights leaders, Elizabeth Cady Stanton and Susan B. Anthony, organized the Woman's National Loyalty League. The word "loyalty" is misleading, since the organization's purpose was to campaign for a constitutional amendment abolishing slavery forever. The league attempted to obtain three million signatures to present to Congress. The women's underlying hope was to encourage Congress to support a similar amendment for woman suffrage by tying its support to northern efforts to free all slaves. But the war's continuing violence also prompted the league's leaders to criticize the Union's war machine. In May 1863, at one meeting, Anthony scolded President Lincoln for not freeing the slaves earlier and transforming them into "a peaceful army for the Union" so that the rebellion in the South could have been avoided. Lucretia Mott, another league supporter, was outspoken in supporting the claims of Conscientious Objectors.

She was also instrumental in helping to establish the Woman's Association for the Aid of Freedmen in Philadelphia.

CONCLUSION

The vast majority of social reformers, though respectful of Christian non-resistance, subordinated their peace commitment to the Union's struggle for survival and the abolition of the slavery system. This was most apparent in the violent utterances of some of Garrison's followers. While still nursing a belief in unconditional non-violence even after the war in the South began in 1861, they condoned the blood-thirsty deeds of others, such as John Brown's fiasco at Harper's Ferry, and retribution after the war ended. "Jeff Davis ought to be hanged if any man should," wrote one of these bellicose non-resistants of the Confederate ex-President. Even Garrison, who was milder than some of his compatriots and never abandoned his faith that non-violence was morally superior to the ordeal of arms, expressed resignation.[62] The war itself generated intense patriotic and emotional loyalty on both sides. It became extremely difficult for anyone, and especially organized groups, to stand apart from the conflict.[63]

Undoubtedly, the Civil War left a legacy of martial enthusiasm which gave credence to the "sacred appeal to arms." The scant 1,500 Conscientious Objectors, brave in their stand and courageous in their unyielding faith in the power of morals, could not compete against Memorial Day, pensions, and the patriotic literature which swamped the popular periodicals of the day. The hearty band of non-sectarian, humanitarian, and romantic peace advocates who dominated the movement for the first half of the nineteenth century faced the stark realization that "For the first time, millions of men discovered that war was terrible but that it was necessary and might be splendid, and found in the Concept of their Nation a cause for which they were really prepared to die."[64]

But perhaps more importantly, the Civil War highlighted two powerful but equally competing traditions: (1) the legacy of glorifying war as a patriotic endeavor; and (2) a growing legacy of peace and feelings of horror about the brutality of war.

The first view can be ably captured by the thoughts and feelings of one of the nation's greatest poets, Walt Whitman. Working in a Union hospital camp outside of Washington, D.C., Whitman saw firsthand war's brutality. Whitman was peace loving and strongly individualistic, possessing an intense democratic faith in the will of the people. This intense faith symbolized the kind of unity and solidarity fostered by the war's patriotic call. The Civil War had convinced Whitman that a strong unified government was essential if democracy was to survive. He looked at this war as a means to a better end. But the hope for true democracy, given the gravity of the present situation, he reasoned, could only be accomplished through the patriotic call to arms. In the midst of postwar reconstruction he penned his famous DemocraticVistas devoted to the dream that perfect individualism as the strength and character of the state would reach its full potential as a matter of patriotic duty.

Whitman had been caught up in the atmosphere of martial enthusiasm. Each year after the war Memorial Day would witness thousands of parades throughout the country. Numerous military leaders were selected to high office such as Medal of Honor winner Governor Joshua Chamberlain of Maine; military training was encouraged in schools and colleges; numerous articles, written by war veterans, managed to find their way into popular journals often with a romantic twist; and the Grand Army of the Republic – forerunner to the American Legion of today – portrayed the conflict with sentimental reverence. The songs, symbols, and flags associated with the martial spirit would portend the late nineteenth century's quest for empire. Inherited in the popular ideology of reunification were a sense of fervent patriotism and an acceptance of the justification in the call to arms.

The other legacy was no less powerful. The Civil War was one of the first examples in the world of modern warfare. Cannon artillery fire, ironclad gunboats, Gatling guns, parrot rifles, and massive bayonet charges reflected the indiscriminate killing encouraged by mechanized warfare, including hand-to-hand combat. In contrast to Whitman's optimistic hopes, the novelist Stephen Crane's The Red Badge of Courage dismisses the sentimental lure of patriotism and the thrill of adventure. The lead protagonist, Henry Fleming's realization that, "He had been to touch the great death, and found that, after all, it was but the great death," captures the level of true reality all soldiers face in combat.[65] Misleading assumptions of a moral crusade, all too often perpetuated by political leaders, became a wakeup call for young men who marched to their deaths.

Friends of the peace movement were disappointed in the war's harshness and its outcome – the war hardly settled issues of racial equality. The revolting descriptions of battles, wounded veterans with their lives destroyed and made public, and fatherless children and husbandless wives being used as examples as to why wars should never be were employed as powerful examples for maintaining peace. The human cost aside, the economic argument that the war was begun by greedy Northern industrialists had its subscribers, like the radical individualist Lysander Spooner. Others pointed out that the postwar depression, marked by widespread unemployment, was directly attributable to an economy of conflict leading to general economic distress. Still many more saw the burden of high taxes, lowering of currency, rising debts, and unchecked prices compelling reasons to wish for lasting peace. There were also military commanders like Generals Thomas Hooker, Philip Sheridan, and William Tecumseh Sherman who admitted that modern warfare was more than the conscience could bear.

In the second half of the century, a new movement would emerge – one more cosmopolitan, urbane, and professional. Reflecting the nation's thrust into the era of scientific reasoning and industrialism, the new peace movement sought to elevate the virtues of logic and reason over ethics and morality. Thus the first movement, born of a semi-religious heart and soul, gave way to a new approach built on professionalism and arbitration. The way to end war was to settle differences in a reasonable manner through cosmopolitan enlightenment, or so it was presumed until expansionism again became a central issue at the end of the nineteenth century.

CHAPTER THREE
PEACE SEEKERS ENCOUNTER THE INDUSTRIAL AGE

> Acknowledging war a horrible evil, and yet accepting it on account of the cause...is not calculated to lessen its enormity....
>
> Alfred Love, 1861

INTRODUCTION

The young Quaker and successful woolens merchant, Alfred Love, declined government contracts and military service in the Union cause believing that a reinvigorated radical pacifist appeal rested upon the Christian ethic of love and non-violence. Reared in the Garrisonian idea of peaceful non-resistance, Love and a few other non-resistants sought to take the peace movement in a more radical direction after the Civil War. Saddened by the movement's inability to prevent violence and the fact that many peace organizations, especially the American Peace Society, supported the war, Love attempted to broaden the meaning of peace as change. For Love, the word "peace" did not just apply to foreign relations; it applied to the whole social fabric – the family, the local community, and even business relations. The Civil War taught him to extend his pacifism to all aspects of living. As an active pacifist, Love vigorously campaigned against American military intervention overseas and studied the ideas of disarmament and arbitration shaping the new industrial age. But, above all, Love was convinced that a fresh injection of radical pacifist non-resistance was the only effective remedy for curing society's ills.

Between 1865 and the beginning of the new century, the peace movement addressed the country's westward movement and its industrialization, becoming involved in a number of peace and justice causes. In an attempt to improve the quality of life and prevent violence at home peacemakers supported the rights of labor, formulated peace education plans in schools, witnessed women's increasing involvement in reform organizations, questioned what it meant to be "civilized" with respect to the plight of Native Americans, and applauded the observations on contemporary life by utopian novelists. Some peace activists also focused on matters abroad, seeking a more organized, practical form of internationalism. These individuals called for a campaign supporting the use of arbitration in international disputes. Whichever channel peacemakers followed, the post bellum peace movement was charged with excitement and hope for the future of humankind.

The post-Civil War peace movement would be linked to a growing international peace movement and tied at home to world-minded industrialists, social reformers, and politicians. Many post bellum anti-war workers, such as American Peace Society leader Benjamin Trueblood, encouraged the development of concrete proposals that linked "true patriotism" with international law and order bonded by an "international conscience." Such ideas seemed more necessary than ever by the end of the century when the Spanish-American War 1898 and subsequent Filipino conflict sparked the development of a strong anti-imperialists movement.[1]

While the government in the post-Civil War era grappled with reconstructing the South, moving westward, and developing its industrial prowess, there were numerous efforts by peace activists to advance a broader notion of peace: that is, the absence of war and the presence of justice. More radical visions of social reform were advanced along with the ideas of traditional peace organizations like the American Peace Society.

The American Peace Society, which still regarded itself as the backbone of the movement, regained much of its spirit and enthusiasm. In the days shortly after Appomattox, the Society regrouped with traditional sectarian pacifists, radical pacifists, and New England reformers. With a renewed sense of purpose, the Society reinstituted friendlier relations with advocates of peace in Britain, which had deteriorated during the War Between the States; it also initiated fraternal correspondence with new continental peace organizations.

But the Society's philosophy, program, and method of propaganda did not substantially change, even after 1865. Ever hopeful that a wider audience could be found despite millions of people lacking in formal education, the Society reprinted old tracts and made familiar appeals once again to the clergy, the press, and educators. Under the leadership of George Beckwith, the Society plodded along, ignoring domestic strife between business and labor and between newly-enfranchised blacks and white supremacists, and failing to articulate its disapproval of the government's militaristic pacification of the Plains Indians. The Society faced an ongoing problem of mounting debts, which increased during the long years of post-war depression. Two years after the Panic of 1873, the debt had risen to $6,000, and it wasn't until a decade had passed that revenue from the permanent fund, amounting to $60,000, rendered the organization solvent.[2]

The mounting financial problems besetting the American Peace Society and its conservative tactics in post-Civil War America proved disconcerting to the more radically-inclined pacifists. Openly critical of the Society's concern for respectability, a group of one-time Garrisonians, including Joshua Blanchard and Ezra Heywood, helped form the Universal Peace Union.

LOVE AND THE UNIVERSAL PEACE UNION

Launched at Providence in 1866 as a result of dissatisfaction with the compromising tactics displayed by the American Peace Society during the Civil War, the Universal Peace Union (UPU) labored "to remove the causes and abolish the customs of war; to discountenance all resorts to deadly force between individuals, states, or nations, never acquiescing in present wrongs."[3] Its scant membership of only ten thousand kept the peace idea alive, demanded total and immediate disarmament, and cooperated with a French peace society. The guiding spirit was Alfred Love, one of the few remaining visible sectarian pacifists of the nineteenth century. As stated earlier, he was a successful Philadelphia Quaker woolens merchant who "emphatically refused both lucrative government contracts and military service during the war."[4]

More than any previous pacifist, this somewhat "modest, shy, eccentric man" dramatized the cause of peace. "Let our halls, churches, and parks," Love proclaimed, "be thrown open to teach the arts of peace. They never yet have been fully developed. They are not confined merely to education and prayer, but comprehend proper amusements, mutual sympathy, cheer, and social life—the development of freedom, the exclusion of caste, and the guarantees of the rights of man." Each summer at Mystic, Connecticut, the Universal Peace Union, led by Love, sponsored a picnic in which thousands of people came for a pleasant exchange of views, the singing of songs, and meetings in the rustic "Temple of Peace." Under Love's personal direction and largely through his journal, The Peacemaker, the Union supported several related forums, including temperance, ensuring the civil rights of freed slaves, improved Native American/white relations, industrial arbitration, and the women's rights crusade.[5]

Though most UPU members were from the northeast, Love established more than forty branches, including one located as far west as California. The earliest members came from the ranks of the "non-resistant abolitionists," as well as some Shakers, Progressive Friends, and Connecticut-based Rogerene Quakers; there were also other Christian groups added to the mix. Some of its best known figures were utopianist Adin Ballou, Lucretia Mott, Henry Clarke Wright, Woman's Christian Temperance Union president Frances Willard and her colleague Hannah Bailey, and women's suffrage activist Julia Ward Howe. They were drawn to the post-Civil War's most radical peace organization because it offered a continuation of the perfectionist principles defining the antebellum reform movements.

Leaders of the Union, including the first woman lawyer to argue a case before the U.S. Supreme Court, noted feminist and effective lobbyist Belva A. Lockwood, petitioned, preached, and employed innovative techniques in attempts to rally public support. In one such picturesque ceremony, "the sword of a veteran officer, who had forsworn his belief in war, was beaten into a plowshare."[6] They enlisted "nearly 200 prominent figures, including Grant and William Howard Taft, as titular vice-presidents." Yet, they failed to expand a base of support beyond a 400-member remnant of Quakers and never raised an annual budget above $1000. The Union's rolls listed some 10,000 supporters, but only slightly over 400 were dues-paying members. The Union faded from existence in 1913 upon the passing of its spiritual leader.[7]

JIM CROWISM AND THE NEW SOUTH

In matters of race one would have thought that the radical utopian vision of Love and the Universal Peace Union should have expanded its vision of social justice to address the plight of blacks in the post-Reconstruction South. After 1877, southern editors and orators constantly promoted the theme of a New South. The New South represented economic hope to a defeated region in the form of cheap resources, railroad expansion, industrial development, and jobs. Yet the New South was based on segregation, not equal opportunity. One of the paradoxes of the region was that political democracy for whites and racial discrimination for blacks originated from the same dynamics. The free blacks, now American citizens, in search of mining and industrial jobs came into greater contact with hill-country whites. The competition for subsistence wages in the mines, cotton fields, and industrial plants led to wage-earning whites demanding the creation of Jim Crow laws.

It was this lost opportunity on the part of the peace movement that deserves greater examination. One particular problem was that many suffragists who were linked closely to peace efforts resented the Fifteenth Amendment granting black men the right to vote before white women. But perhaps the major stumbling bloc was regional rather than global. Peace pioneers had assumed that the bloody Civil War finally addressed the issue of slavery and that the enactments of the Thirteenth, Fourteenth, and Fifteenth Amendments were solid achievements in the struggle for social justice. What they overlooked was the regional implications of segregation once reconstruction was over. They became more focused on world affairs as the industrial impulse grew in importance. Peace pioneers did not share the "scientific racism" of this era. What they did do was place their faith in the role of arbitration on the international sphere rather than pressing the issue of racial equality. Sadly, an entirely separate system of society and economic distribution was established on the other side of "the color line" in the South. Denied access to the white world blacks established their own churches, schools, economic institutions, professions, and other services. Although racism and inequality were not limited to the South, it was more clearly accentuated below the Mason-Dixon Line and defined by its two separate and not equal societies.

Such separateness did little to lessen the hostilities and violence carried out against blacks by white supremacists. With disenfranchisement and segregation came lynchings. From 1889 to 1899 the average number of lynchings per year in the country was about 187. The following decade the number dropped to 92. Yet the percentage of lynchings taking place in the South increased to almost 90 percent during the first decade of the twentieth century. Lynching had become an increasingly Southern and racial problem. Even though there were anti-lynching campaigns led by journalist Ida B. Wells and UPU author Frances Ellen Watkins Harper, who personally used her literary skills to arouse public opposition, at this point in time, the peace movement's efforts as applied to industrial organizing were not extended to African Americans living in the South. Such attention finally came after World War I when members of the peace movement linked their drive for peace with equal treatment for blacks.

PEACE EDUCATION AND POST-BELLUM FEMALE EFFORTS

While the small Universal Peace Union demonstrated its abhorrence of war by using its vocal chords at song festivals and hammer and anvil to beat swords into plowshares, the problem of race relations would continue to haunt the nation. Meanwhile, the peace movement continued focusing on the problem of war and armaments and how the nation was educating students to think about these issues. Peace activists expressed growing concern over the rise of militarism in public education. Peace leaders felt that, in addition to chautauquas, encampments, and organizations speaking the word of peace, colleges and schools were also fortresses to be scaled. In large measure, the movement was reacting to the passage of the 1863 Morrill Act, which called for military training in public colleges and schools. By 1894, eighty-six colleges had army officers as instructors in drill.[8]

Of immediate concern was the impact of the Franco-Prussian War, which broke out in 1870. Considerable American interest was exhibited over the various European systems of military education. The long-standing American admiration for the Prussian plan of state education was carried over to her citizen army, which the American press praised as an educated, thinking army. Many Americans believed the Prussian military system, based on compulsory service, was both democratic and non-aggressive.

The public's favorable perception of Prussian militarism, identifying compulsory military training with democracy, was not received graciously by leading members of the peace movement. The war, with its widespread implications of military education, prompted Charles Sumner to deliver his famous oration, "The Duel between France and Prussia," in which he passed heavy judgment on Napoleon III, pleaded for "sympathy with Republican France, and protested against her dismemberment." This duel, Sumner declared, was "a military despotism enforcing universal military service or 'bondage.'" Unless the war system is abolished, Sumner warned his American audiences, all nations would eventually follow the Prussian example and adopt the hated policy of conscription.

In particular, peace leaders of both genders were concerned about teaching the martial spirit to America's youth. Looking at the post-Civil War records of the National Education Association (NEA), the most prominent national teachers' organization, peace movement leaders were disturbed to find absolutely no discussion of the problem of peace or war at its meetings.[9] They were even more upset by William T. Harris, the dominant figure in public school education in the 1870's and 1880's, who believed that if war came "it was inevitable and functional to some higher synthesis," and whose Darwinian views reached into hundreds of classrooms. Peace movement leaders were also distressed because schools in Boston and New York during the 1870's had overwhelming numbers of war pictures on classroom walls, and pupils were called upon to recite the details of war campaigns, the noble characteristics of military heroes, and the national advantages resulting from America's wars.[10]

Peace advocates thus began making a conscientious effort to influence the curriculum and teaching materials of the public schools. During the Grant Administration, a pamphlet by Joseph W. Leeds argued <u>Against the Teaching of War in History Textbooks</u>, which Columbia University philosopher John Dewey would also urge in the early twentieth century.[11] During the same period, <u>The American Advocate of Peace and Arbitration</u> (organ of the American Peace Society) carried a reprint from the <u>Journal of Education</u> entitled "Teach the Children—a Woman's Word." "This article," peace researcher Clinton Fink notes, "urged school teachers to promote the cause of international arbitration, one of the major goals of the peace movement during this period."[12] In the same issue, the American Peace Society advertised two of its own peace education publications: (1) <u>Topics for Essays and Discussions in Schools, Colleges, and Debating Societies</u>, which presented a list of 200 peace-related topics and a list of relevant reference books, and (2) the <u>Angel of Peace</u>, an illustrated monthly magazine for children. Primarily, peace educators in the post-war period launched a direct attack on school textbooks as a source of international misunderstanding. In the tradition of Benjamin Rush, moreover, APS also recommended "the removal of false ideas about the nature and causes of war, and called for a radical reduction in the amount of textbook space devoted to armies and war."[13]

Women were particularly prominent in promoting peace education. During the last third of the nineteenth century, according to historian Harriet Hyman Alonso in Peace as a Women's Issue, women assembled a wide range of independent reform organizations focused on educating the public about peace. Though their peace efforts received little respect from the traditional all-white male-dominated organizations, one notable feminist, Julia Ward Howe, welcomed the liberal attitude of the peacemakers toward the women's rights crusade and responded in kind. A poet, reformer, and one of the first invited officers of APS, Howe entered the peace movement during the Franco-Prussian War (1870-1871) as a way of uniting the mothers of mankind to prevent future outbreaks of barbarity. The author of "The Battle Hymn of the Republic" issued "An appeal to Womanhood Through out the World"—September, 1870. "Our husbands," she declared, "shall not come to us reeking with Carnage, for caresses and applause. Our sons shall not be taken from us to unlearn all that we have been able to teach them of charity, mercy, and patience."[14] In public meetings in New York and Boston, Howe took steps toward forming a Women's International Peace Association and a World Congress of Women on behalf of International Peace.

In the spring of 1872, she journeyed to England in an attempt to initiate a woman's peace congress and develop "a Woman's Apostolate of Peace." She was unsuccessful, despite a friendly voice of support here and there. An international peace meeting in Paris, the anti-feminist friends of peace refused her an opportunity to speak at their public meetings. Thus, her intended peace congress, Curti so aptly put it, "melted away like a dream."[15]

Still, Howe was the first female suffragist to link early feminist-pacifist ideology into a distinct and separate peace movement for women. Howe was the first reformer to propose a national day honoring mothers, a holiday that in its origins was linked to the cause of peace. As a UPU officer, she proceeded to organize "Mother's Peace Festivals" in various places throughout the globe on June 2, 1873. Gatherings were held in Boston, New York, Connecticut, Pennsylvania, New Jersey, Delaware, Illinois, Missouri, and in Constantinople, Geneva, Rome, and London. At these festivals, women condemned war and military training in schools and urged more political power for females regarding the politics of decision making for war. Each June, as late as 1909, the Festivals attracted numerous participants worldwide.

While Howe tried to carry her peace message across the Atlantic, Quaker feminist Hannah Bailey remained at home and created a peace department within the Woman's Christian Temperance Union (WCTU). Under her capable and efficient direction, the department operated in twenty-eight states—"issuing the Pacific Banner and handing out thousands of Children's Leaflets" in Sunday Schools. Encouraged by Bailey, local members of the WCTU peace department supplied anti-war material to women, who would then present papers to their literary clubs or civic organizations. They also worked to persuade ministers to preach against war, editors to publicize peace propaganda in their columns, and teachers to present the idea of international goodwill in their classrooms.[16]

Inspired by the efforts and determination of other female activists, in particular, May Wright Sewall finally succeeded in bringing into fruition an idea she had long held dear to her heart. Sewall, founder of the Girl's Classical School in Indianapolis and chair of the executive committee of the National Woman Suffrage Association, helped establish the International Council of Women, combining the national councils of women in all countries. At the World Congress of Women, which met in Chicago to coincide with the Columbian Exposition in 1893, the International Council initiated intense efforts to promote peace and arbitration. The purpose of the Council was to encourage a frank exchange of opinions by women throughout the world. During the 1890's Sewall tirelessly worked to get a manual adopted by the schools. The manual was that showed how the popular idea of arbitration could be easily adapted to family situations, school, economic endeavors, and, above all, relations among nations. Later, as president of the Council, Sewall sought to show that might does not always make right when addressing the situation in the Philippines. An effective orator and respected organizer, Sewall succeeded in developing a thoroughgoing educational campaign alerting the public to the dangers of unthinking patriotism and unchecked militarism.

The efforts of Love, Lockwood, Howe, Bailey, and Sewall were instrumental in keeping alive the idea of peace work while also expanding its focus on social justice. As Eleanor Flexner's Century of Struggle points out, the post-Civil War period initiated a widespread domestic revolution freeing many females to pursue other interests outside the home. Women who joined the temperance crusade, for instance, realized that achieving their reform goals required a broader social program. Led by females such as WCTU's president Annie Wittenmeyer, and its secretary Frances Willard, they worked not only for temperance alone, but also a wider welfare program embracing women's suffrage as both an instrument and objective. Inspired by earlier female abolitionists in WCTU, moreover, including Lucretia Mott and Lucy Stone, the crusade attracted the likes of other female activists and supporters of peace and justice. Among them were Mary McDowell, Mary Livermore, labor organizer Leonora Barry, author Frances Harper, and Anna Howard Shaw. What drew them into the public sphere was not just a concern with temperance but a strong desire to improve society through the use of women's organizations. These organizations were instrumental in calling attention to the issues of equal rights, racial justice, abolishment of industrial oppression, and the peaceful resolution of conflicts. Women's revulsion at society's ills went beyond a mere feeling of ethical injustice. It was rooted in the firm belief that all God's children were equal and capable of finding their own destiny. Their actions during this period gave even more meaning to what it meant to be civilized.

COSMOPOLITAN INFLUENCES: INTERNATIONALISM AND ARBITRATION

The post-war peace movement was also influenced by a genuine interest in cosmopolitan concerns for peace. Inspired by prominent thinkers like Francis Lieber and David Dudley Field, a small but influential group of lawyers and businessmen in the 1860's began collaborating with sympathetic European peace advocates. The goal was to encourage governments directly to establish judicial and arbitral means of settling disputes. In doing so it was hoped that order would be brought to the "functional infrastructure of the emerging system of interdependence" (international postal service, trade, communications, and consular services). These cosmopolitan peace seekers in northeastern cities had little use for "panaceas or preachments," which were commonplace among traditional sectarian peace groups still dotting the American landscape. Instead, they believed that America was part of an Atlantic community and that, as Love had suggested, government could serve as a useful instrument for social and economic improvement. In their concern for world politics, the new cosmopolitan peace seekers, who were less concerned about promoting pacifism, concentrated on the development of legal processes that would assist America in its rise to world power; at the same time, it was also their expressed hope to avoid European political entanglements that could cause war.

As events would later show, however, peacemakers who wanted to assist the U.S. in its rise to world power proved quite controversial. By the 1890s assumptions of racial hierarchy and the desire to Christianize "backward peoples" became inextricably tied to notions of American imperialism. Unintended consequences resulted. Those in the peace movement who viewed America's outward thrust as a mechanism for global improvement and stability would find themselves questioning their own justifications for U.S. expansionism.

The initial scholarly expression of the cosmopolitan peace effort came from the pen of the German-American political scientist at Columbia University, Francis Lieber. As author of <u>Instructions for the Government of Armies in the</u>

Field, General Orders No. 100 (1863), Lieber offered a cautionary appeal for the control and containment of war's violence. Even total wars, Lieber emphasized, should not be waged without respect for rules.[17] Lieber's work helped to popularize the need to provide ambulances and military hospitals for wounded soldiers.

Two years later, Lieber's peace interests expanded when he publicly urged arbitration in settling Anglo-American differences. Arbitrationists took his proposal into serious consideration. Anglo-American relations were quite tenuous during the post-Civil War years—a result of disputes pertaining to the North Atlantic fisheries, Irish-American interference in Canada, and, most importantly, the Alabama Claims issue. The Alabama Claims, especially, was an "emotionally charged situation" based on Washington's demand "for indemnity for Union losses suffered from Britain's refusal to prevent the release of Confederate warships from English shipyards."[18] A considerable degree of American animosity had been generated against the British during the Civil War because of England's less than mild endorsement of the Union cause. Nevertheless, in early 1871, British and American diplomats ironed out their differences. The two nations established a Joint High Commission resulting in the Treaty of Washington, which provided for the submission of the Alabama Claims to a five-member international arbitration tribunal that met in Geneva, Switzerland, and handed down its judgment in September 1872.

The Treaty of Washington and the Geneva Claims settlement aroused considerable interest among cosmopolitan peace advocates in the areas of international law and arbitration. David Dudley Field, a prominent American jurist who had led the way in the codification of American criminal and civil law, had previously urged the British Society for the Advancement of Social Science to establish a joint committee for the purpose of drafting a code of international laws. Encouraged by an affirmative response, Field produced in 1872 his Draft Outlines for an International Code, which called for the simultaneous reduction of armaments, followed by the development of peace machinery to solve diplomatic conflicts via a tribunal of arbitration.[19]

While Field was preparing his juridical Magnum Opus, Elihu Burritt and James Miles of the American Peace Society called for the creation of a permanent arbitration system resting upon a government-approved code of international law. Growing support for such means to peace reflected the APS's more "cautionary" approach in the post-Civil War era. It also signaled a shift within the peace movement to allow non-pacifists a louder voice. Following Field's lead, the Society succeeded in convening an international meeting in Brussels in 1873, which ultimately led to the formation of the Association for the Reform and Codification of the Law of Nations. With branches in America and Europe, the Association became the primary vehicle for reforming aspects of international law until 1895 when it was reorganized into the International Law Association.[20]

European peacemaking efforts had a profound impact on the American quest to eliminate war. Efforts to promote the importance of international law in Europe occurred roughly at the same time as the American Peace Society began widespread propaganda for arbitration. At the end of 1873 two academic juridical societies were founded in Europe: the Institute de Droit International at Ghent, devoted to the study of arbitration and private international law, and the Association for the Reform and Codification of the Law of Nations, known after 1895 as the International Law Association, formed at Brussels to promulgate a code. The Zurich meeting of the latter society, in 1877, passed a resolution stating that in future all treaties should contain a clause making arbitration obligatory in certain classes of disputes. This society claimed as a member Sir Robert Phillimore, who later played a major role in shaping the ideas that became the foundations of the Covenant of the League of Nations.

In addition, Randall Cremer, a tireless British peace advocate who was instrumental in furthering Anglo-American arbitration negotiations, organized the vast Peace Congress in Paris in 1878. With spokesmen from thirteen countries, the Congress went on record for a court of arbitration and for an international commission to estimate the armaments of each nation. The congress placed emphasis on the cost of wars to working men and on the need for strike action to prevent war. The proposal that the peace societies in various countries be federated marked a step toward more effective organization. These included Societe Francais des Amis de la Paix of France, Workmen's Peace Association of Britain, the Italian Peace Society, and the Netherlands Peace Society. A conference of representatives from workmen's organizations (from England, France and Italy) to discuss peace proposals was held in Paris in 1879. After this conference, Cremer carried a disarmament proposal through the annual meeting of the British Trades Union Congress. Strikingly, the earlier dialogue Elihu Burritt had developed with the English working classes had a profound impact on Cremer's thinking.[21]

European gestures for peace throughout the 1870's included the establishment of the Institute of International Law (for the scientific training and study of international law) and magnified the new internationalism of American peace seekers like Lieber, Field, Burritt, and Miles. Efforts of European and American arbitrationists and internationalists thus led to the creation of 130 new international nongovernmental organizations in the last quarter of the nineteenth century, and, as many peace scholars have pointed out, the very term "international organization."

The cosmopolitan peace pulse in the U.S. picked up momentum in the 1880's with the formation of the National Arbitration League. The first general convention took place in Washington, D.C., in 1882, where ex-Governor of Kansas Fred P. Stanton was elected president. While a member of Congress, according to DeBenedetti, he had deplored the "havoc, the exhaustion, the taxes, the debt" accumulating from the Mexican War.[22]

But the sparkplug who ignited the League's engine was a Scotch-Irish Philadelphian, Robert McMurdy. In 1837, after graduation from Jefferson College, he engaged in educational forays in Brazil that gained considerable distinction. When he returned to the United States, he aided Dorothea Dix in her prison reform efforts and subsequently became president of a small Kentucky college, an ordained minister in the Episcopal Church, and a very effective lobbyist. A "recognized linguist and journalist," he became a familiar sight in Washington in the 1880s because of his "portly figure, broad waistcoat, high straight collar, and high hat set back on his ears."[23]

Led by Stanton and McMurdy in the early 1880's, the National Arbitration League attempted to popularize "arbitral ideals." In May 1882, during a two-day conference attended by delegates from fifteen states, the league gave as much publicity as possible to the recent move by the Chester A. Arthur Administration for a Pan-American Conference to promote closer relations with the nation's southern neighbors. At the end of the meeting, a committee headed by Edward Tobey, the postmaster of Boston, presented some familiar resolutions calling for American initiative in summoning a congress of nations to limit armaments, to negotiate permanent treaties of arbitration, and set up an international court. League efforts on behalf of arbitral ideals helped establish one aspect of peacemaking in the last quarter of the nineteenth century.

PEACE ACTIVISTS AND THE LABOR MOVEMENT

Though international settlement based on arbitral means occupied some of the peaceseekers' efforts throughout much of the seventies, eighties, and nineties, the peace movement also focused attention on the domestic scene. Between 1865 and the turn of the century, the nation underwent tremendous material expansion. The competitive economy "based on profits that characterized industrial capitalism increased tensions between workers and those who employed them."[24] While advances in transportation brought the nation closer together, the combination of rapid industrialization with growing urbanization and immigration led to a host of conflicts, labor and ethnic tensions being among the most evident.

One of the least explored areas in American peace history has been the relationship to the worker. Post-Civil War advances in industry swelled the ranks of the country's labor force. The low wages, long hours, unsafe factory conditions, and an expanding labor pool fueled by the large number of immigrants coming to America, led to unionization efforts and strikes that were fought bitterly by employers. This era witnessed a number of strikes resulting in bloody encounters between the strikers and strike breakers backed by their allies, local law enforcement agents, and the state militias, and on some occasions federal troops. At times, workers in the peace movement, despite the American Peace Society's concern for respectability and fear of labor radicalism, protested the use of private armies by industrialists to crush strikes and destroy unions

Because of the violent nature of many labor conflicts, the Universal Peace Union offered to moderate wage and working condition disputes. Because of its abhorrence to violence, UPU failed to place the entire blame on the employers' shoulders. However, there were some members who refused to accept the organization's view that workers shared in the blame for violence. One of its founders, Ezra Heywood, became quite active in the labor movement and by the 1880s, to Love's dismay, rejected the doctrine of non-resistance completely. Eventually, he became an avowed anarchist.

Prior to abandoning his belief in non-resistance, Heywood, who followed the example of Josiah Warren and taught Benjamin Tucker, another prominent anarchist, established the Worcester Labor Reform League. He organized it in 1867 in order to educate the public about the rights of labor. By the 1870's the organization evolved into the American Labor Reform League, which encouraged support for women's rights in the area of equal pay and pushed for the eight-hour day. Aligning itself with the Knights of St. Crispin and the Sovereigns of Industry, Heywood's league encouraged working class self-consciousness; it did not, however, subscribe to the Marxist notion of the inevitability of class warfare. From the early 1870's to 1882, Heywood published a four-page monthly, The World, encouraging the idea of a monetary system based upon the value of labor rather than of gold. He also published a number of booklets disseminating the ideas of men and women calling for a restructuring of the nation's economic, social, and political way of life.

Despite Heywood's departure from the UPU, the peace organization continued supporting working-class organizations. During the Erie Railway strikes in 1874, Love condemned the readiness of the military to fire on striking workers: "Where is our boasted inalienable right to life, if we sanction such a course?" he queried. Love objected to standing armies and the military system as means by which despotism transformed workingmen into soldiers to mete out oppression and injustice to their hapless fellow workers. At the time of the 1892 Homestead strike, Love condemned Henry Clay Frick and Andrew Carnegie for employing Pinkerton's private armies to kill strikers: "A monstrous error is committed whenever military force is brought to bear upon the birthright of labor...."[25]

The Pullman strike in 1894 (Jane Addams was also involved in this labor arbitration) caused Love to declare that "lawless capitalism, with mouth dripping with blood, with heel ruthlessly crushing the helpless, must be forced backward." He agreed with Henry George, the social reformer and the author of the enormously popular book Progress and Poverty (1879), that the "vampires in iron heels" applaud the increases in the size of the army, "because the millionaire monopolists are becoming afraid of the armies of poverty-stricken people, which their oppressive trusts and machinations are creating."[26] Love and other peace disciples were quick to point out that the "highest flowering of modern industrial civilization required peace at home before it could be established abroad."[27]

The Universal Peace Union showed its sympathy in action as well as words. Its Massachusetts branch made an informal alliance with the Labor Reform League; the Philadelphia faction extended a friendly overture to William H. Sylvis (organizer of the National Labor Union) and to the Knights of Labor. In 1870 and 1873, agents of the Workmen's Peace Association, the English anti-war movement, took part in Universal Peace Union meetings, and, in 1886, Karl

Liebknecht and Edward Aveling spoke to the union on "How to Abolish Strikes, Boycotts, and Wage-Slavery."

In Love's desire to win the active support of labor and help resolve the basic economic causes of war, he advocated profit sharing and the cooperative management of industrial plants, as well as the idea of arbitration between management and workers. Such efforts were not overlooked by organized labor. In 1887, Samuel Gompers invited Randall Cremer, the visiting English trades-union leader, to address meetings of the American Federation of Labor on war, peace, and arbitration. That same year, the organization Gompers helped establish committed itself, officially, to the cause of peace and arbitration. Men of peace, especially Love, pointed out that the working class bore the brunt of war and so must join hands with peacemakers in the struggle for a warless world.

This notion also helps explain labor's broad concern for justice. The establishment of the Knights of Labor in 1869, led by Uriah Stephens and Terrence V. Powderly, demonstrated one organization's belief in the power of the just cause rather than the use of class war to achieve its goals. During the 1870s and 1880s, the Knights advanced cooperatives and used voluntary arbitration to achieve social and economic justice through non-violence; by the mid-1880s, for instance, it was operating some 140 cooperatives and had mediated over 300 labor disputes in New York alone. The Knights' Preamble specifically called for the substitution of arbitration for strikes. Strikes were considered a last resort and members were told not to use violence.

By the middle of the decade of the eighties the Knights claimed a membership of 700,000 – the height of its influence. African Americans, women, skilled and unskilled workers were all members of this one big union whose main objective was to abolish the wage system through gradualism. The Knights of Labor promoted non-violence through mediation, equality for all races and sexes among the laboring masses, and economic justice for all workers, even preferring the words "Fraternal Order" to union.

One powerful example of the Knights concern for social justice was its organization of women. It welcomed into its ranks females from all types of occupations, including waitresses, textile workers, dressmakers, teachers, clerks, shoe workers, domestics, tailors, farmers, milliners, hatters, all kinds of factory operatives, and even students. Many had never before belonged to a labor organization since most organized labor groups were led by and composed of males. In the Knights a number of women attained leadership positions in various assemblies. Helping to organize women were Miss Mary Stirling, a Philadelphia shoe maker and the lone female delegate at the "General Assembly" of 1883, Miss Mary Hanafin, a charter member of the first woman's assembly to be established, housewife and mother of twelve Mrs. George Rodgers who attained the position of Master Workman of the entire Knights' organization in Chicago, noted suffragist Frances Willard, and Leonora M. Barry, an Irish-born hosiery mill operative from Amsterdam, New York, who became Master Workman of an assembly of almost 1,0000 women and a delegate to the 1886 General Assembly. Barry, as head of the Knights' Woman's Department, traveled around the country, speaking, investigating work-related issues, and organizing women. Her efforts in support of women's issues were equal to that of two earlier female reformers, Susan B. Anthony and Frances Willard.

The accomplishments of the Knights in giving women a voice in the labor movement extended to other reform areas as well. The Knights' peaceful agitation led states to pass labor reform legislation. Some of the laws established boards of arbitration, protections for women in industry, child labor hours, safety inspections, and length of the working day. These early pieces of labor legislation would eventually be strengthened in later years. It was the Knights who led the way.

At the pinnacle of its strength, the Knights commitment to conciliation over violence was seriously challenged as a result of the Haymarket Affair in 1886. Powderly's gradualism led him to withdraw the Knights' support from a general strike for the eight-hour work day called for May 1, 1886. Concerned about increasing animosity toward labor, Powderly's first concern was educating new members and the public about the eight-hour day itself rather than risking a confrontation. By this point in time Chicago had become the nation's center for socialist and anarchist activities. Numerous German immigrant workers joined rifle and marching clubs that were akin to revolutionary cells in the eyes of the city's middle class citizens. On May 4th a large group of workers gathered in Haymarket Square to protest an attack on strikers which took place the day before; during that mêlée one striker was killed and a number were wounded. This all began as a result of a May 1st strike calling for the 8-hour day.

The meeting was orderly. When the crowd began to disperse nearly 200 police officers appeared and charged the crowd. Unexpectedly, a bomb was tossed into the confused and reeling crowd of police and protestors. Seven people were killed, including some policemen. The police retaliated against the fleeing crowd. No one was able to identify the bomb thrower. Yet Chicago authorities and the city's upper and middle classes were convinced that insurrectionary violence was at hand. Eight so-called "radicals" were rounded up in the intervening days and indicted on loosely-drawn up charges of conspiracy. All eight were convicted, with seven sentenced to be hanged. One was given 15 years in prison. After all the judicial appeals were exhausted, one of the convicted committed suicide in jail and four others, including August Spies, a well-known anarchist and agitator, and Albert Parsons were hanged on November 11, 1887. The remaining three were later pardoned by Governor John P. Altgeld in 1884. Altgeld had maintained that the convictions were unjust.

Powderly's timidity during the course of these events and his refusal to support the accused and condemn their eventual executions led to the Knights' demise. Workers by the thousands left the organization thereby paving the way for Samuel Gompers to unionize craft workers and build his own organization, the American Federation of Labor (AF of L).

Despite a propaganda campaign of nation-wide proportions linking unionism with anarchy and criminality, friends of peace immediately condemned the executions. Members of the postwar peace movement like Ezra Heywood railed against the actions of the Chicago Police Department and the actions of the Illinois courts. The executions prompted his support for anarchism. Alfred Love and his UPU lobbied intensely for exoneration of the accused and registered a strong protest after the executions were carried out. The extension of social justice to workers had taken a back seat following the Haymarket Affair and the anti-labor hysteria then sweeping the nation. Even novelists like Edward Bellamy and William Dean Howells could not hide their disappointment at the chain of events. Many of their vitriolic responses were aimed at elected officials and other public denizens who went out of their way to paint the whole labor movement as one big insurrectionary attempt to destroy America. This event also sparked the concerns of utopian novelists who sought to communicate labor's broader concerns for justice.

UTOPIAN THOUGHT IN INDUSTRIAL AMERICA

In the years following the Civil War a number of important novelists concerned with the growing effects of a business civilization painted a generally unfavorable picture of American society. Mark Twain's The Gilded Age (1871) satirized the political corruption engulfing the nation during the "Era of Reconstruction." His close friend William Dean Howells depicted American entrepreneurs as uneducated, crude, unrefined, and seriously lacking in cultural taste. In 1888, Edward Bellamy created the model for utopian novels of social criticism with his futuristic classic, Looking Backward, discussed below, which offered a vision of a more just and peaceful society. Younger novelists of the period such as Stephen Crane, Frank Norris, and Hamlin Garland detailed their own pessimism regarding the fate of the individual in his/her struggle against the uglier aspects of industrial civilization. But it would be Bellamy and Howells, who, using the persuasiveness of their pen and the acerbity of their observations of contemporary society, would pave the way in their commentaries on industrial America.

Howells, who was born and raised in frontier Ohio, became one of the most influential American novelists, editors, and critics of his time. For over fifty years he became the dominant champion of literary criticism—"the truthful treatment of material." Focusing on the normal or commonplace, as opposed to the romantic notions of the ideal or sentimental, Howells was concerned about the views and ideals shaping the actual life of men and women. He was greatly influenced by Leo Tolstoy's ideas about economic equality and non-violence. This was conveyed in his 1886 novel, The Minister's Charge.

Building on the famous Russian novelist's non-resistance philosophy Howell's intense feeling regarding social justice and democratic fairness became most apparent in his defense of the accused Haymarket anarchists. The response of the newspapers and most influential people of the nation at the time were instant and bitterly retaliatory towards the anarchists. Howells believed that the accused were set up by strong feelings of anti-labor hysteria and conspiratorial theories. After the Supreme Court of Illinois denied the appeals on November 2, 1887, Howells sent a letter to the New York Tribune on November 4th. In this letter he urged readers to petition Illinois' governor to commute the sentences; it appeared on November 6th under the heading, "Clemency for the Anarchists/A Letter from W.D. Howells." He immediately became the target of public scorn. But his sense of fairness and justice made him even more determined. After four of the accused were executed Howells wrote a second letter to the Tribune, "A Word for the Dead"; it was never published. In what many critics consider his best novel, A Hazard of New Fortunes (1890), his feelings about the Haymarket executions are conveyed in his portrayal of the German socialist Lindau. The novel powerfully contrasts two prominent and incompatible world views against each other: a narrow-minded capitalist and a cultured socialist. Howells' own distaste for war also finds expression through the actions and thoughts of Lindau, who fought in the Civil War and lost a hand in the fighting, while his capitalist foe brought a substitute.

Howells sympathy for socialistic ideals and world peace, moreover, would find expression in his less successful utopian expose`, A Traveler from Alturia (1894). Influenced by Bellamy's Looking Backward, Howells continued his critique of the Robber Barons of his time. In this particular novel Howells makes clear his complaint that the millionaire now dominated the American way of life, skewing the values of society toward profit-making rather than human welfare.

While Howells earned the reputation as one of America's most important realist writers sympathetic to utopian ideals, it was Edward Bellamy who best popularized the call for social justice. His Looking Backward, 2000-1887 (1887) was the most widely read piece of utopian literature of its time. By 1900 only Uncle Tom's Cabin had sold more copies. It is a work outlining a new type of socialist political order in which the competitive aspects of capitalism are replaced by a culture of economic security, social harmony, and peace. What holds Bellamy's society together is loyalty to the solidarity of the state. He called this philosophy of communal harmony Nationalism.

To a great extent, Bellamy's vision was inspired by Laurence Gronlund, whose 1884 work, The Cooperative Commonwealth in Its Outlines: An Exposition of Modern Socialism , became the basis for establishing a socialistic society. After the appearance of Bellamy's novel Gronlund stopped distributing his tract and began endorsing Bellamy's novel. The two visionaries sparked a Nationalist movement leading to the establishment of several utopian experiments. The most noted of these was the Equality Colony, founded in Washington State in 1897 by activist Norman Wallace Lermond and his Brotherhood of the Cooperative Commonwealth. It was built on 600 acres on the Puget Sound; nearly 3,500 colonists lived there prior to the turn of the new century. The colony's name was derived from Bellamy's last novel.

Shortly after Looking Backward's publication and well before Equality's founding, a number of Bellamy Nationalist clubs were formed. The movement quickly spread throughout the country and received support from writers like Howells and the Harvard sage Edward Everett Hale. Many members of the Nationalist clubs became involved with other reform political groups, including socialist labor leader and head of the Rail Way Car Men Eugene Debs. Many Bellamy Nationalists were also represented at the Populist Party Convention in 1891. The Nationalist movement's call for a new society was to be spearheaded by a group of educated leaders, not the laboring masses. Because of this and the fact that the movement emphasized an evolutionary, not revolutionary, approach to social change, dependent on a strong state, it soon fell out of favor with more radical democratic socialists and populists. Nevertheless, its call for social justice through peaceful means represented one unique and popular aspect to the late nineteenth century crusade for peace and justice.

PACIFISTS AND NATIVE AMERICANS

Champions of justice in the field of labor and novelists who provided an alternative vision of America in the form of a cooperative commonwealth kept alive the peace movement's broader concerns for building a better society. Turning their attention to other oppressed groups, moreover, peace workers also saw the need to assist Native Americans in their fight to survive. The homesteaders' desire for good arable lands in the West, in conjunction with the development of the railroads and various business ventures, intensified white pressure upon Native Americans. This would be the main cause of recurrent Native American wars from 1862 to 1877. It forced a mad scramble for Native American territory until most of this land was preempted for sale to advancing settlers. To the frontiersmen and the railroad magnates, the Native American had always been an obstacle in the path of westward progress; to the Native Americans, the coming of "progress" spelled the doom of the buffalo and other game on which Indian tribes depended for food, and ultimately, the destruction of their culture and way of life.

In the 1860's violence erupted shortly after the "War Between the States" had ended. In the new state of Minnesota, the Eastern (Lakota) Sioux became incensed when they failed to receive their promised payments from the government; they continued to grow angrier at the injustices committed by settlers and agents from the Bureau of Indian Affairs. When they refused to yield, further violence occurred in Minnesota farms and towns. Numerous settlers were killed in the confrontation. In brutal and swift retaliation, the U.S. Army killed numerous warriors, and at Mankato thirty-eight Native Americans were hanged in public.

The new Colorado Territory was also the scene of horrific bloodshed. Arapaho and Cheyenne resented the intrusion of miners and ranchers on their sacred lands. They began raiding stage-coach stations and ranches and murdered a white family. Once again, in reprisal, Colonel J.M. Chivington surprised the Native Americans at Sand Creek where he butchered and killed five hundred, including many women and children. Many of the bodies of those killed were mutilated, prompting Army General Nelson A. Miles to comment that the Sand Creek massacre, also known as the Chivington Massacre, was "the foulest and most unjustifiable crime in the annals of America." Throughout the 1870's highlighted by the Battle at Little Big Horn on June 25-26, 1876 and culminating with the last battle in December 1890 at Wounded Knee, South Dakota, Native Americans fought back against the U.S. military in a vain attempt to keep their lands and preserve their way of life.[28]

It was on the northern plains that the final bloody chapter in the long and tragic history of Native American-white warfare was written. More than any other battle, the massacre at Wounded Knee symbolized the destruction of a civilization. When a unit of the Seventh Cavalry responded to the unfounded fears of white miners and settlers to the "Ghost Dance" sweeping through the Indian tribes, the cavalry began arresting a number of Sioux men, women, and children who were traveling to the Pine Ridge Reservation in search of food and protection. The troops surrounded them and took away their weapons. While disarming them a disturbance broke out after a shot was heard. Without any warning or provocation the troops opened fire with their rifles and Gatling guns into the disarmed Sioux. Some 90 men and 200 women and children were mortally wounded or killed. Many American expressed horror and shame at the brutality.

During the thirty-odd years of the Indian wars, Native Americans desperately tried to hold onto their lands and maintain their distinctive ways of life. The smaller the area in which they were driven, the more desperately they fought back. In Our Hearts Fell to the Ground historian Colin G. Calloway counters the stereotype of the Plains warrior as an implacable foe of the white man. The first encounters were largely peaceful until disease and decline of game resulting from the impact of white migration across the plains made the encounters violent. The resulting friction led to the breaking up of reservations into individual landholdings in the 1880s and 1890s. The federal government imposed compulsory schooling on Indian students in an effort to strip them of their cultural values and abrogated the sense of treaties in Lone Wolf v. Hitchcock (1903), when the Supreme Court upheld the right of the government to deny its obligation to respect the rights of Indian tribes under the treaties.

Examples of Native American non-violence were evident in some instances. Beyond the Rocky Mountains Indian tribes engaged in almost no warfare prior to the arrival of the whites. These tribes developed elaborate ceremonies promoting non-violence between them. In the Northwest the potlatch ritual was established in which noted Native Americans gave away their wealth in return for honor and privilege. This practice reduced the need for warfare by lessening the competition for wealth. One tribe, the Sanpoli, composed of some 200 people in the Pacific Northwest, was a shining example of a consistent attachment to non-violent living. In 1877, for instance, the Sanpoli dreamer-prophet Skolaskin rejected invitations to join the Nez Perces tribes in war against the encroachment of white settlers. Their pacifism did not save them from the heart-wrenching dislocation when the whites took control of their land and forced them to live on a reservation together with other tribes. But in keeping with their tradition of non-violence they did not shed the blood of their enemy conquerors.

The troubling and long history of the white settlers' injustices to the Native Americans did not go unreported by contemporary Americans. Helen Hunt Jackson, in her book, A Century of Dishonor (1881), provided documentary evidence of the federal government's broken promises. While today's scholarship has done much to revise some of Jackson's observations such as Calloway's Our Hearts Fell to the Ground, Paul H. Carlson's The Plains Indians, William Leckie, The Military Conquest of the Southern Plains, and Elliot West's The Contested Plains: Indians, Goldseekers, and the Rush to Colorado, the fact remains that reformers of the period were deeply disturbed by the corruption, inefficiency, and lack of leadership plaguing the Bureau of Indian Affairs and the government's treatment of Native Americans.

Within the peace movement and with the blessings of President Grant and other high officials sympathetic to the plight of the Native Americans, the Quakers' yearly meetings set up a Committee of Friends of Indian Affairs. This body watched over the work of two Quaker superintendents of agencies and the forty Friends associated with them in the work of demonstrating Christian love and kindness to 15,000 Native Americans.

Quaker agents succeeded surprisingly well in dealing with Indian problems. They had been inspired by President Grant's message to Congress that "The Society of Friends is well known as having succeeded in living in peace with the Native Americans in the early settlement of Pennsylvania, while their white neighbors of other sects in other sections were constantly embroiled. They are also known for their opposition to all strife, violence and war, and are generally noted for their strict integrity and fair dealings. These considerations induced men to give the management of a few reservations of Native Americans to them and to lay the burden of the selection of agents upon the Society itself."[29] These agents made substantial contributions to the education of many tribes; they prevented at least one battle between rival Native Americans bands; and they demonstrated the efficacy of the principle of non-violence in dealing with peoples of color. However, their role as friends of the Indians was limited by their view that "civilizing" Native Americans meant insisting they become Christians and independent farmers and give up their traditional ways.

The idea that Native Americans should be treated fairly was shared by others besides the Society of Friends; the Universal Peace Union was most vocal in criticizing military authorities for not adhering to the peace policy between Native Americans and the U.S. government. The Union argued before committees of Congress that various proposed Indian treaties were so unjust that they could only result in uprisings. On one occasion, the UPU helped save Native Americans captured in battle from the death penalty. UPU members sent agricultural implements and other gifts to Indian agents and constantly supported those working for a just and peaceful policy toward Native Americans.

Throughout this period, the UPU passed resolution after resolution calling upon the Federal Government to revise its Indian policy and withdraw troops from the frontier. Inflaming public opinion, the Union blamed the deaths of General George A. Custer and the 264 men of his 7th Cavalry on an unjust and insincere government policy. UPU even accused the War Department of provoking the Sioux War to prevent Congress from reducing the size of the army, a criticism that did little to endear the organization to public officials.

Apart from Love one of the UPU's most ardent defenders of Native American rights was Alfred Meacham, a survivor of the Modic tribal attack on the 1873 peace commission. The attack took the lives of two unarmed peace commissioners, and Meacham barely survived. But as a member of the UPU's executive committee, Meacham recognized the importance of ending hostilities and granting equality to all Native American tribes.

Despite their commitment, the Quakers and the Universal Peace Union's humanitarian gestures proved ineffective in halting the conquest of the Indians. Grant's experimental "Peace Policy" failed. This experiment involved reservations distributed among the major religious denominations, which were given the right to direct educational and other activities on the reservations. The church groups quarreled bitterly among themselves over the disposition of the reservations, and few of the religious groups gave adequate support to the undertaking or questioned its premise that Native religion was inferior. Politicians, eager to gain reservation jobs for office-seekers, finally helped kill the policy under the Hayes administration. Additionally, the peace policy did not bring peace; on the reservations, agents relied frequently on the military to enforce their orders. Indians who refused to submit to life on the reservation were not dealt with peacefully in most cases.

Though more peaceful in their approach, even groups with the noblest of intentions and who were sympathetic to the plight of Native Americans were misled in their efforts to "civilize" them. The voices of Native Americans were loud and clear in criticizing those friends of the Indians who wanted to Christianize them and make them farmers, thus stripping them of their culture. Indian leaders like Sitting Bull and Chief Joseph and those who managed to relate their oral history for future documentation such as Black Elk, explained that their people did not want to give up deeply held values and customs, including the collective or tribal ownership of land, a belief that work was only a means of providing shelter and food, not an end in itself, and numerous religious beliefs and practices that appeared alien to white people. Whites who wanted to "Americanize" the Indians ignored the Native Americans' sense of self-respect and identity.

Many sympathizers should have heeded the warnings of Sarah Winnemucca, daughter of a Nevada Paiute chief and former scout and interpreter for General Oliver Otis Howard. A peaceloving person who called for mutual understanding of the races, Winnemucca presented numerous lectures at Boston, San Francisco, and other cities. At these gatherings she addressed the white's misconception of civilizing her people; she spoke firmly and authoritatively against the injustices to her people and denounced the corruption of agents of the Bureau of Indian Affairs. One of her major concerns was the need for a better distribution of lands to Native Americans rather than placing them on reservations.

Her views were supported by the National Indian Defense Organization. In the name of peace, members of this group argued that the Native Americans should be allowed to retain their own traditions and customs. But most reform groups ignored the pleas of Indian leaders. Caught up in the idea of assimilation many argued that it was in the best interests of the Indians to adopt Christianity, individual land ownership, and American forms of education. It was a misguided altruistic attempt.

THE LIMITS OF COSMOPOLITANISM

While some peace workers focused on domestic issues such as economic inequality, labor rights, and the fate of Native Americans, others continued their efforts on behalf of international mediation as a way to prevent war. In the 1880's, the peace movement expanded upon the world-minded attempts of Lieber, Field, Burritt, Miles, and the National Arbitration League to develop international peacekeeping machinery. It became one of the movement's principal preoccupations in the last two decades of the nineteenth century.

Particularly, growing global interdependence caused a number of American reformers to seek ways of establishing lawmaking machinery for settling international disputes. The increasing development of jurisprudence based upon social interdependence—the subordination of law to morals—reflected the changing status of the science of law itself. Legal as well as political institutions were consciously directed to the furtherance of general human ends. Although the interest of lawyers in peace would become more important after the turn of the century, their concern for developing peacemaking machinery (based upon international law) had already begun to take shape. This was based on the premise that jurisprudence and legislation may not be separated by any hard and fast line since both presuppose political and social ethics.

American business and reform leaders were well aware that improved communications and technology meant the U.S. would become more involved in a shrinking world. On the one hand this gave new life to American peacemaking and the growing cosmopolitan approach to solving international disagreements through political, diplomatic, and legal means; on the other hand, such approaches were limited by social Darwinism, racial assumptions, the search for profits, and the U.S.'s sense of mission. Within these parameters, the peace movement received a boost from government policymakers like James G. Blaine, Secretary of State, who encouraged the creation of international peacekeeping mechanisms.

Concerns about commerce, industry, and economic growth prompted world-mindedness. Blaine promoted peace as a means to increased trade: "Peace is essential to commerce, is the very life of honest trade, is the solid basis of international prosperity...." Ebullient and influential Protestant minister Josiah Strong, despite his strong Anglo-Saxonist religious proclivities, believed American peace seekers were riding the wave of the future, declaring that "We are entered upon the final stage of industrial development, which is the organization of a world-industry. This world-tendency also involves the complete development of a world-life, a world-conscience. And all these involve ultimate international arbitration." A combination of material, political, and moral factors converged upon world-minded Americans fostering a sentiment of cosmopolitanism urging the establishment of new machinery for an international peace movement.[30]

Earlier notions of equality that had animated the Garrisonians, among others, did not interest influential figures who envisaged the "triumph of peace through the domestic and global extension of Anglo-American racial supremacy."[31] Hoping to win public opinion by blending the rhetoric of evangelical Christianity with the scientific idiom of racial Anglo-Saxonism, leading British and American peace seekers promoted the general ideal of international arbitration. In 1887, British peace activist Randal Cremer was given the red carpet treatment by steel king and labor foe Andrew Carnegie—a man opposed to militarism in cases not directly affecting his profits from wages. Cremer and other British legislators had traveled across the Atlantic, visiting many American cities, with a proposal for an Anglo-American treaty agreement to submit to arbitration all future disputes between the powers.[32]

Anglo-American arbitration, initiated by Cremer in the late 1880's, was finally given wide publicity in 1895 when two Quakers, Albert and Alfred Smiley, welcomed to their scenic Lake Mohonk, New York, resort notable national leaders supporting the cause of international arbitration. This would be the first of twenty-two annual conferences to which selected guests were invited; the number of guests grew from fifty to three hundred. Topics most commonly discussed were peace education in the schools and colleges, the role of government in international arbitration, the impact of arbitration treaties, and arbitration as a matter of world politics. The purpose of the discussions was "to help concentrate the public opinion of our own land, which is very largely in favor of peace, and to bring it to bear upon the war system." Although discussions were seldom vigorous or fundamental, the Lake Mohonk Arbitration Conference popularized the idea of a permanent international court and lent a glow of respectability to the peace movement itself. As Benjamin Trueblood noted in his opening address to the first conference: "We shall find another interesting subject of discussion in the proposed establishment of a great international tribunal of arbitration, which shall be to the nations of the world what the United States Supreme Court is to the States of the Union. There is considerable difference of opinion among jurists and even among leading peace men as to the possibility of such a court, and yet it will come legitimately within the range of the discussions of this Conference."[33]

Trueblood, a respected figure at these conferences, emerged as one of the most important peace leaders near the turn of the century. President of Wilmington College in the 1870's and then head of Penn College from 1879 to 1890, Trueblood enthusiastically embraced the cause of peace in the early 1890's after spending one year in Europe as an instrumental figure in European peace councils. Fluent in a number of modern languages, he was selected secretary of the American Peace Society in 1892, a position he held until 1915. For most of that period, he was the only full-time salaried peace worker in the United States. Under his leadership, the Society's membership grew from 400 to close to 8,000 and subscriptions to its journal, the Advocate of Peace, climbed from 1,500 to more than 11,000.

Aside from organizing branch societies and writing about peace, Trueblood popularized the efforts for international arbitration – the "respectable" approach to peace. He was partly responsible for establishing the Lake Mohonk Conferences and also participated in both the International Law Association and the American Society of International Law. In keeping with the cosmopolitan nature of the movement, he insisted that an independent world economy brought about by the Industrial Revolution could hasten the movement in the direction of world federation; such views were discussed in his 1899 book, Federation of the World.

The idea of international arbitration also gained force when the long-simmering border dispute between Venezuela and the British Crown Colony of Guiana erupted into a full-scale diplomatic confrontation in the mid-1890s. The United States, using the pretext of the Monroe Doctrine to assert its imperial preeminence in the western hemisphere, interceded on the Venezuelan side. After weeks of mounting tension, the two powers agreed to submit their differences to an ad hoc tribunal at The Hague. The result was a reinforcement of the Anglo-Saxonist insistence that the two powers settle their differences with olive branch rather than cannon. At the same time, the event also signaled America's imperial dominance in the Latin American hemisphere.

Early in 1897, soon after this settlement, Secretary of State Richard Olney accepted British ambassador Sir Julian Paunceforte's overture for a treaty arrangement. The agreement required the two countries "to submit all financial and territorial differences over a five-year trial period to a complicated system of arbitrated settlement." Peace leaders in America came alive; they vigorously pressed for Senate ratification of the treaty. Their efforts were in vain, however, as the politicians on the Hill were wedded to a "skepticism of British intentions" and "doubtful over the mechanical peace agreements involved in the joint proposal."[34]

Unquestionably, the limits of the cosmopolitan peace impulse were apparent in efforts to assist in American's rise to world power. Despite the earlier historical tradition of isolationism, the years between 1865 and 1900 were marked by notions of commercial destiny and political mission abroad. Although peacemakers did not favor a policy of colonization, promoting instead arbitration conferences giving the U.S. a greater presence on the world stage, American leaders seized upon this effort to insist upon a more commanding role in global affairs. Economic motives, not altruistic feelings for peace, became the primary factor for American expansionism. The growing need of American manufacturers for more markets could only be satisfied by significantly increasing U.S. exports. To a considerable extent, this was precipitated by three decades – 1870s, 1880s, and 1890s – of falling prices, financial panics, and periods of economic depression. The farmer-labor discontent of the period was reflected in the political radicalism of the emerging Populist and Socialist parties. Businessmen, in particular, urged an expansionist policy despite not insisting on territorial acquisitions. Many from this quarter strongly encouraged arbitral means to settle disputes in order to further peaceful trading relations. Interestingly, the most vocal supporters behind the expansionist thrust were publicists, missionaries, politicians, naval officers, and professors, who blended the philosophies of manifest destiny, Darwinian evolutions, Anglo-Saxon racism, militarism and navalism, patriotism, and economic determinism into a unique justification for territorial acquisition. Supporters of territorial expansion argued that it was the duty of Anglo-Saxon nations to exercise political domination over backward areas in order to spread the principles of Christianity and civil liberty. Such rationale would be tested at the end of the 1890s with the war with Spain and then the Philippines.

TOLSTOY'S INFLUENCE IN AMERICA

While some conservative elements within the peace movement pushed for Anglo-American cooperation as part of their cosmopolitan quest for internationalism, a more radical pacifist ideology began taking root in the late 1880's and early 1890's with the appearance of the teachings of the famous Russian novelist Leo Tolstoy.[35] A nobleman by birth who professed his faith "in literal Christian anarchism," Tolstoy will forever be remembered for his classic work War and Peace. In 1888, Tolstoy published What I Believe, climaxing a "long process of spiritual fomentation and growing discontent with orthodox religion and the aristocratic society" of which he had been a member. Reading the New Testament again, Tolstoy reached the conclusion that "Western civilization as a whole was sick" and likely to die unless an effective medication for full recovery was developed. In his view, only the peasants had preserved the gospel spirit in some measure; the cultured classes were hopelessly corrupted by greed. Tolstoy now believed Jesus had taught "non-resistance to evil as a part of a broader philosophy of non-violence that contemporary civilization denied in all its activities." Man, therefore, must renounce all wars.[36]

Tolstoy, like other anarchists, wished to base the organization of society on consent and cooperation, not force. To fight for the nation-state, in his opinion, meant submission to the most powerful organ of human oppression in its most bestial form. The state, he believed, was merely an instrument for waging war against other states, each nation directing its soldiers to kill for the sake of patriotism. Anti-militarism thus seemed to Tolstoy to be both a manifestation of Christian love and an act of defiance directed against the very seat of human evil. On many occasions, he supported the principle of Conscientious Objection: "Universal military service is the keystone of the arch holding up the edifice [of the state], and its removal would bring down the whole building."[37] Acts of individual resistance to militarism, he hoped, would result in the destruction of government and its replacement by the cooperative society based on love.

Though many American reformers did not advocate the overthrow of their government, they were receptive to Tolstoy's pacifist convictions. Chicago settlement house worker and later Nobel Peace Prize winner Jane Addams, lawyer Clarence Darrow (perhaps best remembered for the 1925 Scopes "Monkey Trial" in Dayton, Tennessee), former judge Ernest H. Crosby, American Peace Society president Benjamin Trueblood, and Democratic Party leader and 1896 presidential candidate William Jennings Bryan who later resigned as Secretary of State when the policies of the Wilson administration were leading to war, all were very impressed by Tolstoy's Christian anarchism. Even in Boston, reformers and Brahmin intellectuals organized a Tolstoy Club in 1889 which numbered over a hundred members a decade later.[38]

THE SPANISH-AMERICAN WAR AND ANTI-IMPERIALISM

Through most of the 1890's, reflecting the openness of nineteenth century peace activism, sectarian pacifists, arbitrationists, and Tolstoyans cooperated in polite fashion to achieve international harmony. The issue of territorial expansionism, however, presented a serious challenge to those with a broad view of peace and justice. In April 1898, the United States Government declared war on Spain and launched effective military attacks on Spanish holdings in Cuba, Puerto Rico, and the Philippines.

Initially, many Americans supported the call for Cuban independence along with all the other territories under Spanish rule. But sentiment would quickly change to disgust when it became apparent that the battles to be fought would entail conquest rather than liberation. Howard Zinn's popular narrative A People's History of the United States, points out that business people initially felt inclined to support an "open door" policy rather than military intervention with respect to Spanish possessions. But by the Spring of 1898, business leaders were calling for action. They believed that a war would stimulate business and transportation. Most American labor unions also opposed expansionism until the war fever hit. The majority of Socialists did criticize the war insisting that the government wanted the war to take the worker's minds off their own true interests. Those highly critical of the government's ulterior motives quickly began mobilizing to form their own anti-imperialist movement.

This "splendid little war," fondly referred to by the "yellow journalists" such as William Randolph Hearst and Joseph Pulitzer, followed the failure of a three-year attempt by Spain to crush the Cuban independence movement. A jingoist press inspired by Social Darwinist preachments on behalf of the white man's burden, Alfred T. Mahan's popular book, The Influence of Sea Power upon History, and preservation of the Monroe Doctrine, encouraged American military leaders to make short work of the Spanish resistance. Within ten weeks, the United States had captured Cuba, Puerto Rico, and the Philippines, and facilitated the annexation of Hawaii. Later that year, Spanish and American negotiators worked out a settlement in Paris in which the United States compensated Spain monetarily in return for American occupation of Cuba (to be granted independence in 1902) and the cession to the U.S. of Puerto Rico and the Philippines.[39]

In response to these events, a powerful anti-imperialist movement appeared. Its origins date back to the early 1870's when liberal Republicans like Charles Sumner and Carl Schurz criticized Washington for eyeing the conquest of the Caribbean. In the 1890's, anti-imperialist sentiment was once again finding its way into press and onto podium. Schurz and E.L. Godkin, editor of The Nation, who had rebuked devotees of peace for what he called a lack of realistic insight into the causes of war, opposed plans for naval expansion, increased military budgets, and the seizure of territories such as Samoa and Hawaii.[40] Rejecting the concept of "manifest destiny," anti-imperialists argued that overseas expansion would corrupt America's noble experiment in constitutional republicanism.

The arguments that imperialism was "economically unsound, subversive of the free-trade basis of competitive capitalism, and distracted from the urgent need for domestic reform," were among those that led to the formation of the Anti-Imperialist League in Faneuil Hall, Boston, on June 15, 1898. The leaders were old-fashioned liberals (abolitionist children), endowed with a New England conscience and a determination to keep an industrializing America free from imperial temptations. Though branches were organized in Chicago, St. Louis, San Francisco, and other cities, Boston remained the heart of the movement. Anti-imperialists seriously believed all government derived its power from the consent of the governed. Respected professionals who were towers of strength in the League included Gamaliel Bradford (67 year-old descendant of the Bay Colony's first governor), Moorfield Storey (secretary to Senator Sumner), pacifists Edward Atkinson and Ernest Crosby, clergymen A.A. Berle, reformer and feminist Jane Addams, urban reformers like Hazen Pingree and Samuel "Golden Rule" Jones, African-American activist Booker T. Washington, and educator David Starr Jordan. With such political allies as George S. Boutwell, the venerable Senator George F. Hoar, William Jennings Bryan, and influential supporters like philosopher William James, Andrew Carnegie, Samuel Gompers, Carl Schurz, William Graham Sumner, and General Nelson A. Miles, the Anti-Imperialist League fomented much of the latent opposition to American expansionism.[41]

Men of letters also lent their pens to the cause; perhaps the most famous was Mark Twain. His "The War Prayer," pointing out the hypocrisy of Christian support for imperialism, tells the story of a man in church rising up and shouting sarcastically at the preacher, "O Lord our God, help us to tear their soldiers to bloody shreds with our shells, help us to cover their smiling fields with the pale forms of their patriot dead; help us to drown down the thunder of the guns with the shrieks of their wounded…." And in his essay, "To a Person Sitting in the Darkness," Twain wrote a satirical masterpiece which attempted to open the windows to the light of moderation and restraint: "Extending the Blessings of Civilization to our Brother who Sits in Darkness has been a good trade and had paid well, on the whole; and there is money in it yet, if carefully worked – but not enough in my judgment, to make any considerable risk advisable." Calling into question the rationale behind the "white man's burden," he continued his attack by noting that "The People that Sit in Darkness are getting to be too scarce – too scarce and too shy." People of sound judgment should open their eyes to the realities of the world situation because "…such darkness as is now left is really but of an indifferent quality, and not dark enough for the game. The most of these people that Sit in Darkness have been furnished with more light than was good for them or profitable for us. We have been injudicious." Adding literary weight to Twain's condemnation, moreover, was William Vaughn Moody, whose "haunting lines attempted to persuade the government to turn a deaf ear to the patriotic calls of chambers of commerce, industrial groups and missionary boards"—all of whom saw a "golden opportunity" and a "challenging duty" in empire:

> Tempt not our weakness, our cupidity!
> For, save we let the island men go free,
> Those baffled and dislaureled ghosts
> Will curse us from the lamentable coasts
> Where walk the frustrate dead.

Twain and Moody were particularly outspoken in their objection to the conquest and retention of the Philippines, which "repudiated our traditional tenet of the right of self-determination of peoples."[42]

Organizationally and individually, participants in the peace movement cast their own criticisms, along with those of the anti-imperialists. This was the era of "yellow journalism," when the popular press exaggerated events such as the deLome letter (in communication with a friend in Havana, the Spanish ambassador to the United States, Enrique deLome, had characterized President William McKinley as a "cheap politician") and the explosion of the battleship Maine in Havana harbor, which, without evidence, William Randolph Hearst blamed on the Spanish. In response, Trueblood advised peace advocates to oppose intervention in Cuba. By contrast, the American Peace Society ultimately toned down its criticisms due to the jingoistic press encouraging ultrapatriotic

Americans to view peace organizations as disloyal. This new strategy to discredit the efforts of peace movements would be used repeatedly from then on.

The APS's silence did not stop Love and the UPU from speaking out. UPU continued to urge an arbitrated resolution to the war as well as the entire question of Cuban independence. After the sinking of the battleship Maine in Havana Harbor, Love had sent some letters and cables to the American minister in Madrid, Steward Woodford, urging acceptance of third-party mediation to quell the conflict. But when the U.S. went to war, and it was revealed by a reporter for the Philadelphia Bulletin that the UPU's office and peace museum (located in Independence Hall) had hanging on the wall amid the flags of numerous nations the Spanish colors, anger soon followed. Patriotic supporters of the war were also aroused when the reporter made pubic Love's undelivered April 21st letter to Queen Regent Maria Cristina and Spanish Prime Minister Praxedes Mateo Sagasta. An angry mob entered the office and tore down pictures and banners. Love and other members received death threats and the UPU president was burned in effigy. The peace organization's office was forced to leave Independence Hall. In spite of the harassment, Love continued to oppose the war and the U.S.'s subsequent conquest of the Philippines.

The linkage between commercialism, colonialism, and a rapidly expanding navalism aroused passions on both sides. Those against a growing empire used the argument to highlight the nation's lost sense of purity. Those favoring a more aggressive overseas policy relied on an emerging virulent devotion to patriotism which was used for sinister purposes — to label those opposed to war as disloyal. Many anti-imperialists were afraid that America's "outward thrust" would distract from the more pressing needs of domestic reform. Two things were clear: first, McKinley's policies, especially in the Philippines, represented a marked departure from the U.S.'s past conduct in the Americas; second, such a departure threatened American constitutional principles and the very notion of democratic freedoms. It would be the acquisition of the Philippines that came to represent the most significant development in American foreign policy with respect to past traditions and future behavior. The decision to acquire the Philippines, a result of the 10-week war with Spain, was seen as critical to United States interests in the Far East; however, history would demonstrate that it came at a heavy price.

Two weeks prior to the February 6, 1899, Senate ratification of the Treaty of Paris, which ended the war with Spain, the Filipino-America War broke out. The war would last almost three and a half years; it cost the United States $170 million and caused 7,000 American deaths. Hundreds of thousands of Filipinos were also killed. As the ill-equipped Filipino armies, led by Emilio Aquinaldo, were defeated by superior American-trained troops, they fled into the jungle to wage a vicious guerilla war, with strong popular support. American troops resorted to torture and the slaughter of entire villages and tales of unthinkable atrocities rocked the United States. American soldiers used the painful "water cure" – forcing water down victims' throats until they yielded information or died – and even established re-concentration camps similar to those used by the Spanish Army in Cuba. With the arrival of General Arthur MacArthur, father of General Douglas A. MacArthur, in May 1900, the U.S. had 126,000 troops located on 639 military posts. MacArthur drastically increased troop levels and was unyielding with the Filipinos in revolt. Fighting continued on and off throughout 1900 and 1901, until a cunning ruse led to Aquinaldo's capture and his eventual swearing an oath of allegiance to the U.S. government.

More effective than the peace societies proper was the work of the Anti-Imperialist League. Originally, the Anti-Imperialist League was organized to discourage the McKinley Administration from seizing the Philippines. The League sought to convince the government and the people that war led to imperialism and imperialism led to war in a never-ending cycle, and that both ran counter to the "principles of Christianity and humanitarianism, the dictates of common sense, economic interest, and moral well-being." The brutality of the Filipino-American War and tales of atrocity quickly transformed the Anti-Imperialist League into a national movement with a mass constituency. Working with other anti-imperialist elements, League membership soared to over 30,000 in a growth spurt that made it the largest anti-war organization per capita in American history. Finding receptive audiences, anti-imperialists "distributed literature and placed speakers around the country as they pursued two basic goals: an immediate suspension of hostilities in the Philippines and a Congressional pledge of Philippine independence."[43]

Through the League's periodical, the Anti-Imperialist, and Edward Atkinson's The Cost of a National Crime and The Hell of War and its Penalties, the League exposed repulsive and ghastly brutalities despite official investigations that tried to hide the actions of American military personnel. Much criticism was leveled at the increased power in the executive department and the development of bureaucracy, which further demonstrated how imperialism was contrary to U.S. Constitutional traditions. Recalling the decline and fall of the Roman Empire, anti-imperialists urged Americans to remember that "When Rome began her career of conquest, the Roman Republic began to decay."

Two of the League's most important personalities were the eminent Harvard philosopher William James and the judge turned "Tolstoyan Apostle of Peace," Ernest Howard Crosby. James was for a brief time Vice-President of the Anti-Imperialist League. The Spanish-American War impressed James with the irresistible power of the war fever. He saw imperialism as an outlet for blind passion masked by a professional benevolence and he was not immune to criticizing the U.S.'s vile conduct in the Philippines:

> We gave the fighting instinct and the passion of mastery their outing...because we thought that...we could resume our permanent ideals and character when the fighting fit was done. We now see how we reckoned without our host.... We are now openly engaged in crushing out the sacredest thing in this great human world—the attempt of a people long enslaved to attain to the possession of itself, to organize its laws and government, to be free to follow its internal destinies according to its own ideals.... We are to be missionaries of civilization, and to bear the white man's burden, painful as it often is!... The individual lives are nothing. Our duty and our destiny call, and civilization must go on! Could there be a more damning indictment of that bloated idol termed "modern civilization" than this amounts to?[44]

The Spanish-American War and the suppression of the Filipino revolt aroused Crosby's deepest passions. Crosby was New York City born, a Columbia Law School graduate, Theodore Roosevelt's successor as New York State Assemblyman, and an international judge in Egypt. A member of the American Peace Society and President of the New York and American Anti-Imperialist Leagues, Crosby and other reformers immediately issued "A Declaration of Peace" in the spring of 1898. It was addressed to the "Workers of America," invoking their support for arbitration in settling a senseless war in which "American workmen" would be called upon to shoot "Spanish workmen." The war in Cuba, he wrote, was "a mad orgy of slaughter, it is a grand national 'drunk.'"[45]

Crosby was especially harsh on what he called "the absurdities of militarism." He mocked the empty vanity of military dress and manners and the inane worship of military heroes. In the world, he saw "the military idea of manliness" manifested in "Great Powers" like England and the United States picking on "nations of peasants" like the Boers in South Africa and the Filipinos. "Does any truly military nation ever tackle a nation of its own size? Of course not....They pass their time in searching the ends of the earth for little powers to massacre and rob."[46]

In 1902, expressing his outrage against American imperialism in the Philippines, Crosby wrote a satirical novel, modeled on Don Quixote, entitled, Captain Jinks, Hero. Jinks, who defended "Old Glory" in suppressing the insurrection of "Gomaldo," became a celebrated hero upon his return to the United States, only to go insane because he did not think he was an ideal soldier. He could not imagine killing loved ones on orders; the military creed was that to every command no matter how ludicrous, a soldier's appropriate response was not to "think," God forbid, but to "obey orders."[47]

Crosby also dismissed Theodore Roosevelt's fetish for building a mighty navy, saying that "to substitute a big navy for big ideas is stupid and puerile." He accused the United States of spreading its imperfect institutions by military force, of transporting race hatred to other nations by calling Filipinos "niggers" and "monkeys," and of shaming itself with hypocrisy. When a nation "steals the soil from under your feet and enslaves you," while egotistically boasting about "Christianity and civilization and benevolent intentions, it turns the stomach of an honest man."[48]

Anti-Imperialist arguments and criticisms of the Spanish-American War were not lost on college students either. The editor of the DePauw Palladium (Spring 1898) warned fellow students not to be swept away by the war spirit and quest for overseas territories. 'War may be a quick road to the heights of fame for the brave and capable man, but it is one where he must mount over the bodies of his comrades—it is a gory path to glory." He congratulated his fellow students on "the absence of the cheap patriotism and jingoism which have been so prevalent at many other institutions." He praised those who did not choose "to drop their college work and rush away...." "The duties of peace," he reminded his classmates, "are as sacred as the duties of war. The courage of the citizen must be no less than that of the soldier."[49] So wrote the future eminent historian, Charles Austin Beard.

CONCLUSION

The anti-imperialism movement was based more on abstract political and ideological principles than on shared economic or humanitarian considerations. Some anti-expansionists were even candid racists, who dreaded the prospect of bringing tropical peoples into the U.S. system. "No matter whether they are fit to govern themselves or not," Missouri's Democratic Representative Champ Clark said of the Filipinos, "they are not fit to govern us." Unable to halt war or curb expansionists' appetites through popular agitation, anti-imperialist leaders thus toyed for a brief time with the prospect of mounting a third-party effort for the 1900 presidential election. Surprisingly, most decided to support the Democratic candidacy of the "Great Commoner," William Jennings Bryan, who had lost to

McKinley in the 1896 election; Bryan grudgingly supported Senate ratification of the Paris Treaty granting United States control over the Philippines, believing "that it was easier to persuade the American people to promise independence to the Filipinos in connection with the ratification of the treaty than to continue war and force Spain to recognize a republic in the Philippines." This fact, coupled with the rejection of Bryan's candidacy by conservative anti-imperialists like Andrew Carnegie and Senator Hoar (whom Bryan considered to be a demagogue) and the success of U.S. military forces in grinding down the Filipino insurrection, resulted in a McKinley victory even more decisive than the election of 1896. This proved to be a devastating blow to the anti-imperialist movement, which collapsed by 1902.[50]

Nevertheless, the Anti-Imperialist League left an important legacy, growing from a small group of intellectuals and business leaders in Boston to a large nationwide movement in reaction to the mounting casualties in the Filipino-American War. Those who point out that the Spanish-American War and the U.S. seizure of the Philippines led to the largest American movement up until that period give much credit to the Anti-Imperialist League; however, it is important to point out that the league lost strength after Bryan's presidential defeat in 1900. Two factors help to account for the league's demise: (1) government threats to prosecute anti-war activists for disloyalty; and (2) McKinley's decision to withdraw volunteer troops from the Filipino campaign, thus leading to less upper-class opposition to his policy.

In any case, the rash of annexations accompanying the Spanish-American War quickly subsided as outright colonialism was replaced by indirect forms of political and economic control. In that instance, the Anti-Imperialist League did have a latent effect on the conduct of U.S. foreign policy as it entered the twentieth century.

The forces of peace continued to be heard, despite the peace movement's failure to halt America's imperialist policies. Jane Addams—profound student of urban life, industrialism, pacifism, and feminism—pointed out the ethical disadvantages of the war idea and system as much as Edward Atkinson did the economic and material shortcomings. Though Addams would gain prominence in the new century, she had already begun paving the way for a new attack on war. In modern industrial civilization, she contended, the earlier virtues have no real place. New types of courage and patriotism must be developed to meet these new conditions. "It is the military idea, resting content as it does with the passive results of order and discipline which confesses a totally inadequate conception of the value of power and human life, [and]...is an implement too clumsy and barbaric to subserve our purpose."[51]

From Addams' comments came forth a new peace purpose—one that would be as much "inductive or practical" as "deductive or idealist." Thus, as America entered its second full century of existence, a new peace movement appeared covering a wide range of pragmatic issues: a challenge to the economic benefits of war; an elaboration of the biological losses of war; an analysis of the dangers from competitive armament; an analysis of certain weaknesses of nationalism; and the development of elaborate projects for the reconstruction of society. Gone forever would be the appeal to the Bible and Christianity. In their place, would be trained "experts" whose knowledge of law and practicality in foreign affairs would, in theory, enable them to usher in the peaceful society.

CHAPTER FOUR

APPROACHES TO PEACEMAKING AND CONFRONTING A WORLD WAR AT HOME

It was as if the ancient prophet foresaw that under an enlightened industrialism peace would no longer be an absence of war, but the unfolding of world-wide processes making for the nurture of human life. He predicted the moment which has come to us now that peace is no longer an abstract dogma but has become a rising tide of moral enthusiasm slowly engulfing all pride of conquest and making war impossible.

Jane Addams, Newer Ideals of Peace, 1907

INTRODUCTION

The advent of the reform idealism of the new century, one marked by progressive change, could not have found a more effective spokesperson than Jane Addams. Founder of the educational settlement home for immigrants, Hull House, in Chicago, Addams was drawn to the peace movement as part of her larger vision for social change. Despite the divisive nature of the war in the Philippines, the peace movement emerged from it with some new allies, having captured the attention and support of some of America's most economically and socially privileged leaders. Addams would find such an alliance with America's genteel class somewhat uncomfortable, yet her steadfast conviction that peace as a moral instrument was quickly replacing its abstract idealism proved reassuring. A new national movement, she believed, was now underway; a movement that would build upon the former cosmopolitan faith in progress, Christian idealism, human reason, social justice, and the modern mechanisms of peacekeeping institutions.

By the close of the century the nation was now at a new critical turning point. The bitter class conflict of the 1890s reflected the fact that growing numbers of Americans were not happy with the status quo. Criticisms of the prevailing political and economic institutions were advanced by thoughtful observers who believed that the great concentrations of wealth and power resulting from America's industrial growth threatened individual liberties and stunted the drive for social justice. The fact that the U.S. was now the leading manufacturing nation in the world proved troubling to those reformers who insisted that the dilemma Henry George raised in Progress and Poverty (1879) remained unresolved. More and more Americans were now living in large cities and earning their bread by factory work. Yet ninety-nine percent of the nation's wealth rested in the hands of only one percent of the country's population.

For proponents of peace America's rapid social and economic transformation presented a number of challenges. Reconciling traditional mechanisms of peacekeeping with more radical proposals for social justice consumed the energies and efforts of numerous supporters of the crusade for world peace. Three fairly distinct groups with different approaches to the issues of war and social justice appeared in the early years of the new century: those who supported juridical means to internationalism, supported by endowed foundations, peace educators and thinkers, and church organizations; social progressives who looked for ways to help the newly-arrived immigrants; and labor socialists who focused on violence and war caused by capitalism and the search for profits.

Organized efforts to promote internationalism represented the more limited approach to solving the problem of war. Those who supported this effort were primarily legalists and upper class citizens who shunned more radical solutions in favor of a world body and court. A considerable amount of their time and energy was devoted to studying the causes of war, examining government efforts to develop treaties, relying on church peace organizations, and working with leading educators and jurists. The approach undertaken was somewhat elitist and conservatively pragmatic.

Social progressives who promoted peace did so in a broader sense. These individuals supported juridical peacemaking attempts but also encouraged a wider view of peace. They were active in assisting newly-arrived immigrants adjust to the difficulties of living and working in urban America. Their focus was encouraging the advancement of social justice as the means to building a peaceful society. Consciously and intellectually, they wanted to eliminate the ills associated with the modern industrial state. For peace to exist abroad it had to be established at home first.

The third approach was the most radical in terms of ideological outlook. Socialists opposed to war did so out of distrust and distain for the social Darwinistic practices of the capitalist system. The vanguard for change, they believed, was the laboring masses. What set them apart from European socialists was their acceptance of an evolutionary, as opposed to revolutionary, process for eliminating economic equality. Internationalism and lasting peace could only be achieved successfully when workers throughout the world refused to heed the call of their governments to wage war against one another.

Within each approach to peace one would find pacifists as well as many non-pacifists. All were hopeful that, at last, nations would agree to lay down their arms and work toward mutual understanding. But the forces of imperialism, nationalism, and militarism proved too powerful by the year 1914. It was at that point when peace proponents in America were forced to reveal their true colors. Those internationalists who were not pacifists supported the call to arms and left the peace movement. Those social progressives who wanted peace but could not resist appeals to patriotism also retreated. Those socialists who believed that fighting would finally provide the opening they had been waiting for to change the capitalist system and advance the cause of workers also abandoned the crusade for peace (The Socialist Party, though, did take a strong stance against the war and the draft in support of the People's Council for Democracy and Peace once war was declared – a stand many socialists were punished for). It would be the pacifists, some of whom were aligned within each approach, who would emerge from the conflict and provide the backbone to a rejuvenated peace movement. It would be a movement combining all three approaches to form a more radical pacifist effort; it would also be one proclaiming that peace is built upon social justice and not just treaties and international peacekeeping machinery.

ORGANIZATIONAL EFFORTS FOR INTERNATIONALISM

International peacemaking became a more pragmatic enterprise in the early twentieth century as its leadership passed to business-philanthropists like Andrew Carnegie, influential lawyers like Elihu Root, and educational administrators such as Columbia University President Murray Butler. Under their direction, this branch of the peace movement became a prestigious calling, devoted to the legal settlement of disputes and the "scientific" study of war and its alternatives. Between 1901 and 1914, forty-five new peace organizations appeared—an unparalleled achievement in American peace history. Among the most influential were the American Society of International Law, the Carnegie Endowment for International Peace (CEIP), and the World Peace Foundation (WPF). These were established between 1906 and 1911 as specialized agencies for transmitting the experts' knowledge of peace to the masses and encouraging more conciliatory gestures among governments. Noticeably missing, however, was the moral appeal that characterized the early peace organizations of the nineteenth century.[1] At the same time, interdenominational Protestant leaders joined the peace crusade and helped form the Federal Council of Churches of Christ of America. Another addition was a scattering of militant federalists, such as the magazine editor Hamilton Holt, who sought more stringent forms of world order modeled on the constitutional arrangement of the United States government.[2]

Arguments for juridical peace, international law, arbitration, and European federation proposed by late-nineteenth-century peace advocates were continued by more conservative-minded peacemakers. These peace advocates believed that war and the economies of war stifled prosperity, exacerbated social upheaval, and frustrated the evolution of harmonious social relationships. They maintained that an open commerce in goods and ideas would distribute power equitably, erect systems of exchange, and lessen the threat of military conflict. They regarded peace as the practical expression of social and international order and as largely good in itself, yet they disassociated harmonious social relationships from contemporaneous issues of justice.

Supplementing the concept of juridical peace, these peace advocates also claimed to take a scientific approach to society without falling victim to the tyranny of intellectual systems. Their specialized endowed agencies provided a functional analysis of peace and war in order to deal with the complexity of societies and the processes of change. The emphasis was on contingency for change. They did not offer simple solutions, yet they placed a premium on intelligence and well-planned, organized social forces resulting from thorough scientific investigation and calculated analyses.

This sort of international peacemaking, based on a narrower vision of peace and justice, gained considerable recognition as a respectable calling, having secured the allegiance of many of the country's academic, religious, business, and political organizations. Yet very few members in the movement upheld a "radical pacifist" position calling for the eradication of all forms of violence within socio-economic structures. The vast majority of peace supporters considered war prevention a matter for international relations, and they ignored the arguments socialists and the working class tendered with respect to rival imperialisms as a cause of war, and the relationship between peace and economic justice. For a short period, the wealthy and social elite dominated the drive for world peace.

This more limited approach to ending armed conflict began at the conclusion of the nineteenth century with a brief period of well-publicized international disarmament discussions. The unlikely figure who raised the curtain was the czar of Russia. On August 24, 1898, he issued an invitation to the nations of the world to assemble in a disarmament conference. His motives were not entirely idealistic. The Russian government, like other continental powers, had found expenditures for military equipment rising enormously each year after 1890. New and costly weapons were being introduced such as the field-artillery piece that would later be known as the French 75 and would be indispensable to armies by 1914. Naval expenditures were rising alarmingly marked by the modern battleship. The czar's government did not possess enough funds for both the 75's and the new ship, and, therefore, wished for a moratorium on land ordnance in order to build a modern navy. The czar's invitation resulted in the First Hague Peace Conference, held in the de facto capital of the Netherlands in 1899. A Second Hague Peace Conference would follow eight years later.[3]

The interest aroused by the czar's invitation, though not entirely pacifist, contributed to a revitalization of peace efforts in the United States. In 1904, two notable peace congresses were held in the United States. The first, the Twelfth Inter-Parliamentary Union, was held in conjunction with the World's Fair in St. Louis. This organization had been formed at Paris in 1888 by thirty members of the French Chamber of Deputies and ten members of the British Parliament, and consisted of parliamentary delegates from every European country having a constitutional form of government. This conference in St. Louis provided a ready-made forum for American Peace Society leaders Benjamin Franklin Trueblood and Edwin Mead to encourage America's new industrial elite to lend money and resources to the struggle against war. The second congress was in Boston on October 3rd and once again Mead and Trueblood reiterated their plea for a "high brow" approach to peace and arbitration. One of their disciples captured the spirit of the new approach to peace in these words: "The substitution of justice for force in settling the differences that arise between nations has become a question of practical politics.... This is due...to [sic] the almost unbearable burden of the world's armaments and to the obstacle which their cost offers to carrying out policies of constructive statesmanship in solving the new social and political problems that have arisen everywhere."[4]

Ironically, Mead and Trueblood's efforts led to the demise of the peace movement as they had known it. The nineteenth century U. S. peace movement had been largely an attempt to realize the Christian ideals of love, brotherhood, and the sanctity of life in domestic and international relations. Many of the recruits to the new peace movement were not pacifists, Christian or otherwise. They were "practical" men: academicians, men of Mugwump (liberal Republican) backgrounds, leaders in the business world, and members of the emerging profession of international law. They were not interested in peace because they felt war to be an unmitigated evil. Rather, peace represented a secondary reform to be trumpeted and abandoned according to circumstance.

For many of these positive-minded conservatives the peace movement, at least in their eyes, was not an anti-war crusade. They were not campaigning against the idea of defensive war, or, for that matter, the use of force as an instrument of national policy. Instead, they couched their arguments for world peace in terms of a pro-law movement – one seeking to promote the "non-idealistic" mechanisms of arbitration, courtroom justice, and, if possible, world federation backed by the rules of international law.

A variety of motives brought them to the peace movement. Some were impelled by a sense of civic responsibility and a craving for status and, thus, attracted to peace as a safe, uncontroversial, undemanding cause. "No reform," remarks Merle Curti, "demanded less sacrifice on the part of the American middle class."[5] Others were attracted out of concern for their country's recently acquired position in the world. Between the conquest of the Philippines and the start of World War I, overseas investments multiplied fivefold; for the first time, Americans were extending rather than receiving credit in large amounts. American elites sought a stable international order; long convinced of the moral superiority of the U.S., they doubted the capacity and good will of the international order's chief custodians—the European powers with their cabinet politics and secret diplomacy. They distrusted the balance of power system, sensing its inherent instability. How could the United States retain its purity and at the same time enjoy wealth and power—all without becoming involved in the crises generated regularly by the international system? As a vehicle for expressing their concerns and in terms of practical policies, the peace movement, as they conceived it, held the promise of permitting Americans to have the best of both worlds.

The post-1900 internationalist peace seekers, according to historian David Patterson, were ably represented by Fannie Fern Andrews, organizer of the American Peace League, Arthur Deerin Call of the American Peace Society, Samuel Train Dutton, head of Teachers College, Columbia University, and University of Wisconsin student, Louis Lochner, who wanted the major world powers to establish permanent international institutions that would formalize and regularize the conciliation process. Unwilling to wait for every nation to convert to the goal of world peace, others such as Hamilton Holt, editor of the Independent, Richard Bartholdt, Republican Congressman from St. Louis, and Raymond Bridgman, author and journalist, joined forces with the likes of Nicholas Murray Butler, George Kirchwey, professor of International Law at Columbia, James Brown Scott, international lawyer; and Elihu Root, Secretary of State in Theodore Roosevelt's Administration and later a senator from New York in arguing for the creation of a world court. All of them in one manner or another believed that international congresses, such as the two Hague Peace Conferences, could gradually formulate a code of international law, which justices of a world court could apply in adjudicating disputes between nations.[6]

The years prior to 1914, largely inspired by The Hague Conferences, were filled with ambitious and energetic peacemakers willing to compromise with ideological opponents in the quest for world peace. Thus, between 1906 and 1910, a number of new peace societies emerged. The seriousness of peace organizations as a practical endeavor was best demonstrated by the remarkable growth and activity of the New York Peace Society. Reorganized and reenergized in 1906 by Professor Ernest Richards of Columbia, the Reverend Charles Jefferson of the Broadway Tabernacle, and a group of like-minded reform intellectuals, the

Society within a year numbered about 500 members. It enjoyed the support of many of the most prominent business leaders, philanthropists, journalists, lawyers, and ministers in the city. Carnegie, despite the failure of the anti-imperialist crusade, accepted the presidency and lavished time and funds on the Society. Within four years, the Society was the second largest in the country, surpassed only by the American Peace Society.[7]

During the same year that the New York Peace Society was revitalized, Richard Bartholdt and Nicholas Murray Butler organized the American Association for International Conciliation (as a branch of the French-based Conciliation Internationale) for the purpose of employing "private initiatives" among the world's policy-shaping elite. The American Association for International Conciliation grew out of a friendship between Butler and the Frenchman Baron d'Estournelles. They became close friends: d'Estournelles introducing him to the French statesmen, Butler returning the favor with an honorary degree from Columbia University in 1911.[8]

Many of the legalists who swelled the ranks of peace advocates saw a developing body of international law as an appropriate means for easing tensions among the world's powers. They were inspired by the example of enlightened nations controlling the spread of war. European powers had been successful in avoiding a general war for nearly a century after Waterloo, in some conflicts successfully experimenting with a substitute for war: international litigation. John Bassett Moore, the dean of American authorities on international law, was able to cite "at least 136 treaties or agreements signed during that century which had included comprehensive settlements embracing hundreds of particular cases and involving millions of dollars."[9]

Many of these adjudicators attached themselves to the eminent jurist and politician, Elihu Root, winner of the 1913 Nobel Peace Prize. A somewhat pretentious Wall Street lawyer, "credited with masterminding the country's thrust toward economic centralization," Root was a Republican conservative who believed in law and order and shared Alexis de Tocqueville's fear of the democratic masses.[10] Root's magnetism attracted a number of Republican internationalists who would shape American foreign policy for almost half a century, such as Henry Stimson and James Brown Scott. They agreed with Root's argument, one he related to fellow attorney Theodore Marburg, that "disputes between nations shall be settled by judges acting under the judicial sense of honorable obligation with a judicial idea of impartiality rather than by diplomats acting under ideas of honorable obligation and feeling bound to negotiate a settlement rather than to pass without fear or favor upon questions of fact and law."[11]

Applying the principles of courtroom justice to diplomacy, "peace justices" carried their law books to the Lake Mohonk Conferences where the issue of international law was discussed annually. Acting on these discussions, Columbia University law professor George Kirchwey and law school administrator James Brown Scott worked together in establishing the American Society of International Law in 1906. The basic goal of this Society was to act as a "scientific" clearinghouse for the study of international law and as a means of making the nation's world-minded elite aware of the importance of judicial means of maintaining peace. "It was felt that annual meetings of such a Society at which distinguished persons—statesmen, diplomats, professors of international law—should meet, read papers of an historical or theoretical nature, and engage in the discussion of questions involving international law," James Brown Scott remarked during the Twelfth Annual Conference, "would not only bring international law prominently before the people but [sic] would count for much in the dissemination of those principles of the law of nations which must in the course of time regulate international relations."[12]

To a considerable extent, Scott, the judicialist who helped shape U.S. diplomacy for almost fifty years, became the symbol of the legalist's concern for the importance of international law and courts as the arbiter of disputes. It easily permitted him, and those of like mind, to promote the idea of an independent judiciary as the first bastion in support of private property rights and Anglo-Saxon political authority. A military veteran of the Spanish-American War, Scott insisted that peace came through law and order and that these in turn were premised on the extension of Anglo-American power. His participation in the peace movement was part of the trend from non-institutional pacifism to institutional internationalism.

A prolific writer and author of a massive two-volume text with accompanying documents entitled The Hague Peace Conferences of 1899 and 1907 (1909), Scott upheld the concept of legal equality of sovereign states while also tolerating the inequality of power among them until international conferences could formulate a set code of laws that all nations could accept. While deployed to the Philippines as part of his volunteer service during the Spanish-American War, Scott helped draft the text for governing the islands after Spain surrendered. Influenced by the theological and moralistic views of Francisco de Vitoria and the Dutch jurist Hugo Grotius, Scott maintained that international law would enable nations to function effectively in a "civilized" world, the same way citizens obey the laws in their respective countries. Like many of his colleagues, he had little respect for the term "pacifism." To him, the connotation implied "passivism," hardly a means by which to cage the dogs of war.

Another organization that emerged in these years was the creation of the American Society for the Judicial Settlement of International Disputes in 1910. Formed to promote the second Hague Conference's view that an international court endowed with judicial authority ought to supplement the existing arbitration tribunal, this Society was greeted warmly by political scientists, legalists, and jurists. The leader was Dr. James Brown Scott; he was ably assisted by the Baltimore jurist, millionaire publicist, and subsequent minister to Belgium, Theodore Marburg. The Society not only popularized the idea of an international court comparable to the United States Supreme Court, but considered "other technical matters like sanctions, judiciable and non-judiciable disputes, and advanced the emerging field of international jurisprudence." Though thoroughgoing pacifists believed that this organization of technical experts, one dominated by lawyers and law school professors, overemphasized the value and importance of the juridical technique, they realized this organization did more to make the World Court a reality after World War I than any other single factor.[13]

PRACTICAL PEACE MACHINERY FOR INTERNATIONALISM AT WORK

No central clearinghouse popularized these practical approaches to peace—judicial, diplomatic benevolence, and international machinery. Thus, in an effort to coordinate more efficiently the peace movement's numerous activities, Edwin Ginn, a noted textbook publisher and president of Ginn & Company, took the first step. Ginn's biographer, Robert I Rotberg, insists that the publisher was no starry-eyed peace reformer but rather a hardheaded businessman who upheld the virtues of practicality and efficiency. He fitted nicely into historian Robert Wiebe's description of progressive reformers who formulated their views in order to reshape and refine the established order. Although not a man of ideas, Ginn was able to assemble and popularize others' views. A believer in international compacts, a world court, and enforcement of global harmony backed by an international police force, Ginn established his own major peace organization which attempted to educate people to the importance of peace through more businesslike procedures.

Ginn, who had participated in the Lake Mohonk Arbitration Conferences, became the first American to endow and organize educational peace work on a major scale. The World Peace Foundation was endowed in 1910 with a million dollars—a third of Ginn's wealth derived from his Boston textbook firm. Directed by Stanford University President David Starr Jordan, Dr. Charles Livermore, Edwin D. Mead, and Denys P. Myers, the World Peace Foundation made available both peace classics and important new works like Jean de Bloch's <u>The Future of War</u> and the writings of British pacifist Norman Angell.[14] The foundation also distributed a series of brief, accurate, and informative pamphlets and leaflets.

Operationally, the WPF emphasized the need for research and education as part of the businesslike approach to international harmony. Ginn and his associates believed strongly that educational work for peace would be most effective among youth and, toward that goal, the Foundation generously subsidized the American Peace League—founded in 1908 by Fannie Fern Andrews, a Boston school teacher. It also aided financially the Association of Cosmopolitan Clubs, which originated in 1903 for the promotion of international friendship and understanding among university students.[15]

Not to be outdone by Ginn's magnanimity, Carnegie contributed $10 million in United States Steel Corporation bonds in December 1910 toward the formation in New York of the Carnegie Endowment for International Peace. Carnegie had made part of his fortune by the sale of naval armor plate—some actually of an inferior quality produced during the Cleveland administration. Despite his general appearance of magnanimity the steel magnate had little interest in economic and social justice. His 1886 essay, "The Gospel of Wealth," was a reflection of his appreciation for social Darwinism and his philanthropic charity was dictated by a desire to counter support for socialism rather than a generous desire to assist the less privileged. Carnegie had displayed his contempt for unions during the bitter Homestead steel strike. He had destroyed the Amalgamated Association of Iron and Steel Workers through the use of force and Pinkerton detectives. Disregarding the public outcry against his anti-labor tactics, Carnegie typified the Gilded Age entrepreneurs "public be damned" attitude.

At the same time, he directed the officers of the Endowment to "hasten the abolition of international war, the foulest blot upon our civilization."[16] Their efforts were ably led by Elihu Root as president, Nicholas Murray Butler as head of the Division of Intercourse and Education (he succeeded Root as president in 1925), John Bates Clark as head of the Division of Economics and History, and James Brown Scott as head of the Division of International Law.

Carnegie, who already had spent more than $2 million for the Church Peace Union and $1,500,000 toward the building of the great Peace Palace at The

Hague, was anxious to immortalize his own name under the banner for peace. "What am I good for, anyhow?" he once asked his British friend Lord Morley. "If I'm not willing to sacrifice myself for the cause of peace, for what would I sacrifice?"[17]

The three divisions of the Carnegie Endowment were testimony to the professionalism of peace "experts." Each division had its own special task. The Division of Intercourse and Education was created to maintain agencies throughout the world in order to gather information about other nation's international policies and to promote international goodwill; under Butler's direction, the division arranged for the exchange of eminent scholars and writers among nations. The Division of Economics and History sponsored studies of the conditions –political, social, and economic—that influenced peace and war, and suggested methods of action regarding them. Clark's division encouraged intellectuals to draw upon its findings in accumulating more evidence for additional writings against war. The Division of International Law tried to extend the law of nations to all disputes arising among nations. Faithfully assisted by James Brown Scott as secretary, the division disseminated information on the nations' rights and responsibilities under existing international law and promoted periodic international conferences to amplify and codify that law.

The elitist, establishment-oriented approach to peace was best typified by Carnegie's well-managed foundation. Reluctant to subsidize "peace" societies per se, the endowment spent its money on only the safest peace proposals and the twenty-seven trustees appointed were very conservative in domestic affairs. The Carnegie Endowment remained a detached, businesslike concern. Although Carnegie was a strong supporter of peace societies, the endowment's leaders circumvented his wishes by insisting that the trustees would provide a subvention thereby relieving him of any future financial obligation. CEIP was guided by a scholarly desire to encourage international good will and world peace through an appeal to the intellectual elite of all lands. Seeking to establish "a veritable Faculty of Peace," the popular endowment not only sponsored interchanges of

American and foreign professors, but built up an admirable research library and collected all the learned documents on the development of international law, the causes of war, and the past records of peace efforts. By the 1920's, aided by figures like James Brown Scott and Robert Lansing, the Endowment—with access to top United States policymakers—was operating, DeBenedetti points out, as a virtual "division of the State Department, working in harmony constantly."[18]

RELIGIOUS MECHANISMS SUPPORTING THE DRIVE FOR INTERNATIONALISM

The conservative peace advocates also stirred up the clergy's efforts. The role of church peace groups represented another element to the larger organizational drive favoring the principle of internationalism. For instance, the 1907 Carnegie-sponsored National Peace Congress in New York was "attended by ten mayors, nineteen members of Congress, four Supreme Court justices, two presidential candidates, thirty labor leaders, forty bishops, sixty newspaper editors, and twenty-seven millionaires." Between 1910 and 1915, Protestant peace movers were active, coordinating efforts for peace. The impetus had been provided earlier when H.W. Stuckenburg, a Lutheran clergyman, wrote in 1903 that "war would be an increasingly alien aspect of society as it evolved from tribalism to cosmopolitanism." Although "war had value in fostering unity and creating order," the brutality of modern war, the "development of scientific, cultural and political bonds," and the "emergence of international law" now made war anachronistic. University of Chicago theologian Shailer Matthews declared in the Social Gospel (1910) that war, "a hideous thing," was rooted in greed and pride. "All the world, and especially a woman, loves a uniform," he insisted, and it would take nations, "just as it takes plain folks, a long time to grow sensible." War would cease when "the question of war ceases to be merely economic and becomes one of morality."[19]

It would be interesting to see how many of the clergy fit the profile of the type of progressive reformer the late historian Richard Hofstadter referred to in his The Age of Reform as "status quo revolutionists." Compelled less by financial necessity than by their own dissatisfaction with the society they were living in, how many adopted the cause of peace as a means of satisfying their deep psychological and moral needs to be heard and respected? It is possible that they may have resembled the abolitionist sons and daughters of the New England clergy, who, in the mid-nineteenth century, no longer commanded the prestigious positions they once enjoyed in Colonial America. Civic responsibility compelled duty and commitment and the peace movement served as a convenient option for many. Was this their way of countering the emerging influence of a post-civil War nouveau-riche business class in their efforts to influence the direction of the peace movement? Was this the new avenue of self-fullment and respectability they could travel?

Whatever the case may be it is obvious that, while devoting a considerable amount of writing to the subject of war, Protestant clergymen also worked for the creation of religious mechanisms to build peace. Many were willing to encourage stronger legal means for establishing internationalism. The interdenominational Protestant preacher Charles Macfarland, with the help of Carnegie confidante Frederick Lynch, encouraged the Federal Council of Churches of Christ in America to establish in 1911 a Commission on Peace and Arbitration. With a $2 million endowment from Carnegie, the Church Peace Union (CPU) was founded during the same period as an interfaith front of prominent religious peace seekers interested in building a more organized and effective crusade against war. In the summer of 1915, the Church Peace Union organized an American branch of the London-based World Alliance for International Friendship in an effort to promote the twin goals of Christian federalism and global harmony. Unfortunately, their efforts were too late, for the war in Europe had already broken out and the Protestant effort did little to prevent European Christians from using swords instead of plowshares.[20]

PEACE EDUCATION FOR INTERNATIONALISM

While conservative peacemakers relied on their expert knowledge of courtroom justice and Protestant clergymen were reexamining the Book of Isaiah in light of current events, both groups recognized the fundamental importance of peace education. In 1905, the Lake Mohonk Conference on International Arbitration appointed a committee on colleges and universities that subsequently induced many institutions to hold regular observances of Peace Day (May 18th, anniversary of the first Hague Conference for World Peace), debates, and oratorical contests, and special lectures on the peace movement. During the conference Dr. Henry M. McCracken, Chancellor of New York University, issued the following observation: "The utmost stretch of imagination would not lead me to find that anything that these universities and colleges can do would banish the possibility of war. . . ," he stated. "But if, on the other hand," he continued, "we can imagine that throughout a generation the higher schools of learning. . .had done the utmost possible in teaching a right doctrine respecting national obligations. . .then. . . governments. . . would never dream of arriving at a settlement of their differences by the use of the cannon and the sword." In the same year, President Noah Byers of Goshen College and Professor Elbert Russell of Earlham College founded the Intercollegiate Peace Association (IPA) to promote peace-oriented activities among faculty and students. By 1912, the IPA had conducted "intercollegiate and interstate oratorical contests" involving "at least 300 undergraduates from 80 colleges in some 16 states."[21] In 1907, several campus clubs with foreign and American student members formed the National Association of Cosmopolitan Clubs, whose aim was to promote international understanding and friendship.[22]

The American School Peace League held its annual meetings in conjunction with the National Education Association, the largest teaching organization in the United States, beginning in Denver in 1909. Its state branches held meetings in conjunction with state teachers' associations. The League "distributed literature, supplied speakers, gained observance of Peace Day in the schools," developed curriculum materials. It organized "peace study groups for teachers," and held essay contests on peace issues for high school students. Through these and other activities, the American School Peace League became "perhaps the most influential of all the juvenile propagandist bodies in the world."[23]

Educators such as John Dewey understood the importance of teaching peace. Although he would forsake his peace principles in favor of Wilson's call to arms during World War I, Dewey's concern for social democracy was borne out in many of his pre-war writings on democracy and progressive education. Books such as The Ethics of Democracy, Psychology, Outlines of a Critical Theory of Ethics, The School and Society, My Pedagogic Creed, The Child and the Curriculum, Ethics, Moral Principles in Education, How We Think, and his most noted work completed prior to American military intervention, Democracy and Education, demonstrated Dewey's concern for suggesting new ideas for solving social, political, and economic problems through the use of intelligence and the scientific method. Dewey envisioned his democratic ideals as part of a moralistic-educational crusade attempting to inculcate in the American mind the values of reason and understanding as opposed to those of armed force and violence. Industrial ills, war, open class conflict, imperialism, and poverty, he believed, could be eliminated through the democratic processes of social cooperation and human understanding. In his writings and teachings he pressed the desirable qualities of a peaceful and intelligent solution to domestic and international problems. Peace societies were inspired by Dewey's progressive education ideas and adapted them to the cause of international harmony.

A 'MORAL EQUIVALENT FOR WAR'

If Dewey's instrumentalism – his brand of pragamatism related to ends and means – urged the use of intelligence to solve social ills, it was William James who used his pragmatic philosophy to address head-on the issue of human nature and aggression. One of the more interesting educational peace proposals ever put forth was James' "Moral Equivalent." When his essay was introduced during a speech at Stanford University in 1906, it was considered one of the most important addresses on one of politics most classic problems: how to maintain political unity and civic virtue without war or the threat of war. In the past James noted, the traditional way the U.S. had maintained civic bonding was through the militia system. But by the early 1900s that system had declined for lack of an outside enemy. The Civil War had set the militia institution on a downward path because many militiamen were killed, wounded, or demoralized. In lieu of the militia promoting social unity, James came up with the brilliant idea; he proposed a form of national service that would wage warfare against nature.

James realized that nature itself was not the enemy; it was man's own darker human nature. No one had been able to establish an alternative to the strong life of war. Men, it seemed, were drawn to physical contact and less reluctant to resist the call to arms. His speech highlighted the gender assumptions of this era and his attempt was to pose an alternative use of male energies for constructive rather than destructive purposes.

His vision of a means toward a peaceful society was designed around organizing an army of workers to work in the coal fields and industries of America. Rather than being conscripted for military service male youths would serve in an army of economic and reconstruction builders. One of the foremost philosophers of his time, James was a Harvard professor and pioneer in the field of pragmatism. He examined why the impulse for heroism through "individual sacrifice for the tribal good" was a basic instinct guiding human behavior. Reacting to the psychological values of manliness and physical vigor encouraged by war, James developed a counterweight by providing what he called the "moral equivalent of war" encompassing the military virtues of "intrepidity, contempt of softness, surrender of private interest, [and] obedience to command." He argued, "It is only a question of blowing on the spark until the whole population gets incandescent, and on the ruins of the old morals of military honor, a stable system of morals, of civic honor, builds itself up...." Furthermore, he opined, "war has been the only force that disciplines a whole community, and until an equivalent discipline is organized, I believe that war must have its way." As a substitute for military conscription, he urged the drafting of all youth to form for several years an "army enlisted against nature," to contend with the "sour and hard foundations of his Higher life." He would draft them "to coal and iron mines, to freight trains, to fishing fleets in December, to dishwashing, and window washing, to road-building and tunnel making, to foundries and stoke-holes, and to the frames of the sky-scraper." As a medium of discussion in the classroom, James' essay was a topic of hot debate and this idea would later be used as the basis for the creation of the Civilian Conservation Corps during the Great Depression of the 1930s.[24]

PROGRESSIVISM AND SOCIAL JUSTICE

James' proposal should be viewed in the context of the Progressive Era search for order, which also spawned a number of grassroots activists and muckraking writers who promoted social justice reforms. These individuals represented a second approach to prewar peacemaking, one that did not cater to the elite-minded internationalists. Rather, it was an approach that looked inward for the root causes of injustice and one that would provide the basis for the post-World War I "modern" peace movement. Progressivism went beyond previous periods in its broad call for social and political change. It was frequently embedded with the strong moral overtones of a religious crusade. In a vigorous crusade for social and economic justice, reformers demanded that the principle of democracy be applied to meet the challenges of modern industrialization and urbanization. Calls for social justice were mounted from two fronts: private philanthropy and the use of public power and governmental planning. One of the most noticeable efforts, one which peace workers endorsed, was the settlement house movement.

Peacemakers endorsing the settlement house movement premised their goals on the idea of wholeness; that is, the concept of reform must be comprehensive and ongoing rather than intermittent. The full needs of the individual and society must be met if a peaceful order was to be established. This view was popularized by Robert Treat Paine, an active member of the American Peace Society. Speaking for many of his colleagues Paine, who headed the Associated Charities of Boston in the 1890s, insisted that uplifting the general level of life must be examined as one whole problem. He and other peace activists believed that one of the most practical ways of enlightening the community to the cause of social justice was through the neighborhood settlement house (a program to assist newly-arrived immigrants by providing educational and cultural awareness to their new environs) in impoverished urban areas.

The settlement house idea appealed to middle-class and upper-class individuals, many of them women, whose humanitarian conscience sought constructive outlet. No one was more qualified to lead this venture than Jane Addams. She became the leading spirit behind the settlement house movement at the turn of the new century. Not supported by tax funds and liberated from the philistine goals of church home missions, the settlements captured the imagination of progressive reformers and exemplified the wider goals of the crusade for social justice.

Peace activists who flocked to the settlement house movement were youthful and well-educated. Many came from middle-class families and were determined to bridge the gulf between the rich and the poor; they wanted to lessen the social and economic problems associated with an emerging industrial-urban society, such as unsanitary housing, raw sewage in streets, contaminated water, high infant mortality rates, impure foods, ill-ventilated factories, heavy pollution filling the air of neighborhoods from nearby factory smokestacks, juvenile crime, child labor, and unhealthy overcrowding.

As the settlement idea spread throughout urban America, its influence expanded. Promoting peace and justice became synonymous as the settlement workers tried to help working class people meet basic needs. Hull-House, among others, established a lecture series, amateur theatricals, vocational classes, and nursery schools for mothers working in the factories. Even neighborhood needs like nursing care, playgrounds, and parks incorporated settlement solutions to the problems of public health, housing, and city planning. Throughout the country the social justice movement of the early 1900s began to achieve some of its more important objectives. Those in the peace movement, like Addams and Paine, for example, were delighted when some of the more noted progressives and social reformers addressed the issues of crowded tenement houses, abuses in child labor, public health, working hours for women, and even workers' compensation for accidents in the factory or workplace. In many respects, those engaged in peace work were some of the first reformers to point out that domestic social and economic justice are prerequisites for the idea of genuine internationalism.

Noteworthy contributions to the cause of social justice were made by Ida B. Wells (Frances Harper also worked with UPU's anti-lynching campaign). Born in Mississippi during the Civil War to slave parents Wells was an intelligent and perceptive young female. She attended Rust College until her parents died in 1878. Yet education was important and she continued her efforts teaching school. In 1884, when removed from the "ladies' car" on a train, Wells initiated her own campaign for equal justice for blacks and females. She sued the railroad, but even though she lost the case it did not deter her from pursuing justice.

Turning to journalism she eventually became editor of the Memphis Free Speech. After a close friend was lynched in Memphis in 1892, Wells wrote a series of editorials exposing the myth that lynching was caused by black men's rape of white women. The local white citizens were incensed and drove her out of the city. She moved to New York City where she continued her crusade against lynching and all other forms of social injustice. In 1895, she married and settled in Chicago. There she joined Susan B. Anthony's crusade for woman suffrage, followed Jane Addams' lead in establishing a black settlement house, and continued her investigations of lynchings and race riots plaguing the nation. First and foremost, she was a shining example of African American females' struggle for equality and social justice. Her settlement house served as an inspiration to urban blacks seeking an opportunity to better their lives.

Establishing settlement houses was one concrete example of the drive for social justice in the pre-World War I years. At a more ideological level the publication of muckraking articles and novels succeeding the critical or utopian works of the 1880s and 1890s represented another byproduct of positive reform. Muckraking literature encouraged the movement for greater social justice while sharing some of the evangelical fervor of the contemporary Social Gospel movement. Despite the unfair application of the term as applied to all the popular reform literature of the 1900s, muckraking as the practice of sensational literary exposure of corruption and evil was an important component behind the push for greater social justice in America.

During this period of progressive reform hundreds of muckraking articles and books appeared. Ida Tarbell's commentary on the Standard Oil monopoly and Lincoln Steffens Shame of the Cities, exposing the corruption of American urban government, initiated the progressive reformers' attack on trusts and the concentration of wealth and power. Ray Stannard Baker's Following the Color Line called attention to the plight of rural African Americans who left the impoverished and segregationist rural South in search of better economic opportunities in the industrial North. Novelist Frank Norris' powerful book, The Pit, examined the harsh working conditions in coal mines. His criticisms of railroad monopolies were the subject of discussion in The Octopus. John Spargo's The Bitter Cry of Children emotionally describes the work of cold breakers, children as young as eight-years-old losing their fingers and hands while sorting and grading the cola outside the mineshafts. Jack London's socialism was perhaps best reflected in his Iron Heel. Jacob Riis' How the Other Half Lives added to this growing body of literature through narrative and illustrations depicting the squalid conditions of immigrant tenement houses in New York City.

No one better captured the muckraking spirit than Upton Sinclair. In the early 1900s, having spent seven weeks investigating the unsanitary conditions in Chicago meatpacking houses, Sinclair's observations originally appeared in the Socialist periodical, Appeal to Reason. His efforts were inspired by the actions of Mary E. McDowell, the "Angel of the Stockyards." McDowell was one of the founders of the Women's Trade Union League and president of the Illinois branch. She had assisted Michael Donnelly, organizer of the Amalgamated Meat Cutters and Butcher Workmen, and played a vital role during the bitter 1904 Packinghouse strike. Sinclair's articles based on these events and his recording of conditions in the meatpacking industry were quickly picked up by a major publishing house. In 1905, Doubleday and Company published his accounts as The Jungle. The book became an immediate best seller. To his dismay, however, the socialist commentary filling the pages of the book – aimed at exposing the atrocious working conditions and harsh treatment of immigrant workers – went ignored in favor of his descriptions of the food handling and contaminated meat. In his own words, "I aimed at the public's heart and by accident hit it in the stomach." Nonetheless, his hope for a peaceable society and calls for economic justice were expressed in a series of later novels, including the Metropolis (1908) examining upper-class New York Society and its derision of poor people, The Money Changers (1908) discussing the economic consequences of the Panic of 1907, and King Coal (1917) criticizing the working conditions in the coal mines.

SOCIAL GOSPEL ADVOCATES AS PART OF THE RELIGIOUS PROGRESSIVE REFORM ERA

The muckrakers gave an added boost to the peacemakers of this period. So, too, did the Social Gospel preachers. The Social Gospel movement, apart from the organized Protestant church's attempts at peace, was representative of grassroots progressive concerns for social justice. Led by Washington Gladden and Walter Rauschenbush, religious preachers exemplified the influence that radical Christianity was able to exert on progressive reform. In their sermons and writings they contrasted the teachings of Jesus with the materialism of modern society and the corruption of American cities.

In the case of Gladden, pastor for almost forty years of the First Congregational Church in Columbus, Ohio, he encouraged Christian unity as a middle way to salvation between the extremes of individuality and state conformity. His sermons attacked "the ethics of luxurious expenditures" (later popularized by University of Chicago economist Thorstein Veblen in The Theory of the Leisure Class) and the evils of "tainted money." He questioned whether John D. Rockefeller's Standard Oil funds should be given to foreign missions and was sympathetic to the needs of the working class. In Applied Christianity he called upon the church to distance itself from predatory wealth and embrace the call for social reform.

This message was expressed even more forcibly by Rauschenbush, a Baptist clergyman whose first pastorate was in a New York City slum area. The search for peace and justice led Rauschenbush to criticize the churches' traditional conservative role in relationship to wealth, labor, and social change. Not a scientific Marxist by any stretch of the imagination, Rauschenbush argued that the U.S. could never be Christian until it reorganized its entire economic life on a democratic, cooperative basis. In calling for change Rauschenbush elevated peace consciousness by insisting that America's reorganization would only come about through a non-violent, though still revolutionary, socialist movement. Later, while teaching at the Rochester Theological Seminary, he expanded his ideas in a number of books: Christianity and the Social Crisis (1907); Christianizing the Social Order (1912), and A Theology for the Social Gospel (1917).

Unlike the more formal, institutionalized peace machinery of the pre-World War I years, the efforts of social progressives and Social Gospel preachers to improve American society represented a more grassroots attempt to achieve domestic justice. It represented another dimension to the richness and diversity of the peace crusade at this time. One of its most important representatives was America's foremost social reformer, Jane Addams.

JANE ADDAMS: PROGRESSIVE REFORMER FOR PEACE AND JUSTICE

Jane Addams also articulated important ideas about peace in this era. Already respected for her leadership role in the feminist movement and her establishment, along with Ellen Gates Starr, of Hull-House in Chicago, Addams' interest in peace surfaced as a result of her opposition to the Spanish-American War. Having immersed herself in the works of Tolstoy, she went even further in "arguing that uncontrolled industrial capitalism was the primary cause of domestic and international violence." In Newer Ideals of Peace (1907), her most comprehensive prewar peace tract, Addams rejected "idealistic" pacifism and argued that only a "dynamic" version was natural or rational for the modern world. She similarly rejected, "a priori, artificial, idealistic, and deterministic accounts of human nature as static," and she demanded that the personality be regarded as "incalculable." Her reform program changed from relief to "nurture" and to an emphasis on "life and its possibilities." She called for a "genuine evolutionary democracy" that would expand to meet the constant growth of human needs and relationships. She contrasted social orders founded upon "law enforced by authority" with social orders founded upon "liberty of individual action and complexity of group development," and she stated her preference for the latter.[25]

Addams' devotion to the twin causes of peace and social justice was easily revealed in her lectures and writings. Before the outbreak of World War I she had already published several books and articles on subjects ranging from unemployment insurance to child labor. The first book she published, Democracy and Social Ethics (1902), became the clarion call to all progressive reformers. Social ethics for her demanded that business leaders and politicians to develop plans for meeting the social and economic needs of the lower working-class in modern industrial society. It meant a redistribution of the profits for the general welfare. A few years later she received high acclaim when her autobiography, Twenty-Years at Hull House, appeared in 1910. In this work Addams examined her own efforts to eliminate barriers between classes that were caused by industrialism and how best to promote harmony among all nationalities and races. Her notion of social ethics reverberated to the international sphere as well. It was her constant belief that all national leaders have a moral obligation to address economic and territorial disputes leading to war. The average citizen is always called upon to fight wars but is never responsible for starting them. She also insisted that wars would inevitably lead to adverse reactions at home under the false pretense of patriotic allegiance.

The notion of people, women in particular, nurturing all of human life rather than just looking out for their own family was an important part of her peace thought. Challenging social Darwinist assumptions, inspired by her own objections to the Spanish-American War and the brutal suppression of the Filipino insurrection, Addams called for international cooperation in economic, social, and political interactions. With the establishment of international peace, governments would be in a stronger position to devote their resources to the basic needs of all its citizens, not just the privileged few. Because of women's historic role in nurturing, protecting, and conserving human life, Addams made it her life's work to extend these traditional values to the international sphere.

Addams avoided connection with the dominant conservative peace organizations and international law societies, perceiving peace as a social dynamic based on individual acts of common decency rather than cold, detached stipulated agreements among nation states. At the same time, she was mildly ignored by socialists, despite the similarity of views regarding social and political reform. She had worked tirelessly to promote the goals of organized labor and to expose working conditions in sweatshops. Unlike conservatives who heaped constant accolades on her doorstep, however, the socialists refused to approach her sidewalk. For Addams, war was unnatural, anti-progressive, and immoral. It precluded spontaneity; it was a throwback to an archaic stage of social history; and "it was fought to maintain the balance of power, a concept that glorified stasis and left no room for innovation."[26]

THE SOCIALIST APPROACH TO PEACEMAKING

The third avenue of expression to prewar peacemaking was offered by socialists, primarily those in the labor movement. By the Progressive period, as hundreds of thousands of workers left Europe for America, socialists began pointing out that U.S. capitalism was becoming more ruthless. Yet America did not appear to be on the brink of a socialist revolution. American socialists, thus homegrown, who were not tied to orthodox Marxism, developed their own plan for social and economic change: a slower, evolutionary process that would be hastened by a strong trade union movement and participation in electoral politics.

The Socialist Party of America was founded in 1901, but its origins date back to the 1880s and 1890s with the rise of labor and social protests by immigrants who were sympathetic to socialism. In the aftermath of the Pullman Car Strike in Chicago in 1893, union leader Eugene Debs successfully merged his followers from the American Railway Union and the Social Democrats of America with disaffected members of the more radical Socialist Labor Party. With the collapse of the Socialist Labor Party Debs managed to solidify his hold over labor socialists and in 1900 ran for president of the U.S. Although he was unsuccessful, Debs began establishing a home-grown political party with socialist roots.

Debs and the Socialist Party epitomized the twin causes of class solidarity and world peace in America. Debs, in particular, as so aptly described in Nick Salvatore's Eugene Debs: Citizen and Socialist, personified native protest against the forces of industrial capitalism that dehumanized the workplace and attacked individual self-worth. Debs'concept of socialism crossed class boundaries and became popular with non-politically-minded workers. Rather than specifically promoting the idea of class war Debs offered a broader vision of peace based on social justice. Embracing the concept of industrial unionism, the Socialist Party and Debs toned down the militantly anticapitalist rhetoric in favor of a more gradual approach to economic change. Throughout the prewar years, Debs and the party gained the respect and support of nonsocialist middle-class reformers. His argument that peace was more than the absence of war enabled him to develop an even larger base of support extending beyond the labor movement proper.

Socialist leaders like Debs were neither unpatriotic nor undemocratic. Their immediate focus was on advancing the rights of American workers. Higher wages and shorter hours took precedence over direct attacks on the government. Philosophically against the whole system of private ownership, socialists were more concerned with organizing industrial workers. It was Debs, who, in 1906, rallied a million men to march against the mine owners in Idaho by evoking the memory of John Brown. It was Debs who spoke out against both individual terrorism and acts of sabotage. He carried his message further in the years ahead even though his party would be wracked with internal dissension. It was his commitment to justice that symbolized best the socialist effort to create an environment receptive to international worker solidarity. Though that solidarity broke down, when World War I began in Europe in 1914, many American socialists were among the most persistent opponents of the war as noted by their active participation and support for the People's Council.

PEACE TREATIES AND RENEWED HOPE

The efforts of social progressives and socialists to debunk militarist thinking and expand the notion of social justice in America coincided with the attempts by more conservative peace workers to continue the struggle against war. Prior to the start of the World War I, judicialists devoted their greatest efforts in moving Washington in the direction of world peace. The field of arbitration held some promise and hope. At a peace banquet in New York on March 22, 1910, and again a few months later on a similar occasion in Washington, President Taft proposed that questions involving national honor be submitted to the juridical process. Friends of peace were delighted. By midsummer of 1911, treaties had been negotiated with both England and France; the treaties "declared that all judiciable questions were to be arbitrated, and all other questions submitted to a joint commission of inquiry." This commission was composed of six nationals designated by the signatories and if all, or all but one agreed that "the controversy was a judiciable one, it was to be submitted to arbitration." If they could not agree then recommendations for resolving it peaceably were to be recommended.[27]

Throughout the nation, peace groups, trade unions, college presidents and women's organizations pushed for Senate ratification. Arbitration treaties became the buzzword within professional circles as more than three hundred chambers of commerce sent resolutions favoring Senate ratification. In addition, according to one unofficial estimate, "three-fourths of the clergy preached and prayed on behalf of the treaties."[28]

However, not all Americans approved of Washington's dove-like position. Theodore Roosevelt attacked the treaties as meaningless, sentimental promises that carried no weight on the scales of diplomacy. West Coast senators were fearful that the treaties would lead to an arbitration question of the Panama tolls. Others were uneasy over compromising the Monroe Doctrine, while many more were upset that U.S. restrictionist immigration policies would be hampered if the treaties were ratified. Taft's efforts proved fruitless when "amendments to the treaties robbed them of their arbitral effectiveness."[29]

OPPOSING CONFLICT WITH MEXICO

The election of Woodrow Wilson to the presidency in 1912 renewed the hopes of peacemakers. Wilson, former president of Princeton University and then governor of New Jersey, had joined the American Peace Society in 1908. On numerous occasions, he declared himself in favor of a certain kind of war, "not the senseless and useless shedding of human blood, but the only war that brings peace, the war which is that untiring and unending process of reform from which no man can refrain and get peace." His appointment of William Jennings Bryan, the Christian pacifist, as Secretary of State indicated strong evidence of his intentions to battle for peace.[30]

Before long, however, Wilson learned that majestic pronouncements were easier to make than keep. He began to interfere in the Mexican Revolution soon after he came to office, with General John Pershing's forces landing at Vera Cruz. From Wilson's inauguration until the war in Europe became too hot in June 1915, Mexico was the chief international problem of the U.S. As President Wilson believed that Mexicans were ready to accept democracy in the American way. His initial policies were based on the belief that if Mexicans would hold free elections and follow constitutional practices their troubles would disappear. He soon learned that this would not be the case.[31]

Wilson was an idealistic nationalist; he was neither an imperialist nor a pacifist. His program of moral imperialism was designed to force the Mexican nationals to comply with his stated goal of constitutional democracy. Americans were somewhat divided over the Mexican civil war and whether U.S. leaders should continue to support Victoriano Huerta's government or the Constitutionalists led by Venustian Carranza. Either way, the efforts at intervention to stabilize Mexico began in earnest when Wilson decided to rid the country of Huerta. This action evoked strong protests from various quarters in the U.S. Many Americans were critical of previous policies in Latin America, especially the Monroe Doctrine and the Roosevelt Corollary, which claimed U.S. intervention in Latin America as legitimate. The anti-foreignism that had been a major factor in the overthrow of Porfiro Diaz also worried American anti-interventionists. The overall concern that any interference in Mexican affairs would be interpreted negatively by large numbers of Mexican-Americans living on the borders inside the U.S. was another factor peacemakers raised in their objections.

In this situation, the more conservative arm of the peace movement remained silent. This wing was more focused on matters related to Europe, while considering President William Howard Taft's policy of "Dollar Diplomacy" in Latin America a welcome substitute for the more bellicose "Big Stick Policy" of Teddy Roosevelt. When American Marines first landed at Vera Cruz on April 21, 1914, there were only modest protests by traditional peace groups. The American Peace Society's organ, the Advocate of Peace, published several resolutions from peace groups under the heading "Protests against War with Mexico." Edwin Mead and his Boston colleagues sent a number of telegrams calling upon Wilson to prevent war. Mead also telegraphed "his fellow peace workers in Philadelphia to preach against war at that critical juncture." Oswald Garrison Villard, descendant of the famed non-resistant abolitionist, William Lloyd Garrison, a peace leader and editor of the New York Evening Post, took his own protest to Washington by seeking out members of Wilson's cabinet such as Commerce Secretary William Redfield, Treasury Secretary William McAdoo, and Franklin D. Roosevelt of the Navy Department.

More determined protest came from outside the traditional peace movement. A committee of women organized an overflow meeting at Cooper Union in New York in the spring of 1914 in which suffragist leaders and women who had been reluctant or unwilling to join the suffrage movement joined together, calling upon Wilson to withdraw American troops immediately from Mexico. Even more outspoken were the socialists, who displaced the peace movement as the center of war opposition. Socialists were concerned that a war with Mexico would mobilize the forces of government and big business and use war as a pretext for silencing labor dissent. The Socialist Party, skeptical of the traditional peace movement's emphasis on arbitration, took the lead in advocating peace as an instrument for domestic social reform. "Big" Bill Haywood, fiery leader of the Industrial Workers of the World and head of the Western Federation of Miners, declared at a Carnegie Hall rally that a war against Mexico would be the signal for a general strike. The nation's mine workers would lead the strike by folding their arms and refusing to take up weapons. Rallies organized by the socialists and protests from labor leaders clearly stressed a familiar theme that war would spill the blood of workers, not capitalists.

The invasion at Vera Cruz allowed the Huerta regime to assume the role of defender against the Yankee imperialist aggressors after two years of conflict. It was not so much an outpouring of public sentiment for peace that shaped Wilson's decision to accept the mediation proposals tendered by the envoys of Argentina, Brazil, and Chile. It was the reality that the presence of American forces on Mexican soil had unleashed a torrent of nationalistic feelings reinforcing Huerta's power, producing the exact opposite of what Wilson had hoped to achieve.

In the immediate years before U.S. intervention in World War I labor leaders in the U.S. supported efforts for world peace, including improving relations with Mexico. The obvious reason was to strengthen international working-class solidarity. Military conflict would not serve the worker's interests for the focus would shift from achieving long-awaited economic concessions to patriotic conformity. In early 1916, the Mexican crisis prompted Samuel Gompers, president of the American Federation of Labor, to initiate a call for closer cooperation between the AFL and Latin American workers. Throughout the summer and fall of 1916, Gompers began instituting plans for the formation of the Pan American Federation of Labor (PAFL). As Chairman of the PAFL Conference Committee, Gompers put forth proposals "to secure better understanding between the workers of the United States and Mexico and improve the economic, political, and social conditions of the workers of both countries through economic action." He also hoped to extend the PAFL to the labor movements of all the Latin American countries and "safeguard as far as possible the principles of autonomous, independent and democratic Pan-American countries from open or insidious attempts to impose autocratic forms of government." Finally, in February 1919, the PAFL began operation for "bringing about mutual goodwill, cooperation and confidence among the workers, peoples and governments of Pan America."[32]

OPPOSITION TO WORLD WAR I AND BIRTH OF THE MODERN PEACE MOVEMENT

The Mexican Revolution was hardly the peace movement's or the Wilson administration's most formidable challenge. Growing nationalism, militarism, imperial conflict, and an alliance system enabled the assassination in 1914 of Archduke Franz Ferdinand, heir to the throne of Austria-Hungary, at Sarajevo to spark what we now call World War I. Europe experienced the worst bloodbath humankind had ever encountered. Almost ten million men lost their lives. With the use of tanks, 75mm guns, submarines, machine guns, and poison gas, modern technology proved its effectiveness in killing soldiers in unprecedented numbers. Civilian casualties were also enormous. Disease and unsanitary conditions also contributed to the high death toll on the part of soldiers and innocent victims of warfare.

Ultimately, a great majority of prewar peace workers abandoned their interest in international peacemaking mechanisms and followed the flag in defense of American nationhood. Still, a number of peace reformers attempted to keep the peace vision alive. When the limitations of the conservative peace organizers became apparent, a progressive new coalition was formed to try to keep the U.S. out of war. This coalition of feminists, social workers, and Social Gospel clergymen joined to form an anti-preparedness (or anti-militarist) campaign, then split into two groups when the United States entered the war. One group, the liberal internationalists, supported the war, ever hopeful that from it would develop a democratized, stable, and reformed post-war world order; the other group, a contingent of pacifists, withdrew to continue to fight a major enemy: war.

It would be this fight against war that led to the birth of the modern peace movement, a movement that understood peace in terms of social justice rather than surface order. Leaders of the new movement understood international justice as the "amelioration of social wrongs rather than the adjudication of courts," valued nationalism as "a cultural diversity rather than some form of Anglo-Saxon exclusivity," and saw war as a by-product of militarism, nationalism and imperialism rather than an irrational outburst of mass ignorance. They sought a reformed and democratized international system by which responsible policy-makers would manage peace through applied social justice. "More than ever," Charles DeBenedetti notes, "peace was to be known as a literal social reformation."[33]

A more ample discussion of this new movement will be provided later. But it is important to address certain components now since its seeds were developing even prior to U.S. military intervention. During World War I a number of pioneers for peace recognized the need to combine their absolute pacifism with a commitment to social reform based on a realistic appraisal of the horrors of this war. During the war the progressive values of their generation heightened their pragmatic approach to choices involving the ultimate worth of the individual in society. By distinguishing violence from other instruments of power, their opposition to war and social injustice became more pronounced because it is "destructive and perverts power from a relative to an absolute value." While not only opposing the war, they began preparing themselves to work as non-violent agents of social change, building peace through humanitarian and political efforts both at home and abroad.[34]

The search for a lasting peace in the midst of the world's most destructive conflict up to that time began in earnest in early 1915 as proponents of peace began developing their own plans for stabilizing the world situation. Borrowing from earlier ideas proposed by judicialists and internationalists a call was issued for creating a new type of international peacekeeping machinery. Peace proponents of all persuasions had always been sympathetic to such proposals, and it would be no different after the cessation of hostilities.

Led by ex-President Taft, Harvard University president A. Thomas Lowell, diplomat Oscar Strauss, and Hamilton Holt, the League to Enforce Peace was formed at an impressive meeting in Independence Hall, Philadelphia on June 17, 1915.[35] The campaign for a league of nations endowed with the power of military sanctions satisfied their advocacy of preparedness with their public pronouncements against; this idea was closely akin to that outlined in the Covenant proposal incorporated into the 1919 Treaty of Versailles.

According to the plan of the League to Enforce Peace, the signatories were to bind themselves to submit all justifiable questions to a judicial body for a hearing and subsequent judgment. All other questions not settled by negotiation were to be sent to a council of conciliation for "hearing, consideration, and recommendation." The signatory powers were to use both their economic and military might against "any one of their number which might go to war or commit hostile acts against any other signatory without first having submitted the issues to a judicial hearing or to the council of conciliation."[36]

Despite opposition by prewar legalists such as James Brown Scott, who disliked sanctions, or progressive peacemakers such as Jane Addams, who opposed the League's preference for the international status quo, the League became, by 1916, the most powerful wartime pressure group favoring the ideal of a post-war league of nations. It operated on a budget of nearly $300,000 with 23 full-time staff workers. It even managed to move the President, in May of 1916, into favoring a post-war league of nations—despite Wilson's refusal to endorse its program publicly.

Peace groups with a stronger social justice focus were also established that same year. On January 10, 1915, the Woman's Peace Party (WPP) was launched in Washington; it was inspired by Jane Addams, Anna Garlin Spencer, Carrie Chapman Catt, and Charlotte Perkins Gilman. Prompted by University of Wisconsin English professor Julia Grace Wales' proposal for a Conference of

Neutral Nations, Addams led the way for a meeting of top female pacifists at The Hague to end the war through neutral mediation.

In April of that same year, forty-five delegates, including the Hungarian pacifist Rosika Schwimmer and the British political activist Emmeline Pethwick Lawrence, attended an International Congress of Women. The Hague conferees, after some discussion, "called for a peace built upon national self-determination, international organization, and democratic control of policy." Though unsuccessful in their lobbying world leaders for mediation, they proved to be the source of the creation of the Women's International League for Peace and Freedom (WILPF) in 1919—the first female-pacifist organization to "promote the idea of transnational peace through social justice."[37]

In December 1915, Louis Lochner, Executive Secretary of the Chicago Peace Society, and Jane Addams convened an Emergency Peace Federation of veteran peace activists, feminists, and social reformers. Convinced that "the real enemy was militarism," the Federation pressed for neutral mediation (as contained in Julia Grace Wales' earlier proposal) and opposed preparedness. The organization's "primary fear was that overseas war would destroy reform opportunities at home." [38]

WOMEN'S PEACE ACTIVISM GROWS

Female socialists provided the initial impetus to women's opposition to war. A thorough examination of their role can be found in Mary Jo Buhle's Women and American Socialism. "Can we,...as mothers and teachers, instill into the minds of our growing generations the horror and cruelty of war?" asked a Driftwood, Oklahoma, woman in 1912. She answered with an all too familiar affirmation: "We as mothers of the race should stand with helmet and shield, at the head of the procession, marching and educating toward the Grand Union for a World of Peace." As early as May 1911, the Women's National Council (WNC), an appendage of the Socialist Party, urged women to form an anti-war campaign in their home towns. By 1914, in sharpening their attack against war patriotism and preparedness, Socialist women had filed the first of many petitions with President Wilson. They asked him to guard the neutrality of the United States and to act forcefully upon the food shortage and inflation by seizing resources from capitalist profiteers. In September 1914, the WNC produced a special anti-war edition of the American Socialist, unofficial organ of the national office. By the end of the year, the WNC had established a subcommittee on disarmament and militarism, and urged Socialist women to cooperate with all local "peace forces." Much like the mainstream suffragists at this point, Socialist women interpreted the conflict as the apotheosis of male domination at its last historic moment prior to women's political coming-of-age. Socialist trade union activist Meta Stern suggested, after the outbreak of war in Europe, that "soon will women, the peaceful producers, the homemakers, the mothers of men, help to conduct the affairs of the world....They will compel governments to settle their disputes."[39]

Whether socialist or not, female pacifists were finally emerging as a significant force within the peace movement. Notable women pacifists like Jane Addams and Belva Lockwood, Secretary of the International Peace Bureau, had been the exception rather than the rule when it came to visibility and influence in the organized peace movement. However, with the advent of World War I and its aftermath, women pacifists built their own separate organizations for peace. The emphasis on motherhood and instruction, echoed by the female socialist from Oklahoma, became a hallmark of the women's peace movement during and after the war.

Historian Linda Schott has persuasively argued that women pacifists rejected traditional peace organizations because of male dominance and the modern view of an absence of world unity, marked by acceptance of violent conflict and disintegration of moral certainty. Nourished by Victorian ideology and maternal practice, female pacifists developed a different world view from that of their male counterparts: for women pacifists, peace was part of a socio-cultural movement designed to guarantee women suffrage, the elimination of racial discrimination, and the upgrading of living standards for the working class.

In explaining the development of four female peace groups growing out of World War I—the Women's International League for Peace and Freedom, the Women's Peace Union, the National Committee on the Cause and Cure of War, and the Women's Peace Society—Schott maintains that women pacifists argued against war from three distinct ideological positions that sometimes overlapped. First, female pacifists argued that human life must be preserved. As nurturers of human life, Schott suggests, women were more sensitive than men. The New England-based writer Agnes Ryan, as well as Jane Addams, strongly supported this conviction. Second, female peace activists like Lucia Ames Mead, Congresswoman Jeannette Rankin, Florence Tuttle, Dorothy Detzer, and Lillian Wald emphasized the humanitarian aspect of life. Countering the Social Darwinist position on moral relativism, these women asserted that each individual deserved the best quality of human life. The commercial appeal to war was base and denigrated the fundamental importance of humanitarianism. Third, and most importantly, the women's peace movement asserted the ethical imperative of moral distinctions between killing and preservation of life. The relationship of women to children was in the context of family. Just as families settle disputes, women argued, so should nations. The male argument favoring war or its preparation in order to protect the home—security for wife and children—had little to do with actual results in war. War, in fact, destroys the happiness and security of families whose husbands are killed in battle. Thus, in disagreeing with the modern world view as established by male rulers, and in delineating the women's peace movement as cultural reform, Schott argued that female pacifists were more committed to the quality of life and well-being of all peoples. It was up to the women of the world to change men's minds regarding the necessity of war to protect one's homeland.[40]

A number of important studies by female historians have reinforced this analysis, examining ways in which women connected international peace with domestic justice issues. In the process, these studies have posited four major themes which have become the basis for female peace activism. Led by Harriet Alonso and others these themes are as follows: (1) women who saw the relationship between women's rights and peace issues were able to make the connection "between institutional violence and violence against women"; (2) feminist pacifists defined this connection by "condemning militarism and government oppression as well as the social and economic exploitation of women"; (3) the cause of sexual, physical, and psychological abuse of women was placed at the doorstep of the male power structure; and (4) there were clearly defined philosophical premises suggesting that non-violent resistance must be "a means and a measure of determining relationships" and women must become responsible citizens by gaining the vote. These scholars discarded the old Victorian notion that women were simply the guardians of moral standards in society and sought nothing more; instead, their political agendas for full equality rested on a broader notion of morality that was directly linked to a warless world.[41]

The increasingly active role played by female peace activists was clearly illustrated by the Emergency Peace Federation's (EPF) establishment, noted earlier. At the urging of Rebecca Shelly, Lella Secor, and Emily Greene Balch, EPF formalized a program that included defense of constitutional rights, opposition to compulsory military training, the right to advocate terms of peace, opposition to the adoption of any treaty, alliance or policy that would keep the United States from making an independent peace, and support for government actions to bring about early peace negotiations. The latter three were included in case the U.S. entered the war.

Following the Federation's lead, female opponents of war in the New York City branch of the Woman's Peace Party not only criticized the war in its periodical, Four Lights, but also sponsored a series of classes taught by Balch that dealt with peace proposals and international organizations. The classes, attracting many non-pacifists, concluded with three lectures by the distinguished British peace expert Norman Angell. Such educational programs provided the NYC-WPP greater exposure in its fight against conscription and possible intervention.

World War I provided women's peace organizations with a distinct identity, not previously afforded them. According to Barbara Steinson's American Women's Activism in World War I, female opponents of war argued that their "sex had responsibility for the nurture of all civilization and that they would no longer tolerate barbaric wars." Female pacifists stressed woman's "special relationship to war and expressed their determination to have a voice in decisions pertaining to war." Thus it was not surprising that pacifism and women's rights went hand-in-hand.[42]

ANTI-PREPAREDNESS

A month before EPF's creation and the NYC-WPP's sponsorship of peace lectures, a group of Quakers, Social Gospel clergymen, and YMCA officials met in Garden City, New York. Inspired by the newly formed British Fellowship of Reconciliation and its tireless and indefatigable leader Henry T. Hodgkin, they unanimously agreed to form an American Fellowship of Reconciliation. Adopting absolute pacifism as the means toward human healing, the Fellowship, at first, was not an active agency—since most liberal Protestants (as Devere Allen had pointed out) were not familiar with the pacifist ethic. Yet it proved in time, as Charles Chatfield so eloquently recounts, to be the "first agency in modern liberal pacifism which touched the nerve center of all Christian social awareness." It provided the perfect meeting place for social progressives (who discovered in pacifism an active instrument of reform) and traditional sectarian pacifists (basically Quakers) who realized that "peace could not sustain itself without the benefits of broader social change."[43]

A more symbolic form of peacekeeping activity of 1915, which captured the heart of many idealists and even some cynics, was Henry Ford's peace ship. Ford was devoted to holding on to old ways – he hated unions and was extremely anti-Semitic. But the Detroit car magnate had been horrified at hearing that in a single day 20,000 men had been killed without affecting the military situation. Prompted by Hungarian pacifist Rosika Schwimmer and Louis Lochner, Ford poured $500,000 into the idea of making a bold, novel stroke for peace. The plan was to organize a crusade of distinguished publicists and opinion leaders, place them on board the Oscar II, and arouse the peaceful sentiments of European neutral and belligerent governments alike. It was a noble, if totally idealistic, undertaking of "noisy adventurers and ludicrous dreamers."[44]

Still, some fifty volunteer peace voyagers set sail on December 4, 1915, and then proceeded to Hamburg, Copenhagen, The Hague, and Stockholm. Unfortunately, these itinerant peacemakers were divided for a variety of reasons, causing even Ford himself to desert the expedition in late December. Yet despite group cleavages and fractionalization, the adventure, thanks to Schwimmer and Lochner's persistence, succeeded in establishing in Stockholm, a year later, a Neutral Conference for Continuous Mediation.

Anti-preparedness efforts received a boost in April 1916 when members of both the Anti-Preparedness Committee and Anti-Enlistment League—including Tracy Mygatt, Jessie Wallace Hughan, John Haynes Holmes, Lillian Wald, and Crystal Eastman—established the American Union against Militarism (AUAM) (forerunner of the American Civil Liberties Union – ACLU). With close to 1,000 members in 22 cities and led by David Starr Jordan and Oswald Garrison Villard, editor of The Nation, the Union raised $50,000 in a year-long campaign to fight plans for conscription by distributing literature, petitioning legislators, and dispatching speakers across the country. Perhaps the most notable achievement of the Union was "its intermediary efforts to calm Mexican-American relations" in the summer of 1916 when General Pershing's forces crossed into Mexico in an attempt to capture the Mexican rebel Pancho Villa. In The Days of a Man, David Starr Jordan described the physical dangers he and his colleagues faced in the city of El Paso during his successful effort to conciliate differences between the Pancho Villa and American citizens.[45]

Such successes were only temporary, however. In May 1916, Congress approved all administration requests for military preparedness. In the early stages of the European war Wilson shared the widespread disposition of most Americans that the conflict was an inevitable result of years of militarism and imperialism of the great powers. Wilson, at first, had opposed the demands for a rearmament program. He had been anxious to preserve American neutrality. But during his 1916 re-election campaign his posture became clearly ambivalent. When he spoke for more arms he did so in the language of pacifist progressives. Yet when he marched in preparedness parades he was in the front of the line. Leaders in the crusade for peace and social justice had put their trust and hope in Wilson's increased preparedness as a means of avoiding U.S. entrance into the war. Only the most radical pacifists and socialists criticized Wilson's preparedness program as incompatible with pacifist neutrality.

America's firm policy against German submarine warfare deprived Wilson the diplomatic flexibility he earnestly desired. Because the U.S. refused to curb its trade and financial support to the Allies, German naval leaders were able to persuade their government that it had little to lose by deploying its submarines for total warfare against all Allied and American shipping across the Atlantic. In defense of protecting the rights of American citizens Wilson chose to see this war as a great moral struggle between good and evil.

Though peace apostles questioned Wilson's sincerity, few abandoned him during the 1916 presidential election; many more supported Wilson's re-election campaign promise, "He kept us out of war." But it was only a brief and heady intoxication. Reality struck quickly. In April 1917, German resumption of submarine warfare (a bold repudiation of the Sussex Pledge of 1916) and the publication of the Zimmerman note in the American press (compliments of British Office of Secret Intelligence) led Wilson to ask Congress for a declaration of war. Congress granted his request on April 2, 1917. The concept of a crusade for peace and democracy with the ultimate goal of a league of nations proved acceptable to those who argued that the ends were now justified by the means.

But the greater notions of what democracy really stood for would be severely tested. Not all Americans were willing to embrace Wilson's message. Dissident individuals and minority groups were bound to suffer from pressures of conformity and blind allegiance enforced in time of war. As some members of Congress expressed their reservations about a declaration of war one compelling reason stood out: war is the supreme example of the conflict between individual freedom and tyranny of the majority.

THE UNITED STATES ENTERS WORLD WAR I

There were some fifty elected officials who felt honor-bound to vote against the declaration. Jeannette Rankin of Montana, the first woman to be elected to the House of Representatives, voted "no." A woman of peace, Rankin reflected on that somber moment: "During my first week as a freshman in Congress," she observed, "the atmosphere was tense and emotional as people everywhere discussed the pending war vote....Speeches and editorials repeated over and over again the idea that to vote against war would be unpatriotic....The galleries were packed with spectators when, on the second roll call, I stood and said, 'I want to stand by my country, but I cannot vote for war. I vote NO.' In the Senate, Robert F. LaFollette of Wisconsin proclaimed: "We should not seek to hide our blunder behind the smoke of battle, to inflame the mind of our people by half truths into the frenzy of war, in order that they may never appreciate the real cause of it until it is too late. I do not believe that our national honor is served by such a course." Despite the noble objections of Rankin and LaFollette, "Peace Through Victory" became the slogan of prominent pre-war peace advocates who now supported American intervention.[46]

This was especially true of liberal internationalists, many of whom supported Wilson because they believed American intervention was the quickest and most realistic way toward achieving international reform. The possibility of creating a world agency for peace outweighed warnings like the one offered by

Senator George W. Norris of Nebraska: "We are going into war upon the command of gold....By our action, we will make millions of our countrymen suffer, and the consequences of it may well be that millions of our brethren must shed their lifeblood, millions of broken-hearted women must weep, millions of children must suffer with cold and millions of babes must die from hunger." Some blood-letting was necessary, according to progressives who supported Wilson's policies, no matter how distasteful it appeared. Those who supported the establishment of the League of Free Nations Association in 1918 (later the Foreign Policy Association) maintained that a post-war international organization, "run by administrative experts and regulatory agencies, would sustain peace through planned reconstruction, liberalized trade, and social democratization." Those who took this position included Lillian Wald; Paul Kellogg, editor of Survey; Columbia University philosopher John Dewey; Herbert Croly, editor of The New Republic; New York attorney and Assistant Secretary of War Raymond B. Fosdick; Walter Lippmann, noted journalist; Harvard law professor Manley O. Hudson; and Columbia historian James T. Shotwell as well as his distinguished colleague, Charles A. Beard. All felt some hope in Wilson's liberal promises to "Make the World Safe for Democracy" and prove this to be, in the words of H.G. Wells, a "War to End all Wars."[47]

Not all Americans were convinced as to the correctness of Wilson's position. As will be discussed in more detail later a number of anti-war groups quickly surfaced once the declaration of war was approved by Congress. In an effort to counter the insidious aspects of militant propaganda supporting the war – the Wilson administration established the Committee for Public Information (CPI) under the leadership of George Creel – anti-war organizations mobilized efforts to opposed the draft and challenge the illiberal measures of a democracy at war. The American Union against Militarism, which had been formed in November 1916, at a meeting in the Henry Street Settlement House in New York City, was led by Wald, Holmes, Eastman, and Mygatt, and was soon joined by Stephen Wise, and Paul U. Kellogg. Anti-war groups, such as the Union, had previously campaigned against drafting men into the military and now became even more active in conducting a vigorous campaign against universal compulsory military training. Its efforts were now directed at slowing down the implementation of the Selective Service and Training Act of 1917. Socialists and members of the radical syndicalist Industrial Workers of the World also resisted conscription, arguing that the war was waged by capitalists for capitalists and fought by workers who received no measure of economic justice. Workers were being forced to fight for a system that oppressed them.

The People's Council of America for Democracy and Peace was another anti-war organization; it acted as an umbrella for all propeace opinions. Rallying support from radicals, socialists, labor leaders, pacifists, and left-wing intellectuals the People's Council rallied thousands of individuals to its cause. Its primary goal was to prevent wholesale military or industrial conscription. In the early stages of American military intervention the People's Council spent considerable capital seeking the support of the laboring masses.

PATRIOTIC LOYALTY AND SUPPRESSION OF ACADEMIC FREEDOM

Of the more notable liberal thinkers in American society who supported the war, no one captured the public's attention more than John Dewey. Before American intervention, Dewey declared all forms of militarism "undemocratic, barbaric, and scholastically wholly unwise." Now he was looking for his own suit of armor. As a practicing pragmatist and instrumentalist, he reasoned that war might serve as a useful and efficient means for bringing about the desired end of a democratically organized world order. It was not that Dewey enjoyed the fruits of war; however, given the circumstances in 1917, he reasoned that war could not be separated from the system of power politics in international relations nor disconnected from the ends it sought to achieve. Although war on the whole was undesirable, it might nonetheless be made useful and educative, or so he thought.[48]

Perhaps even more disconcerting was the way in which the leading pre-war peace activist Nicholas Murray Butler conducted himself once the sword was unsheathed. "This ground offers no room for compromise or for equivocation," one of the leaders of the Carnegie Endowment for International Peace proclaimed, "because it goes to the very bottom of human life and of human government. It must be prosecuted until the world can be made secure."[49] And prosecute he did! During 1917 and 1918, Butler saw to it that no one at Columbia University dissented. In one of the worst violations in the history of academic freedom in higher education, some of the country's top scholars were told either to leave or be dismissed, while others resigned in protest because of Butler's patriotic highhandedness. For Butler, caught in the war fever, loyalty to his views became synonymous with national patriotism: "Men who feel that their personal convictions require them to treat the mature opinion of the civilized world without respect or with contempt may well be given an opportunity to do so from private station and without the added influence and prestige of a university's name."[50] Consequently, James McKeen Cattell, Leon Fraser, Henry R. Mussey, and Ellery C. Stowell were told to leave—while the eminent historian Charles Beard, who supported the war, resigned in protest over the dictatorial actions of the Columbia Board of Trustees and its president.[51]

The Columbia University experience was reflected in a number of other academic freedom cases. In 1918, the Nebraska State Council of Defense submitted to the University of Nebraska Board of Regents a list of twelve professors who were accused by this organization of promoting indifference or opposition to the war. The Board of Regents conducted an investigation. The Board disclosed that three of the professors believed in internationalism, refused to promote the sale of liberty bonds, and openly criticized some of their more patriotic colleagues. After a Board trial those three professors were dismissed. At the University of Virginia, Leon R. Whipple, Director of the School of Journalism, was charged with disloyalty for a speech he made in which he declared that the war would not remove the specter of autocracy nor make the world safe for democracy. After a trial by the state's Board of Visitors Whipple was given his pink slip. The University of Minnesota's Board of Regents dismissed the chairman of its Political Science department, William A. Schaper, for stating that he did not wish to see the Hohenzollerns completely destroyed. In Maine the Dean of the University's law school was removed by the Board of Trustees on the grounds that his lectures were tinged with pro-German sentiments. Cornell University was a bit more humanitarian; Henry W. Edgerton, a young professor of law, was granted an indefinite leave of absence because he had registered as a conscientious objector.

Attacks against educators came from all quarters and were not limited to professors. As H.C. Peterson and Glibert Fite have shown in their work, Opponents of War, 1917-1918, every effort was made by federal and state governments to convert schools into "seminaries of patriotism." More than 100,000 school districts became receptive instruments to all ideological forms of guerilla warfare. Led by the National Education Association and the Committee on Patriotism through Education, district after district banned the teaching of German and demanded loyalty oaths of school teachers and support personnel. The New York Legislature, for instance, went so far as to create a commission to hear and examine complaints about "seditious" textbooks in subjects like civics, history, economics, and English literature. In elementary schools teachers were instructed to teach the themes of patriotism, heroism, and sacrifice as well as learning about the differences between German autocracy and the American democratic way of life.

While Peterson and Fite pointed out the number of instances where teachers were fired for refusal to support the war, nowhere was this more apparent than in New York City. One Board of Education member, General Thomas Wingate, proclaimed that "the teacher who teaches pacifism and that this country should not defend itself is a thousand times more dangerous than the teacher who gets drunk and lies in the gutter." Despite elaborate hearings, defense counsel and all the elaborate appearances of a trial, the decision to fire teachers had been largely predetermined by the hysteria of the men in charge of conducting the proceedings. Throughout the city's school system, teachers were suspended or dismissed for questioning American military involvement, refusing to teach patriotism in their classes, or not taking the recently-enacted loyalty oath. Thus, three teachers from De Witt Clinton's High School in Brooklyn were fired because of their socialist opposition to the war. A German-born elementary school teacher, Gertrude Pignol, was fired for wearing a locket engraved by her father and having a picture of the Kaiser's grandfather on one side and the cornflower on the other.

Perhaps nothing exemplified the height of patriotic intolerance in public schooling more than the dismissal of Phi Beta Kappa, Swarthmore College graduate, and Quaker Mary Stone McDowell from Brooklyn's Manual Training High School. When she refused to take the loyalty oath because of her Quaker faith, school officials promptly gave her a hearing and then fired her anyway. Little consideration was given to the historic protections of the Society of Friends' religious opposition to war. McDowell chose to challenge her dismissal in state court, but she lost. Her challenge was the first case in American legal history involving the issue of religious freedom in public education that went to a state court.

The hysteria spread far and wide. Another example of the abuses within school house gates occurred in Bucksport, Maine. There, veteran middle school teacher Lucina Hopkins was fired from her job because she took driving lessons from a German immigrant! Her husband had purchased a new car for her so that she could visit her ailing mother on the way home from work. Since she did not know how to drive, her husband hired a driving instructor, who was a German alien, to teach her. Hopkins did sue in court, but the lower court ruled against her. The Maine Court of Appeals overturned the decision and awarded her $400; however, she was never reinstated in her teaching position.

The liberal internationalist John Dewey and the conservative legalist Nicholas Murray Butler both misjudged the war's impact on the American psyche. Their attempts to use the universities and school systems as vehicles of patriotic instruction caused them to ignore the power of anti-democratic forces at work. If the war was being fought for patriotic reasons as Butler believed or for social reform in Dewey's estimation, neither was prepared for the scathing attack Randolph Bourne leveled against their misguided reasoning.

This brilliant student of John Dewey turned the pro-war internationalist logic upside down. He was virtually alone in calling attention to the fact that many who shouted loudly in behalf of the freedom and democracy for which the Allies stood were contemptuous of democratic strivings in their own backyard. How was one to channel "the fierce urgencies" of the war into positive democratic outlets? To Bourne, the pro-war liberal internationalists' excessive optimism led them to overestimate the power of intelligence and underestimate the force of violence and irrationality. Indeed, "war is the health of the state," Bourne asserted. "the moment war is declared…the mass of people, through some spiritual alchemy become convinced that they will have willed and executed the deed themselves." Adding insult to injury, he continued: "They then with the exception of a few malcontents, proceed to allow themselves to be regimented, coerced, deranged in all the environments of their lives, and turned into a solid manufactory of destruction…."[52]

DISSENT AND CONSCIENTIOUS OBJECTION

The demand for patriotic conformity overshadowed whatever semblance of democratic freedoms existed in the U.S. at this time. Schools were not alone in efforts to teach obedience to the state. Creel's committee was charged with "selling" the war and CPI's advertising executives did everything in their power to portray the war a crusade against the evil "Huns." Millions of pamphlets, posters, and newsreels were made trumpeting the pro-war cause. The home-front atmosphere was one of political repression and widespread abuse of civil liberties.

Despite the pressure to go along with the war, there were many who accepted Bourne's indictment of it. Hard-core anti-war socialists, some urban intellectuals, and FOR-related liberal pacifists composed the majority of stubborn American opponents of war.[53] Opposition took the form of both individual and organized resistance. Approximately four thousand Conscientious Objectors were recorded, most of whom went into non-combatant military service; five hundred were court-martialed and imprisoned, 17 were sentenced to death, but never executed, and 142 were given life terms but released by 1921.[54] World War I prisoners of conscience included civil libertarian Roger Baldwin who helped found the American Civil Liberties Union (1920) and socialist leader Eugene V. Debs. Jailed twice for war opposition and in prison during the election of 1920, Debs received nearly a million votes as the socialist candidate for president. "I am not a capitalist soldier," he proclaimed. "I am a proletarian revolutionist. I do not belong to the regular army of the plutocracy, but to the irregular army of the people. I refuse to obey any command to fight from the ruling class, but I will not wait to be commanded to fight the working class." Anarchists Emma Goldman and Alexander Berkman, who formed a No-Conscription League in 1917, were sentenced to two years in jail and later deported. Tom Mooney and Warren Billings, accused of setting a bomb near a "preparedness parade" in 1916, were released from prison in 1939 after serving twenty-two years. "Big Bill" Haywood, Elizabeth Gurley Flynn, and other labor organizers were indicted for war opposition under the Espionage Act.[55]

The heart and soul of the anti-war movement was, of course, conspicuously exemplified by Conscientious Objectors. Apart from the 4,000 classified as Conscientious Objectors, approximately 20, 873 were granted non-combatant classification by their local draft boards. Among them were various types of opponents of war: religious objectors – opposed to all wars and human killing; humanitarian or liberal objectors who believed that all men were brothers and that fraternal blood should not be shed; and political objectors—Socialists, anarchists, syndicalists, and other radicals—who promoted an international revolution of the working class but who objected to participating in a "capitalist" war.

To be sure, the problem of Conscientious Objection was an old and difficult one. It raised the important question of the relationship between the state and an individual's conscience. However, the military was unprepared at first to handle the issue with humanitarian compassion. When the CO's arrived at an army camp, the general practice was to get as many of them as possible to accept combatant duty. Labeling them as cowards and shirkers, military officials used all kinds of pressures to break the convictions of the objectors. In some camps, they were "enticed, jeered, hosed, beaten, placed in solitary confinement, and given other rigorous and inhumane treatment." Army officers often looked upon "physical punishment and a policy of pressure as the best means of testing the genuineness of a man's convictions." In one of the more egregious examples of mistreatment, Molokans, Christian pacifists and emigrants from Russia, were sent to Ft. Leavenworth in October 1918. They were thrown into a hole where they were manacled to cell bars in a standing position for nine hours each day; they were not even allowed to receive or send mail. At Alcatraz, some non-resisters were placed in straitjackets and locked to a ball and chain in a damp and dreary dark cell for five consecutive days. Two of them, brothers, eventually died after being transferred to Leavenworth.[56]

Despite such treatment, many held firm. Sheldon W. Smith recounted his own experience when he refused to put on a uniform or to sign the clothing slip; despite the grammatical errors, he captures the indignities of the punishment meted out: "When finally dressed in blue denhams (sic), part of the noncommissioned officers took me to the house which was soon well occupied with spectators or would be assistants. They again stripped their victim, put him under a shower and scrubbed him with a broom; then whipped him with their belts; put a rope around his neck and drew it up to a pipe until he could not breathe; all the while renewing their question about giving in." And if that was not sufficient enough, "One would cry one thing and one another so they did not stick to one form of punishment very long only the bathing was continued until I was chilled and shook all over, part of the time they had me on my back with face under a faucet and held my mouth open. They got a little flag ordering me to kiss it and kneel down to it." At Camp Upton, Long Island, an objector refused to obey orders and "was struck and cut across the knees and shins repeatedly with a bayonet. For two hours, he was beaten with fists and rifles." From other camps came similar reports of the objector's treatment by the military.[57]

Those suffering the greatest indignities were absolute pacifists. A normal prison sentence for absolutists was from twenty to twenty-five years. One CO avoided execution by volunteering to retrieve wounded soldiers from the battlefield. It was not until November 1920 that all objectors were released from prison.

The government was slow to respond to pacifist criticisms. John Nevin Sayre, brother-in-law to one of President Wilson's daughters, an Episcopal priest, and a member of the Fellowship of Reconciliation, called upon the president to intervene on behalf of better treatment for CO's. He provided the president with a list of abuses committed against imprisoned COs. After reading Sayre's documentation, the president immediately ordered all military personnel to cease and desist the application of inhumane treatment meted out by soldiers at federal prisons. Emphasizing the democratic nature of American society and its support for differing viewpoints, noted socialist clergyman Norman Thomas proclaimed: "If this is indeed a people's war for freedom, the people can be trusted to see it through, without any coercion of conscience. To deny this is either to distrust democracy or to doubt the validity of war as its instrument. Justice to the Conscientious Objector secures, not imperils, the safety of the democratic state." In most instances, pacifists from the historic peace churches took it upon themselves to establish their own forms of non-combatant relief work. A notable example is Rufus Jones and Philadelphia-area Friends creating the American Friends Service Committee in April 1917. It was specifically formed to engage Quaker non-combatants in volunteer work in the areas of war relief and reconstruction. Numerous AFSC volunteers grew crops and rebuilt villages in war-torn France; after the war, they fought disease and famine in Central Europe.[58]

ORGANIZATIONS DEFEND DISSENT AND SPEAK OUT

The treatment of COs strengthened the doubts and suspicions peace and anti-war groups expressed towards military intervention in Europe. The American Union Against Militarism protested the violence accompanying the administration's appeals to patriotic Americans to fight what Wilson had called the "sinister intrigue" of German dupes and the equally, dangerous dissenters. Some manifestations of that violence were limited to words, such as former ambassador James Gerard's declaration that "we should hog-tie every disloyal German American, feed every pacifist raw meat, and hang every traitor to a lamp-post to insure success in this war." Other forms of violence were physical. The anti-militarists were convinced that the U.S. had witnessed the first victories of Prussian militarism when in Boston "thousands of peaceful citizens" who had a permit to assemble "were attacked by lawless soldiers and sailors in uniform" as the police stood by "apparently over-awed [sic] by the uniform and did nothing except to arrest the victims." The AUAM noted that this scene had already occurred in "a dozen American cities" only three months after America's entrance into the war.[59]

Much of the abusive treatment accorded critics of the war, Peterson and Fite have pointed out, cannot be justified as a response "to violent acts endangering national security." In only one instance was there an organized effort to overthrow governmental authority: the Green Corn Rebellion in Oklahoma. In early August 1917, about five hundred tenant farmers and sharecroppers opposed to conscription planned to march on Washington. The march was designed to take over the machinery of government and declare the war over.[60] However, these "malcontents were easily rounded up by the state police" and their leaders were sent to the federal penitentiary at Leavenworth, Kansas, to serve sentences of three to ten years.[61]

Meanwhile, organized resistance was manifested by anti-war socialists who were also interested in reforming the society in which they lived. For them a decent future required "a basic change in values and power." An important outcome of such advancement would also be the abolition of war—which they considered, perhaps too narrowly, as "an aspect of capitalism and imperialism." But, as supporters of the international working class, they could not sanction a war against their fellow workers in other nations.[62]

Large meetings in support of this position were commonplace at socialist rallies. The passage of the Espionage Act of 1917 and Sedition Act of 1918 were intended to stifle socialist dissent. Both laws were designed to silence free speech. Government disregard for protecting civil liberties were most pronounced. In one of the most egregious examples of government oversight Postmaster General Albert S. Burleson approved the opening of mail of groups and organizations opposed to the war. Any evidence obtained was then used for prosecutorial purposes.

In one prominent case, Russian-born Jew Rose Pastor Stokes, who had worked in the U.S. as a cigarmaker and became an important propagandist for the socialists, was sentenced to ten years in prison (later reversed by a higher court) for writing a letter to the Kansas City Star in which she stated that the soldiers were not fighting for democracy but for protecting Morgan's millions.

The most noted free speech case involving socialists was that of Charles T. Schenck. In August 1917, Schenck, the general secretary of the Socialist Party in Philadelphia, and some of his comrades planned to mail a leaflet to men whose names were published in the newspapers as having passed their draft board physicals. The leaflet Schenck and his comrades printed had "Long Live the Constitution of the United States" on one side and "Assert Your Rights!" on the other. Each side of the leaflet attacked the Constitution for its repudiation of free choice as guaranteed in the laws of the country. The key phrase in the leaflet stated: "A conscript is little better than a convict. He is deprived of his liberty and of his right to think and act as a free man." Some 15,000 copies of the leaflet were printed, but a large number were not mailed. Schenck and four other Socialist Party members, including Dr. Elizabeth Baer, were subsequently charged with conspiring to obstruct the draft. In December 1917, Schenck and Baer were found guilty. Schenck received a six-month prison sentence and Baer three months. Both appealed their convictions.

In January 1919, the U.S. Supreme Court heard their appeal. On March 3, 1919, Justice Oliver Wendell Holmes, Jr., announced his "clear and present danger" test defining when speech can be the basis for criminal punishment. His oft-quoted statement read: "The most stringent protection of free speech would not protect a man in falsely shouting fire in a theatre and causing a panic...." The Supreme Court upheld Schenck's conviction on the grounds that his leaflet intended to cause harm to the government's effort to prosecute the war. Interestingly, Court testimony at the initial trial revealed that few of the inductees received the leaflet. Of eleven witnesses called to testify for the prosecution, eight never received the leaflet, one never read it, and eight read it for the first time under questioning at the trial. Nevertheless, the Schenck case established serious limitations on freedom of speech.

The government also worked to silence radical labor unions. For the Industrial Workers of the World (IWW), the most noted radical labor organization, the war represented nothing more than an "opportunity of certain groups of American capitalists to coin old profits out of the blood and suffering of our fellowmen in the warring nations of Europe." In fact, the Industrial Worker, the official journal of the IWW, offered a poetic remedy:

I love my flag, I do, I do,
Which floats upon the breeze,
I also love my arms and legs,
And neck, nose and knees,
One little shell might spoil them all

Or give them such a twist,
They would be of no use to me;
    I guess I won't enlist.
I love my country, yes I do
I hope her folks do well.
Without our arms, and legs, and things
I think we'd look like hell.
Young men with faces half shot off
Are unfit to be kissed.
I've read in books it spoils their looks,
    I guess I won't enlist.

The Wilson Administration did not take kindly to such satirical observations. On September 5, 1917, federal agents raided IWW headquarters in 33 different cities between Chicago and Los Angeles. Three weeks later, one hundred and thirteen IWW leaders were arraigned in Chicago federal court; they were charged with obstructing the war effort. Within one year, following a dramatic trial in the summer of 1918, ninety-six of them were tried, convicted, and sent to prison. Among those convicted was "Big Bill" Haywood, a legendary figure of the IWW.[63]

The IWW's feelings were well elaborated upon in more eloquent fashion by the founder of the American Railway Union and Socialist Party leader Eugene Debs. From almost the beginning of his career, Debs argued that "modern wars were invariably the result of economic competition and commercial rivalry among nations in their struggle for world power." For Debs, war was "a survival of the black ages of slavery, superstition, and ignorance." The workers, rather than letting the government and capitalists make cannon fodder of them, should "be aroused to grapple [sic] with and overthrow" this unfortunate and terrible blight on mankind. "Without the workers, who are at the same time its misguided supporters and its mutilated and bleeding victims," Debs passionately maintained, war would disappear and become "a horrid nightmare of history." Workers must come to the full realization that they do possess enormous power: "The working class alone can put an end to war." For speaking his conscience in Canton, Ohio, Debs drew a ten-year jail sentence for an anti-war speech in violation of the Espionage Act.[64]

The notion of workers as particular victims of war became the battle cry of the People's Council of America for Democracy and Peace. Tentatively organized May 30, 1917, in New York City and officially established in September of that year, "amid turmoil, public denunciation, and armed repression," this coalition of radicals, labor leaders, and bohemian intellectuals insisted that the worker despised war, recognized it as a conspiracy against his own fundamental interests, and sought brotherhood and cooperation with workingmen in other parts of the world. At the Madison Square Garden Rally of May 30th some 20,000 people were in attendance. The Council's program was a direct response to the Russian Revolution: Russian workers threw down their weapons and refused to continue fighting against German workers.

The basic argument of the People's Council was socialist. Support came from trade unions, pacifists, suffragists, and the Socialist Party's left wing. It endorsed the Socialist Party's pledge to "continuous, active, and public opposition to the war." It also called for "...unyielding opposition to all proposed legislation for military or industrial conscription...vigorous resistance to all reactionary measures, such as censorship of the press and mails, restrictions of the rights of free speech, assemblage...constant propaganda against military training...and widespread educational propaganda to enlighten the masses as to the true relation between capitalism and war." Modern wars, the Council argued, were "an integral and inevitable part" of the capitalist system. Under capitalism, industrial oppression is manifest; the worker is incapable of commanding wages for the full value of his labor. The accompanying "unequal distribution of income meant that capitalists, or the owning class, would acquire more than they could profitably invest at home" and produce more goods than the workers could afford to buy. The end result was increased competition between the industrialized nations for empires and spheres of influence—imperialism—which would "serve as new investment and marketing areas."[65]

It was not until September 1917 that the People's Council finally began to formulate its opposition to war. James Maurer, President of the Pennsylvania Federation of Labor, forcefully stated the membership's views: "The very same interests which in the past corrupted our courts, denuded our forests, polluted our streams, robbed us of our lands and mineral deposits, exploited, imprisoned, starved, and in industrial disputes unhesitatingly murdered the toilers—these are the people who are opposing the People's Council...."[66] Earlier, the resolutions of the May 30th Madison Square Garden People's Council Conference underscored its basic theme: "Industrial plutocracy makes for war—industrial democracy for peace." A subsequent broadside clearly spelled the difference between the People's Council's position and that of the official war ideology: "The President has said that it is our purpose to help make the world safe for democracy. We would like to make democracy safe in our own country."[67]

This was the direction the People's Council proposed to follow in the fall of 1917, but by spring of the following year, the Council's strength and popularity diminished considerably. Domestic pressures for patriotic conformity presented the most serious obstacle to keeping members. Increasing wartime prosperity played a part as well. Overt government suppression of dissenting groups by state and federal court action—as in the case of the IWW and Socialist Party—also effectively checked the Council's union support. By spring of 1918, almost "one-third of the Party's leadership was sentenced to federal prison." Meanwhile, with Wilson's approval, Burleson barred from the mails all socialist anti-war publications—thereby, as Frank L Grubbs points out, "cutting the intellectual lifeline of organized socialism in the United States, the largest single source of wartime dissent." The concept of democracy was being severely tested, and the People's Council discovered how difficult it was to carry out its highest ideals.[68]

Many African Americans faced the same pressures as the working class and members of organized labor. Little attention was given to W.E.B. Du Bois' initial argument that racism and colonialism were basic sources of war. In an early essay, "Credo," first published in The Independent on October 6, 1904 and widely distributed throughout the world, Du Bois openly criticized militarism and war and called for global justice, equality, and world peace. Du Bois continued hammering home the connection between racism and colonialism as instruments of war. In a New York Times editorial on December 12, 1909, and in another editorial entitled "Peace" appearing in the May 1913 issue of The Crisis, Du Bois maintained that the van of human progress must ride on the hopes for female emancipation, universal peace, political democracy, human brotherhood, and, most importantly, the socialization of wealth. But once world war commenced pressures for conformity and government efforts to unite the nation under the banner of patriotic loyalty proved too much for Du Bois and those sympathetic to race relations.

Eventually, many African Americans followed Du Bois' lead after he was pressured by President Wilson, supporting the war and putting black rights second to demonstrating their loyalty (a position for which they were not rewarded). But there was black opposition to the war. A good example is the monthly publication of The Messenger, an anti-war socialist periodical published by African-American intellectuals, including A. Philip Randolph of the Brotherhood of Sleeping Car Porters, which questioned how the country could fight for democratic freedoms overseas while choosing to ignore such rights at home. The Messenger urged blacks not to fight, enlist, or be drafted into the army. Many African Americans believed that the war was started because nations like England, France, and Germany were fighting over the riches they could obtain from their colonial possessions and to see who would rule over the darker peoples of Africa and Asia. For Randolph the war was also about cheap labor. A socialist and pacifist, Randolph insisted that the war was one way in which white capitalists could continue to oppress minorities and keep them from achieving economic equality.

The war years inflamed already existing sentiments of racism, nativism, and anti-unionism. It still remained a time of terrorism and segregation against people of color. In July 1917, for example, while Wilson praised the virtues of democracy, random white attacks on blacks in East St. Louis, Illinois, resulted in racial rioting that left 38 African-Americans and eight whites dead, along with hundreds injured. It was the worst case of interracial violence in American up until that time. It led Debs to reflect somberly that "Had the labor unions ever opened the door to the Negro, instead of barring him . . . the atrocious crime at East St. Louis would never have blackened the pages of American history."[69] This atrocity was soon followed by the hanging of thirteen African American soldiers in Houston, Texas. After a riot occurred in September 1917, involving a number of black soldiers unjustly accused, the 13 were quickly executed and another 41 sentenced to life imprisonment. When the next world war came around, many more African Americans insisted on continuing their own fight for democratic and human rights.

CONCLUSION

The patriotic hysteria of World War I and its aftermath is unparalleled in American history, and many members of the various peace societies jumped enthusiastically on the caissons. Many others remained firm in their convictions and suffered from both informal and governmental repression. The degree and severity of repression was dramatically illustrated in terms of pubic hysteria against all things German. Food names were changed: frankfurter became hot dog and sauerkraut became liberty cabbage. In St. Louis, home to a large number of German Americans, street names were arbitrarily changed to erase any vestiges of German influence. German books were burned by vigilante groups who also took sadistic pleasure in harassing German Americans.[70]

While the majority of Americans lined up behind the war effort, significant groups did not. Among Irish-Americans, for example, there was some chagrin at the prospect of a war on the side of hated England. German-Americans and emigrants from the Austro-Hungarian Empire were also dismayed at the prospect of a war with their mother countries. The war was never accepted in areas like rural Wisconsin where German immigrants were numerous.

The greatest opposition to World War I was not a pacifist movement but a radical one. It taught pacifists to pay more attention to the long-neglected economic causes of war and diverted them from their pre-war conservatism to a closer relationship with radical groups. The American Civil Liberties Union—founded in reaction to the wartime mockery of civil liberties—defended both religious and radical pacifists. During and after the war new organizations replaced the American Peace Society, which now became a mere shell of its former self. The Fellowship of Reconciliation, War Resisters League, and Women's International League for Peace and Freedom maintained close relations with radical organizations and incorporated radical thought into their programs.

The wartime xenophobia, something Bourne accurately noted, but Dewey and his apostles unfortunately underestimated, destroyed the underpinnings of the conservative elements within the peace movement. During World War I, the suppression of freedom enjoyed the almost unanimous support of the patriotic populace and the various agencies of the government—national, state, and local. Before the war was over, almost every major Socialist Party official had been indicted for anti-war activity. Enraged mobs had also cracked down on radical dissent everywhere. Throughout the country, IWW headquarters were raided. In Oklahoma, Wobblies were rounded up and tarred and feathered; in Arizona, they were packed into cattle cars and abandoned in the desert; and in Montana, Frank Little, a crippled IWW leader, was kidnapped and hanged from a railway trestle.

Ironically, while many peace workers who were not absolutists stood by Wilson's internationalism and witnessed society's repressive tactics, their own foundation crumpled in the process. Their individualistic, moral sensitivities surrendered to a collective mentality that demanded conformity at the cost of personal freedom. Clarence Darrow, the famed attorney and former disciple of Tolstoyan pacifism, reflected somberly: "Wars always bring about a conservative reaction. They overwhelm and destroy patient and careful efforts to improve the condition of man. Nothing can be heard in the cannon's roar but the voice of might." He continued his thoughtful analysis by arguing that "All the safeguards laboriously built to preserve individual freedom and foster man's welfare are blown to pieces with shot and shell. In the presence of the wholesale slaughter of men the value of life is cheapened to the zero point."[71]

The inability of the peace movement to prevent mass killing and bloodshed on the field of battle strengthened its resolve and redefined its mission. Supporters of peace would regroup and reassess their strategies for building a more humane society. Building upon these various strains of opposition to war, pioneers for peace would construct a stronger and more pro-active peace movement. Disillusioned at the results of the war and domestic intolerance, they restructured their efforts to make the crusade for world peace not only a mission eradicating the evils of war but also a crusade for social and economic justice.

CHAPTER FIVE
INTERNATIONALISM AND PEACE REFORMERS IN ACTION

> The willingness to sacrifice one's individual self is the affirmation of the greater unity, and therefore attracts the support of many forces, by themselves subtle and seemingly weak but together in organized unity immensely strong. Thus the giving up of the smaller original self is the first necessary step toward the creation of a richer, more inclusive and more permanent self.
>
> Richard Gregg, "The Pacifist Program in Time of War, Threatened War, or Fascism," 1939.

INTRODUCTION

Gregg's words aptly sum up the post-war liberal peace movement's commitment to social justice. Son of a Congregational minister and Harvard-trained lawyer, Gregg, perhaps more than any other figure, save for A.J. Muste, taught pacifists and social reformers that non-violence was a lot more than a religious or ethical way of life. Immersing himself in Gandhi's non-violent way of social change, Gregg's radicalism was a self-conscious method of social action with a clear-defined logic and strategy. For Gregg, as well as for generations of pacifists in the past, the rejection of violence had been "a fundamental religious imperative." Yet, in the aftermath of the most destructive and violent confrontation in history up to that time, the method of non-violence would blend itself with the techniques of modern psychology and mass media influences to create the most militant grass-roots movement in the name of peace and social justice.

What gave impetus and meaning to this drive for militant non-violence was the Red Scare of 1919-1920. During the postwar years, federal and state governments conducted a vigorous drive against anarchists, Communists, and socialists spurred on by fears that radicals in the United States might try to imitate the Russian Bolshevik Revolution of 1917. The Espionage Act, passed in wartime to punish treasonable or disloyal activities, remained in effect after the war. Pacifist and radical opponents of the war were refused amnesty, and Eugene Debs remained in a federal prison in Atlanta, even as he was nominated to the presidency by the Socialist Party in 1920. In the fall of 1919, Attorney General A. Richard Palmer instructed Department of Justice agents to arrest radicals throughout the country. Several hundred were arrested in these mass raids and deported after cursory hearings to countries where they had not resided for many years. Among those deported aboard the "Russian Arc" were Emma Goldman and Alexander Berkman.

The Red Scare was also a byproduct of the intensification of American nationalism resulting from the war. Those who saw themselves as 100% Americans sought to limit American citizenship and the benefits of democracy to those meeting the tests of race, creed, color, and political and economic desirability. Fostered by an atmosphere of political conservatism and general disillusionment with World War I, Congress took matters into its own hands by halting the tide of immigrants seeking entrance into the United States. The issue of immigration and radicalism became linked in the popular mind. In a series of measures designed to promote 100% Americanism, Congress passed the National Origins Act of 1924. It reversed the liberal immigration policy of more than a century. This new legislation was specifically designed to cut drastically the numbers of those arriving from Southern and Eastern Europe or from Italy and the Slavic regions. It was racially motivated.

Newly-created patriotic groups such as the American Legion, an organization composed of veterans of military service, expressed strong reservations about immigrants from Southern and Eastern Europe for fear that they would bring with them socialist and anti-capitalistic ideas. Such fears linking immigration and radicalism would manifest themselves with the 1927 executions of the Italians Nicola Sacco and Bartholomeo Vanzetti. Asian immigrants would also find themselves singled out for discrimination based on competition for jobs. Their discrimination pre-dated the World War I period, but continued nonetheless. In sum, a strong prejudice against foreigners based on their national origins was derived from old fears of radicalism and competition for jobs.

For peace pioneers, seeking to expand the definition of peace to include justice at home became a tall order. Their efforts were greeted rudely by the rebirth of the Ku Klux Klan. The Klan, in particular, was the most extreme organization hostile toward African Americans and other minorities during the postwar years. Although the organization was not directly connected with the original group which flourished during the Reconstruction era, its revival borrowed much of the nativist philosophy of the Know-Nothing movement of the antebellum years. The revived Klan incorporated into its program the most intolerant and illiberal features of the cult of postwar nationalism. Viciously and without regard for human decency, members of the Klan carried out multiple acts of violence. Its slogan of "native, white, Protestant" supremacy represented the most sinister aspects of ultranationalism. Hiding behind the cult of patriotism, the Klan despised all things foreign, all who were black, as well as Jews and Roman Catholics.

Although the revived Klan promoted white supremacy, it moved beyond the bludgeoning and lynching of blacks to also attacking white people who openly criticized their actions. It also condemned any citizen who favored peace and social justice. Klan members continued criticizing communists and questioned the virtues of labor organization. The Klan's warped view of patriotism, rooted in rural suspicions of an urban society, was built on racial purity and military supremacy. It was not unusual to witness Klan parades with American flags. It was its way of masking intolerant acts, which symbolically captured the whole range of post-1919 nativism.

Despite the Red Scare's legacy of suspicion of aliens, dislike for reformers, distrust of organized labor, and an emphasis on political conformity, along with the appearance of the super-intolerant Klan, the decade of the 1920's did witness a growing sympathy for world peace. The poet Austin Dobson's "WHEN THERE IS PEACE" aptly characterized American post-war sentiment:

When there is Peace, our land no more
Will be the land we know of yore."
Thus do our facile seers foretell
The truth that none can buy or sell
And e'en the wisest must ignore.
When we have bled at every pore,
Shall we still strive for gear and store?
Will it be heaven? Will it be hell?
When there is Peace?
This let us pray for, this implore:
That, all base dreams thrust out at door,
We may in loftier aims excel
And, like men waiting from a spell,
Grow stronger, nobler, than before,
When there is Peace.[1]

Disillusionment with World War I left a determination in millions of Americans never to fight again; no one was willing to stand up now and sing songs like "Rally Round the Flag" or attend romantic plays like "The Drummer Boy of Shiloh." The Unknown Soldier—the American doughboy whose very identity remained buried beneath the rubble of the war's destruction—symbolized that this was a fight to forget. At no time in U.S. history was the hold of pacifism, or disdain for war, as strong or compelling as it was between the first and second world wars.

World War I was never idealized by the American people as earlier wars had been; the magnitude and severity of death and destruction had much to do with that feeling. The revisionist historians strengthened the commonly felt attitude that the war had been a complete mistake. In 1926, Harry Elmer Barnes, professor of Sociology at Smith College, published his Genesis on the World War, an attack on the widely accepted idea of German responsibility for the conflict. Two years later, Sidney B. Fay's two-volume Origins of the World War left little doubt that the official Allied propaganda did not square at some points with a critical analysis of archival and other material. The fact that scholars, including those who had supported it in the name of progressive social reform, were weighing in on the issue gave greater credence to those who openly questioned Wilson's reasons for going to war.

Feeding into this postwar disillusionment, moreover, were the revelations of the Nye Committee of the mid-1930s. In September 1934, Republican Senator Gerald P. Nye of North Dakota convened a Senate investigation to look into allegations that manufacturers of armaments had unduly influenced the American decision to go to war. According to reports, weapons suppliers had reaped enormous profits at the cost of over 53,000 American battlefield casualties. Publicity regarding the role of munitions makers in the war was aroused due to the publication of sensationalist works such as Seymour Waldman's Death and Profits (1932) and Book-of-the Month club selection Merchants of Death (1934) by H.C. Englebrecht and F.C. Hanighen.

Over a period of eighteen months the Nye Committee held 93 hearings and questioned over 200 witnesses, including J.P. Morgan, Jr., and Pierre du Pont. Based on these hearings the Nye Committee charged that private armament interests worked contrary to arms embargoes and treaties, sold weapons to both sides in World War I, stimulated arms races between friendly nations, and benefited from excess profits with government blessings. Although the committee uncovered little hard evidence of an arms makers' conspiracy, its disclosures aroused great public interest and added to the public's distrust for war.

In addition to historians questioning the rationale behind the war and congressional committees looking into the role of arms makers, virtually all American literary men and women who wrote about the war also expressed severe disappointment; examples include Willa Cather in One of Ours, John Dos Passos' Three Soldiers, What Price Glory by Stallings and Anderson, and A Farewell to Arms by Ernest Hemingway. The prevailing antipathy toward the war also found expression in the popularity of former German soldier Erich Remarque's All Quiet on the Western Front, which produced enormous sales in the United States.

THE DRIVE FOR PEACE BEGINS AND THE MODERN MOVEMENT TAKES SHAPE

During the 1920s peace reformers, acting "out of a creed of liberal humanism" and revulsion for war, were deeply involved in promoting the goals of internationalism and economic and social justice.[2] Throughout this period there were liberal internationalists, pacifists, socialists, communists, labor activists, educators, clergy, and supporters of civil rights, to name a few, who touted the goals of world peace through internationalism and social and economic justice at home. Such would be the two dominant currents of the postwar peace movement. While more conservative peace advocates pushed the goal of internationalism there were others within the peace movement who insisted that a militant approach to peace and justice was necessary in order to achieve the larger goal of social reform at home. It would make for a very dynamic and, at times, exciting struggle against war and social injustice.

Very early in the decade some advocates of harmony asserted that their purpose was to move the American people into cooperative action with peoples and governments abroad through international peace treaties and disarmament agreements.[3] Peace activists quickly took the lead in urging government officials to carry through with promises to limit the expansion and growth of naval armaments as the first step in stabilizing world peace.

Peace advocates were thus pleased when the Washington Naval Conference of 1921-1922 succeeded in halting the construction of capital ships and aircraft carriers—which was more than any other disarmament conference had been able to do. It eliminated the objectionable Anglo-Japanese alliance; it reduced tension in the Far East, albeit briefly; and it provided a more hopeful atmosphere for peace throughout the world. Most important of all, the treaty helped erect a new peace structure for the Far East that seemed to make it possible for Britain, the United States, and Japan to live and work together in mutual trust and respect. A number of historians have pointed out that "the Washington Conference signaled the finest achievement of positive citizen peace action in the interwar period."[4]

Throughout the decade, supporters of peace also encouraged the new policy of sending "unofficial observers" to speak for the United States in various League of Nations agencies and commissions. Although the United States still refused to join the League, this new policy developed rapidly. The U.S. government cooperated in conferences to control the traffic of arms and participated in the work of the Reparations Committee, League Health Organizations, and the International Labor Organization. By 1930, the United States had been involved in forty League conferences and, even more importantly, had constructed machinery for cooperation with the League Council in any crisis menacing the peace of the world. Such involvement, including questionable acts of intervention in Latin America, makes it reasonable to question just how isolationist was American foreign policy in the 1920's.

Signing of the Kellogg-Briand Pact in 1928 signaled the climax of official peace efforts during the twenties. The idea of a treaty to outlaw war as an instrument of national policy was the brainchild of a wealthy civic-minded Chicago lawyer, Salmon O. Levinson, who won the support of John Dewey and Idaho Republican Senator William E. Borah. At the same time, a group of peace foundation officials—led by Nicholas Murray Butler and his successor as president of the Carnegie Endowment for International Peace, James T.

Shotwell—were interested in the plan. However, they did not approach the scheme from the same point of view as the Levinson faction. With Butler's CEIP contacts, he did help obtain a hearing in the United States for French Foreign Minister Aristide Briand, the European sponsor of the outlawry plan. Consequently, on August 27, 1928, the Pact of Paris (popularly known as the Kellogg-Briand Pact) was signed by the United States and fourteen other nations: the treaty bound signatory nations to renounce war as an instrument of national policy except in the case of self-defense. Although idealists romanticized the significance of the pact and cynics sneered at what they called an "international kiss," it nevertheless placed important moral obligations on the American government to cooperate with existing peacekeeping machinery—the League and World Court—in the event that some aggressor violated the pact.[5]

The Washington Naval Conference, United States cooperation and participation in the League committees, and the Kellogg-Briand Pact represented serious efforts by peace supporters to promote a level of common understanding among the nations of the world. These efforts were partly responsible for pushing the government to act on behalf of world peace and reflected a growing awareness of the devastating effects of modern warfare. All were ready to accept Saturday Evening Post reporter and former war correspondent Will Irwin's judgment that "anyone who says that the average man is a better man because of the war of 1914-1918, is lying consciously or unconsciously to himself":

> If war were what old-fashioned theology we used to call a 'means of grace,' if it sent its victims to death and its survivors back to civil life better men, it would be your [the churches'] business to support it, no matter how great its physical agencies. But I who saw the late war from its first battle to its last, who saw it in six nations, who saw it front and rear, am here to tell you that it is not....From first to last during the great war, a thousand soldiers of all nations asked me what it is all about, anyhow? And this, mind you, was not a straight inquiry of one who wants to know, but a rhetorical question, plainly put by way of eliciting the answer, "Nothing!"[6]

Clearly, World War I would mark the birth of the modern American peace movement. Aside from encouraging the government to enter into peace agreements with other nations, pioneers for peace and social justice became involved in numerous causes during the postwar years; among the causes they became associated with were support for a World Court, arbitration treaties, disarmament, the Outlawry of War Crusade, stable economic agreements, nonviolent action in defense of social justice, unionization of industrial workers and progressive labor education programs, the Committee on Militarism in Education (C.M.E.) in its fight against the recently-established Reserve Officers Training Program (R.O.T.C.) in colleges and universities, improved relations with Latin American countries, adopting Madison Avenue advertising techniques to promote internationalism, and working with clergy to encourage their flock not to take up arms. While there may not have been one single American search for peace during this period, there was a strong, active peace movement. It would become a movement largely defined by the efforts of "modern" activists, many of whom adopted non-violent resistant strategies such as sit-downs during the labor organizing drives of the interwar period, campaigning and organizing support against the lynching of blacks in the segregated South, calling for a general strike against war, and college students peacefully marching against war and signing the Oxford Pledge.[7]

What the "modern" activists shared was a belief that the United States had to bear some responsibility for maintaining world peace. They asserted that this could best be achieved by participating with other states in collective efforts—League of Nations, World Court, disarmament, and arbitration—to avoid war and settle disputes through pacific means. But they also approached the peace problem from a domestic perspective. They considered peace as a process fostering individual and group cooperation based upon a common set of values and beliefs. Before world peace could be achieved it was imperative to address the social and economic problems at home. A touch of humanism dictated how they would direct efforts to secure world understanding. In line with this aspect of their thinking they also understood peace to be a condition that followed the destruction of the war system through the establishment of a lasting international peacekeeping organization and the abolishment of pernicious social institutions.

Simply put, the modern peace movement would be spearheaded by those espousing a faith in the ability of a people to change conditions and achieve a stable world order based on cooperation rather than force through the establishment of world agencies and those emphasizing the importance of social and economic change through radical non-resistance.[8] During the interwar period their approaches to peace would often intersect, thereby strengthening the movement's public appeal.

The World War I era gave birth to peace organizations whose activities continue to this day, groups influenced by both internationalism and social justice pacifism. The most visible of them were the following: Women's International League for Peace and Freedom; American Friends Service Committee (AFSC); War Resisters League (WRL) founded in 1923, not during or right after the war; and American Fellowship of Reconciliation (FOR).[9] With the exception of the American Friends Service Committee, founded by the Quakers during the war without any political agenda, these new organizations developed a radically conscious position linking peace with domestic social reform.

Much attention has been devoted to the contributions of the interwar radical peace organizations. Yet, the American Friends Service Committee also marked an important change in the Quaker peace witness. Although Friends had remained involved in the American Peace Society, the emergence of the pre-war cosmopolitan and practical peacemakers supplanted the role sectarian/religious pacifists had played in the historic struggle against war. During World War I, Friends decided to take a more active role demonstrating their peace witness. Once the United States entered the war, members of the Society of Friends established AFSC as a sanctuary for young Quakers and other Conscientious Objectors willing to perform non-combatant service in wartime. Specifically, the Committee focused its efforts on relief and rehabilitation for war victims. During the war the Committee sent many young men and women to France where they worked in cooperation with British Friends to feed and care for refugees, build a maternity hospital, and repair and rebuild destroyed homes. Reconstruction and medical care represented a major part of the Committee's relief efforts. Once the war ended, the Committee extended its work in Russia where relief workers helped fight famine and disease; in Serbia and Poland where they assisted in agricultural development and constructed orphanages; and, finally, into Austria and Germany where they fed hungry children.

Other organizations emerged as well. In 1922, Quaker activist Frederick Libby formed the National Council for Prevention of War (NCPW), aimed at building peace through the construction of an overwhelming popular consensus against war. It was Libby's strategy to combine what he saw as the best of various peace strategies in order to accomplish disarmament, U.S. participation in the World Court and, ultimately, membership in the League of Nations.[10]

Two years later, Tracy Mygatt, Frances Witherspoon, and founder Jessie Wallace Hughan combined a cross section of absolute pacifists and workers into the American branch of the War Registers League, whose motto "Wars Will Cease When Men Refuse to Fight," expressed its emphasis during its early history. This diverse group of pacifist socialists planned to stop the next war through a massive general strike. With a total membership of about 19,000 in 1924, they held firmly to their conviction that war was "a crime against humanity."[11]

That same year, Carrie Chapman Catt, still pushing forward her desire for lasting peace, assembled the National Committee on the Cause and Cure of War (NCCW) as a forum for annual conferences of women's organizations. From 1924-1936, hundreds of concerned female peace seekers met annually in the nation's capitol to debate and propose peace objectives within an internationalist framework. Although they had achieved their most important objective, suffrage, they were unable to agree on how to go about establishing a united women's coalition against war.

Part of the reason why Catt and her conferences failed to enjoin women of all peace persuasions was the nagging issue of respectability. More conservative female peace activists were suspicious of socialist critiques of capitalist war and feared that such arguments would dilute the "sanctity" of their efforts. They were also determined to push an agenda more compatible with the government's way of thinking when it came to the goal of internationalism. Female radicals' prescriptions for peace involved much bolder remedies for social and economic justice at home, including equal rights for African-Americans and support for labor. "Respectable" female peace activists could not find an acceptable mechanism for fostering the larger goal of peace as social justice.

THE NEW ORGANIZATIONS AT WORK

Characteristically, peace organizations of the modern era developed distinctive aims with modest budgets, coordinating agencies and effective propaganda and congressional lobbying tactics. One organization typifying the modern peace movement was Libby's National Council for Prevention of War, established as a cooperative agency with a budget of over $100,000 per year. Most contributions, however, were relatively small. Its journal, Peace Action, had a circulation of over 20,000; it published several books, more than 1,000 pieces of literature—its main vehicle of communication – and conducted a regular radio program. It even had a motion picture department. NCPW had an energetic staff that was able to mobilize broad support from farm and labor organizations; it encouraged national legislators to voice their opinions on its radio program. The council achieved some success in 1927 when it provided the initiative and organization for mobilizing public opinion that forced President Coolidge to arbitrate differences with Mexico and thus avoid possible armed conflict. NCPW's experience exemplified the post-war peace movement's all-encompassing relationship between specific publics like farm, labor, civic organizations, politicians, and peace activists.[12]

The belief that objection to war must be buttressed by an effort to transform society became the trademark of another noted peace organization, the Fellowship of Reconciliation. Though there were numerous interwar peace groups, none was more committed to the Christian idea of peace than the FOR, which drew its main inspiration from one particular stream in modern American Protestantism, the "Social Gospel." FOR peace activists shared the hopes of the protagonists of the Social Gospel to be able to transform human society so that it approximated the Kingdom of God. The coming of the Kingdom was, for them, no utopian dream but a real possibility open to all people. The elimination of war between nations and the ending of economic exploitation within society were merely different aspects of one struggle—the struggle for the realization of a peaceable kingdom.

FOR pacifists advocated varying degrees of social reform as an integral part of their peace testimony. Since capitalism appeared to them to be a primary cause of human conflict, they increasingly detected the seeds of war in the exploitation of labor by capital and in the brutal suppression of the workers' efforts to organize backed by local, state, and federal governments. "Capitalism is based on coercion and violence," wrote John C. Bennett in 1933, "it is destructive of human life and human values on a colossal scale...a ruthless system which results in starvation, disease, death, and warped bodies and souls for millions." FOR members no longer considered themselves as an elect minority leavening the world but as the non-violent vanguard of those political forces whose task it was to inaugurate the classless society. From this new Christian social order, capitalist exploitation would be banished along with international war.[13] This vision was not unlike that of socialists and communists, the difference was FOR's commitment to non-violent means of social change.

In the twenties and early thirties, the main dynamic of the FOR's thinking was directed toward exploring the relationship between violence and an unjust domestic order. But as the depression and its aftermath worsened, it seemed clearer than ever to many FOR members, despite their middle-class origins and status, that the fight against the worker oppression could, paradoxically, be pursued only by means of class war. But could the class war be waged with the weapons of non-violence alone? It was the use of physical force in class war that continually haunted the FOR during the depression. It was not the problem of the magistrate's sword turned against a foreign aggressor that generated heated debates in the Fellowship but that of the policeman's baton raised against workers struggling to throw off the yoke of capitalism.

Of course, no one symbolized better the FOR's dilemma than A.J. Muste, labeled by Time magazine as "the Number One U.S. Pacifist." Born in the Netherlands, but raised in Michigan and educated at the Dutch Reform Hope College and later at New Brunswick Theological Seminary, Muste exerted enormous influence on U.S. social movements during the first two-thirds of the twentieth century. Over the course of his adult life, he became directly involved in the interwar labor struggles, post-World War II civil rights and economic justice movements, support for civil liberties and, most importantly, in the campaigns for peace through active non-violence and civil disobedience. World War I drew him away from his pulpit and into the arms of the peace movement; he soon joined the FOR in order to usher in the kingdom of peace and justice.

The Great Depression caused Muste to rethink his commitment to non-violence and civil disobedience. Like some other absolute pacifists ("absolutes") who had repudiated all aspects of organized violence, class revolution, and war, Muste took a brief detour to the left in the 1930s. For a short time, he affiliated with the American Workers Party, adopting more radical, armed tenets of Marxism. In the summer of 1936, after returning from a summer trip to Europe, he once again embraced the philosophy of non-violence. Having been overcome by a feeling of not belonging among secular revolutionaries, Muste became reacquainted with the Fellowship of Reconciliation: he and John Nevin Sayre, would guide the FOR during some of its most challenging times.

While the FOR served as a clearinghouse for religiously-affiliated pacifists, its secular counterpart, the War Resisters League, was more willing to participate in coalitions promoting peace and justice. WRL was founded in 1923 by socialist-pacifist Jessie Wallace Hughan in an attempt to unite political, humanitarian, and philosophical objectors to war. Hughan, a high school English teacher from Brooklyn who obtained her Ph.D. in economics from Columbia University before World War I, was drawn into socialist circles while researching the industrial and urban problems associated with modern America.

During World War I, Hughan, along with her close friends, Frances Witherspoon and Tracy Mygatt, created the Anti-Enlistment League, an organization for war opponents who had no traditional religious basis for their pacifist beliefs. Operating out of Hughan's apartment, the organization managed to enroll 3,500 men who willingly signed a declaration against military enlistment. The pledge read: "I, being over eighteen years of age, hereby pledge myself against enlistment as a volunteer for any military or naval service in international war, either offensive or defensive, and against giving my approval to such enlistment on the part of others."[14] When the U.S. entered the war, the organization folded. Attacked for her opposition to war on socialist grounds, Hughan was allowed to keep her teaching job because charges of disloyalty had been leveled prior to the actual declaration of war. During the Red Scare, however, the Lusk Committee of the New York State Legislature denied her the Certificate of Character and Loyalty because she deliberately added the following words to the state's teacher loyalty oath: "this obedience being qualified always by dictates of conscience." Listed a dangerous radical by the U.S. Senate Judiciary Committee, her name was included along with Jane Addams, Lillian D. Wald, and Oswald Garrison Villard.

In Radical Pacifism: The War Resisters League and Gandhian Non-violence in America, 1915-1963 Scott Bennett points out that the absolute or radical pacifists enabled the WRL to transform the meaning of pacifism into more than just repudiation of war. The WRL worked in conjunction with the religious FOR, the newly-created Women's International League for Peace and Freedom, and other groups, enrolling anarchists, socialists, radicals, and even capitalists who rejected all war. WRL became part of a non-violent social movement – a secular pacifist/anti-war one. The organization popularized the modern peace movement's goal of resisting the evils of war by demanding a just social and economic order at home. During the WRL's early years, Hughan delivered numerous speeches and wrote pamphlets and tracts on the use of active non-violence. She organized various public protests to war and militarism, including some New York "NO MORE WAR" parades. Much of the WRL's support came from pacifist members of the Socialist Party when it became apparent that the FOR could not relate to nonreligious Conscientious Objectors. Anyone was eligible to become a member of the WRL if he or she signed a pledge renouncing participation in war. The WRL did most of its interwar work in the education field as well as providing legal support to Conscientious Objectors.

Resisting war also became part of the Women's International League for Peace and Freedom's agenda. As noted earlier, in January 1915, at the request of female suffragists and peace leaders, Jane Addams and Carrie Chapman Catt established the Woman's Peace Party in the United States. Three months later, April 1915, members of the WPP traveled to The Netherlands and met with European female peace advocates calling for an end to World War I. This meeting eventually led to the creation of the Women's International League for Peace and Freedom.

Although independent female attempts to end the hostilities failed, WILPF was formally established in Zurich, Switzerland, in May 1919. Jane Addams was elected its first president and Emily Greene Balch, who lost her position as professor of political economy at Wellesley College due to her anti-war activities and later was co-recipient of the Nobel Peace Prize, was chosen secretary-treasurer. The specific objectives of the new organization were to unite women throughout the world in opposition to war, exploitation, and oppression. During the interwar years WILPF promoted universal disarmament through conciliation and arbitration and sponsored programs calling for the establishment of social, political, and economic justice for all regardless of creed, sex, or class. Numerous branches of the U.S. Section were formed, along with many others in various nations. The organization, headquartered in Geneva, sent peace missions to areas of tension and promoted peace education by creating created Summer Schools for young people. In its campaign for disarmament, the League's efforts sparked the widely-publicized Nye Committee Investigations of the munitions industry. In 1932, while supporting the World Disarmament Conference, WILPF organized a Peace Caravan that started out from Hollywood, California, and stopped at nearly 125 cities along the way to collect petitions for world peace before delivering them to elected officials on the capitol steps in Washington, D.C.

In promoting an agenda that included equal treatment for women of color, WILPF made yet another contribution to the peace movement. In the 1920s, when the International Council of Women of the Darker Races was unable to move beyond self-education to public action, African American female pacifists turned to WILPF. They encouraged WILPF to widen its agenda to include attacks on racism, especially lynchings and a resurgence of Klan activity, though such work was often frustrating at the local level. At the national level, however, many African American women, such as Addie Hunton, who was the first chairperson of WILPF's Interracial Committee during this period, succeeded in obtaining influential positions within the organization. African American women of WILPF also took on the challenge of explaining the aims of anti-war work to a black community that regarded such efforts as irrelevant to its most pressing goal of eradicating all forms of racial injustice. In the long run, WILPF's efforts in the area of racial equality would ultimately push the more traditional male-dominated white peace organizations to take a closer look at the issue of race relations.[15]

The newly formed peace organizations of the "modern" movement sought to eradicate the ravages of war, but also to address its causes, such as economic inequality.[16] Yet the rapid economic and industrial success of the twenties only made Americans more protective of their gains, thereby stimulating the powerful appeal of nationalism at the expense of internationalism.[17] For peace workers, the job was difficult. How could they convince fellow Americans that their nation's security could be served best by sacrificing for international harmony? Much of their dynamic thrust would be based on that very question.[18]

MARKETING PEACE

One of the more interesting schemes to create greater awareness to peace and justice were efforts to advertise their importance. The new peace organizations created in the wake of total war enthusiastically endorsed this strategy. In June 1923, Ladies Home Journal editor and millionaire Edward M. Bok offered a $100,000 prize for the best plan involving the United States in maintaining a cooperative international peace. More than 22,000 plans were submitted to a panel of noted luminaries—including Elihu Root, Colonel Edward M. House (one of President Wilson's advisers in Versailles), and Henry Stimson—who served as judges for the American Peace Award. In February 1924, Bok presented the official award to longtime peace activist and one-time president of Adelphi University, Charles Levermore. The 69 year-old peace advocate collected the first $50,000, half of the award, but died before the second installment arrived. His plan proposed an international system backed by the legal authority of a world court. In some respects, his ideas largely followed the principles previously espoused by the League to Enforce Peace. However, he waited somberly for the American government to adopt his winning plan as official policy. At least he had enough money to be accorded a proper burial.[19]

The idea of a prize coincided with peace organizations' efforts to adopt Madison Avenue advertising techniques to their agenda. Chatfield has argued that selling world peace was an acceptable idea in the "roaring twenties," a period when advertising was becoming a significant part of national culture. The Brooks-Bright Foundation in New York and Boston's American School Citizenship League sponsored a series of oratorical and essay contests, each backed by generous prizes from numerous sponsors. Many businesses were serious about peace. One of the more interesting attempts to de-commercialize martial values took placed in Cincinnati, Ohio. There the Peace Heroes Memorial Society, resurrecting Benjamin Rush's long-forgotten proposal, requested that stores substitute the battle-dressed uniforms of military toy soldiers "with equally heroic civilians." Stores along the Ohio Riverfront were encouraged "not to stock military toys." The high point of peace advertising occurred in 1931, when Estelle Sternberger of World Peaceways employed commercial advertising techniques that included a newspaper column on world issues, a weekly radio news program, posters, and free advertising space in magazines in an effort to bolster sales and increase exposure to peace issues.[20]

CLERGY FOR PEACE

Support for world peace was also strongly encouraged within Protestant churches in this era. Led by John Haynes Holmes, Kirby Page, the brilliant Reinhold Niebuhr, and Sherwood Eddy, Protestant leaders throughout the country preached the message of global harmony. The Christian Century, liberal Protestantism's most influential weekly, was filled with pages calling to mind the necessity for international harmony; not a week went by without demands for peace action to inform anxious readers. It even expressed outrage at the postwar treatment of CO's. The paper summed up its views in a blistering editorial written in the early part of the 1920s entitled, "Political Prisoners and the Christian Conscience": "The record of our attitude toward those who 'for conscience sake' refused to support the war is a matter which Christian intelligence can no longer decline to contemplate. We passed laws depriving such men of what they had supposed were their constitutional rights of freedom of speech and press. We enforced those laws with a degree of passion in excess of that obtaining in any other country, not excepting even Germany itself."[21] The YMCA held numerous meetings condemning war, while the FOR offered its intellectual and spiritual arm to extend the handshake of peace.

Noted clerics were now willing to admit that the churches possessed a special obligation to overcome the war menace. Many were willing to move beyond gospel pages and offer concrete criticisms of social and economic injustices created by modernization. Harry Emerson Fosdick, who had enthusiastically "presented arms" in 1917, took a solemn vow from the pulpit that he would never again come to the support of war. Charles Clayton Morrison, irascible editor of The Christian Century, became one of the most outspoken clerical critics of post-war American foreign policy. Disturbed by the injustices of the Versailles Treaty, he opposed the League of Nations, calling it an instrument of European reactionaries bent on frustrating America's world peace mission. In Morrison's opinion, America had to play an active, independent role in rescuing Europe through moral vigor and the proven power of law.

In general, Protestant churches, remorseful about excessive militarism exhibited during the war, followed Fosdick and Morrison in accepting a commitment to Christian pacifism. Christian peace groups (like the Church Peace Union and World Alliance for International Fellowship) flourished in such an atmosphere, especially in the seminaries. Countless Protestant ministers had sworn that they would never again support a war. Two of the most prominent preachers, Ernest F. Tittle and Ralph W. Sockman, were taking pacifist positions. Many wondered if even police forces could be justified and, among radicals, the question of justifying violence in the class struggle became divisive. So committed were the churches to world peace that by 1929 the Federal Council of Churches greeted the United States Senate's consent to the Kellogg-Briand Peace Pact with jubilation: "Let Church bells be rung, songs sung, prayers of thanksgiving be offered, and petitions for help inform God that our nation may ever follow the spirit and meaning of the Pact."[22] Thus, the recurring campaigns among Protestant peace agencies and clergy for disarmament, the World Court, peace education, and outlawry of war created a spirit of immediacy and hope that had not been felt since the guns of August resounded throughout the European countryside.

SUPPORT FOR A WORLD COURT AND THE GENEVA PROTOCOL

Prompted by the groundswell of support for peace by liberal Protestantism in the early twenties, pacifists, feminists, and internationalists, in particular, jumped aboard the World Court train as the most promising route for peace success. Capturing the popular mood of world peace through legal mechanisms, the Court cause stood as the largest common denominator of peace activism throughout the 1920's. Support for the Permanent Court for International Justice at The Hague, or its modification based upon the American Supreme Court, seemed to many the best working basis for cooperative peace action. Because of its essential modesty, which was also its most critical shortcoming, the World Court issue attracted the support of peace factions that otherwise clashed over the nature of the country's global responsibilities. Pacifists and nationalists, militarists and internationalists—all favored the ratification of the Court Protocol.

Even the business community, not known for its support of pacifist causes, promoted the World Court idea. This represented a carryover from the pre-war days when world court proposals and international arbitration, rather than disarmament, had been very popular among members of peace societies. Republican businessmen and lawyers had dominated these societies, and many individual Republican business leaders continued to advocate a judicial approach to world peace after the war. Business groups like the United States Chamber of Commerce and the American Manufacturers Export Association consistently supported adherence to the World Court in the 1920's. In 1922, the International Chamber of Commerce established the International Court of Business Arbitration to encourage business support of the World Court. Throughout the decade, businessmen were generally convinced of the advantages of settling international disputes through a judicial body. They also harbored the vague hope, far from altruistically, that somehow the World Court would be able "to facilitate debt agreements between nations and create a positive feeling necessary for good trade relations." All in all, a sense of euphoria characterized business support for the World Court proposal of the twenties. Edward W. Bok, leading Philadelphia publisher and businessman, did not exaggerate when he said in 1925: "The World Court is essentially our idea. We proclaimed it for years.... It is of American origin. It came into world consciousness because of American initiative; it is American in its conception and in its reflection of our strong national belief in courts of justice."[23] In Bok's opinion, it was time to abandon Old World suspicions or fears of foreign entanglements and work to solidify the enforcement of international law.

Harmony among those seeking United States participation in the World Court and official diplomatic activities for peace at home and abroad also bolstered the hopes of American peace seekers. Anti-war groups were encouraged by the 1926 Geneva Conference for the Supervision of International Arms—where the United States government took the initiative in seeking to prohibit the export of gases for use in warfare. The Geneva Protocol signed on June 17, 1925, restated the prohibition previously set down by the Versailles and Washington treaties. Yet their happiness was short-lived; two years later, the Geneva Naval Conference turned out to be a complete failure. It had been called by President Coolidge, who is perhaps remembered best for his truisms—"when more and more people are out of work, unemployment results"—than lasting statesmanship. Even Senate ratification of the World Court bill remained in abeyance, as it would throughout the thirties, due to an internal struggle for control of the Republican Party. The Senate's failure to ratify the bill prompted Nicholas Butler to call such inaction "the most discreditable thing in the recent history of the United States."[24]

ISSUES IN LATIN AMERICA

While the issues of World Court participation and arms control garnered some optimism, pioneers for peace and justice expressed serious concerns over American intervention in parts of Latin America. In the 1920s America's economic superiority was being felt throughout the world, but in Latin America it was clearly backed by force. Twice between 1910 and 1920, U.S. military troops were deployed to Nicaragua and Honduras in order to maintain a large measure of economic and political control over these republics. The policy of dollar diplomacy, instituted during the Taft Administration, was most apparent in Colombia, Costa Rica, and Guatemala. Under this policy, American bankers, often at the invitation of the State Department, loaned money to Caribbean governments. When they failed to repay their debts or the interest on their loans, the U.S. government intervened under the pretext of protecting American investments. Often the intervention led to the landing of marines as was the case in Haiti and Santo Domingo, the supervising of elections, and even supporting the political group favoring the United States.

It was somewhat preposterous, peacemakers argued, that, while the United States government talked in terms of peace and support for the League of Nations' work, World Court, naval armament limitations, and outlawry of war, American leaders condoned imperialist policies south of the border. For some time, American investments had created a political stranglehold on the actions of these Latin American countries. When Emily Balch and WILPF leaders conducted a thorough investigation of America's informal control of Haiti, they were pleased when University of Chicago economist Paul Douglas' draft of their findings condemned neo-colonial rule in the Caribbean. They were also worried "that America may well be at a point where it must decide whether it shall be an empire or a democracy."[25]

After marines landed in Nicaragua in December 1926 to crush a revolt detrimental to American economic interests, the Fellowship of Reconciliation sent a commission to investigate American military involvement. Led by John Nevin Sayre, the commission members included Professor Elbert Russell of Duke University, Professor Robert Jones of the University of Chicago, and socialite Caroline Wood of New York. The report that they issued, "Democracy Called Farce in Nicaragua," was not very comforting. It reported that 300 Nicaraguans had been killed by U.S. marines during the political turmoil. Sayre was so concerned that, during a speech at Brookwood Labor College, he condemned the presence of U.S. marines in Nicaragua and pressed for their immediate withdrawal: "If we are going to do anything to bring order out of the chaos, we must get on the job. We must take away from the President his power to send marines to Nicaragua—or anywhere else for that matter. It is not so much Nicaraguan democracy that is at stake as it is our own."[26] Due to increased pressure from a broad collection of peace activists, the Coolidge Administration softened its hard-line position in the Caribbean.

WORKERS FOR PEACE AND JUSTICE: BROOKWOOD LABOR COLLEGE

If problems involving U.S. military presence in Latin America presented a stiff challenge to peace activists in the 1920s, attempts to unionize workers proved just as daunting. Labor historian Irving Bernstein correctly referred to this period as the "lean years." Efforts by Gompers and other labor leaders to curry favor from the government for supporting the war quickly went unfulfilled in a decade marked by racial intolerance and business conservatism. While traditional labor unions found it tough sledding when it came to organizing workers, more progressive-minded labor reformers decided to support the establishment of labor colleges in order to link unionization with broader social and economic concerns. During the 1920s and 1930s a progressive workers' education movement was started in the United States to encourage domestic economic and social reform. Workers' education promised unions an avenue in which to develop more socially-minded laborers.

One of the most noted workers' education experiments was at Brookwood Labor College in Katonah, New York. Nestled in a pastoral setting, Brookwood was labor's most noticeable peace representation during the interwar period. Led by the respected pacifist clergyman, A.J. Muste, Brookwood was America's first and most famous residential labor school. Its primary goal was to train workers in the crusade for unionization, but Brookwood also stood out for its attempt to educate workers about the link between industrial oppression with war. Primarily through lectures, class discussions, and plays, Brookwood created an intellectual environment thoroughly sympathetic to world peace. Norman Thomas, Scott Nearing (author of The Great Madness and noted anti-war critic), and John Nevin Sayre were frequent visitors at Brookwood. The college received a large endowment from liberal bohemian and anti-war philanthropist Charles Garland. Yet, the college's most impressive display for peace was its traveling Chautauqua.

Throughout the college's existence, 1921-1937, students and faculty carried on a theatrical program designed to dramatize their concern for world peace. Performing in New York, St. Paul, Detroit, Baltimore, Toledo, Boston, Philadelphia, and 30 other major cities, the Brookwood players satirized the folly of war in front of enthusiastic labor audiences in performances like "Coal Digger Mule Goes to War," which depicted the "false glamour and folly of war," and "Uncle Sam Wants You," warning workers "against a coming war with its lure of pay after years of unemployment." Others included: "Guncotton," describing a "plea for peace through a young worker in a munitions factory;" and "God and Country," illustrating the fate of four soldiers (a cockney cab driver, a German woodcarver, a French small farmer, and an American mechanic) who are "blown to nowhere and proceed to talk it over." At the conclusion of each performance, the audience would be asked to sing the "D.A.R. Song" with the players. Verse 5 went as follows:

"My sons were moved to Wilson's Plea
To end all strife they bore guns.
They fought to save democracy
(They saved the Fords and Morgans).
"You say their ardors banished war
Dictators barred forevermore:
That now not want or woe is seen?"
That was nineteen seventeen! [27]

Significantly, the plays encouraged unionists to campaign for mass action against the forces of war, forces which had contributed to oppression of the worker. Brookwood's dramas reflected an abiding interest in the importance of popular action that might affect the decisions of government and the structure of society as a whole—and perhaps create a spirit of social awareness within the ranks of labor.

THE SCHOOLS AND WORLD PEACE

Such spirit within the non-traditional realm of academia provided renewed hope to the established branches of America's educational system. The post-war period witnessed a vast expansion of peace education activities. The American School Peace League became the American School Citizenship League. The WILPF began a new multifaceted program in 1919 through its education committee. In 1923, the World Federation of Education Associations was established, whose central purpose was "the mobilization of teachers of all lands, most immediately in America, in order that their combined influence and that of their pupils may be thrown solidly on the side of peace." Stanford University president David Starr Jordan was awarded a $25,000 prize (a lot less than Charles Levermore's $100,000) offered under the auspices of the Federation for the best educational plan designed to produce international harmony.[28]

School textbook revision became a notable byproduct of the peace crusade as educators began to see nationalistic tendencies as an important factor leading to war. At Columbia University, John Dewey argued for "a curriculum in history, geography, and literature which will make it more difficult for the flames of hatred and suspicion to sweep over this country in the future, which will indeed make this impossible, because when children's minds are in the formative period we shall have fixed in them through the medium of the schools, feelings of respect and friendliness for the other nations and peoples of this world."[29] In line with Dewey's call for "transnational patriotism," the Association for Peace Education published a report in 1924 on the impact of curriculum materials related to war and peace—based on a quantitative and qualitative content analysis of typical school histories in the United States. Based on this report Paul Klapper, Dean of the School of Education at CCNY, published a text in 1926 entitled, The Teaching of History. This text was widely used to prepare Social Studies teachers. A section, "History and World Peace," noted that "instruments thus far devised to answer humanity's prayer for the abolition of war" include international treaty agreements and the reduction of armaments. But the real solution, according to Klapper, is for "Teachers of history and the social sciences" to "picture vividly the human cost of war, and that war persists only because some of the leading nations are not ready to maintain justice in international affairs on as high a plane as in individual matters." To accomplish this requires the elimination of "bigoted nationalism and martial propaganda from history."[30]

The belief that schools had a primary responsibility toward peace was widely shared by members of the educational establishment. Dewey's colleague, William H. Kilpatrick, gave an address at a Quaker school in Philadelphia in 1921 on the subject "Our Schools and War" which reasoned that just as "learning to kill" requires "careful teaching," it can be unlearned in the name of peace. Teachers trained in America's normal colleges must be taught the new bible: that war is not inevitable; that the "social integration" of mankind is inevitable; that competitive armament is folly; and that if war was a form of learned behavior, it could be unlearned, as dueling had been unlearned. These new educators must teach the children committed to their charge that modern war is horrible; that war is unnecessary; that world integration is the shape of the future; and that unlimited national sovereignty is out of date. Teachers, Kilpatrick stressed, should downplay in their lesson plans the German atrocity stories that had been the staple of the Allied press during the war: "We have too many children of German parentage in our midst." He suggested that educators cautiously endorse the

League of Nations: "When finally we have settled our partisan disputes...about the League, then the teachers must do their utmost to make it work."[31]

Echoing Kilpatrick's faith in the possibilities of education for peace was Army Reserve Major General John F. O'Ryan. In a 1923 article in the National Education Association's journal, O'Ryan proposed the substitution of "peace heroes" for "war heroes" in the schoolbooks children use. His idea was novel and gave rise to further studies regarding chauvinistic textbooks. In 1924, three university professors studied twenty-four standard public school American history texts and twenty-four popular supplementary readers. They concluded that the books glamorized and glorified war—so much so that military exploits rivaled civilian achievements in terms of their descriptions and proportionate space allotted. The Nation called for the replacement of war propaganda with peace propaganda: "The future demands a type of history that will not exaggerate the place of war, which will show its true nature, and which will develop in children the will to peace. Parents should demand such histories…."[32]

College students took these arguments seriously and with conviction. World War I had elevated their interest in international affairs and concern for peace and justice. The death and destructiveness wrought by modern weaponry had made an unforgettable impression upon their minds – one that was not so easily dismissed. Questioning the virtues of the martial spirit while not fully embracing pacifism, college students were determined to be heard. Close to 7,400 students from a thousand American colleges and universities attended the 1924 international convention of the Student Volunteer Movement whose slogan was: "The Evangelization of the World in This Generation." Rejecting both nationalistic "preparedness" (300 votes) and "absolute pacifism" (500 votes) most delegates embraced a principle of international order: "We believe that war is un-Christian, and that the League of Nations is the best means of preventing it, but we would resort to war in case an unavoidable dispute had been referred to the League or World Court without peaceful settlement."[33] A decade later students were prepared to take a much stronger stand against war.

COMMITTEE ON MILITARISM IN EDUCATION

By 1925, a number of peace pioneers had also established the Committee on Militarism in Education in response to the National Defense Act of 1920, an ambitious plan for bolstering the nation's military might in order to be prepared for war. World War I had demonstrated to War Department officials the inadequacies of the officer corps, and many government officials believed that degree-bearing officers would add quality and intelligence to military leadership while advancing the military's stature in the public's eyes. The act provided for the establishment of more than 300 Reserve Officers Training Corps (R.O.T.C.) units with about 125,000 students participating in the program on college campuses throughout the country. The program was a two-year course in military subjects with weekly drill instructions. Upon graduation, an individual trainee would automatically receive a commission in the United States Army.[34]

Led by Frederick Libby, E. Raymond Wilson, Kirby Page, John Nevin Sayre and Oswald Garrison Villard, the Committee on Militarism in Education was composed mainly of pacifists, religious leaders, and liberal educators. Its primary purpose was to act as a lobbying group seeking legislation to prohibit federal funds for compulsory military training courses for R.O.T.C. units on campus.[35] A secondary function was its role as an educational propaganda agency. The C.M.E.'s main argument, which it regularly sought to publicize, rested upon its belief that, in order for war to be abolished, American students would have to be trained to think in terms of peace and internationalism, rather than spit-shined shoes and polished brass. The conspiratorial view that R.O.T.C. was merely a covert method for universal conscription added to the Committee's anti-militarist prestige.[36] In numerous pamphlets written by leading educators, including John Dewey, and noted pacifists, and distributed throughout the colleges and universities in the United States, the Committee on Militarism in Education deliberately tried to counteract the military influence then being generated by R.O.T.C. units on campus.[37]

Leading the charge on behalf of the committee was Sayre. Although he did not object to government-backed military schools – West Point and Annapolis – he expressed grave concerns about establishing military training units in civilian educational institutions. On June 15, 1926, Sayre testified before the House Committee on Military Affairs in favor of the Walsh Bill, which proposed to strike out the word "compulsory" from the 1920 Defense Act. In numerous arguments Sayre insisted that the public educational system of America ought to be the "holy" place of our democratic way of life. Freedom and adventurous thinking in America's universities and schools should be encouraged and not interfered with by a military machine. In Sayre's opinion democracy and militarism were incompatible. The most pressing need in the world was for better and wiser thinkers and statesmen who were willing to address conflicts by less destructive means than war.

Opponents of militarism also brought legal challenges to the R.O.T.C. program, though these were unsuccessful. During the 1930's, as the program became entrenched in many college and universities, two cases questioned the impact of militarism on free thought in a democratic society. In University of Maryland v. Coale, a Methodist and a Unitarian student challenged their expulsions in 1932 for refusing to take the compulsory R.O.T.C. course. Ennes H. Coale, the lead petitioner, challenged the requirement on the grounds that the university charter permitted exemptions for Conscientious Objection. The State Court of Appeals backed the lower court's decision to uphold the expulsions. Two years later, in 1934, the University of California suspended two Methodist students, Albert Hamilton and Alonzo Reynolds, for similar reasons. Both students claimed that the university's actions denied them their constitutional rights. Attempting a different legal approach than Coale's legal team, Hamilton and Reynolds rested their claim on Senate ratification of the 1928 Kellogg-Briand Pact outlawing war as an instrument of national policy which, they maintained, superseded state law. The Court, once again, ruled against the plaintiffs, declaring that the privilege of attending a university came from the state, not the federal government.

Naturally, the military and other patriotic groups did not sit idly and permit these criticisms, legal or otherwise, to go unchallenged. There were many defenders of the program who directly challenged Sayre and the committee's position. In addition to portraying pacifists as impractical idealists, critics also accused them of being members of a dangerous left-wing conspiracy.

As early as 1922, the head of the War Department's Chemical Warfare Services, General Amos A. Fries, linked anti-militarist criticisms to an alleged Communist conspiracy. In an elaborate scheme to silence critics of the program, Fries introduced his spider web chart: a complex graph linking peace groups, social welfare organizations, and religious societies and their leaders to a broad pacifist-socialist cabal. Legionnaires and R.O.T.C. officers undertook a concerted campaign in the 1920s to prevent anti-militarists from speaking out on college campuses. In 1926, John Nevin Sayre was banned from presenting a speech at the University of Oklahoma; a U.S. Army lieutenant colonel, speaking as a civilian, considered Sayre "more dangerous than an open Communist." Ohio State's R.O.T.C. unit attacked a student pastor for his criticisms of compulsory military training. The R.O.T.C. fraternity, Scabbard and Blade, circulated warnings to other campus units to be on the lookout for Communists and left-wing organizations who were attempting to undermine the country's national security. Kirby Page was constantly harassed on campuses throughout the nation and accused of disloyalty – a very common charge. Critics found pacifist ideas threatening and constantly tried to silence them by accusing them of being cowards.

PROMOTING PEACE AND NON-VIOLENT ACTIVISM

Despite vocal opposition, by the end of the 1920s, pioneers for peace and justice were able to look back and take heart at the growing popularity of pacifist ideals. It was a remarkable decade of peace action, even if their assessment of the Kellogg-Briand Pact was overly optimistic. For example, attached to the Senate passage was a rider calling for the largest naval appropriations bill in peacetime American history. Still, Peacemakers were confident that the day was not far away when peace would indeed be given its chance. Even the new decade held promise. In April 1931, leaders from many peace organizations established the Emergency Peace Committee as "a springboard for rallying left-wing pacifist opinion on disarmament and related issues."[38] At the same time, Carnegie Endowment leaders Nicholas Murray Butler and James T. Shotwell organized a special internationalist committee to develop plans for strengthening the Pact of Paris by committing all signatories to join in supporting economic sanctions against an aggressor state. These leaders attempted to adjust American neutrality to the needs of the League system.[39]

The new decade also witnessed the expansion of the popular peace caravan program. In 1926, in an effort to create intelligent public concern for world affairs, the Peace Section of the American Friends Service Committee started a summer program in which students were sent out to speak on the subject of peace. During the next fifteen years, some 1,200 young people gave their summers to such voluntary work for world peace. The program was directed by Ray Newton, a former teacher at Phillips Exeter Academy who lost his job during the war because of his pacifism. In 1927, Newton conducted a three-day training conference at Haverford College, Pennsylvania, for twenty-one college students and then sent them off in used model-T Fords. They traveled from town to town throughout the nation, distributing peace literature while addressing people in clubs and churches, wherever an audience could be found.

Under Newton's direction, the peace caravan program began operating on a year-round basis, sending field secretaries to colleges during the winter to form study groups and recruit summer volunteers. The caravan program reached thousands of people, mainly in the rural Midwest. In 1930, the caravan leaders estimated that "each of twelve teams reached about 6,000 people." In 1931, as noted earlier, Mabel Vernon, inspired by Newton and under the auspices of the United States section of WILPF, organized a peace caravan in order to gather signatures for a petition on behalf of international disarmament. Vernon, along with Katherine Devereux Blake and other student volunteers, started their long journey from Hollywood, California, to Washington, D.C. Along the way they held numerous rallies addressing the importance of world peace. From place to place, fearing attacks from ultra-nationalistic groups such as the Klan and American Legion, they were often escorted by local police cars. Five caravans that had gathered signatures in Pennsylvania, "joined the long parade of mobile opponents of militarism and war" to the national capital, where the petition was presented to President Hoover. The following year, the petition was sent to the Geneva Disarmament Conference. By 1940, in the shadow of war, the peace caravan program still managed "to sponsor 119 students from fifty-five colleges, representing 26 states, 20 denominations, and 8 nationalities."[40]

No less ambitious were the efforts of individual pacifists of the early thirties, such as the respected writer and editor, Devere Allen. Receiving a subvention from the American Friends Service Committee, Allen established the No Frontier News service (later renamed the Worldover Press) in 1933. It had two basic goals, according to Charles Chatfield. First, it provided "peace constituencies with new peace efforts abroad and a rigorous, clear analysis of world events." Second, it reached people outside peace groups by providing valuable information to religious papers, labor journals, rural weeklies, and city presses. It even initiated a two-way flow of information by exchanging periodicals in Europe and Latin America. Allen believed it was essential for citizens to develop a capacity for independent judgment and action; the peace movement and the public alike needed additional information that often was not carried by the major news outlets. Similarly, in a world where news was defined largely by its relationship to governments, popular and peace movements needed independent information about one another. By 1935, Allen's project was serving papers with a total circulation of nine million readers.[41]

Print culture for peace was also advanced the following year by Gandhi disciple Richard Gregg. A Harvard-trained lawyer, Gregg wrote an appealing and engaging book, The Power of Non-violence, which became the virtual manual of action for non-violent activists over the next generation. In this book, Gregg advocated coercive, but non-violent techniques—fasts, mass protests, sit-downs—in order to affect domestic and international relations. "The aim of the non-violent resister," Gregg argued, "is not to injure, or to crush and humiliate his opponent, or 'to break his will,' as in a violent fight. The aim is to convert the opponent, to change his understanding, and his sense of values so that he will join wholeheartedly with the resister in seeking a settlement truly amicable...to both sides." He attempted to trace the practice of non-violence in the history of modern Western Civilization—pointing to such incidents as the Magyar struggle against Hapsburg autocracy in the 1860's—to support his contention that non-violence was something more than a peculiarly Hindu practice. His proposal for a new mode of conflict resolution was applied to all aspects of disagreement in order that truth speaking to power would resolve differences through "a mutually satisfactory approximation of justice."[42]

Gregg's non-violent philosophy also became the trademark of the fledgling Catholic peace movement. Peace activists among U.S. Catholics adopted an evangelical pacifism which culminated in the Catholic Worker Movement. It was founded on Manhattan's lower East Side in 1933 by Catholic convert and journalist Dorothy Day and the French pacifist Peter Maurin. Born into a lower middle class family in Brooklyn, New York, in the late 1890's, Day grew up in New York, Oakland, California, and Chicago. In 1914, she entered the University of Illinois, where she found comfort in the ideas of the Socialist Party. She did not graduate, but instead returned to New York City where she resided in the immigrant quarter of the Lower East Side. There she began working as a reporter for socialist newspapers and journals, while becoming involved in the suffrage movement. In 1932, Day met Maurin, who championed the notion of

Catholic populism, voluntary poverty, and small cooperative communities void of political regulations.

The Catholic Worker Movement expanded the definition of peace work by feeding the hungry, nursing the sick, and aiding the homeless and destitute. The Catholic Worker established its first "house of hospitality" in 1933, a shelter providing direct relief to the unemployed. It became a movement composed of lay people who established farming communes and hospitality houses in both rural and urban areas. Relying on her journalistic skills, Day traveled about the nation lecturing and reporting on the organizing drives in America's growing industrial sectors. Maurin, likewise, did his part by lecturing on the evils of industrial capitalism – arguing that war could only be eliminated by a total transformation of society into a free association of communities established on the acceptance of voluntary poverty – and writing free verse "Easy Essays" for the organization's monthly paper, The Catholic Worker.

With its official organ, The Catholic Worker, the movement was involved in supporting organizing drives in the mass production industries and a back to the land movement based on subsistence farming. It was not until 1935 that the Movement adopted an explicitly pacifist position when it renounced war in principle as well as in practice. Throughout the thirties, Catholic Worker pacifism became more articulate as it argued against the necessity of violence in the labor movement while urging Catholic Conscientious Objection against all war. The Catholic Worker movement was not well received by a majority of America's Roman Catholics. But it persisted and poverty and pacifism became integral to its social philosophy. The attempt to make the life-giving love of Christ real and to turn the other cheek is most tellingly expressed in the words of Dorothy Day: "….St. Peter disobeyed the law of men and stated that he had to obey God rather than man. Wars today involve total destruction...killing of the innocent....When one is drafted for such war,...when one pays income tax, eighty percent of which goes to support such war, or works where armaments are made, one is participating in this war. We are all involved in war these days. War means hatred and fear. Love casts out fear."[43] In her view, a social order which depends on profits and which does not consider the nature of human beings' needs, as to living space, food and work, is a bad one and totally inadequate in the modern world.

THE GREAT DEPRESSION, PACIFIST ACTION AT HOME, AND COMBATTING RACIAL INJUSTICE

Day's compassionate plea for social reform through peaceful means and greater human understanding came in the face of the twin blockbusters of economic catastrophe and international conflict. First and foremost, the magnitude of the depression led interwar peace advocates to establish summer Work Camps. The camps were organized by the AFSC and were based on the conviction that pacifism applies not only in case of international war, but also in new ways of bringing about essential changes in the social order through methods and devices which are creative rather than destructive. Pacifists applied James' "moral equivalent of war" to the nation's greatest economic catastrophe.

The Work Camps, as Sherwood Eddy and Devere Allen explain in their book, Peaceful Pioneers, were composed mainly of college-age young men and women; they were set up in various areas of the country in order to provide large numbers of poor and unemployed people with food and shelter. During the winter of 1931-32, for instance, the AFSC fed 42,000 children in the bituminous coal areas.

Additionally, young people worked in groups at physical tasks which needed doing and would otherwise have not been undertaken. The activities were wide-ranging: a group of high school seniors helped to construct a tourist camp in the TVA region; fifty college students and others built a dam for a fish-growing pond in the Tennessee Valley area; forty people assisted in building roads and chicken houses and installing a water system in a homestead community in Fayette County, Pennsylvania; one work camp did a house-renovating job in

Philadelphia; another work camp did some house construction and built a bridge on the Delta Cooperative Farm in Mississippi; and a group of volunteers repaired buildings and did farm work on an Indian reservation near Quaker Bridge, New York. In each case, an adult educational program was implemented to bring students into touch with the local problems of conflict or of experimentation in the community where they were working, together with some study of the technique of social change without the use of violence. "We are not interested merely in finding jobs for peace," proclaimed supporters Sherwood Eddy and Devere Allen. "We are interested only in the building of a new order, a socialized, planned economy that will provide not only work for all, but [also] openings for creative pioneers determined to build this new world in the midst of the old."[44]

Building a new order also required an intense commitment to racial justice. Peace pioneers of the modern movement extended their analyses of conflict to include racial justice. In this respect the FOR led the way and Howard Kester of its Youth Section assumed command. In the late 1920s, he spent considerable time in the South promoting interracial contacts among college students. He continued his journey with even more conviction in the 1930s. During the Great Depression Kester addressed racial inequality by emphasizing the region's social and economic problems.

Kester's efforts had been inspired by the work of young African Americans such as Hosea Hudson and Angelo Herndon. Both had joined the Communist Party. As will be noted shortly, the Communist Party in America had taken the lead in the fight for racial justice after nine black male youths were accused of raping two white girls in Scottsboro, Alabama, in 1931. The black youths were convicted on slim evidence by all-white juries and members of the Communist Party continued the battle for their release. Grateful for their efforts, Hudson joined the party and began organizing unemployed blacks in Birmingham, Alabama; Herndon soon joined the effort and assisted with the creation of the Unemployment Council. The efforts of communists and Hudson and Herndon's work in the Unemployment Council went a long way in bringing to the attention of white peace activists the connection between economic depression and racial injustice in the south.

Kester's most dramatic and dangerous encounters took place in Arkansas and Tennessee. In making moral pilgrimages across the South he constantly drew attention in his reports to the social and economic bases of racial disharmony. His most damning reports dealt with lynchings. In August 1931, he investigated a lynching that took place the previous spring in Union City, Tennessee. Shortly after he reported on the Scottsboro affair in Alabama and the lynching in Tennessee, the National Association for the Advancement of Colored People (NAACP) took notice of Kester's knowledge and understanding of race relations in the South. His most productive report was about the 1934 lynching of Claude Neale, which proved crucial to the NAACP's antilynching campaign.

Neale was accused of murdering a nineteen-year-old white female from Marianna, Florida. A small group of vigilantes from Florida crossed into Alabama where Neale was being held in a local jail due to the publicity surrounding the alleged murder. There they overpowered the local sheriff and took Neal from the jail. In the intervening hours, as state authorities argued over jurisdiction, the ruthless mob tortured and hanged him. The lynchers then took the mutilated body back to Marianna and suspended it from a tree in front of the courthouse. Angry whites who were not part of the execution felt deprived and began attacking blacks throughout the town until the Florida National Guard was called in to restore order.

Kester's report, The Lynching of Claude Neale, was distributed widely by the NAACP in 1934 and 1935. It helped push forward the Costigan-Wagner anti-lynching bill that had been introduced in Congress in early 1934. What enabled Kester's report to become so powerful was his interpretation that the lynching of Neale represented a manifestation of deeper economic problems in the South. The pressing issue of jobs, bread, and economic security were directly related to the lynching. Later, Kester would also report on the double lynching near Duck Hill,

Mississippi, in the spring of 1937. This event finally sparked both federal and state authorities to use their authority to enforce new anti-lynching laws.

As a representative of the FOR and crusader for social justice Kester, uplifted by the actions of the Unemployment Councils, communists, and brave African American organizers who shunned violence, represented the expanding dimensions of modern peace activism. Through his efforts, in particular, Kester was able to bring to the attention of lawmakers and reformers the dynamics behind the violence and prejudice plaguing race relations in America. For Kester, building a new social order required more than just education and economic reform. It demanded an enlightened conscience dedicated to the welfare of all citizens regardless of the color of their skin.

What cannot be ignored is that racial discrimination and segregation continued to haunt African Americans during the interwar period. Black veterans found it especially hard to comprehend that the rights for which they were sent to Europe to fight and die for – "to make the world safe for democracy" – were still denied to them at home. Some of the more noted African American thinkers and activists such as Richard Wright, Hudson, Herndon, Paul Robeson, and Souls of Black Folk author W.E.B. Du Bois supported communist activities to combat racial injustice in the 1930s. It was the Communist Party that defended young black men imprisoned due to southern injustice, most notably the Scottsboro boys. In the early years of the depression it was the Communist Party that organized Unemployment Councils in order to get relief for needy people, regardless of color.

Despite New Deal labor policies and the organizing efforts that led to greater recognition for blacks in the labor movement, the American peace movement had a long way to go in terms of race relations. It found itself troubled by seeking its own respectability while watching the Communist Party take the lead in the struggle for racial justice and equality. Within the peace movement it was the FOR that brought to light the seriousness of racial discrimination between the wars. In so doing, it provided the impetus for peace activists to play a greater role in racial justice work during the Second World War.

SIT-DOWN, CLASS STRUGGLE, AND TESTING PACIFIST CONVICTIONS

Peace pioneers' concern for labor organizing was also dramatically illustrated during the industrial organizing drives in the auto industry of the mid-thirties. The magnitude of the depression and labor setbacks during the 1920s necessitated the need for more innovative ways to organize the unorganized. The conservatism of the craft unions had been one of the major criticisms of labor progressives at workers' colleges such as Brookwood, Commonwealth, Works' People College, and Highlander. Students and educators at these schools supported the industrial unionizing drives of the mid-to-late 1930s. These schools were instrumental in promoting the establishment of the Congress of Industrial Organization and helped to popularize the sit-down tactic during the automobile plant strikes in early 1937.

Efforts by the Congress of Industrial Organization to unionize auto workers took an important turn in January 1937 at the Fisher Body Plants of General Motors in Flint, Michigan. Without any warning the assembly line's production came to a complete standstill. Quickly, the strike spread to auto plants in Detroit, Cleveland, Toledo and other parts of the country. Some 112,000 of General Motors 150,000 workforce became immobilized.

The strike at Flint was totally new to plant managers and employers. It took the form of a sit-down, a tactic that had been taught at Brookwood. Two fundamental ideas related to non-violence had been stressed in classes dealing with labor organizing: non-violence tends to throw the aggressor off balance, and the strikers become the innocent victims of brutality and physical oppression, thereby forcing employers to negotiate. Led by United Auto Worker organizers and former Brookwood students, Roy Reuther and Merlin Bishop, the laborers at the Fisher Body Plant refused to leave the plant; they simply sat at their work benches. Plant managers were dumbfounded and caught totally off guard.

Bishop, who was by then the educational director of the United Auto Workers, helped organize the sit-down strike by leading the workers in singing within the cold confines of brick walls and with nothing to stare at but the instruments of their oppression. The plant managers were not sure how to handle the situation. The sit-down was not an act of violence but one of passive resistance. It was doubly effective in that the strike could only be broken by the forcible removal of the workers from company premises. General Motors management and the Flint Alliance, a company-sponsored association supposedly made up of loyal employees but most likely consisting of small merchants in town, immediately assailed the non-violent tactic as an unlawful invasion of property rights and called for the immediate ejection of the strikers. But the strikers demonstrated their unyielding determination not to be dislodged from the occupied plants.

In an effort to force the strikers out, all heat in the plant was cut off. When the police tried to rush the Fisher Body Plant No. 2, using billy clubs and tear gas bombs, the strikers retaliated by turning streams of water on the charging blue suits from the plant fire hoses. The forces of law and order were finally compelled to make a hasty retreat in what the exultant workers proudly called the "Battle of Running Bulls."

Plant No. 4, where all Chevrolet motors were assembled, was strategically crucial to the union's efforts. Not far from this plant was the personnel building, headquarters of the company police and hired gunmen. In an effort to divert the union workers from expanding the sit-down, a sham attack was planned for plant No. 9 where a sit-down was already in progress. When union men started running to plant No. 9 to assist they were instead directed to No. 4 where they immediately started a sit-down. The Company police arrived too late and the union completely shut down all production.

The Women's Emergency Brigade, composed of wives, mothers and sisters of the strikers, played a key role in the battle, especially at plants No. 9 and No. 4. Demonstrating their own special brand of fortitude and determination they smashed windows to keep the men from being suffocated by tear gas, and with locked arms prevented the police attack upon the main gate of plant No. 4. As the sit-downs spread throughout the auto industry women became an important force behind the struggle for social and economic justice. Females who also worked in the plants stood side-by-side with their fellow male co-workers in an effort to establish the right to organize and to fight for higher wages and safe working conditions.

The strike at General Motors dragged on for weeks during one of the coldest recorded winters for that area. Finally, on February 4, 1937, with the sit-downers barricaded in the factories and protecting themselves against the expected tear gas with skimpy cheesecloth masks, the impasse between General Motors and the United Automobile Workers was broken. GM management decided to recognize the United Auto Workers as the bargaining agent for its members, to drop injunction proceedings against the strikers, to refrain from discriminating in any way against union members, and to take up such grievances as the speed-up and other matters. Although the UAW failed to achieve a minimum wage and thirty-hour work week it succeeded in capturing another anti-union stronghold. Its success was attributable to the discipline exhibited during the sit-down and the avoidance of bloodshed.

The actions and efforts of industrial organizers, progressive labor educators, and peace activists of the 1930s had a profound influence on the post-World War II non-violent movement. In fact, the anthem of protest, "We Shall Overcome," had previously been sung by striking textile workers in the Piedmont region in the late 1920s and early 1930s when labor organizers from workers' education colleges participated in their struggles. The sit-in tactic was also partly inspired by the sit-down strikes in the automobile plants in the mid-thirties. Even Rosa Park's actions which sparked the Montgomery Bus Boycott in 1955 were partly due to her attending a leadership seminar for training union organizers. It was at Highlander where Parks was exposed to music, games, storytelling, and making skits as a way of assisting poor people to learn the power of unity and organization. Many of Highlanders' tactics such as voter drives, music festivals, blockading strip mines, and environmental cleanup took center stage in the social reconstruction efforts during the latter half of the twentieth century. With the assistance of non-violent activists, the peace movement in the wake of World War I had expanded its focus and the labor movement stood as a shining example of pioneers for peace putting in place a course of non-violent action in the name of social justice.

But the country's worst economic depression in history, 1929-1941, also led many pacifists to a greater concern with class conflict. Many questioned whether or not America's industrial order could be humanized without resorting to violence. According to Charles Chatfield, the more deeply they became involved in social justice struggles, the more they questioned their pacifist convictions. As mentioned earlier, the magnitude of the depression caused A.J. Muste to abandon his pacifism, as well as Brookwood Labor College, for the militancy of the Trotskyist Workers Party; it was a brief flirtation in which he became absorbed in the endless factional in-fighting among Trotskyists. In the end, he found little in Marxism-Leninism to meet his personal needs to live according to the principles of peace and justice. He returned to his Christian pacifist principles in 1936, while visiting a Parisian church. "Peace is indivisible," he now believed, "not only in the geographical and diplomatic sense...but in the sense that the way of peace is really a seamless garment that must cover the whole of life and must be applied in all its relationships."[45] Some pacifists took longer to reach this position as they faced urgent issues of unemployment, hunger, and the rise of fascism.

A number of pacifists accepted Muste's temporary doubt regarding the effectiveness of non-violence as an instrument for social reform in the 1930s. They were willing to forsake their pacifist views for the righteousness of class conflict as advocated by the left. Given the existing power structure in America, these pacifists argued, non-violence would most likely operate to confirm economic justice. Violence was undesirable and should be minimized, but it would inevitably occur where there was basic social change. Justice was more fundamental than peace because it was a prior condition of peace. Thus, the duty of pacifists was to support revolutionary change even if it was somewhat violent.

Most pacifists puzzled over the larger questions that troubled people of conscience throughout the tumultuous thirties. In The Peace Reform in American History, the late peace historian Charles DeBenedetti raised a number of provocative questions. Could pacifists instill a non-violent ethic in matters pertaining to class conflict? Could domestic reform progress while checking the spread of fascism? What is the ultimate worth of the individual in a society in which economic power is highly concentrated?

This very issue involving the relationship between violence and an unjust domestic order was at the heart of a heated debate within FOR circles in the early 1930s. On which side, if presented in politics, must a Christian choose between justice and love? Joseph B. Matthews, a Protestant minister and FOR's Executive Secretary, accused absolute pacifists of selling out to the owning class. Struggling with his conscience, Matthews felt compelled to argue that coercive rather than persuasive techniques were now necessary to bring about the desired social reconstruction. In 1933, the FOR decided to poll its membership on the issue of class war. To the key question – "Should the FOR hold on to non-violence in the class war as well as in international war?" 877 respondents answered *yes*, 97 *no*. Although less than half of the FOR membership responded to the questionnaire, the organization remained in favor of non-violence in the class war as well as in international war. Matthews left the FOR in early 1934 after his term as executive secretary expired.

For some pacifists, such as Norman Thomas, domestic reform was most important. For him, the realities of economic determinism and class struggle were apparent. Unlike Muste, he considered his socialist ideals to be a vital instrument relevant to America's democratic principles. Thus he clung to his pacifist faith as a technique of social action. World War I had convinced him that violence and authoritarianism were precisely what threatened his democratic socialist values. But he considered domestic reform from a political perspective that was pragmatic and, therefore, changeable.

A noted clergyman and peace worker, Thomas had been editor of the FOR monthly, World Tomorrow, since 1918. Throughout the twenties, he was more active in socialist and pacifist affairs than he was in saving souls. Long active in socialist politics, he finally renounced his ministerial vows in 1931. A year later, as Socialist Party presidential candidate, he ran against Herbert Hoover and Franklin D. Roosevelt, polling 900,000 votes. Yet within two years, factionalism ran rampant throughout his party because of internal quarreling and growing popular support for FDR's New Deal.

Nevertheless, the Socialist Party remained a bulwark of anti-war sentiment throughout the 1930's. Thomas' pacifism and social reform views also led him to criticize many of the paramilitary aspects of the New Deal. Conscious of the fact that New Deal spokesmen "compared the economic crisis of the 1930's to the war emergency of 1917," Thomas cautioned Americans about the use of the war metaphor and World War I precedents as measures for achieving domestic reform. He was quite critical of the Civilian Conservation Corps (CCC)—a symbol of the New Deal's deliberate effort to permeate the country with "a spirit of devotion and sacrifice customarily known only in war." The fact that wartime models were employed so intentionally for the sake of reform was dangerous, Thomas believed, for the future of democracy in America.[46]

Critics of the CCC saw parallels between the corps and the Nazi work camps. Unlike the public-works programs, CCC camps did not employ many industrial workers who had lost their jobs, nor were they expected to have much of a stimulating effect on private business. Both the Nazi work camps and the CCC employed enrollees at forestry and similar projects to improve the countryside and were essentially designed to keep young men out of the labor market.

Both types of labor had been organized on semi-military lines with the subsidiary purposes of improving the physical fitness of potential soldiers and stimulating public commitment to national service in the emergency. Paramilitary and patriotic functions, not essential to its announced purpose, became part of the CCC's overall objectives. Corpsmen were required to stand "in a position of alertness" while speaking to superiors and to address them as "sir." Camp commanders possessed mild but distinctly military powers to discipline their men, including the right to issue dishonorable discharges. Morning and evening flag-raising ceremonies were held in order to foster patriotism, solid citizenship, and appreciation for the government's concern for their welfare. Army authorities soon concluded that six months' CCC service was worth a year's conventional military training, and Secretary of War George Dern claimed that running the camps provided the army with the best practical experience in handling men it had ever had.[47]

THE RISE OF FASCISM AND DISARMAMENT ATTEMPTS

The resort to reform through war analogue certainly annoyed some peace seekers. But nothing was more upsetting than the events taking place overseas. The rise of Japanese militarism in the Far East and the rapid spread of fascism in Italy and Nazism in Germany added to their woes. The American public also recognized that the depression was not the only major problem the nation now faced.

Alarmed by the political instability and rising militarism in Europe and Asia, beginning with the Japanese invasion of Manchuria in 1931, the American people were even more convinced that "isolation from war, rather than collective efforts to prevent war, was now the most realistic policy for the United States."[48] Support for the idea of collective security – nations entering into treaties of mutual support or implementing the use of sanctions against aggressor nations – was popular among liberal internationals and among communists concerned abut the fate of the Soviet Union. But the fear of a coming war in Europe in the early thirties strengthened isolationism as much as peace activism. Given the seriousness of the world situation, peace workers were willing to try anything in order to check the growing tide of war.

They had already tried challenging the government's legal right to conscript non-religious Conscientious Objectors. Hoping to capitalize on strong anti-war sentiments in the wake of World War I, peace groups took their case to court. The question of the constitutionality of federal conscription laws dated back to the Civil War. In the widely-discussed 1863 Pennsylvania Supreme Court decision of Kneedler v. Lane, the Union's draft act was at first ruled to be unconstitutional on the basis that it violated the states' authority over their militias. But when the case was reargued, the earlier decision was reversed. A similar ruling favorable to the draft was finally determined almost seventy years later. In the 1930 case of Macintosh v. United States, the United States Supreme Court ultimately determined that the constitution does require citizens with conscientious reservations not based in religious principles to bear arms. The Court noted that the privilege of native-born Conscientious Objectors to avoid conscription derives not from the constitution but from acts of Congress. In this particular case, the ruling barred American citizenship to pacifist immigrants. Macintosh was a Canadian. The ruling was then applied to the matter of a draft and permitted Congress the right to initiate a draft anytime it saw fit to do so.

In April 1931, upset over the spiraling arms race, representatives from 28 different organizations, ranging from the Women's International League for Peace and Freedom to the Carnegie Endowment for International Peace, agreed to establish the Interorganizational Council on Disarmament (ICD). At first, as long as they kept to disarmament, leaders of various peace persuasions were able to act with near unanimity, framing resolutions of support, sending delegations to the White House, State Department, and Congressional hearings, sponsoring demonstrations, and supporting observers in Geneva. Even after Japanese aggression in Manchuria, a majority of the Council agreed on a number of propositions, including an embargo on arms to Japan and China, support for the Stimson doctrine of non-recognition of territorial changes made by force of arms, and close cooperation with the League of Nations. Yet by 1933, this loose coalition of peace groups collapsed over the disagreement on basic issues such as Japan, inter-Allied war debts, and America's relationship to the League.

The ICD failure did not diminish peace activism: to the contrary, it became stronger. On behalf of one hundred college presidents and out of concern "for the well-being of the tens of thousands of young men and women to whom we stand in loco parentis," Ernest H. Wilkins of Oberlin College transmitted an open letter to President Roosevelt in 1934 urging his support for "the passage of legislation intended to keep this country clear, so far as is humanly possible, of all circumstances and forces that draw nations into war...."[49] Much of Wilkins' concern had been prompted by a number of articles and best-selling books that gave detailed accounts of the international traffic in arms carried on by the so-called "merchants of death."[50]

The strengthening of peace activism in the early 1930s was due largely to the number of broad-based alliances among pacifists, internationalists, socialists, and communists. At the height of peace sentiment in the mid-1930s, many within the "modern" movement, including communists, feared that another world war would benefit only the bankers and munitions makers. Communists were the dominant group on the American left in the 1930s, yet their role in the peace movement had not received much attention. Their involvement in the peace movement has been largely overshadowed by increased fascist aggression and the onset of the Spanish civil war in 1936, when antifascism, rather than peace, became their major goal.

Nevertheless, it is also important to point out that they played a seminal role in peace groups such as the American League Against War and Fascism (ALWF) and the American Student Union (ASU). Before communists began supporting the need for collective armed action against the fascists many party members were serious about peace and participated in causes on its behalf.

Serious scholars recognize that the Communist Party was the driving force behind ALWF. Created in September 1933, the organization, which later changed its name to the American League for Peace and Democracy, claimed a rank-and-file membership of over two million at the height of its popularity in 1935. Many of its members came from organized labor and were genuinely interested in peace, despite the organization's concerns with Soviet security. Its 1933 manifesto warned against a new imperialist war and the dangers of capitalistic monopolies. The League's position against war was to use the Soviet Union as an example of how the basic cause of war could be removed. Since the Soviet Union had no classes or groups which could stand to benefit from war or war buildups, the League argued, it was best suited to pursue a policy of peace and disarmament. Interestingly, those in the peace movement who did not trust communists did not take issue with their position at this time.

The League also had many non-communists in its leadership like Roger Baldwin of the American Civil Liberties Union as well as communists such as general secretary Earl Browder. Until the later part of the decade when the Nazi-Soviet Non-Aggression Pact led to serious problems for communist peace backers, ALWF continued calling for a halt to the sale of arms to Japan, support for the Spanish Republic against the fascists, and bringing together trade unionists with members of the peace movement's middle class.

In a similar vein, the 1935 establishment of the American Student Union represented a determined effort by young communists and socialists to perpetuate the goal of left-wing politics. Like the ALWF, ASU was composed of communists, socialists, pacifists, and internationalists concerned about war. These student radicals went even further in modifying the British-created Oxford Pledge which will be discussed below. Specifically, they changed it to read as a refusal to support the American government in any war it may conduct. While the ASU adopted a more nonpacifist stance by qualifying the Oxford Pledge, it was responsible for taking the lead in organizing and carrying out numerous anti-war strikes on college campuses throughout the country.

Yet it also encountered the very same problem as the ALWF. The Nazi-Soviet Pact and the Soviet invasion of Finland witnessed the organization's leadership remaining silent on the matter. By not condemning these actions by the Soviet Union ASU sacrificed its reputation. By the end of the decade it no longer was a force for peace not a serious instrument for promoting left-wing political action in the United States.

At least until the mid-1930s, then, the peace movement managed to accommodate a wide variety of political persuasions. When their views coincided on certain issues it was thus not out of the ordinary to witness pacifists, socialists, internationalists, and communists working in harmony for the cause of peace.

STUDENT ACTIVISM AND THE OXFORD PLEDGE

Moved by fresh signs of mounting conflict and inspired by left-wing activism on many campuses, student activists began ramping up their own campaign for world peace. The Student League for Industrial Democracy and the National Student League organized a "Student Strike Against War." The event took place on April 13, 1934, precisely at eleven o'clock—thus commemorating the entrance of the United States into the First World War. It was a simple demonstration, scheduled for one hour, with students instructed to go to their class, get up and leave the room, and join the strike. Twenty-five thousand students participated in the strike, most of them from schools in New York City. At City College, the scene of the largest demonstration, students paraded for peace throughout the campus and signed petitions condemning war. Also, more than 3,500 activists participated in the first anti-war strike at the University of California at Berkeley. One of the significant moments of the strike occurred when activists everywhere affirmed their hatred of war by taking the Oxford

Pledge—a statement first passed by the Oxford Union in Britain in February 1933—that "this House refuses to fight for King and Country in any war."[51]

A year later, April 12, 1935, a second student strike against war took place. The number of participants increased dramatically, with more than 150,000 undergraduates leaving class to demonstrate. The scope of the strike had become nationwide, with anti-war protests occurring on over 130 campuses across the country. The largest strike meetings were once again in New York City where ten thousand students attended demonstrations at City College, Columbia University, and Hunter, and Brooklyn Colleges. At American University in Washington, D.C., five hundred striking students listened attentively to an address by Congresswoman Jeannette Rankin, who had voted against the declaration of war in 1917; three thousand activists at the University of Pennsylvania cheered Socialist leader Norman Thomas who urged them to "have the guts to stay out of war"; at UCLA five hundred students attended the first peace strike ever held at the school, stirred on by the school's own student leader, Celeste Strack; and the entire student body of eight hundred struck at the College of the Ozarks in Arkansas thereby irritating some razorback patriots.[52]

Finally on April 22, 1936, the third and largest student anti-war strike took place. Activists claimed a record of 500,000 students from all over the country participated, although a more accurate estimate is about 350,000. On the eve of the strike, a student journal declared that the leaders of America "Seem[ed] to be paralyzed in the face of the terrific war catastrophe that confronts us all. For us the strike has become one measure with a chance of success.... We must not hesitate. Strike against War!"[53]

The strike was enlivened on many campuses by the activities of members of the Veterans of Future Wars—an intercollegiate organization whose first chapter was formed at Princeton University in early 1936. The club's proclaimed purpose was to enable young men to collect their entire war bonuses in advance. Their motto was "hand outstretched, palm up, expectant." Drawing upon the fate of the World War I veterans, who were promised a bonus for fighting in the war but never received it and were driven out of Washington, D.C., by General Douglas MacArthur after they had set up an encampment on Constitution Mall, the group's primary purpose was to satirize war and its military virtues. Membership spread rapidly among undergraduates throughout the nation. During the strike, some twelve hundred "veterans" (dressed in uniforms decorated with medals and ribbons) at the University of Washington took part in the funeral services "of the unknown soldier of tomorrow," with students dressed as Hitler, Mussolini, and J.P. Morgan as pallbearers. At Columbia University, two hundred members of the Randolph Hearst Post of the "Veterans of Future Wars" marched in a strike parade, led by a student using a crutch for a baton.[54]

What is most interesting about the student peace movement in the 1930s was that it was not composed only of pacifists. Robert Cohen's When the Old Left Was Young: Student Radicals and America's First Mass Student Movement, 1929-1941, points out that the student movement welcomed into its ranks (and was often led by) those young radicals interested in developing a more caring society based on social change and who were willing to participate in campaigns against world war and fascist aggression. He deals extensively with many different student organizations but his discussion of the American Youth Congress (AYC) is particularly instructive.

Until the 1960s, the student movements of the Great Depression represented the most compelling organizations of political activity on the part of America's youth. In 1934, with the establishment of the American Youth Congress, historian Eileen Eagan notes, it represented the first example of the popular front among the nation's youth. Local youth organizations melded into a national federation and lobby to promote the goals of progressive government. Specifically, AYC championed the goal of a meaningful jobs program for low-income students and unemployed youth. Linking peace with social justice and seeking to energize student activism, AYC issued its own "Declaration" on July 4, 1936. In its Declaration it promised to promote free speech on college campuses, work against the threat of war and the draft, assist in the industrial organizing drives of the Congress of Industrial Organization, build campus cooperative and student unions, campaign against all forms of racism in America, get the government to create an unemployment and social insurance program, abolish child labor, and prevent the destruction of crops and livestock that could be provided for the undernourished and underfed.

Between 1936 and 1939 the student movement's appeal for full educational opportunities, steady employment with adequate wages, civil rights, and peace resulted in a membership of almost 4, 700,000 in 513 affiliated groups throughout the country. One of its specific targets was ending mandatory participation in the Reserve Officers Training Corps for male college students. The AYC was one of the first student groups to sponsor peace strikes on campus during the month of April. In 1937, for instance, it was a prime sponsor behind the national United Student Strike Committee's call for change. The national call urged the "demilitarization" of universities and colleges, passage of the Nye-Kvale Bill (elimination of compulsory R.O.T.C. for male college students), reaffirmation of the Oxford Pledge, reduction in military spending, and courses in the economic and psychological causes of war.

What AYC did to assist the student youth movement of this era was to expand the idea of peace and connect it to matters of justice. During these years it lobbied the government vigorously for more federal spending on education instead of the military and to end racial discrimination. One of its leading members was Joseph Lash who described the organization as the "student brain of the New Deal." Within the White House its biggest supporter was Eleanor Roosevelt. She courted the organization by convincing its leaders that it could be more effective if it supported the objectives of the National Youth Administration rather than criticizing the New Deal. In return for AYC's support, Mrs. Roosevelt protected it from Congressional attacks on the right.

The organization did have communists within its leadership, which finally opened the door for an attack by the House Committee on Un-American Activities. But its demise was largely due to the bitter divisiveness among young

American radicals that resulted from the Nazi-Soviet Non-Aggression Pact of 1939. Some AYC communist leaders were able to convince the organization to officially support the non-aggression pact. This resulted in large-scale defections by its most important allies, Eleanor Roosevelt among them. Shortly thereafter the organization died a quiet death, a tragic blow to the student activism of the decade.

THE ISSUE OF NEUTRALITY

While the student peace movement was reaching its height, however, the depression mood of hostility to business leadership and the continuing publication of critical historical works revising official accounts of the origins of the World War added further weight to general demands for congressional legislation to protect the peace and neutrality of the United States.[55]

The impetus to keep America neutral had historical roots in the American policy of isolationism, encouraged by the disillusionment that followed World War I. Americans believed their nation's leaders had misled them by calling it a crusade for democracy. Many were also disappointed by the vindictive peace the victors had imposed at Paris in 1919; others were upset by the pernicious aspects of American propaganda, the work of unscrupulous Wall Street bankers, and the controversy over war debts. All of these factors accounted for a general sentiment on the part of Americans to avoid the next European war.

The desire for neutrality galvanized peace groups of all persuasions, who shared common interests in disarmament and economic conciliation. This partnership was solidified in early 1935 because of the Senate's rejection of U.S. membership in the World Court. They feared that the United States might withdraw entirely from promoting international programs for peace upon which they did agree. Peace groups like the Carnegie Endowment for International Peace, League of Nations Association, Foreign Policy Association, the World Peace Foundation, and the Woodrow Wilson Foundation, which previously confined themselves to educational campaigns designed to check isolationist sentiment, began promoting the neutrality laws as a barrier against involvement in a new war.

The Neutrality Acts, beginning with the temporary measure of 1935 and culminating in the modifications affected by the "cash-and-carry" provisions of the law of 1937, were designed to isolate America from another world war. But the were hardly satisfactory nor comforting to dedicated peacemakers.[56] Confronted by acts of fascist aggression, civil war in Spain, and persecution of Jews in Nazi Germany, supporters of world peace and justice anguished over the policy of strict neutrality. How can one not get involved and permit fascism to take over? How does one stay "neutral" in the face of such an obvious evil? How can one allow for the possible extermination of a group of people based on their culture and religious beliefs?

Pioneers for peace and justice were faced with numerous challenges as the peace process began to unravel in the mid-1930s. Many of those in the peace movement were forced to re-examine their position on neutrality and abstention from the use of collective force as news spread that Francisco Franco and his fascist allies were committing untold acts of brutality against the Loyalists.

The case of Socialist Party leader Norman Thomas, who temporarily gave up his pacifist stance because he strongly believed that Franco had to be defeated and the Loyalist government preserved, is instructive here. Thomas went so far as to appeal this cause to President Roosevelt, asking him to lift the arms embargo. Thomas was also instrumental in helping to organize a volunteer unit of Americans to fight in Spain with the Loyalists.

Ironically, even communists supported the notion of neutrality despite their antifascist stance (for a short time they shared the isolationist position of America First, a right-wing group). But the dilemma they faced was promoting peace in order to defend the Nazi-Soviet Pact. It cost them dearly with the collapse of the united-front organizations they worked so hard to establish. When the Nazis invaded the Soviet Union in 1941, the communists were no longer isolationist or neutralists, but interventionists. Their commitment to peace disappeared when the Soviet Union came under attack.

DRIFT TOWARD WORLD WAR

The Administration's neutrality policy and the worsening situation in Europe highlighted the complexities the "modern" peace pioneers faced. Pacifists, on the one hand, clung ever so tightly to what Chatfield termed, "committed neutralism."[57] Internationalists, on the other hand, were not as hopeful and pressed for "more Presidential discretionary authority in case of a worsening of international tension." They were convinced that Mussolini and Hitler would eventually wage war to destroy the Versailles system. Many within the peace movement's ranks, whether or not they were pacifists, internationalists, or critics of capitalist wars called upon American officials to cooperate more fully with League powers in maintaining the current European order against the threat of fascism.[57]

Peace action continued, nonetheless.[58] In December 1935, Kirby Page and Ray Newton rejuvenated the National Peace Committee by creating an extension to it, the Emergency Peace Campaign (EPC). Its intended purpose was to offer an outlet to anti-communist liberals and conservatives who wanted to keep America neutral. Receiving support from other peace groups, such as the FOR, the Emergency Peace Campaign got under way in April 1936 with "a $130,000 budget and the support of the widest peace coalition of the interwar period." Under Page's leadership, ministers, educators, feminists, and social activists presented lectures throughout the country; 3,500 clergymen pledged to deliver sermons in support of the Committee's foreign policy objectives: U.S. membership in the World Court and International Labor Organization, governmental control of the munitions industry, and cooperation with the League of Nations regarding non-political issues. During the year of its inception anti-war activities were conducted in close to 278 American cities and citizens in twenty-four states were treated to peace skits performed by traveling theatrical companies. EPC speakers also toured the country campaigning for peace candidates on November election slates.[59]

Encouraged by its initial success, the committee began creating a large coalition of established peace organizations. On the twentieth anniversary of America's entrance into World War I, April 6, 1937, the No-Foreign-War Crusade was launched. Its "pacifist-neutralist message" elevated pacifist influence in the anti-war movement of the 1930's "to its highest level." But as quickly as its message spread, signs of dissatisfaction appeared. Some pacifist members quit on the grounds that "their principles were being watered down by the coalition's consensual strategy." Some internationalists also begged off because of the Campaign's firm commitment to strict neutrality and its opposition "to providing the President with greater discretionary authority in matters related to foreign affairs." Clearly, the fractious nature of the attempted peace coalitions became visible as international tensions mounted.[60]

Another effort to rally pacifist groups was the Ludlow Amendment – inspired by the Women's Peace Union. This was a bill which would have required a popular referendum prior to a congressional declaration of war. A number of pacifists, neutralists, and right-wing isolationists supported Congressman Louis Ludlow's (Republican-Indiana) attempt "to secure a constitutional amendment requiring a popular vote before Congress declared war, except in the case of an invasion of the United States." Hundreds of peace workers "lectured and distributed literature in an effort to mobilize public support for the bill." However, the Roosevelt Administration exerted strong pressure against the impending legislation. The bill was defeated in the House by a vote of 209-188.[61]

The defeat of the Ludlow Amendment led to a rapid deterioration of pacifist influence within the anti-war movement, but some refused to quit. John Nevin Sayre worked through the National Peace Conference with internationalists like Clark Eichelberger in calling for an international economic conference. Numerous others, such as Frederick Libby of NCPW and Dorothy Detzer of

WILPF, joined Norman Thomas in the neutralist "Keep America Out of War" campaign.

Founded in February 1938, with pacifist and socialist support in particular, Thomas' organization developed into the Keep America Out of War Congress (KAOWC). Its slogan conveyed its neutralism: "The maximum American cooperation for peace; the maximum isolation from war." But the Congress, while sponsoring a few mass meetings and a few student strikes in 1938, never effectively functioned as a political force; it was incapable of raising enough money, nor could it prevent factionalism within its ranks. Yet, it was the only national anti-war coalition in existence at the time war in Europe broke out on September 1, 1939.[62]

The tenuousness of the peace coalitions reflected how ineffective they became after 1935. As Lawrence Wittner points out, the organized peace movement underwent a disastrous split in 1935 when the obvious collapse of the League of Nations and heightened European militarism created fears of another great war. For example, the National Council for Prevention of War, the Women's International League for Peace and Freedom, and other staunchly pacifist groups, realizing their inability to prevent war in Europe, focused their attention on isolating America from that war. Other peace groups, including the Carnegie Endowment for International Peace, the Church Peace Union, World Alliance for International Friendship through the Churches, the Catholic Association for International Peace, and the League of Nations Association, gradually shifted to doctrines of collective security. In the heated neutrality debates, the former pacifist groups supported the maintenance of mandatory neutrality; while the latter worked for the modification of the neutrality provisions and, eventually, for their repeal.[63]

The interwar peace movement, far from being a coherent social movement as originally hoped for, was essentially a collection of disparate public interest groups—each with specific programs, priorities, and constituencies. On some key issues such as the Outlawry of War Campaign, these groups were able to establish broad coalitions and mass constituencies that proved effective in addressing foreign policy matters. But as soon as the single uniting issue was no longer politically viable, the movement collapsed into its constituent elements. This resulted in public misperception of "peace advocacy as merely sporadic, crisis-provoked and inconsequential."[64]

Along with Muste, perhaps no one individual more accurately captured the peace movement's dilemma regarding non-violence than the distinguished Protestant theologian, Reinhold Niebuhr. Faced with the choice between fascism and war, Niebuhr eventually accepted force as an instrument of necessity under the given circumstances. Over the course of his religious life, Niebuhr crafted an ethics of Christian realism that ultimately sharpened the social ethics of pacifism while giving new meaning and support to the just war theory. After publishing Moral Man and Immoral Society in 1932, he began arguing that social and political choices require a realistic assessment of their consequences, as well as taking into account the role of power in human affairs. In terms of society, justice can only be obtained through an equitable distribution of power. Although comfortable with the social consciousness of reform pacifists like Sayre and Page, Niebuhr gradually challenged the question of non-violence in the throes of the depression. He eventually defected from the FOR's repudiation of any form of violence, insisting that the religious-pacifist organization's position was arbitrary.

As he kept questioning his position, he finally determined that non-violence was justifiable as a social strategy in relative political terms, but not on absolute religious principles. In other words, there were times when the use of violence was acceptable for improving social conditions. Pacifism was a personal philosophy of non-violence, not a "prescription for public policy." Although his ideas on social action strategy anticipated Gregg's non-violent resistance theory, Niebuhr's paradoxical views on the social ethics of pacifism brought to the forefront the dilemma facing absolute war resisters and anti-war peace advocates.[65] By the late 1930's he openly criticized the absolute pacifist position. After the failure of the 1938 Munich Conference, he abandoned pacifism entirely.

He argued that it was no longer relevant to the existing situation. Armed force, not morality, was the only way to stop Hitler and totalitarian aggression.

By 1939, with pacifists retreating inward and neutralists faltering, many internationalists who did not subscribe to the ethic of non-violence began to adorn themselves in interventionist clothing. They were not deterred by the American Federation of Peace's blood-curdling injunction—"THERE IS A SANTA CLAUS! You, men and women of America are the suckers who filled up the stockings of the profiteers, propagandists and foreign politicos with your own blood—your own brain—your own money!...WHAT ARE YOU GOING TO FILL THEM WITH THIS TIME? With the flesh of your wives? With the bowels of your children?..." Nor were they persuaded to sing along to the tune financed by the meat packing giant and right-wing isolationist George A. Hormel entitled, THIS AIN'T OUR WAR!

> We don't want that kind of trouble any
> more.
> A lot of us remember when we went across
> to France,
> And what did we get? What did we get?
> We got a kick in the pants.
> No! THIS AIN'T OUR WAR!
> If they want to fight each other, well, it's
> none of our affair,
> We haven't any mothers with an extra son
> to spare,
> Let's sing "God bless America" instead of
> "Over There,"
> THIS AIN'T OUR WAR!

To leading liberal internationalists, who previously had aligned themselves with the peace movement and were now critical of any isolationist talk, the enemy was not war but the undesirable Nazi menace and growing fascist threat.[66]

On November 11, 1940, therefore, James T. Shotwell, John Foster Dulles, Owen Lattimore, and Max Lerner formed an organization called the Commission to Study the Organization of Peace; the title was deceiving. It was an organization that supported armed intervention to secure peace; it did not seek to make armed violence or the use of power accountable to the people. Publicly it called upon the American people to cooperate in the destruction of fascism and to help create a post-war international security system to suppress future aggression. The organization's leaders may have been realistic in their assessment of the current situation; they were certainly not, however, committed to their reform-minded visions of an earlier era. These liberal internationalists were now moderate interventionists until American entrance into the war; at that point, they became confirmed interventionists seeking some form of *Pax Americana*.

Clark Eichelberger, a World War I veteran and respected organizer of internationalist causes, also rallied his interventionist troops within the League of Nations Association to place American resources at the disposal of the Allied powers. FDR must have been smiling, for this is exactly what he hoped for when proposing Lend-Lease and the Destroyer-for-Bases deals with the Allies in the same period. Eichelberger was so convincing that he managed to secure the services of the noted and respected Midwestern Republican journalist, William Allen White, in creating the Committee to Defend America by Aiding the Allies. The Committee's campaign ranged from all aid short of war to outright military involvement. White, though, did not feel comfortable with this new position and resigned his chairmanship in late 1940. Eichelberger then led internationalists into a working partnership with militant interventionists. In forming a new group, Fight for Freedom, they urged sending U.S. supplies to beleaguered Britain, stepping up U.S. patrols in the Atlantic, instituting an embargo on Japan, and repealing all neutrality legislation. Obviously, they were no longer looking for ways to ensure world peace; they were seeking ways to insure American involvement in war in order not to lose the second peace.

CONCLUSION

In the context of war and fascism – Nazi advances into Belgium and France, the extermination of Jews in Germany and Poland, and the imminent attack on Russia by Germany – the American people, peace advocates included, had much cause for concern. What about Japanese advances in Asia? Would the Japanese military remain content knowing full well that only the United States stood in its way of imperial conquest of the Pacific? By the beginning of 1941, most Americans were convinced that, though the option was not very appealing, the only way to peace was by going to war. Maybe it was Archibald MacLeish, Librarian of Congress, at one time a bitter anti-war critic, who erased all doubts when he wrote the following: "If the young generation in America is distrustful of all words [and] distrustful of all moral judgments of better and worse, then it is incapable of using the only weapon with which fascism can be fought—the moral conviction that fascism is evil and that a free society of free men is good and is worth fighting for." Then, on December 7, 1941, the Japanese attack on Pearl Harbor removed all doubts. Most Americans were convinced that this was a war, in MacLeish's own words, "worth fighting for."[67]

A tiny group of Conscientious Objectors and organizations such as the WRL and FOR maintained their commitment to non-violence. More so than the FOR in the 1930s, the WRL consistently repudiated violence in the class struggle and objected to armed force to defeat fascism during the Spanish Civil War. Its position never wavered nor was compromised after Pearl Harbor. WRL's leaders remained steadfast in their radical opposition to all wars. During the war years its membership increased at a modest rate, especially among Conscientious Objectors, and its operating budget rose from less than $5,000 in 1939 to close to $21,000 in 1943. During the war years WRL organized local chapters promoting peace activity and education. At numerous peace meetings anti-war and labor songs were sung, money raised to assist COs in their legal battle with the government, and pacifist literature, including newspapers and periodicals, was distributed. One of the League's most important anti-war efforts was providing financial support, office space and writing articles for the Conscientious Objector, a newspaper devoted to covering international and national pacifist activities. The WRL even went so far as to issue a pamphlet calling for an immediate negotiated peace.

The FOR also refused to be roped into supporting the war or the belief that war was necessary to save democracy and preserve international harmony. Its Executive Committee hoped, in the words of the founder of the Society of Friends George Fox, that "all men might come to a conscientious renunciation of war and might enter into that spirit 'which taketh away the occasion for all war'...."[68] The Fellowship's resistance would thus consist of helping to organize nonpartisan refugee and P.O.W. relief work and supporting the Feed Europe Fund. The FOR's passive resistance to war carefully emphasized the right of dissent to protect Conscientious Objectors. Consequently, in opposition to the internationalist-interventionist line of reasoning, historian Glen Zeitzer argued that the FOR developed carefully planned strategies and techniques which would eventually have great impact on the civil rights and end-the-war-in-Vietnam movements in the 1960's. In choosing non-violence as their form of dissent, they directly challenged the interventionist position with regard to the best approach to lasting peace.[67] The WRL's and FOR's positions foreshadowed the increasing radical pacifist concern with the growing power of the garrison state.

(Figure 1) David Low Dodge, Founder of New York Peace Society

Papers of David Low Dodge, Swarthmore College Peace Collection

(Figure 2)Elihu Burritt, "The Learned Blacksmith

Papers of Elihu Burritt, Swarthmore College Peace Collection

(Figure 3)Alfred Love, Founder of the Universal Peace Union

Records of Universal Peace Union, Swarthmore College Peace Collection

(Figure 4) Benjamin F. Trueblood, President of the American Peace Society circa 1900

Records of American Peace Society, Swarthmore College Peace Collection

(Figure 5) WWI CO Detachment, Camp Dix, New Jersey

Records of the New York Bureau of Legal Advice, Swarthmore College Peace Collection

(Figure 6) America's "Beloved Lady," Jane Addams

Jane Addams Collection, Swarthmore College Peace Collection

(Figure 7) Tracy Mygatt, Frances Witherspoon, and Mercedes Randall

Papers of Mercedes Randall, Swarthmore College Peace Collection

(Figure 8) Jessie Wallace Hughan, Leader in War Resisters League

Papers of Jessie Wallace Hughan, Swarthmore College Peace Collection

(Figure 9) Jeannette Rankin, Only Member of U.S. Congress to vote against the World Wars

Records of the National Council for Prevention of War, Swarthmore College Peace Collection

(Figure 10) Emily Greene Balch, Second American Female after Jane Addams to win the Nobel Peace Prize

Papers of Emily Greene Balch, Swarthmore College Peace Collection

(Figure 11) Abraham Johannes Muste, "America's Number One Pacifist"

Records of the War Resisters League, Swarthmore College Peace Collection

(Figure 12) Dorothy Day, Founder of the Catholic Workers Movement

Papers of Dorothy Day, Swarthmore College Peace Collection

(Figure 13) AFSC 1930s Peace Caravan

Records of the American Friends Service Committee, Swarthmore College Peace Collection

(Figure 14) 1947 Journey of Reconciliation, Richmond, Virginia, April 1947. Left to Right: Worth Randle, Wally Nelson, Ernest Bromley, Jim Peck, Igal Roodenko, Bayard Rustin, Joe Felmet, George Houser, and Andrew Johnson.

Records of Congress of Racial Equality, Swarthmore College Peace Collection

(Figure 15) Bayard Rustin teaching at School of Nonviolence

Papers of Bayard Rustin, Swarthmore College Peace Collection

(Figure 16) 1950s Civil Defense Protest in New York City

General Miscellaneous Photographs, Swarthmore College Peace Collection

(Figure 17) Anti-Vietnam Protest in Washington, D.C.

Records of Clergy and Laity concerned, Swarthmore College Peace Collection

(Figure 18) 1970s Civil Disobedience Protest at the Pentagon

Records of Mobilization for Survival, Swarthmore College Peace Collection

(Figure 19) Seabrook, New Hampshire, Clamshell Alliance Protest

Records of Clamshell Alliance, Swarthmore College Peace Collection

(Figure 20) Martin Luther King, Jr.

Records of Fellowship of Reconciliation, Swarthmore College Peace Collection

(Figure 21) Erna Harris, 3rd from left, Conference of Soviet and American Women

Records of Women's International League for Peace and Freedom, Swarthmore College Peace Collection

(Figure 22) Coretta Scott King

Records of Women's International League for Peace and Freedom, Swarthmore College Peace Collection

(Figure 23) Bertha Mc Neil, 3rd from left, Delegation to Cuba

Records of Women's International League for Peace and Freedom, Swarthmore College Peace Collection

ANTI-ENLISTMENT LEAGUE

Working Men and Women of the United States:

Your brothers in Europe are destroying each other; the militarists in this country may soon try to send you to the trenches. They will do so in the name of "Defense of Home" or "National Honor," the reasons given to the people of every one of the twelve nations now at war.

But **DO NOT ENLIST.** Think for yourselves. The Workers of the World are YOUR BROTHERS; their wrongs are your wrongs; their good is your good. War stops Trade, and makes vast armies of Unemployed.

DO NOT ENLIST. The time for Defense by Armies is over. Belgium, Germany and Great Britain have defended themselves with the mightiest of fortresses, armies or navies; and today each country suffers untold misery. War can avenge, punish and destroy; but war can NO LONGER defend.

DO NOT ENLIST. Your country needs you for PEACE; to do good and USEFUL work; to destroy POVERTY and bring in INDUSTRIAL JUSTICE.

WOMEN, REFUSE your consent to the enlistment of your men; the TRUE COURAGE is to STAND FOR THE RIGHT and REFUSE TO KILL.

PEACE IS THE DUTY—NOT WAR
MIGHT IS NOT RIGHT
USE YOUR LIGHT
DO NOT FIGHT

Join the ANTI-ENLISTMENT LEAGUE, 61 QUINCY ST., Brooklyn, N. Y.

I, being over eighteen years of age, hereby pledge myself against enlistment as a volunteer for any military or naval service in international war, either offensive or defensive, and against giving my approval to such enlistment on the part of others.

Name ....

Address ....

Committee, JESSIE WALLACE HUGHAN, Secretary,
TRACY D. MYGATT.

Forward to the Anti-Enlistment League,
61 Quincy Street, Brooklyn, New York.

(Figure 24) World War I Anti-Enlistment League Registration Form

Records of the Anti-Enlistment League, Swarthmore College Peace Collection

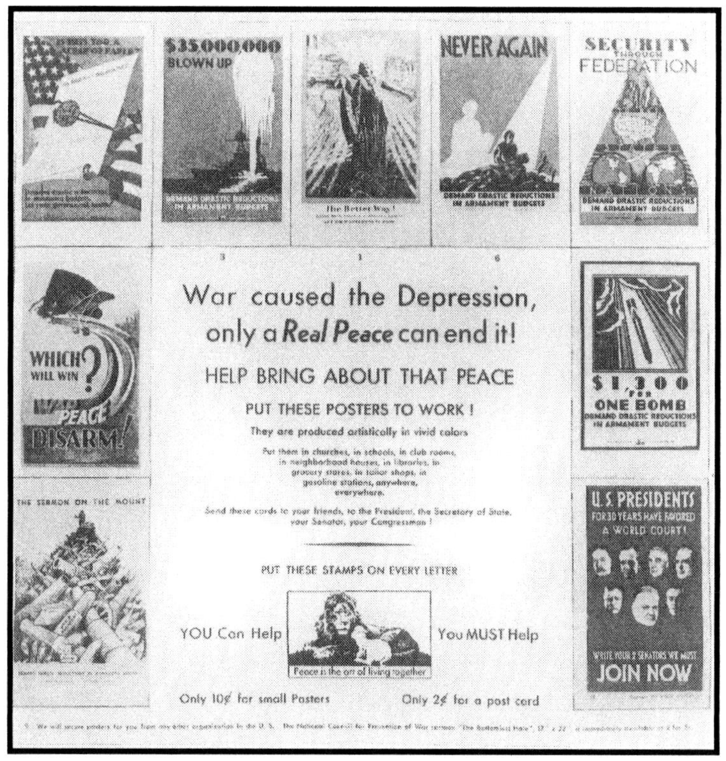

(Figure 25) Interwar Peace Posters and Peace Stamp

General Miscellaneous Photographs, Swarthmore College Peace Collection

(Figure 26) BOOTS 2007 Anti-Iraq War Demonstration

Photo Courtesy of Diane Lent

CHAPTER SIX
WORLD WAR, COLD WAR AND DIRECT ACTION

> The problem which the bomb poses to the world cannot be solved except by abolishing war, and nothing less will do.
>
> Leo Szilard, 1959.

INTRODUCTION

Szilard, one of the most prominent physicists of his time, was more than capable of explaining the devastating impact the bomb posed for the future of civilization. It was his desire, along with many other notable scientists of that generation, including Albert Einstein who had helped create the Atomic Bomb, that nations and their military leaders avoid further attempts to create more dangerous weapons of mass destruction. Clearly, there would be no turning back. The only hope was to provide the forces of peace with enough support so that humankind would survive. The Cold War brought civilization to the brink of extinction, while leading to more dramatic forms of peace protest. Before such events would unfold, the peace movement once more had to confront a nation mobilized for total war.

The Japanese attack on Pearl Harbor led dedicated peace pioneers to protest the war by refusing induction into the armed forces, volunteering for noncombatant service in the Civilian Public Service camps (CPS) or accepting a federal prison term upon conviction, aiding Conscientious Objectors, arguing against the military strategy of saturation bombing, and calling for the Allies to pursue a negotiated settlement. They also called for a more lasting peace; in their view this could come about through the establishment of a new, more workable, international organization which would be acceptable to the American public.

By the close of 1941, they had little to cheer about. The onset of World War II shattered the peacemakers' optimism of the thirties, when they had developed a program of non-violent social change that seemed feasible. In the face of such intense international conflict, that program could not be sustained. Pacifists, in particular, retreated to a defensive position with the approach of war; "they reasserted the essential religious quality of pacifism and emphasized personal resistance to war."[1]

The pacifists' defensive posture surfaced early and was most pronounced during the congressional hearings on the Burke-Wadsworth Bill, popularly known as the Selective Training and Service Act of 1940. The vagueness of pacifist thought on the eve of World War II and the reemphasis of the religious orientation of pacifism, according to historian John M. Glen, proved detrimental to the pacifists' struggle to win recognition for the full range of Conscientious Objections to war and military service. During congressional hearings, many questions were raised and left unanswered by those opponents of the war who testified. The pacifist position seemed unclear, confusing, and muddled. Could objection be based on personal religious belief? What constituted a valid basis for objection – philosophical, humanitarian, or political beliefs? Could religious COs recognize the precepts of secular objectors as comparable to their own? Since no satisfactory answers were supplied, congressmen concluded that they themselves would have to devise a workable formula defining the terms of sincere Conscientious Objection.[2]

The Selective Training and Service Act of 1940 expanded the classification of Conscientious Objectors to include any person who opposed participation in war because of religious training and belief (not just members of the Historic Peace Churches—Society of Friends, the Mennonite Church, and the Church of the Brethren—as was the case in World War I). It also provided for alternative service work under civilian direction (the 1917 law only allowed

Conscientious Objectors the option of non-combatant military service such as the medical corps). Still, pacifists were unsuccessful in their fight to expand the secular connotations of Conscientious Objection. Thus, the small number of pacifists and committed opponents of war during the Second World War may have been a result of their own inability to reconcile "the ethical side of pacifism which sought more political relevance and social usefulness with its more traditional Christian cast."[3]

Compounding this dilemma was an even more troubling issue for them. The persecution of Jews in Nazi Germany proved extremely difficult to deal with. Pacifists were ready to stand on principle and conviction when it came to war. But watching millions of innocent people being discriminated against did little to assuage the underpinnings of what to do when the values of peace are in apparent conflict with decency, humanity, and justice. The argument that violence would only beget more violence led many to offer alternatives to the use of force. It was of little consolation and consequence. But in dealing with this problem the one thing they did try to do was provide war relief supplies and assist in the effort to provide a safe haven for Jews. Religious pacifists in the FOR were quite active in relief efforts and they helped European members of the FOR provide sanctuary to refugees through monetary support. Clearly, it was far easier for members in the peace movement to justify why they would refuse to fight or support war than it was for them to provide a moral justification why they should not take up arms to stop the eventual slaughter of millions of Jews. Some pacifists even went so far as to call for a quick and negotiated peace to save the Jews.

WORLD WAR II AND OPPONENTS OF WAR

In general, the protest against war and militarism in 1941 was much weaker than in 1917. This was attributable not so much to popular enthusiasm for the war than to a kind of public apathy that settled over the American people once they had recovered from the initial shock of Pearl Harbor. More outspoken war opponents who had stood out against war in 1917, especially socialists were divided and less effective. There was also no counterpart in the labor ranks of the mass protest carried out in World War I by the IWW. American communists, who had been active in the peace movement of the 1930's, strongly supported the Roosevelt policies after Russia entered the war in June 1941. They were sorely disappointed at such turn of events and felt betrayed.

The anti-war movement during the Second World War was small but dynamic and intense. Those who chose the course of peace were strong and passionate. Hitler and Mussolini were real threats and the Japanese did strike first; however, that did not hinder the efforts of strongly-committed pacifist groups such as the War Resisters League. Despite constant and unrelenting harassment by the Federal Bureau of Investigation on the grounds of evasion of the Registration Act (Selective Service Act, 1940), the WRL's pamphlets, speeches, and counseling services were not aimed at blatantly obstructing the draft during the war years. They were principally interested in informing pacifists and other individuals of available choices. Believing in the First Amendment's guarantee of freedom of speech, the League's pamphlets criticized the imprisonment of Japanese-Americans for so-called security reasons and insisted "that in this war as in the first World War all nations must share responsibility for the causes leading up to that struggle." One of its leaders, Evan Thomas (Norman's brother) correctly, but impetuously, accused the Allies of having secretly prepared for war. Whatever the case, the WRL, like its ally the FOR, continued the struggle on behalf of peace and respect for individual conscience.[4]

As early as 1937, more than 12,000 Americans had signed the WRL pledge "War is a crime against humanity. I, therefore, am determined not to support any kind of war, international or civil, and to strive for the removal of all causes of war." During the war, WRL had a core base of 2,300 active members who were united in their humanitarian, political, and philosophical objections to war. These hard-core radical pacifists would help spark a more militant civil disobedience movement during the early Cold War years.

JEWISH AND NATIVE AMERICAN OBJECTORS

Equally important were the anti-war efforts of a small number of Jewish pacifists. Approximately two hundred and fifty-one Jewish men refused to comply with induction and spent the war years either in a Civilian Public Service camp or in prison. Some derived their objection from a pacifist interpretation of the Jewish tradition but most based their stand on either political or humanistic grounds. As Jews, they all experienced subtle and sometimes not-so-subtle pressures that distinguished them from their fellow pacifists. Because of Nazi atrocities committed against Jews, they felt more isolated from their communities than the others—as many were ostracized by their friends and neighbors and some were disowned by their own families.

Though Jewish pacifists joined anti-war groups like the WRL and FOR, their recognition of the unique burden they carried led some to work towards the establishment of a separate Jewish peace organization. The original impetus for what would be the Jewish Peace Fellowship was supplied by a Philadelphia resister, Bernard Gross, who felt the need to maintain his Jewish identity in spite of the pro-war stand and intolerance displayed by his fellow Jews. Led by Rabbi Isidor B. Hoffman and a group of Columbia University graduate students, they joined together with pacifist members of the Central Conference of American Rabbis to organize the Jewish Peace Fellowship. The group started out with about forty members and one chapter in New York City. Within a year, New York membership increased to one hundred. New chapters were also established in Philadelphia and Los Angeles. According to its "Statement Of Purpose," the JPF would venture to apply the pacifist way of life to all human affairs, both public and private, to assist financially and spiritually the Jewish conscientious objector in camps or in prison, and to engage in constructive social action on behalf of peace and justice. "No self-respecting member of the JPF can merely <u>refrain</u> from buying war bonds," the statement began. "If his neighbors are giving 10% to this cause, he must give more than 10% to the feeding of the victims of war, to the relief of civilian populations, to the support of CPS [civilian pubic service] and to all the manifold causes which look to us for aid," it continued. Clearly and unequivocally, "We can answer the charge that we are 'aloof pacifists' only by being vigorous 'activists' in service and sacrifice. This is why our organization is exploring opportunities for social action."[5]

No less remarkable was the record of a small number of Native Americans. The Hopi tribe's trouble with the draft began, ironically, with a 1924 Act of Congress granting citizenship to all Indians. When conscription was ordered to meet the need of American entry into World War II, the Hopis were placed in an awkward, ambiguous position. The People of Peace, as they called themselves, had received none of the privileges of citizenship, yet they were expected to deny their belief in non-violence and accept the citizen's responsibility to fight when called upon. Six Hopis from Hotevilla, Arizona, led by Paul Siwingayawma, elected to resist on essentially religious grounds: "For when we came to this continent, we promised our Guardian Spirit to never show our weapon to anyone to destroy him. If we did show our weapon, we would not inherit any land when the next world was established and would lose our chance."[6]

These six Indians were arrested for refusal to register for the draft and were shunted from one jail to another. The court which tried the six, after three months of confinement, ruled that Hopi belief was not a recognized church and provided no grounds for conscientious objector status. The sentence was three years hard labor. They were put to work first at rock-breaking and then farming. It was to the bleakest of prospects that the six Hopis returned from prison as confinement had nearly drained them of the strength needed to carry on their daily struggle to survive.

COs AND CIVILIAN PUBLIC SERVICE CAMPS

The stand by Jewish pacifists and the anti-conscription protest by the six Hopi Indians were characteristic of much of the peace activism during the Second

World War. During World War II, almost 43,000 Americans were Conscientious Objectors: 25,000 received non-combatant status, 11,950 did alternative service work in Civilian Public Camps, and 12,662 draft violators were imprisoned or forced to enter the armed forces. Approximately 6,600 were found guilty and sent to prison because they were unable to meet the requirements for conscientious objector status under the narrow provision of the Selective Service Law. Many were objectors not only to war but also to conscription as well. Refusing to register for the draft, they charged that conscription was incompatible with human freedom. Two-thirds of those sent to prison were Jehovah's Witnesses.

Significantly, this number of 43,000 was three times higher than in the last war. The number who went to prison was almost four times higher than World War I. In A People's History of the United States, Howard Zinn notes that out of every six men sent to federal prison, one was a CO. He also points out that the government listed close to 350,000 cases of draft evasion. For a nation almost unanimously for war, this observation should not be so easily dismissed.

Attorneys who defended COs in court, moreover, were quick to point out that the draft law fell far short of the British policy, enacted and implemented in the National Service Act of 1939, which provided the absolutist objector, whose conscience would not permit him to yield to the dictates of the military state, full exemption from service. According to the counsel of the National Committee on Conscientious Objectors of the American Civil Liberties Union, Julien Cornell, whose widely read works, The Conscientious Objector and the Law (1943) and Conscience and the State (1944), pointed out the shortcomings of the Selective Service Law, alternative service in work of national importance, even under civilian direction, was no substitute for conscientious war resisters.

In October of 1940, eight students at Union Theological Seminary in New York City who had been living in voluntary poverty in Harlem while pursuing their studies initiated the legal confrontation when they refused to register for the draft. The court testimony, given the following year, of Donald Benedict, Joseph J. Bevilacqua, Meredith Dallas, David Dellinger, George M. Houser, William H.

Lovell, Howard E. Spragg, and Richard J. Wichlei expressed their belief that conscription was definitely a part of the institution of war. Their dissent was in keeping with the fundamental American belief in individual conscience. War, they felt, would strip them of that cherished right. Dellinger, Houser, Lovell, Spragg, and Wichlei conveyed their feelings in the following words: "The deeper issue is not that some of the warring nations have a bit more democracy than others, but that all nations are caught in a war system that damns them all equally and will do so eternally unless we do everything in our power now to bring an end to the conditions that breed war. . . ."[7]

For these objectors, it was extremely important to fight against the "totalitarian" nature of conscription and its related institutions, military training and large-scale industrial production. Their stand as objectors was not simply a negative reaction to an unpleasant situation; rather it was an attempt to establish a movement trained in the techniques of non-violent opposition to the encroachments of militarism and fascism. It was, in their opinion, the only possible way to stall the war machine at home.

As the war proceeded, their ranks were swelled by many within the CPS camps. Initially, the major pacifist groups, WRL and FOR, had cooperated in the establishment of an alternative service program for objectors (in 1940 the Historic Peace Churches created a National Service Board for Religious Objectors under the chairmanship of a French Quaker, Paul Comly French; the Board assumed financial responsibility despite military supervision and control of the camps). In fact, when Congress was about to vote on the Selective Service Act in 1940, polls indicated that a third of all Americans called for either forcing COs to fight in combat units or be imprisoned. Congress went along with the plan for alternative service conceived by the various religious groups. Peace groups were convinced that it was the best option that could be salvaged under the circumstances and that CPS camps would render a humanitarian service in a world at war. Yet military control, inconsequential work projects, and a sense of futility led many in the camps to believe their basic principles had been ignored by officials. What surfaced was resentment of the regulations; bitter distrust of the Church for entering into such an alliance; disdain toward the staff, and vociferous demands to set up their own regulations." The poor morale was also reflected in "an astonishing amount of physical incapacitation." The freedom to hold on to one's personal beliefs was gradually dissipating in the seas of authoritarian conformity. One CO, later a noted American historian, Arthur Ekirch, Jr., drew a fitting historical analogy between CPS camps and slavery: "....[T]he pacifist threatens the existing order. His stand may sway some wavering, unenthusiastic supporters of the war. His example is an unpleasant exception to the cult of national unity."[8]

The exact details of the CPS program had not been ironed out until the early months of 1942. Supervision of the program was left in the hands of Quakers, the Brethren, and the Mennonites. The costs of the program were paid by the Historic Peace Churches at the rate of $35 per month for each CO. CPS members received a few dollars each month from church groups; otherwise, they were not paid nor did they seek money from the government for to do so would have implied their tacit acceptance of the war.

In many parts of the country, CPS workers assumed tasks previously assigned to the Civilian Conservation Corps. Those tasks included reforestation, road building, and irrigating areas damaged by drought. The almost 12,000 men conscripted for CPS work performed labor from forty to ninety-six hours a week. Apart from reforestation and soil conservation projects, as well as building roads, they also battled forest fires, constructed sanitary facilities for communities riddled with hookworm, and tended dairy cattle.

The daily life of the CO was strictly regimented. The CO was ordered to remain in his assigned camp or unit at all times except when on duty or given leave. Whenever so ordered he could be moved to another camp. All assigned work was to be carried out promptly and with the utmost efficiency. The CO was responsible for taking care of all government property in his possession. His living quarters, including his person, clothing, and equipment had to be "neat and clean." Lastly, his personal behavior had to be beyond reproach and bring no discredit to himself or to the CPS program.

Apart from physical tasks, men volunteered for dangerous and painful experiments in hospitals and research facilities. There were typhus tests in which the "volunteers"—ironic since they refused volunteering for military service—had to wear lice-infested clothing for three weeks while continuing their usual work day, were placed in semi-starvation diets, and participated in atypical pneumonia experiments that involved drinking throat washings from infected soldiers. Thirty men in CPS died; more than 1,500 were discharged for physical disabilities, and yet their families were not granted any form of compensation for their suffering. "This refusal of the government to provide minimal financial support," historians Heather Frazier and John O'Sullivan argued, "rendered the claim that C.P.S. was a noble exercise in affirming freedom of conscience 'a virtual farce.'" Thus walkouts began in 1942. Arthur Wiser, a son of American missionaries who was schooled in India and who was interred at CPS Camp No. 94 at Trenton, North Dakota, walked out in protest because he felt that "CPS, as the internment of Conscientious Objectors by a wartime government, exists only to assert the state's authority to final jurisdiction over the individual to direct his living, even though professing to recognize a particular scruple of conscience." Soon, the trickle of illegal walkouts broadened into a steady stream, while inside the camps objectors began campaigns of non-violent resistance which spread from coast to coast.[9]

The most notable walk-out took place on October 16, 1942, when Stanley Murphy, Louis Taylor, and George Kingsley walked out of CPS camp No. 46 at Big Flats, New York, to protest the camp system as a form of conscription. Tried in January 1943, each was given two and a half years in the Danbury prison in Connecticut. At the time of his conviction, Kingsley insisted that the CPS program was a "definite compromise" with the system of war.

Rebellious COs brought to the fore the controversy over the CPS program within the pacifist community. The camp militants and those in prisons felt that their leaders and organizations had compromised their beliefs and abandoned them. Pacifists in the peace organizations believed it was their responsibility to aid COs, even at the cost of supporting the CPS program, and not to side with those who adopted a position of non-cooperation; to them, that issue was beside the point. CPS supporters insisted that this program was a far better cry than what took place during the First World War. The objective on the part of peace organizations and religious pacifists was to create an alternative to military service short of going to jail. Those choosing prison over CPS, however, considered their actions in keeping with matters of conscience.

Upon their arrival in prison, as Mulford Q. Sibley and Philip E. Jacob pointed out in their revealing book, Conscription of Conscience: The American State and the Conscientious Objector, 1940-1947, CPS resisters joined their counterparts in organizing an unprecedented revolt behind bars. Fasts, strikes, and programs of total non-cooperation cropped up in the federal penitentiaries at Danbury, Connecticut; Springfield, Missouri; Lewisburg, Pennsylvania; Petersburg, Virginia; Nulan, Michigan; Sandstone, Minnesota; and Ashland, Kentucky.

Significantly, events at the Danbury federal prison initiated the fight against segregation in the nation's prisons. Some of the modern civil rights struggles were foreshadowed during World War II, when imprisoned COs acted to challenge Jim Crow. To many COs who were in jail this "social evil" – segregation in dinning halls and dormitories – elevated their resistance as much as their opposition to war. For black COs such as Wally Nelson and Bayard Rustin it was inconceivable to submit to being forced to sit at segregated tables or to remove themselves from "whites only" tables and rooms.

While watching African Americans like Nelson and Rustin refuse to accept such practices, white COs began joining in by refusing to eat and work until the practice of segregation was abolished. By mid-1943, prolonged hunger strikes were going on throughout the federal prisons. At Danbury striking COs were summarily placed in administrative segregation for 135 days. Prison officials sought to isolate them from the rest of the prison population and from one another. But the separation actually had the reverse effect. Instead of breaking their spirits it actually strengthened it and bonded them even closer. Confined to their own cell and wing of the prison, the COs developed their own sense of community and unique ways of communicating with each other: hollering through the ventilators, talking through the tiny open space below cell doors, and sliding messages to one another in the form of metal disks tied with string. Supporters on the outside managed to acquire appeals from the prisoners that were smuggled out. Once the appeals were distributed and made public to the press, prison officials at Danbury were quickly forced to end the Jim Crow system.

After the 135-day strike shattered Danbury's system of racially segregated dining halls, objectors moved on to new programs of resistance; in early 1946, the prison was "picketed inside and outside by hundreds of sign-carrying pacifists demanding amnesty for all Selective Service violators and war resisters." Some pacifists even "refused parole, rejecting release from prison on any terms except absolute freedom."[10]

This growing radicalization led to major changes within the pacifist movement as the militant non-cooperatives, released from the camps and prisons, began swelling the ranks of many of the non-violent organizations and transforming them into more radical, activist-oriented groups. Similar to what had happened during World War I, the peace movement would undergo another transformation. While upholding the banner of non-violent resistance, militants would also engage in civil disobedience tactics thereby challenging the very basis of law and order.

STRUGGLE FOR RACIAL EQUALITY

As the COs resistance to segregation in prison suggests, the issue of racial justice drew peace activists into the black freedom struggle. Unlike World War I when African Americans were relatively quiet and supported the conflict, the Second World War witnessed a different attitude. Although African Americans generally supported the war they were more determined than ever to continue the struggle for full equality. During the war membership in the NAACP increased from 50,000 to 450,000 thus reflecting a growing insistence to be heard. The double V campaign (victory against the fascist powers and victory for racial justice at home) and the call by A. Philip Randolph to organize a March on Washington to protest racial discrimination in defense industries were clear indications of rising racial militancy.

In an effort to maintain consistency with their commitment to social justice pioneers for peace were more than eager to act in concert with their black brethren. Sensing the mood of black activism and a growing understanding of international affairs and Gandhian non-violence on the part of blacks – Randolph, among others began promoting Gandhian non-violence as an important political tool for advancing civil rights – peace activists considered the struggle for racial justice part of their larger program for universal brotherhood and global harmony.

The connection between peace workers and black activists would prove to have long-lasting implications. One root of the modern civil rights struggle can be traced to actions initiated by a Chicago pacifist group in 1942. It is noteworthy that their efforts to combat racism began in the North. When the Chicago Committee of Racial Equality organized sit-ins by small interracial groups at Stoner's—a white tablecloth restaurant in the heart of Chicago's Loop—the participants little dreamt that within two decades this type of action would have changed the entire face of the South regarding segregation in public places.

So successful was the Committee in cracking the color line along Chicago's Loop that a national conference of persons and groups interested in this technique was called the following year. The result was the establishment of CORE (Congress of Racial Equality), a federation of local interracial groups using the tactic of non-violent direct action. National coordinators George Houser and Bayard Rustin worked out of the Fellowship of Reconciliation office in New York.

During its early years, local CORE groups picketed restaurants, amusement parks, swimming pools, barber shops, hotels, bowling alleys, playgrounds, and theaters in northern cities; local groups targeted one at a time. All the groups were small, comprising fewer than fifty persons, and sometimes as few as a dozen. But while progress was slow, it was steady. Rarely did a campaign fail, thanks in large part to the non-violent pursuit of racial justice.[11]

Determined to fight racial injustice "without fear, without compromise, and without hatred," CORE members pioneered in their efforts to apply Gandhian methods in opposition to discrimination and segregation. FOR leaders George Houser, who was also Executive Secretary of CORE, A.J. Muste, and James Farmer (FOR's Race Relations Secretary), along with Rustin, supported the establishment of CORE groups in Detroit, Syracuse, and New York City. Through its summer workshops and direct actions, CORE successfully trained hundreds of organizers in the techniques of non-violent action. By 1948, CORE had integrated theatres in Denver, restaurants in Detroit, a public bath in Los Angeles, and Palisades Amusement Park in New Jersey.

CORE also took the issue of racial injustice to the national level after the U.S. Supreme Court's 1946 decision outlawing segregation in interstate travel. In the spring of 1947, CORE and FOR co-sponsored the first freedom ride, known as the Journey of Reconciliation. An interracial group of protestors that included George Houser, Bayard Rustin, Jim Peck, and Ernest Bromley, among others, hopped aboard Greyhound and Trailway buses in order to test the Court's decision. The freedom riders rode through the upper South where they encountered little harassment, but some arrests. Rustin, Igal Roodenko, and Joe Felmet were arrested and given thirty-day sentences on segregated North Carolina chain-gangs for sitting together in the front of a Greyhound bus. This Journey of Reconciliation garnered national publicity for CORE and served as a model for later non-violent direct action efforts.

The Journey of Reconciliation also cast light on one of the more important African American figures in both the peace and civil rights movements: Bayard

Rustin. Rustin, a CO in World War II and close associate of Martin Luther King, Jr., A.J. Muste, and A. Philip Randolph, was an important theoretician and organizer of the late 1950s and early 1960s civil rights movement. Rustin was raised in West Chester, Pennsylvania, a suburb of Philadelphia. In the thirties, he moved to New York where he sang with Leadbelly and Josh White. In 1938, he became an organizer for the Young Communist League but resigned after the 1939 Nazi-Soviet Non-Aggression Pact. He then joined the FOR and, for the next twelve years, served as Field Secretary and then Race Relations Secretary. Along with Muste and Farmer, he helped create CORE.

During World War II, Rustin spent twenty-eight months in prison. He condemned the pacifist community for supporting the CPS program. When he was released from prison in 1946, he led the Free India Committee and later spent six months in India learning about Gandhi's non-violent direct action techniques. He then served as Executive Secretary of the War Resisters League from 1953 to 1965; his work moved the League in a more radical direction in such areas as disarmament and civil rights. In 1955, Rustin helped King dramatize the Montgomery bus boycott (organized by women) and was responsible for developing the plan that led to the creation of the Southern Christian Leadership Conference (SCLC). He is given credit for organizing the massive 1963 civil rights March on Washington where King delivered his famous "I Have a Dream" speech. A coalition builder, Rustin was one of the major architects of the modern civil rights movement -- a movement built upon the principles of non-violent direct action.[12]

The inspiration provided by African American COs like Rustin convinced other white peace activists to extend the struggle for racial justice beyond American shores. One such person was John Nevin Sayre of the FOR. After World War II, black intellectuals led the way in drawing links between decolonization and black rights at home. Black pacifists such as WWII COs Bill Sutherland and William Worthy were quick to point out the problem of U.S. support for apartheid in South Africa, while noting that the struggle over Africa's future in the context of the Cold War could become the spark for igniting nuclear war between the United States and the Soviet Union.

Mindful of African American concerns in Africa, Sayre and the FOR encouraged other peace pioneers to work for the abolition of apartheid. He followed the lead of Bill Sutherland who was deeply involved in linking African American concerns to the problems in South Africa. Sayre was also alerted to Worthy's efforts on behalf of the UN's Economic and Social Council to address the growing issues of African nationalism and the end of colonialism in the post-World War II period, and he acquainted himself with the emerging writings of Pan Africanist scholar John Henrik Clarke.

In South Africa there were 2,500,000 whites who kept themselves apart from and restricted basic rights of some 9,500,000 Africans and Asian Indians. Demonstrations using non-violence to protest apartheid were taking place when Sayre arrived in 1951-1952. Meeting with the Reverend Arthur Blaxall, secretary for the Christian Council of South Africa, Sayre used Fellowship resources on behalf of the fight for racial justice. Initiated by the FOR, a public campaign began in which both whites and minorities opposed to apartheid placed a piece of white cloth over a button and then sewed it to their coat or blouse. Those wearing the white button agreed not to resort to violence when conducting their protests. Anyone wearing the white button would be greeted with a smile. It turned out to be a very successful campaign not only in support of non-violence but also in throwing off attempts to suppress opponents of racial injustice. As more and more people were arrested for protesting apartheid by wearing the buttons, the campaign gained more attention on the world stage.

The efforts by Sayre and the FOR, African Americans such as Sutherland (in 1959 he traveled with Rustin and Muste to the Sahara Desert to protest France's nuclear testing program), Worthy (he distributed leaflets at the UN calling for mediation rather than intervention at the start of the Korean War), and Clarke (a prolific writer who spent his scholarly career discussing the role of Africans in Africa to black Americans), as well as black activists in South Africa, set the stage for the long struggle ahead. Equally important, peace pioneers in the United States were quick to recognize that the struggle for racial justice at home and around the world was an important component to the campaign for world peace. What they realized was that you could not achieve one without the other.

JAPANESE-AMERICANS AND INTERNMENT CAMPS

The courage CPS war resisters displayed and civil rights and anti-apartheid activists demonstrated was matched by that of Japanese-Americans. Their internment represents one of the most serious constitutional breaches in American history. The U.S. government and citizens treated Japanese and Japanese-Americans living mainly on the West Coast as a threat to the country. Panic-stricken citizens feared that the Japanese were agents of the emperor and could do immediate harm. Action taken by the United States government was swift, efficient, and unremorseful. First, all Americans of Japanese descent were asked to move voluntarily from strategic coastal areas. This alone was devastating. Time was short and property was sacrificed. Stricter measures followed, and all Japanese and Japanese-Americans, despite their loyalty to the U.S., were assembled at "Concentration points," with military guards to hold off resentful inland whites still mourning over losses at Pearl Harbor.

After President Roosevelt signed Executive Order 9066 in February 1942, some 110,000 men, women, and children were taken from their homes and transported by Army convoys into the interior of the U.S. where they found themselves forced to live in internment camps. Three-fourths were Nisei – children born in the United States of Japanese parents. Not only did they lose their homes, property, and businesses totaling in the millions of dollars, but they were confined to cramped barracks in bleak conditions.[13]

Conditions of overcrowding, unsanitary toilet and bathing facilities, curfews, and other forms of military control were both degrading and humiliating. At many of the internment camps strikes, petitions, refusal to sign loyalty oaths, and riots took place. Although there were some who questioned the legitimacy and wisdom of the forced evacuation of Japanese and Japanese-Americans on the West Coast, the majority of Americans remained silent and took comfort under the umbrella of national security.

That was not the case, however, for the FOR's Co-Executive Secretary, Sayre. In numerous reports to his council Sayre urged the FOR to monitor the forced internment and to assist Japanese Americans who had lost all their possessions. Under his guidance Sayre sent letters to American officials on behalf of the FOR seeking relief for those kept in the internment camps and to make sure that they were being treated properly. The FOR and other pacifist groups also condemned the forced internment as a violation of American civil liberties. What is most important is that pacifists encouraged Japanese-Americans to challenge this policy in court in the same manner that COs fought to protect their consciences.

Three Japanese-Americans refused to buckle under to forced internment. Gordon Hirabayashi, a Quaker law student, refused to cooperate with curfew and evacuation orders, which he labeled the poisoning of human personality. He was found guilty and jailed for his violations. Despite a spirited defense, he failed to convince the Supreme Court, which unanimously upheld the curfew measures.

Fred Korematsu tried another approach, one that a few Japanese-Americans used in their struggle to avoid forced internment: he Americanized his last name. When he was finally caught, court-supervised probation was ordered, but the Army seized him and shipped him off to camp. Again the Supreme Court upheld detention by a 6-3 decision.

The Korematsu case is particularly disturbing since, as Peter Irons shows in Justice at War, two key government lawyers, Edward Ennis and John L. Burling, knowingly permitted Solicitor General Charles Fahey to submit mendacious material to the court. Had these lawyers resigned in protest, the case might have gone the other way.

Though the legal system failed Korematsu in 1942, Irons' research convinced him that there were grounds for a writ of error, coram nobis. Working with a group of primarily Asian American lawyers, Irons helped secure a reversal of Korematsu's conviction in federal district court in November 1983. Judge Marilyn Hall Patel pointed out rather tellingly that Korematsu "should continue to stand for a caution that in times of war, military necessity or national security, our institutions must be all the more vigilant of protecting constitutional guarantees."[14]

Korematsu's fate was not shared by Mitsuye Endo, who petitioned for a writ of habeas corpus. Endo claimed that as a loyal citizen she could not lawfully be contained in a camp. In late 1944, two years after the suit had been filed, the Supreme Court handed down a unanimous verdict that the government had no right to confine citizens without due process of law. The very next day the mass exclusion orders were revoked. It ended one of the most blatant cases involving the denial of the fifth and fourteenth amendments in American history.

PEACE NOW MOVEMENT

Notable efforts of organized and individual war resistance did inspire some attempts by groups such as The Peace Now Movement of 1943. PNM members argued that a negotiated peace was more humane, more politically astute, more economically viable, and more capable of guaranteeing a lasting peace than a settlement forced by the victors on the defeated nations.[15]

George W. Hartmann (a thirty-eight year old professor of psychology at Columbia University Teachers College, Director of the Jane Addams Peace School at New York City's Labor Temple, and Vice-Chairman of the WRL) and Dorothy Hewitt Hutchinson (a Quaker) initiated the "peace now" campaign, organizing a meeting of people interested in a negotiated peace at Philadelphia's Hotel Whittier on July 10 and 11, 1943.[16] In addition to Hartman and Dorothy

Hutchinson, participants included Frederick Libby, Hannah Clothier Hull (WILPF), Mark Shaw (NCPW), Theodore Walser (FOR), and two non-affiliated pacifists, Bessie Simon and John Albert Collett. An organizing committee was formed to promote the prospects of a negotiated peace within the existing peace organizations and to seek the help of non-pacifists who wanted to end the war.

What motivated them was a desire to resurrect the anti-war coalitions of the late 1930s in an attempt to bridge the gap between isolationist desires and internationalist concerns for a lasting world order. What distinguished their efforts from previous ventures was their determination to seek political solutions for the cessation of all military action in exchanged for a negotiated peace. Instead of just opposing war or speaking out against it, "peace now" wanted to bring all warring factions to the bargaining table. They specifically wanted to avoid duplicating the efforts of the existing peace organizations by trying to resurrect the pre-war coalition of both pacifists and non-pacifists. Before adjourning, they chose the name Peace Now Movement and approved a tentative $25,000 budget.[17]

The primary goal of PNM was to garner support for an earnest Allied peace aims statement containing plans for simultaneous demobilization and disarmament, food for the hungry, an economic organization of Europe with Germany as the dominant member, freedom for all ethnic groups, international currency stabilization, a world bank, creation of an Asian and American federation, and continuing discussions aimed at designating new national boundaries in Europe. The organization argued that nationalism and absolute sovereignty were outdated concepts that should be replaced by a postwar internationalism. The one instructive lesson this anti-war organization attempted was to convince the American people that peace without military victory was a more palatable alternative to the continuing brutality of the world war. Uppermost to Collett and Hartmann was the view that a negotiated peace did not mean "abject surrender." What an immediate peace would do was confirm the positions of Germany and the United States as the two dominant world powers and provide all the belligerents the opportunity to transcend petty discussions of war guilt in favor of making a permanent peace.

No sooner was this non-member organization established than disagreement arose between pacifists over strategy and personalities. The personal idiosyncrasies of some PNM advocates, like Collett and Hartmann, precluded their acceptance by such groups as the Fellowship of Reconciliation, the Women's International League for Peace and Freedom, and the American Friends Service Committee. A.J. Muste became fearful that the whole peace movement would be discredited for giving up its opposition to all forms of war as a result of the PNM's actions. These factors, along with a hostile press and congressional harassment, caused the demise of the Peace Now Movement.

OPPOSITION TO OBLITERATION BOMBING

Consistency among pacifists was dramatically demonstrated by their public castigation of the Allied saturation bombing of European cities. In March 1944, John Nevin Sayre, editor of the FOR's organ Fellowship, pulled off the editorial *coup* of his career when he published a vigorous denunciation of the bombing of German cities. The publication in Fellowship, "Massacre by Bombing," was written by the English pacifist and noted author Vera Brittain. This masterful piece singled out for particular attention the bombing of innocent women and children. With factual precision, Brittain listed the number of civilian casualties city by city. "It is only when the facts are collected, and the terrible sum of suffering. . . estimated as a whole," Brittain wrote, "that we realize that, owing to our raids, hundreds of thousands of helpless and innocent people. . .are being subjected to agonizing forms of death and injury comparable to the worst tortures of the Middle Ages." Brittain's article was signed by twenty-eight American religious leaders including Harry Emerson Fosdick, John Haynes Holmes, Kirby Page and publisher Oswald Garrison Villard, and it was widely distributed among anti-war advocates in a plea for compassion toward non-combatants.[18]

The publication of Brittain's article in an American periodical drew a furious response. Letters arriving to the New York Times were reported as fifty-to-one opposed to the pacifist appeal to stop the bombing campaign. The noted journalist and author of the popular Berlin Diary, William L. Shirer, publicly denounced Brittain and called into question the authenticity of her facts and figures. President Roosevelt issued his own "stinging rebuke" to the twenty-eight Americans who signed the manifesto against mass bombing. Brittain herself estimated that she had been condemned in at least two hundred articles. But, in "Not Made in Germany," a specific response to Shirer's and Roosevelt's remarks, Brittain heroically defended her arguments against obliteration bombing. She upheld the integrity of the twenty-eight persons who signed the manifesto. She argued that they were "helping to preserve the highest traditions of that Western Civilization which the President entered the war to defend," and asked, "If the State is indeed all, and those who criticize its policy must be ranked with its enemies," Brittain pleaded, "for what are we fighting the Nazis?"[19]

RELIEF TO WAR VICTIMS

While the rhetoric and publicity surrounding the pacifist condemnation of mass bombings had no effect on the Allied war policy, war resistors, led by the major peace groups, had more impact when they turned their attention to the administration of relief and rehabilitation programs during and after the war. Relief to war victims had become a basic part of the "modern" peace movement's agenda. After World War I the American Friends Service Committee played a vital role in the reconstruction of war-torn Europe. Many Quakers rebuilt homes and schools in northern France and Belgium. During the Spanish civil war the AFSC and Fellowship sent food and medical supplies to the victims of fascist aerial bombings. Left-wing sympathizers in America collected money to aid the

Spanish Republic and organized the Abraham Lincoln Brigade, which fought alongside the Loyalists in Spain. Famous writer Ernest Hemingway, whose work For Whom the Bells Toll is based on the civil war, served as an ambulance driver in the conflict.

Perhaps relief work was the peace movement's way of trying to salve its conscience when its came to the persecution of Jews in Germany. It may also have been in response to the U.S. policy of not allowing many refugees to seek asylum in America. AFSC and the WILPF were particularly active in rendering relief and assistance. Other peace organizations such as the FOR would also lend its resources in the cause of humanity. There would be many examples of humanitarian assistance by American peace groups.

Replacing the tactic of militant opposition to war with a more "positive pacifism," war resistors used their collective efforts to help the victims of war. Peace groups worked assiduously in Congress to secure authorization to send shipments of food and relief supplies to famished European nations occupied by German troops. Although the humanitarian plan made some inroads within political circles, the Administration refused to endorse it, maintaining that Germany should be made to bear full responsibility for her captive territories.

Working without political endorsement, the Historic Peace Churches by 1942 had provided over $300,000 in assistance to war-torn areas in Poland, France, India, China, and England while also sending relief workers and supplies to France and China. The AFSC operated the Friends Ambulance Unit in China, aided in relief in India, cared for war victims in France, and assisted the United Nations Relief and Rehabilitation Administration in the Mediterranean area. John Nevin Sayre headed up a War Victims Fund during the war, with aid going to individuals and organizations such as the school and community at Le Chambron headed by Andre Trocme and Edouard Theis. Premsyl Pitter's homes for children from concentration camps in Czechoslovakia also received much needed funds. Pressured by the WILPF, Roosevelt accepted a plan to expand the number of refugees admitted to the country by establishing the War Refugee Board.

INTERNATIONALISTS AND PEACEKEEPING MACHINERY

Meantime, internationalists working under the slogan "Win the War, Win the Peace," formed a coalition of old-line Wilsonians, one-world federalists, and Protestants like John Foster Dulles for developing a new post-war league. With Eichelberger and Shotwell at the helm, a Commission to Study the Organization of Peace was established. With the aid of the Federal Union, Inc., a world federation group formed in 1941 as an outgrowth of Clarence Streit's call for a new world order in Union Now (they employed the term "One World" and boasted among their ranks Dorothy Thompson, Clare Booth Luce, and Robert Sherwood). So, too, did former Republican presidential candidate Wendell Willkie's One World (an immensely popular pamphlet). Along with the Woodrow Wilson Foundation (established in 1923 in honor of the ex-President's ideas) and the conservative peace organizations (like CEIP and LNA), the commission was successful in pushing the administration in the direction of forming a new organization for peace, the United Nations (UN). In 1944 at the Dumbarton Oaks Conference, preliminary plans for the United Nations were drawn up. A year later in June, internationalists were elated at the birth of the UN in San Francisco.[20]

The creation of the UN was spearheaded by the United States and peace groups like WILPF—Detzer went to Dumbarton Oaks. When President Roosevelt entered the White House in March of 1933, he was intent upon establishing a new international organization to replace the failing League of Nations. In 1920, as the Democratic nominee for vice-president, Roosevelt had presented more than eight hundred speeches supporting U.S. membership in the League of Nations. Despite Senate rejection of the Treaty of Versailles and failure to participate in the League, Roosevelt persisted in offering his own ideas on the topic of international peacekeeping machinery. In 1923, he submitted his own ideas for the Edward Bok Peace Award that was won by Charles Levermore. His plan was somewhat similar to the one put forward at Dumbarton Oaks twenty-one years later.

During the war Roosevelt continued to promote the idea of an international peace organization. He also believed that the balance-of-power approach to world order was insufficient. Incorporating ideas he first proposed in the late 1930s during the neutrality debates, the wartime president insisted that real peace could only be achieved and secured through an interstate organization that could rapidly and quickly "quarantine" aggressor countries. The UN Charter ultimately contained two central and very important principles that differentiated it from the League. First, the use of force was banned in interstate relations unless in self-defense or authorized by the Security Council. The UN also had its own military force, composed of member states, to strengthen the notion of collective security through centralized control. Second, the League's principle of unanimity was replaced with a majority vote, but permanent members of the new Security Council, which included the United States, Soviet Union, France, Great Britain, and Nationalist China, at the time, had the right to veto substantive decisions of the entire body. The main purpose of the UN, as conceived by the wartime allies, was to promote international peace and security. Although Roosevelt did not live to see the implementation of the UN, internationalists praised his efforts and pacifists cautiously endorsed the new organization's attempt to maintain world peace.

The importance of the UN to African Americans is also a critical story in the struggle for peace and justice. The postwar civil rights movement witnessed a growing link between black freedom at home and human rights abroad. Not only did prominent African American spokesmen such as W.E.B. Du Bois, A. Philip Randolph, and Paul Robeson hailed the UN's creation but also mainstream members of the black community. The African American community believed that the new international organization would lead the way in ending colonialism and bring forth a new era of human rights. It was hoped that by garnering an international perspective the issue of human rights would extend beyond the narrower definition of civil rights, which many understood to be political and legal equality. The African American community began urging the UN to play a pivotal role in defining the notion of rights to include social and economic justice. Domestically, this notion encompassed better educational facilities, housing, health care, and employment. For African Americans and many other peace and social justice activists the UN's creation was more than just an instrument to maintain world peace. It was also an organization that was designed to expand the world's understanding of the true meaning of human rights.

A WEAPON TO END THE WAR

While the United States talked about winning the peace through international cooperation and peacekeeping, it had begun covert work on developing the most destructive weapon in history: the Atomic Bomb. Though some atomic scientists such as James Franck and Leo Szilard expressed concern for humanity's future, the immediate government objective was to win the war. With Roosevelt's death in April 1945, Harry S. Truman of Missouri assumed the presidency and with it responsibility for America's war aims.[21]

Truman, who was not well prepared for the presidency, was faced with the most difficult choice of his political career. With the war in Europe virtually at an end in May 1945, the question arose as to how many men would have to be sacrificed before Japan finally surrendered. With the successful testing of the A-bomb at Alamogordo, New Mexico, he believed he had his answer: not that many.

Historians such as Gar Alperovitz, Martin J. Sherwin, and Barton Bernstein, among others, have contributed to the historiographical debate over whether or not the bomb was necessary for ending the war and thus eliminating the need for an invasion of Japan. This position was raised by top-ranking military officers during the war and peace groups after the war ended. Moreover, peace groups argued that though the bomb may have ended the war it now placed the entire world at risk.

Ironically, while the United States hosted the founding of the UN in June, two months later it dropped two A-bombs on the Japanese cities of Hiroshima and Nagasaki. With the push of two release buttons, America ended the Second World War but put in doubt the effectiveness of any peacekeeping organization.

Many Americans rejoiced when the war ended and two Japanese cities were spectacularly destroyed by a formidable new weapon. Newspaper headlines everywhere throbbed with excitement over the untold promise represented by the opening of the nuclear age. But the editor of the Catholic Worker recognized immediately what the awesome new weapon portended: "....We have killed 318,000 Japanese...they have vaporized our Japanese brothers, scattered men, women and babies to the four winds, over the seven seas. Perhaps we will breathe their dust into our nostrils, feel them in the fog of New York on our faces, feel them in the rain on the hills of Easton."[22]

Other peace activists also condemned the Atomic Bomb. One was Norman Cousins, who would later become the moving force behind the Committee for a Sane Nuclear Policy (SANE). At this time Cousins was serving as the young editor of the Saturday Review. The night of the bombing he sat down and composed a noted editorial, "Modern Man Is Obsolete." The thrust of his article was quite simple: humankind's survival is now totally contingent upon avoiding a new, more catastrophic, war. He quickly became a new recruit for the peace movement. Others would follow, such as liberal news commentator Raymond Gram Swing, who was so concerned that he devoted one out of every five of his radio broadcasts to serious discussions on the ramifications of atomic energy and what it meant to civilization's future.

RISE OF A GARRISON STATE

The end of the war brought only temporary peace. It also brought forth a national-security state of enormous proportions, as well as a permanent wartime economy. The heightening tensions between the United States and the Soviet

Union, formally called the Cold War, led to the following government actions: creation of the National Security Council, Central Intelligence Agency, National Security Resources Board, extension of the Selective Service Act; and the appropriation of billions of dollars for the development of a nuclear arsenal. The peacemakers' attempts to establish a cooperative peace beyond the reach of Great Power predominance became ever more challenging.

The predominance of a new militarism in post-war America had widespread repercussions. In The Economic Basis of Politics (1945), Charles Beard emphasized the role of the military as an independent interest commanding power in the modern state. Like Marx's "economic man," Beard's "military man" would plot an expanding role in the public and foreign affairs of the United States. He warned that the prospect of Universal Military Training—something that had been discussed during the war and its aftermath—would result in large numbers of persons with armed services careers. Though the "military man" may not be more warlike than civilians, he nevertheless possesses a set of values which differs greatly from civilian values. The "military man" with his insatiable demand for materials would be heavily dependent on economic production, Beard noted, and this would lead to the "economic underwriting" of the modern state. Thus, as the power of the military extended into areas of American life previously reserved for civilians, the contrast between the citizen and the soldier would become less and less apparent.

Moreover, as the noted British political scientist Harold J. Laski pointed out in fervent overtones: "In the United States as elsewhere, the technological implications of modern warfare may make possible a new type of militarism unrecognizable to those who look for its historical characteristics." "Anyone who thinks for one moment of the effort involved in building the atomic bomb," Laski added, "will not find it difficult to realize that, in the new warfare, the engineering factory is a unit of the army, and the worker may be in uniform without being aware of it." The new militarism, he continued, "may clothe itself in civilian uniform, and, if the present relations of production are maintained, it may be imposed upon people who see in its development no more than a way to full employment."[23] The time-honored historical distinctions between military and civilian affairs in American life became less and less obvious.

With Beard and Laski leading the way others picked up the pace. One of the more important critics was Columbia University sociologist C. Wright Mills. In his powerful work, The Power Elite, he charged that significant connections had been established between the Pentagon, defense industry, and universities in support of Cold War policies furthering the militarization of society. Mills' argument was controversial, but similar concerns were raised by President Dwight D. Eisenhower in his Farewell Address. The distinguished General of the Army during World War II and former West Point graduate also warned Americans about the threat posed to democracy by the expanding military-industrial complex.

The new militarism was most apparent in the large percentage of the national budget devoted to war preparation and in the close connection between the armed forces and American industry. Prior to World War II military expenditures constituted less than one-quarter of the total national budget. Concerns for disarmament and disillusionment with World War I led to reduced military spending despite the creation of the R.O.T.C. program and support for naval preparedness. The Second World War and continuation of a peacetime draft due to Cold War fears saw military expenditures increase dramatically; expenditures for military prepredeness would continue to grow during the Cold War.

To support the largest peacetime military establishment in American history, approximately one-third of the Federal budget, $12 billion, was appropriated in 1947 for the armed forces.[24] Most certainly, it had frightening implications for a democratic society. The conversion of the War Department to Department of Defense, the creation of a separate military branch for the Air Force, and the classified document NSC-68 in 1950 that set Cold War policy firmly in place with a large-scale military budget presented serious challenges.

Even if the new-war type economy could be maintained without impairing the American standard of living, it created other problems. The inflationary economics of preparedness disregarded the individual consumer, except as his or her interests served those of the state. As the government entered private business and industry, it was involved also in practices incompatible with free and responsible self-government. It became a partner and accomplice in some of the illegal and monopolist techniques of big business. Morality in American politics was subject to a new kind of institutionalized graft dependent on securing governmental contracts. Although the standards of individual government employees were often high, the maze of government-business relations fostered the rise of a new profession of high-powered lobbyists bent on securing federal spoils for their wealthy clients. As vocal activists in the 1960s would point out, the university also became more concerned with gaining government contracts than promoting free inquiry.

CONCERNED ATOMIC SCIENTISTS

One important example of the way the traditions of free economic enterprise and scientific inquiry were subordinated to the demands of modern state capitalism was the passage of the Atomic Energy Act of August 1946. When the United Nations—chartered in San Francisco in 1945 with full U.S. support to create a new international peacekeeping organization—proved unable to agree on a plan of international control satisfactory to both Russia and the United States (specifically the U.S. proposal drawn up by Bernard Baruch), the continued production of atomic bombs and other nuclear material remained in the hands of the United States. To administer the United States monopoly, Congress gave the Atomic Energy Commission full control of nuclear power development. Even though the Commission "planned for the eventual private use of some forms of atomic energy, considerations of national security required that the military retain control over all major work in the field of nuclear fission." The Atomic

Energy Commission in closely guarding its mission also took satisfaction by claiming that the "chief fruits of the greatest discovery of modern science were the constant production of instruments of military import."[25]

Concerned atomic scientists and engineers, led by Leo Szilard and Eugene Rabinowitch, formed the Federation of Atomic Scientists in November 1945; in early 1946, it broadened its base and became the Federation of American Scientists. Knowing there was no defense against nuclear annihilation and looking back on their scientific achievement with chagrin, members of the FAS called upon the government to promote international control of atomic weapons. Their interest had been reinforced by the May 29, 1946, radio address of the esteemed pacifist physicist Albert Einstein, who announced categorically that "The development of technology and military weapons has resulted in what amounts to a shrinking of our planet. . . . The offensive weapons now available leave no spot on earth secure from sudden, total annihilation." With approximately 3,000 members FAS sought to make clear the threat posed by atomic weapons. J. Robert Oppenheimer, chief scientist of the Manhattan A-Bomb project, popularized the message by stating that "I do not believe . . . that we can...measure...the defense of our people, our lives, our institutions, our cities," by relying on the use of the atom for the nation's security. It was a chilling and frightening prospect.[26]

Though the post-war scientists did alert the public to the dangers of atomic and later nuclear warfare in the pages of The Bulletin of the Atomic Scientists, their influence in politics was weak contrasted with their effectiveness in thermonuclear physics.[27] The intensification of Cold War hostilities caused a schism in the scientific community over whether the United States should develop the hydrogen bomb. The success of the communists in China, Russia's first atomic explosion in September 1949, the onset of the Korean War in June 1950, and Truman's decision to detonate an H-bomb of untold dimensions in 1951, left pro-peace scientists were left with "the realization that they could move mountains—replacing them with craters—but not the political machinery which governs society."[28] Overseas events and a tightening dragnet placed on so-called subversives (alleged communist sympathizers) by the FBI silenced the scientific critics along with others who shared their views.[29]

PROGRESSIVES, COMMUNISTS AND THE PEACE MOVEMENT

The Cold War and the accompanying new Red Scare put peace proponents on the defensive. The 1948 presidential election, for instance, led the government and public to renew the 1920s charges of grass-roots peace activism as subversive. As the Cold War intensified, a group of concerned citizens formed the Progressive Citizens of America in 1946. By mid-1947, the organization had about 25,000 members with chapters in 19 states. The organization had developed from a working class base; many came from the industrial organizing drives of the 1930s and had been affiliated with the Congress of Industrial Organization. In the 1948 presidential election, the group supported Franklin D. Roosevelt's former vice president Henry Wallace. This group created the Progressive Party with a platform calling for a repeal of the draft, negotiating with the Soviet Union to resolve the arms race and secure a permanent peace and an end to military and economic support for anti-democratic forces in China, Greece, Turkey, the Mideast, and Latin America. Running on a peace platform, Wallace and his Progressive Party also called for self-determination for all colonial areas, support for national liberation struggles in Africa and racial justice at home, strengthening the United Nations' ability to secure peace, and outlawing the atomic bomb.

Wallace created quite a stir, drawing large crowds to hear his message of "Peace, Freedom, and Abundance." but by the time the November 1948 elections rolled around, anti-communist sentiment was so pervasive that Wallace received only a million votes for president. The CIO, led by Walter Reuther, and the Association of Catholic Trade Unions launched an all-out campaign to defeat Wallace. "Redbaiting" increased at an alarming rate. Both the Left and the peace movement came under constant attack from newspapers and the government, especially from the House Un-American Activities Committee and the Senate Internal Security Committee, led by Richard Nixon and Joseph McCarthy respectively. Even liberals joined the witch hunt, attacking the Progressive Party and working to rid their own organizations of any communist ties or influence. This strategy backfired as peace efforts in the United States became so narrowly construed as to imply that any attempts to achieve world harmony were inextricably linked to communism. Communists in America were very active in the campaign for world peace as evidenced by their support for Wallace and the Progressive Party, their participation at the Scientific Conference for World Peace held at the Waldorf-Astoria Hotel in Manhattan in March of 1949, and their work with the Peace Information Center, which circulated the Stockholm Peace Petition calling for a ban on atomic weapons.

The problem was that, although American communists had a genuine interest in peace, they connected it with the fortunes of the Soviet Union. Thus, anyone promoting peaceful co-existence became suspected of disloyalty. Peace groups such as the FOR and WILPF, searching for respectability during these troubling times, did everything in their power to distance themselves from anything remotely connected to communist efforts for peace. One of the great ironies of this period was that Cold War liberals, fearful of a return to a post World War I pattern of isolationist pacifism, now resorted to a militant, interventionist internationalism. Another irony was that in the name of defending democracy, many liberals acted in undemocratic ways to keep their organizations free of any accusations of communism. Organizations such as the ACLU, NAACP, WILPF, and Committee for a SANE Nuclear Policy were examples of such house cleaning. In defending Cold War America many left intellectuals cut peace activists off from their traditional bases of support and created a large credibility gap. Undeniably, former war liberals were now competing with conservatives for leadership in the battle against communism. Nowhere was this more glaringly apparent than in the efforts of patriotic nationalists to denigrate those who supported both peaceful co-existence with the Soviet Union and civil rights in America. The experience of noted African-American singer Paul Robeson, at Peekskill, New York, in 1949 served as a wakeup call of just how vicious the second Red Scare had become.

PEEKSKILL RIOT OF 1949

In April 1949, Paul Robeson presented a speech at the Paris Peace Congress. American newspapers, though misquoting Robeson, reported that he said American blacks would not go to war against the Soviet Union. Robeson's remarks were considered tantamount to treason and his loyalty to the United States government was put under the microscope.

Previously, Robeson had performed concerts in Westchester County, New York. Another concert was scheduled in Peekskill for August 27th. Because of his Paris speech, pro-Soviet sentiments, outspoken criticism of U.S. Cold War and racial policies, and growing pressure to demonstrate loyalty on the part of all American citizens, a number of local veterans were determined to prevent Robeson's concert. The sponsor of the concert was the "People's Artists, Inc.," an organization listed as subversive by the Attorney General. The funds to be collected from the sale of tickets were intended to benefit the "Harlem Chapter of Civil Rights Congress," another organization branded as subversive by former U.S. Attorney General Tom Clark. On the day of the scheduled concert, the Peekskill Evening Star aroused the local citizenry with its comment that "The time for tolerant silence that signifies approval is running out."

Aided by the local police force, the veterans succeeded in preventing the concert. They barricaded the roads leading to the concert grounds and burned the platform, chairs, songbooks, and programs. Immediately after the initial riot, a number of Robeson's supporters formed the Westchester Committee for Law and Order and decided to hold the concert a week later. The concert was rescheduled for the 4th of September. Although the local police promised protection, the organizers were accompanied by 250 trade unionists acting as guards that day.

Twenty thousand people attended the Sunday-Afternoon concert. When it was over, angry mobs, mostly veterans, overturned cars, dragged people out of their cars, and beat them. Along the highways, a number of vehicles were also stoned. Some 150 people received treatment at local area hospitals. Those witnessing the events reported that during the violence racial slurs and anti-Semitic remarks were hurled at the concertgoers. For instance, the angry mob also shouted, "Hey, go on back to Russia, you niggers!" Despite a strong police presence, the authorities did little to stop the violence as the concertgoers exited the grounds.

New York Governor Thomas Dewey ordered a grand jury investigation of the Peekskill Riot. To no one's surprise, the jury found that "The fundamental cause of resentment and the focus of hostility was Communism . . . and Communism alone." That was as far as it went.[30] As noted earlier, Robeson was denied a passport, as were many others on the left who joined the causes of peace and freedom, so that they could not criticize U.S. policy from abroad.

UNITED WORLD FEDERALISTS

Although peace scientists became victims of their own experimental success and Communist "redbaiting" frightened anti-war groups fearing guilt by association, there were other Americans who believed that they could win the day for lasting peace. Representing the internationalist wing of the peace movement, they embodied many of the former ideas and principles of the pre-World War I cosmopolitan peacemakers. War was a reality that could only be brought under control by the rule of law, they believed. Spurred on by student activists like Harris Wofford, Jr., University of Chicago President Robert Maynard Hutchins, and New York lawyer Grenville Clark, a call went out among federalists to establish an organization that would solidify "world peace through world law." In February 1947, five federalist groups combined to form the United World Federalists for World Government with Limited Powers Adequate to Prevent War, more popularly called United World Federalists. Their shared aim was to mobilize public opinion and use its political weight at all levels in order to create a world government.[31] It was supposed to be more than just an international peacekeeping organization. These groups—Americans United for World Government, World Federalists, Mass Committee for World Federation, Student Federalists, and World Citizens of Georgia—proclaimed that the United World Federalists "believe that peace is not merely the absence of war but the presence of justice, of law, of order—in short, of government and in the institutions of government; that world peace can be created and maintained only under world law, universal and strong enough to prevent armed conflict between nations."[32]

The growth of the United World Federalists was remarkable. Led by Cord Meyer, Jr. (an ex-Marine and Yale University Phi Beta Kappa) and Norman Cousins, the UWF announced the expenditure of $550,000 in an expansion program developing the already existing six hundred chapters in the United States toward the goal of one chapter in every community. In 1948, North Carolina attorney Robert Lee Humber, described by contemporaries as a one-man UWF lobby on the state government level, had managed to persuade sixteen state legislatures to ratify resolutions urging the federal government to officially support the idea of world federation. By June 1949, there were 45,000 members in 720 local chapters; 8,000 people came to Madison Square Garden in New York for a UWF rally supporting a congressional resolution that "advocated the official State Department announcement that the goal of American foreign policy involved the development of the United Nations into a world federation."[33] The main speaker of the evening was Supreme Court Justice William O. Douglas; also on the podium were Cord Meyer, Jr. and former isolationist and critic of munitions makers Senator Charles W. Tobey (R-NH), the elected official who joined with twenty-one other colleagues in sponsoring the resolution in the Senate and who received endorsements from well over one hundred members in the House of Representatives. But as quickly as the UWF movement rose, its descent was even more startling. In less than two years the movement collapsed – a victim of the haplessness of American liberalism in the immediate post-World War II years. Eventually, UWF members became trapped between their desire to achieve total peace and their determination to check the spread of communism with the outbreak of war in Korea in 1950.

The war in the Far East that began in June 1950 was an enormous obstacle to the peace movement and its supporters. World government organizations generally supported the "police action," as it was labeled by the United Nations. Justifying a world police to use intervention, federalists insisted, was not about communism, but stopping aggression. Of course, it was more complicated than that. The Soviet Union's "peace offensives" that began in the late 1940s resulting in ventures such as the Cultural and Scientific Conference for World Peace, the American Peace Crusade, and the Stockholm Peace Petition campaign, put traditional peace groups in an awarkward position. Searching for respectability while agreeing with Soviet-sponsored peace initiatives, the American peace movement could not have it both ways.

African Americans also found themselves at odds with U.S. foreign policy and the war in Korea. Many were critical of the war because they felt that it had distracted the nation from addressing their own pressing concerns at home and the emergent world problem of postcolonial nationalism in Africa. Efforts had been made by African Americans to use the UN and international declarations on human rights to pressure U.S. officials to work for an end to discrimination at home and colonialism abroad. The notion that blacks were uninterested in foreign policy matters unless it dealt with segregation at home and matters directly related to Africa is a misleading one. Many African Americans, and not just the elite, saw a strong correlation between racism at home and how European colonization had degraded people of color. Lukewarm at best about the war in Korea, a decade later African Americans would play key roles in the Fair Play for Cuba group. The biggest obstacle they faced during the early Cold War era was fending off the tidal wave of anticommunism that identified the crusade for human rights with Soviet peacemaking ventures.

Prospects of a garrison state and atomic annihilation also worried educators. The AFSC's 1955 pamphlet "Speak Truth to Power" inspired educators to critique the Cold War and a U.S. military-industrial complex. On the elementary and secondary level, many members of the National Education Association upheld the traditional banner of anti-militarism. Concerned with the economic and political costs of a peacetime draft, educators raised the familiar anti-conscription arguments along with two new ones. They maintained that "in an age of war through complex machines and sophisticated technology," the nation's security rested less upon mass citizen armies than upon a well educated citizenry. They also felt atomic weaponry would give new force to their warnings that "compulsory military training would speed the corrosion of American democracy and cause a greater decline of liberal values."[34] Fearful that the development of atomic power was increasing the concentration of power in centralized authority, educators worried about a possible monopoly of decision-making controls placed in the hands of the army and government rather than the populace.

Moved by the threat of humanity's possible extinction, educators insisted that democracy revitalize itself through affirmative acts of purposeful control. According to David Lilienthal, the noted scientist associated with the atomic program, atomic energy posed a threat to basic liberties. Unless democracy was invigorated through "aggressive public education to establish popular control over the new power at the expense of self-serving national security bureaucrats," the preservation of democratic liberties was at best questionable. Until the Korean War, which diminished considerably their enthusiasm for lasting peace, educators stressed the fundamental need to work in the classroom for the purpose of highlighting the necessity of tolerance, the burdensome costs of war, the United Nations' new peace machinery, the importance of global interdependence, and the need for a sense of world community.[35]

While educators and the UWF initially generated a warm response from sympathetic audiences, the Cold War froze all liberal tendencies for a world federation. Between 1947 and 1949, events in Europe and Asia counteracted its appeal. Noted earlier, in March 1947, Truman issued his doctrine committing the U.S. to an active policy of fighting communism. Events abroad unfolded quickly. In January 1948, Czechoslovakia fell to communist rule. A half year later, the Russians blockaded Berlin, which led to a massive eighteen-month Allied airlift. In September 1949, Russia exploded its first atomic device, while Mao Tse-tung's Red Army in China forced Chaing Kai-shek and his nationalists to flee to the island of Taiwan. In June 1950, North Korean communist forces invaded South Korea. Almost overnight, the UWF became trapped between its One-world ideals and its fear of revolutionary communism.

As leading federalists agonized over these fears of communism, Senator Joseph McCarthy's (R-Wisconsin) accusations that communists were hiding in the closets of the State Department, along with the intensification of the Korean War, cemented the belief that the peace movement was an agency of communist subversion.[36] With Congress and the country apparently convinced that communism was a conspiracy, the only remaining task was to formalize the procedures for uncovering persons suspected of disloyalty or subversion. This exercise in thought control, which reflected growing nationalism and centralization was achieved through congressional investigations, loyalty-security programs, and official registration or listing of organizations deemed subversive.[37]

The second Red Scare was devastating to the UWF cause. Other groups were also affected. The jailing of Communist Party leaders under the Smith Act (enacted in 1940 as part of the new conscription law) and the problems experienced by peace groups such as the Women's International League for Peace and Freedom highlighted just how tenuous it was to protect civil liberties during this period. In 1950, the Senate Foreign Relations Committee heard testimony branding the UWF as subversive from witnesses representing the Women's

Patriotic Council on National Defense, National Society of New England Women, National Society of Women Descendants of the Ancient and Honorable Artillery Company, Dames of the Loyal Legion of the United States of America, The American Coalition, The Veterans of Foreign Wars, and the Society of the War of 1812.[38] Joseph P. Kamp published a book in 1950 titled We Must Abolish These United States, claiming this was the essential message of the UWF.[39] Two years later the Senate Appropriations Committee, with Pat McCarran as chairman, approved a bill banning federal funds from any organization which "directly or indirectly promoted one world government or world citizenship."[40] The McCarran Act was instrumental in silencing people who questioned the government's policies directed at communism. Thus it was up to Norman Cousins, the new UWF president, a few remaining atomic scientists, and world government activists to pursue total opposition to atomic warfare throughout the 1950's. In 1957 they decided to form the National Committee for a SANE Nuclear Policy to prevent a future holocaust.[41]

NON-VIOLENT DIRECT ACTION

Unsuccessful efforts by scientists and world federalists to push forward the goal of world government and world citizenship demonstrated the inherent weakness of pacifism's political thrust. It is extremely difficult to generate moral values through politics and protests. Committed pacifists who opposed the UN's collective security policies remained the only segment of the anti-war movement to survive the fifties without being bruised by the failures of peace politics. Between 1945 and 1948, Gandhian activists such as David Dellinger and Jim Peck kept alive the vision of spiritual non-violence. These radical pacifists encouraged an "inner revolution" within peace-minded individuals as a way of organizing a popular movement against war and institutionalized violence. They helped form Peacemakers and the Committee for Non-Violent Action, two organizations "bound by the creed of individual resistance as a form of social protest."[42]

Radical pacifists like Peck and Dellinger, recently released from prison or CPS camps, initiated a series of demonstrations calling for amnesty for COs, opposition to atomic testing, elimination of permanent conscription, an end to racial discrimination, and cessation of the growing militarization of society. In Peck's case, labor events in the 1930s radicalized his social consciousness. Dropping out of Harvard after his freshman year, Peck's career would be marked by putting his life on the line in support of trade unionism, civil rights, and world peace. Joining WRL in 1940, he was later sentenced to jail for twenty-eight months for opposing World War II. While imprisoned at Danbury, Peck was one of the leaders behind the 135-day strike against racial segregation in the mess hall. After his release from prison, he edited publications of CORE and WRL. In February 1947, he was one of a group who burned their draft cards in front of the White House. During the 1950's Peck was instrumental in organizing numerous demonstrations against civil defense drills.[43]

Like Peck, Dellinger emerged from prison to become involved in active non-violent protests against war and nuclear testing. Born in Wakefield, Massachusetts, he attended Yale College and Union Theological Seminary. Before the war, he helped set up a communal colony in Newark, New Jersey; he also devoted time as a community organizer in the slums of Harlem and Newark. In 1940, while studying at Union Theological Seminary, Dellinger refused to register for the draft. He was imprisoned for two years in the Lewisburg Penitentiary in Pennsylvania. There, he took part in a 65-day fast protesting racial segregation. After his release from prison, Dellinger helped organize other radical pacifists in order to establish a strong non-violent movement for economic and political change. In a similar vein to Peck, Dellinger helped edit radical periodicals like Direct Action and Alternative while participating in peace groups such as WRL, Peacemakers, and the Committee for Non-violent Action.[44]

Peck and Dellinger, along with a number of other radical pacifists, notably Bayard Rustin, were important for translating Gandhian tactics to the American Left from the 1950's to the 1970's. Groups like CORE, WRL, FOR, and CNVA played key roles in establishing the tactics, structure, and culture of post-World War II social movements. Influencing Cold War dissent, radical pacifists defined protest movements through direct action and an agenda that placed race and militarism as the most important social issues in America. These individuals were also responsible for creating a protest style that used the media and employed confrontational symbolism aimed at oppressive institutions in order to highlight dissatisfaction with the power elite. Direct actionists relied on a decentralized movement based on consensus decision-making. But, above all, they readily used the tactic of non-violent individual resistance characterized by a willingness to put "one's body on the line." In many ways, their actions and forms of protest were remarkably similar to the ideals of American individualism (as expressed by non-resistants and abolitionists) in the antebellum period.

What types of non-violent demonstrations were thus undertaken by these organizations and their members shortly after the conclusion of World War II? The first of a series of protests – always symbolic in form and substance and referred to as direct action – took place in the summer of 1946, on the occasion of the first Bikini atomic bomb test explosion. Pacifists held a demonstration in Times Square, New York. Because goats were being used as guinea pigs to test the effects of the blast, Peck and other demonstrators rented a stuffed goat, placed it on wheels, and led it down 42nd Street with a sign that read, "Today Me, Tomorrow You." Non-violent activists also carried out Amnesty protests at the White House on Christmas Day in 1946 and 1947, wearing black and white-striped prison suits to call attention to their message. On February 12, 1947, the first draft card burnings took place, one in front of the White House, the other at the Labor Temple in New York City. One of the more innovative forms of symbolic protest was goose-stepping in rented Uncle Sam costumes in front of the White House wearing placards that read, "The Draft Means a Goose-Stepping

Uncle Sam." As in most of these early demonstrations, the numbers of protestors were small, usually no more than thirty; however, their message was loud and clear.[45]

Committed to direct action tactics, more than one hundred war resisters formed the Committee for Non-Violent Revolution in February 1946. This loosely organized group urged a democratic, decentralized socialist society. It held a few minor demonstrations urging closure of the Big Flats CPS camp in upstate New York. Its actions symbolized a growing awareness of the importance of direct action techniques. Their theoretical position would eventually reach a wider audience in the late 1950's when the fear of nuclear weapons provided radical pacifism more of a fair hearing.

MUSTE AND WAR TAX RESISTANCE

In the face of the loyalty-security era and government attempts to silence dissent, the conscience of radical pacifism was best personified by the FOR's long-time secretary, A.J. Muste. Distraught over the Hiroshima and Nagasaki bombings, Muste argued that "No political or moral appraisal of our age is adequate, no attempt to find an answer to its dilemmas and destiny offers hope, which does not take adequate account of that fact."[46] Extolling love as the countermeasure to the awesome power of the modern state, Muste led pacifists in many direct action protests in postwar America.

One of the most daring of these was Muste's income tax resistance policy. The idea had already been carried out during the Second World War. In early 1945, the WRL distributed a sticker to be attached to tax payments: "This tax goes chiefly for war purposes; as a pacifist, I pay it only under protest." During World War II, a law requiring employers to withhold taxes from their employees caused particular difficulties for pacifists. Some pacifists asked their employers to refuse cooperation with this law since it made tax refusal practically impossible. Groups with tax exempt status—non-profit organizations—were often reluctant to jeopardize this status by disobeying the law. As a result, some pacifists resigned their positions rather than permit the money to go to the military.

These concerns led Muste and others to form the Peacemakers in 1948, a group whose main thrust was in the area of war tax resistance. At a national conference held in Chicago, Marion Coddington, Ernest Bromley, Caroline Urie, Walter Gormly, Valerie Riggs, and Ralph Templin were designated as a committee to promote tax refusal. For many years, they provided research, literature, action suggestions, and publicity for those in the tax-resistance movement. They were moved by Muste's Thoreau-like message that "They who profit by violence though it be indirectly, unwillingly, and only in small measure, will always be under suspicion and rightly so of seeking to protect their profits, and of being selfishly motivated, if they address pious exhortations to those who suffer that violence."[47]

Over the next 15 years after 1948, hundreds of people followed Muste's call to refuse paying income taxes. The government prosecuted and imprisoned only six: James Otsuka, Indiana; Maurice McCrackin, Ohio; Eroseanna Robinson, Illinois; Walter Gormly, Iowa; Arthur Evans, Colorado; and Neil Howorth, Connecticut. Rather than risk a greater reaction the government selectively chose whom to prosecute in order to set an example and intimidate others into complying with the tax law. These imprisonments and the seizure of a few cars and houses by the Internal Revenue Service highlighted the tax refusal testimony and established it as a major anti-war position.

KOREAN WAR

The war tax resistance movement certainly had historic roots: the debates among Pennsylvania Friends during the French and Indian War and the Revolutionary War and the courageous stand Thoreau took at Walden Pond in Concord, Massachusetts, were refined and implemented with some success. The growing popularity of direct action protests, led by former imprisoned COs and war tax resisters, indicated that the peace movement might regain some of its appeal as it had done after World War I. But just when it appeared as if the movement would regain its momentum, the outbreak of war in Korea dashed all hopes. The organized anti-war movement had almost no impact during the Korean War. The overwhelming majority of Americans endorsed United States' participation. Eighty-one percent of the nation's countrymen agreed with Truman's decision to send ground units to the peninsula to repel the North Korean attack; they foresaw an intense but short conflict to stem the spread of communism.[48]

Only a few anti-war groups managed to express their objections publicly. The FOR, WRL and WILPF called for an immediate ceasefire and a UN-negotiated settlement. The FOR pronounced that "What is taking place in Korea is not 'police action.'" The newly established National Council of Churches—an integration of previously extant Protestant denominational agencies composed of thirty million church members mostly from the old, long-established "mainstream" churches—criticized the war. Further, in a public statement, they called for a standard of life "without hysteria, without hatred, without pride, without undue impatience, without making national interest our chief end, but shaping our policies in the light of the aims of the United Nations, without relaxing our positive services to the other peoples of the world, and in complete repudiation of the lying dogma that war is inevitable."[49]

Muste led the anti-war crusade. In 1950, he penned a serious indictment of the American military positioned in Asia entitled, <u>Korea: Spark to Set a World Afire?</u> In his message to anti-war supporters, Muste quickly dispelled the notion that the United States was preventing a war in Asia by "applying force in time." "Whatever further analysis may show, what we have already recorded makes it clear," he asserted, "that American troops in Korea are hardly engaged in a perfectly simple police action to save an innocent pedestrian, on a lawful and beneficent errand, from a bandit." Fearful that World War III might result if the

American government viewed the Korean conflict as part of the "power struggle between Russia (and itself)," Muste argued that "war does not stop Communism." To the contrary, "war gives Communism its chance. The psychological tension, the social upheaval, and the material destruction of war prepare the soil in which Communism flourishes." Muste offered five reasons why the United States should cease military operations: (1) the U.S. was at a military disadvantage; (2) it was interfering in a civil war; (3) its actions symbolized a "white" nation identified with Western conquest; (4) it was supporting a corrupt and repressive puppet regime; and (5) the U.S. moral position in the eyes of the world was untenable because of a superiority in atomic weapons and a failure to use our technology and resources to raise the world standard of living. Muste's solution was simple: "Uncle Sam, the Soldier, should get out of Korea, Japan, and the rest in order that Uncle Sam, the friend and enormously skilled fellow worker, may get in."[50] So compelling were Muste's arguments that the anti-establishment journalist I.F. Stone incorporated them into his own weekly periodical.

Most of the peace workers' staunchest allies, however, accepted Truman's policy. The Federal Council of Churches and the Socialist Party's National Action Committee backed the dispatch of troops to Korea. Norman Thomas became a vocal supporter of efforts "to beat back that aggression." A number of Progressive Party leaders, including Henry A. Wallace and O. John Rogge, repudiated their party and its Communist support and affirmed their faith in Uncle Sam. Even the traditionally anti-war Progressive expressed enthusiastic and sustained approval of the Truman move and criticized "true-blue pacifists," whose devotion to peace "robs them of capacity to see how meeting force with force can result in anything but war." As a result, according to one pacifist leader, pacifists were "reduced pretty much to talking to themselves."[51]

Some within the left opposition refused to be intimidated or cajoled into silence. Communist peace groups, in particular, rejected outright the military occupation of North Korea. African Americans such as DuBois and Robeson criticized American military intervention as an imperialist plot to subjugate another race of people. As director of the Peace Information Center, DuBois openly attacked the "police action." To make his point he ran for the Senate in New York on the American Labor Party ticket in the fall of 1950. His expressed purpose was to raise the issues of "Peace and Civil Rights." In retaliation the Justice Department indicted DuBois for circulating a petition calling for the abolition of atomic weapons and linking the war to a U.S. imperialistic-led crusade under the pretext of defeating the communists. DuBois' position was remarkably consistent to the one he held during World War I. In a 1915 article entitled "The African Roots of War," appearing in the Atlantic Monthly, he equated the struggle between Germany and the Allies as a symbolic contest over the spoils of Africa. This time the struggle extended to the Far East.

Although the Korean War quickly became the most unpopular war fought up until that time in American history – one which cost the U.S. approximately $100 billion, some 37,000 soldiers killed and 103,000 wounded – traditional protest groups, including the emerging civil rights movement, the left, and the pacifist wing of the peace movement, became hopelessly divided. Unlike later years, there was no organized draft resistance movement and draft evasion and desertion were no higher than during World War II. The only ones who remained true to form in their steadfast opposition to the war were dedicated neo-isolationists, some communists, and committed pacifists like Muste. Even liberal intellectuals and those in the academy desirous of criticizing the war were muzzled by the rising tide of McCarthyism.

The peace movement reached rock bottom in the early 1950s. Its leaders were confused; the coalitions it had generated split apart as fast as the atom. As a result, diehard pacifists began to concentrate, not on war itself, but on social justice; at least they could work on eradicating some of the economic and social causes leading to war. The civil rights issue would now become one of their most important campaigns, thereby linking together the twin issues of peace and justice.[52]

A BURGEONING CIVIL RIGHTS MOVEMENT

After the cessation of hostilities in Korea in 1953, peace activists shifted into high gear their commitment to social justice. In large measure they responded to the debates within the civil rights movement over strategies and tactics. Seeking to overcome the status quo segregationists who equated the drive for civil rights with communism, mainstream black leaders encouraged the civil rights movement to drop the international focus and concentrate solely on domestic issues. Aware of this fact, many in the organized peace movement looked to implement direct action non-violence in an effort to raise the public consciousness about race relations in the United States.

The civil rights movement was given an added boost in 1954 after the U.S. Supreme Court decision in Brown v. Board of Education of Topeka, Kansas. The abolition of segregation in public schools was a shot in the arm to traditional civil rights groups like the NAACP. For years this organization relied on the law and court decisions as an instrument of justice. Peace activists, holding on to the actions employed by CORE and FOR, encouraged African Americans to adopt non-violent tactics in the struggle for racial equality. A year later the tactic would be tested when Rosa Parks, an African American woman and NAACP member who honed her skills on non-violent civil disobedience at Highlander Folk School, refused to move and take a seat in the back of a Montgomery city bus in Alabama.

Non-violent acts in the American civil rights struggle were first used on a mass basis beginning in late 1955 when, for an entire year, 42,000 blacks in Montgomery simply ceased riding the city's buses rather than be humiliated any longer by segregated seating. Their successful boycott, in which women played a key organizing role, catapulted to fame a 26-year-old Baptist minister originally from Atlanta, Martin Luther King Jr. Until his assassination in April 1968, King was the outstanding leader of the non-violent wing of the civil rights movement.

Money and advisers from CORE and the FOR poured into the Montgomery Improvement Association. Radical pacifists quickly began drilling local blacks in the techniques of non-violent resistance to sanctioned abuse. At the same time, King studied the writings of Gandhi and Tolstoy and underwent "a complete conversion to non-violent resistance that fused Christianity and peaceable mass protest." Reflecting later on the Montgomery boycott, King said: "Christ furnished the spirit and motivation, while Gandhi furnished the method." Ultimately, he merged the concerns of middle-class northern whites and liberals throughout America with the needs of forgotten southern blacks. He also channeled "oppressed black outrage into a massive, non-violent movement" that made manifest the relevance of Gandhian techniques in the crusade for social justice. "The non-violent approach," King so often stated eloquently, "does not immediately change the heart of the oppressor. It first does something to the heart and souls of those committed to it. It gives them new self-respect; it calls up resources of strength and courage that they did not know they had. Finally, it reaches the opponent and so stirs his conscience that reconciliation becomes a reality."[53]

In attempting to promote non-violent resistance, King joined clergymen Fred Shuttleworth and Ralph Abernathy in forming the Southern Christian Leadership Conference in January 1957 to mobilize southern blacks for the peaceable overthrow of institutionalized racial segregation. He also worked closely with northern white pacifists associated with WRL, CORE and the FOR to prove that mass non-violent resistance was "the sole authentic approach to the problem of social injustice."[54]

Some concerned Americans thought the Montgomery boycott might set off similar mass protests, however, that did not happen until four years later. On February 1, 1960, a sit-in by four black college students at a Woolworth's lunch counter in Greensboro, North Carolina, sparked a wave of sit-ins—which within a month had spread to twenty-five cities in five states. Within the first year of the sit-ins, lunch counter desegregation came to 134 southern communities.

The sit-ins inspired activists like Julian Bond, SCLC organizers such as Ella Baker, and other blacks like Bayard Rustin and James Lawson to establish the Student Non-violent Coordinating Committee (SNCC) in May 1960. In large measure Ella Baker, for many years a staff member on the NAACP and then SCLC, was the real driving force behind the student civil rights organization. She nurtured the vision of grassroots, decentralized democracy. Promoting the notion of social change "from the bottom up," SNCC drew on Ella Baker's vision and the peace and justice traditions of CORE, FOR, and SCLC.

The youthful activists in SNCC rejected the path of political caution practiced by the NAACP and SCLC. Instead, they favored a more immediate end to segregation through adherence to the religious or philosophical principles and practices of non-violence. Using a communitarian-anarchist foundation, SNCC downplayed national control in favor of functioning through a "group-centered leadership." It favored developing local leadership in different communities rather than the top down model of SCLC. Over time choosing not to look respectable in a purposeful attempt to accentuate their struggle, members of SNCC dressed down. The committee also did not act sheepishly by directly challenging the powers that be.

During the early sixties, SNCC volunteers organized sit-ins throughout the South and joined other civil rights organizations in sponsoring voter register campaigns. During the 1964 presidential campaign, its members helped organize the Mississippi Freedom Democratic Party, whose challenge to the all-white Mississippi delegation eventually led to increased minority participation within the Democratic Party. In its early years, SNCC was, by far, the most radical, and perhaps the most influential civil rights group (later infighting over the question of "black power" and harassment by the government led to its demise). SNCC staff members, who worked for about $10 a week under dangerous circumstances, included the former divinity school student (and later U.S. Congressman) John Lewis, Bob Moses, who left Harvard Graduate School to join the movement, Fisk University student Diane Nash, and others. With a small membership, minimum budget, and decentralized structure, SNCC's efforts captured a great deal of public sympathy for the cause due to the commitment of its members and their willingness to make sacrifices for the cause of racial justice.

Another successful tactic to abolish social injustice was the freedom rides. In the summer of 1961, blacks and whites from all parts of the country converged to challenge travel segregation in the South. In contrast to the First Freedom Riders of 1947, these fearless activists decided to penetrate the Deep South. Coordinating this mobilization were CORE, SCLC and SNCC. Facing violent opposition along the way, a group of riders eventually made it to Jackson, Mississippi, where the Kennedy administration had agreed to have them arrested and jailed in order to prevent the violence that had greeted the riders elsewhere. Government, it seems, valued order over justice. In certain instances, the freedom riders were beaten before being put in jail. However, in September, the Interstate Commerce Commission issued new regulations prohibiting interstate carriers from segregating. The movement also received more national attention in the spring of 1963 when young people protesting segregation in Birmingham, Alabama, were attacked by police dogs and high-powered water hoses.

On August 28, 1963, a quarter of a million people participated in the March on Washington, and King delivered his eloquent speech, "I have a Dream." Though violent opposition to the movement continued, milestone victories were achieved with the passage of the Voting Rights Acts of 1964 and 1965. As part of President Lyndon Johnson's Great Society, the civil rights acts provided a greater measure of social and political justice. But there remained a long way to go. Discrimination continued in many parts of the United States and staunch segregationists in the South did everything in their power to deny blacks the right to vote. Poverty remained visible among African Americans and the inner cities became a battleground as high unemployment and deplorable living conditions were the norm. These more intractable problems, reflected in the urban rebellions of the mid to late 1960s, along with King's assassination in April 1968, brought home just how difficult it would be to bring the nation forward.

The African American protest movement addressed not only the segregation of public accommodation, but also "the twin levers of power in American society, the vote and the job." In the modern civil rights struggle, non-violence was referred to both as a "tactic" and a "way of life." Though relatively few activists accepted the philosophy of non-violence, it was a vital and effective tactic; the protestors were outnumbered and outgunned, and their refusal to retaliate when attacked won them necessary and devoted sympathizers. In terms of political strategy, civil rights direct action was a form of non-violent revolution.

AIR RAID DRILLS

Before the Vietnam War took center stage among non-violent resisters, pacifists used civil disobedience to protest atomic bomb tests and express their displeasure with mandatory air raid drills. Dissent against civil defense drills began in earnest and with fervor on a warm day in 1954. On June 14th, air raid sirens wailed throughout the United States signaling millions of Americans to take "shelter" —a mass burial—from a mock nuclear attack. This was the first nation-wide air raid civil defense drill; such drills continued for the next eight years. The most common air raid drill was called "duck and cover," supposedly for protection if the enemy attacked without warning. The drills were directed primarily at schools, and students dropped to the floor or crawled under their desks at the teacher's command and took what a professor of education called "the atomic head clutch position": backs to the windows, faces buried between their knees, hands clasped on the back of their necks, ears covered with their arms, and eyes closed. The "atomic clutch" was supposed to protect children from the bomb flash, flying glass, and falling timbers -- from what a civil defense proponent called "life in a meat-grinder." The National Education Association warned teachers to have their students take the "atomic clutch" position immediately if a "sudden dazzling light" appeared outside the school to indicate the bomb's arrival. A Los Angeles school administrator explained that this emergency position was approved as medically sound by doctors because "it provides the desired protection for the back of the neck. . . It compressed by some degree the organs of the abdomen, decreasing the effects of the blast on these organs."[55]

During this period numerous federal and state civil defense programs appeared. The government was faced with an impossible task: convince the public that it was possible to survive an atomic and subsequently a nuclear attack. Behind this campaign was a hidden agenda. Policymakers wanted to pacify the population and legitimize its own deterrence policy. They also wanted to justify the billions of dollars being spent on elaborate and secret underground bomb shelters set aside for the government elite.

To peace-seekers this logic belied reality. The civil defense program, in the opinion of labor pacifist and The Progressive editor Sidney Lens, represented "another manifestation of a man's present frustration" in "his quest for elusive panaceas." Such a program blinds Americans "from an objective examination of the totality of the problem."[56] Consequently, after a modest start in opposing the drills in 1954, when a few pacifists distributed leaflets, the WRL and other peace groups organized in 1955 a non-violent disobedience action. Twenty-eight people (including A.J. Muste and also Dorothy Day of the Catholic Worker Movement) sat in City Hall Park, New York, during the drill holding signs that read "End War—The Only Defense Against Atomic Weapons." All were arrested, tried, and convicted. Supporters organized a defense committee to carry out an appeal in the courts.

The legal defense was that the arrests were a denial of the defendants' rights of free speech and assembly, right to petition, and rights of conscience under the provisions of both the state and federal constitutions. The moral defense, as remembered by one of the defendants, Ralph DiGia, stated in part: "The kind of public and highly publicized drills held on June 15 (1955) are essentially a part of war preparation. They accustom people to the idea of war, to acceptance of war as probably inevitable, and as somehow right if waged in 'defense' and 'retaliation'....They create the illusion that the nation can devote its major resources to preparation for nuclear war and at the same time shield people from its catastrophic effects...."[57]

Though the appeal was in the courts for about four years and was lost, civil disobedience protests and arrests continued in New York and elsewhere—usually involving small numbers of participants. By 1960, however, the protesters numbered in the hundreds, and in 1961, the demonstrations were larger and more widespread than ever. That year in City Hall Park more than a thousand people refused to take shelter. This demonstration marked the last of compulsory public air raid drills.

The air raid drills lost public credibility as nuclear weapons grew larger and the time for defense preparation grew shorter. In reality, the civil defense program turned out to be a complete failure. The protests increased pubic awareness of the suicidal nature of a nuclear exchange. But one question that pacifists kept asking remained unanswerable: How do you influence government policies to make the bomb's use less likely?[58] In the late fifties, new groups of nuclear pacifists emerged, questioning the morality of America's military superiority.

CONCLUSION

During World War II and the early years of the Cold War, the crusade for peace underwent dramatic changes. Pioneers for peace and justice expanded their humanitarian impulse in the area of social service programs. The war, however, put them on the defensive. Their political energy was sapped by popular support for the war. In response, radical pacifists sharpened their forms of protest while serving in CPS camps or in prison. In the aftermath of war, they would find expression in civil rights campaigns and in acts of civil disobedience. But the

1950's were far from kind to peacemakers as the Cold War and second Red Scare nearly shattered the peace movement.

Nevertheless, dedicated peace and justice activists kept alive the spirit of non-violent civil disobedience in their continued and determined civil rights protests during the latter part of the 1950s. At the same time they also continued to dramatize their opposition to the threat of nuclear war, while refining direct action techniques that became central to their strategies and protests. Their efforts would spark a new, more militant wave of anti-war protests in the 1960's as American troops were shipped to Southeast Asia.

CHAPTER SEVEN
THE BOMB, CIVIL DISOBEDIENCE, AND THE WAR IN VIETNAM

..... With nuclear energy whole cities can easily be powered, yet the dominant nation-states seem more likely to unleash destruction greater than that incurred in all wars of human history. Although our own technology is destroying old and creating new forms of social organization, men still tolerate meaningless work and idleness. While two-thirds of mankind suffers undernourishment, our own upper classes revel amidst superfluous abundance. Although world population is expected to double in forty years, the nations still tolerate anarchy as a major principle of international conduct and uncontrolled exploitation governs the sapping of the earth's physical resources. Although mankind desperately needs revolutionary leadership, America rests in national stalemate, its goals ambiguous and tradition-bound instead of informed and clear, its democratic system apathetic and manipulated rather than 'of, by, and for the people.'

SDS, Port Huron Statement, 1962.

INTRODUCTION

In June of 1962, approximately sixty members of the newly-formed Students for a Democratic Society gathered at Port Huron, Michigan, to participate in a conference sponsored by the United Auto Workers. Michael Harrington, whose 1962 book, The Other America, inspired President John F. Kennedy to take an interest in the issue of poverty, revived the ideological roots of the old League for Industrial Democracy – a socialist institution that had claimed as members Jack London and Upton Sinclair. Student radicals who were attracted to Harrington's vision formed the Student League for Industrial Democracy, which evolved into the Students for a Democratic Society (SDS). While attending the conference at Port Huron the student radicals proclaimed their own manifesto of the New Left. The 64-page document, written by Tom Hayden, then the editor of the University of Michigan's student newspaper, condemned the growing ties between the universities and the military-industrial establishment. The realities of life in Cold War America, marked by the threat of extreme extinction, violations of civil liberties, discrimination against African Americans, and academic acquiescence to a large military presence called for a re-examination of America's social structure. What troubled SDS members most was that the ties among the military, industrial, and academic sectors that bolstered the social structure undermined democracy and led to a sense of apathy among the nation's youth. At first, their efforts focused on issues of racial and economic equality through non-violence. Creating a New Left movement, SDS became the initial vanguard in calling for a complete overhaul of American values and institutions. As the war in Vietnam gripped the nation's attention, SDS turned more of its efforts to organizing against the war. Its actions helped create the largest anti-war movement in twentieth-century U.S. history.[1]

While the 1950's offered a glimmer of hope which flickered on and off, the next decade provided an ideal opportunity for the new peace activists, whose views were shaped by two post-World War II developments: the use of atomic warfare, especially the volatile issue of atmospheric testing, and non-violent resistance by Conscientious Objectors and political protestors of war. Those focused on nuclear warfare characterized one branch of the peace movement known as nuclear pacifists; the non-violent resisters, better known as radical pacifists, made up another branch. When communists, student radicals, and black power advocates were added to the mix – all strongly opposed to the Vietnam War – a dynamic movement resulted.

As historians like Milton Katz, James Tracy, Scott Bennett, and Charles DeBenedetti point out, nuclear pacifists were more conservative in their peace making. They concentrated on the dangers of nuclear war—using public opinion, impressive credentials, and political strategy to try to influence policymakers on war-related issues. Radical pacifists were less patient; they were opposed to all wars and pushed for major societal reform by developing a non-violent action plan through non-traditional means.

All this would change somewhat in the 1960s, as both groups would find common ground against the war in Vietnam. Clearly the decade of the sixties witnessed a remarkable confluence of events and situations. First, there would be the emergence of the SDS calling for a social, political, and economic transformation of power to the "have-nots." Second, the appearance of the women's liberation movement changed the character of the peace movement. Feminists seeking their own avenue of power became associated with the anti-Vietnam War movement and reshaped the thinking of longtime women's peace organizations. In some ways, it was remarkably similar to the women's rights movement and those who opposed World War I. Many women opposed to the war in Southeast Asia carried signs that read, "Support the troops, Bring them home." Third, the anti-Vietnam War movement had an original ally in the black community. That changed over time as more militant blacks, though angry at the war and the draft, questioned how the anti-war movement would address other pressing concerns such as discrimination in jobs and eliminating poverty in urban areas. For many, the battle was not the war but eliminating racism. Fourth, the anti-war movement consisted of unusual combinations of individuals; there were those opposed to the war from the beginning based on moral and ethical beliefs to those who protested later when it became obvious that the war was unwinnable and a drain on the economy. Fifth, additional tensions were created by the sixties counterculture. Many liberals and pacifists, as was the case with the Committee for a Sane Nuclear Policy, were uncomfortable marching alongside young people with long hair and dirty jeans fearing they would enable pro-war supporters to discredit the anti-war protests because of the "hippies" appearance and demeanor. Sixth, while leaders of various organizations have been cited in this book and were responsible for receiving most of the media attention, the sense of empowerment within the anti-war movement was largely the result of lesser known individuals; the anti-war movement was more about collective effort than charismatic leadership. Lastly, the massive protests against the Vietnam War turned out to be some of the most dramatic in American history. The war came to dominate the attention of American society. But for a brief period in the late 1950s and very early 1960s all eyes were focused on the threat of nuclear annihilation.

SANE AND CNVA

The same year that the Soviet Union launched the Sputnik rocket, 1957, nuclear and radical pacifists formed two interdependent organizations. The nuclear pacifists set up the National Committee for a Sane Nuclear Policy (SANE) and the radical pacifists founded the Committee for Non-violent Action (CNVA).[2]

Concerned over the atmospheric testing of hydrogen bombs, Lawrence Scott, American Friends Service Committee Peace Education Director in Chicago, organized an April meeting in Philadelphia to plan a strategy for stopping H-bomb tests. He gathered the support of A.J. Muste, Bayard Rustin, and Robert Gilmore, AFSC New York secretary. From that meeting emerged a three-pronged coalition: an ad-hoc liberal, nuclear pacifist organization referring to itself as SANE; an ad-hoc radical pacifist, direct-action oriented group to be known as CNVA; and the older peace organizations, like FOR, WILPF and AFSC, which would concentrate on the nuclear testing issue while giving support and encouragement to ad-hoc committees. Scott and Muste, both of whom relished activism, organized CNVA. Robert Gilmore, Norman Cousins, and Clarence Pickett, secretary emeritus of the AFSC, formed SANE.

A fall 1957 SANE advertisement in the New York Times garnered overwhelming response to its plea for "an immediate suspension of atomic testing," and by the summer of 1958 SANE had about 130 chapters consisting of 5,000 members.[3] According to sociologist Nathan Glazer, SANE was "based on a coalition of two major groupings, both of which had their origins in older issues: the proponents of world government on the one hand and the pacifists on the other."[4] A number of prominent people filled its ranks, including some old-line United World Federalists: Oscar Hammerstein, the music composer; Walter Reuther, head of the United Auto Workers; and Donald Keys, SANE's first full-time executive director, and former First Lady, Eleanor Roosevelt.

When the United States and the Soviet Union voluntarily suspended nuclear tests, SANE broadened its goal to include a general disarmament treaty. During the 1958-59 Geneva talks on disarmament, SANE gathered thousands of signatures urging a test ban. It initiated peace demonstrations modeled after Britain's Aldermaston's March, and worked in support of a Senate resolution endorsing efforts to secure a test-ban treaty.

But at the height of SANE's success, red-baiting attacks on the organization drastically curtailed its effectiveness. The Senate Internal Security Committee, headed by Thomas Dodd (D-Connecticut) "publicly accused SANE of harboring avowed Communist sympathizers," sending shock waves throughout SANE's organizational structure.[5] A respectable group like this could not tolerate such an accusation, according to its leadership, and the Board worked to purge the organization of suspected communists. Yet radical pacifists like Muste accused SANE of catering to the very hysteria it was supposed to prevent: McCarthyism and the Cold War. Other activists agreed that SANE was passing up a golden opportunity to challenge the characterization of peace efforts as subversive activity. Linus Pauling dropped his sponsorship of SANE, Robert Gilmore resigned from the Board, and several branches protested the purge. SANE's actions stood in marked contrast to other newly-emerging groups such as Women Strike for Peace (WSP) and SDS that avoided exclusionary tactics in order to achieve the common goal of peace and justice. The political climate was changing in any case; the 1961 creation of the semi-autonomous Arms Control and Disarmament Agency and the American-Soviet accord on a nuclear test-ban treaty two years later, led many within SANE to question whether the organization still had a significant purpose. The war in Vietnam provided an answer.

While SANE was experiencing setbacks and advances, its cousin, CNVA, moved ahead regardless of the consequences. CNVA was a loosely organized group of radical pacifists committed to non-violent direct action against nuclear testing. Enamored of civil disobedience, the group formed in 1957 as an ad hoc committee, known as Non-Violent Action against Nuclear Weapons. Veteran activist George Willoughby was its chairman and Lawrence Scott its coordinator. Two years later, the organization adopted the name Committee for Non-violent Action and received endorsements from FOR, WILPF, and WRL. Working closely with other pacifist organizations, CNVA included among its ranks Ralph DiGia, Lillian Willoughby, Dagmar Wilson, Bradford Lyttle, Jeanne Bagby, Eleanor Garst, and A.J. Muste. Originally located in Philadelphia, its headquarters moved to New York City in 1960.

Before the Vietnam War moved the peace movement as a whole to endorse the techniques of non-violent direct action, CNVA's separate efforts were widely regarded. Through peace walks, vigils, voyages by peace ships into nuclear test sites in the south Pacific, and other forms of civil disobedience, CNVA activists were able to express their own personal commitment to Peace & Change while educating the general public about peace issues.

Its first significant act took place on August 6, 1957, twelve years after the Hiroshima bombing. Eleven radical pacifists, including Lawrence Scott, were arrested at an Atomic Energy Commission bomb test project in Nevada for deliberately trespassing onto government property. Their Prayer and Conscience Vigil, historians Robert Cooney and Helen Michaelowski noted, was "the first anti-nuclear demonstration to be conducted at an actual site of nuclear explosions."[6]

The next year, CNVA undertook a far more ambitious project, the protest voyage of the Golden Rule. This ketch, with four Quakers aboard, attempted to sail into the restricted area of the Pacific where the Atomic Energy Commission was conducting hydrogen bomb tests. Prior to the journey, the boat's captain, former World War II naval commander Albert Bigelow explained: "When you see something horrible happening, your instinct is to do something about it... I have to act. This is too horrible." His wartime experiences and conversion to Quakerism convinced him "to find ways to make our witness and protest heard":

> I am going because, as Shakespeare said, 'Action is eloquence.' Without some such direction, ordinary citizens lack the power any longer to be seen or heard by their government....
>
> I am going because, like all men, in my heart I know that all nuclear explosions are monstrous, evil, unworthy of human beings.. I am going because it is now the little children and, most of all, the as yet unborn who are the front line troops. It is my duty to stand between them and this horrible danger....
>
> I am going because however mistaken, unrighteous, and unrepentant governments may seem, I still believe all men are really good at heart, and that my act will speak to them.
>
> I am going in the hope of helping change the hearts and minds of men in government. If necessary I am willing to give my life to help change a policy of fear, force and destruction to one of trust, kindness, and help.
>
> I am going in order to say, 'Quit this waste, this arms race. Turn instead to a disarmament race. Stop competing for evil, compete for good.'
>
> I am going because I have to if I am to call myself a human being.[7]

Although the Golden Rule was stopped in Hawaii and its crew sentenced to sixty days in jail, the Phoenix, with Barbara and Earle Reynolds and their children and a Japanese mate aboard, picked up and carried on the protest.[8] The Reynolds were not arrested until well inside the forbidden zone and his trial, helped by the supportive activities of CNVA, gained world-wide attention. As a result of these actions, the public was made increasingly aware of the dangers of radioactivity resulting from nuclear tests.

As Gandhian non-violence became more popular in the United States, the CNVA gained more momentum. To protest atmospheric nuclear testing CNVA conducted a month-long vigil in front of the White House in early 1959. At Cheyenne, Wyoming, concerned pacifists took part in non-violent intervention in the path of construction equipment where missile bases were being built. Two similar projects were undertaken at the Cape Canaveral Missile Base in Florida. CNVA eschewed traditional approaches designed to inform and persuade in favor of more militant actions. Its members sought to confront and coerce by staging sit-ins in front of military bases and blocking cars and trucks from entering. Upon arrest, they did not resist; they surrendered peacefully. These tactics were designed to maximize public awareness of the dangers of nuclear testing and proliferation.

In the summer of 1959, an offshoot of CNVA, Omaha Action (Non-violence against Nuclear Missile Policy) staged a series of demonstrations against intercontinental ballistic missile bases in Nebraska. Starting with official meetings in Lincoln and Omaha, the project continued during the summer with vigils, leafleting, and direct action involving civil disobedience; these actions resulted in a number of protestors being arrested, including A.J. Muste and Brad Lyttle, a young scholar and disciple of Gandhian non-violent action. Uplifting to these demonstrators was 73-year-old Muste climbing the fence and penetrating the Omaha base while awaiting arrest.

By 1960, a permanent Committee for Non-violent Action had been formed, with Muste as national chairman and George Willoughby as executive committee chairman. In Connecticut, New England CNVA undertook an ongoing program of education and training for direct action to protest the building of Polaris subs. Direct action techniques, such as picketing and a person-to-person educational campaign were combined with David-and-Goliath encounters, "as individuals in canoes and rubber rafts confronted the Navy each time a newly-commissioned submarine slid down the ways and into the Connecticut River." These actions gained widespread media coverage for the cause and hostile reaction from the townspeople whose livelihoods depended on defense contracts.[9]

While symbolically firing peashooters at the massive Polaris subs at New London, Connecticut, CNVA also organized the San Francisco to Moscow Walk for Peace. This culminated in October 1961 with a demonstration in Red Square protesting the buildup of nuclear weapons of both East and West.[10] CNVA was the first group to carry such a message to both sides of the Iron Curtain, but its call for disarmament had no immediate effect on the superpowers. Much to its disappointment, in August of 1961, the Soviet Union announced the resumption of nuclear testing and the United States followed suit early in the following year.

CNVA did not quit, however. During 1962, it conceived and sponsored protests and sail-ins in a number of directions. Everyman I, skippered by pacifist Hal Stallings, sailed for Christmas Island in the Pacific Ocean to protest U.S. nuclear tests, only to be stopped before it got well under way. Everyman II succeeded in reaching its target, Johnston Island, before its captain, Monte Steadman, was put under arrest. Everyman III, under Earle Reynolds, sailed from England with an international crew and messages of protest for the Soviet Union. In Russia, as Milton Katz and James Tracy have pointed out, "they had one or two days of worthwhile exchanges with members of the Soviet Peace Committee" before the Cuban missile crisis broke in October. Kennedy's ultimatum to Khrushchev to remove Soviet missiles from Cuba and the American naval blockade ruined Reynolds' mission. With no knowledge of what had occurred, his group was kept incommunicado for about a week in the harbor of Leningrad before he and his crew were released without explanation and ordered to sail at once.

The increasing violence used against the civil rights struggles, combined with the United States-Cuba confrontations, caused CNVA to reassess its perspective on the relationship between non-violence and liberation. With Muste's call to "radicalize the peace movement" in order to "relate non-violence... to the dynamics of social change rather than to a personal philosophy or way of life," CNVA became involved in a major civil rights struggle in Albany, Georgia.[11] In 1963, during another CNVA Walk for Peace, civil rights activity increased and the arm of the law moved quickly. Fourteen pacifists were jailed for up to 56 days. They ignored a court order prohibiting an integrated protest march through the city's main street. After eight weeks of publicized fasting by the pacifists, a compromise was reached. Five members of CNVA, three black and two white, marched through the predominantly downtown white area. The question of how peace and freedom were related continued to be an issue throughout the 1960s.[12]

With SANE and CNVA, along with newly-emerging civil rights groups such as the Southern Christian Leadership Conference (SCLC) and Student Non-Violent Coordinating Committee (SNCC), and others, leading the way towards a more humane world, other concerned activists drew attention to the abolition of war. In 1959, Chicago-area pacifists and socialists formed the first major student peace organization of the era, the Student Peace Union.[13] Some months later, noted intellectuals opposed to the arms race, such as Harvard sociologist David Reisman, the renowned psychologist Erich Fromm, and the urban prophet Lewis Mumford, established the Committee of Correspondence. Nostalgic about their country's revolutionary heritage, they wanted to know how mankind could "survive with honor and human dignity."[14] The following year, the World Law Fund was created as an educational branch of the 13-year- old Institute for International Order.[15] Only two months later Washington, D.C.-area activists, headed by Dagmar Wilson, organized the national Women Strike for Peace as a means of mobilizing women in protest against the arms race. In November 1961, they put together protest demonstrations in more than twenty cities. Politicians became aware, very quickly, of the persuasive powers a mother can exert in looking out for her children's future.

WOMEN STRIKE FOR PEACE

The increasing role of female direct action in protesting the bomb is engagingly recounted in Amy Swerdlow's Women Strike for Peace: Traditional Motherhood and Radical Politics in the 1960s. Established in the early 1960's, WSP began as a grassroots, lobbying force protesting the nuclear arms race, but within a few years was engaging in civil disobedience, including the politics of protest, against the Vietnam War. WSP first made its presence known on

November 1, 1961 when thousands of mostly white middle class women engaged in, as Swerdlow, a participant herself, observed, an "unprecedented nationwide strike for peace." Throughout American cities, women carried placards with slogans reading "Pure Milk – Not Poison" and "No Tests – East or West." Reacting to a radioactive cloud from Soviet atomic tests passing over American cities, these protestors visited mayors, governors, congressional members, and even school board officials to express their fears regarding "pollution of children's milk from radioactive fallout."[16]

The November strike for peace encouraged WSP to develop more innovative and spontaneous forms of political protest. Employing a loosely structured, decentralized format enabled the women activists to utilize direct action tactics at the grassroots level. Between 1961 and 1962, WSP captured headlines through debates, walks, vigils, marches, local meetings, and letters to newspaper editors. Shunning the traditional politics of Left and Right, WSP leaders relied on "maternal rhetoric," criticizing the ways in which men in power undermined "the capacity of mothers to carry out their socially assigned roles of nurturance and life preservation." WSP's declaration of its makeup was simple and direct: "We are women of all races, creeds, and political persuasions." Despite an investigation by HUAC, WSP leaders seized the moment during congressional testimony by noting that as mothers for peace they were the most loyal and patriotic of all Americans: "With the fate of humanity resting on the push button, the quest for peace has become the highest form of patriotism."[17]

By 1963, WSP's membership counted close to 150,000 women. Most had a high level of education, but chose to identify themselves as housewives first. Its most successful campaign was in support of the nuclear test ban treaty. Mobilizing tens of thousands of women, WSP exerted intense political pressure by lobbying in Washington and at the UN, handing out leaflets at supermarkets, and marching in New York, Geneva, and Washington, D.C. WSP's efforts would also encourage many members of the university community to actively engage in research efforts to bring about world peace.

ACADEMICS FOR PEACE AND TURN TOWARD PEACE

The fear of a Third World War revitalized the academic approach to peace in the early sixties. The best known effort was that of the distinguished economist, Kenneth Boulding. While at the University of Michigan, Boulding published a theoretical analysis of conflict resolution entitled Conflict and Defense (1962). Basically a work of statistical compilation, Boulding's work was the first of its kind in America to analyze social and international conflicts by means of formal analytical models, derived from a large number of disciplines. With Boulding's leadership, a Center for Research in Conflict Resolution was formally established at the University of Michigan devoted to peace research and conflict resolution.[18]

The Center reflected three major beliefs of its founder: humanity is good, the war system is evil, and more powerful knowledge is necessary to transform the system, thus it represented an unusual alliance between humanistic wisdom and social science data. The primary purpose of the Center, according to DeBenedetti and other scholars, was to apply quantitative knowledge to social forces in order to build upon the premise that the national state is obsolete and that reliance on research, statistics, and information represents a way out of reliance on military force. Combining statistical data with skillful literary prose, Boulding's Center reached the same conclusion Randolph Bourne noted forty-odd years earlier: the state should be the servant, not the master of humanity.

Another attempt to change the course of American foreign policy was the creation of the umbrella organization Turn Toward Peace. It was formed in the fall of 1961 as forty peace, church, and labor organizations sought to reposition the peace movement in the direction of social change and curtail America's Cold War militarization. The New York Times described it as the largest single force in the peace movement. Ranging from the militantly pacifist CNVA to the American Veterans Committee, and, finally, to the Church of the Brethren, its aim was to devise an alternative to the threat of war as the primary means of American foreign policy. Led by Norman Thomas and coordinated by pacifists Robert Gilmore and Robert Pickus, TTP attempted to win over the communications media to its peace cause. Despite noble intentions, it was an organizational failure. TTP never established educational forms or sustained meaningful tactics to channel mass peace sentiment into a force that would gain the attention of government officials.[19]

NEW LEFT AND STUDENTS FOR A DEMOCRATIC SOCIETY

More effective at getting the government's attention was the emerging group of student radicals, civil rights workers, and action-minded intellectuals that became known as the New Left. Its primary interest was in participatory democracy, whereby people would actually participate in the decisions that shaped their lives. Their vision was of a more decentralized, socialist society. They differed from the Old Left of the previous era in that they were less likely to look to the traditional working class as an agent of social change; instead they looked to the young intelligentsia.[20]

SDS was the major organized expression of the New Left, and its Port Huron Statement made an explicit connection between an end to the Cold War and advancing domestic reform. Two factors troubled this generation: first, "the permeating and victimizing fact of human degradation, symbolized by the Southern struggle against racial bigotry"; second, the Cold War, "symbolized by the presence of the Bomb, brought awareness that we ourselves, and our friends, and millions of abstract 'others' we know more directly because of our common peril, might die at any time." Part of what was needed to achieve a truly democratic society, SDS asserted, was universal controlled disarmament: "disarmament to be discussed as a political, not technical, issue...and disengagement and demilitarization as part of the total disarming process." Only a New Left of young people, committed to political action, could succeed in providing "alternatives to helplessness."[21]

The majority of New Left participants were white, upper middle class, and well-educated. They came from the very segment of American life that had reaped the most benefits from the American system, both materially and educationally, yet they challenged the system. They were receptive to C. Wright Mills' The Power Elite (1956), which argued that centralized decision-making power was actually concentrated in the hands of small cliques in government, the economy, and the military, which together formed an interlocking directorate, a "power elite." Mills' concept of power elite struck a responsive chord among those who were concerned about the size of the military establishment, the concentration of economic power in great corporations, the growing bureaucratization of public and private institutions, and the indifference of the national government to these concerns. To those who felt estranged by the drift of American politics – especially left-leaning youth who sought some way to understand their sense of ineffectualness – Mills' interpretation proved a useful and worthwhile explanation. SDS was ideologically diverse, though America's Third World policies moved the SDS closer to anti-imperialists remnants of the Old Left such as the pro-Maoist Progressive Labor Party, the Trotskyist Socialist Workers Party, and the Young Socialist Alliance. It ran the gamut from center-left to communist to anarchist, and encompassed exponents of the tactics of direct action as well as those of more moderate persuasion. The national organization had a highly decentralized structure barely kept together by a small, constantly traveling, and underpaid staff (located in Chicago from 1965 on). Distrusting bureaucratic structures, SDS insisted that each local chapter work out its own programs. Most SDS members approached peace and social justice issues with high moral convictions and emotional commitment, but no grand theory held the organization together.[22]

In its early pre-Vietnam War years, SDS undertook a series of Economic Research and Action Programs. These programs promoted community organization in ghettos, both north and south. SDS members, working for almost no pay, moved into slums to help organize an "interracial movement of the poor" that could define and analyze outstanding problems, and pressure the established power structure into dealing with these problems. One of the best publicized ERAP ventures took place in Newark, New Jersey, under the leadership of Tom Hayden, a founder and prominent spokesman of SDS.[23]

As the Vietnam War became more of a focus in 1965, SDS introduced such tactical innovations as anti-war teach-ins and sit-ins, draft-counseling, "free schools" and "resistance" campaigns. Yet its original vision of participatory democracy, according to some observers, was one of the many casualties of the Vietnam War.[24]

CESAR CHAVEZ AND NON-VIOLENT UNIONISM

Although opposition to the war would take center stage in 1965, inspired by the actions of SDS, the connection between organizing workers and proponents for peace did not go unnoticed by social justice activists. It represented an ongoing commitment dating back to the post Civil War years. From the Knights of Labor to Cesar Chavez's United Farm Workers the peace movement supported non-violent unionism. With regard to migrant farm workers along the West Coast things began to heat up the very same year the U.S. became directly involved in the war in Vietnam. On September 8, 1965, Filipinos who were members of the Agricultural Workers Organizing Committee of the American Federation of Labor-Congress of Industrial Organizations, conducted a strike in the grape fields of Delano, California. The following week they were joined by the Mexican-American laborers of Chavez's National Farm Workers Association. It signaled the first successful strike by farm workers for union recognition in U.S. history.

What precipitated this action was the fact that large landowners controlled most of the agricultural land in California. The living and working conditions for the migrant workers were deplorable. They lived in shacks with no heat, walked on dirt floors, and the showers were outdoors. There were no plumbing facilities in these shacks – outhouses were used and were extremely unsanitary. Throughout the day they worked in the searing heat for up to 12-14 hours a day. They were paid less than minimum wages. Throughout the years numerous efforts had been made by migrant workers to organize, but in every instance their efforts were violently beaten down. The owners consistently sought cheap labor that was drawn from the poorest populations, including the Filipinos, Chinese, Japanese, Chicanos, and Mexicans. Since migrant farm workers were generally considered incapable of being organized many politicians and growers were satisfied with the status quo. By the early 1960s, coinciding with civil rights and the anti-war movements, efforts were underway to organized the migrant laborers.

The person most responsible was Chavez. Chavez's NFWA and the AWOC's Filipinos joined hands in mounting a 300 mile march from Delano to the state capital of Sacramento, publicizing their strike against the fruit growers. The walk ended on Easter Sunday, 1966, with the announcement of the very first farm worker contract. The large wine grape grower Schenley Industries, entered into the contract. On August 22, 1966, the two union groups merged to form the United Farm Workers' Organizing Committee. Chavez was selected as director.

Chavez brought to the farm labor organizing struggles a personal commitment to non-violence. Only in this manner was it possible for the migrant workers to maintain respect for their cause. With Chavez in the lead the protests took the forms of pickets, sit-ins, and processions, which were distinctly marked by strong religious overtones. Catholic masses were often conducted to boost the morale of strikers. Many clergy also joined the movement. Perhaps the new union's most effective tactic was the grape boycott. In February 1968, in an effort to prevent protestors from resorting to violence and to draw national attention to the boycott and strike, Chavez began a twenty-five–day fast. The International Grape Boycott organized that year also resulted in organizers canvassing over 100 cities in the U.S. and Canada. The loss of sales from the boycott, combined with strong public pressure and clergy backing, forced the twenty-six Delano growers to sign the first wide scale union contracts in California on July 26, 1970.

Chavez remained the leading figure in the UFW until his death in the early 1990s. Throughout the 1970s and 1980s he used his personal commitment to non-violence to publicize and promote the cause of the migrant farm workers. Relying on boycotts and non-violent strikes the UFW reached agreements the lettuce growers in Salinas in the early 1970s and with Coca-Cola's Minute Maid subsidiary in Florida (covering orange pickers who were mostly African American) in 1972. In June 1975, marking the first time in American history, the California legislature granted the right of agricultural workers to vote for the union they wanted to join. The efforts of Chavez and the UFW bore testimony to the effectiveness of non-violence in the struggle for economic and social justice in America. It represented another side to the tumultuous sixties which was largely dominated by the massive anti-war protests and demonstrations.[25]

THE VIETNAM WAR AND EARLY YEARS OF PROTEST

A few months before Chavez broke onto the scene as an important figure in the peace and justice movement, anti-war activists were already banking the flames of dissent against growing military involvement in Southeast Asia. Failing to learn from the French colonial failure and in violation of the Geneva Accords, which had set elections for a unified Vietnam to take place in 1956, the United States agreed to support Ngo Dinh Diem when he proclaimed himself president of a newly-created Republic of Vietnam (South Vietnam) in 1955. By that time, peace groups in America had been calling for a ceasefire in the war between Diem's Republic of Vietnam and the communist-backed National Liberation Front since hostilities had broken out in August. The U.S. continued its support of Diem's repressive regime until it became so embarrassing that the American government acquiesced to his assassination in 1963, just weeks before President John F. Kennedy's assassination in Dallas, Texas. In March 1964, Senate Foreign Relations Committee Chairman J. William Fulbright, Democrat from Arkansas and former Rhodes Scholar, called for a complete military disengagement from

Vietnam. No response was forthcoming from Lyndon Johnson's administration, which came into power after the Kennedy assassination. Then, some months later, the Gulf of Tonkin incident became Johnson's excuse for implementing military force. In August 1964, the U.S. claimed that two North Vietnamese gunboats had fired at an American naval ship off the coast of North Vietnam in the Gulf of Tonkin. Although there was some speculation about whether or not the ship had been fired upon (based on former Secretary of Defense Robert McNamara's The Fog of War, it is now widely accepted that there was no attack), it was enough for President Johnson to appear before Congress and request a formal resolution to commit military troops to Vietnam in the name of saving the South Vietnamese from communism.[26]

During the winter of 1964-65, the anti-war movement, countering the Johnson administration's charge of communist aggression, argued that the conflict was, in reality, a civil war not directed from Moscow or Beijing and that the U.S. had no right to be involved. According to various historians, the movement assumed three distinct parts as the war dragged on. First were the anti-imperialists who believed that the real enemy was America's corporate ruling class; for these protestors the war represented a revolutionary struggle for Vietnamese liberation against American imperialism. Second were the radical pacifists who saw the war as the real enemy, and advocated non-violent means to encourage immediate withdrawal of American troops. Last were the main-line peace liberals who emphasized the traditional means of political pressure to compel U.S. policymakers to negotiate an end to the war by providing for American withdrawal and a governmental role for the National Liberation Front in Saigon. Despite differences in substance and style, the most significant characteristic of the anti-war movement was its ability to coalesce and form new coalitions, which enabled the movement to sustain its momentum.[27]

The protestors were also as heterogeneous as American society and not all would fit nicely into the three general categories mentioned above. Small town demonstrations were likely to include housewives, business people, doctors, dentists, ministers, and workers. Demonstrations in large cities added students, college professors, bohemians, clergy, teachers, veterans in uniforms, and show-business celebrities. Most importantly, at the movement's grassroots, anti-war groups from pacifists to liberals viewed collaboration with American communists as far less heinous than the actions of their government and the indolence of the American people. Pacifists and political moderates saw the presence of radical activists or anarchists in their ranks as a tactical handicap but regarded the cause of ending the war as worth the association.[28]

Regardless of strategy, tactics, and composition, opposition to the war was first tragically dramatized on March 16, 1965, shortly after Johnson announced the bombing of North Vietnam and major troop increases. That day 82-year old Alice Herz, a survivor of Nazi terror, set herself on fire in Detroit and lingered in the hospital for ten days before dying. Eight months later two other self-immolations occurred: Quaker Norman Morrison set himself on fire before the Pentagon on November 2nd ; Catholic Worker volunteer Roger LaPorte torched himself in front of the United Nations in New York on November 9th. Their actions prompted distinguished peace advocate A.J. Muste to comment sarcastically: "But ours is a society composed of people who somehow feel that...the deaths of hundreds, thousands, millions in war is...somehow moral, human, civilized.... Even more, this is a society in which people contemplate, for the most part calmly, the self-immolation of the whole of mankind in a nuclear holocaust."[29]

By the summer of 1965, leading Americans were beginning to speak out against the war thus energizing the emerging student anti-war movement. I.F. Stone, the noted journalist, called for an immediate withdrawal. Senator Ernest Gruening (D- Alaska), Senator Wayne Morse (D-Oregon), both had voted against the Tonkin Gulf Resolution, political theorist Hans Morgenthau, George F. Kennan, father of the American containment policy, pediatrician Benjamin Spock, and retired Lt. General James Gavin either called for a ceasefire and negotiated settlement or urged the Johnson Administration to limit the U.S. military role in Vietnam and turn the war over to the Vietnamese.

Their respectable protest coincided with the anti-war "teach-ins" (informative programs held at universities throughout the country debating and questioning the merits of U.S. military involvement) that swept through the nation's colleges and universities in 1965. Having supported Johnson in 1964 as the "peace candidate," many faculty members and students felt betrayed as he adopted the Vietnam policies of his opponent Barry Goldwater. On March 24th, an all-night teach-in at the University of Michigan attracted 3,000 participants. This event touched off a series of teach-ins across the country. "We are using our [U.S.] power to thwart and abort an indigenous social and political revolution," charged Professor William Appleman Williams at the University of Wisconsin. Speaking at the University of Oregon, Senator Wayne Morse predicted: "Twelve months from tonight, there will be hundreds of thousands of American boys fighting in Southeast Asia—and tens of thousands of them will be coming home in coffins." At the University of Michigan, Arthur Waskow of the Institute of Policy Studies—condemning militarism and conscription—cited Jefferson on slavery: "I tremble for my country when I reflect that God is just." Artists, writers, and intellectuals were in the forefront of the protest.[30]

Between early 1965 and late 1967 there was a flurry of anti-war activity taking place on a number of fronts. For instance, college students were mobilizing efforts to put an end to the expanding military involvement in Vietnam. The commencement of Operation Rolling Thunder, in which B-52s dropped thousands of tons of bombs on North Vietnam, led SDS to call for an immediate March on Washington. Organizers Paul Booth and Todd Gitlin agreed that they would not exclude anyone, meaning communists, from the planned protest. Their decision drew criticism from longtime peace advocates such as Norman Thomas, Bayard Rustin, Robert Gilmore, and A.J. Muste. Leaders of SANE had already gone on record as being opposed to communist involvement in the peace movement. Seeking to circumvent SDS's role in the scheduled demonstration leaders of the established peace groups called for an independent peace movement with no ties to any form of totalitarianism or direction from foreign governments.

SDS leaders were miffed, but went ahead with the march anyway. It was the largest single anti-war demonstration yet conducted in the U.S. Some 20,000 demonstrators, mostly young people, arrived in Washington, D.C. on Easter Saturday, April 17th. A picket line encircled the White House and then the picketers marched to the Washington Monument where folksingers Judy Collins, Joan Baez, and Phil Ochs performed. In between their performances speeches were presented by Yale historian Staughton Lynd, I.F. Stone, civil rights leader Robert Moses, SDS president Paul Potter, and featured speaker Ernest Greuning. Potter was especially effective in pointing out the violence in Vietnam and in the U.S. as symptoms of a "deeper malaise." His speech was in keeping with the historic goal of peace pioneers calling upon reformers to make the U.S. a better place in which to live. Anti-war protestors need "to build a more decent society," Potter proclaimed, "a democratic and humane society in which Vietnams are unthinkable, in which human life and initiative are precious."[31] After the speeches and music ended the protestors marched eight abreast down the Mall to the Capitol steps. There petitions were handed over to elected officials calling for immediate withdrawal or a new Geneva Conference negotiating an end to the conflict.

The student anti-war movement that formed around the Vietnam War displayed some significant departures from previous anti-war student activism and was inspired by SDS's leadership and policy of nonexclusion. The movement that emerged was not as dependent on "parent groups" such as the Communist or Socialist Parties or the FOR as were the movements of the thirties. It was prompted by neither internationalist nor pacifist sentiments, although its critique of American society contained many similar objectives. A new group of intellectuals led the movement as part of a broader revolt against the values of Cold War America. As the war dragged on, students turned to more confrontational tactics, challenging the right of companies such as Dow Chemical, maker of napalm, to recruit on campus and targeting symbols of university complicity with the "war machine." Some of the most dramatic campus confrontations involved student opposition to R.O.T.C. programs (these increased in intensity after 1968 when a new draft law went into effect). Very often these were loud and boisterous, involving, in certain cases, the burning down of the R.O.T.C. building on campus. Unlike previous wars, the Vietnam War did not weaken protest, but rather invigorated it. The anti-war movement among students in the 1960's had more significant political impact than any of the earlier student movements.[32]

Peace groups also began picking up momentum as the war escalated. SANE sponsored a march on Washington for Peace in Vietnam on November 27, 1965. Two new groups—the pacifist Catholic Peace Fellowship and the interfaith Clergy and Laity Concerned about Vietnam (CAL-CAV)—joined SANE's anti-war march. Publicized as "A Call to Mobilize the Conscience of America," the action attracted a crowd estimated at 35,000 "moderate and respectable" war protesters. SANE-approved signs dominated the picket lines and read: "Stop the Bombings," "Respect 1954 Geneva Accords," "War Erodes the Great Society," and "Self-Determination – Vietnam for the Vietnamese." In this way, it strove to moderate both the demonstration's tone and to preserve its general atmosphere of dignity and restraint.

Attempting to create mainstream support for the anti-war movement became the object of Clergy and Laity Concerned about Vietnam. Initially, the National Emergency Committee of Clergy Concerned About Vietnam was organized in late 1965 by John C. Bennett, head of the National Council of Churches, Roman Catholic activist priest Daniel Berrigan, Yale minister William Sloane Coffin, Jr., its first Executive Secretary, Rabbi Abraham Heschel who became Executive Secretary, and Lutheran minister Richard John Neuhaus. Mobilizing religious leaders' opposition to the war, this committee quickly developed a national organization of Roman Catholic, Jewish, and Protestant clergy and laity. It officially adopted its formal name of Clergy and Laity

Concerned about Vietnam in 1966. Historian Mitch Hall notes that CAL-CAV provided the anti-war movement with broad access to religious leaders in large and small communities alike. Networking with religious leaders in local communities enabled CAL-CAV to get the anti-war message out to its followers. The organization began sponsoring delegations to North Vietnam and joined other anti-war groups in rallies and mass demonstrations throughout the nation.

At the same time peace groups were mobilizing the masses, opposition to the war within the ranks of the military and former veterans began to grow. Many of the soldiers were draftees who came from lower-income groups and the inner cities. Not all, however, fit this category. In June 1965, for example, Richard Steinke, a West Point graduate stationed in Vietnam, refused to board a helicopter bound for a remote village in the lowlands. His individual act of resistance, one coming from the officer corps, sent shock waves through the military and signaled how divided many soldiers felt about the war in general. For his own actions Steinke was subsequently court-martialed and summarily dismissed from the military.

Steinke's action was soon followed in February, 1966, when over one hundred veterans, accompanied by a few hundred supporters, marched to the White House where they gave back their medals. Their action prompted other veterans' groups to stage their own local protests in communities throughout the nation. An Ad Hoc Committee of Patriots for Peace in Vietnam conducted a two-day demonstration in Gainesville, Florida. This was followed by other small veterans' groups such as the Veterans for Peace and Veterans and Reservists to End the War in Vietnam.[33]

Perhaps the most dramatic act of GI resistance in the early years of the war was that of the "The Fort Hood Three." James Johnson, a black American, Dennis Mora, a Puerto Rican, and David Sambas of Lithuanian-Italian parentage announced to a stunned military that they would refuse their orders to report to Vietnam. On June 30, 1966, these three GI's arranged a press conference in New York, aided by the Fifth Avenue Peace Parade Committee, SNCC, and CORE.

Having made their announcement public, the draftees then pleaded with the peace movement to reach out to the other "trapped" and "helpless" enlisted men. The peace movement responded. A.J. Muste and Staughton Lynd co-chaired "The Fort Hood Three" Defense Committee.

Each member of "The Fort Hood Three" had his own reasons for opposing the war. Johnson saw a direct relationship between the peace movement and the civil rights movement. "The South Vietnamese are fighting for representation, like we ourselves. The South Vietnamese just want a voice in the government, nothing else. Therefore the 'Negro' in Vietnam is just helping to defeat what his black brother is fighting for in the United States." Mora would "not fight for the blood money of war industries" nor give his "life so that U.S. corporations can claim as their property the people and resources of Vietnam." Sambas relied on a comparison to America's War for Independence, maintaining that "We are telling them, we are instructing them by force...to live the way we want them to live.... I believe the war to be immoral, unjust, and illegal." Despite the vigorous efforts of the Committee to halt their prosecutions, all three men were tried and convicted: on September 9, Johnson and Sambas were given maximum sentences of five years at Leavenworth and Mora was given a three-year sentence. All of the men were given dishonorable discharges resulting in forfeitures of their pay.[34]

The strategy of building coalitions to protest the war continued unabated during the years 1965-1967. In February, 1966, the Fifth Avenue Peace Parade Committee, organized by Muste and the National Coordinating Committee to End the War in Vietnam (NCCEWV) based in Madison, Wisconsin, brought out 5,000 pickets in New York City opposing the presentation of a Freedom House Award to President Johnson. The following month between 20,000 and 25,000 marchers participated in another demonstration under the leadership of the National Committee. The New York <u>Times</u> reported that the parade was led by "a sizeable contingent of disillusioned American war veterans and Afro-Americans against the war," and participants were "a racially and politically mixed lot." At a rally in Central Park Mall, Muste, Vietnam veteran Donald Duncan and writer Norman

Mailer attacked Johnson's war. They were not without their "hecklers and egg-throwers," however, which proved the pro-war forces were not about to lie down and die.[35]

A month later, under CNVA sponsorship, A.J. Muste, veteran activist Barbara Deming, Brad Lyttle, anti-nuclear activist Karl Meyer, outspoken anti-war scientist William Davidson, and peace movement novice Sherry Thurber flew to Saigon to show the South Vietnamese that some Americans opposed the war. The Americans held cordial meetings with the underground South Vietnamese peace movement but were harassed by Vietnamese youth at public meetings. The peace contingent believed the harassment had been ordered by the South Vietnamese government, with the approval of the United States. Thus, they returned home to eliminate the chance of further misunderstandings.[36]

Many anti-war activists went to Vietnam during the war. In some instances it was to find out what the facts were and return to the United States with the information in the hopes of encouraging a negotiated settlement. In other instances it was to try to reach North Vietnamese officials and work as intermediaries to further the peace process. And in certain situations it was to bring humanitarian aid to the victims of the conflict such as the efforts by the Society of Friends.

On July 13, 1966, A Quaker Action Group was formed with Larry Scott and George Willoughby as co-chairs. Seeking to work apart from the yearly meeting's control and support for funding, a number of radical Quakers joined the group. Among them were Lillian Willoughby, Barbara Deming, Albert Bigelow, Viola Scott, Bob Eaton, Ross Flanagan, George Hardin, A.J. Muste, Robert Gilmore, George Lakey, Wilmer Young, and Charles Walker. The group's first major action was to send medical supplies to North Vietnam.

Despite opposition from the federal government, AQAG went ahead with its plans to bring medical supplies to North Vietnam by sailing its own ship into Haiphong Harbor. The vessel they chose to sail was the yacht, Phoenix. When word got out that the vessel was ready to sail the State Department refused to issue passports to the intrepid crew. Undaunted by this action a crew of Quakers from around the U.S. was assembled. It consisted of the following: a mother of six from Madison, Wisconsin; Bob Eaton, a Philadelphia draft resister; men from Massachusetts and California; and a 61-year-old printer from northern Ohio.

With its crew's action considered to be civil disobedience against the U.S. government, the Phoenix arrived in Hiroshima on February 18, 1967. The woman from Wisconsin, Betty Boardman, first flew to Hiroshima with $100,000 to buy medical supplies for the trip to North Vietnam. While the boat was docked in Hiroshima, Dr. Tomin Harada, a supporter of this mission, managed to cobble together some one hundred medical kits. On March 1, 1967, the Phoenix set sail down the coast for Hong Kong before arriving at its final destination: Haiphong Harbor. The American consul in Hong Kong sternly warned the crew that sailing into Vietnamese waters could lead to prosecution and possibly jail terms. The event garnered worldwide attention and came to symbolize peaceful acts of civil disobedience on the part of the anti-war movement. As the vessel continued on its course, White House presidential aide Walt Rostow avoided a public-relations disaster by ordering the American navy to allow the peace-supply boat to pass. Without any fear for their lives the Phoenix crew sailed into Haiphong Harbor during an intense American air raid. The supplies were delivered amid North Vietnamese lectures on U.S. atrocities and viewing of children who were severely wounded from American bombing raids. This mission was warmly received by veteran peace activists and demonstrated that opposition to the war was coming from many different fronts.

Building coalitions against the war was also aided by the actions of female and African American protestors. As in other periods of U.S. history, women played a significant role in the peace movement. WSP, for example, expanded its activities to call for an end to the war. Concerned women carried banners and signs throughout many of the peace parades urging that the soldiers be supported by being brought home. Their sympathies were aimed at the young men who were drafted to fight in a brutal, unjust war, and innocent Vietnamese civilians.

During the formative years of anti-war opposition WSP escalated its tactics, participating in more acts of civil disobedience. WSP activists staged sit-ins in congressional offices and die-ins at draft boards and at the corporate headquarters of major defense contractors. WSP participated in marches, as well as counseling more than 100,000 young men about their legal rights under the selective service law. Women of all ages were present at draft card burnings, appeared at armed forces induction lines where they distributed flyers urging men not to go, and even sat in at trials of draft resisters. WSP also arranged three conferences with leading North Vietnamese women and the National Liberation Front of South Vietnam. The slogan at these gatherings was "Not Our Sons, Not Your Sons, Not Their Sons." One of the organization's most famous tactics took place in 1967 when close to 2,500 members went to Washington, D.C., and removed their shoes and banged them on the doors of the Pentagon. In another instance, invoking a sense of humor, the Los Angeles section published a cartoon in its local paper Peace de Resistance Cookbook #1, depicting a mother in a delicately patterned apron carrying a sign which read, "Bring the Boys Home for Dinner." Remarkably, the issues of nuclear proliferation, above-ground nuclear testing, and the war in Vietnam were responsible for an organization that transformed, Swerdlow maintains, the image of the "concerned mother from private to public and from passive victim of war to active fighter for peace."[37]

In March 1967, inspired by WSP's actions, fifteen women on the West Coast created Another Mother for Peace. Founded by Academy Award-winning screenwriter Barbara Avedon after the birth of her son, Another Mother for Peace argued that war was obsolete and civilized methods must be created to end the conflict in Vietnam and prevent future wars. Avedon and her female companions such as TV star Donna Reed printed 1,000 Mother's Day cards and sent them to Congressional representatives urging them to talk peace, not war. The response was so overwhelming that by the end of May they had sold over 20,000 cards. The money they raised from selling the cards was then used to support legislators who were willing to vote against future appropriations for the war.

Meanwhile, the African American protest movement brought other issues, personnel, and tactics into the anti-war movement. In January 1966, linking the war to domestic oppression, the Student Non-violent Coordinating Committee's leaders declared their support for draft resisters – "Hell No, We Won't Go" – and attacked President Johnson for violating international law overseas while neglecting to enforce civil rights ordinances at home. In June, Stokely Carmichael, the new leader of SNCC, led civil rights demonstrators in the streets of Atlanta, encouraging black youths to refuse military induction. Most importantly, Martin Luther King, Jr.—the civil rights movement's spiritual leader and 1964 Nobel Peace Prize recipient—accepted the co-chairmanship of CALCAV in 1966 and proceeded to dispute the war policy of the Johnson White House. His 1967 speech condemning the war linked the issues of peace and civil rights together, a connection that some in both movements resistated.[38]

In an important recent book entitled Peace and Freedom: The Civil Rights and Anti-war Movements in the 1960s, British historian Simon Hall notes that the failure of the peace and freedom movements to work together as one continuous force was reflective of an increasingly segmented left. During the war, conservatives, especially, were able to achieve remarkable electoral success by tapping into white working class and ethnic discontent. They did so by focusing on issues such as black power, the anti-war movement, liberal welfare programs, and countercultural hedonism. More to the point, Hall also argues that traditional African-American organizations like the National Urban League and the NAACP were slower than the newer groups such as SNCC, SCLC, and CORE, to get on board the train. The question of priorities, racial equality first and ending the war second, was always evident. A meaningful coalition between civil rights organizations and the mainstream peace movement never fully materialized, even though proportionally more African Americans than whites were opposed to the war. The major problem was that of multi-issuism: how to link an immediate withdrawal from Vietnam with racial equality and an end to poverty.

To some extent, blacks and whites emphasized different issues; whites focused mainly on Vietnam, American imperialism, and student issues, while black activists were not only anti-imperialist but also focused on eradicating a culture of oppression within the framework of a new identity for African Americans. The bottom line, according to Hall, was that the peace movement's own leftist infighting, exacerbated by the white counterculture movement and failure to relate to African Americans in a meaningful way, accounted for the widespread lack of African American participation in the peace movement.[39]

In this context, King's 1967 speech is even more noteworthy. "Beyond Vietnam: A Time to Break Silence," delivered at Riverside Church in Manhattan urged civil rights activists to speak out against the war. Against the advice of many of his colleagues, including the board of SCLC, King explained to his attentive audience why it was necessary to connect civil rights, opposition to the Vietnam War, and economic exploitation. These represented the "triple evils" destroying the soul of America. Silence could no longer be tolerated nor accepted despite his critics' worry that his talking about the cause of peace would hurt their struggle by alienating the Johnson administration and opening African Americans to charges of being unpatriotic.

King was not the first activist to link peace and civil rights. Black women in WILPF – Erna Harris, Flemmie Cottrell, Enola Maxwell – had struggled to make these connections clear to fellow activists in an earlier era, as had Bob Gore, an African American pacifist who was part of CNVA's 1963 Quebec-Washington-Guantanamo Walk for Peace. For him, as well as many others, the connection between civil rights, peace and poverty represented a fight for democratic rights and individual empowerment.

It was this tradition King drew upon to further the cause of peace and justice. In his analysis, ending the war in Vietnam, which wasted valuable economic resources and hurt U.S. society spiritually, was an important step toward achieving justice and ending economic exploitation. That was the message he held on to until his untimely death a year later.

WAR TAX RESISTANCE

Protesting the war through coalitions, GI dissent, veterans' groups, and gaining support from females and African Americans characterized one aspect of the peace movement during the early years of the war. Yet there were also other forms of opposition in addition to speeches and demonstrations. Tax resistance became a popular tool to oppose the war. In 1966, the federal telephone tax was raised and, in a rare moment of candor, the federal government admitted that the additional money would be used to help subsidize the war. Peacemakers, War Resisters League, CNVA, FOR and other peace groups urged nonpayment of this tax. In fact, in 1965, the Peacemakers formed the "No Tax for War in Vietnam Committee" calling upon signers to take the pledge "I am not going to pay taxes on 1965 income." This was followed by a committee led by A.J. Muste that obtained 370 signatures (including Joan Baez, David Dellinger, Dorothy Day, Noam Chomsky, Nobel Prize-winner Albert Szent-Gyorgyi and Staughton Lynd), and which placed an ad in The Washington Post proclaiming their intention not to pay all or part of their 1965 income taxes. By 1967, nearly 500 people had signed the Peacemakers pledge. Also in that year writer Gerald Walker of The New York Times Magazine began organizing the Writers and Editors War Tax Protest. Some 528 writers and editors pledged themselves to refuse the ten percent war surtax – just added to income taxes – and "possibly" the twenty-three percent of their income tax allocated for the war.

The IRS's discomfort with the burgeoning movement grew and, as the government's reprisals became more frequent, the need for legal information within the tax resistance community became manifest. To disseminate information about which taxes opponents of war could refuse to pay and who would represent their case in tax court, War Tax Resistance was formed. Under the leadership of Bob and Angie Calvert, it devoted itself to all the aspects and ramifications of conscientious tax refusal. WTR's first press conference included

Allen Ginsberg's reading of a tax resistance poem and a musical plea for peace by Pete Seeger.

One interesting tactic of tax resistance was for an individual to claim enough dependents on his or her forms to prevent an employer from withholding any income taxes. The idea was first introduced by Ken Knudson in a 1965 letter to the Peacemaker. Groups such as Peacemakers, Catholic Worker, and WRL, along with other groups, promoted the idea of inflating W-4 forms. This tactic brought particularly strong counteraction by the government and a number of people were prosecuted and imprisoned, including a 64-year old grandmother named Martha Tranquilli. Despite such acts of retribution, the number of known income tax resisters grew from 275 in 1966 to almost 20,000 by the early 1970's. Participants in the telephone tax resistance numbered in the hundreds of thousands. Other groups subsequently formed "people's life funds," which sent war tax money to fund community development and other social programs (in 1972, Congressman Ronald Dellums (D-California) introduced legislation promoting the World Peace Tax Fund Act designed to create a conscientious objector status for taxpayers. One of its major supporters was folksinger Joan Baez, who established her own peace awareness program, the Institute for the Study of Nonviolence, in Carmel Valley, California.[40]

PROTESTS AND OPPOSITION TO THE DRAFT CONTINUES

While war tax resistance was gaining in popularity, opposition to the war kept growing along with increasing numbers of Conscientious Objectors and draft evaders. By 1967, anti-war sentiment in America was at fever pitch. A series of events that year magnified the intensity with which organizations and individuals were protesting the war. First, A.J. Muste, German pastor Martin Niemoller (aged 75), Anglican Bishop Ambrose Reeves (aged 67), and American Rabbi Abraham Feinberg (aged 67 and serving a congregation in Toronto) spent ten days in North Vietnam (January 9-19). In outright contradiction to statements from Washington denying American air attacks in the area around Hanoi, Muste wrote from that city to the CNVA that no more than three or four blocks from his hotel in the center of town there were civilian neighborhoods reduced to rubble. Based on what they were seeing, Muste directed Americans back home to convey a message to Washington: "For God's sake stop lying!...Let us stop this bombing practice or else say honestly to our government, to the world, and to ourselves, 'We are trying to bomb the hell out of the Vietnamese people.'"[41] Second, on the heels of Muste's trip to Hanoi a group of trade unionists organized the National Labor Leadership Assembly for Peace, hoping to convince workers in defense plants of the war's immorality. The spring March on the Pentagon, sponsored by CNVA, went right to the doorstep of the nation's military might. Activists surrounded the building and some even splattered blood and red paint on entrances. Third, in the summer, heavyweight boxing champion Muhammad Ali was sentenced to five years in jail and a $10,000 fine for refusing induction on the grounds of his Black Muslim beliefs precluding him from fighting in a white man's war. Fourth, army surgeon Captain Howard Levy made public his refusal to train combat first aid teams for action in Vietnam. Finally, respected Harvard liberal economist and former ambassador to India in the Kennedy Administration, John Kenneth Galbraith, bluntly published a little pamphlet arguing that "it is reasonable, indeed an inescapable, assumption that we are in conflict not alone with the communists but with a strong sense of Vietnamese nationalism. If so, a further and massive conclusion follows. It is that we are in a war that we cannot win and, even more important, one we should not wish to win."[42]

By this time, the rate of Conscientious Objection was four times as large as World War II, while levels of draft evasion, violations, and exile to Canada or into the domestic underground reached record heights. The country had never seen such a serious challenge to the Selective Service Law. Though many young men volunteered for military service or accepted the draft willingly, unprecedented personal anti-war decisions became more and more commonplace. For instance, a University of Rochester student, Vincent Francis McGee, not only burned his draft card but sent the following missive to the President of the United States: "....I am very much aware of the consequences of the deed done today [April 15, 1967], but find no other way in which to effectively protest what seems to be the decision of our government concerning the future. I cannot participate in this evil and must cry out against it.... I consider this act not only non-treasonous but completely patriotic. Blind patriotism would be treason here for me...."[43] Thus did many draft resisters express their commitment to personal liberty and the dictates of conscience in a democratic society.

Fleeing to Canada became another visible manifestation of opposition to the war. For many resisters it was a tough decision to abandon home and family, and in some cases it would take many years for the healing to occur. Many fathers who served during World War II found it difficult to accept their sons' reasons for refusing to serve. During the first couple of years of the war Alice Lynd compiled We Won't Go, an anthology in which she discusses the reasons for young American men fleeing to Canada and includes their own personal statements.[44] Richard Paterak, a graduate of Marquette University, observed that the "unavoidable conclusion was that we [U.S.] were being politically impractical, internationally as well as domestically, and, at the same time, immoral." To David Taube, an Army reservist, the thought of killing "innocent Vietnamese" was a reality with which he could not live. "I was about to go to jail. Although this wouldn't be as good as active rebellion for the anti-war cause, it would have at least made the U.S. feed and clothe me for five years....Canada seemed to be nicer than a jail, however, [so] I chose to opt out of the struggle."[45] For the British subject Ivan Petrokovsky, who had been living in the United States for ten years, the draft and the Vietnam war were reasons to leave. "I am not a pacifist, but I do not like violence or killing." Petrokovsky's move to Canada, more than an act of political resistance, was in his eyes a psycho-social form of liberation: "...if there is one thing I would like to say to my people...it is that it is possible to act independently, that it feels good if you are strong enough to follow through on your act...it will be a better world."[46]

THE MOBES AND OPERATION CHAOS

There were also brief, but spectacular, coalitions such as the National Mobilization. Originally called the Spring Mobilization to End the War in Vietnam, it was a loose coalition of groups that sought to stoke the flames of escalating opposition to military involvement. Its greatest success was organizing massive anti-war marches in New York and San Francisco on April 15, 1967. As usual, estimates of attendance varied according to the source; anywhere from one hundred thousand (police estimate) to four hundred thousand (mobilization estimate) turned out in New York and probably about fifty to one hundred thousand rallied in San Francisco.

Throughout the war years, the “Mobes” and their organizers coordinated thousands of anti-war groups into massive and demonstrative nationwide protests. The leadership consisted of a wide range of peace groups from communists and socialists to Quakers. “Mobes” such as the Spring Mobilization (1966), Student Mobilization (1966), National Mobilization (1967), and the New Mobilization (1969) called for an end of American military involvement in the war and the withdrawal of American troops.

Perhaps the highlight of the year’s 1967 anti-war activities occurred during the weekend of October 21-22, when approximately 100,000 Americans came to Washington, D.C. to protest the Vietnam War. It was the largest anti-war protest in the history of the United States. After a Saturday morning of speeches and song near the Lincoln Memorial, 35,000 protesters crossed the Potomac River to the Pentagon—where they confronted close to 3,000 U.S. troops and federal marshals dispatched to protect the Capitol from American citizens (for the first time since the depression-era 1932 Bonus March of World War I veterans). During that hectic weekend, confrontations between the two opposing factions resulted in 47 injuries and 683 arrests. From that point on anti-war militants expressed more determination than ever to escalate their opposition from simple dissent to outright resistance.[47]

The Johnson Administration, however, initiated its own attack. In an effort to discredit the peace movement by linking it to communism, Johnson prodded the Central Intelligence Agency (CIA) to investigate the underpinnings of the anti-war dissent. Johnson was well aware that domestic spying on the civil rights movement had been going on since the mid-1950s. Between the mid-1950s and 1971 the Federal Bureau of Investigation (FBI) conducted an elaborate Counterintelligence Program (COINTELPRO) that harassed and attempted to discredit African American groups. Some of the most intense counter-intelligence operations were directed at the Black Panther Party, which the FBI considered a serious threat to internal security. Although the anti-war protests were a matter of domestic surveillance, administration officials selected the CIA under the pretext that foreign operatives were responsible for many of the domestic disturbances related to the opposition to the war.

With Operation CHAOS in full swing in August 1967, the CIA undertook surveillance of domestic dissidents. According to the agency's report, "International Connections of U.S. Peace Movement," some 7,200 Americans had been "bugged" by 1970, with a computer index to the names of an additional 300,000 individuals and groups. Yet, with all this sophisticated equipment, CIA director Richard Helms admitted that communist control of domestic dissent was more myth than reality. In fact, scholarly research makes it clear that there never was outside control.

The very notion of CIA spying on American citizens had been an ongoing enterprise by the American government since 1959, during the Communist Revolution in Cuba. In 1964, President Johnson permitted then-CIA director John McCone to establish a new super-secret branch called the Domestic Operations Division (DOD). A year later, Johnson instructed McCone to provide an independent analysis of the growing student anti-Vietnam War protest movement. Previously, the president had relied primarily on J. Edgar Hoover and the Federal Bureau of Investigation for such information. What prompted Johnson's actions was Hoover's insistence that international communism was manipulating student protests for its own purposes. Johnson wanted the CIA, whose primary responsibility was overseas surveillance, to confirm or deny Hoover's assertion.

In June 1966, Richard Helms was appointed the new Director of the CIA. He slowly expanded the CIA's domestic intelligence operations by conducting covert surveillance intelligence gathering on college and university campuses. The CIA implemented two new domestic operations. The first, Project Resistance, was set up to provide security to CIA recruiters on college campuses. The program sought active cooperation from college administrators, campus security, and local police to assist in identifying anti-war activists, political dissenters, and "radicals." Information on thousands of students and dozens of groups was given to DOD and government recruiters on campus. The second project, MERRIMAC, was designed to provide warnings about demonstrations around CIA facilities or personnel in and around the nation's Capitol. The fear that the movement would move from dissent to resistance and disrupt the machinery of government had created a sense of urgency within Johnson's inner circle.

In 1968, Helms consolidated all CIA domestic intelligence operations under one program – CHAOS. Some fifty CHAOS agents, after several weeks of training to act like student radicals, promptly enrolled in colleges and universities working under cover. By 1970, more sinister operations were underway including "black bag operations" (planting false but incriminating evidence and infiltrators), wiretappings, and mail-openings investigating all forms of actions: protests, travel to international peace conferences, and movements of members of various dissident groups, etc.

An agency document, "International Connections of the U.S. Peace Movement," released years later revealed how extensive domestic spying had been during the war. The document showed that surveillance of domestic dissidents had burgeoned into matters regarding the financing of anti-war groups, the day-to-day activities and itineraries of leaders in the peace movement, and the daily functioning of peace groups on college campuses. The CIA spied on some of the more noted organizations such as SDS, WSP, the American Indian

Movement, SNCC, FOR, WILPF, the Nation of Islam, the Youth International Party, the Women's Liberation Movement, Black Panthers, and CAL-CAV. But for all its efforts, Operation CHAOS never established a direct link between the peace movement and the Communist International because there was none. In 1973, newly-appointed CIA Director William Colby terminated the operation.[48]

DRAMATIC ACTS OF CIVIL DISOBEDIENCE

Spying on American protestors and anti-war organizations strengthened the resolve of pioneers for peace and justice. By 1968, public opposition to the war was at an all-time high and events that year turned out to be some of the most dramatic in American history. The year began with the Tet offensive in which a surprise attack was carried out against the American Embassy in Saigon and Johnson's decision not to run for reelection – "If nominated I will not run, if elected I will not serve." Between April and September, the nation witnessed the assassinations of Martin Luther King, Jr. and Robert F. Kennedy, violent strikes on college campuses, raids on draft boards, the My Lai incident (not made public at the time, however, in which Lt. William Calley and other soldiers massacred innocent men, women and children in a Vietnam village sparking outrage and embarrassment for the U.S. military when it was revealed), and the violence that marked the Democratic National Convention in Chicago. Such events further polarized people's views of the war and the peace movement.

The Democratic Convention was one example of how explosive things had become in the U.S. Protestors in Chicago hoped the Democrats would nominate a peace candidate. When Mayor Richard Daley refused to grant permits for demonstrations in the city, many people stayed away during convention week knowing that violence was likely. The battles in the streets that did, indeed, take place were later termed a "Police riot" by an investigating commission. Nevertheless, eight activists were put on trial in 1969 for conspiracy to incite a riot, including Yippie founders Jerry Rubin and Abbie Hoffman. Dave Dellinger, who had assumed the mantle of pacifist leadership after A. J. Muste's death in 1967, was also one of the Chicago Eight (which became seven after Black Panther leader Bobby Seale was severed from the trial). At the end of what became the most celebrated political trial of the era, just prior to sentencing, Dellinger was given the chance to speak. Judge Julius Hoffman tried to cut him off, but he responded by shouting: "You want us to be like good Germans, supporting the evils of our decade, and then when we refused to be good Germans and came to Chicago and demonstrated, now you want us to be like good Jews, going quietly and politely to the concentration camps while you and this court suppress freedom and the truth." The convictions were later overturned.[49]

For radical students at Columbia University, it seemed time to up the ante in the face of the university's military research and its building a gym in Harlem that locals would have no access to. In April 1968 they took over administrative offices in Low Library. Convinced it was necessary to stop business as usual and challenge the powers that be, SDS and the Student Afro-American Society (SAS) led 700 to 1,000 students in the seizure of five university buildings. The spark that set off the explosion was an SDS rally called to protest Columbia's relation to the Institute for Defense Analysis (IDA), the university's racist policies, and the administration's placing of six SDS leaders, including Mark Rudd, on probation for violation of a rule against indoor demonstrations. After six days, with the aid of more than 1,000 policemen, the buildings were cleared, but the campus was in chaos. For the rest of the academic year, education was at a standstill.[50]

While confrontation on college campuses became a regular occurrence, many Catholic peace activists showed their disdain for the war in another way – their means was destroying draft board files. The Catholic Left sparked a long series of draft board raids that began in 1967 and did not terminate until 1972. From coast to coast, similar raids occurred in Boston, New York, Milwaukee, Chicago, Los Angeles, Evanston, Illinois, and San Jose, California. Linking corporate activity to the war, activists also raided corporation offices and factories following much the same style as action against draft boards. In 1967 in

Washington, D.C., a group of nine Catholics raided the offices of Dow Chemical Company and exposed official documents tying Dow directly to the manufacture of napalm used in the war. Some months later, another group, calling itself The Beaver 55, scrambled computer tapes at Dow's Midland, Michigan, research center.

The inspiration for these raids had come from the establishment of the Catholic Peace Fellowship (CPF) in the summer of 1964. The organization was founded by Daniel and Philip Berrigan and three former Catholic Worker editors, Thomas Cornell, James Forest, and Martin J. Corbin. Its sponsors included Dorothy Day, John Deely of Commonweal, Gordon Zahn, Thomas Merton, and Msgr. Paul Hanley Furfey. Formed in the spirit of Vatican II, CPF became the only Catholic peace group that was institutionally connected to non-Catholics—namely, the primarily Protestant, ecumenical Fellowship of Reconciliation. CPF emphasized the pacifist traditions of the Catholic Church, participated in direct, non-violent anti-war protests, organized study conferences, and counseled Conscientious Objectors.

CPF's success in attempting to disrupt the draft and show the connection between the war and corporate America was in large part due to the efforts of Daniel and Philip Berrigan. They were the first Roman Catholic priests to receive federal prison sentences for their anti-war activities. Daniel was ordained as a Jesuit and Philip was a former Josephite. Influenced by Martin Luther King Jr., and Day's Catholic Worker Movement, the Berrigans increasingly turned to active non-violence in response to the escalation of U.S. military involvement in Vietnam. In the summer of 1965, much to the chagrin of the hawkish Francis Cardinal Spellman, Daniel helped to found the interdenominational Clergy and Laity Concerned about Vietnam.

Philip would soon follow in his older brother's footsteps. On October 27, 1967, he and three associates carried out a planned raid upon an inner city draft board in Baltimore. The "Baltimore Four," as they were dubbed, entered the office and grabbed a number of records and poured containers of duck blood on

Selective Service files (not digital then). Shortly after accompanying the historian and activist Howard Zinn to Hanoi, North Vietnam, Daniel joined his brother and seven others in destroying Selective Service files in Catonsville, Maryland. After alerting the media about their raid, on May 17, 1968, the "Catonsville Nine" entered the draft board and seized some 1-A files. They escaped to an adjacent parking lot, placed the documents in trash containers they had brought, and burned the files using homemade napalm while reciting the Lord's Prayer. The police then rushed in and arrested them. Their actions gained national attention.

Scheduled to report to federal authorities on April 9, 1970, the brothers chose to go underground. Daniel had been sentenced to three years in jail; Philip had been given three and one-half years, to run concurrently with the six years he had already begun serving for his first draft board incident. After only twelve days Philip, along with a companion from the Baltimore Four, was picked up by authorities. Daniel was later arrested on Block Island (off Rhode Island), having avoided capture for several months. The Berrigans were paroled in 1972.

Throughout these years, the Catholic Left, inspired by the Berrigans' actions, resorted to other targets. An anonymous group raided the Media, Pennsylvania, office of the FBI, expropriating documents that proved the FBI was conducting covert and illegal surveillance of groups and individuals working for social change. Other groups dismantled bomb casings at a York, Pennsylvania, manufacturer, and at Hickam Air Force Base in Hawaii poured blood on secret documents concerning electronic warfare, which was reducing the government's need for conscripts to continue the war.

Participants in the various raids based their rationale on several events in both religious and secular history. They cited the clearing of moneychangers from the Temple by Jesus and the Boston Tea Party preceding the American Revolution. They held that nothing short of civil disobedience and direct interference with the war machine would be effective. Their most commonly used phrase was, "...some property has no right to exist," as draft records, computer tapes, surveillance files, industrial war research, and secret files used to further the war and stop the peace effort became fair game for destruction. In the words of one pacifist priest, "It was saner to burn papers rather than children."[51]

Generally, the action communities resisted openly by destroying property and waiting for arrest. Many were willing to follow in the words of Day: ". . . I wish to place myself beside A.J. Muste to show solidarity of purpose with these young men and to point out that we, too, are breaking the law, committing civil disobedience." In many cases, activists invited members of the news media to view the event, so that the group would receive as much publicity as possible. Protestors then used the trials that followed as forums to discuss the war, raise the question of property rights, focus public attention on Vietnam, and challenge the Judiciary to take legal responsibility where the Executive and Legislative would not. Those who went to jail considered incarceration as an essential part of their resistance.[52]

In time this style of disobedience was replaced by more covert activity. Anonymous groups carried out raids taking responsibility at a later date or, in certain instances, not at all. Covert action was just another step in their resistance. Rather than go to jail willingly, they preferred to make the government work for arrest and conviction, thereby demonstrating "that personal and public inconvenience works both ways." If it was an inconvenience to be drafted, it was also an inconvenience to be prevented from implementing such policy. These hit-and-run raids were experiments with "styles of resistance that held the line at destroying property rather than people."[53] While the issue of property destruction did raise many eyebrows within pacifist circles, the question of property rights versus human rights was brought to the attention of millions of Americans in a very dramatic way.

So, too, did the issue of equal rights for women and the notion of empowerment. Inspired by the publication of The Feminine Mystique by Betty Freidan, women looked to increase their visibility in the anti-war movement. One innovative and useful strategy occurred in January 1968. Coalitions of women's groups, led by members in WSP and WILPF, formed the Jeannette Rankin

Brigade. A year earlier Rankin publicly stated that if thousands of women were willing to go to jail in opposition to the war then the conflict would end. When the new Congress convened on January 15, 1968, thousands of women marched with Rankin to the steps of the Capitol where she and Coretta Scott King presented a petition to the Speaker of the House and the Senate Majority leader demanding an end to the war in order to heal the divisiveness at home.

During this demonstration another interesting development occurred. A group calling itself the New York Radical Women and some members of the Rankin Brigade broke ranks and continued their protest at Arlington National Cemetery. Apparently, presenting a petition was not enough. At Arlington this group performed a moving ceremony that not only included criticisms of the war but also demanded for full equality for women. One of the New York Radical Women's spokeswomen, Kathie Amatmiek, later Sarachild, pointed out that the drafting of men actually fostered second-class citizenship upon women. Young men were in a better position to exert power over their own lives by refusing to be drafted whereas females were only capable of supporting draft resistance. How were they going to exert real pressure on government leaders?

During this same period the recently-established Another Mother for Peace held its first annual Mother's Day Assembly in Los Angeles. At this gathering the group unveiled its new logo. The logo was created by Lorraine Schneider and remains one of the most famous in American peace history. The logo has large flowers surrounded by the words, "War is not healthy for children and other living things." It is an icon in today's popular culture.

Separate acts of GI resistance were also on the rise in the late sixties. An African-American private from Oakland would not board his troop plane bound for Vietnam. Navy Lieutenant Susan Schnall, a nurse, was court-martialed for marching in a peace demonstration in uniform and dropping anti-war leaflets on navy installations from a plane. An Army lieutenant was arrested in early 1968 for picketing the White House with a sign questioning the war and noting that already there were over 100,000 casualties. Two black marines, George Daniels and

William Harvey, were given extended prison terms for encouraging other black marines to criticize the war; later their sentences were reduced due to a public outcry of injustice.

One of the most dramatic incidents of GI dissent was that of eighteen-year-old Army deserter Ray Kroll. Desertions were a serious problem as many soldiers fled to Canada. Others, like Kroll, took "Sanctuary" in churches where they waited to be captured and court-martialed. In Kroll's case he took "Sanctuary" at the chapel at Boston University. Close to a thousand students kept a vigil over Kroll for five days. When federal agents showed up on Sunday morning they forced their way down the crowded aisles, smashed down the doors and carried Kroll away to the stockade.

Dissent also manifested itself in other unique ways. Until it was declared a "public nuisance" and shut down by order of the court at the end of 1968, a "GI Coffeehouse" was set up outside Fort Jackson, South Carolina. Soldiers who came to get coffee and doughnuts also found plenty of anti-war literature for consumption. Other GI Coffeehouses sprang up near military bases to the consternation of the commanders. Underground newspapers such as About Face, Fed Up!, Short Times, and Last Harass printed stories, alerted soldiers about harassment cases against other GIs, provided legal advice, and suggested ways to resist orders short of court martial. In Vietnam some soldiers wore black armbands to show their support for the proposed October 1969 Moratorium.

THE NEW MOBE, THE MORATORIUM AND KENT STATE

The fiasco at the Democratic Convention that ended with the nomination of Johnson's vice president Hubert Humphrey, helped Richard Nixon to capture the White House. Nixon successfully campaigned on two issues: law and order and ending the war by winning the peace. Nixon had no intention of ending American military involvement until the South Vietnamese could hold their own. Using Spiro Agnew (his vice-president) as a foil, Nixon sought to circumvent and undermine peace groups while pressing North Vietnam to negotiate on American terms. Consequently, anti-war dissidents found a new basis for a coalition. Frustrated by the failure to capture the Democratic Party nomination for peace candidate Eugene McCarthy or to get the party to repudiate the war, they had reformed as the New Mobilization Committee by late summer 1969.

At the same time, another coalition developed a new tactic known as the Moratorium. The Moratorium involved a popular strike against business-as-usual for one day beginning in October 1969, and to expand in duration each month as long as the war continued. The object of this form of protest was to lessen profits by major corporations who supported the war. This was a form of consensus politics—the creation of an expanding base of popular awareness and opposition to exert pressure through economic means.

The Moratorium, however, was faced with a critical choice of tactics. The New Mobe called for mass marches in Washington, D.C., and San Francisco at the same time as the Moratorium program. Again issues of strategy and tactics plagued peace coalitions as radical and liberal anti-war activists debated the merits of their approaches. In this particular case, Moratorium leaders realized that they could ill afford to lose the support of the left wing of the anti-war movement and thus agreed to cooperate with the March in "the hope of averting either a fiasco or violence."[54]

In Washington on November 15, 1969, between 250,000 and 500,000 war protesters marched down the streets of the nation's capital. Millions watched what seemed to be a cohesive coalition—little knowing that "the platform and speakers' policy had been determined through frantic talks between staffs of organizations that differed in their aims and tactics. Clearly, the coalition organizers had not agreed on a "vision of peace much beyond the curtailment of American involvement in the Vietnam War."[55]

The anti-war movement lost momentum early in 1970 as the peace coalitions broke up after the march. Their diffusion was in part a result of the new Selective Service Law passed by Congress. In November 1969, the Nixon administration set up a lottery system, which succeeded in separating the twin issues of opposition to the draft from opposition to the war. Since World War II men between the ages of 18 to 36 were subjected to military induction. In most cases, college students were granted an education deferment until graduation. During the first two years of the Vietnam War most draftees came from poor backgrounds with only a high school diploma, if that. The vast majority were nineteen years of age. Exemptions were granted to those with children or because of family hardship). The master-stroke of the new law was limiting all men—students and non-students alike—to one year of draft vulnerability after their nineteenth birthday. Consequently, the anti-war movement lost one of its most compelling issues. But a series of White House decisions regarding military moves in Southeast Asia led to yet another eruption on college campuses, this time with consequences that were tragic and irreparable.

On April 30, 1970, Nixon announced the invasion of Cambodia and the renewed bombing of North Vietnam. Immediately, his actions touched off a roar of anti-war demonstrations on college campuses across the country. Students were angry based on the president's earlier remarks that it was time to withdraw troops from Vietnam and end the war; many felt betrayed and misled by his remarks The most traumatic events took place at Kent State University, where on May 4th Ohio National Guardsmen were given the order to lock and load, aim, and fire; they shot down thirteen students, four of whom died (not all protestors). A few days later, Mississippi National guardsmen shot and killed two students at Jackson State University. In response to the killings nearly 470 colleges and universities struck or closed; anti-war demonstrations were reported on nearly 60 percent of the country's campuses. In retrospect, these protests appear as the last gasp of the student movement – though the demonstrations did take place sporadically after 1970, student anti-war sentiment seemed to decrease in the face of fears of violence and the end of the draft system.[56]

VIETNAM VETERANS AGAINST THE WAR

The anti-war movement, however, received an added boost in September 1970 when Vietnam Veterans against the War (VVAW), a three-year-old organization, launched Operation RAW (Rapid American Withdrawal). The organization began in June of 1967, when six former Vietnam War veterans, including Jan "Barry" Crumb, Mark Donnelly, and David Brown met in New York City to form VVAW. The organization grew to a membership of more than 40,000 at its height. A grassroots organization, VVAW organized its own actions exposing the truth about U.S. military action in Southeast Asia.

Careful to distinguish its action from the more publicized radical anti-war groups, VVAW's first major action took place on Labor Day weekend of September 4-7, 1970, when Operation RAW witnessed over 150 veterans marching from Morristown, New Jersey, to Valley Forge State Park. More than 1500 people attended that rally at Valley Forge, where speakers included VVAW leader John Kerry, Jane Fonda, Mark Lane, Donald Sutherland, and New York Congressman Allard Lowenstein. In January 1971, VVAW sponsored the Winter Soldier Investigation in order to highlight war crimes committed by U.S. troops. The testimony that was gathered from former veterans willing to talk about their experiences exposed a number of transgressions, including search and destroy missions, crop destruction, and mistreatment of prisoners of war. The investigation testimonies were later read into the Congressional Record by Senator Mark Hatfield.

The VVAW's most dramatic protest occurred in Washington, D.C., from April 19 through April 23, 1971. Dubbed Operation Dewey Canyon III, based upon two short military incursions into Laos, the protesting veterans referred to their action as "a limited incursion into the country of Congress."[57] With Gold Star Mothers leading the protest march, more than 1,100 veterans walked across the Lincoln Memorial Bridge to the Arlington National Cemetery. Though refused entrance into the cemetery, they conducted a memorial service outside the gates. That evening, protesting veterans defied a Justice Department injunction banning them from setting up camp at The Mall. On April 20,th some 200 members of VVAW listened to hearings by the Senate Foreign Relations Committee on proposals to end American military involvement, while others marched back to Arlington National Cemetery where they were now permitted to enter as a result of public criticisms of the government's actions against the veterans. Additional members performed guerrilla theatre on the Capitol steps depicting combat scenes and search-and-destroy missions. On April 21,st more than fifty veterans marched to the Pentagon and attempted to surrender and turn themselves in as war criminals. The following day, large numbers of the organization's members demonstrated on the steps of the Supreme Court demanding to know why it had not ruled on the constitutionality of the Vietnam War. The final day of protest culminated with more than 800 veterans tossing their medals, ribbons, and combat badges on the steps of the Capitol as a show of defiance and anger at the war.[58]

Basically, VVAW contributed to the anti-war movement by forcing middle-class America to face the possibility that the war was forcing clean-cut young men to commit war crimes and resort to drugs because of the horrors they had witnessed and the purposelessness of their sacrifice. VVAW, along with the Concerned Officers Movement in the navy during 1971, visibly demonstrated the erosion of morale and lack of respect for authority within the armed forces.

MAY DAY, PENTAGON PAPERS, AND WAR POWERS ACT

The failure of the U.S.-sponsored ARVN (Army of the Republic of Vietnam) and the invasion of Laos in early 1971 led to further anti-war actions. In March, a group of Madison Avenue advertisers started the "Help Unsell the War Campaign" in an effort to turn public opinion against the war. If Ivory Soap, Crest, and Mustangs could be bought and sold, why not "unsell" the war? On May 3, 1971, previously mentioned, the radical May Day Collective attempted to blockade entrance to Washington, D.C., by using stalled cars, garbage cans, broken fences, and even their own bodies. David McReynolds and the WRL helped organize this protest. Nixon imposed martial law, and under the direction of the Justice Department the police arrested more than 12,000 people, detaining them at RFK Stadium. It was the largest mass jailing in American history. Four years later, a Washington federal court ordered the government to pay $10,000 total to 1,200 of those arrested for violation of their civil rights.[59]

The publication of The Pentagon Papers in 1971 also aroused more anti-war sentiment. Daniel Ellsberg, a former Pentagon official and policy analyst who spent considerable time in Vietnam gathering intelligence information and advising top military leaders on the course of the war, became deeply troubled by U.S. military actions. In the summer of 1969, Ellsberg attended a War Resisters' International Triennial conference at Haverford, Pennsylvania. While there a young draft resister named Randy Kehler, who was on his way to jail, made a special impression on Ellsberg. When he returned from the conference, he read Thoreau's "On the Duty of Civil Disobedience" and proclaimed to his son that "This may be the most important essay I've ever read." For someone whose specialties had been guerilla warfare, counterinsurgency, nuclear planning, and crisis decision-making, this was quite a revelation. A few days later, Ellsberg, his son Robert, and a friend, Tony Russo, copied the documents which showed that Vietnam was a well-planned program of U.S. policy in Southeast Asia dating back to the early sixties and that the government had lied about the reasons for the war, among other things. When the documents were leaked to the press and Nixon's attempts to block their publication failed (Nixon's downfall began with his attempts to discredit Ellsberg; he created the "plumbers" to break into Ellsberg's psychiatrist's office thus foreshadowing the Watergate events), millions of Americans felt betrayed.[60]

Throughout 1972, although the war raged on and the Watergate crisis began to unfold, Nixon solidified his hold on the presidency with some impressive foreign policy coups. In February, he visited the People's Republic of

China thereby ending over two decades of Sino-American distrust. In June, he traveled to Moscow for the conclusion of the first phase of a strategic arms limitation agreement. Though his democratic challenger, George McGovern of South Dakota, tried to portray the upcoming November election as "the clearest choice in the century" between peace and war, Nixon won easily. Finally, after having reassured the Thieu government in Saigon of post-war protection, the U.S. officially signed the Paris Peace accords on January 27, 1973. American involvement in the Indochina war was now over. The war cost more than 58,000 Americans and millions of Vietnamese their lives.

Congress tried to pass legislation that would prevent another such war, most notably the War Powers Resolution of 1973. Specifically, under the War Powers Act, the president had to consult with Congress before introducing the armed forces "into hostilities or into situations where imminent involvement in hostilities is clearly indicated by the circumstances." Trying to curb the Executive Branch's war-making powers, the 1973 law required that American troops could be on foreign soil for no more than 90 days before the President had to seek Congress' permission to keep them there. Though its effectiveness is questionable, the purpose of the law was clearly to prevent future Vietnams.[61]

OTHER ASPECTS RELATED TO THE ANTI-VIETNAM WAR PROTESTS

THE JUDICIAL SYSTEM AND THE DRAFT

During the Vietnam War U.S. courts were faced with a plethora of law suits involving the draft and the war's constitutionality. Initially, in United States v. Mitchell (1967), David H. Mitchell III was tried and convicted of refusing induction into the military. He unsuccessfully challenged the verdict, calling Vietnam an illegal war of aggression and a violation of the Nuremburg War-Crimes Treaty. The government readily used Selective Service reclassification power to silence dissident speech and symbolic acts of protest. One of the more interesting cases was Oestereich v. Selective Service System (1968). Since the

World War I era the Supreme Court upheld convictions under the espionage and sedition laws. James Oestereich, a full-time student at Andover-Newton Theological School, had already received an IV-D exemption (a religious deferment) from induction. His conscience, however, moved him to protest the draft publicly and to turn in his registration card. At that point he was reclassified and subject to the draft. His actions constituted a crime under the Selective Service Act. His case tested the government's authority "to use Selective Service reclassification and induction regulations to punish war and draft protestors." Though the facts were different than that of Mitchell, the predisposition of the lower courts was to uphold convictions for willful obstruction of the draft. But Oesterich was successful in his challenge. He could have remained in a safe haven due to his religious exemption, yet he withdrew his previous registration as a symbolic gesture to oppose the war and dared his local board to try and draft him. The Supreme Court ruled that "the draft board's reclassification of Oestereich was a clearly lawless attempt to silence dissent."[62]

Despite Oestereich's legal victory, the court system was ambiguous in its rulings. This was especially so with judging the war's constitutionally. In Berk v. Laird (1970), the plaintiff, David Berk, charged that "the American involvement in Vietnam lacked constitutionally sufficient authorization, that New York State law forbade his shipment to Vietnam, and that the United States and South Vietnam were prosecuting the war in violation of binding international agreements." It was an interesting argument but it failed to pass the legal litmus test. In Holtzman v. Schlesinger (1973), a New York district court enjoined the U.S. bombing of Cambodia "as an unconstitutional presidential invasion of congressional prerogative under Article I, section 8, clause 11 of the Constitution." However, the Court of Appeals for the Second Circuit stayed the injunction, and Justice Thurgood Marshall refused to vacate the court's stay on the grounds of "profound effects upon the maintenance of social order," arguing that it could lead to violence. In other words, the national military program did not violate international law.[63]

Court dockets were filled with draft cases concerning violations of First Amendment rights. For instance, in 1967, two University of Michigan students, reclassified by their New York draft boards, brought suit to compel the boards to restore their student deferments. Both had been part of a group that staged a sit-in at a local draft board in Ann Arbor, for which they were convicted of trespass. The State of Michigan Selective Service headquarters thereupon sent the names of the students involved to their local draft boards, at which time the students were reclassified 1-A, subject to immediate induction. The district court dismissed the complaint, but the Court of Appeals reversed the opinion noting that such actions represented a direct threat to their constitutional right protected under the First Amendment. Faced with numerous challenges to the constitutionality of the draft, particularly the burning of Selective Service cards, the high court finally established guiding principles for determining free expression in opposition to the draft. In United States v. O'Brien (1968), the Supreme Court established a four-part test for determining when a governmental interest sufficiently justified the regulation of expressive conduct. The defendant, David O'Brien, was convicted in federal court for violating section 462(b) of the 1948 Universal Military Training Service Act. O'Brien had burned his Selective Service card on the steps of the South Boston Courthouse. Although O'Brien's conviction was upheld, this case redefined the "clear and present" danger application. A stricter definition was set down limiting the right of government to regulate expressive conduct.[64]

The O'Brien decision was ultimately applied in numerous cases as the war grew more unpopular. One of the more interesting ones took place in 1971 when a young man was arrested in front of the Los Angeles County Courthouse for wearing a jacket upon which were written the words, "F--- the Draft." In Cohen v. United States, defendant Cohen testified that the jacket was his way of expressing his feelings about the draft and the war. He was convicted of violating a statute prohibiting "malicious and willful disturbance of the peace" by conduct considered "offensive." In a 5-4 decision, the State Supreme Court struck down the statute. The court ruled that words, not conduct, were the issue and that a state has no right to excise epithets as offensive by functioning as a guardian of public morality. It should be noted that the controversy over the draft convinced the government to institute a different form of conscription in 1969 when the lottery was introduced. Eventually, conscription would be done away with as the government instituted an all-volunteer army in 1975.

Criticism of the war even penetrated schoolhouse gates. In 1969, the Supreme Court ruled in Tinker v. DesMoines that public school students would be allowed to wear black armbands as a symbolic protest against the war. In its decision, the nation's highest court proclaimed: "In our system, state-operated schools may not be enclaves of totalitarianism. School officials do no possess absolute authority over their students. Students in school, as well as out of school are 'persons' under our Constitution. . . .In our system, students may not be regarded as closed-circuit recipients of only that which the State wishes to communicate." Although symbolic protests disrupting the learning environment would not be condoned, the Court gave wider latitude to the principle of free expression as a forum for criticizing the war.[65]

ANTI-WAR PROTEST SONGS

While the U.S. court system grappled with the draft and opposition to the war, dissidents sang in protest. Protest songs quickly entered the realm of popular music. A number of songs criticizing the war hit the airwaves: P.F. Sloane's "Eve of Destruction," Donovan's "The War Goes On," and Buffy Saint-Marie's "Universal Soldier" all made the Top Forty Charts. Beatle John Lennon's simple chant "All we are saying is give peace a chance" was perhaps the most popular and frequently heard at anti-war moratoriums and rallies in the later stages of the war. Pete Seeger's "Waist Deep in the Big Muddy" and "Bring Them Home" were popular songs played at anti-war gatherings, although he still had trouble with record distribution and television appearances – a lingering effect of the 1950s blacklist. Eric Burden's "Sky Pilot" was a ringing condemnation of military chaplains who sent soldiers out to die, while Earth Opera's "American Eagle

Tragedy" indicted the president as a king preoccupied with wealth while the "kingdom is rumbling." The nation, the song repeats, is falling as "the King" sends our "lovely boys to die in a foreign jungle war."[66]

A great variety of artists sang about the war and the draft as well as social justice more generally. The Young Rascals produced a popular song called "People Got to Be Free." Credence Clearwater Revival's "Fortunate Son" was a refusal of induction into the armed forces with "some folks...made to wave the flag...It ain't me, it ain't me." It pointed to the hypocrisy of those pulling the war strings. Flag waving came easier for the "senator" and "millionaire's son." They were deemed "fortunate" in that they wouldn't be serving or dying for their country. In "American Woman" the Canadian rock group, the Guess Who, sang "I don't need your war machine, I don't need your ghetto scene." Even black "Soul" singers questioned the efficacy of the war. The Temptations' "Ball of Confusion" included a list of grievances against American society, including "end the war," and Freda Payne's "Bring the Boys Home" was popular on Soul and Top 40 stations. In 1970 Edwin Starr's "War" was the Number One song. The chorus repeated the following refrain:

> War...HUH! What is it good for?
> Absolutely nothing!

One striking cultural response to the tragedies of war at home was captured by musicians Crosby, Stills, Nash, and Young. To condemn the events that took place at Kent State University in May 1970, the group quickly composed the song, "Ohio." The recording leaped to the top of the charts in a matter of weeks after its release. The words to the song clearly depict the sense of anger, frustration, and bewilderment millions of American felt:

> Tin soldiers and Nixon's coming'.
> We're finally on our own.
> This summer I hear the drummin'.
> Four dead in Ohio.

Gotta get down to it.
Soldiers are gunning us down.
Should have been done long ago.
What if you knew her and
Found her dead on the ground?
How can you run when you know?[67]

MOVEMENT FOR A NEW SOCIETY

While opposing the war occupied most of the attention and resources of peacemakers, the commitment to social justice and community building was never abandoned. Efforts to develop more comprehensive frameworks of action and to establish organizational structures promoting non-violent change different from the peace movement's national committees' work was noticeably apparent in a number of alternative community settings. One of the best known was the creation of the Movement for a New Society (MNS). In 1971, led by Lillian and George Willoughby, Susan Gowan, George Lakey, Bill Moyers, Richard Taylor, Ross Flanagan, Berit Lakey, and Gail Pressberg, MNS set up projects and community centers promoting political and economic analysis of society, providing food and assistance to impoverished communities, collective work projects, and a broader conception of political action which called for the sharing of material resources by government and industry. Modeled after the Brook Farm experiment in antebellum Massachusetts, MNS lasted longer than the communitarian efforts of Emerson and his fellow transcendentalists.

The creation of MNS was due largely to the efforts of a loose community of West Philadelphia activists. The movement eventually spread to eight cities in the U. S. including Denver, Boston, and San Francisco. It also established worldwide connections for non-violence training and acting in such places as India, Sri Lanka, and Malaysia. The activists for social justice lived as groups, bought food through cooperatives, engaged in sharing child care, and had few large appliances or automobiles. Holding part-time jobs members were able to write training manuals and participate in political and social actions. Dancing and group singing was one way in which social harmony was promoted.

All of MNS's actions were guided by its founding philosophy: "living simply that others may simply live." The group's non-violence training and action was based on Gandhian and Quaker practices aimed at systematizing past experiences through single-issue campaigns. The visible aspect of its existence was the non-violence training and action; the internal component was to create a community in which members interacted and learned to live and work with one another peaceably on a sustained basis.

Like many of the progressive social experiments at that time, MNS was founded on a leaderless, consensus decision-making basis. These principles were applied to social issues such as racism, sexism, ethnocentrism, and class conflict. Unfortunately, the group's failure to utilize and develop fully its leadership basis – influenced by the anti-leader attitudes of the period – undermined coherence and stability. Collective agreements were hard to achieve when sensitive discussions unmasked the prejudices of many of its members regarding those controversial social issues.

MNS's most dramatic and well-organized non-violent action took place in the same year as its founding. It involved the blockade of U.S. arms exports to West Pakistan, which was engaged in a bitter civil war with East Pakistan (now Bangladesh). Over two hundred people participated in this campaign all along the East Coast of the U.S. Marching, picketing, paddling canoes in front of Pakistani ships, and all-night prayer vigils in front of the White House were conducted. Working closely with the head of the International Longshoreman's local in Philadelphia, MNS also succeeded in getting the dockworkers to refuse to load the freighters. The activists managed to blockade Philadelphia's port, thus preventing the shipment of arms until the conflict finally ended in 1972. MNS's campaign helped educate the public thus leading to a cutoff of U.S. government military aid to Pakistan.

In 1988 the Movement for a New Society ended. A number of former members such as the Willoughbys, Lakey, and Taylor continued participating in non-violent acts of civil disobedience. Some served as consultants; others joined action groups like Witness for Peace, which sought to bring peace to Latin American countries such as Nicaragua. Whether it was Hopedale, Bellamy's Nationalist experiment, the Settlement House movement, or the Movement for a New Society proponents for peace continued the historic effort to create a better America through non-violence and justice. MNS's creation and lengthy existence was largely a result of peace activists' determination to provide an alternative to the violence and disruption caused by the war in Vietnam.[68]

CONCLUSION

The anti-war demonstrations of the sixties and early seventies were unique in American history. Strongly antimilitarist and anti-imperialist—concentrating on reversing U.S. war policy in Asia—the size of the protests indicated how strong anti-war feeling was during this period. Previous anti-war movements such as the War of 1812, the Mexican War, and the Spanish-American and Filipino Wars were smaller in size but just as effective. Yet none were able to mobilize such diverse coalitions on a grand scale like the anti-Vietnam War protests. So massive was the protest that no single group can be singled out for credit.

Based on the research of noted historians such as Charles DeBenedetti, Charles Chatfield, Tom Wells, and Mel Small, among others, it is reasonable to argue that the anti-war movement became institutionalized as a result of Vietnam. Some have even argued that American protests against the Vietnam War proved to be the most effective anti-war movement in U.S. history. Wells, for instance, offers three tenable reasons: first, the anti-war movement played a major role in constraining the war and caused the Johnson administration to reverse its policy in 1968; second, it hastened U.S. troop withdrawals and promoted congressional legislation severing U.S. funds for the war during the Nixon years; and third, it "fostered aspects of the Watergate scandal" (the seeds for such behavior were hatched in his earlier efforts to discredit Ellsberg) by undermining Nixon's authority in Congress and hindering his ability to continue the war.

The anti-war movement was successful in its ability to politicize public opinion against the war and force policymakers to reconsider their options. One should not forget, however, that the anti-war movement was not a single, harmonious force. The movement was distinguished by internal tensions and numerous shifting coalitions that quickly appeared and just as rapidly disappeared. Within the broad movement, there was always disagreement involving tactics, values, and the priority of peace versus wars of liberation. There were serious disagreements between pacifists who valued non-violence above all and anti-war activists who supported more forcible resistance. There were also strategic debates over a negotiated settlement versus an immediate troop withdrawal. Perhaps the best way to describe this movement is that it was more assembled than organized. What enabled the movement to survive for as long as it did was its resiliency and the commitment of its constituent parts on the local and regional levels.

Charles DeBenedetti's An American Ordeal, which was completed after his death by Charles Chatfield, pointed out that the anti-war movement was composed of many independent interests, in most instances vaguely allied and at odds with each other on numerous issues. What united them was their strong opposition to the Vietnam War. The movement, consisting of college students, middle-class suburban families, unionists, and others gained national prominence in 1965, reached its zenith in the late sixties, and remained a powerful political force throughout the war's duration. Although the anti-war movement generally declined between 1971 and 1975 as a result of the troops coming home and the implementation of the lottery system, peace activists continued to protest U.S. bombing and the government's funding of the war. At the very least, the anti-war movement did three things: it clarified the political and moral issues involved in the conflict; it set parameters on the war policy by mobilizing significant opposition; and it added to the war's social cost due to the large-scale controversy it caused.

Equally significant, as Chatfield argues elsewhere, the anti-Vietnam War movement altered the historic foundation of the peace movement in a number of ways. Actions against the war provided flexibility to local branches and individuals through a wide range of options. Innovative forms of dissent and protest were carried out, from acts of civil disobedience to street theatre. Mass demonstrations were controlled through discipline and conviction. activists also practiced party politics at both the electoral and congressional levels. One of the most significant contributions the movement made was challenging the Cold War policy of containment and calling into question the desirability of emphasizing national security over social welfare concerns. Lastly, by adopting a decentralized base the anti-war activists created forms of networking to replace the "directive style of earlier campaigns." Perhaps the most telling legacy is that not only did the activists of this period have a profound impact on U.S. foreign policy, but also by the policies and strategies they chose to carry out, they dramatically changed the course and outlook of the peace movement itself.

In June 1975, two years after American military involvement ended, the FOR's magazine of print, Fellowship, declared that "The war is over, the problem of war remains intact."[69] Yes, the war in Indochina officially came to an end when Nguyen Van Thieu left Saigon (on April 21) and the American embassy closed its doors (nine days later). But to veteran peace workers, the struggle continued. It was time to respond to the spiraling arms race, nuclear war, environmental pollution, and social and economic injustice. These were realities peace seekers could not ignore.

CHAPTER EIGHT

THE PEACE MOVEMENT SINCE THE VIETNAM WAR

We were all working in unison, we were all motivated. The primary motivation was stopping the nukes, the secondary one how good it felt. That secondary motivation became the primary for a lot of people....For a lot of people, the process became more important than the product, the means became an end. People said, 'I just want to lay my body on the line.' They got involved as an opportunity for community, for self-expression, for a sense of purpose....

1985 Interview with Cathy Wolff of the Clamshell Alliance

INTRODUCTION

Calling for a transformation of society extending beyond traditional political and economic structures is one of the primary themes of the peace movement in the 1970s and after. As Cathy Wolff points out in the above quote, members of the Clamshell Alliance bonded in their efforts to establish a broad redefinition of social values. These activists who protested the construction of a nuclear power plant in Seabrook, New Hampshire, captured the new direction peace and justice movements would follow in the aftermath of the Vietnam War. The new direction would be characterized by the formation of small communities governed by mutual participation. They would be communities shunning the use of violence and ones devoid of special privilege and power elites. Consensus and non-violent direct action based on grassroots affiliation, not national organizations and media attention, highlighted the efforts peace pioneers would undertake in the struggle against war and social injustice as the nation prepared to enter a new millennium.

Lessons had been learned by peace and justice activists after the Vietnam War. The evolution from large-scale protests and bureaucratic organization to local and personal efforts for social change dictated the pace and activity in the struggle to build a better society. Major national demonstrations and groups – divided by internal disagreement and government harassment – took a back seat to more local activity for social change in the context of a growing conservatism. In the 1970s and 1980s, peace activists focused their energies on such issues as saving the environment, promoting a policy of divestment to combat South African apartheid, opposing nuclear power, combating homelessness, continuing the struggle to unionize farm workers, and providing sanctuary for Central American refugees. A new generation of non-violent resisters, many of whom did not consider themselves pacifists, began proclaiming the doctrine of individual responsibility for one's actions. Initially, however, it had to overcome the inertia that came in the wake of the post Vietnam War anti-war movement.[1]

DOMESTIC PROTESTS AGAINST NUCLEAR POWER PLANTS

The role of citizen activists in attempting to control and halt the construction of new nuclear power plants reflected some of the lessons learned by the movement against the Vietnam War. Barbara Epstein's Political Protest and Cultural Revolution: Non-violent Direct Action in the 1970s and 1980s offers an important insider's account of the no-nukes reformers and their efforts to build communities based on shared beliefs and values. These activists, using non-violent direct action, presented a new style of politics shaped by "a vision of an ecologically balanced, non-violent egalitarian society." In practicing mass civil disobedience in opposition to the development of nuclear power plants, these action groups expanded their efforts to the arms race of the early eighties.[2]

But before the arms race of the Reagan years occupied their time and attention, these new style political activists focused all of their attention on the issue of nuclear power. The movement started in 1976 when some forty protestors in New England sought to halt the proposed construction of a nuclear power plant at Seabrook, New Hampshire. Calling themselves the Clamshell Alliance (in deference to the clams, living in sand and mud flats along the seacoast, which would be destroyed by nuclear wastewater), some six hundred activists gathered at the construction site on August 1, 1976. Employing non-violent civil disobedience, eighteen members walked along the railroad tracks to the site and were arrested. During the last week of August, the number of protestors arrested for trespassing grew to 178, while 1,200 rallied to their support.[3]

During the winter months, the Clamshell Alliance grew to a coalition consisting of some thirty-five New England action groups. The Alliance established a small-group structure with a spokesperson who served on a "spokes-council." There, by consensus, all decisions were made. On April 30, 1977, for a period lasting 24 hours, two hundred "Clams" occupied the parking lot of the construction site. On May 1st the police moved in and arrested almost 1,500 protestors who refused to post bail, forcing the State of New Hampshire to incarcerate them in National Guard armories. It was a costly and embarrassing move on the part of state authorities. They were forced to release the activists without collecting any bail. This particular strategy, "Bail Solidarity," became a new and effective strategy within the non-violent direct action movement. On June 24-25, 1978 the protests, having gained national attention, grew even larger. Some 6,000 "Clams" camped at the Seabrook site, accompanied by 14,000 members from the general public. To that point in time it was the largest anti-nuclear power rally in American history. Speakers at this rally included Dr. Benjamin Spock, actor and comedian Dick Gregory, and representatives from the National Organization for Women (NOW). Music was provided by Pete Seeger and Arlo Guthrie. One of the more novel acts of protest was an offshore "boat picket" blocking the plant's drilling platform.

The Clamshell Alliance sparked other direct action groups across the nation. The protests at Seabrook added more innovative styles including mandatory non-violence training for acts of civil disobedience, and copying the

"Clams" politics of protest became the order of the day for direct action against nuclear power plants.[4]

Another spectacular demonstration was organized by the Abalone Alliance in California. In August 1977, forty-seven people were arrested as 1,500 demonstrators organized a non-violent occupation of the Diablo Canyon plant. The following year, over 6,000 people mobilized at the site while 490 occupiers entered the plant and were arrested. Throughout the late seventies the anti-nuclear campaign, inspired by non-violent direct action, had taken on the vigor of the demonstrations a decade earlier.

What really provided the spark igniting the anti-nuclear movement was the accident at the Three Mile Island nuclear power plant on March 28, 1979. A partial meltdown of one of the reactors created widespread fear among the residents living near the plant. Concern over radioactive contamination in nearby rivers and streams engendered a nationwide call for halting the construction of new plants. Even though the movement was already highly visible, this incident outside Harrisburg, Pennsylvania, touched off a wave of protests and demonstrations. Some 125,000 "No Nukes" protestors made their sentiments felt in Washington, D.C. in May of that year. On Long Island, in June, 600 protestors were arrested at the Shoreham power plant construction site. In September close to 200,000 people rallied in New York City to oppose the nuclear power plant program in the United States.

Stepped-up demonstrations continued into the 1980s. A number of demonstrations, leading to hundreds of arrests for civil disobedience, were conducted at the Shoreham site. In September 1981, in California, the Abalone Alliance conducted a two-week "human blockade" to prevent the startup of the diablo plant. Over ten thousand demonstrators showed up: some 1,900 occupied the plant and were arrested in the largest anti-nuclear civil disobedience action ever conducted. Those arrested used ladders to climb over the fence from many different directions and hiked over rugged terrain to the plant. Other protestors, aided by the environmentalist action group Greenpeace, approached the plant by sea. The degree and extent of the mass civil disobedience protests at Diablo Canyon ultimately came to represent the high point in the "plant occupation" movement.[5]

The growing support for anti-nuclear action seriously crippled the nuclear power plant industry. Although some plants went online, including Diablo Canyon, no new construction plants were ordered after the late 1970s. Peace activists can point to this particular movement as one example of the success of non-violent direct action. Concerns about not only nuclear weapons development but also an overriding desire to protect the environment provided peace and justice activists with the necessary ingredients for success.

One important byproduct of the anti-nuclear movement was the establishment of the Livermore Action Group (LAG), which was spawned as a result of the September 1981 Diablo Canyon plant blockade. Some of the protestors at Diablo were part of a Berkeley-based affinity group. After serving their jail sentences they connected with an ongoing campaign headed by the Labs Conversion Project, challenging the Livermore Lab work on nuclear weapons design. An important think tank for the military, many of the lab's scientists had been working on the MX missile project.

LAG began in earnest on June 21, 1982. Over 40,000 people demonstrated outside the lab. Many of the protestors, who had been trained previously in the tactics of non-violent civil disobedience, sat down in the road to block cars and buses from entering the lab. Among the protestors were grandmothers, social workers, doctors, students, and ministers. A vast majority were "respectable" citizens and not part of any radical or dissident group. During the two-day demonstration, more than 1,400 people were arrested. In June of 1983, another blockade was carried out in which about 1,000 protestors were arrested for acts of civil disobedience. The LAG was a prime example of how effectively direct action groups were able to link the issues of nuclear power and nuclear weapons as one.

PERSONAL AND COMMUNITY ACTION

In the 1980s peace groups, more establishment-oriented than their predecessors of the Vietnam War era, sprang to life. Randall Forsberg—who headed an organization called the Institute for Defense and Disarmament Studies (IDDS) in Brookline, Massachusetts—noted that from 1979 to 1981 there were more than 200 church-based community conferences on the theme of the nuclear arms race. Forsberg was an arms control expert not affiliated with mainstream arms control groups. Her IDDS served as a clearinghouse for spreading the word about arms control. She proposed that a bilateral nuclear freeze on the testing, production and deployment of nuclear weapons should be the focal point of a new antinuclear campaign, an idea that reached fruition in the early 1980s.[6]

An important strain of the post-Vietnam War peace movement was a grassroots anti-nuclear weapons movement mixing religion and politics. In Let Your Life Speak, political scientist Robert D. Holsworth examined the origins of what he terms the "personalist" approach to politics—one emphasizing the responsibility of the individual, the close relationship between personal and political life, and the significance of local community action. Using as his case study the role of anti-nuclear activists in Richmond, Virginia, Holsworth detailed the development of communal action as an approach to political reform in America. As part of the broader context of social reform movements, anti-nuclear activism had its roots in local communities throughout the nation. The wellspring for this action was from religious leaders and church groups who possessed a deep and abiding respect for human life and social justice. The movement for halting the construction of nuclear power plants and nuclear weapons proliferation, Holsworth insisted, can only be understood in terms of the activists' individual ideas about citizenship, in their efforts to rebuild local communities based on peace and justice, and in the choices that they made. One new direction the 1980's peace movement took was the way in which activists internalized their approach to political change—one often guided by religious and moral values.

Groups such as the Movement for a New Society, the Atlantic Life Community, and the Community for Creative Non-violence were dependent on community-based organizing and personalized decision-making. Direction and organizing was done on the local level and members clung to their grassroots approach, namely working for a larger goal within their very own communities. Whether it was protesting nuclear power plants or campaigning against the arms race the organizing, distribution of literature, and mobilization began in the backyards and not the national headquarters in urban centers.

In early 1980, inspired by the personalist and community-based approach to change, a new organization was formed under the working rubric of the Committee to Prevent World War III. It subsequently changed its name to the Committee for National Security. This particular group promoted the position that, beyond a certain point, weapons can be a source more of insecurity than security. What was needed, in this organization's analysis, was a broader definition of national security in contrast to military preparedness. Since its inception the committee had enlisted a broad range of prominent Americans as active members—including Paul Warnke (former diplomat and Director of the U.S. Arms Control and Disarmament Agency during the Carter administration), Wassily Leontief (an expert on Soviet arms), Harrison Salisbury (the first New York Times correspondent to Moscow and author of numerous books on the Soviet Union and China), and Hodding Carter III (journalist and former Assistant Secretary of State in the Carter administration). What they attempted to do was to lend a degree of intellectualism and governmental experience to the push for arms reduction.

EFFORTS FOR DISARMAMENT

Personal and community-based action was due in large measure to the reality that the anti-war, student, and black power movements had been harassed and intimidated during the Vietnam War. By the mid-to-late 1970s some things had changed due to their efforts while movements such as personal and community-based action were just hitting their stride. At the end of the war, a contracting economy, less media attention to protests, and more and more activists turning to local organizing – less visible but just as active – peacemakers began setting their sights on the continuing problem of nuclear proliferation.

Pioneers for peace and justice were thus responding to the increasing intervention of conservative corporate elites into the political arena during this period. This intervention was most strongly felt in foreign and military matters. By the mid-1970s conservative policymakers were attempting to convince the American public that there were two trends seriously eroding American military dominance. One was the "Vietnam syndrome": public disillusionment with the Vietnam War. Conservatives feared that this sentiment would make future military interventions, particularly in the Third World, almost impossible to wage. In other words, the government would have to prove to the American public that the next war would not exact a large amount of blood and treasure. The other concern was that the Soviet Union had continued to expand its nuclear arsenal and was nearly at parity with the U.S.

Responding to conservative policymakers and lobbyists calling for greater military spending peace activists stepped up their campaign for disarmament. Activists were now engaged in a variety of peace projects focused on the threat of nuclear destruction and military expansion. They worked to halt production of the costly B-1 bomber and the Trident Missile Project, and to halt deployment of Pershing missiles in Europe. More and more demonstrations appeared in the early 1980s in opposition to the proliferation of nuclear weapons. The government's imposed registration for 18-year old males led to a revival of draft counseling. By this time, numerous actions had also taken place exposing the institutionalized sexism and racism in American society.

One of the greatest areas of concern was that of military overkill and the effects of huge increases for military appropriations.[7] During the post-Vietnam War, period nearly fifty percent of every tax dollar collected was allocated for military purposes. In fact, from the conclusion of the Second World War to the 1980's, the United States had expended over $1 trillion (one thousand billion) on military programs; almost $250 million per day was spent for militarization. On a more personal level, it meant that the average American family spent close to $1,500 a year on military programs as compared to $200 on education and less than $50 on all environmental programs.[8]

One of the major reasons for such expenditures was economic profitability. Armaments were big business, whether for national supplies or foreign sales. In the latter case, this evolved into a $15-20 billion annual business, primarily to third world countries. Linked to this was the matter of national industry and jobs at some $30-50 billion annually contracted to private business by the Pentagon. As the traditional manufacturing sector decline or moved overseas, military spending became one of the foundation blocks of the U.S. economy.

Such expenditures produced an arsenal of awesome proportions. The escalation in nuclear armaments was matched equally in the arena of conventional weaponry. American nuclear capacity to destroy and kill was calculated to be some 30-40 times greater than every human being on the planet. New and deadlier weapons in the conventional field included super napalm, and napalm-phosphorus (Thermite bombs which disperse over a wide area and burn at a higher temperature). There were also "improved" anti-personnel (fragmentation) bombs which had a higher kill ratio and which could be released from supersonic aircraft. Another new weapon was the Fuel Air Explosive Weapon which dispersed fuel over a large area and then ignited it with grenades thereby incinerating everything in that area.

High on the Pentagon's priority list was the Hard Structure Munitions (HSM) bomb. This weapon had the capacity to penetrate hard targets (e.g., bridges, foundations, dikes, cement bunkers, etc) and release its energy inside. There were also new "smart" bombs, which had their own TV guidance system—

the 7.5 ton bomb used in Vietnam that could flatten everything within 10 city blocks—and continuing perfection of the electronic/computerized battlefield.

Intellectuals and activists sought to expose the myth that the genocidal weapons offered more national security. In reality, humankind had never been less secure than it was. In the mid 1970's, the Bulletin of Atomic Scientists changed the famous symbol on its cover. The drawing had been a clock which in 1948 displayed the time as twelve minutes to midnight, symbolizing the nearness of a possible nuclear holocaust. The time had now been changed to nine minutes to midnight in response to the new escalations of the arms race. By the 1980s it had been reduced to six minutes.

Both within and outside the peace movement many people, representing a diversity of perspectives and values, were thinking about the bomb again. The haunting nuclear specter was a recurring theme in many books, articles, and TV specials in the eighties. These included the following: Larry Collins and Dominique LaPierre, The Fifth Horseman; Nigel Calder, Nuclear Nightmares; Jonathan Schell's The Fate of the Earth; Louis Rene Beres, Apocalypse; Eisei Ishikawa and David L. Swain, eds., Hiroshima and Nagasaki; E.P. Thompson, Beyond The Cold War; Bernard J. O'Keefe, Nuclear Hostages; Fred Kaplan, The Wizards of Armageddon; Harvard Magazine's "The First Nuclear War"; The American Journal of Public Health's "Addressing Apocalypse Now"; and television specials "First Strike," "Nuclear Nightmares" and "The Islamic Bomb." An off-Broadway play, "Dead End Kids" was an impressionistic and satirical production. It climaxed with someone brandishing a dead chicken—while an unperturbed announcer reads a National Academy of Sciences report, entitled "Effect of Radioactive Fallout on Livestock in the Event of a Nuclear War." Media outlets were raising greater awareness to the issue and in the process providing legitimacy to the peace movement.[9]

As in the fifties, the political debates surrounding the nuclear arms race were given renewed impetus because of the nuclear and radical peace activists. As early as 1976, the WRL organized a Continental Walk for Disarmament and

Social Justice. Marching from Vancouver, British Columbia to Washington, D.C., leaders emphasized the need to replace weapons systems with useful jobs and public services. In May 1978, Mobilization for Survival, an umbrella organization uniting traditional peace groups and many of the new grassroots anti-nuclear organizations, staged a march of thousands in New York City to call attention to the U.N. General Assembly special session on disarmament. That spring, peace and anti-nuclear activists conducted protests, rallies and parades at the Trident submarine base near Bremerton, Washington, the Hollywood Bowl in Los Angeles, the nuclear weapons plant at Rocky Flats, Colorado, and in San Francisco.

PHYSICIANS AND EDUCATORS FOR SOCIAL RESPONSIBILITY

The threat of nuclear war activated a new constituency: the medical profession. It began devoting considerable attention to what doctors were calling "the final epidemic." "The Medical Consequences of Nuclear Weapons and Nuclear War" was the theme of three conferences held in 1980, all heavily attended by healthcare professionals and medical students. Organized by the Physicians for Social Responsibility (a group of activist anti-war doctors led by Helen Caldicott) the conferences were held in Cambridge, Massachusetts, New York and San Francisco and drew more than 2,000 people. They were sponsored by prominent medical institutions in each region, including Harvard Medical School, Columbia University College of Professional Physicians and Surgeons, School of Public Health at Berkeley and Stanford University Medical School.

Behind the physicians' concern was the stark realization that conventional projections of death and destruction were likely to be vastly exceeded in the event of an actual nuclear attack. "In addition to the tens of millions of deaths during the days and weeks after the attack," Jennifer Leaning, a member of the Physicians for Social Responsibility, stated, "there would probably be further millions (perhaps tens of millions) of deaths in the ensuing months or years. Nobody knows how to estimate the likelihood that industrial civilization might collapse in the area attacked; additionally, the possibility of significant long-term ecological damage cannot be excluded." Administration and Pentagon officials who argued that a nuclear war was winnable committed the worst possible kind of sin: creating false hope. In Leaning's opinion, a survivalist movement was unrealistic: "In the setting of nuclear war...a circumstance which engulfs us all in devastation of unprecedented scale, we must submit that civil defense cannot ensure conditions for post-attack survival. To persist in planning as if it could," she argued, was at best "unrealistic," and "extremely dangerous." It diverted "the nation from its major task, the pursuit of a sound, comprehensive, bilateral disarmament agreement and the prevention of nuclear war," she proclaimed.[10]

Following the lead of the Physicians for Social Responsibility were members from the teaching ranks: Educators for Social Responsibility (ESP) was established in 1981. Operating mainly from Columbia University Teachers College—with Betty Reardon, Doug Sloan, and Willard Jacobson leading the way—this organization relied on Nikolai Berdyaev's psychology of fear analysis in order to make peacemaking a positive force rather than an ideological reaction to possible nuclear annihilation.[11] In attempting to reveal and tap the energies and impulses that make possible the full human capacity for a meaningful and life-enhancing experience, Educators for Social Responsibility utilized classrooms to convey the notion that problems of war and peace should be studied in connection with other related issues: economic development, economic aspects of the arms race, social justice, human rights, ecological balance, and conceptions of a just world order. The interrelations among military spending, economic development, and human rights, the organization maintained, are fundamental and demand analysis and understanding. In the opinion of one of its leaders, "a peace not grounded in a just political and economic order, and impervious to ecological destruction, is unsustainable, and for the exploited, famished, and the oppressed is no peace at all."[12]

Other organizations followed ESP's lead. The Student/Teacher Organization to Prevent Nuclear War (STOP), a national network of high school students and teachers, sponsored events, presentations, and projects in schools, churches, and communities. The Federation of American Scientists (FAS) instituted a Nuclear War Education Project in 1981. The United Campuses to Prevent Nuclear War (UCAM)—a nationwide association of college and university chapters—was composed of students, faculty and campus community members dedicated to ending the threat of nuclear annihilation. The Performing Artists for Nuclear Disarmament, a loosely organized contingent of classical and commercial artists who opposed nuclear war, expressed the belief that education is the foundation for all efforts towards reducing the threat of nuclear war. Specifically, their primary thrust was to encourage citizens to obtain the information necessary to evaluate policies and proposals about nuclear weapons while judging political candidates on the basis of facts rather than campaign rhetoric.

THE FREEZE

Highlighting all these organizational activities was the push for a nuclear freeze. What provoked such a sharp response was the growth of anti-nuclear movements in Western Europe. In 1981 massive protests were carried out in various Western European cities aimed at stopping a NATO plan to deploy intermediate-range nuclear missiles in five European nations. Major demonstrations were conducted in Paris, Rome, London, Amsterdam, Brussels, and Bonn. Inspired by activists like the British historian E.P. Thompson, American pacifists initiated a series of direct action campaigns aimed at defense plants, submarine bases, missile sites, and the Pentagon.

Still very much active in the peace movement after their release from prison, Daniel and Philip Berrigan formed a new action group in 1980 called "Plowshares" (following the biblical injunction to "beat swords into plowshares") in order to bear witness against the arms race. With a group of Catholic activists, the Berrigans broke into a General Electric plant in Pennsylvania and smashed computer keyboards and missile nosecones with hammers, and then waited there to be arrested. Elizabeth McAlister, wife of former priest Philip Berrigan, illegally entered Griffiss Air Force Base in upstate New York on Thanksgiving Day in 1983. With other protestors she entered the hangar where a B-52 was being outfitted with cruise missiles. Some of the protestors hammered on the bomb bay doors, others poured their own blood on the fuselage, another group spraypainted the phrases "320 Hiroshimas," "Thou Shalt Not Kill" and "If I Had A Hammer" on the bomber, and some taped photos of their children and a "people's indictment" of the air base on the plane's wings. These "ultra-resisters" were carrying out non-violent acts as part of their own doctrine of individual responsibility.

Another dramatic protest was the Women's Pentagon Action, in which hundreds of feminists inspired by Grace Paley, demonstrated outside America's military headquarters shouting and chanting to end the arms race. As part of their protest, they boldly attempted to "weave a web of life" around the Pentagon in order to block all the entrances. As one protestor was arrested, another would jump in to keep the weave going. Weapons laboratories in Berkeley, California and Cambridge, Massachusetts, were also the targets of vigils and site invasions. During these particular protests, the direct actionists used the tactic of "competing harms" defenses. At their trials, they compared the dangers of nuclear war against the dangers of trespass. Another dramatic action was that in which direct actionists began sprouting up all along the "White Train" route, sitting on the railroad tracks in order to slow down and even stop trains from delivering nuclear warheads to Trident missile submarines. During one of these incidents, a protestor lost both legs when he refused to move and was run over by a train.

The idea of a "nuclear freeze" was initiated by Forsberg in 1980. What prompted her action was President Jimmy Carter's Presidential Directive 59, endorsing plans for a first strike nuclear option backed by a massive diversion of federal funds to finance the development of new technological weapons. The newly-elected president Ronald Reagan added to growing concerns when he presided over the largest peacetime military buildup in U.S. history in the early 1980s.

The Freeze campaign was bilateral in intent, calling on the U.S. and the Soviet Union to adopt a mutual and verifiable freeze on the testing, production, and deployment of nuclear weapons and of missiles; it also called for a halt to new aircraft designed to deliver nuclear weapons. As a spiraling arms race greeted the new decade, Forsberg's call for a "freeze" became more urgent. When the Soviet invasion of Afghanistan occurred in late December 1979, President Carter immediately pulled the SALT-II Treaty from the Senate. He then halted all high technology sales and grain shipments to the USSR. Carter also spelled out other military measures such as arms supplies to Pakistan, including support for the Afghan rebels and followers of Osama Bin Laden, building U.S. naval facilities in Oman, Kenya, Somalia, and Egypt, and forming a rapid deployment force for use in the Middle East. On January 24, 1980, he also announced the Carter Doctrine which proclaimed that any nation seeking control of the Persian Gulf region would be repelled by any means necessary, including the use of military force. Such measures quickly led to a deterioration of Soviet-American relations.

Additionally, the North Atlantic Treaty Organization's (NATO) decision to deploy a new set of missiles along the borders of Eastern Europe raised fears in both Europe and the United States. President Reagan did little to alleviate these fears. Reagan and his administration assumed that the Soviet Union outspent the U.S. on armaments and development of nuclear weapons. He had campaigned on an anti-SALT-II platform and expressed disdain for nuclear-arms control talks. After his election he replaced arms experts in the Arms Control and Disarmament Agency with like-thinking individuals who had no use for mutual self-restraint. Statements by administration officials about winning a nuclear war stirred up a transatlantic debate and created the necessary political fodder for the emerging Freeze Campaign.

Organizations quickly responded to the freeze idea. Ground Zero, an anti-nuclear organization founded in 1980, staged a series of peace protests in the spring of 1982.[13] Three factors contributed significantly to the motivation behind these protests: the Senate's failure to ratify the 1979 SALT II treaty limiting strategic offensive nuclear weapons; President Reagan's talk about fighting and winning a nuclear war; and his administration's push for a vastly increased Pentagon budget. Backed by such groups as the American Association for the Advancement of Science, the National Education Association, the United States Catholic Conferences, the United Steel Workers of America, the United Automobile Workers and the United Food and Commercial Workers, Ground Zero (the flash point where the nuclear bomb detonates) began a week of anti-nuclear war protests in mid-April.[14]

The week opened nationwide with films, foot races, bicycle tours, concerts, lectures and debates designed to stimulate discussions about the possibility of nuclear war and its effects. Throughout the week such activities involved 10-20 million people in 650 communities and on 350 college campuses. For instance, people gathered in cities like Cincinnati and Austin, Texas, to hear the ultimate horror story of what would happen if a nuclear bomb landed in the center of their towns. In Boston, signs were displayed along the route of the Boston Marathon showing the destruction that would occur if a nuclear bomb were dropped on the finish line. Simulated nuclear bombs or banners describing potential destruction, death and disease appeared at the Daley Center in Chicago, in front of an Episcopal church in downtown Indianapolis and in other cities. In Columbus, Ohio, Ground Zero coordinators displayed maps showing what would be left of the city after a nuclear attack. A silent vigil was held in Bangor, Maine. A 370-mile bicycle ride took place around Whiteman Air Force Base in Missouri. Runners ran for one-half hour (the amount of warning a person would get in case of nuclear attack) in "Run From Ground Zero" in Salt Lake City and "Run For Your Life" in Winston-Salem, North Carolina, and "Run for Peace" in New York City. At Columbia University rock concerts, lectures, slide shows and dramatic presentations were held—highlighted with readings by entertainers Tammy Grimes, Michael Moriarty, and Kitty Carlisle.[15]

The Freeze represented a broad public response that was coordinated by the Nuclear Weapons Freeze Campaign (NWFC). NWFC linked local groups to the wider national campaign. In less than a year the Freeze had a rank-and-file force of 20,000 activists in some 40 states. Although NWFC coordinated all effort, the campaign was enriched by local community efforts. Numerous community groups set up their own "nuclear free zones" and held referenda to support the larger goals of the campaign.

Despite the lack of media coverage the Freeze benefited from the massive European demonstrations as well as Jonathan Schell's best-selling Fate of the Earth and the television drama, The Day After. The TV show was actually slammed by the White House leading to NWFC's label as a communist dupe. Nonetheless, the campaign continued focusing on electoral politics and congressional support to pass Freeze legislation.

In June, 1982, the popularity of the movement for a nuclear freeze was dramatically illustrated at a disarmament rally in New York City. Over 700,000 people participated, making it the largest political demonstration in U.S. history. The campaign's grassroots impact was enormous as the Freeze referendum appeared on state ballots across the nation. "It represented," in the words of one reporter, "the largest referendum on any issue in American history; sixty per cent of the voters supported the resolution."[16] One measure of the Freeze's success was its ability to spark so much activism on the local.

On the national level things were more complicated. Within the Freeze campaign were establishment supporters who considered the Freeze a tool to save the arms control regime. They were backed by powerful economic and military interest groups. Peace activists had a wider vision. They wanted the Freeze to constrain the administration as well as look at the issue of national security beyond arms control; they wanted to examine how money could be spent on education, health care, and the environment. The problem was trying to balance entrenched institutional concerns with grassroots reformism.

Meanwhile, within the halls of the U.S. Congress the Freeze Campaign began picking up political momentum. In the winter of 1982 Edward Markey (D-MA) and Mark Hatfield (R-OR) introduced a Freeze Resolution in the House of Representatives. Edward Kennedy (D-MA) did the same in the Senate. In May 1983, the House of Representatives finally did pass Freeze legislation, only to see it defeated in the Senate; it did receive 40 votes in the upper house.

What accounted for the failure to approve legislation in both houses? There were sinister forces at work. Those within the White House were not afraid to raise the Cold War specter of communism and anti-Americanism. In concerted efforts to smear the campaign White House officials succeeded in portraying the Freeze as a campaign for unilateral disarmament. In the end Euro missiles were deployed in 1984. However, a few years later, in 1987, the missiles were removed under the terms of the new INF Treaty (Intermediate Nuclear Forces Treaty).

In the end, arms control groups with a long history of institutional ties to the establishment tried to influence Congress on budgetary matters and pushed the President on arms reduction. These groups preferred this approach to political influence than the art of mass demonstrations. Pacifists and other activists, while continuing the Freeze Campaign were disappointed at the campaign's leadership to refuse to employ tactics like non-violent direct action. For his own part, President Reagan skillfully maneuvered his campaign so that his 1984 re-election was not a referendum on either the Freeze or the United States' own national security program. In 1984, Reagan proclaimed a new commitment to arms control negotiations and offered to restore summit meetings with the Soviet Union. Pressure in Europe and the U.S. helped bring the Cold War to an end by the end of the decade.

Though the Freeze movement did not achieve its ultimate goal, the anti-nuclear arms movement did result in a change in attitude, both at home and abroad. It provided a badly-needed political platform in support of arms control and disarmament. More importantly, though designed to gain congressional support for its legislative agenda in order to avoid public condemnation based on Cold War assumptions, the campaign ultimately helped force Reagan to adopt a more peace-oriented style in the latter half of his second term in office.

Historians like Martin Sherwin, Paul Boyer, Robert Divine, and Donald Meyer among others, have offered compelling and worthwhile accounts of the history of the bomb in the second half of the twentieth century. Perhaps the most exhaustive study of the movement is Lawrence Wittner's trilogy, The Struggle Against the Bomb. According to Wittner's analysis, the rising tide of popular protest against Western powers and their decision to build and deploy more nuclear weapons, as well as the movement's challenge to similar policies in communist-ruled Eastern Europe prior to the end of the Cold War, resulted in a modification of hawkish positions on both sides. What emerged was a strong global anti-nuclear protest movement, resulting in further arms control and reduction agreements. The movement in the 1980s became the largest grassroots citizens' movement in modern history. What this movement accomplished was creating a compelling vision shared by the worldwide community. The movement's focus was not only on educating elites, but also on informing all citizens. As a powerful social movement, the anti-nuclear campaign forced political leaders to consider undertaking newer and bolder steps to reduce armaments of mass destruction. Mobilization of public opinion remains the key to controlling nuclear weapons. Citizen activism, Wittner maintains, can and does work. But one should not forget that the threats caused by nuclear weapons had strengthened, not diminished, the power of the nation-state. Therein remains the dilemma facing all peace activists.

COMMUNITY FOR CREATIVE NON-VIOLENCE

Anti-nuclear activism was not the only endeavor peace proponents engaged in during this period. In 1970 a small group of activists with deep religious convictions and a strong commitment to social justice had established the Community for Creative Non-Violence (CCNV). But it found its true calling in the 1980s, when it took the forefront of the movement to combat homelessness. The economic policies of the Reagan administration – reversing New Deal measures for social programs by reducing the federal budget through tax cuts for the large corporations and requiring states to assume more of the costs for social welfare programs – resulted in rising poverty and homelessness rates, especially among families. While cutting taxes which normally funded social welfare programs and at the same time increasing federal spending for his military buildup, Reagan's fiscal polices created an additional burden on low income families.

In keeping with the expanding peace movement's emphasis on equality and economic and social justice, CCNV's leader, Mitch Snyder designed a series of non-violent actions in order to raise the nation's consciousness regarding the plight of poor people. During this decade CCNV's activists launched a series of acts of civil disobedience aimed directly at the Reagan administration and the nation's seemingly insensitivity to the homeless and destitute. In 1981, a group of activists erected a tent city in Lafayette Park, directly across from the White House. The encampment was called "Reaganville," evoking less than fond memories of the Hoovervilles set up during the early years of the Great Depression. CCNV's tent city was clearly an eyesore to some of Washington's most powerful politicians. It became the site of ongoing protests, numerous press conferences, and, at times, massive rallies and demonstrations marked by well-publicized fasts. Frequently, the park police were dispatched to dismantle the tent city. In the process news media attention grew.

Perhaps the organization's most dramatic form of protest, rich in Gandhian tradition, was the fast. In July 1983, CCNV members fasted for a month in Kansas City to protest the federal stockpiling of surplus agricultural products. This action was taken to demonstrate the widespread hunger in America. The Reagan administration, embarrassed by this, acknowledged the reality of the situation and released some of the government-owned food for the poor in urban areas and some of the more depressed agricultural areas in the South. CCNV's most significant fast occurred in September 1984 when twelve members, including Snyder and Carol Fennelly, started an open-ended fast in conjunction with a sit-in in the tent city at Lafayette Park. This action also coincided with CCNV's "Call to Civil Disobedience," in which small groups of demonstrators engaged in direct action. Their arrests garnered the organization even more media coverage. Some of the direct action tactics included raising a scarecrow effigy of President Reagan, laying sleeping mats across the White House driveway, declaring it a homeless shelter, and releasing paper bags of cockroaches on one White House tour.

While all this was going on Snyder's fast continued. The White House was acutely aware of Snyder's actions and did not want to make a martyr of him. Negotiations got underway and after fifty-one days without solid food, Snyder agreed to end his fast in return for an administration pledge to fund needed renovations of "Reaganville." For the next two years Snyder's group engaged the Reagan administration over the promised funds which had yet to be delivered. In June 1985, two hundred people marched with CCNV members to the White House demanding that the president follow through on his promise and release the funds for the tent city. In November 1986, Snyder decided to begin fasting again in order to get the money. After only four days into his fast, Congress released $1.5 million in renovation funds for homeless shelters.

From that point on, and into the 1990s, the Community for Creative Non-Violence acted as both a service provider and a political action group. CCNV maintained administration of the fifteen-hundred-bed Federal City Shelter in Washington, D.C., and also provided education and drug-treatment programs, and ran an in-house health clinic and day care center. The organization's crowning achievement took place with the passage of the Stuart-McKinney Homeless Assistance Act in 1987. Passage of the act followed in the wake of CCNV's "Great American Sleep-Out," in which Hollywood celebrities and noted politicians gathered over heating grates on a cold night in the nation's capitol demanding passage of the bill.

CHALLENGING U.S. INTERVENTION IN CENTRAL AMERICA AND THE RESISTANCE MOVEMENT

While the Freeze issue occupied the greater part of peace activism in the early eighties and social justice groups such as the Community for Creative Non-Violence called for an alternative to structural violence in society, President Reagan's escalation of the Cold War led to the birth of several other peace groups. One of these was the Women's Encampment for a Future of Peace and Justice. In late July and early August 1983, a large contingent of women peace campers was charged with disorderly conduct during a march to the Seneca (NY) Army Depot. The group – protesting the storage of nuclear weapons, Reagan's pro-militaristic policies, and the administration's policy of "constructive engagement" rather than outright condemnation of apartheid in South Africa – created quite a stir when approximately 2,000 feminists formed a tent city on a 52-acre farm abutting the huge depot. According to Newsday, the depot was "one of the nation's largest storage and trans-shipment centers for nuclear warheads destined for Europe." At the height of the demonstrations, which lasted three days, more than 300 female peace activists were arrested by either the local authorities or the military police. In one instance, "two-hundred and forty-four women were arrested by military police as they climbed over the fence into the heavily guarded depot." The large demonstrations and arrests were reminiscent of the anti-war protests that marked the Vietnam War. As the Associated Press story in Newsday recounted, military officials realized that it would be unwise to underestimate the power of women and downright stupid to ignore their strength in numbers.[17]This encampment served as a model for others across the country. In Puget Sound, Washington, Tucson, Arizona, Sperry, Minnesota, Palo Alto, California, Savannah, Georgia, and other places, peace encampments were set up and represented one of the most novel efforts undertaken by female peace activists. After the INF Treaty the peace encampment movement became inactive.

On August 23, 1983, in commemoration of the twentieth anniversary of Martin Luther King, Jr.'s "I Have a Dream" speech, some 250,000 marchers walked through the sweltering, humid 90 degree weather of Washington, D.C., on behalf of social and political change. Though the primary thrust of the march was to rekindle the civil rights movement, the theme of peace became a major focal point of the march. Leaders included the Reverend Joseph E. Lowery, president of the SCLC, Coretta Scott King, longtime member of WILPF and inspirational leader for black females, Atlanta mayor Andrew Young, Jesse L. Jackson, and Democratic senators Alan Cranston and Senator Gary Hart, and former Vice President Walter Mondale. There were speeches at the Washington Monument on civil rights, the Nuclear Freeze, American involvement in El Salvador and Nicaragua, and the proposed Federal Equal Rights Amendment. The highlight of the march was Coretta Scott King's declaration: "We still have a dream. We are all here to reaffirm our commitment to peace, justice, brotherhood and equality. We gather together today in non-violent solidarity." The March for Jobs and Peace and Freedom, moreover, "awaits fulfillment of the dream."[18]

One of the overriding issues among peace and justice activists in the 1980s was the controversy provoked by Reagan's interventionist policies in Central America. A number of beliefs were responsible for Reagan's foreign policy actions. In his compelling work, <u>Meeting the Communist Threat: Truman to Reagan</u>, diplomatic historian Thomas G. Paterson persuasively argues that American leaders had a consistent penchant for exaggerating the threat of communism. Among these exaggerated beliefs were: an evil-minded Soviet Union was responsible for fomenting international insecurity; the Soviets were engaged in the largest military buildup in history; the need to whip up an emotional patriotism in order to shake off the public's post-Vietnam suspicions about military intervention; and the need to support anti-communist freedom fighters as well as to draw a clear distinction between "authoritarian" and "totalitarian" regimes (authoritarian regimes were composed of strong leaders who held power under a democratic pretext in order to oppose socialist rule while totalitarian regimes were governments that relied on a socialist/communist model to control all aspects of society). For Reagan and his allies Central America became the battleground for testing these assumptions, ones that led the U.S. into Indochina.[19]

To put it simply, the Reagan administration viewed Central America in Cold War terms. Reagan attempted to explain away popular uprising against political repression and economic exploitation as sinister plots instigated by Soviet and Cuban forces. Thus the U.S. extended CIA covert action, military aid and training, and economic and diplomatic pressure were all extended in support of elitist regimes in Costa Rica, El Salvador, and Guatemala.

In El Salvador, for instance, the Reagan administration charged that armed aggression was being carried out against the small country by communist powers working through Cuba. In 1979, the U.S. supported Christian Democratic Party leader Jose Napoleon Duarte. His military organized "death squads" to assassinate moderates and radicals, including Catholic clergyman Archbishop Oscar Romero despite his own objections. In 1980, the right-wing military force raped and killed four American nuns; the officers who ordered the murders were never prosecuted. Blaming much of the civil war in El Salvador on Cuba and Nicaragua, Reagan dramatically increased military assistance to the right-wing regime.

The main country in Central America Reagan targeted for intervention was Nicaragua. The popular revolutionary force, the Sandinistas, had gained control of the government. They had fought against the repressive rule of General Anastasio Somoza. Once in office Reagan immediately began putting pressure on the small socialist government of Daniel Ortega. The Sandinista government was being forced to either capitulate or seek outside help. Reagan first cut off all foreign aid and then in November 1981 he ordered the CIA to train and arm the anti-Sandinista contras (the former National Guard troops of Somoza) in what became referred to as a low-intensity strategy. Using bases in Honduras, where

American military maneuvers were conducted thus suggesting the threat of more direct intervention, and Costa Rica, contras raided Nicaragua blowing up oil facilities, bridges, and burning crops. The fighting continued even when Congress banned aid to the contras in mid-1984 and the World Court charged that the U.S. breached international law. Reagan ignored both the World Court and Congress. Only when the Iran-Contra scandal surfaced – the U.S. secretly sold weapons to Iran and then funneled the money to the contras – did the American public seriously question Reagan's policies in Central America.

As if covert CIA-sponsored operations were not enough, Reagan was also determined to employ "Gunboat Diplomacy" in the Banana Republics. In late October 1983, the Reagan Administration dispatched 1,900 marines and army paratroopers to the tiny Caribbean island of Grenada. The Reagan administration claimed that an airstrip being built on the island was to serve the military needs of Cuba and the Soviet Union. The real reason was to intimidate Castro and send a message that Cuba might be next. Another reason troops were dispatched was to oust a Marxist regime currently in power. The pretext the Reagan administration used to justify the invasion was in order to protect American lives, principally those American students at St. George's Medical College and to "restore order and democracy." More than 100 people died as a result of American military operations, including close to 25 Cubans helping to construct an airstrip. Militarily, the operation was a complete success. Reagan and the military basked in the glory of armed victory, despite claims by British engineers that the purpose for building the airstrip was to boost the tiny island's tourism. Equally important, word of the invasion did not reach the American pubic right away. Plans for the attack were kept secret until the operation was well underway, which prevented the media from sparking opposition (a role the government believed it had played during the Vietnam War).

Yet, not all Americans greeted the surprise invasion with joy. Hundreds of sign-waving, chanting demonstrators marched in New York, Detroit, Boston and Berkeley protesting the invasion of Grenada. In Ann Arbor, Michigan, 250 people carried signs protesting the invasion and rallied at the Federal building, then moved to the ROTC building on the University of Michigan campus. Another 350 people gathered in front of the Federal courthouse in Minneapolis to protest the invasion. In Rochester, New York, "banners denouncing the action were hung from bridges over approaches to the city from Interstate 490." In mid-November, approximately 20,000 protesters gathered at the nation's capital in opposition to the invasion. Led by the November 12 Coalition—a group of peace, civil rights and disarmament groups—the demonstrators listened to speeches and protest songs on a cold, blustery afternoon. The featured speaker, Jesse Jackson, accused Reagan of "increasingly using military might as a first resort rather than a last resort," and using "poor blacks, whites and Hispanics...as cannon fodder in Grenada...."[20] Many critics argued that the U.S. faced no immediate danger. When the UN Security Council called for a resolution disapproving the invasion, the U.S. promptly vetoed it.

Opposition to American foreign policy in Latin America continued throughout 1984. The most visible demonstration occurred on June 9, 1984, when more than 10,000 people rallied and marched across midtown Manhattan criticizing American involvement in Central America and the Caribbean. The demonstration was organized and coordinated by Plowshares.

Challenges to these policies are the subject of sociologist Christian Smith's Resisting Reagan: the U.S. Central America Peace Movement. Smith's study examines why more than 100,000 Americans marched in the streets, traveled to Central American war zones, housed illegal refugees, committed acts of civil disobedience, and openly opposed the Reagan administration's program of sponsoring wars in El Salvador and Nicaragua. Although the "Central America peace movement failed to force the Reagan administration to end its low-intensity wars in Central America," Smith argues, it did make the "wars exceedingly difficult to conduct, and, as a result, substantially limited the severity of their destructiveness."[21]

The Reagan administration's intervention in Central America thus sparked the rise of the U.S. Solidarity Movement and other resistance movements. Solidarity grew over time as an informal coalition of over 150 national groups and thousands of activists. Organizationally, it was a grassroots initiative involving extensive networking among church and like-minded justice groups. In many ways Solidarity adapted the Freeze Campaign structure. What kept this loosely scattered activist network functioning was the phone, personal computer, and the U.S. Postal Service.

Solidarity had a strong religious component comprised of the following factors: the role of U.S.-based churches in Central America; the influence of the Catholic Church, which condemned the 1980 murders of Romero and the four nuns; the role of "liberation theology" (the gospel call for social justice through the use of non-violent action and for the Catholic Church to become more active in making governments accountable); and a strong and well-staffed Church-based human rights lobby in Washington, D.C. Solidarity was primarily a middle-class movement aimed at promoting religious and humanitarian awareness of the repressive regimes in the region. It maintained that the administration's policies interrupted the economic and political modernization taking place in Central America. Instead of promoting the welfare of the people, Solidarity charged, White House policies have instead resulted in paramilitary death squads, poverty, and repression. What Solidarity actually accomplished was giving rise to a number of coordinated groups employing acts of non-violent civil disobedience in order to highlight the oppressive tactics and policy of intervention in Central America.

One of the more dramatic acts of civil disobedience peace activists carried out was the sponsorship of the Sanctuary Movement. The idea of sanctuary – the practice of offering a place of refuge, usually a church, for individuals fleeing persecution – was born during the Vietnam War. On April 20, 1968, the historic Arlington Street Church in Boston reached out and provided sanctuary to a draft resister who had recently lost his appeal to the U.S. Supreme Court and to an

AWOL soldier who had served in Vietnam. The movement then spread throughout the country.

The movement gained even more visibility when peace activists began using sanctuary to meet the growing crisis in Central America. Because of civil strife, violence, and governmental repression in El Salvador and Guatemala in the late 1970s, numerous refugees fled to the United States. Throughout this period, the authoritarian governments in El Salvador and Guatemala received political and economic support from the U.S. government, which considered Central America a Cold War front.[22] The U.S. government would not grant political asylum to fleeing refugees from these countries citing that many had supported the revolutionary movements in opposition to these authoritarian rulers.

When the flow of refugees from El Salvador and Guatemala increased dramatically in 1980, peace and justice organizations in the U.S. stepped up their activity. In March 1982, for instance, a Presbyterian church in Tucson, Arizona, proclaimed itself to be the first official sanctuary. During the next several years, the sanctuary movement "grew into a network of several hundred churches, synagogues, and communities with the support of tens of thousands of individuals."[23] Initially, the Tucson Ecumenical Council established weekly prayer vigils outside the Immigration and Naturalization Service office, created community-based legal services to assist refugees regarding their rights, and raised money for bonds and legal expenses. One successful effort was adopting shareholder resolutions forcing "all U.S. airlines to refuse to carry any Salvadoran refugees back to their country, where many would face death."[24]

When all applications for political asylum were being rejected and the INS continued deportations and increasing bond amounts, the Sanctuary Movement changed tactics. Activists in the movement began smuggling Salvadoran and Guatemalan refugees into the U.S. This tactic was largely supported by the Committee in Solidarity with the People of El Salvador (CISPES), formed in 1980, composed of its own local chapters and base of activists mainly in the southwest United States. Reminiscent of Harriet Tubman's 19th Century

Underground Railroad CISPES helped transport refugees were then transported to a safe haven in order to prevent their arrest and deportation. Hundreds of church and community-based organizations established networks from Arizona to Boston. In almost every instance, fleeing refugees were housed in churches or religious places. By the mid-1980s, the Sanctuary Movement became the largest grassroots civil disobedience action in the United States since the Vietnam War. In an effort to halt the movement's success, the INS arrested some of the movement's leaders on charges of conspiracy, concealing illegal aliens, and unlawful entry of immigrants. Harassment by other government agencies, including the Internal Revenue Service, local police departments, and the state police, made CISPES a constant target—a recurring theme in American history with regard to dissenting groups. By the late eighties, as the repression in both Latin American nations subsided, the flow of refugees gradually declined.

In many ways the Sanctuary Movement was, according to historian Sharon Nepstad, "both a humanitarian effort to assist victims of war and an act of political protest against the Reagan administration's policy toward Central America."[25] This movement successfully "expanded the idea of sanctuary to be a holy and protective community for people whose basic human rights were being violated" by government officials and military regimes.[26]

While the Sanctuary Movement was in full swing, an interfaith movement—Witness for Peace—formed in 1983 to challenge Reagan's policies in Nicaragua. Beginning in October 1983, Witness for Peace placed volunteers trained in non-violence in the besieged town of Jalapa, which was surrounded by Contra forces. The Contras, heavily-financed by the U.S., did not want to risk losing their financial backing by killing American citizens. By December teams of twenty to eighty volunteers came to Jalapa and other threatened communities for two-week stays. While there, members of Witness for Peace would meet with the victims of the war and with civic, religious, and political leaders. They rebuilt damaged schools and clinics and planted crops in burned-out fields.[27] They also returned home with documented stories of rape and murder committed by the

Contras. Thus, Witness for Peace served as an unarmed peace monitoring force in southern Nicaragua's demilitarized zone.

Throughout much of the 1980s Witness for Peace activists protested, lobbied, used the media to expose atrocities, and employed non-violent actions to "stop a war that would eventually claim more than thirty thousand Nicaraguan lives."[28] In 1984, in one of its most important confrontations, a peace delegation riding aboard a small shrimp boat motored its way in front of a U.S. destroyer off the coast of Corinto. The efforts of WFP to investigate and record the Contra atrocities directly challenged the misinformation put out by the U.S. government regarding involvement in Nicaragua. The thousands of noncombatant pacifist observers who traveled to Nicaragua as part of the short-term delegations eventually helped bring about an end to military aid to the Contras in the last year of Reagan's presidency.

In the 1990s WFP continued its mission of helping the oppressed in Central America. In early 1994, when the Zapatista rebels living in abject poverty in Chiapas, Mexico, criticized government leaders for their economic policies and willingness to participate in the North American Free Trade Agreement (NAFTA), WFP was there to help them. The rebels insisted that NAFTA hurt the indigenous peoples of the region by encouraging the development of the land for corporate profit. The leadership of Witness for Peace joined in solidarity with Latin Americans by protesting in the U.S. problems associated with economic globalization. For rich countries and elites these new economic arrangements proved beneficial. But for poorer nations, WFP protested, it accelerated poverty, created greater economic instability, and led to further oppression. For many in Witness these newer forms of globalization policies were a historical extension of Dollar Diplomacy enacted during the Taft administration. Little consideration was given to how living standards in Central America were declining.

While WFP vigorously criticized American policies in Central America well into the 1990s, other groups of activists also raised strong objections to what was taking place once Reagan set in motion plans to oust the Sandinistas from

Nicaragua. In 1984, Christian peace groups announced “A Pledge of Resistance,” designed to dissuade the United States from invading Nicaragua. Specifically, it called for “a coordinated plan of massive public resistance . . . that would undertake non-violent direct action against congress on the largest scale possible.”[29] In the event of an invasion some seventy thousand people signed the pledge, and “Urgent Action” networks were quickly established to provide information to every congressional district should the U.S. act aggressively towards Nicaragua. Local Pledge of Resistance affinity groups were also established. These groups acted out their resistance to Reagan’s policies by staging sit-ins, vigils, blockades of munitions trains to Central America, and other acts of civil disobedience. Peace activists were thus able to curb the Reagan administration’s efforts to dictate policies in Central America by force.

SOUTH AFRICAN APARTHEID, STUDENT ACTIVISM AND THE DIVESTMENT MOVEMENT

While Central America received attention from peace activists and prior to the start of the 1991 Gulf War, there were also other world problems to contend with. The longstanding problem of apartheid (the policy of strict segregation and racial discrimination against people of color) in South Africa remained a thorn in the side of American peace proponents. Challenges to U.S. policy in South Africa went back a long way. African Americans, noted earlier, had demonstrated against apartheid as far back as 1948 when they called upon the UN to take a more active role in abolishing this policy. In the early 1960s African Americans demonstrated against Chase Bank which had numerous dealings with South African businesses. American corporations which had business ties or investments in South Africa became the target of activists who called upon the American government to force U.S. businesses and others from investing in South Africa.

Divestment was the strategy employed to bring about an end to apartheid. In 1970, Ron Dellums was the first African American elected to Congress from

Northern California. During his terms in Congress he called for a series of hearings on alleged war crimes in Vietnam, criticized the United States for its complicity with the apartheid government of South Africa and led numerous campaigns against military projects that included the Pershing and MX missiles, and the B-2 "stealth bomber." Pressing the campaign to end U.S. support for South Africa turned out to be his most effective effort.

In 1972, Dellums started his congressional campaign to end the practice of apartheid in the Republic of South Africa. Over the next fourteen years he continuously introduced anti-apartheid legislation. Finally, in 1986, his legislation calling for a trade embargo against South Africa and immediate divestment by American corporations was passed with broad bipartisan support. The Comprehensive Anti-Apartheid Act of 1986 specifically called for sanctions against South Africa and established preconditions for lifting the sanctions. One of the preconditions was the release of all political prisoners, especially Nelson Mandela who had been in prison since the 1960s. Although President Reagan vetoed the bill in favor of a policy he called "constructive engagement," his veto was overridden by a wide majority. This was the first override of a presidential foreign policy veto in the twentieth century.

Dellums' and his colleagues' efforts in Congress were complemented by student activists on campus. In the late 1970s students at Dartmouth College in New Hampshire created a stir when they built shanties symbolizing the policy of apartheid in South Africa. Of course, lessons in history oftentimes provide the inspiration. During the early 1930s, World War I veterans demanding their bonus built their own "Hooverville" on the Mall in Washington, D.C. A stunned nation read in horror about President Hoover's decision to use military troops under the command of General Douglas MacArthur to destroy the shanties and drive the men out of the Capitol.

In the 1980s students from elite eastern colleges and universities like Columbia, Dartmouth, and Cornell as well as large public universities such as the University of Wisconsin, University of California at Berkeley, University of

Missouri, and University of Illinois at Urbana-Champaign, and others built shantytowns to highlight the oppressive conditions of apartheid. The strategy was twofold: (1) to heighten student awareness of racial segregation and the evils of apartheid, and (2) to expose their own institutions financial investments in South Africa. What the divestment movement really accomplished was calling into question what their colleges and universities were supposed to do and what they stood for.

Eventually, pressure from within and without succeeded in bringing to an end the policy of apartheid in South Africa. A full history of these efforts has been compiled by David Hostetter in Movement Matters: American Antiapartheid and the Rise of Multicultural Politics. Hostetter traces the efforts behind the United States fight to end apartheid and white minority rule in South Africa. Concentrating on the history and organizational efforts of the American Committee on Africa (ACOA), AFSC, and TransAfrica, Hostetter highlights the tensions between those calling for a more gradual approach for ending apartheid and those advocating an immediate total disengagement through divestment and economic pressures. What stood out were the efforts of "liberation pacifism" in building transatlantic links and support for leaders such as Archbishop Desmond Tutu as well as direct action protest supported by elected African American officials, particularly the Congressional Black Caucus. These efforts not only helped end apartheid in South Africa but also provided a clear path unifying African Americans from all walks of life.

Success in South Africa, however, has not been matched in other parts of the continent. At the start of the 21st century a different sort of crisis in Africa emerged. The enormity and severity of the current crisis in the Sudan remains unresolved. A bitter civil war wreaked havoc on this country and led to the establishment of a repressive regime. The result has led to a near genocide in which non-Muslim tribal peoples are starving to death and being forced to live in camps as they migrate throughout the region. In response, a new divestment movement recently led to a yearlong national student movement which was aimed at universities and major corporations. The atrocities in Darfur sparked a form of student activism comparable to what took place twenty years earlier when numerous corporations with ties to South Africa began pulling their investments. What prompted the present movement was opposition to the Sudanese government, which was accused of sponsoring militias responsible for killing, raping, and abusing thousands of non-Arabs living in the region.

Colleges, once again, proved fertile ground for the divestment wakeup call. Student activists questioned how higher-education money managers, whose primary goal is to look for the best returns on investment, were conducting their policies. Throughout 2005 and 2006, peace and justice advocates aroused student awareness to the concept of socially responsible investing. When it became public knowledge that almost seventy-two percent of college investments did not take social responsibility into account, students began creating campus chapters to address the matter. National umbrella groups like Students Taking Action Now on Darfur, which originated at Georgetown University, and the Sudan Divestment Task Force, formed at the University of California at Los Angeles, placed tremendous pressure on colleges and universities to reconsider their investments. These efforts had an impact, as numerous college officials made a series of investment-policy changes. In April 2005, for instance, due to student pressure, Harvard University divested stock in the China National Petroleum Corporation, a business partner of the Sudanese government. Harvard owned some $4.3-million shares in PetroChina. In 2006, Harvard also withdrew almost $8.3-million in holdings in another Chinese oil company, Sinopec.

Harvard's actions led other institutions of higher learning to follow suit. Among them were Brown, Stanford, Yale, Amherst, Dartmouth, Smith, and Swarthmore. In March of 2006 the University of California System decided to divest shares of nine public companies with connections to the Sudanese government. Such action was also undertaken by the University of Pennsylvania, Princeton University, and Williams College.

Like the earlier divestment movement, this one also based its appeal on non-violent strategies. In the more recent case, research, rather than protest, was the students' most effective instrument. Student groups like the Sudan Divestment Task Force did most of the research that led to colleges reconsidering their investment policies. Two student leaders, Adam Sterling at UCLA and Daniel Millenson at Brandeis, were instrumental in arousing student awareness. But rather than using events like rallies they opted, instead, to wear business suits and present reports to colleges across the country. This non-confrontational approach proved exceedingly effective. The student divestment groups decided early on that undertaking a moderate approach that is urging colleges and universities to sell off their shares in companies that are most harmful to the Sudanese people, would be far more effective than demanding a sell-off of holdings in companies that were providing needed services in the region. The student divestment groups specifically targeted those companies which were the worst offenders.

The initial success of these student-led divestment groups also took them to state and local legislatures. In calling for barring investments of public money in Sudan the state legislatures of Illinois, New Jersey, and Oregon, along with the California State Teachers' Retirement System, entered into the divestment movement. At the present time, student leaders continue to approach large institutional shareholders, encouraging them to get rid of their Sudan-related assets. In so doing, it is hoped that the demand for share companies will evaporate thereby forcing them to stop helping the Sudanese government sponsor violent militias. Indeed, despite so much attention being devoted to the war in Iraq, students concerned about peace and justice in North Africa have made an important contribution.

PERSIAN GULF WAR

Despite the continuing crisis in Darfur, the end of the Cold War had ushered in new prospects for peace in the Middle East, an end to apartheid in

South Africa, and to lengthy civil wars that superpower rivalry had complicated. In the U.S., people had high hopes for a "peace dividend," meaning that government spending priorities might shift to domestic issues that had been put on hold in the face of the enormous Cold War military budget. But just as poverty, education, and the environment were poised to receive more attention, Saddam Hussein's invasion of Kuwait breathed new life into the military-industrial complex.

In reaction to the Iraqi invasion of the small oil-rich country of Kuwait, the United States chose to drive Hussein's army out by force. "No negotiations" was part of the official U.S. position. While not condoning Saddam Hussein's actions and not informed about the reasons or the possibilities of negotiating, much of the American public opposed military intervention. Prior to the commencement of the war opinion polls suggested that around 50% of the population opposed the use of force, and months before "Operation Desert Storm" unfolded, an anti-war movement organized. On October 20, 1990, some 15,000 protestors marched in New York and fifteen other cities across the country. Between October of 1990 and January 1991, when the war began, there were various forms of protest. In San Francisco, for instance, a TV station was interrupted and the Golden Gate Bridge was blockaded on several occasions. In New York city groups of protestors, organized by WRL, marched outside the stock exchange on Wall Street to condemn a possible war fought in the name of oil. Other protestors also gathered outside the UN carrying signs urging the Security Council to disapprove a U.S.-sponsored resolution calling for military force.[30]

As peace activist and historian Barbara Epstein later observed, "…there was a strong protest until the war began; when public opinion in the United States turned decisively in favor of the war, the anti-war movement collapsed."[31] A major reason for this was government control over information. Despite constant TV coverage of the war the amount of information provided as to the number of civilian causalities or the amount of damage inflicted by the bombing raids was kept to a minimum. A concerted effort by President Bush I and the military was made to avoid the "Vietnam Syndrome." A quick war with little information provided to the public did not give the anti-war movement a chance to grow.

At the same time, in obvious reference to the Vietnam debacle, government publicists generated a huge public relations campaign in support of the war by encouraging citizens to tie a yellow ribbon around trees in their yards – the yellow ribbon was a symbolic gesture supporting the troops. The Bush I administration purposefully conflated supporting the troops with supporting is war policies. The president floated various reasons for military intervention: (1) military intervention would provide jobs in defense plants which had downsized due to the end of the Cold War; (2) employing propaganda techniques such as his comparing Saddam to Hitler based upon the Iraqi leader's execution of those who opposed his rule; and (3) encouraging the public to make connections to the oil-rich country of Kuwait and how its resources were a key to U.S. economic needs. In addition, once the UN Security Council endorsed the use of arms and other nations became part of the coalition against Hussein, the American public dramatically switched in favor of removing Hussein's forces from Kuwait.

However, when the war was first launched, January 16, 1991, over 3,000 Bostonians immediately turned out to protest the war. Members of the Initiative for Peace led a rally which began with speeches at the government center and continued at Boston Common. Speakers at this rally considered the Persian Gulf War a conflict over oil.[32] On January 26th, a week after 15,000 turned out in force for a demonstration in Washington, D.C., a much larger crowd returned; estimates ranged from 70,000 to as high as 250,000. This turnout prompted Newsweek to state the following: "and there was, finally, undeniably, the presence of more than 150,000 Americans on the Mall last Saturday, little more than a week into a war whose worst horrors surely lie ahead of us. The peace movement, like the troops themselves, has barely begun to fight."[33]

Yet no sooner had the troops begun to fight and the anti-war movement to mobilize than the war ended after one month. A massive air attack demoralized the Iraqi forces and the vaunted Republican Guard retreated to Baghdad when faced with a superior American military force. For five weeks Americans watched on satellite television (CNN) Tomahawk cruise missiles hit Iraqi targets and Patriot missiles intercepted Iraqi Scud missiles. As Iraqi forces retreated from Kuwait, Allied aircraft flew hundreds of missions along the "highway of death" killing Hussein's soldiers as they fled from Kuwait City to Basra. After only one hundred hours of fighting on the ground, Iraq accepted an UN-imposed cease-fire.

Destruction from the war, particularly in Kuwait, was enormous. The infrastructure around the city of Baghdad was also severely damaged. Some 800 oil fields in Kuwait were destroyed. Although estimates vary, Iraqi casualties numbered about 25,000 dead. U.S. losses were 148 killed and 458 wounded. Some 140,000 U.S. service personnel were exposed to low levels of sarin and by 2002 more than half had sought medical care or some type of disability assistance. The Iraqi people were subsequently forced to battle typhoid fever, cholera, and imposed UN sanctions – military and economic – resulting in many more deaths and depravity. For peace activists the region was still considered a powder keg.

OPPOSITION TO THE IRAQ WAR

The First Gulf War was a military success even though Hussein remained in power. But by the fall of 2002, in the wake of 9/11 patriotic fervor, the Bush II administration decided it was time to use military force against Iraq. The justification for the attack was that Hussein possessed weapons of mass destruction. Evidence later revealed that such was not the case. Military plans were prepared and the war would eventually begin in March of 2003.

Thus, even before the invasion began peace groups quickly mobilized to try to prevent war. As early as October 3, 2002, an anti-war group, Americans Against War With Iraq (AAWWI) ran a full page ad in the New York Times with blaring headlines, "Bush's Weapons of Mass Distraction: War With Iraq." The subtitle read: "Is the Bush administration pushing this war because . . . war will take our minds off our failing economy, our broken education system, the environmental meltdown, the healthcare emergency, the raids on social security, the corporate scandals, the new $157 billion deficit? And we won't notice the loss of our civil liberties."[34] Surrounding the ad were hundreds and hundreds of names endorsing it as well as encouraging Americans to call upon their senators and congressional representatives to vote against an invasion of Iraq. Three weeks earlier, September 13, 2002, U.S. Catholic bishops had signed a letter sent to President Bush stating that any "pre-emptive unilateral use of military force to overthrow the government of Iraq" could not satisfy the criteria for just war according to Catholic theology.[35]

By October anti-war coalitions were appearing and putting pressure on government officials to stop talk of an invasion. On October 6, 2002, thousands rallied at Central Park's East Meadow in New York City. Speaker after speaker denounced the impending invasion. The event was organized by the anti-war group, NOT IN OUR NAME. Throughout the crowds were signs and T-shirts reading "It Takes Courage NOT TO MAKE WAR" and "Imagine," an obvious reference to the popular song sung by John Lennon that had been banned by Clear Channel after the attacks on the U.S. on September 11, 2001. One individual, John Earl, a salesman from Greenville, New York, held a sign that read, "EXXonerate" and "BPrepared"—an obvious reference to the suspicion many people had that the war about about securing more oil for the U.S.[36] On October 26, 2002, a massive anti-war rally, with the anti-war International ANSWER acting as the clearinghouse, was held in Washington, D.C. One protester on her way to the rally, Wendy Fuchberg, a student at SUNY Stony Brook, commented that President Bush's push for a pre-emptive strike "together with his neglect of bread-and-butter domestic issues, has politicized folks on campus." Others expressed their opposition differently, like the Reverend Mark Lukens who believed he was joining other "loyal, patriotic Americans in urging the president to seek peaceful solutions in consort with our allies."[37] In December, ninety-nine people were arrested in front of the U.S. mission to the UN for protesting the impending war in Iraq; they were arrested for disturbing the peace. Among those arrested were Daniel Ellsberg of the Pentagon Papers case and Ben Cohen, co-founder of Ben and Jerry's Ice Cream.[38]

One of the salient aspects of this anti-war movement has been the sheer size of protests and its global scale. Prior to the commencement of military action, anti-war demonstrations were larger than those that opposed the Vietnam War at its height. Increasing criticism of the Bush II administration's plans for war was based on the following concerns: (1) the war would lead to the killing of thousands of U.S. soldiers, Iraqi soldiers, and civilians; (2) it would have a negative effect on stability in the Middle East; (3) it was generated by imperialistic desires, especially the protection of oil interests; (4) without UN approval it violated international law; (5) U.S. military action in Iraq would not put an end to terrorist acts and would likely breed more terrorists who resented U.S. actions; (6) Bush's claim that as part of the "Axis of Evil" – Iran and North Korea – Iraq threatened the peace of the world with weapons of mass destruction was false; and (7) misleading and unsubstantiated attempts to link Hussein's regime with 9/11 and Al-Qaeda were misleading and unsubstantiated.

Based on these arguments, peace activists undertook their own courageous acts of resistance prior to the invasion. During a large demonstration in Washington, D.C., on January 15, 2003, sixteen protestors were arrested across from the White House while others, invoking the spirit of Martin Luther King, Jr., in observance of his birthday, shouted a familiar refrain from the Vietnam period, "Give Peace a Chance." A week later, a group of fifty volunteers from various nations departed from London and headed to Baghdad to act as human shields. Eventually, 200 to 500 people made their way to Iraq before the March invasion. The primary organizer was Kenneth O'Keefe, a former U.S. Marine who served in the 1991 Gulf War and subsequently renounced his citizenship. Many of the shields were deployed throughout key areas in Iraq; some eighty remained in Baghdad during the "Shock and Awe" bombing campaign.[39]

Meanwhile, in the United States, rallies and demonstrations continued. On February 15, 2003, a crowd estimated at between 100,000 to 250,000 marched through the streets of New York, making it the largest political demonstration the city had seen since the anti-nuclear proliferation movement two decades earlier. One protestor, Glenn Tepper, an English teacher at Jane Addams High School in the Bronx and a member of New York Teachers Against the War, stated, "I'm not giving my students everything I have for the last 29 years only to have them spill blood on the sands of Iraq." The New York City demonstration coincided with huge anti-war protests in London, Paris, and Berlin. Although the media reported this and other such protests there was very little follow-up by the press to generate more pubic interest. Nevertheless, the spontaneity of the protests, size, and ability to mobilize on such short notice was a reflection of how unpopular the war was. In early March hundreds of high school and college students sponsored a "Books not Bombs" walkout from their classes in opposition to the possibility of war. It was organized by the National Youth and Student Peace Coalition. On March 9, 2003, remarkably similar to WSP's actions in the sixties, some 3,000 pink clad activists, women who were organized by the feminist anti-war group, Code Pink for Peace, marched around the White House. One of the organizers, Kim Gandy, president of NOW, told protestors: "Instead of dealing with the tyranny of poverty," Bush will "rain destruction on a poor country in order to settle a score," an obvious reference to the first President Bush and a later plot to assassinate him while visiting Kuwait after he was out of office. On March 15th, the last massive demonstrations before the war began witnessed tens of thousands of protestors participating in anti-war rallies from Portland, Oregon to Los Angeles to Washington, D.C., in a final attempt to head off war.[40]

The magnitude and size of the protests increased exponentially once the U.S. attack began. Peace groups such as United for Peace and Justice continued urging acts of non-violent civil disobedience. In all of these protests throughout the remainder of 2003, the anti-war coalitions were composed of people from all walks of life. There were the elderly, former veterans young and old, college students, and people from all races. Opposition to this war cut across all race and gender lines. Rich and poor also came out to protest the war. Most noticeable, perhaps, were women and men who were in their seventies and eighties. They either fought in previous wars – World War II, Korea, or Vietnam – or were parents of a child who served in the military. At one New York anti-war demonstration, for example, 87-year-old Moses Fishman, who was wounded during the Spanish Civil War, remarked that he had been protesting wars since Vietnam. Back then, he added, "the first demonstrations very few people came out. If we had this many people, imagine what we could have done." On October 25th more than 100,000 marched in Washington and other cities carrying signs reading "No Blood for Oil" and "Bring Them Home Alive," reflecting the movement's focuses on preventing war and saving soldiers' lives. Activists worked hard to avoid the charge of being "unpatriotic" that veterans groups attached to anti-war protest during Vietnam.[41]

From 2004 to 2007, large anti-war demonstrations continued as did smaller ones in towns and communities across the nation. In January 28, 2007, an anti-war rally in Washington, D.C. saw thousands of peaceful protestors listen to Hollywood celebrities such as Jane Fonda, Sean Penn, Danny Glover, Susan Sarandon, and Tim Robbins condemn the war. In most instances, large crowds gathered at places such as New York City, San Francisco, and Washington, D.C. Although some people were arrested, these anti-war rallies were remarkable in their discipline and adherence to the principle of non-violent civil disobedience. The January 2007 rally on the National Mall, for example, unfolded with no serious incidents or arrests. What makes this even more remarkable is that the numbers of protesters in the current anti-war demonstrations have been larger than those during the Vietnam War.

As the number of American soldiers killed in action mounted (presently, the number is over 4,000), the American Friends Service Committee initiated its own novel protest. This popular strategy has been copied by other anti-war groups. Called "False Pretenses," AFSC first introduced the idea of a memorial by placing 500 pairs of boots at the Federal Building Plaza in Chicago to symbolize graphically the number of soldiers killed at that point in the war. Other anti-war activists built mock coffins and stretched out on busy roads. During the 2004 Republican Convention in Manhattan, hundreds of demonstrators carried coffins down 7th Avenue. During the convention one member of Code Pink disrupted Vice President Dick Cheney's speech. Jodie Evans, co-founder of Code Pink, was forcibly removed from the convention floor when she showed off her pink slip with anti-Bush slogans on it.[42] Between 700-800 people were arrested at the convention. Once again, despite the size of the protests, media and press coverage remained somewhat subdued.

Individual acts of resistance have also sprung up. David Gross, a San Francisco technical writer, requested that his employers drastically cut his pay so he wouldn't have to pay taxes to the support the war. In 2007, according to Ruth Benn, who is coordinator of the National War Tax Resistance Coordinating Committee located in Brooklyn, New York, an estimated 8,000 to 10,000 Americans refused to pay some or all of their federal taxes because of war objections. The summer of 2007 also witnessed two teenagers, Ashley Casale, 19, from Clinton Corners, New York, and Michael Israel, 18, from Jackson, California embarking on a 3,000 mile march from San Francisco to Washington, D.C. Casale set up her own Web site, "March for Peace," and, along with Israel, began the continental walk on May 21st and completed it on September 11th. Like War Tax Resistance, the continental peace march is a throwback to the 20th century when peace groups initiated these very same activities. Typifying local community action groups an organization calling itself East End Vets participated in a July 4th parade in Southampton, New York, one of the most popular summer East Coast resorts for the rich and famous. Their peace march was in keeping with the long tradition of democratic dissent against unpopular wars.

One anti-war group that did capture the national media's attention is Grandmothers against the War. This organization is primarily a local, responsive coalition in New York. In late 2005, seventeen grandmothers, ranging in age from

49 to 90, were arrested. On October 17th, these aging but fiercely determined activists attempted to enlist in the military at New York City's Times Square recruiting station. When they were refused entry into the station, they then sat down and were promptly arrested. At their arraignment one of the protestors, sixty-five-year-old Eva-Lee Baird, called her arrest "a badge of honor."[43] Their actions inspired other elderly females to take up the cause in cities such as Chicago, San Francisco, and Los Angeles.

Perhaps no one individual did as much to call attention to the anti-war cause than Gold Star Mother Cindy Sheehan from California. Her personal campaign began in 2004 after her son, Army Specialist Casey Sheehan, was killed in Iraq. She first attracted worldwide attention when, in August of 2005, she conducted a 26-day vigil outside President Bush's Texas ranch at Crawford. Her goal was to meet and talk with the president; however, as the days went by and she did not receive a response, more and more supporters traveled to Crawford in support of her efforts. She never did get to meet with the president to ask him "why we went to war." In September she was arrested while protesting outside the White House. She was among several hundred demonstrators who marched around the White House and then sat down on the pedestrian walkway on Pennsylvania Avenue. As the police came to arrest the demonstrators, all were singing and chanting "Stop the war now." Her most dramatic act of civil disobedience to date took place at the 2006 State of the Union Address. Sheehan was removed from the chambers wearing a T-shirt that read: "2245 Dead. How many more?" As one observer noted of her actions: "She has been a kind of lightning rod for the anti-war effort. . . ."[44]

Numerous peace groups, including CODEPINK for Peace, World Can't Wait, ANSWER, Veterans for Peace, Peace Action and Not in our Name have undertaken traditional and not-so-traditional forms of protests. These include staging a war-crimes tribunal in New York City to look into abuses in the "war on terror," independent filmmaking such as Michael Moore's controversial movie, "Fahrenheit 911," bringing Iraqi women to the United States to explain the horrors of the war, guerrilla theatre, opposing military recruiters on campus, mass letter-writing to members of Congress as well as to news and media outlets, extensive use of blogging, and protest music such as the Dixie Chicks and Raging Grannies. Peace activists were encouraged when, in November of 2005, Representative John Murtha (D-PA), a highly decorated Marine Corps officer in Vietnam, introduced a resolution in the House of Representatives calling for U.S. forces in Iraq to be "redeployed at the earliest practicable date" to bases in neighboring countries such as Kuwait and Qatar. By the end of 2007, a majority of Americans favored establishing a timetable for withdrawal, but are still opposed to an immediate withdrawal. Polls showed that almost 64% of Americans are against the war, while 72% of U.S. troops say the war should be ended within a year and 25% favor immediate withdrawal. An ABC News/Washington Post Poll showed Bush's disapproval rating for handling the Iraq War at 68% in contrast to the 22% disapproval rating taken on April 27-30, 2003. The cost of the war to date is well over 500 billion dollars. The hidden total cost of the wars in Iraq and Afghanistan (oil market disruptions, foregone investments, long-term healthcare for veterans, and interest payments on borrowed funding for the war) is expected to balloon to $3.5 trillion in the decade after 2010 and it is estimated that from the period 2002 to 2008 it will cost a family of four an average of $20,900.[45]

One of the more subtle and telling examples of present-day war resistance can be surmised from the actions of the African American Community. In a very compelling commentary by Kenyon Farrow that appeared in the March/April 2006 issue of The Nonviolent Activist entitled "Not Showing Up: Blacks, Military Recruitment and Anti-War Movement," he noted while African Americans were not visibly present at many of the protest marches – in most cases their actions are routinely criminalized – their opposition to the war can be ascertained by their refusal to enlist in the military. Why is this significant? Historically, one of the largest employers of African American youth has been the armed forces. For many black youths the military has served as an avenue out of the depressed economic conditions – the large inner cities or rural areas of the

the South. It became of way of economic and social uplift for those seeking some form of self-respect.

At home, passage of the Patriot Act has also mobilized the intensity of and civil libertarian groups. The current law significantly expanded U.S. law enforcement's power by removing the warrant requirement for communications taps as long as the government could certify that the information likely to be obtained would be relevant to an ongoing investigation against international terrorism. FBI electronic surveillance powers were significantly increased. Though the issue of civil liberties during wartime has always remained a troubling issue in American history, the extent to which the current policies have been undertaken represent the most serious invasion of personal liberties this country has experienced. In the past the government usually singled out groups and individuals who spoke out against government policies. Warrants were required by order of the court. At the start of the Iraq War millions of phone lines were tapped secretly with permission of the court. Every American citizen was subject to an unlawful invasion of their privacy without their knowledge.

At the same time a federal program to collect and process massive amounts of data to identify certain patterns was widely criticized as a threat to civil liberties. Millions of Americans have had their phones tapped for the purpose of gathering data. In 2007 the government finally suspended its secret program TALENT, a covert operation designed to gather information on organizations and groups critical of the war. Still, many Americans have been concerned over the prospects of "Orwellian" mass surveillance by the federal government in its war on terror. At what point do national security interests outweigh the right to privacy?

Another troubling aspect for peace proponents has been the issue of torture. The revelations at Abu Ghraib in Iraq and Camp X-Ray at Guantanamo Bay, Cuba, were troubling to human rights activists. While the CIA does have a long history of employing torture from the Cold War to the present, peace activists and the American public were stunned to learn of the mistreatment of prisoners at both detention camps. Forcing captives to undress and pose in indecent positions at Abu Ghraib shocked American sensibilities. Photographs showing shackled captives with their eyes covered with no-see goggles and their ears and noses muffled kneeling before American soldiers as they were about to board a plane for Guantanamo has exposed another side of this war. Employing sensory deprivation measures, long a favorite of the CIA, revealed a disturbing trend of the U.S. failing to practice what it preaches. One of the most troubling aspects is that these captives, prisoners of war, have not been afforded legal counsel as required by the Geneva Convention. The mistreatment of Taliban (opponents of U.S. in Afghanistan) and Al Qaeda (Osama Bin Laden's followers) captives has undermined the credibility of the American government among the Arab states and the world community. For a democratic government that prides itself on securing the blessings of liberty, its actions at home and abroad continued to leave much to be desired.[46] How are these activities making America safer and how are they detracting from the goal of a society all should emulate?

CYBERACTIVISM AND THE WAR

One of the unique aspects of the current peace movement has been its online organizing, which has helped many anti-war groups succeed in their efforts to mobilize at the grassroots. College campuses have become one of the primary components of today's anti-war movement. It has emerged as a force for organizing, raising money, and influencing politicians and the media through blogs and e-mail messages. One recent anti-war organization relying heavily on Internet usage is Americans Against Escalation in Iraq. AAEI is a broad-based coalition of activists, policy outfits and labor unions which were brought together in 2007 by MoveOn.org, the 3.4 million-member-strong liberal advocacy group. Using conference calls and e-mail messages to Congress this organization represents the new wave in protest movements – one aimed at influencing votes in Congress rather than street theater and mass demonstrations.

Though it is too soon to assess the full impact of domestic and international anti-war organizing through the Internet, it has had a big effect on the nature of protest. According to New York Times reporter Jennifer Lee, "the Internet has become more than a mere organizing tool; it has changed protests in a more fundamental way, by allowing mobilization to emerge from free-wheeling amorphous groups, rather than top-down hierarchical ones." One example of these new types of decentralized networks, or, as social theorists call them, heterarchies, dedicated to a "global movement toward peace and justice" is the web-based anti-war network, WHY WAR? It provides news and analysis, along with strategies to political activists. Another popular group, United for Peace and Justice, encourages campus activism by offering updates as to what other student activists are doing around the nation. There are also sites encouraging veterans to participate in a campaign to bring the soldiers home. While some of the anti-war organizations are more than online organizations such as the Iraq Veterans against the War, their efforts to mobilize quickly and over a large geographic area have been aided by internet emails and message boards. Among these organizations that mobilize online or received their initial start through the internet are Veterans for Common Sense, Operation Truth, and Iraq Veterans against the War.[47]

Another group that mobilizes via the Internet is Peaceful Tomorrows, founded by family members of 9/11 victims in order to encourage non-violent solutions to terrorism and "consciousness-raising regarding civil liberties being lost in the United States as well as U.S. foreign policy." Another organization, ANSWER, consists of hundreds of groups and individuals seeking "to promote mass action that opposes imperialist wars anywhere, occupation of any country, and the attack on civil liberties in the United States." ANSWER has emerged as a powerful umbrella organization because of its philosophies and strategies, which have enabled the global justice movement to transcend both national and interest-group boundaries through "creating common interests (peace, respect for environmental issues, and worker and human rights)."[48] ANSWER's particular strategy is to mobilize the masses for protest demonstrations in order to bring about an end to the war in Iraq and to prevent future wars of intervention. It has adopted letter writing campaigns to government officials via emails and has encouraged members of Congress not to grant additional monies for fighting the war. The group also used the Internet to mobilize support for a revision of the Patriot Act which took place in 2007.

These cyberspace organizations are noteworthy for creating and employing new concepts in their efforts to bring about change. Groups such as WHY WAR?, MOVE ON, and Win Without War, primary online organizations, have effectively utilized new social movement strategies like "radical empathy" and "swarming." Sociologists Victoria Carty and Jake Onyett describe these terms in the following fashion: "radical empathy" encourages individual ownership in all aspects of peace activism while "swarming" enables the individual to move from ownership to collective participation in the larger movement. Thus, with "radical empathy" groups are able to immerse the individual in the struggle of another in order to share authentic life-experiences bringing different aspects of the global effort for world peace. With "swarming" there is an involvement with a spontaneous effort on the part of anti-war groups willing to engage in acts of civil disobedience. Both strategies are designed to maximize and personalize the activist's involvement in the struggle. It is done through Internet communication and the sharing of information for the purposes of mobilizing rapidly and dispensing with an authoritarian structure.[49]

As noted, more scholarly research is needed to assess the role of Internet organizing and its impact on the anti-war movement. Carty and Onyett have introduced the topic to a wider audience. But it is worth observing that not everyone is enamored of internet organizing and debates continue to persist about whether it does more for the government's ability to keep tabs on people and thereby effectively monitor their actions. Nevertheless, research seems to suggest that the peace movement that emerged after 9/11, spurred on by the Iraq War, has embraced the notion of "international collective political struggles in novel and traditional ways." New opportunities have emerged as a result of the interconnectedness associated with globalization and new communication technologies; forging a global collective identity has become more of a distinct possibility due to modern technology. In this context, issues are now being framed under the rubric of global standards of justice and peace and people from other countries are sharing "oppositional consciousness in accordance with international norms." While military theorists state that the future of warfare will revolve around social and communication networks worldwide, anti-war groups are echoing the very same theme and using them to get out the message of peace and justice.[50]

CONCLUSION

From the anti-nuclear campaigns of the early 1970s and 1980s to the present war in Iraq, the peace movement has continued to play an important role in American society. The Freeze campaign, the anti-interventionist movement, and the anti-apartheid organizing of the 1980s all provided a modicum of hope. The peace movement's near collapse during the first Gulf War was a cause for concern; however, the more recent anti-Iraq War movement has been the largest ever.[51]

The apparent strength of the current peace movement is "the sophistication of its perspective." According to Epstein, "understanding of the war in Iraq as imperialist has been very widespread."[52] Many activists have willingly joined the movement because they have perceived this war as "a grab for world power, an attack on democratic rights in the United States and abroad."[53] A consensus of opinion among pioneers for peace and justice is that the current war is a serious threat to the stability of the international order and the economic development of societies who need global financial support the most. This broad perspective constitutes an advance beyond previous anti-war movements, which have been based primarily on opposition to particular wars.

What the current peace movement has done is to incorporate newer means of technology such as the Internet in order to promote its historic mission of ending wars forever in the hopes of establishing an equal and just society for all. From the beginning of the sectarian quest for peace to the 21st century opponents of the Iraq War the movement continues to awaken the public for the need to address the huge gap between the rich and poor, face up to racial hate crimes and discrimination based on ignorance, and move governments to tackle one of the world's most pressing problems: climate change. The history of the peace movement demonstrates its emergence as one of the most important forces for social and political change in the U.S. Pioneers for peace and justice have never abandoned their goal and making American a better place to live along with achieving global harmony in the name of humankind.

CONCLUSION

It is true that there is an infinite human capacity for violence. There is also an infinite potential for kindness. The unique ability of humans to *imagine* gives enormous power to idealism, an imagining of a better state of things not yet in existence. That power has been misused to send young men to war. But the power of idealism can also be used to attain justice, to end the massive violence of war.

Howard Zinn. Passionate Declarations, 2003.

While the peace movement will continue to have both its supporters and detractors, it has become apparent that the movement has developed more sophisticated forms of political and moral relevance. Particularly, over the last eighty-five years the peace movement has been effective in analyzing global conflicts, lobbying for legislation (e.g., War Powers Act of 1973), and election campaigns for "peace candidates" (e.g., Vietnam War and the current Iraq War), and mobilizing large numbers of Americans for efforts on behalf of peace and justice, with tactics ranging from militant civil disobedience (e.g., draft board raids, Plowshare actions, and Nuclear Power Plant protests) to unprecedented mass protests (e.g., Vietnam War, Freeze Campaign, Iraq War). In efforts to construct a safer world, the peace movement has continued to grapple with ways to secure a greater measure of justice in accord with most basic human values society cherishes, while avoiding the mass slaughter wrought by advances in scientific and technological development. The movement's historic goal has always been making peace, at home and abroad, a more realistic option than large-scale violence.

Obviously, war or the threat of war has been responsible for the establishment of an organized peace movement in the U.S. But it is also important to note that pioneers for peace and justice have extended their analysis of society beyond just warmaking. In fact, the peace movement has always been and always will be more than just opposing war. The struggle against slavery, support for women's rights and equality, involvement in the organized labor movement, building alternative communities that are based on economic equality and justice, and fighting against discrimination and segregation have also been part of the larger story of the peace movement in American history. If one looks at these aspects of the movement it is easy to comprehend the motivation and behavior of those who desire to make this nation a better place in which to live. Pioneers for peace and justice are facilitators, not obstructionists, of the American democratic tradition.

Zinn's plea for a dose of idealism merits serious attention. For many years peace historians have argued that activists for economic and social justice have presented many compelling and significant observations on the state of American society and beyond. It has been their vision that has inspired them to make a realistic critique of current situations. Without that idealism it would not have been possible for them to present viable alternatives which ultimately were translated into realistic solutions. Beginning with the Populist Revolt of the late nineteenth century, for instance, pioneers for peace and justice have been successful in calling attention to the need to limit the concentration of economic power. Activists attached their efforts to the reform mentality of the Progressive Era, and continue to spread the word about predatory corporations who remain determined to avoid social controls. Peace pioneers broadened their focus over the years to examine political, economic, and military hegemony, not just territorial. They maintained that the U.S. was compromising its own principle of self-determination by trying to impose its will on other nations, from Cuba and the Philippines at the turn of the twentieth century, Central America in the 1980s, to Iraq in the early twenty-first century. As the U.S. increasingly became a dominant world power throughout the later half of the twentieth century to the present, peace activists have served as a valuable check on executive authority, such as

Johnson and the Gulf of Tonkin, Reagan and the Iran-Contra Affair, and Bush and his preemptive war against Hussein (unilateral warfare in direct defiance of the UN and NATO allies). At least since World War I the peace movement and its supporters have raised concerns about civil liberties. The present war in Iraq, for instance, has led to serious questions about the Patriot Act in relationship to U.S. foreign policy and the state of individual rights in a democracy. Lastly, when it has come down to national interests and values, peace and justice activists have been quite vocal. From the War of 1812 to the Iraq War the peace movement insisted that war and militarism have been counterproductive to U.S. interests and to fundamental American values.

Its persistence in addressing structural violence as well as war remains one of the great contributions of the American peace movement. It self-consciously has injected a dose of idealism to counter entrenched institutions such as war and economic oppression. Where would American society be today if it were not for the efforts of peace and justice activists in the abolitionist and civil rights crusades? How far along would the women's rights and feminist movements be if it were not for the contributions of peace activists who criticized the inherent structural violence in American society that caused women to be treated as second class citizens? What if the peace movement had not called a halt to the development of weapons of mass destruction? Who has presented the more realistic alternative for the preservation of humankind: the peacemakers or the governments and their armies? It needs to be pointed out that what changes we now take for granted were largely attributable to these courageous pioneers for peace and justice.

Nor should readers of history ignore the peace movement's important dissemination of information, its appeals to conscience and public opinion. Consider the role of the Garrisonians and The Liberator when it came to publicizing the abolitionist cause. One should not forget the publicity attracted by Mark Twain, William Dean Howells, and other anti-imperialists who soundly criticized the motives and conduct of the Spanish-American and Philippine Wars.

In spreading the ideals of peace and expanding its international appeal, the record shows that Burritt's League of Universal Brotherhood in the nineteenth century and Devere Allen's No Frontier News of the twentieth century were important and innovative efforts for their times. In recent history one can draw upon the publicity generated by the Freeze, Solidarity Movement, and cyberactivism in mobilizing public opinion against nuclear proliferation, support for authoritarian regimes in Central America, and the Iraq War. In the past twenty-five years, more sophisticated efforts at grassroots mobilization (lobbying, media skills, and Internet) and raising large amounts of money in support of political and humanitarian causes have changed the character of the peace movement.

It is revealing that the architects of war and structural violence have made concerted efforts to silence dissent in American society. If the peace movement presented no real challenge then why did we have Espionage and Sedition Acts during World War I, silencing of voices for peace in the early Cold War years, COINTELPRO during the Vietnam War, and the passage of the Patriot Act and the Pentagon's TALENT database during the current war? At what point should American society sacrifice its personal liberties in the name of "national security" based solely on military victory and conquest?

One of the peace movement's most important contributions has been to redefine national security in broader terms. The creation of a national security state in the aftermath of World War II was couched in terms of military readiness to counter the threat of the Soviet Union and communism. Military preparedness and anti-communism defined both foreign policy – Korea and Vietnam – and domestic security – McCarthyism. But if national security is about protecting the homeland, peacemakers argue, than why not apply it to problems plaguing American society such as health care, education, and the environment? Why is it not possible to divert monies into these concerns in an effort to improve the quality of life of all Americas, not just those who profit from the national security state? Presently, many Americans have come to believe that the militarization of U.S. foreign policy has increased not lessened, feelings of insecurity.

Throughout American history there has been a vibrant peace movement. A careful examination of this book will also show that peace movements in American history have dealt with many pressing economic and social issues, not just war. That being the case, why, then, has the peace movement not received the attention it deserves in history books? Why has it not been placed alongside the abolitionist, suffragist, prohibitionist, and civil rights movements? The peace movement may be the most important social movement in American history in the last century.[1]

The fact remains that little is being done to describe and explain in school texts **all** the contributions peacemakers have made, apart from their opposition to wars. In recent surveys of eleven widely used junior and senior high school history texts, for example, the overwhelming conclusion was that they failed to challenge militaristic values. Not one of the eleven texts raised philosophical questions about the acceptability of war; war as a social institution remains unchallenged. In the detail given to military strategy, in the adjectives used to describe particular wars, and in the way U.S. war leaders are extolled, the texts did little to counter militaristic values. Reporting about the anti-war protest movements as well as involvement in social justice causes was practically nonexistent.[2]

Such documentation poses a fundamental problem for peacemakers. How can they convince people of the real value of peace when the concrete ideal of nationalism and patriotism is embodied in armies, national defense contracts, past wars, medals and ribbons, and the supposed righteousness of America's foreign policy objectives?[3] As this work demonstrates, peacemaking has been and always will be tied to social change, and it is important that the historical record be set straight.

But what can peacemakers do today that could lead to greater global security while solidifying their rightful place in the history texts? Retired State Department historian David S. Patterson suggests two avenues. One is to work to restrain the militarized version of security, which "might lead to the negotiation of comprehensive international arms control accords" (to regulate the arms race in general and the development of more lethal weapons in particular). In this way a greater part of the populace could join hands with the dedicated activists working for a less violent if not completely non-violent world. Second, peace workers must develop "new perspectives on national security which would place less emphasis on conventional military aspects of the concept and more on the psychological, social and economic dimensions." A constant reliance on military power to settle differences will only alienate America's allies and weaken its leadership of the western world.[4] Peace and justice pioneers must return to their colonial roots and reconstruct the "citty [colonial spelling] on a hill" model. Rather than being the "empire of the globe," a phrase popularized by the late diplomatic historian William Appleman Williams, the U.S. should resist using force as the means for controlling other peoples' destinies. Pioneers for peace and justice have always preached this message.

Years earlier, one of the nation's foremost peace historians, Charles Chatfield, argued that the peace movement has been "innovative, believing that it prefigured social values and norms. . . . From the Garrisonians to the New Left, individuals and groups attempted to act out behavior they associated with peace, whether in Conscientious Objection to militarism, humanitarian service across boundaries, or attempts to make power accountable to human values." Other innovations have ranged from the codification of international law and human rights, treaties of arbitration, international organization and collective security agreements, to "disarmament, decolonization, and international measures to make the world economy more accessible and stable." Given the realities of an increasingly global society, moreover, the peace movement has attempted to take the "idealism out of war." Peace advocates have relied on empirical realism in their argument that "war was no longer a viable extension of politics, nor imperialism a valid form of economics." Most importantly, throughout the peace crusade, activists have successfully "reformulated the problem of peace in terms of the process of social change and the accountability of power." This view has proved appealing to non-pacifists and pacifists alike, and has become a major reason "for the attractiveness of Gandhi's example in the interwar period and for the application of non-violent direct action techniques in civil rights, anti-war, and antinuclear campaigns" as well as the current opposition to the war in Iraq. Finally, peace activists have been "directly responsible for popularizing otherwise inaccessible information" or challenging deliberate misinformation in past wars such as the Philippine-American War, Vietnam War, activities in Central America, and the Iraq War. "By unveiling them in the public arena, often against the resistance of decision makers," Chatfield concludes, "peace advocates participated in the political process and made it more democratic."[5]

Concern for democracy has dictated the conscience and actions of peacemakers. In this respect, peace and justice advocates have looked at government spending and other priorities. The commitment and zeal the government has displayed when waging war far exceeds its devotion to assist the poor and those suffering from natural calamities. One of the ironies peace reformers point to is the government's indifference to the plight of the victims of Hurricane Katrina with its obsession for waging war in Iraq.

This is the very point made by David Callahan, director of research at Demos, a public policy group. Only one week after the U.S. launched its invasion into Iraq, he commented that while anti-war movements are "rarely successful in their immediate goal," they have "always put forth larger critiques of how American society is organized, and have often been entwined with powerful social movements focused on domestic problems." Today's anti-war movement has unveiled two powerful undercurrents involving a larger critique of American society: a mounting public concern over consumption and waste and democratic dissent involving the obvious "disconnect between the will of the ordinary people and the elites in Washington." As these two currents continue to swirl around, the fate of the nation may very well hang in the balance.[6]

The late Alan Dawley once suggested that his fellow historians examine how peace movements have shaped the American past in order to demonstrate their importance. He argued that peace movements have been successful in setting limits on war-makers. After World War I, for example, pacifists and anti-war activists played an important role in establishing the Geneva Conventions banning the use of chemical weapons. After the creation of the Atomic Bomb peace activists worked diligently at cultivating a climate of opinion resulting in a series of nuclear arms limitation treaties starting with the 1963 atmospheric test ban and continuing through with the 1970s and 1980s Strategic Arms Limitation agreements and the Comprehensive Test Ban Treaty in the 1990s. One area where peace movements have been most consistent throughout U.S. history is in the struggle over the distribution of resources. In this respect, the peace movement has been in the forefront in its demands for social justice. According to Dawley, during World War I the American Union against Militarism opposed the creation of a 400,000 man army and navy maintaining that such a course of action would drain badly needed resources from the civilian sector. Between the world wars the peace movement extended its reach to the industrial sector. It endorsed the organization of workers, pointing out that many of them were employed in munitions plants, were patriotic, but were not receiving adequate compensation for their labors. Peace activists tried to make the point that it was hypocritical to ask factory workers to make new tanks, bombs, and machine guns, and then deny them the right to organize in order to obtain fair wages.

Dawley also observed that during the Vietnam era peace and justice activists called for redirecting funds away from overseas military bases toward urban renewal projects, enforcement of civil rights laws for people of color, and other Great Society programs urged by the Johnson Administration – a sound example of making the United States a better place in which to live and a principal thesis of this survey. In the Reagan era the nuclear freeze movement pushed for "economic conversion" from the military-industrial complex that developed in the 1950s to school construction and health care improvements. Proponents of peace also played significant roles in support of anti-interventionist campaigns in the early twentieth century in the Philippines, Mexico, Bolshevik

Russia, and the Caribbean region; they unmasked the sinister influence of finance capital at the expense of the humanitarian well-being of the native populations. By linking peace to justice and democracy the peace movement has been able to mobilize a large segment of the population to question motives for war as well as the growing militarization of American society. Its efforts should be remembered and its ideas considered as we continue moving toward an uncertain future.

END NOTES

INTRODUCTION

1. Charles F. Howlett & Glen Zeitzer, The American Peace Movement: History and Historiography (Washington, D.C.: American Historical Association, 1985), 1-2. There are some excellent surveys to consult. A superb overview of the various strategies to peace is found in Charles DeBenedetti, The Peace Reform in American History (Bloomington: Indiana University Press, 1980). The ideas of peace activists are beautifully discussed in Merle Curti's pioneering work, Peace or War: The American Struggle, 1636-1936 (New York: W.W. Norton & Co., 1936). An important study exploring public attitudes toward peace and war and the shifting constituencies of peace coalitions is Charles Chatfield, with the assistance of Robert Kleidman, The American Peace Movement: Ideals and Activism (New York: Twayne Publishers, 1992). Chatfield introduces social movements as part of his analysis. David Cortright's Peace: A History of Movements and Ideas (New York: Cambridge University Press, 2008) examines the rise of peace action and internationalism from its religious origins of earlier centuries to the mass movements of recent decades.See also, Alice and Staughton Lynd, eds., Nonviolence in America: A Documentary History (Maryknoll, NY: Orbis Books, 1998). Our analysis explores how activists attacked the issue of war in the name of peace and social justice. In a special issue of the Peace History Society's journal Peace & Change, editors Wendy E. Chmielewski and Michael S. Foley compiled a collection of essays exploring the different political venues peace and social justice activists have created to develop alternative means of conflict resolution. Apart from traditional paths to power such as legislative politics, political parties, and bureaucracies peace and justice activists have also utilized non-governmental organizations. In the latter half of the twentieth century to the present NGOs have played an increasing critical role in working to achieve peace and justice. Consult, Wendy Chmielewski and Michael Foley, eds., "The Politics of Peace Movements," Peace & Change 26 (July 2001), 277-391 and special issue, "Non-Governmental Organizations and the Vietnam War," with an introduction by George C. Herring, Peace & Change 27 (April 2002), 161-300.

2. Howlett and Zeitzer, The American Peace Movement, 2-3; Jeffrey Kimball, "Alternatives to War in History," OAH Magazine in History 8 (Spring 1994), 5-9.

3. Harold Josephson, ed., Biographical Dictionary of Modern Peace Leaders (Westport, Conn.: Greenwood Press, 1985), 14-15.

4. Ibid., 15-16. Also consult the efforts of economist Kenneth Boulding and psychologist Charles Osgood. Both applied social scientific techniques toward the resolution of global warfare. This field emerged in the 1950's. For further information see, Charles DeBenedetti, "Peace History in the American Manner," History Teacher 18 (November 1984), 75-100.

5. DeBenedetti, The Peace Reform, 11.

6. For a complete discussion, consult the introduction to Warren F. Kuehl, ed., Biographical Dictionary of Internationalists (Westport, Conn.: Greenwood Press, 1983).

7. DeBenedetti, The Peace Reform, 12.

8. Charles Chatfield, ed. Peace Movements in America (New York:Schocken Books, 1973), 26-28.

9. Ibid., 26-27.

10. Charles Chatfield & Peter van den Dungen, eds., Peace Movements and Political Cultures (Knoxville: University of Tennessee Press, 1988), 14-18; Chatfield, The American Peace Movement, 165-185; Quincy Wright, A Study of War: An Analysis of the Causes, Nature, and Control of War (Chicago: University of Chicago, 1942), passim; See also the interdisciplinary work by Kenneth N. Waltz, Man, the State, and War: A Theoretical Analysis (New York: Columbia University Press, 1959).

11. Lawrence S. Wittner, Rebels, Against War: The American Peace Movement, 1941-1960 (New York: Columbia University Press, 1968), vii; Howlett & Zeitzer, The American Peace Movement, 6-7. See also, Charles DeBenedetti, ed., Peace Heroes in Twentieth Century America (Bloomington: Indiana University Press, 1986), 2-4, 19. It should be noted that, unlike peace historians, diplomatic scholars cover events until the moment when the belligerents broke diplomatic relations and then continued the story once the peace process got underway. Diplomatic historians have been good at telling how wars began and ended, but have not offered much in the way of explaining the economic, social, political, and cultural aspects of war itself. In contrast, peace historians are much more interested in ways to prevent war and in how mobilized groups have attempted to counter the powerful symbols of patriotism and power politics among nation states.

12. Curti, Peace or War, 13-14.

CHAPTER ONE

1. A sect, unlike a church, is distinguished by its voluntarism, exclusivity, a perfectionist bent toward pure beliefs and practices, an intense abnegation of the world and its attractions, and an eschatological sense of Christ's imminent Second Coming to earth. See, Sydney E. Ahlstrom, A Religious History of the American People. (New Haven: Yale University Press, 1972) 230-231. For an excellent analysis of the origins of British pacifist ideas consult, Ben Lowe,

Imagining Peace: A History of Early English Pacifist Ideas: 1340-1560 (University Park: Pennsylvania State University Press, 1997). For a Medieval discussion on conflict resolution consult, Roscoe Balch, "The Resigning of Quarrels: Conflict Resolution in the Thirteenth Century," Peace & Change V (Spring 1978), 33-38.

2. Curti, Peace or War, 17. See also, James Turner Johnson, Ideology, Reason, and the Limitation of War: Religious and Secular Concepts, 1200-1740 (Princeton, NJ: Princeton University Press, 1975), 18-24; Donald A. Grinde, Jr., and Bruce E. Johannsen, Exemplar of Liberty: Native America and the Evolution of Democracy (Los Angeles: American Indian Studies Center, UCLA, 1991), 118-125; 230-244.

3. Ibid., 17-18.

4. DeBenedetti, The Peace Reform, 5-7.

5. Curti, Peace or War, 16. For additional insights consult, Alden T. Vaughan, New England Frontiers: Puritans and Indians, 1620-1675 (New York: W.W. Norton & Co., 1979), passim.

6. Quoted in Perry Miller, The New England Mind: From Colony to Province (Boston: Beacon Press, 1961), 370-71; see also, Jon A.T. Alexander, "Colonial New England Preaching on War As Illustrated in Massachusetts Artillery Election Sermons," Journal of Church and State 17 (Autumn 1975), 423-42; Jill Lepore, In the Name of War: King Philip's War and the Origins of American Identity (New York: Vintage Books, 1999), 1-8, 84-91. One of the more controversial perspectives was put forth by Francis Jennings in The Invasion of American Indians, Colonialism, and the Cant of Conquest (New York: W.W. Norton & Co., 1975). For a challenging response to Jennings' view consult, Stephen Saunders Webb, 1676: The End of American Independence (New York: Alfred A. Knopf, 1984). For the Puritan view consult, Douglas Edward Leach, Flintlock and Tomahawk: New England in King Philip's War (New York: Macmillan & Co., 1958).

7. Arthur H. Buffinton, "The Puritan View of War" (Colonial Society of Massachusetts, Transactions. December 1930-April 1931, Boston, 1932), 67-86; Blanche Wisen Cook, "American Justifications for Military Massacres from the Pequot Wars to Mylai," Peace & Change III (Summer/Fall 1975), 4-20; quoted in Poems in American History. (New York: Macmillan Co., 1916), 50-51; see also, Lowe, Imagining Peace, 307-314. For a richer understanding of religious views see, Roland H. Bainton, Christian Attitudes Toward War and Peace: A Historical Survey and Critical Evaluation (New York: Abington Press, 1960).

8. The most authoritative study of the sectarian basis of non-resistance in Colonial America is Peter Brock, Pacifism in the United States: From the Colonial Era to the First World War (Princeton: Princeton University Press, 1969).

9. Buffington, "The Puritan View of War," 68-69; See also, Richard Slotkin, Regeneration Through Violence: the Mythology of the American Frontier, 1600-1860 (Middletown, Conn.: Wesleyan University Press, 1973), 4-6.

10. Peter Brock, ed., Liberty and Conscience: A Documentary History of the Experiences of Conscientious Objectors in American Through the Civil War (New York: Oxford University Press, 2002), 7-8.

11. Quoted in Gara, War Resistance in Historical Perspective., 4; Roger Williams, "Mr. Cotton's Letter Examined and Answered.," Publications of the Narragansett Club. First Series, I (Providence: Providence Pres Co., 1966), 328.

12. DeBenedetti, The Peace Reform. 9; William Penn, "Address to the American Indians," in Peter Mayer, ed., The Pacifist Conscience (Chicago: Henry Regnery Co., 1966), 93.

13. For a lengthy annotated sketch of Penn's treatise see, Staughton Lynd, ed., Non-violence in America (Indianapolis: Bobbs-Merrill Co., 1966); see also, William Penn, "The Rise and Progress of the People Called Quakers" in Frederick Tolles & E. Gordon Alderfer, eds., The Witness of William Penn (New York: Macmillan Co., 1957).

14. Howard H. Brinton, The Peace Testimony of the Society of Friends (Philadelphia: American Friends Service Committee, 1958), 7-9.

15. Quoted in Gara, War Resistance in Historical Perspective. 4; Lynd, ed. Non-violence in America., 11; Frederick Tolles, ed., The Journal of John Woolman (New York: Corinth Books, 1961).

16. Tolles, ed., The Journal of John Woolman. 130-131.

17. Ibid. 120-123.

18. Claude H. Van Tyne, The War for Independence (Boston: Houghton, Mifflin Co., 1929), 271-275. Also consult the following: Gordon S. Wood, The Radicalism of the American Revolution (New York: Vintage Books, 1991) and the Creation of the American Republic, 1776-1787 (Chapel Hill: University of North Carolina Press, 1969), 23-34; Ray Raphael, A People's History of the American Revolution: How Common People Shaped the Fight for Independence (New York: Oxford University Press, 2002); Thomas S. Martin, Minds and Hearts: The American Revolution as a Philosophical Crisis (Lanham, MD.: University Press of America, 1984); Gary B. Nash, Urban Crucible: Social Change, Political Consciousness and the Origins of the American Revolution (Cambridge, MA.: Harvard University Press, 1979); and Stanley Weintraub, Iron Tears: America's Battle for Freedom, Britain's Quagmire, 1775-1783 (New York: Free Press, 2005).

19. Peter Brock, The Roots of War Resistance: Pacifism from the Early Church to Tolstoy (Nyack, NY: Fellowship Press, 1981), 52-54.

20. Ibid., 53.

21. Anthony Benezet, Thoughts on the Nature of War (Philadelphia, n.p., 1776), 1-5; George S. Brookes, Friend Anthony Benezet (Philadelphia: University of Pennsylvania Press, 1937), 324-326, 356; Nancy S. Hornick, "Anthony Benezet: Eighteenth-Century Social Critic, Educator, and Abolitionist" (Ph.D. thesis, University of Maryland, 1974).

22. Anthony Benezet to George Dillwyn, July 1781, quoted in Brookes, Friend Anthony Benzet, 356; Carter G. Woodson, "Anthony Benezet, Journal of Negro History 2 (January 1917), 39-40.

23. Arthur J. Mekeel, The Relation of the Quakers to the American Revolution (Washington, D.C.,: Public Affairs press, 1979), 76-88; Brent E. Barksdale, Pacifism and Democracy in Colonial Pennsylvania (Stanford, CA: Stanford University Press, 1961), passim.

24. Brock, The Roots of War Resistance, 54.

25. Brock, Pacifism in the United States, 246.

26. Jefferson, "The Declaration of Independence", in Henry Steele Commager, ed., Documents of American History 2. Vols. (New York: Meredith Publishing Co., 1963), i-ii, 100. The three best accounts of the American anti-militarist tradition are: Arthur A. Ekrich, Jr., The Civilian and the Military (New York: Oxford University Press, 1956); Walter

Millis, Arms and Men: A Study of American Military History (New York: New American Library, 1956); and Marcus Cunliffe. Soldiers and Civilians: The Martial Spirit in America, 1775-1865 (Boston: Little Brown & Co., 1968).

27. Merle Curti, The Growth of American Thought (New York: Harper & Row, 1943), 136.

28. Benjamin Rush, "A Plan for a Peace-Office, for the United States" in Benjamin Banneker, Almanack and Ephemeries for the Year of Our Lord in 1793. (Philadelphia, n.p., 1794); Dennis D'Elia, "Benjamin Rush: Philosopher of the American Revolution," Transactions of the American Philosophical Society 64, part 5 (Philadelphia: American Philosophical Society, 1974), 97-98.

29. Richard H. Kohn, Eagle and Sword: The Federalists and the Creation of the Military Establishment in America 1783-1811 (NewYork: Free press, 1975), xii-xiii, 88,137-139. See also John E. Freeling,"' Oh That I Was a Soldier': John Adams and the Anguish of War," American Quarterly 36 no. 2 (Summer 1984), 258-275.

30. An interesting perspective on female citizenship in the young republic is offered by Linda Kerber. She notes that after the revolution "Many women's self-perception had changed, but the mechanisms for collective action by women had not been developed....It would be for the succeeding generations of American women to institutionalize their political identity." See, Linda K. Kerber, "'May all our Citizens be Soldiers, and all our Soldiers Citizens': The Ambiguities of Female Citizenship in the New Nation" in Joan R. Challinor and Robert L. Beisner, eds., Arms At Rest: Peacemaking and Peacekeeping in American History (New York: Greenwood Press, 1987), 1-22. Placing women at the center of the American culture and politics is the theme of Sara Evans' Born for Liberty: A History of Women in America (New York: Free Press, 1989). For the colonial perspective and the reconstruction of gender and myth among Native American tribes consult chapters one to three. For an interesting perspective on female Quaker activism consult, Sandra Stanley Holton, Quaker Women: Personal Life, Memory and Radicalism in the Lives of Women Friends, 1780-1930 (New York: Routledge, 2007), passim.

CHAPTER TWO

1. On Jefferson's ambivalent attitude toward war and the Embargo of 1807 as an Instrument of neutrality consult, Reginald C. Stuart. The Half-Way Pacifist: Thomas Jefferson's View of War (Toronto: University of Toronto Press, 1978), 2-5, 59-66; L.M. Sears. Jefferson and the Embargo (Indianapolis. IN: Bobbs-Merrill Co., 1966), passim.

2. Samuel Eliot Morison, "Dissent in the War of 1812" in Samuel Eliot Morison, Frederick Merk, & Frank Freidel, Dissent in Three American Wars (Cambridge, MA: Belknap Press, 1970), 3-20.

3. William Gribben, The Churches Militant: The War of 1812 and American Religion (New Haven: Yale University Press, 1973), 102-104; DeBenedetti, The Peace Reform, 30-31: Nathan O. Hatch, The Sacred Cause of Liberty: Republican Thought and the Millennium in Revolutionary New England (New Haven: Yale University Press, 1977), 138-140; Richard Archer, "Dissent and Peace Negotiations at Ghent," American Studies 18, no.2 (Fall 1977), 15.

4. Morrison, "Dissent in the War of 1812," 22-24.

5. Charles F. Howlett, "Anti-war Sentiment, 1812-1815" in David & Jeanne Heidler, Encyclopedia of the War of 1812 (Santa Barbara, CA.: 1997), 8-9. See also, Richard Buel, America on the Brink: How the Political Struggle over the War of 1812 Almost Destroyed the Young Republic (London: Palgrave Macmillan, 2004), 12-25.

6. Ibid., 8-10.

7. Patrick C. T. White. A Nation on Trial: America and the War of 1812 (New York: George Wiley & Sons, 1965), 33-41. A peace-oriented perspective is offered by Ralph Beebe, "The War of 1812" in Ronald A. Wells, ed., The Wars of America (Grand Rapids, MI.: Eerdmans, 1981), 26-35. For Thomas Jefferson's views on relations with Great Britain see, Reginald C. Stuart, The Half-way Pacifist: Thomas Jefferson's View of War (Toronto: University of Toronto Press, 1978).

8. DeBenedetti, The Peace Reform. 32-33.

9. Merle Curti, The American Peace Crusade, 1815-1860 (Durham, NC: Duke University Press, 1929), passim: DeBenedetti,. The Peace Reform, 34; Charles Chatfield with Robert Kleidman, The American Peace Movement, 14-22. A scholarly discussion of European peace movements can be found in Sandi E. Cooper, Patriotic Pacifism: Waging War on War in Europe, 1815-1914 (New York: Oxford University Press, 1991).

10. Gribben, The Churches Militant, 137-139: Donald Matthews, "The Second Great Awakening as an Organizing Process, 1780-1830," American Quarterly XXI, no. 1 (Spring 1969), 30-41; Don H. Doyle, "The Social Functions of Voluntary Associations in a Nineteenth -Century American Town", Social Science History 1, no.3 (Spring 1977), 333-355..

11. Curti, Peace or War, 36.

12. Curti, The American Peace Crusade, 6-8.

13. For a comprehensive analysis of the pre-Civil War peace movement consult, David C. Lawson, "Swords into Plowshares, Spears into Pruninghooks: The Intellectual Foundations of the First American Peace Movement, 1815-1865" (Ph.D. thesis, University of New Mexico, 1975), passim.

14. Noah Worcester, A Solemn Review of the Custom of War: Showing That War Is The Effect of Popular Delusion, and Proposing a Remedy (Hartford, CT: n.p., 1815), reprinted in Peter Brock, ed., The First American Peace Movement (New York: Garland Publishers, 1972), 2-4.

15. Clinton Fink, "Peace Education and the Peace Movement since 1815," Peace & Change VI (Winter 1980), 66.

16. Curti, The American Peace Crusade. 11.

17. Fink, "Peace Education and the Peace Movement since 1815," 67. In 1838, the Bowdoin Street Young Men's Peace Society in Boston issued a pamphlet entitled, Dialogue between Frank and William, Illustrating the Principles of Peace, which was "seemingly the first attempt at peace education of youth in a consciously pacifist spirit." Consult, Brock, Pacifism in the United States, 512-516.

18. Curti, Peace or War, 37.

19. Memorial of Mr. David L. Dodge (Boston: S.K. Whipple & Co., 1854), passim.

20. Worcester, A Solemn Review, in Brock, ed., The First American Peace Movement, 17-18; David I. Dodge, "By Gospel Authority," in Mayer, ed., The Pacifist Conscience, 113.

21. David L. Dodge, War Inconsistent with the Religion of Jesus Christ, also reprinted in Brock, ed., 57-59, 76, 138-140. See also, DeBenedetti, The Peace Reform. 36-37; Chatfield, The American Peace Movement, 3-15.

22. Ekrich, The Civilian and the Military, Chapt. 4.

23. William Ladd, The Essay of Philanthropos on Peace and War (New York: Garland Publishers, reprint, 1971), 8-10, 81-83; quoted in Lila & Arthur Weinberg, eds.. Instead of Violence (Boston: Beacon Press, 1963), 389; Chatfield, The American Peace Movement, 5-9.

24. William Ladd, The Harbinger of Peace. Vol. I, 10, quoted by James Brown Scott in his introduction to Ladd, An Essay on a Congress of Nations for the Adjustment of International Disputes Without Resort to Arms (New York: Oxford University Press & Carnegie Endowment for International Peace, 1916), 10.

25. Ladd. An Essay on a Congress of Nations, xlix, 6,100-101.

26. Robert Cooney & Helen Michalowski, eds., The Power of the People: Active Non-violence in the United States (Philadelphia: New Society Publishers, 1987), 28-30.

27. Arthur A. Ekrich, Jr., ed., Voices in Dissent (New York: Citadel Press, 1964), 80.

28. Louis Ruchames & Walter Merrill, eds., The Letters of William Lloyd Garrison, 4 vols (Cambridge, MA: Belknap Press, 1971), Vol. II, 30-32,146-147.

29. Curti, The American Peace Crusade. 75-77; Lewis C. Perry. Childhood, Marriage and Reform: Henry Clark Wright. 1777-1870 (Chicago: Univ. of Chicago Press, 1980), 65-7.

30. "Non-resistance Society: Declaration of Principles, 1838," in Mayer, ed., Pacifist Conscience, 124-127. See also, James Brewer Stewart, William Lloyd Garrison and the Challenge of Emancipation (Arlington Heights, Ill.: Harland Davidson, 1991), and Henry Mayer, All on Fire: William Lloyd Garrison and the Abolition of Slavery (New York: St. Martin's Press, 1998).

31. Curti, The Growth of American Thought , 310; Arthur A. Ekrich, Jr., The Idea of Progress in America, 1815-1860 (NY: Columbia University Press, 1944), 28-37; Alice Felt Tyler, Freedom's Ferment: Phases of American Social History from the Colonial Period to the Outbreak of the Civil War (New York: Harper & Row, revised, 1962), 365-405.

32. William Reichert, "Adin Ballou (1803-1890)" in Larry Gara, ed., To Secure Peace and Liberty (New York: War Resisters League, 1976). This is a peace calendar with no page numbers. See also, Thomas F. Curran, Soldiers of Peace: Civil War Pacifism and the Postwar Radical Peace Movement (New York: Fordham University Press, 2003), 1-16; Valerie H. Zeigler, The Advocates of Peace in Antebellum America (Bloomington, IN: University of Indiana Press, 1992), 65-73.

33. Adin Ballou, Christian Non-Resistance (Boston, n.p., 1846), reprinted in Mayer, ed., The Pacifist Conscience, 130-138.

34. Quoted in Kathryn Kish Sklar, ed., Women's Rights Emerges within the Antislavery Movement, 1830-1870 (Boston: Bedford/St. Martins, 2000), 142-145; see also, Larry Ceplair, The Public Years of Sarah and Angelina Grimke`: Selected

Writings, 1835-1839 (New York: Columbia University Press, 1989); Gerda Lerner, The Feminist Thought of Sarah Grimke` (New York: Oxford University Press, 1998); Sara Evans, Personal Politics: The Roots of Women's Liberation in the Civil Rights Movement and the New Left (New York: Vintage Books, 1979), 8-16; and Ellen Carol Du Bois, Feminism and Suffrage: The Emergence of an Independent Women's Movement in America, 1848-1869 (Ithaca, NY: Cornell University Press, 1978). See also, Wendy C. Chmielewski, "Binding Themselves the Closer to their Own Peculiar Duties: Gender and Women's Work For Peace, 1818-1860," Peace &Change 20 (October 1995), 466-490.

35. Sojourner Truth, "Aren't I am Women," in Margaret Washington, ed., Narrative of Sojourner Truth (New York: Vintage Books, 1993), 117-118.

36. See, Robert Trendel, "William Jay and the International Peace Movement," Peace & Change 2 (Fall 1974), 17-23. .

37. The two best accounts of Burritt's life are Peter Tolis, Elihu Burritt: Crusader for Brotherhood (Hamden,CT: Shoestring Press, 1968), and Merle Curti, The Learned Blacksmith: The Letters and Journals of Elihu Burritt (New York: Garland Publications, revised, 1972). Quoted in Weinberg, eds., Instead of Violence, 344.

38. Advocate of Peace and Universal Brotherhood (February 1846), 56.

39. Elihu Burritt, "Manuscript Journal", March 31, 1851; there are 28 volumes (1837-60) in the library of the Institute of New Britain, Connecticut.

40. Ekrich, ed., Voices in Dissent, 88, 91-93. See also, David Herbert Donald, Charles Sumner and the Coming of the Civil War (New York: Fawcett Columbine, 1960), 140-142.

41. Frederick Merk, "Dissent in the Mexican War", in Morison et al., Dissent in Three American Wars, passim; Zeigler, The Advocates of Peace in Antebellum America, 91-92, 109-115.

42. Ibid., 38-40.

43. Merk, "Dissent in the Mexican War," 46-52.

44. Ibid., 54; quoted in Weinberg, eds., Instead of Violence, 378-382; quoted in Alice Tyler, Freedom's Ferment, 416.

45. Carl Bode, ed., The Portable Thoreau (New York: Viking Press, 1971), 109-138.

46. Quoted in Bradley, Beatty & Long, eds., The American Tradition in Literature, I (New York: W.W. Norton & Co., 1967), 1504-1505.

47. Merk, "Dissent in the Mexican War", 35-63; Zeigler, The Advocates of Peace in Antebellum America, 112-115.

48. John H. Schroeder, Mr. Polk's War: American Opposition to Dissent. 1846-1848 (Madison, WI: University of Wisconsin Press, 1973), passim.

49. Merle Curti, "Elihu Burritt," Dictionary of American Biography Vol. 2, 329.

50. Tolis, Elihu Burritt, passim: see also, Peter Brock, Radical Pacifists in Antebellum America (Princeton: Princeton University Press, 1968), passim.

51. Curti, The Learned Blacksmith. 10-11; & The American Peace Crusade, 150.

52. Curti, The American Peace Crusade. 221-230. On the earliest stages of female peace activism consult, Harriet H. Alonso, Peace as a Women's Issue: A History of the U.S. Movement for World Peace and Women's

Rights (Syracuse: Syracuse University Press, 1993), Chapt. 1, passim. A rather interesting perspective of the tradition of radical Christian liberalism has been presented in Dan McKanan, Identifying the Image of God: Radical Christian and the Non-violent Power in the Antebellum United States (New York: Oxford University Press, 2002). In his opinion, this tradition has not fully rebounded from the setbacks incurred at the time of the Civil War. To a great extent, nineteenth-century liberalism was victim to an excessive belief in human nature: "…radical Christian liberals did *not* ignore the widespread violence and oppression in their society. They were deeply attuned to the violence of slavery, the tyranny of addiction, and the horrors of war. When they flattered in their responses to evil, it was because they were so dazzled by its ubiquity that they forgot its contingency. Their sin was a lack, not an excess, of faith in human nature" (pp.215-216).

53. Josiah Warren, True Civilization: An Immediate Necessity (Boston, n.p., 1863), 14-24, 47-52, 68-69,107-109; Robert Cooney & Helen Michalowski, eds., The Power of the People, 33-35; Charles F. Howlett, "Josiah Warren," American National Biography Online (3/28/2005).

54. J.M. Hofer, "Development of the Peace Movement in Illinois During the Civil War," Journal of the Illinois State Historical Society. XXIV (April 1931), passim; Curti, Peace or War. 64.

55. J.T. Headley, Pen and Pencil Sketches of the Great Riots (NY, n.p., 1877), 136-184; Elbert J. Benton, The Movement for Peace Without a Victory During the Civil War (Cleveland: World Publishing Co., 1918), passim; Georgia Lee Tatum, Disloyalty in the Confederacy (Chapel Hill, NC: University of North Carolina Press, 1935), passim J. Hugh McTeer, "A Fife and Drum Began to Play; Music and the Civil War," Curriculum Review (May 1985), 159-70.

56. It is worth noting that in the case of the Quakers they failed to contribute significantly to the emerging peace societies of the early nineteenth century because of their absorption in internal religious schisms and a "narrowly conceived separatism." See, Brock, Pacifism in the United States, 376-377.

57. The Civil War Diary of Cyrus Pringle (Wallingford, PA: Pendle Hill Press, 1962); Edward Needles Wright, Conscientious Objectors in the Civil War (New York: A.S. Barnes, 1961); Brock, The Roots of War Resistance, 58-61. After the Civil War the Quakers' distinctive peace commitment narrowed. Partly, their commitment diminished because the absence of wartime governmental pressure loosened the communal bonds of the Society and eased sectarian demands upon younger members. Also the Quakers' success in missionary activity in the West won to the group new members who valued the experiential Inner Light but ignored the testimony of active nonresistant love. See also, Curran, Soldiers of Peace, 50-68; Zeigler, The Advocates of Peace in Antebellum America, 158-59; and James O. Lehman & Steven M. Nolt, Mennonites, Amish, and the American Civil War (Baltimore: The Johns Hopkins University Press, 2007), passim.

58. Brock, Pacifism in the United States, 88-89.

59. Ibid., 788.

60. Ibid., 789-90.

61. Ibid, p. 810. For the Mennonites' position during the Civil War I have relied heavily on Brock's superb analysis, especially pages 780-821. Also consult Samuel Horst, Mennonites in the Confederacy: A Study in Civil

War Pacifism (Scottsdale, PA: Herald Press, 1967.), and James O. Lehman and Steven M. Nolt, Mennonites, Amish, and the American Civil War (Baltimore, MD: The Johns Hopkins University Press, 2007).

62. Brock, The Roots of War Resistance. 70-71; Lewis Perry, Radical Abolitionism: Anarchy and the Government of God in Antislavery Thought (Ithaca, NY: Cornell University Press, 1973), passim; Curran, Soldiers of Peace, 23-44. For the radical Christian liberal perspective consult, McKanan, Identifying the Image of God, 174-214.

63. Merle Curti, The Roots of American Loyalty (New York: Athenaeum, revised, 1968), 68-72; Brock, Pacifism in the United States, 689-710.

64. Michael Howard, War and the Liberal Conscience: The George Macaulay Trevelyan Lectures in the University of Cambridge (London: Temple Smith, 1978), 47.

65. Quoted in Robert Spiller et al., eds., Literary History of the United States (New York: The Macmillan Co., 1963), 1023.

CHAPTER THREE

1. Benjamin Trueblood, in First Annual Report of the Lake Mohonk Conference on International Arbitration 1895 (n.p., lake Mohonk Arbitration Conference, 1895), 8; DeBenedetti, The Peace Reform, 59

2. Edson L. Whitney, The American Peace Society: A Centennial History (Washington D.C.: American Peace Society, 928), 115-25.

3. Proceedings of the Peace Convention held in Providence, May 16,1866 (Boston, n.p.); Advocate of Peace (May-June 1866), 84, 143-4.

4. Robert Doherty, "Alfred H. Love and the Universal Peace Union" (Ph.D. thesis, University of Pennsylvania, 1962), passim; Curran, Soldiers of Peace. 106-112; 124-28; Cooney & Michalowski, eds., The Power of the People, 34-37.

5. Not all European visitors delighted in the Union's propaganda techniques. One Englishman was shocked by the "tomfoolery" at a meeting of the UPU during the Philadelphia Centennial of 1876. He reported that a large sprinkling of Spiritualists detracted from the dignity of the proceedings; the young woman in short petticoats and Turkish trousers who mounted the platform and read badly a school-girl declamation plainly jarred on his nerves; and others indulged in long-winded subjects on tiresome subjects. See, Herald of Peace XV (September 1, 1876), XXIII (November 1893), 317, quoted in Weinberg, eds., Instead of Violence, 334.

6. Women made up at least one-third of the Union's membership. Yet feminists, despite assembling a wide range of independent reform organizations in the last third of the nineteenth century, failed to sustain organized peace activism among women in the early postwar years. See Curran, Soldiers of Peace, 158-89.

7. DeBenedetti, The Peace Reform, 60-61.

8. Ekrich, The Civilian and the Military, passim.

9. Howlett, "Nicholas Murray Butler's Crusade for a Warless World," Wisconsin Magazine of History 67 (winter, 1983-84), 99-120.

10. Herald of Peace XX (September 1886), 115; (May 1888), 68; XXII (September 1891), 294; Century Magazine XLVII (January 1894), 468-9; XL, no.VIII(June 1894), 318-9; Peacemaker XII (May 1894), 203-04; Josiah Leeds, Against the Teaching of War in Historical Textbooks (Philadelphia, 1896), 93-104, et. passim.

11. Charles F. Howlett, Troubled Philosopher: John Dewey and the Struggle for World Peace (Port Washington, NY: Kennikat Press, 1977), 58-60.

12. Fink, "Peace Education and the Peace Movement since 1815," 67.

13. Howlett & Zeitzer, The American Peace Movement, 17-21.

14. Laura Richards and Maud Howe Elliott, Julia Ward Howe. 1819-1900 (Boston: Houghton Mifflin Co., 1915), 160, 300-04; Julia Ward Howe, Reminiscences. 1819-1899 (Boston & NY: Houghton Mifflin Co., 1899), 325-36; Voice of Peace III (November 1876), 127, 310-45; Wendy Chmielewski, "'Mid the Din a Dove Appeared': Women's Work in the Nineteenth Century Peace Movement," Over Here: A European Journal of American Culture 17 (1997), 71-98.

15. Curti, Peace or War, 115.

16. Peacemaker XX (March 1901), 50; Advocate of Peace LXI (November 1899), 237-8.

17. DeBenedetti, The Peace Reform, 64-5; James P. Piscatori, "Law, Peace and War in American International Legal Thought" in Ken Booth and Moorhead Wright, eds., American Thinking About Peace and War (New York: Barnes & Noble, 1978), 135-7.

18. The Alabama Claims is well documented in Curti, Peace or War, 91-98.

19. H.M. Field, Life of David Dudley Field (New York: Macmillan Co., 1898), 220-42: Herald of Peace XVIII (April 1882), 41-2.

20. Advocate of Peace VI (December 1875), 76 ff; Herald of Peace (January 1876), 2; Burritt-Miles Mss.(American Peace Society, Washington, D.C.); Louis Sohn, "The Growth of the Science of International Organizations," in Karl Deutsch and Stanley Hoffiman, eds., The Relevance of International Law (New York: Doubleday Anchor edition, 1971), 328-30.

21. Curti, Peace or War, 154-55; DeBenedettti, The Peace Reform, 65-67.

22. DeBenedetti, The Peace Reform, 65.

23. The Peacemaker I (August 1882), 40; R. McMurdy, The Arbitration League (Washington, D.C., n.p., 1885), passim.

24. The attack on capitalism as a merchant of death, though not popular until the 1930's, did not go unnoticed at this time. The muckraking liberal, John Clark Ridpath, declared that capitalism had been the immemorial policy of the "Money Power" to foment wars, to egg on combatants, until frightened by bankruptcy, were willing to sell their debt for a painful of gold after which, to the tune of patriotic proclamations for preserving national

honor, these sheep in wolfs clothing raised the debt to par. See, John Clark Ridpath, "Plutocracy and War," Arena XIX (January 1898), 97-103.

25. Voice of Peace I (May 1874), 25-6; Peacemaker XIII (July 1894), 7-8.

26. Peacemaker XIII (December 1894), 117; XIV (January-February 1896), 139.

27. Peacemaker I (December 1882), 89; Advocate of Peace LXI (December 1899), 258; Herbert Spencer, The Principles of Sociology (NY: Appleton & Co., 1897), II, 242, 594; III, 599-611; John Fiske, The Destiny of Man (Boston & NY: Houghton Mifflin Co., 1884), xi; Excursions of an Evolutionist (Boston: Houghton Mifflin Co., 1884), xi; Excursions of an Evolutionist (Boston: Houghton Mifflin Co., 1883), 208-28; Lester Ward, Dynamic Sociology (New York: D. Appleton & Co., 1894), II, 87-9, 237-9; Pure Sociology (New York: Macmillan Co., 2nd edition, 1925), 238-40; Richard Hofstadter, Social Darwinism in American Thought (Boston: Beacon press, 1955), passim.

28. Helen Hunt Jackson, A Century of Dishonor (New York: Indian Head Books, 1994, originally published in 1881), 88-96. Recent scholarship on Native Americans is quite extensive. Some of the more representative works include the following: Colin G. Calloway, ed., Our Hearts Fell to the Ground: Plains Indians View of How the West was Lost (Boston: Bedford/St. Martins, 1996), 12-36; Paul H. Carlson, The Plains Indians (College Station: Texas A&M Press, 1999); William Leckie, The Military Conquest of the Southern Plains (Norman: University of Oklahoma Press, 1963); Elliot West, The Contested Plains: Indians, Goldseekers, and the Rush to Colorado (Lawrence: University of Kansas Press, 1998); Angie Debo, And Still the Waters Run: The Betrayal of Five Civilized Tribes (Princeton, NJ: Princeton University Press, 1973); and an updated reprint, Black Elk, Nicholas, Black Elk Speaks: Being the Life Story of a Holy Man of the Oglala Sioux (Lincoln: University of Nebraska Press, 2000). Richard Slotkin's Regeneration Through Violence: The Mythology of the American Frontier, 1600-1860 (Middletown, CT.: Wesleyan University Press, 1973) provides a valuable passageway for examining the historical justification for expansionism through conquest.

29. M.E. Hirst, Quakers in Peace and War (London: Swarthmore Press, 1923) 449.

30. Warren F. Kuehl, Seeking World Order: The United States and International Organization to 1920 (Nashville, TN: University of Tennessee Press, 1969), passim; David S. Patterson, Toward a Warless World: The Travail of the American Peace Movement, 1887-1914 (Bloomington, IN: University of Indiana Press, 1976), passim; Chicago Tribune, Sept. 1,1882; Fourth Annual Report of Lake Mohonk Conference, 74. Also refer to, Cecilie Reid, "Peace and Law—Peace Activism and International Arbitration," Peace & Change 29 (July 2004), 527-548.

31. DeBenedetti, The Peace Reform, 66.

32. Patterson, Toward a Warless World, 18-24.

33. First Annual Report of Lake Mohonk Conference, 9.For a discussion on the role of female participation at the Lake Mohonk Annual Conferences refer to Charles F. Howlett, "Women Pacifists of America: Women's

views at the Lake Mohonk Conferences for International Arbitration, 1895-1916," Peace Research 21 (January 1989), 27-32, 69-74.

34. Ibid, 36-44.

35. For Tolstoy's wide appeal consult, Peter Frederick, Knights of the Golden Rule: The Intellectual as Christian Social Reformer in the 1890's (Lexington, KY: University of Kentucky Press, 1976), passim.

36. Arthur A. Ekrich, Jr., "Reflections on Problems of Militarism and History in Tolstoy's War and Peace," Peace & Change VIII, no. 4 (Fall 1982), 1-5.

37. Quoted in Brock, The Roots of War Resistance, 73.

38. Curti, Peace or War, 114.

39. For background information consult the following works: Julius Pratt, The Expansionists of 1898 (Chicago: Quadrangle Books, rev., 1964); Walter LeFeber, The New Empire: American Expansionism, 1860-1898 (Ithaca: Cornell University Press, 1963); Frank Freidel, Splendid Little War (New York: Doubleday, 1958); William E. Leuchtenburg, "Progressive Movement and American Foreign Policy, 1898-1916," Mississippi Valley Historical Review 39 (1952); Thomas A. Bailey, "America's Emergence as a World Power," Pacific Historical Review 30 (1961).

40. Nation XXVII (November 7, 1878), 28.

41. For discussions on the role of the Anti-Imperialists refer to the following sources: Robert L. Beisner, Twelve Against Empire: The Anti-Imperialists, 1898-1900 (New York: McGraw-Hill, 1968); Sondra R. Herman, Eleven Against War: Studies in American Internationalist Thought. 1898-1921 (Stanford, CA: Hoover Institution Press, 1969); C. Roland Marchand, The American Peace Movement and Social Reform. 1898-1918 (Princeton: Princeton University Press, 1972); E . Berkeley Tompkins, Anti-Imperialism in the United States: The Great Debate. 1898-1920 (Philadelphia: University of Pennsylvania Press, 1970); Frank Friedel, "Dissent in the Spanish-American War and the Philippine Insurrection," in Morison, Merk & Freidel, Dissent in Three American Wars, passim; Fred H. Harrington, "The Anti-Imperialist Movement in the United States, 1898-1900," The Mississippi Valley Historical Review XXII, no. 2 (September 1935); John M. Craig, Lucia Ames Mead (1856-1936) and the American Peace Movement (Lewiston, NY: The Edwin Mellen Press, 1990), 54-56.

42. Bernard DeVoto, ed., The Portable Mark Twain (New York: Viking Press, 1946), 582-84,599. For greater insight into Twain's anti-imperialist sentiments consult, Jim Zwick, Mark Twain's Weapons of Satire: Anti-Imperialist Writings on the Philippine-American War (Syracuse: Syracuse University Press, 1992).

43. Howlett & Zeitzer, The American Peace Movement, 18-20.

44. Letter to Boston Evening Transcript. March 1, 1899, quoted in Ralph Barton Perry, The Thought and Character of William James (Cambridge, MA: Harvard University Press, 1948), 245-6.

45. Ernest H. Crosby, "War and Christianity," Social Gospel 1 (July 1898), 5-6. See, Peter Frederick, "Ernest Howard Crosby: Tolstoyan Apostle of Peace," in Charles F. Howlett, ed., "Apostles of Peace," Peace Research 15. no.2 (May 1983), 28-35; and Perry E. Gianakos, "Ernest Howard Crosby: A Forgotten Tolstoyan Anti-Imperialist and Anti-Militarist," American Studies (Spring 1972), 11-29.

46. Crosby, "The Absurdities of Militarism," an address in Boston, June 16, 1901 (American Peace Society Pamphlet), 7-11; "War from the Christian Point of View", Boston, 1901 (APS Pamphlet); "The Military Idea of Manliness," The Independent 53 (April 8, 1901), 874-5; Frederick, "Ernest Howard Crosby," 27-28.

47. Ernest H. Crosby, Captain Jinks Hero (New York, 1902), 12, 227, 323, also noted in Frederick, "Ernest Howard Crosby," 33-5.

48. Ernest H. Crosby, "Why I am Opposed to Imperialism," Arena 28(July 1902), 10-11; Frederick, '"Ernest Howard Crosby," 33-34; Gianakos, "Ernest Howard Crosby," 26-29.

49. Quoted in Ellen Nore, Charles Beard: An Intellectual Biography (Carbondale, IL: Southern Illinois University Press, 1983), 33-35.

50. Mary Baird Bryan, The Memoirs of William Jennings Bryan (Philadelphia: J.B. Lippincott Co., 1925), 122; see also, Merle Curti, Bryan and World Peace (Northampton, MA: Smith College Studies, 1931), passim; Paolo Colletta, William Jennings Bryan 2 vols (Lincoln: University of Nebraska Press, 1968, 1969); Lawrence W. Levine, Defender of the Faith: William Jennings Bryan, The Last Decade, 1915-1925 (New York: Oxford University Press, 1965); Kendrick A. Clements, William Jennings Bryan, Missionary Isolationist (Knoxville: University of Tennessee Press, 1983); and Robert W. Cherny, A Righteous Cause: The Life of William Jennings Bryan (Boston: Little Brown & Co, 1985), 88-94.

51. Quoted in Charles E. Merriam, American Political Ideas: Studies in the Development of American Political Thought (New York: Macmillan Co., 1923), 260; Alien F. Davis, American Heroine: The Life and Legend of Jane Adams (New York: Oxford University Press, 1973), passim; Steven A. Kesselman, The Modernization of American Reform: Structures and Perceptions (New York: Garland Publishers, 1979), 196-261.

CHAPTER FOUR

1. For the dominating role the Carnegie Endowment played see, Michael A. Lutzker, "The Formation of the Carnegie Endowment for International Peace: A Study of the Establishment-Centered Peace Movement, 1910-1914," in Jerry Israel, ed.. Building the Organizational Society (New York: Free Press, 1972), 143-62; and Nicholas Murray Butler, "The Carnegie Endowment for International Peace," Independent LXXVI (November 27, 1913), 397-8.

2. Warren F. Kuehl, Hamilton Holt (Tallahassee, FL: University of Florida Press, 1960), passim.

3. For a scholarly analysis of the Hague Conference consult, Calvin C. Davis, The United States and the First Hague Conference of 1899 (Ithaca, NY: Cornell University Press, 1962), and The United States and the Second Hague Peace Conference: American Diplomacy and International Organization. 1899-1914, (Durham, NC: University of North Carolina Press, 1976).

4. David S. Patterson, "An Interpretation of the American Peace Movement, 1898-1914" in Chatfield, ed., Peace Movements in America. 20-38. This is an extremely important article from a sociological standpoint. Patterson's examination focuses on the social background of thirty-six leaders of the American peace movement. Whereas Michael A. Lutzker's "The 'Practical' Peace Advocates: An Interpretation of the American peace Movement, 1898-

1917" (Ph.D. Thesis, Rutgers University, 1969) concentrates almost exclusively on fifty-three so-called practical peace workers, most of whom were tardy recruits and who managed wealthier peace organizations like the Carnegie Movement, Patterson's index was based on long-term membership in peace or international list organizations and/or fairly consistent participation in peace congresses in the United States.

5. Curti, Peace or War, 196-227; Albert Marrin, Nicholas Murray Butler (Boston: Twayne Publishers, 1976), passim.

6. Patterson, "An Interpretation of the American Peace Movement," 23-4.

7. David S. Patterson, "Andrew Carnegie's Quest for World Peace," Proceedings of the American Philosophical Society CXIV, no.5 (October 20, 1970), 371-80; The Peace Society of New York. Annual Reports. Constitution. List of Meetings (NY, 1907), 6-22; Year Book, 1912, 6 ff

8. Nicholas Murray Butler, Across the Busy Years (NY: Charles Scribner's Sons, 1939), II, 86-8; Michael A. Lutzker, introduction, in reprint of Hayne Davis, ed., Among the World's Peacemakers (NY: Garland Publishers, 1972), 8-9,139.

9. "The Federal Tendency," The Independent LXX (March 23, 1911), 601-4; John Bassett Moore, "International Arbitration," Harper's CX (March 1905), 610. See also, Michael A. Lutzker, "The Pacifist as Militarist: A Critique of the American Peace Movement, 1898-1914," Societas V, no. 2 (Spring 1975), 87-97.

10. Richard W. Leopold, Elihu Root (Boston: Little Brown & Co., 1954), passim.

11. Charles F. Howlett, "Nicholas Murray Butler's Crusade for a Warless World," Wisconsin Magazine of History 67 (Winter, 1983-1984), 104, Fn. 10.

12. Marchand, The American Peace Movement and Social Reform, 1898-1918 (Princeton: Princeton University Press, 1972), 39-73; David S. Patterson, 'The United States and the Origins of the World Court," Political Science Quarterly 91, no. 2 (Summer 1976), 279-95; Twelfth Annual Report of the Lake Mohonk Conference. 150; Chatfield, The American Peace Movement, 18-26..

13. Patterson, "The United States and the Origins of the World Court," 293-5; Proceedings of the Second National Conference for the Judicial Settlement of International Disputes (November 7-8, 1911, 90-5); Proceedings of the Third Conference for the Judicial Settlement of International Disputes, (December 21-2, 1912), 195 ff.

14. For an informative article on de Bloch see, Peter van den Dungen, "Jean de Bloch: 19th Century Peace Researcher" in Howlett, ed., "Apostles of Peace," Peace Research, 21-27.

15. Peter Filene, "The World Peace Foundation and Progressivism, 1910-1918," New England Quarterly XXXVI, no. 4 (December 1963), 484-501; Patterson, Toward a Warless World, 134-137.

16. Yearbook for 1912 of the Carnegie Endowment for International Peace (New York, 1913), 1-3.

17. Patterson, Toward a Warless World, 141-47; Joseph F. Wall, Andrew Carnegie (New York: Oxford University Press, 1970), passim.

18. Nicholas Murray Butler, The International Mind: An Argument for the Judicial Settlement of International Disputes (New York: Charles Scribner's Sons, 1913), 75-83; Butler, "The Carnegie Endowment for International Peace," 396-400. Quoted in Charles DeBenedetti, The Peace Reform, 85, and DeBenedetti, "The

American Peace Movement and the State Department in the Era of Locarno" in Solomon Wank, ed., Doves and Diplomats: Foreign Offices and Peace Movements in Europe and America in the Twentieth Century (Westport, CT: Greenwood Press, 1978), 209; Chatfield, The American Peace Movement, 19-21; Joseph W. Winn, "Nicholas Murray Butler, the Carnegie Endowment for International Peace, and the Search for Reconciliation in Europe, 1919-1933," Peace & Change 31 (October 2006), 555-584..

19. The National Arbitration and Peace Congress (New York, 1907), passim; Advocate of Peace LXIX (May 1907), 97. See also, Darrel E. Bigham, "War as Obligation in the Thought of American Christians, 1898-1920, Peace & Change V (Winter & Spring 1979), 45.

20. The American pacifist minister Kirby Page reflected upon the folly of prewar Christian discussions for peace: "The problem of war had been entirely academic in our infrequent discussions of it. In all those years I had never met an informed and determined pacifist." Quoted in Harold E. Fey, ed., Kirby Page, Social Evangelist: The Autobiography of a 20th Century Peace Prophet Nyack, NY: FOR Press, 1975), 70.

21. Eleventh Annual Report of Lake Mohonk Conference, 115-116; Louis P. Lochner, "Internationalism among Universities," World Peace Foundation Pamphlet Series. Part II. 3 (July 1913), 2-4.

22. Julius Moritzen, The Peace Movement of America (New York: G.P. Putnam's Sons, 1912), 150-2.

23. A.F.C. Beales, The History of Peace (London & NY: Dial Press, 1931), 259. Also consult, Patterson, Toward a Warless World, 130-140; Susan Zeiger, "Teaching Peace: Lessons from a Peace Studies Curriculum in the Progressive Era ," Peace & Change 25 (January 2000), 52-69; Julie Taker Weber, "The Reign of Peace We Hoped For: A History of the American School Peace League" (Ph.D. diss, Penn State University, 1997); and Ann Marie Pois, "Perspectives on 20th Century Women's International Activism," Journal of Women's History 11 (Autumn 1999), 213-222.

24. William James, "The Moral Equivalent of War" in Ralph Barton Perry, ed., Essays on Faith and Morals (Cleveland & NY: World Publishing Co., 1967), 311-28.

25. Jane Addams, Newer Ideals of Peace (New York: Macmillan Co., 1907), 3, 27-30, 60-5, 86, 119, 124, 213. The study by Louise W. Knight must be consulted for its insightful analysis of Addams' "hardheaded progressivism." See, Knight, Jane Addams and the Struggle for Democracy (Chicago: University of Chicago Press, 2005), passim.

26. Jane Addams, "The Revolt Against War" and "Factors in Continuing the War," in Jane Addams et al., Women at the Hague (New York: Macmillan Co., 1915). See also, Sondra R. Herman, Eleven Against War, 115-128; and Allen F. Davis, American Heroine, 140-9.

27. See E. James Hindman, "The General Arbitration Treaties of William Howard Taft," The Historian XXXVI, No. 1 (November 1973), passim; Arbitration and the United States IX (Boston: World Peace Foundation, 1926), 521 ff; William H. Taft, "The Proposed Arbitration Treaties with Great Britain and France," Judicial Settlement of International Disputes, no. 7 (Baltimore, 1912); William I. Hull, "The International Grand Jury," no. 9, Judicial Settlement of International Disputes Series (Baltimore, 1912), 6 ff.

28. Peacemaker XXX (June-July 1911), 152.

29. Proceedings of the Second National Conference of the American Society for the Judicial Settlement of International Disputes, November 7-8, 1911, 75; William Howard Taft, The United States and Peace (New York. 1914), 105-132, 180-2.

30. Quoted in Curti, Peace or War, 225; Paolo E. Coletta, "William Jennings Bryan's Plans for World Peace," Nebraska History 58, no. 2 (Summer 1977), 193-217.

31. Michael A. Lutzker, "Can the Peace Movement Prevent War?: The U.S. -Mexican Crisis of April, 1914," in Wank, ed., Doves and Diplomats, 141-7.

32. Sinclair Snow, The Pan-American Federation of Labor (Durham, NC: Duke University pres, 1964), passim; Philip Taft, The AF of L in the Time of Gompers (NY: Harper & Row, 1957), 320-333. Also consult, Philip Foner, History of the Labor Movement in the United States Vol 8 (New York: International Publishers, 1988), and Arthur S. Link, Woodrow Wilson: Revolution, War, and Peace (Arlington Heights, ILL.: AHM Publishing, 1979).

33. DeBenedetti, The Peace Reform. 91-2, and The Origins of the Modern American Peace Movement (Millwood, NY: KTO Press, 1978), passim: see also, Charles Chatfield's For Peace and Justice, Chapt. 1; Chatfield, The American Peace Movement, 27-50. The term "pacifism" was first coined by Frenchman Emile Arnaud in the 1890s. It was a description of those involved in anti-war efforts. By the time of World War I it came to imply all those steadfastly opposed to the use of force or violence for solving disputes. For more information on Arnaud see Cooper, Patriotic Pacifism, 58-64, 93-95.

34. Walter Rauschenbush, Christianity and the Social Crisis (New York: Macmillan Co., 1908), 306-309.

35. League to Enforce Peace, American Branch (New York: League to Enforce Peace, 1915), 3 ff; Theodore Marburg, League of Nations, A Chapter in the History of the Movement (New York: Macmillan Co., 1917), 23 ff.

36. Program and Policies of the League to Enforce Peace (New York, 1916), passim: Ruhl J. Bartlett, The League to Enforce Peace (Chapel Hill, NC: University of North Carolina Press, 1944), passim. Scholarly peace histories addressing the subject are: Chatfield & Kleidman, The American Peace Movement, 30-31; Patterson, Toward a Warless World, 244-54; and Marchand, The American Peace Movement and Social Reform, 168-182.

37. Consult the following works: Gertrude Bussey & Margaret Tims, Women's International League for Peace and Freedom. 1915-1965: A Record of Fifty Years' Work (London: Alien & Unwin, 1965); Barbara Steinson, "Female Activism in World War I: The American Women's Peace, Suffrage, Preparedness, and Relief Movements, 1914-1919" (Ph.D. thesis, University of Michigan, 1977), published as American Women's Activism in World War I (New York: Garland Publishers, 1982); Marie L. Degen, The History of the Women's Peace Party (New York: Garland, reprint 1971), 38-63; Jane Addams, Emily G. Balch, Alice Hamilton, Women at the Hague (New York, 1916), 1-19; Jane Addams, Peace and Bread in Time of War (New York: King's Crown Press, rev. 1945), 12-19; Alonso, Peace as a Women's Issue, 34-56, 92-104; Craig, Lucia Ames Mead, 113-158; Catherine Foster, Women for All Seasons: the Story of the Women's International League for Peace and Freedom (Athens: University of Georgia Press, 1989), 2-14; Margaret Hope Beacon, One Woman's Passion for Peace and Freedom: the Life of Mildred Scott Olmstead (Syracuse; Syracuse University Press, 1993), 12-19; Joyce Blackwell-Johnson, "African American Activists in the Women's International League for Peace and Freedom," Peace & Change 23 (October 1998), 466-482; Kathleen

Kennedy, "In the Shadow of Gompers: Lucy Robbins and the Politics of Amnesty, 1918-1922," Peace & Change 25 (January 2000), 22-51.

38. Blanche Wiesen Cook, "Woodrow Wilson and the Anti-Militarists, 1914-1917" (Ph. D. thesis, The Johns Hopkins University, 1970), 10; Cook, "Democracy in Wartime England and the United States, 1914-1918," in Chatfield, ed., Peace Movements in America, 39-55.

39. Mary Jo Buhle, Women and American Socialism (Urbana: University of Illinois Press, 1983), 52-68, 88-92, 114-28, 210-216.

40. Linda K. Schott, Reconstructing Women's Thoughts: The Women's International League for Peace and Freedom before World War II (Stanford, CA.: Stanford University Press, 1997), 55-78.

41. Kathleen Kennedy, Disloyal Mothers and Scurrilous Citizens: Women and Subversion during World War I (Bloomington: Indiana University Press, 1999), 44-56; Frances Early, World Without War: How U.S. Feminists and Pacifists Resisted World War I (Syracuse: Syracuse University Press, 1997), 62-74; Harriet H. Alonso, Peace as a Women's Issue, 125-56.

42. Barbara Steinson, American Women's Activism in World War I, 88-112. See also, Frances H. Early, A World Without War:, 51-63; and Kathleen Kennedy, Disloyal Mothers and Scurrilous Citizens, 79-85.

43. Charles Chatfield, "World War I and the Liberal Pacifist in the United States," American Historical Review LXXV, no. 7 (December 1970), 1920-37.

44. Barbara S. Kraft, The Peace Ship: Henry Ford's Pacifist Adventure in the First World War (New York: Macmillan Co., 1978), passim; see also, New York Tribune. December 7, 1915; New York Sun, January 20, 1915.

45. John Patrick Finnegan, Against the Specter of the Dragon: The Campaign for American Military Preparedness. 1914-1917 (Westport, CT: Greenwood Press, 1974), 141-57; New York Times, June 22, 27, 1916; Lillian D. Wald, Windows on Henry Street (Boston: Little Brown & Co., 1934), 291-4; David Starr Jordan, The Days of a Man (Yonkers, NY: World Book, 1922), 690-703.

46. Quoted in Don Lawson, Ten Fighters for Peace (New York: Lothrop, Leer & Shepard Co., 1971), 87, 74; Kevin Giles, Flight of the Dove: The Story of Jeannette Rankin (Beaverton, ORE: Touchstone, 1980), 33 & ff; and Arthur S. Link, Woodrow Wilson and the Progressive Era,. 1910-1917 (New York: Harper & Row, 1963), passim.

47. John Whiteclay Chambers II, ed., The Eagle and the Dove: The American Peace Movement and the United States Foreign Policy. 1900-1922 (New York: Garland Publishers, 1976), passim: George W. Norris, Fighting Liberal (New York: Macmillan Co., 1946) 195-196.

48. Charles F. Howlett, Troubled Philosopher: John Dewey and the Struggle for World Peace (Port Washington, NY: Kennikat Press, 1977), 20-42.

49. New York Times, September 27, October 19,1917, & September 4, 18, 1918; Nicholas M. Butler to master of Balliol College, Oxford, April 17 & September 30, 1917, Nicholas M. Butler Papers, Special Collections, Butler Library, Columbia University.

50. Nicholas M. Butler, Scholarship and Service (New York: Charles Scribner's Sons, 1921), 115.

51. Walter P. Metzger, Academic Freedom in the Age of University (New York: Columbia University Press, 1961), 225-9; Marrin, Nicholas Murray Butler, 84-92; Howlett, Troubled Philosopher, 33-4; Carol S. Gruber, Mars and Minerva: World War I and the Uses of Higher Learning in America (Baton Rouge, LA: LSU Press, 1976), passim. Also worth consulting is Donald Johnson, The Challenge to American Freedoms: World War I and the Rise of the American Civil Liberties Union (Lexington: University of Kentucky Press, 1963), 78-84.

52. Louis Filler, Randolph Bourne (Washington, DC: American Council on Public Affairs, 1943); Carl S. Resek, ed., War and the Intellectuals (New York: Harper & Row, 1964), 60-1.One of the finest discussions of the First World War's impact on society is David M. Kennedy, Over Here: The First World War and American Society (New York: Oxford University Press, 1980). His descriptions of patriotism in the schools deserve serious reading. Also noteworthy is Henry May, The End of American Innocence: A Study of the First Years of Our Own tome, 1912-1917 (New York: Oxford University Press, 1959). .

53. H.C. Peterson & Gilbert C. Fite, Opponents of War. 1917-1918 (Madison, WI: University of Wisconsin Press, 1957), passim.

54. Ann Davidon, "Resistance to World War I," in Larry Gara, ed., To Secure Peace and Liberty.

55. Quoted in Frederick C. Giffin, Six Who Protested: Radical Opposition to the First World War (Port Washington, NY: Kennikat Press, 1977), 2728. Consult the following works: Ronald Shaffer, America in the Great War: The Rise of the Warfare Welfare State (New York: Oxford University Press, 1991); William Preston, Aliens and Dissenters: Federal Suppression of Radicals, 1901-1933 (New York: Harper & Row, 1963), passim; Geoffrey R. Stone, Perilous Times: Free Speech in Wartime From the Sedition Act of 1798 to the War on Terrorism (Chicago: University of Chicago Press, 2004), 135-202; Stephen M. Kohn, Jailed for Peace: The History of Draft Law Violators, 1658-1985 (Westport, CT: Praeger, 1986), and American Political Prisoners: Prosecutions under the Espionage and Sedition Acts (Westport, CT: Prager, 1994); Ernest L. Meyer, Hey! Yellowbacks! The War Diary of a Conscientious Objector (1930; reprint, New York: J.S. Ozer, 1972); Norman Thomas, The Conscientious Objector in America (New York: B.W. Huebsch, 1923); Frederick C. Giffin, Six Who Protested: Radical Opposition to the First World War (Port Washington, NY: Kennikat Press, 1977), passim.

56. Thomas, The Conscientious Objector, 34-42; Kohn, Jailed for Peace, 25-43; Cooney & Michalowski, eds., The Power of the People, 44-46.

57. Quoted in Opponents of War. 178.

58. Chatfield, For Peace and Justice. 50-1; DeBenedetti, The Peace Reform. 103; Weinberg, eds., Instead of Violence, 257.

59. Cook "Democracy in Wartime" 47-48. AUAM Papers, Swarthmore College Peace Collection.

60. Peterson & Fite, Opponents of War, 40-41.

61. Ibid., 40-41.

62. James Weinstein, The Decline of Socialism in America, 1912-1925 (New York: Monthly Review Press, 1967), 78-81; Weinstein, " Sentiment and the Socialist Party, 1917-1918," Political Science Quarterly 74 (June 1959), 215-39.

63. Snow, The Pan-American Federation of Labor. 60-73; David A. Shannon, The Socialist Party of America (Chicago: Quadrangle Books, 1967), 94-6; James Weinstein, The Decline of Socialism in America, Chapt. 3; Melvyn Dubofsky, We Shall Be All: A History of the IWW (Chicago: Quadrangle Books, 1969), 335, 376-444.

64. Eugene Debs, "Soldiers, Slaves and Hell," Iron City Socialist (March 14, 1914); American Socialist (September 5, 1914).

65. Marchand, The American Peace Movement and Social Reform, 266-80. Lillian Symes & Travers Clement, Rebel America: The Story of Social Revolt in the United States (Boston: Beacon Press, rev. 1972), 293.

66. James H. Maurer, "Maintenance of Labor Standards" (Pamphlet reprint of address to People's Council Convention, Chicago, September 2, 1917), Box 1, People's Council Papers, Swarthmore College Peace Collection; Marchand, The American Peace Movement and Social Reform, 311-2.

67. "Resolution of the First American Conference for Democracy and Terms of Peace" (Pamphlet), 7, and "To Men and Women Everywhere Who are Allies of True Democracy," Box 1, PC Papers, SCPC.

68. Grubbs, The Struggle for Labor Loyalty, 131-45.

69. "The People's Council of America, 1917-1919." http://www.culture-of-peace.info (cited December 8, 2005); Jennifer D. Keene, "W.E.B. Du Bois and the Wounded World: Seeking Meaning in the First World War for African-Americans," Peace & Change 26 (April 2001), 135-152; Edward J. Blum, W.E.B. Du Bois, American Prophet (Philadelphia: University of Pennsylvania Press, 2007), 87-101. It should be pointed out that within the labor movement Debs' African American counterpart, A. Philip Randolph, was certainly an influential figure critical of war. For historical perspectives on Randolph's life and career consult the following works: Jarvis B. Anderson, A Philip Randolph: A Biographical Portrait (New York: Harcourt Brace Jovanovich, 1972); Daniel S. Davis, Mr. Black Labor; Father of the Civil Rights Movement (New York: E.P. Dutton, 1972); Philip S. Foner, Organized Labor and the Black Worker, 1619-1981 (New York: International Publishers, 1982); Barbara Kaye Greenleaf, Forward March to Freedom: The Story of A. Philip Randolph (New York: Grossett & Dunlap, 1971); Sally Hanley, A Philip Randolph, Labor Leader (New York: Chelsea House, 1988); Calvin Miller, A Philip Randolph and the American Labor Movement (Greensboro, NC: Morgan Reynolds, 2005); and Benjamin Quarles, "A. Philip Randolph: Labor Leader at Large," in John Hope Franklin and August Meier, eds. Black Leaders of the Twentieth Century (Urbana: University of Illinois Press, 1982).

70. A very interesting commentary reflecting a largely untold aspect of war can be found in Philip Knightley, The First Casualty: The War Correspondent as Hero and Myth-maker from Crimea to Kosovo (Baltimore, MD.: The Johns Hopkins University Press, 2002), passim. Knightley's work

provides telling observations on issues such as censorship and suppression, the advent of myth-making propaganda, and the evolution of governments managing the media. Certainly, World War I offers some concrete examples with Creel's Committee on Public Information. The ability of the press to provide objectivity in time of war has become even more challenging.

71. Clarence Darrow, The Story of My Life (New York: Charles Scribner's Sons, rev., 1960), 210, 219.

CHAPTER FIVE

1. Paul A. Carter, Another Part of the Twenties (New York: Columbia University Press, 1973), 26-28. In the context of discussing the nativist reaction in post-World War I United States consult, John Higham, Strangers in the Land: Patterns of American Nativism, 1860-1925 (New York: Athenaeum, 1968). A must read on the rebirth of the Ku Klux Klan is David Chalmers, Hooded Americanism (Garden City, NY: Doubleday & Co., 1965) The impact of the war on Europe was devastating as well. According to Alan Kramer, the post--world War I led to a culture of annihilation throughout Europe. Two effects on the mind and body occurred: (1) a strong feeling of pacifism as well as appeasement developed in countries such as Britain and France; and (2) worship of violence and brutality in the form of Fascism, Bolshevism, and Nazism in Italy, Russia, and Germany. Consult, Alan Kramer, Dynamic of Destruction: Culture and Mass Killing in the First World War (New York: Oxford University Press, 2007), passim..

2. Chatfield, For Peace and Justice, passim.

3. Charles DeBenedetti, "The American Peace Movement and the State," passim; see also, Richard W. Fanning, "Peace Groups and the Campaign for Naval Disarmament, 1927-1936," Peace & Change 15 (January 1990), 26-45.

4. William Leuchtenberg, The Perils of Prosperity, 1914-1932 (Chicago: University of Chicago Press, 1958), 17-34; Paul A. Carter, The Twenties in America (Northbrook, IL: HMS Press, rev., 1974). passim.

5. Howlett, Troubled Philosopher, Chapters VI-VII.

6. Quoted in Paul A. Carter, Another Part of the Twenties, 27.See also, Warren F. Kuehl and Lynne K. Dunn, Keeping the Covenant: American Internationalists and the League of Nations, 1920-1939 (Kent, OH: Kent State University Press, 1997), passim.

7. DeBenedetti, The Peace Reform, Chapter VI, passim.

8. Harold Josephson, James T. Shotwell and the Rise of Internationalism in America (Rutherford, NJ: Fairleigh Dickinson Press, 1976); Bernard Johnpoll, Pacifist's Progress: Norman Thomas and the Decline of Socialism in America (Chicago: Quadrangle Books, 1970); Jo Ann O. Robinson, Abraham Went Out: A Biography of A.J. Muste (Philadelphia: Temple University Press, 1980). Harold Josephson, "Outlaw War: Internationalism and the Pact of Paris," Diplomatic History, 3 (Fall, 1978) 377-90.

9. Charles DeBenedetti, "Alternative Strategies in the American Peace Movement in the 1920's" in Chatfield, ed., Peace Movements in America, 57-67; Betty L. Barton, "The Fellowship of Reconciliation: Pacifism, Labor and Social Welfare, 1915-1960" (Ph.D. thesis, Florida State University, 1974). See also, Chatfield, The American Peace Movement, 53-58. The most comprehensive history of the WRL is found in Scott H. Bennett, Radical Pacifism: the War Resisters League and Gandhian Nonviolence in America, 1915-1963 (Syracuse: Syracuse University Press, 2003). There are a number of important studies discussing the role of the Women's International League for Peace and Freedom. Among them are the following: Catherine Foster, Women for all Seasons: The Story of the Women's International League for Peace and Freedom (Athens: University of Georgia Press, 1898); Margaret Hope Beacon, One Woman's Passion for Peace and Freedom: The Life of Mildred Scott Olmstead (Syracuse: Syracuse University Press, 1993); and Joyce Blackwell, No Peace without Freedom: Race and the Women's International League for Peace and Freedom (Carbondale: Southern Illinois University Press, 2004), Rosemary Rainbolt, "Women and War in the United States: The Case of Dorothy Detzer, National Secretary Women's International League for Peace and Freedom," Peace & Change IV (Fall 1977), 18-22.

10. George P. Marabell, "Frederick Libby and the American Peace Movement, 1921-1941" (Ph.D. thesis, Michigan State University, 1975), passim.

11. Charles Chatfield, ed., International War Resistance Through World War II (New York: Garland Publishers, 1975), 22-9.

12. Frederick J. Libby, To End War (Nyack, NY: FOR Press, 1975), 22-9. An excellent analysis of Congressional views on foreign policy can be found in Robert David Johnson, The Peace Progressives and American Foreign Relations (Cambridge, MA: Harvard University Press, 1995). The strength of this work is Johnson's examination of the peace progressives' anti-imperialist position in the 1920's and how it was transformed into an isolationist sentiment in the following decade.

13. John K. Nelson, The Peace Prophets: American Pacifist Thought, 1919-1941 (Chapel Hill: University of North Carolina Press, 1967), 83-85.

14. Charles F, Howlett, "Jessie Wallace Hughan" in Bernard Cook, ed., Women and War: A Historical Encyclopedia From Antiquity to the Present , Vol. I (Santa Barbara, CA.: ABC-Clio, 2006), 292-94. The fullest discussion of Hughan in the WWI period is Bennett's Radical Pacifism, Chapt. 1.

15. For links to isolationist sentiment and peace activity consult the following: John D. Hicks, The Republican Ascendancy. 1921 -1933 (New York: Harper & Row, 1960); Foster Rhea Dulles, America's Rise to World Power (New York: Harper & Row, 1954); Selig Adler, The Isolationist Impulse (New York: Free Press, rev. 1964). For a challenge to the isolationist argument, see William Appleman Williams, 'The Legend of Isolationism in the 1920's," Science and Society XVIII (Winter 1954). Regarding the growing influence of feminist peace activism in the 1920s see Linda Schott, Reconstructing Women's Thoughts , 67-89; Alonso, Peace as a Women's Issue, Chapts. 2-3; Beacon, One Woman's Passion for Peace and Freedom, 18-34; Foster, The Women and the Warriors, Chapts 1-3; and Robert Booth Fowler, Carrie Catt: Feminist Politician (Boston: Northeastern University Press, 1986), passim.; Joyce Blackwell, No Peace without Freedom, 57-72.

16. Paul A. Murphy, "Sources and Nature of Intolerance in the 1920's," Journal of American History LI (June 1964).

17. DeBenedetti, "Alternative Strategies in the American Peace Movement in the 1920's," 57-60; Robert H. Ferrell, "The American Peace Movement" in Alexander DeConde, ed., Isolation and Security (Durham, NC: Duke University Press, 1957), Chapter IV.

18. The best works on outlawry of war and the Committee on Militarism in Education are: John E. Stoner, S.O. Levinson and the Pact of Paris (Chicago: University of Chicago Press, 1943); Robert H. Ferrell, Peace in Their Time: Origins of the Kellogg-Briand Pact (New Haven: Yale University Press, 1952); John C. Vinson, William E. Borah and the Outlawry of War (Athens, GA: University of Georgia Press, 1957); Ekrich, The Civilian and the Military, Chapter XIV; Charles F. Howlett, "John Dewey and the Crusade to Outlaw War," World Affairs 138 (Spring 1976), 336-65, and "Dissenting Voice: John Dewey Against Militarism in Education," Peace & Change III (Spring 1976), 49-60.

19. Charles DeBenedetti, "The $100,000 American Peace Award of 1924," The Pennsylvania Magazine of History and Biography 98, no.2 (April 1974), 224-49.

20. Chatfield, For Peace and Justice, 95-97

21. "Political Prisoners and the Christian Conscience," The Christian Century XL (March 20, 1922), 834.

22. Robert M. Miller, How Shall They Hear Without a Preacher?: The Life of Ernest Fremont Tittle (Chapel Hill, NC: University of North Carolina Press, 1971), 390-403.

23. Dana F. Fleming, The United States & The World Court (Garden City, NY: Doubleday, 1945), 22-23.

24. Robert Ancinelli, "The United States and the World Court, 1920-1927" (Ph.D. thesis, University of California at Berkeley, 1968). Quoted in Dana F. Fleming, The United States and the World Court (Garden City, NY: Doubleday, 1945), 111.

25. Paul H. Douglas, "The American Occupation of Haiti, II," Political Science Quarterly XLII, no.3 (September 1927), 396. Merle Curti and Kendall A. Birr's Prelude to Point Four (Madison, WI: University of Wisconsin Press, 1954) offers some interesting observations. See Chapter IV, humorously titled "The Dominican Republic and Haiti: 'Marines and Latrines.'"

26. "Democracy Called Farce in Nicaragua," 1927 report by John Nevin Sayre, F.O.R., Brookwood Labor College Papers, Tamiment Library, New York University; Charles F. Howlett, "Brookwood Labor College and Worker Commitment to Social Reform," Mid-America 61, no.l (January 1979), 47-66.

27. Charles F. Howlett, Brookwood Labor College and the Struggle for Peace and Social Justice in America (Lewiston, NY: Edwin Mellen Press, 1993), passim.

28. David Starr Jordan, "A Plan to Develop International Justice and Friendship: The Raphael Herman $25,000 Award" (Augusta, ME: World Federation of Education Associations, 1925), 25 pp., reprinted in Advocate of Peace Through Justice 87 (May 5, 1925), 287-93.

29. Charles F. Howlett, "John Dewey's Views on Peace Education in America," Peace Research 10 (April 1978), 39-46.

30. Mary Alice Matthews, History Teaching and School Text-Books in Relation to International Understanding: Select List of Books. Pamphlets, and Periodical Articles (Washington, D.C.: CEIP Library, 1931), 14 pp; Paul Klapper, The Teaching of History (New York: D. Appleton & Co., 1926): 114-116.

31. Carter, Another Part of the Twenties, 35; William H. Kilpatrick, "Our Schools and War," Educational Review 61 (March 1921).

32. John F. O'Ryan, "Teachers and World Peace," NEA Journal 12 (May 1923); The Nation 119 (September 17, 1924) contains the 1924 study of hyper-patriotism in American history textbooks.

33. "Youth's Decision Against War," Literary Digest 80 (February 2, 1924).

34. Ekrich, The Civilian and the Military, 219; Michael S. Neiberg, Making Citizen Soldiers: ROTC and the Ideology of American Military Service (Cambridge, MA.: Harvard University Press, 2000), 1-12.

35. Chatfield, For Peace and Justice. 155; Neiberg, Making Citizens Soldiers, 6-9.

36. Ekrich, The Civilian and the Military, 220; Chatfield, The American Peace Movement, 54-55; Charles F. Howlett, "John Nevin Sayre and the American Fellowship of Reconciliation," Pennsylvania Magazine of History and Biography CXIV, no. 3 (July 1990), 399-422.

37. See the following C.M.E. pamphlets: Military Training in Schools and Colleges of the United States; Militarizing Our Youth: The Significance of the Reserve Officers Training Corps in Our Schools and Colleges; Brass Buttons and Education; The Camel and the Arab (a survey of college catalogues); So This Is War; The War Department as Educator. Copies located in C.M.E. Papers, DG 24, SCPC.

38. Chatfield, For Peace and Justice, 162.

39. John F. Greco, "A Foundation for Internationalism: The Carnegie Endowment for International Peace, 1931-1941" (Ph.D. thesis, Syracuse University, 1971), 38-61; Charles DeBenedetti, "The Origins of Neutrality Revision: The American Plan of 1924," The Historian XXXV, no. 1 (November 1972), 75-89.

40. John K. Nelson, The Peace Prophets, 134-139; Bennett, Radical Pacifism, 33-48.

41. Chatfield, For Peace and Justice, 138-41; Charles Chatfield, ed. Devere Allen: Life and Writings (New York: Garland Publishers, 1976), 31-35. An excellent analysis of Allen's post-World War II views is Barbara E. Addison, "Cold War Pacifist: Devere Allen and the Postwar Peace Movement," Peace & Change 32 (July 2007), 391-414 and "Pragmatic Pacifist: Devere Allen and the Interwar Peace Movement, 1918-1940," Peace & Change 29 (January 2004), 81-105.

42. Charles Chatfield, ed., The Americanization of Gandhi: Images of the Mahatma (New York: Garland Publishers, 1976), 58-61; quoted in Mayer, ed., The Pacifist Conscience. 234; Bennett, Radical Pacifism, 46-47; Joseph Kosek, "Richard Gregg, Mohandas Gandhi, and the Strategy of Non-violence," 1329-1337.

43. Quoted in Mayer, ed., Pacifist Conscience. 234; consult, Paul Elie, The Life You Save May Be Your Own: An American Pilgrimage (New York: Farrar, Straus & Giroux, 2003); Nancy Roberts, Dorothy Day and the Catholic Worker (Albany, NY: State University of New York Press, 1984), passim.

44. Sherwood Eddy & Kirby Page, Creative Pioneers (New York: Association Press, 1937), 1-28.

45. Nat Hentoff, ed., The Essays of A.J. Muste (New York: Simon & Schuster, 1967), 200. In line with Muste's commitment to racial justice were those of a fellow FOR member, Howard Kester. Kester, who was born in Virginia, became a leading opponent of the lynching of blacks in the South during the Great Depression. For a sound biography, consult Robert F. Martin, Howard Kester and the Struggle for Social Justice in the South, 1904-1977 (Charlottesville: University of Virginia Press, 1991)..

46. The Roosevelt Administration's deliberate deployment of the "analogue of war" against the depression in a conscious effort to permeate the country with devotion and sacrifice generally felt only in wartime is effectively analyzed by William Leuchtenberg, "The New Deal and the Analogue of War" in John Braeman, ed.. Change and Continuity in Twentieth-Century America (New York: Harper & Row, 1966), 81-143.

47. This information was imparted to be by my late father, John E. Howlett, who worked in the CCC camps in New York. Much has been similarly recorded. See, for instance, Lawrence Cremin, The Transformation of the School: Progressivism in American Education, 1876-1957 (New York: Vintage Books, 1961), 318-22, and Arthur A. Ekirch, Jr., Ideologies and Utopias: The Impact of the New Deal on American Thought (Chicago: Quadrangle Books, 1969), 278-84.

48. The best bibliographic guide to isolationism is Justus D. Doenecke, The Literature of Isolationism: A Guide to Non-Interventionist Scholarship, 1930-1972 (Colorado Springs, CO: Ralph Myles, 1972). The standard scholarly works on isolationism are: Manfred Jonas, Isolationism in America, 1935-1941 (Ithaca, NY: Cornell University Press, 1966) ; and John E. Wiltz, From Isolation to War, 1931-1941 (New York: Thomas Y. Crowell, 1968)..

49. Quoted in Arthur A. Ekrich, Jr., Ideologies and Utopias, 214.

50. Wayne Cole, Senator Gerald P. Nye and American Foreign Relations (Minneapolis: University of Minnesota Press, 1962), Chapter V; John Wiltz, In Search of Peace: The Senate Munitions Inquiry, 1934-36 (Baton Rouge, LA: Louisiana State University Press, 1963), passim.

51. New York Times, April 14, 1934; "Student Strike Against War," Student Outlook II (May 1934), 13; Ralph S. Brax, "When Students First Organized Against War: Student Protest During the 1930's," New York Historical Society Quarterly (1979), 228-54. One of the best studies on the student movement remains Robert Cohen, When the Old Left Was Young: Student Radicals and America's First Mass Student Movement, 1929-1941 (New York: Oxford University Press, 1993). Worth consulting for its incisive analysis as found in chapter one of her book is Robbie Lieberman, The Strangest Dream: Communism, AntiCommunism and the U.S. Peace Movement, 1945-1963 (Syracuse: Syracuse University Press, 2000).

52. James A. Wechsler, Revolt on the Campus (NY: Macmillan & Co., 1935), 132-75; "The Great Student Strike," Student Outlook III (May 1935), 3-8, 16.Dennis Mihelish, "Student Anti-war Activism During the Nineteen Thirties," Peace & Change II, no. 3 (Fall 1974), 29-40; Eileen M. Eagan, "War Is Not Holy - The American Student Peace Movement in the 1930's," Peace & Change II (Fall 1974), 41-7. Eagan expanded

her analysis in Class, Culture, and the Classroom: the Student Peace Movement of the 1930s (Philadelphia: Temple University Press, 1981).

53. Joseph P. Lash, "500,000 Strike for Peace: An Appraisal," Student Advocate I (May 1936), 3-5.

54. Lash, "50,000 Strike for Peace," 4-5; Joseph P. Lash, "The Student Strike," Fellowship II (May 1936), 6.

55. See, Charles A. Beard, The Devil Theory of War (New York: Vanguard Press, 1936), passim. Historical scholarship on Beard's theory is plentiful. Consult the following; Ellen Nore, Charles A. Beard , 148-57; Wittner, Rebels Against War, Chapter I, passim; Wiltz, From Isolation to War, pp. 136-45; Chatfield, For Peace and Justice, pp. 232-55; and Ekirch, The Civilian and the Military, pp. 234-53.

56. Consult Robert A. Devine, The Illusion of Neutrality (Chicago: University of Chicago Press, 1962), passim. An important work introducing sociological perspectives, particularly with the Emergency Peace Campaign, is Robert Kleidman, Organizing for Peace: Neutrality, the Test Ban, and the Freeze (Syracuse: Syracuse University Press, 1993), 58-88.

57. Chatfield, For Peace and Justice, 211.

58. The term "collective security" did not become current until 1934—the idea of independent states cooperating automatically in the impartial enforcement of peace. Recently historians have suggested the terms "collective concern" or "collective responsibility" to more accurately convey the many-sided effort to move the United States after 1928 into some mutual defense of the Versailles system. See, Warren F. Kuehl, "The Principle of Responsibility for Peace and National Security, 1920-1973," Peace & Change III, nos. 2-3 (Summer/Fall1975), passim.

59. Robert E. Bowers, "The American Peace Movement, 1933-1941" (Ph.D. thesis, University of Wisconsin, 1950), 15-20 See also, Chatfield, For Peace and Justice, pp. 114-115, and Robert Kleidman, Organizing for Peace, pp. 58-88.. .

60. Chatfield, For Peace and Justice, 269-78; DeBenedetti, The Peace Reform, 131-32.

61. Ernest Bolt, Ballots Before Bullets: The War Referendum Approach to Peace in America, 1914-1941 (Charlottesville,VA: University of Virginia Press, 1977), 152-185.

62. Justus Doenecke, "Non-intervention of the Left: 'The Keep America Out of the War Congress,' 1938-1941," Journal of Contemporary History 12, no.2 (April 1977), 221-36.

63. Lawrence S. Wittner, Rebels Against War, Chapter 1.

64. Chatfield, For Peace and Justice, 320-27; Wittner, Rebels Against War, 28-37; DeBenedetti, The Peace Reform, 134-40.

65. On this score refer to Joseph Kip Kosek, "Richard Gregg, Mohandas Gandhi, and the Strategy of Non-violence," Journal of American History 91 (March 2005), 1318-1348.

66. Mark L. Chadwin, The Warhawks: American Interventionists Before Pearl Harbor (New York: W.W. Norton & Co., edition, rev., 1970), 173-89,230-36. The song, This Ain't Our War! was due to the effort of Jay Catherswood Hormel. This tempestuous high-browed president of the George A. Hormel Meat

Packing Company hired songwriter Harry Harris to write the words and music as a reminder to fellow Americans not to become involved in the European conflict. Consult Time, October 23, 1939, 75.

67. New Republic CII (June 10, 1940), 789-90. The famous playwright, Robert E. Sherwood, also took the same path as MacLeish. For an instructive lesson consult, Harriet Hyman Alonso, "The Transformation of Robert E. Sherwood from Pacifist to Interventionist," Peace & Change 32 (October 2007), 467-498 and Robert E. Sherwood: The Playwright in Peace and War (Amherst: University of Massachusetts Press, 2007).

68. Glen Zeitzer, "The Fellowship of Reconciliation on the Eve of the Second World War," Peace & Change III, nos. 2 & 3 (Summer/Fall 1975), 46-51.

CHAPTER SIX

1. Chatfield, For Peace and Justice, 300.
2. John M. Glen, "Secular Conscientious Objection in the United States: The Selective Service Act of 1940," Peace & Change IX, no. 1 (Spring 1983), 55-71; Chatfield, The American Peace Movement, 78-80.
3. Glen, "Secular Conscientious Objection," 65-6; John Joseph O'Sullivan, "From Voluntarism to Conscription: Congress and Selective Service, 1940-1945" (Ph.D. thesis, Columbia University, 1971); Theodore R. Wachs, "Conscription, Conscientious Objection, and the Context of American Pacifism, 1940-1945" (Ph.D. thesis, University of Illinois, 1976); Heather T. Frazer & John O'Sullivan, "We Have Just Begun To Not Fight": An Oral History of Conscientious Objectors in Civilian Public Service During World War II (New York: Twayne Publishers, 1996), passim.
4. Susan Dion, "Pacifism Treated as Subversion: The FBI and the War Resisters League," Peace & Change IX, no. 1 (Spring 1983), 43-54; Bennett, Radical Pacifism, Chapt 4.
5. Quoted in Michael Young, "Facing a Test of Faith: Jewish Pacifists During the Second World War," Peace & Change III, nos. 2 & 3 (Summer/Fall 1975), 34-40.
6. Frank Waters, Book of the Hopi (NY: Vintage Books, 1963), passim, and Stan Steiner, The New Indians (NY: Collier Books, 1967), passim; quoted in To Secure Liberty and Peace.
7. James Tracy, Direct Action: Radical Pacifism From the Union Eight to the Chicago Seven (Chicago: University of Chicago Press, 1996), 1-3. See also, "The American Churches and the International Situation," John Nevin Sayre Papers, Swarthmore College Peace Collection. Clearly, these religious objectors were defining individual conscience as a challenge to the dictates of the state. Knowing that if they registered they would receive a deferment on religious grounds they chose instead to challenge the war system itself by total refusal. It was, to them, a very powerful symbolic act. They sought to extend conscience beyond its religious protection. They also wanted to call out the churches for their equivocation on the matter of war. During World War I many preachers heeded the call to arms

under the pretext of nationalism and patriotism which they felt ran contrary to matters of conscience and morality.

8. Arthur A. Ekrich, Jr., "CPS and Slavery", Pacifica Views II. no. 12 (August 25, 1944), 3. Anton T. Boisen, "Conscientious Objectors: Their Morale in Church-Operated Service Units," Psychiatry VII (August 1944), 215-224; Frazer & O'Sullivan, "We Have Just Begun Not To Fight", 79-110. For an excellent discussion regarding regimentation in CPS, see "Daily Schedule and Rules for CPS Camps Administered by the Mennonite Central Committee" (Appendix C, pp. 320-323), Scott Bennett, ed., Army GI, Pacifist CO: The World War II Letters of Frank and Albert Dietrich (New York: Fordham University Press, 2005).

9. Heather T. Frazier & John O'Sullivan, "Forgotten Women of World War II: Wives of Conscientious Objectors in Civilian Public Service," Peace & Change V nos. 2&3 (Fall 1978), 46-51. The reluctance by pacifists to accept government money was due largely to AJ. Muste's personal conviction that "Not only must we not ask for government funds for maintenance of C.O.'s , administration, and education in the camps; we must, it seems to me, refuse them. 'Alternative service' government financed and controlled would not be a genuine pacifist alternative at all. It would represent an almost complete absorption into the program and machinery of a government engaged in war preparation and probably war and tending increasingly toward dictatorship." A.J. Muste, The World Task of Pacifism (Wallingford, PA: Pendle Hill Pamphlet No. 13, 1941), 39-40.

10. Mulford Q. Sibley & Philip E. Jacob, Conscription of Conscience: The American State and the Conscientious Objector, 1940-1947 (Ithaca, NY: Cornell University Press, 1952), passim; Bennett, Radical Pacifism, 79-88; Julien Cornell, The Conscientious Objector and the Law (New York: John Day Co., 1943) and Conscience and the State: Legal and Administrative Problems of Conscientious Objectors, 1943-1944 (New York: John Day Co., 1944); Wittner, Rebels Against War, 70-84. On amnesty, the amnesty campaign, and the Committee for Amnesty consult, Scott Bennett, "'Free American Political Prisoners': Pacifist Activism and Civil Liberties, 1945-1948," Journal of Peace Research 40 (July 2003), 413-433.

11. August Meier & Elliott Rudwick, "The Origins of Non-violent Direct Action in Afro-American Protest: A Note on Historical Discontinuities," in Meier & Rudwick, Along the Color Line: Explorations in the Black Experience (Urbana, IL: University of Illinois Press, 1976), 344-89. There are some excellent studies on the origins of pacifism and civil rights action during World War II: see Tracy, Direct Action, 20-35; Marian Mollin, Radical Pacifism in Modern America: Egalitarianism and Protest (Philadelphia: University of Pennsylvania Press, 2006); Brenda Gayle Plummer, Rising Wind: Black Americans and U.S. Foreign Affairs, 1935-1960.(Chapel Hill: University of North Carolina Press, 1996); and Carol Anderson, Eyes Off the Prize: The United Nations and the African American Struggle for Human rights, 1944-1955 (New York: Cambridge University Pres, 2003). Consult also, Bennett, Radical Pacifism, 96-98; Chatfield, The American Peace Movement, 83-87.

12. Cooney & Michalowski, eds. The Power of the People, 97-139; Charles F. Howlett, "Bayard Rustin" in James Ryan & Leonard Schlup, eds. Historical Dictionary of the 1940's (Armonk, NY: M.E. Sharpe, 2006), 342.Refer to the excellent biography recently published by John D'Emilio, Lost Prophet: The Life and Times of Bayard Rustin (New York: Free Press, 2003).as well as Jervis Anderson, Bayard Rustin: Troubles I've Seen (New York: Harper Collins, 1997). See also, Leilah Danielson, "The 'Two-ness' of the Movement: James Farmer, Nonviolence, and Black Nationalism," Peace & Change 29 (July 2004), 431-452; Bennett, Radical Pacifism, chapts 5-8. Bennett also notes that during this period the protest team distributed a flyer – "PEOPLE OF AFRICA! AFRICA IS IN DANGER! – fusing nonviolent revolution and decolonization with nuclear disarmament.

13. See the following: Harry Kitano, Japanese Americans: The Evolution of a Subculture(Chicago: University of Chicago Press, 1969); Bill Hadakawa, Nisei: The Quiet Americans (New York: G.P. Putnam's Sons, 1969); and Jacobus ten Brock, Edward N. Barnhart, & Floyd W. Matson, Prejudice, War and the Constitution (Berkeley, CA: University of California Press, 1954); Roger Daniels, "Bad News from the Good War: Democracy at Home During World War II," in Kenneth Paul O'Brien & Lynn Hudson Parsons, eds., The Home-Front War: World War II and American Society (Westport, CT: Greenwood Press, 1995), 157-172 and Daniels, Concentration Camps USA: Japanese Americans and World War II (New York: Holt, Rinehart & Winston, 1972), 70-81, 115-130.

14. Information on the Japanese-American situation is found in Gara, To Secure Liberty and Peace and Peter Irons, Justice at War (New York: Oxford University Press, 1983). See also, Roger Daniels' review of Irons book in the American Historical Review 89, no. 3 (June 1984), 871-2.

15. Glen Zeitzer & Charles F. Howlett, "Political Versus Religious Pacifism: The Peace Now Movement of 1943", Historian XLVIII No. 3 (May 1986), pp. 375-393.

16. See, George W. Hartmann, "A Plea for an Immediate Peace by Negotiation" (August 1943) and Dorothy Hutchinson, "A Call to Peace Now: A Message to the Society of Friends" (February 1943), American Friends Service Committee, Swarthmore College Peace Collection, "Peace Now" Folder.

17. Peace Now Papers, SCPC, Box 1.

18. Vera Brittain, "Massacre by Bombing," Fellowship (March 1944), Sayre Papers, SCPC. Brittain and other FOR pacifists were clearly concerned about the trend in 20th century warfare with respect to civilian casualties. Unquestionably, military technology was becoming more and more sophisticated as well as deadlier. While strategic military plans were drawn up to limit civilian casualties, more often than not massive property damage and loss of lives became part of the collateral damage excuse in an effort to break the enemy's will power. See also, Eric Markhusen & David Kopf, The Holocaust and Strategic Bombing: Genocide and Total War in the Twentieth Century (Boulder, CO: Westview Press, 1995), 2-12.

19. Vera Brittain, "Not Made in Germany," Unpublished paper, Sayre Papers, SCPC.

20. Robert A. Divine, Second Chance: The Triumph of Internationalism in America During Word War II (NY: Athenaeum, 1967), 38-9; 101-104; Clark M. Eichelberger, Organizing for Peace: A Personal History

of the Founding of the United Nations (New York: Harper & Row, 1977), 206-17; Josephson, James T. Shotwell, 250-8; E. Timothy Smith, Opposition beyond the Water's Edge: Liberal Internationalists, Pacifists, and Containment, 1945-1953 (Westport, CT: Greenwood Press, 1999), passim; Wesley T. Wooley, "Finding the Usable Past: The Success of American World Federalism in the 1940s," Peace & Change 24 (July 1999), 329-339.

21. Alice Kimball Smith, A Peril and a Hope: The Scientists' Movement in America, 1945-1947 (Chicago: University of Chicago Press, 1965), 40-8. Additional works one must consider are: Michael Bess, Realism, Utopia, and the Mushroom Cloud: Four Activist Intellectuals and the Strategies for Peace, 1945-1989 (Chicago: University of Chicago Press, 1993); David Holloway, Stalin and the Bomb (Stanford, CA: Stanford University Press, 1994); Barton J. Bernstein, "Roosevelt, Truman, and the Atomic Bomb, 1941-1945," Political Science Quarterly XC (Spring 1975) and "Understanding the Atomic Bomb," Diplomatic History XIX (Spring 1995); and Gar Alperovitz, Atomic Diplomacy (New York: Simon & Schuster, 1985), and The Decision to Use the Bomb (New York: Alfred A. Knopf, 1995).

22. Dorothy Day, "We Go on Record", Catholic Worker (Sept. 1945), 1; See also, Martin J. Sherwin, A World Destroyed: The Atomic Bomb and the Grand Alliance (New York: Alfred A. Knopf, 1975), passim; Michael Yavendetti, "The American People and the Use of Atomic Bombs on Japan: The 1940's," The Historian XXXVI, no.2 (February 1974), 239-41..

23. Harold Laski, Liberty in the Modern State (New York: Macmillan, 1949), 20; Charles A. Beard, The Economic Basis of Politics, 3^{d} ed. (New York: Knopf, 1945), 101-3, 107.

24. Arthur A. Ekrich, Jr., Man and Nature in America (Lincoln: University of Nebraska Press, rev. 1973), 179.

25. Arthur A. Ekrich, Jr., The Challenge of American Democracy (Belmont, CA: Wadsworth Publishers, 1973), 266-69.Consult Michael Sherry's important book, In the Shadow of War: the United States Since the 1930s (New Haven: Yale University Press, 1997)..

26. J. Robert Oppenheimer, The Open Mind (New York: Simon & Schuster, 1955), 75; quoted in Weinberg, eds., Instead of Violence, 124-5.

27. Morton Grodzins & Eugene Rabinowitch, eds., The Atomic Age: Scientists in National and World Affairs (NY: Basic Books, 1963), passim. An excellent examination of this issue is found in Michael Bess, Realism, Utopia, and the Mushroom Cloud, 24-36.

28. Federation of American Scientists, "Survival Is at Stake," in Dexter Masters & Catherine Way, eds., One World or None: A Report to the Public on the Full Meaning of the Atomic Bomb (New York: McGraw Hill, 1946), passim.

29. Max Lowenthal, The Federal Bureau of Investigation (New York: William Morrow, Inc., 1950), 420 & ff; Sanford J. Ungar, FBI (Boston: Little Brown & Co., 1975), 104-33; Lieberman, The Strangest Dream, 43-50 and passim. For Dorothy Day's views on the Cold War, consult Nancy L. Roberts, "Journalism and Activism: Dorothy Day's Response to the Cold War," Peace & Change XII (1987), 13-28.

30. Lieberman, The Strangest Dream, 74-78; Charles F. Howlett, "Peekskill Riot of 1949" in Ryan & Schlup, eds. Historical Dictionary of the 1940's, 298. An important analysis of the African American views to the Cold War is found in Gerald Horne's work on W.E.B. Du Bois, Black and Red: W.E.B. Du Bois and the Afro-American Response to the Cold War, 1944-1953 (Albany: State University of New York Press, 1986).

31. New York Times, February 24, 1943, 3. The UWF Executive Council included Cord Meyer, Jr., President, Mark Van Doren, Raymond G. Swing, Norman Cousins, T.F. Finletter, Edgar Ansel Mowrer, and Helen Ball. Other notable UWF's were atomic scientist Harrison Brown and California youth leader Alan Cranston. See also, Chatfield, The American Peace Movement, 94-109.

32. New York Times, February 23, 1947, 25; Wittner, Rebels Against War, 17-2; Harrison Brown, "The World Government Movement in the United States," Bulletin of Atomic Scientists III (June 1947) 156; Cord Meyer, Jr., Peace or Anarchy (Boston: Little Brown & Co., 1947), passim. Works on Henry A. Wallace are Norman D. Markowitz, The Rise and Fall of the People's Century: Henry A. Wallace and American Liberalism, 1941-1948 (New York: Free Press, 1973), especially pages 324-331, and J. Samuel Walker, Henry A. Wallace and American Foreign Policy (Westport, CT.: Greenwood Press, 1976); and Lawrence S. Wittner, The Struggle Against the Bomb: One World Or None: A History of the World Nuclear Disarmament Movement through 1953 Vol 1 (Stanford, CA.: Stanford University Press, 1993), 67-70, 269 ff.

33. Jon A. Yoder, "The United World Federalists: Liberals for Law and Order" in Chatfield, ed. Peace Movements in America, 95-115; Kleidman, Organizing for Peace, 82-106; Chatfield, The American Peace Movement, 94-97.

34. Ekirch, The Civilian and the Military, 276-84.

35. Ibid., 276-78; DeBenedetti, The Peace Reform, 148-150.

36. Ellen Schrecker, Many are the Crimes (Boston: Little Brown & Co., 1998) and No Ivory Tower: McCarthyism and the University (New York: Oxford University Press, 1986), passim.

37. Arthur A. Ekirch, Jr., The Decline of American Liberalism (New York: Athenaeum, rev. 1967), Chapter XVIII, passim Also consult the following: Richard Hofstadter, Anti-Intellectualism in American Life (New York: Vintage Books, 1963); Michel Rogin, The Intellectuals and McCarthy: the Radical Specter (Cambridge, MA.: MIT Press, 1967); David Caute, The Great Fear: the Anti-Communist Purge under Truman and Eisenhower (New York: Simon & Schuster, 1978); and Athan Theoharis, Seeds of Repression: Harry S. Truman and the Origins of McCarthyism (Chicago: Quadrangle Books, 1971).

38. New York Times, February 21, 1950, 11.

39. Yoder, "The United World Federalists" in Chatfield, ed., Peace Movements in America, 106.

40. New York Times, June 25, 1952, 18.

41. Milton S. Katz, "Peace, Politics, and Protest: SANE and the American Peace Movement, 1957-1972" (Ph.D. thesis, St. Louis University, 1973), 50-9. Katz's dissertation was published as Ban the Bomb: A History of SANE, the Committee for a SANE Nuclear Policy (Westport, CT: Praeger, 1986).

42. Dwight McDonald, "The Bomb" in Politics Past: Essays in Political Criticism (New York: Viking Press, 1970), passim. Also refer to Robert A. Divine, Blowing on the Wind: the Nuclear Test Bam Debate, 1954-1960 (New York: Oxford University Press, 1978). A very fine overview is also provided by James Farrell, The Spirit of the Sixties: The Making of Postwar Radicalism (New York: Routledge, 1997).

43. Cooney & Michalowski, eds. The Power of the People, 106-110; Bennett, Radical Pacifism, 113-119; James Peck, Underdogs Vs. Upperdogs (New York: AMP&R Publisher, 1980), and Peck, We Who Would Not Kill (New York: Lyle Stuart, 1958).

44. Andrew Hunt, David Dellinger: The Life and Times of a Non-violent Revolutionary (New York: New York University Press, 2006), 38-62. Also consult Dellinger's autobiography, From Yale to Jail : Life of a Moral Dissenter (New York: Pantheon, 1993), and Bennett, Radical Pacifism, 126-131.

45. Cooney & Michalowsji, eds., The Power of the People, 112-123; Bennett, Radical Pacifism, chapters 4-8.

46. Quoted in DeBenedetti, The Peace Reform, 153; A.J. Muste, "Sketches for an Autobiography" in Nat Hentoff, ed., The Essays of A.J. Muste (New York: Simon & Schuster, 1970), 12 & ff. the authoritative biography on Muste is Jo Ann O. Robinson, Abraham Went Out: A Biography of A.J. Muste (Philadelphia: Temple University Press, 1981).

47.Muste, "Sketches for an Autobiography," 16-18; Howlett & Zeitzer, The American Peace Movement, 34-36.

48. Wittner, Rebels Against War, 203.

49. Ibid., 203-4; Ekirch, The Civilian and the Military, 280-89. For debates involving the causes and impact of the Korean War on American society some of the more representative works are: John Halliday and Bruce Cumings, Korea: The Unknown War (New York: Pantheon Books, 1988); I.F. Stone, The Hidden History of the Korean War, 1950-1951 (Boston: Little, Brown, 1988); and William Stueck, The Korean War: An International History (Princeton: Princeton University Press, 1995).

50. Muste, "Korea, Spark to Set the World on Fire," in Hentoff, ed., The Essays of A.J. Muste, 349-54; Halliday and Cumings, Korea, 23-31.

51. Wittner, Rebels Against War, quoted from p. 202; New York Times, July 7, 1950, 3.

52. Wittner, Rebels Against War, 201-202.

53. David L. Lewis, King: A Critical Biography (New York: Praeger, 1970), 87-90.

54. Lewis, King, 86, and DeBenedetti, The Peace Reform, 159; quoted in Weinberg, eds., Instead of Violence, 73. Also consult, Barbara Ransby, Ella Baker and the Black Freedom Movement: A Radical Democratic Vision (Chapel Hill: University of North Carolina Press, 2003), and Clayborne Carson, In Struggle: SNCC and the Black Awakening of the 1960s (Cambridge, MA: Harvard University Press, 1981). King worked closely with the WRL. Rustin was WRL's

executive secretary from 1953 to January 1965, and he was released half-time to work with King. Rustin wrote SCLC's founding documents. For more on this score consult, Bennett, Radical Pacifism, 216-226.

55. James A. Ridgway, "School Civil Defense Measures," Elementary School Journal (May 1954), 501-3; Raymond E. Polich, "The Defense Program of the Los Angeles City Schools," The National Elementary Principal (June 1951), 22; Paul Boyer, By the Bomb's Early Light: American Thought and Culture at the Dawn of the Atomic Age (New York: Pantheon Books, 1985), passim.; Dee Garrison, Bracing for Armageddon: Why Civil Defense Never Worked (New York: Oxford University Press, 2006), 14-29 and passim.

56. Quoted in Weinberg, eds., Instead of Violence, 42-3.

57. Quoted in Gara, ed., To Secure Peace and Liberty.

58. Michael J. Carey, "The Schools and Civil Defense: The Fifties Revisited", Teachers College Record, 84, no. 1 (Fall 1982), 124.

CHAPTER SEVEN

1. "The Port Huron Statement," SDS Papers, Hoover Library, Freedom Foundation, PA., and in James Miller, "Democracy in the Streets": From Port Huron to the Siege of Chicago (New York: Simon & Schuster, 1987); Todd Gitlin, The Sixties: Years of Hope, Days of Rage (New York: Bantam Books, 1987); Alexander Bloom & Wini Breines, eds., Takin' It To the Streets: A Sixties Reader (New York: Oxford University Press, 1995); Lyman T. Sargent, New Left Thought: An Introduction (Homewood, Ill.: Dorsey Press, 1972); Wini Breines, Community and Organization in the New Left, 1962-1968 (New Brunswick, NJ: Rutgers University Press, 1989); Robbie Lieberman, "Prairie Power": Voices of the 1960s Midwestern Student Protest (Columbia: University of Missouri Press, 2004); Doug Rossinow, The Politics of Authenticity: Liberalism, Christianity, and the New Left in America (New York: Columbia University Press, 1999); and Milton S. Katz and Neil H. Katz, "Pragmatists and Visionaries in the Post-World War II American Peace Movement: SANE and CNVA," in Wank, ed., Doves and Diplomats, 265-88.

2. Initially CNVA was an ad-hoc group known as Non-violent Action Against Nuclear Weapons; it became a permanent organization in 1959. Tracy's Direct Action offers a complete account. See, 51-61, 104-109. Consult, as well, Bennett, Radical Pacifism, 222-38; Kleidman, Organizing for Peace, 89-113.

3. "Pragmatists and Visionaries," 268; SANE members were upper class, professional and semi-professional, white collar, Protestant and Jewish. They represented the respectable side of the peace movement proper; Katz, Ban the Bomb, Chapts. 1&2.

4. Nathan Glazer, "The Peace Movement in America," Commentary XXXI (April 1961), 290-1.

5. U.S. Senate, Internal Security Sub Committee of the Judiciary, "Communist Infiltration in the Nuclear Test-Ban Movement," 86th Cong., 2nd Sess., 1960, pt. 1, & 87th Cong., 1st Sess., 1961, pt. II.; see also, Lieberman, The Strangest Dream, 143-157; Katz, Ban the Bomb, .87-92; 123-126.

6. Cooney & Michaelowski, *Power of the People*, 127-131; see also the CNVA Manuscript Collection, DG 17, Fl 2,3-5, Swarthmore College Peace Collection.

7. "May 7 Press Release," Voyage of the *Golden Rule*, CNVA Mss., SCPC, Box 3; Quoted in Lynd, ed., *Non-violence in America*, 346-7; Tracy, *Direct Action*, 102-104.

8. Howlett & Zeitzer, *The American Peace Movement*, 34-5.

9. "Reports" Polaris Action Mss, Box 1, SCPC. See also, Robert D. Holsworth, *Let Your Life Speak: A Study of Politics, Religion, and Antinuclear Weapons Activism* (Madison: University of Wisconsin Press, 1989), *passim*.

10. "A Long March," *New York Post*, October 6, 1961; "The San Francisco to Moscow Walk," CNVA Mss, Box 2, SCPC; Tracy, *Direct Action*, 120-21; Kleidman, *Organizing for Peace*, 98-103; Bradford Lyttle, *You Come with Naked Hands: The Story of the San Francisco to Moscow March for Peace* (Raymond, NH.: Greenleaf Books, 1966), 48-57.

11. A.J. Muste, "Lets Radicalize the Peace Movement," *Liberation* VIII (June 1963), 26-30; Barbara Deming, *Prison Notes* (New York: Grossman Publishers, 1966), *passim*.

12. "Pragmatists and Visionaries", 280; Katz, *Ban the Bomb*, 45-51.

13. George R. Vickers, *The Formation of the New Left: The Early Years* (Lexington, Ms: DC Heath, 1975), 50-61; Terry H. Anderson, *The Movement and the Sixties: Protest in America from Greensboro to Wounded Knee* (New York: Oxford University Press, 1995), 43-62.

14. Pamphlet, *The Committee of Correspondence: A Statement*, The Committee of Correspondence Folder, Social Protest Project, Box 4, Bancroft Library, University of California at Berkeley.

15. See Records of the World Without War Council, Carton 7, Bancroft Library, UC at Berkeley.

16. Amy Swerdlow, *Women Strike for Peace: Traditional Motherhood and Radical Politics in the 1960s* (Chicago: University of Chicago Press, 1993), 6-9.

17. *Ibid*., 12-18, 224-26. For more commentary on SANE's quest for respectability and exclusion of Communists refer to Lieberman, *The Strangest Dream*, 143-147.Also refer to Swerdlow, *Women Strike for Peace*, 28-34, *passim*.

18. Kenneth Boulding, *Conflict and Defense* (NY: Harper & Row, 1962), *passim*.

19. *New York Times*, October 17, 1961, 32; DeBenedetti, *The Peace Reform*, 166-69.

20. See the following works: Irwin Unger, *The Movement: A History of the American New Left. 1959-1972* (New York: Dodd, Mead & Co., 1974); James Weinstein, *Ambiguous Legacy: The Left in American Politics* (New York: New Viewpoints, 1975), 115-59; Edward J. Bocciocco, Jr., *The New Left in America: Reform to Revolution, 1950-1970* (Stanford, CA: Hoover Institution Press, 1974); Maurice Isserman, *If I Had a Hammer: the Death of the Old Left and the Birth of the New Left* (New York: Basic Books, 1987).

21. "The Port Huron Statement," SDS, Hoover Library, Freedoms Foundation, Pennsylvania, 30-5; Anderson, *The Movement*, 63-65; Tracy, *Direct Action*, 111-114.

22. DeBenedetti, *The Peace Reform*, 171-2.

23. Tracy, Direct Action, 112-113, 126; Cooney & Michalowski, eds., The Power of the People, 184-87; DeBenedetti, The Peace Reform, 167-72, 182-85; Gitlin, the Sixties, 24-26; Breines, Community and Organization in the New Left, 38-42; Miller, "Democracy in the Streets," 48-57.

24. Fred Halstead, Out Now! A Participant's Account of the American Movement Against the Vietnam War (New York: Monad Press, 1978), 12-22; Anderson, The Movement, passim; David Dellinger, From Yale to Jail: Life of a Moral Dissenter (New York: Pantheon, 1993).

25. Information on Chavez can be found in Cooney & Michalowski, The Power of the People, 175-181; Mark Day, Forty Acres: Cesar Chavez and the Farm Workers (New York: Praeger, 1971), passim; and Ronald B. Taylor, Chavez and the Farm Workers (Boston: Beacon Press, 1975), 52-65.

26. William J. Fulbright, The Arrogance of Power (New York: Vintage Books, 1966); Stanley Karnow, Vietnam: A History (New York: Viking Press, 1983), Chapt. 2; George C. Herring, America's Longest War: The United States and Vietnam, 1950-1975 (New York: McGraw-Hill, Inc, 1996), passim.

27. Joseph R. Conlin, American Anti-War Movements (Beverly Hills, CA: Sage Publishers, 1968) passim. See also, DeBenedetti, The Peace Reform, Chapt. 8. Se also, Tom Wells, The War Within: America's Battle over Vietnam (Berkeley: University of California Press, 1994), 28-38; Mel Small, Johnson, Nixon and the Doves (New Brunswick, NJ: Rutgers University Press, 1988), 78-84, passim; and DeBenedetti & Chatfield, An American Ordeal, 387-408.

28. Conlin, American Anti-War Movements, 18-24.

29. Quoted in Jo Ann Robinson, Abraham Went Out, 202. See also, George F. Kennan, American Diplomacy, 1900-1950 (NY: Mentor Books, 1962). See also, Lawrence S. Wittner, Cold War America (New York: Praeger Publishers, 1974), passim.

30. Patti McGill Peterson, "Student Organizations and the Movement in America, 1900-1960" in Chatfield, ed., Peace Movements in America, 116-32; Kenneth J. Heineman, Campus Wars: The Peace Movement at American State Universities in the Vietnam Era (New York: New York University Press, 1993); Marc Jason Gilbert ed., The Vietnam War on Campus: Other Voices, More Distant Drums (Westport, CT: Praeger, 2001). James Eichsteadt, "Shut It Down," New York Archives 7 (Fall 2007), 8-12; Robbie Lieberman, "'We Closed Down the Damn School': The Party Culture and Student Protest at Southern Illinois University during the Vietnam War Era," Peace & Change 26 (July 2001), 316-331.

31. Quoted in James J. Farrell, The Spirit of the Sixties: The Making of Postwar Radicalism (New York: Routledge, 1997), 182-183.

32. New York Times, March 27, 1966, p. 1; Wells. The War Within, 76-89; DeBenedetti, An American Ordeal, 56-62; Farrell, The Spirit of the Sixties, 144-68.

33. Zinn, A People's History of the United States, 482-483.

34. Fort Hood Three, pamphlet, July 1966, A.J. Muste Mss, SCPC; New York Post. October 10, 1966; Alice Lynd, ed., We Won't Go (Boston: Beacon Press 1968), 181-202; Zinn, A People's History of the United States, 482-486; Andrew Hunt, The Turning: A History of Vietnam Veterans against the War (New York: New York

University Press, 1999), 14-24; Richard Moser, The New Winter Soldiers: GI and Veteran Dissent during the Vietnam War (New Brunswick, NJ: Rutgers University Press, 1996), 56-58, 96-100, 123-124, 165-71.

35. Ibid, April 21-22, 1966; "The Saigon Project," A.J. Muste Papers, Box 43, SCPC; Charles F. Howlett, "A.J. Muste: Portrait of a Twentieth-Century Pacifist," in Donald W. Whisenhunt, ed., The Human Tradition in America Between the Wars, 1920-1945 (Wilmington, DE.: Scholarly Resources, 2002), 1-20; Robinson, Abraham Went Out, 201-214.

36. New York Times, February 27, 1966.; Charles F. Howlett, "Fellowship and Reconciliation: a Pacifist Organization Confronts the War in Southeast Asia," The Maryland Historian 25 (Spring/Summer 1994), 1-24; Farrell, The Spirit of the Sixties, 172-183; DeBenedetti, An American Ordeal, 112-121.

37. Swerdlow, Women Strike for Peace, 188-191; Alonso, peace as a Women's Issue, 212-216; Mary Hershberger, "Peace Work, War Myths: Jane Fonda and the Anti-war Movement," Peace & Change 29 (July 2004), 549-579.

38. Martin Luther King, Jr., "Declaration of Independence from the War in Vietnam," in Lillian Schlissel, ed., Conscience in America: A Documentary History of Conscientious Objection in America, 1757-1967 (NY: EP Dutton & Co., 1968), 426-33. An excellent account of the inability of the civil rights and anti-war movements to meld is Simon, Hall, Peace and Freedom: The Civil Rights and Anti-war Movements in the 1960s (Philadelphia: University of Pennsylvania Press, 2006). See also, Tracy, Direct Action, 124-53; Anderson, The Movement, 135-55. For difficulties black females faced in the anti-war movement refer to Joyce Blackwell, No Peace without Freedom, passim. Another important study is Michael B. Friedland, Lift Up your voice Like a Trumpet: White Clergy and the Civil Rights and Anti-war Movements, 1954-1973 (Chapel Hill: University of North Carolina Press, 1998); Thomas J. Noer, "Martin Luther King, Jr. and the Cold War," Peace & Change 22 (April 1997), 111-131, Robbie Lieberman, "Peace and Civil Rights Don't Mix, They Say": Anticommunism and the Dividing of U.S. Social Movements, 1947-1967," (forthcoming).

39. Hall, Peace and Freedom, 118-34; Lieberman, "Peace and Civil Rights Don't Mix, they Say," (forthcoming).

40. Cooney & Michaelowski, The Power of the People, 198-203; Robert Calvert, ed., Ain't Gonna Pay for War No More (New York: War Tax Resistance, 1971); Ed Hedemann, War Tax Resistance: A Guide to Withholding Your Support from the Military (New York: War Resisters League, 1981), passim. .

41. Quoted in Robinson. Abraham Went Out, 217; A.J. Muste, "Last Words," Liberation (September-October 1967), 52-7; Philip S. Foner, American Labor and the Indochina War: Growth of Union Opposition (NY: International Publishers, 1971), 48-59.

42.John Kenneth Gailbraith, How to Get Out of Vietnam (New York: New American Library, 1967), 22. Also refer to Mitchell K. Hall, Because of their Faith: CALCAV and Religious Opposition to the Vietnam War (New York: Columbia University Press, 1990).

43. Quoted in Ten Fighters for Peace, 113-114; See also, Michael Useem, Conscription. Protest, and Social Conflict: The Life and Death of a Draft Resistance Movement (New York: John Wiley & Sons, 1973); Alice

Lynd, ed., We Won't Go: Personal Accounts of War Objectors (Boston: Beacon Press, 1968); David M. Mantell, True Americanism: Green Berets and War Resisters (New York: Teachers College Press, 1974); Renee G. Kasinsky, Refugees from Militarism: Draft-Age Americans in Canada (New Brunswick, NJ: Transaction Books, Inc., 1976); Michael Ferber & Staughton Lynd, The Resistance (Boston: Beacon Press, 1971); Michael S. Foley, Confronting the War Machine: Draft Resistance during the Vietnam War (Chapel Hill: University of North Carolina Press, 2004), 131-160.Foley's work is by far the most comprehensive study of opposition to the draft.

44. Lynd, ed., We Won't Go, 206; Foley Confronting the War Machine, 48-75.

45. Lynd, ed., We Won't Go, 109-119; Morgan David Arant, Jr., "Government Use of the Draft to Silence Dissent to War: A Case of Punitive Reclassification," Peace & Change 17 (April 1992), 147-171..

46. Ibid., 108-112. Historian Mel Small has made a major contribution to our understanding of the anti-war movement. Consult his following works: Johnson, Nixon, and the Doves.; Covering Dissent: The Media and the Anti-Vietnam War Movement (New Brunswick, NJ: Rutgers University Press, 1994); and Antiwarriors: The Vietnam War and the Battle for America's Hearts and Minds (Wilmington, DE: Scholarly Resources, 2002).

47. Charles DeBenedetti, "A CIA Analysis of the Anti-Vietnam War Movement: October 1967," Peace & Change. IX, no. 1 (Spring 1983), 31-41

48. Wells, The War Within, 276-301; DeBenedetti, "A CIA Analysis of the Anti-Vietnam War Movement," 33-39; Geoffrey R. Stone, "Civil Liberties in Wartime," Journal of Supreme Court History (November 2003), 238-242.

49. David Walker, later the governor of Illinois, headed a commission that concluded that the Chicago Police had provoked the crowd. His commission labeled it a "Police riot." Refer to Rights in Conflict: The Violent Confrontation of Demonstrators and Police in the Parks and Streets of Chicago (New York: E.P. Dutton, 1968) with an introduction by Max Frankel. See also, Jon Wiener, ed, Conspiracy in the Streets: The Extraordinary Trial of the Chicago Eight (New York: New Press, 2006), David Farber, Chicago '68 (Chicago: University of Chicago Press, 1998); Farrell, The Spirit of the Sixties, 197-223;.Hunt, David Dellinger, 218-220.

50. The Cox Commission Report, Crisis at Columbia (New York: Vintage Books, 1968),passim; Miller, "Democracy Is in the Streets," 289-93; Farrell, The Spirit of the Sixties, 166-167.

51. Quoted in Gara, ed., To Secure Peace and Liberty.

52 Quoted in Nancy L. Roberts , Dorothy Day and the Catholic Worker, 78, 163; See also, Anne Klejment & Alice Klejment, Dorothy Day and the Catholic Worker: A Bibliography and Index, (New York: Garland Publishers, 1986); Anne Klejment, The Berrigans: A Bibliography of Published Works by Daniel and Philip, and Elizabeth McAlister Berrigan (New York: Garland Publishers, 1979); Patricia McNeal, Harder than War: Catholic Peacemaking in Twentieth Century America (New Brunswick, N.J.: Rutgers University Press, 1992); Penelope Moon, "Loyal Sons and Daughters of God?" Peace & Change 33 (Jan. 2008):1-30.

53. Paul Hoffman, Moratorium: An American Protest (NY: Tower Publications, Inc. 1970), 32-34; Anderson, The Movement, 328-31, Chatfield, The American Peace Movement, 117-45.

54. Ken Hurwitz, Marching Nowhere (New York: W.W. Norton & Co., 1971); Sam Brown, "The Politics of Peace," The Washington Monthly II, no.6 (August 1970), 24-46; DeBenedetti, An American Ordeal, 269-281; Wells, The War Within, 290-294; Halstead, Out Now!, 439-441.

55. For solid discussions and analyses of peace coalitions, including the Mobes, see Chatfield, ed., Peace Movements in America, xxvii-xxviii. There are also a number of important works which add to Chatfield's analysis. Among them are: Charles DeBenedetti, with the assistance of Chatfield, "Retrospect" in An American Ordeal; Melvin Small, Anti-warriors, 128-134; Mary Susannah Robbins, Against the Vietnam War: Writings by Activists (Syracuse: Syracuse University Press, 1999); Nancy Zaroulis & Gerald Sullivan, Who Spoke Up?: American Protest Against the War in Vietnam, 1963-1975 (New York: Holt, Rinehart & Winston, 1984); Tom Wells, The War Within; Guenter Lewy, Peace and Revolution: the Moral Crisis of American Pacifism (Grand Rapids, MI: William B. Erdmans Publishing Co., 1998); Adam Garfinkle, Telltale Hearts: The Origins and Impact of the Vietnam Anti-war Movement (New York: St. Martin's Press, 1995).

56. Wells, The War Within, chapt. 10; DeBenedetti, An American Ordeal, 387-408; Farrell, The Spirit of the Sixties, 254-258; Kenneth Heineman, Campus Wars: The Peace Movement at American State Universities in the Vietnam Era (New York: New York University Press, 1993), passim.. For a scholarly assessments of Kent State consult, "Special Forum Issue: The Greater Kent State Era," Peace & Change 21 (April 1996), 149-207, Scott Bills, Kent State/May 4: Echoes Through a Decade (Kent, OH: Kent State University Press, 1998); and Mel Small, Johnson, Nixon and the Doves, 204-215.

57. VVAW History, Box 6, Records of the Vietnam Veterans Against the War, The State Historical Society of Wisconsin; See also, David Cortright, .Soldiers in Revolt: The American Military Today (Garden City, NY: Doubleday & Co., 1975), Chapter I; Edward M. Opton, Jr., & Robert Duckless, "Mental Gymnastics on Mylai," The New Republic 162, no.8 (February 21,1970), 14-16. See also, Andrew Hunt, The Turning, 89-92 and Richard Moser, The New Winter Soldiers, 67-74.

58. Hunt, The Turning, 122-131; Moser, The New Winter Soldiers, 74-81.

59. See Wells, The War Within, 501-505, 572-74; DeBenedetti, An American Ordeal, 299-307.

60. New York Times, May 4-6, 1971; The Pentagon Papers (New York: Bantam Books, 1971). The secret papers were leaked to New York Times reporter Neil Sheehan. The memo about why the war was fought – to avoid humiliation – became a flashpoint among critics of the war and further justification of their position. Sheehan would later win the Pulitzer Prize for his biography of Colonel John Paul Vann, A Bright and Shinning Lie.. See also, "On Daniel Ellsberg: Remembering the Pentagon Papers," in Gara, ed., To Secure Peace and Liberty , and Daniel Ellsberg, Papers on the War (New York: Simon and Schuster, 1972).

61. Jacob K. Javits, "Who Decides on War?," New York Times Magazine, October 23, 1983, 92 & ff; Newsday, September 16, 1983, 3; Wells, The War Within, 572-575; DeBenedetti, An American Ordeal, 405

62. Charles F. Howlett, "Case Law Historiography in American Peace History," Peace & Change 22 (January 1997), 59-61.

63. Ibid., 60.

64. Ibid., 62.

65. Ibid, 62-63.

66. R. Serge Denisoff, ed., Songs of Protest, War and Peace (Santa Barbara, CA: ABC-CLIO, 1973), 4-5.and Great Day Coming: Folk Music and the American Left (Urbana: University of Illinois Press, 1971); Pete Seeger, The Incomplete Folksinger (New York: Simon & Schuster, 1972); David K. Dunaway, How Can I Keep from Singing: Pete Seeger (New York: McGraw-Hill, 1982); Anderson, The Movement, 171-91 and his useful article, "Pop Music and the Vietnam War," Peace & Change XI (1986), 51-66.

67. Denisoff, ed., Songs of Protest, War and Peace, 5-6..

68. For more information consult, Richard Taylor, Blockade (New York: Orbis Books, 1977), passim.

69. "At Last, At Last...," Fellowship 41, no. 6 (June 1975), 3. In addition, consult Robert Schulzinger, special editor, "The War in Vietnam and its legacy," Peace & Change IX, nos. 2/3 (Summer 1983).

CHAPTER EIGHT

1. Quotations found in Paul S. Boyer, "From Activism to Apathy: The American People and Nuclear Weapons, 1963-1980," Journal of American History. 70, No.4 (March, 1984), 821-844. Consult the transnational triology by Lawrence S. Wittner, The Struggle Against the Bomb: a History of the World Nuclear Disarmament Movement, 3 vols. (Stanford, CA: Stanford University Press, 1993-2003) provides a very thorough history of nuclear pacifists in SANE and CNVA prior to Vietnam, how the war provided an unwelcome distraction, and how the anti-nuclear movement reenergized afterwards and linked their efforts to community and personalist politics while not abandoning traditional strategies.

2. Barbara Epstein, Political Protest and Cultural Revolution: Non-violent Direct Action in the 1970s and 1980s (Berkeley: University of California Press, 1991), 58-91. See also, Natalie Patricia Atkin, "Protest and Liberation: War, Peace, and Women's Empowerment, 1967-1981" (Ph.D. diss, Wayne State University, 1999), passim.

3. Ibid., 61-62; Cooney & Michalowski, eds., The Power of the People, 224-27. See also, Michele S. Gerber, On the Home Front: The Cold War Legacy of the Hanford Nuclear Site (Lincoln, NE: University of Nebraska Press, 1992) passim.

4. Epstein, Political Protest and Cultural Revolution, 66-72.

5. Cooney & Michalowski, eds., The Power of the People, 226-27; Patrick Novotny, "The Peace and Justice Movement in the South in the 1980s," Peace & Change 22 (April 1997), 154-174.

6. Wade Green, "Rethinking the Unthinkable," 47.

7. A fine overview of the peacetime military buildup in the Carter and Reagan years is found in Thomas G. Paterson, et al., American Foreign Relations Since 1895, Vol. 2 (Boston: Houghton Mifflin Co., 2005), 414-445. See also, Thomas G. Paterson, Meeting the Communist Threat: Truman to Reagan (New York: Oxford

University Press, 1988), passim. This work is a collection of essays Paterson wrote questioning how American leaders exaggerated the Soviet threat.

8. Douglas Mattern, "The Economics of Death", Commonweal, CI, No. 2 (October 11, 1974), 31-34; Seymour Melman, "Looting the Means of Protection," New York Times (July 26, 1981), Section 2, 21.

9. See the following articles: Wade Green, "Rethinking the Unthinkable," New York Times Magazine (March 15, 1981), 45-7, 66, 68, 70; Al Martinez, "A New Image for Peace," Newsday (March 19, 1983), pt. II, 2-3; Kai Erikson, "A Final Accounting of Death and Destruction," book review of Hiroshima and Nagasaki in New York Times Book Review (August 9, 1981), 1, 22-4; Barbara Tuchman, "The Alternative to Arms Control," New York Times Magazine (April 18, 1982), 44-5, 90-100; Leon Wieseltier, "Nuclear War, Nuclear Peace," The New Republic (January 10 & 17,1983), 9-18; Leslie H. Gelb, "A Practical Way to Arms Control" New York Times Magazine (June 5,1983), 33-42; Robert Jay Lifton, "Beyond Nuclear Numbing" and Randall Forsberg, "A Nuclear Freeze and a Noninterventionary Conventional Policy." in Teachers College Record 84. No. 1 (Fall 1982), 15-29, and 65-78.

10. Prepared Statement by Jennifer Learning, "Civil Defense in the Nuclear Age: Strategic, Medical, and Demographic Aspects," United States and Soviet Civil Defense Programs, Hearings, 97th Congress, 2nd session., March 16 & 31, 1982.

11. The noted Russian philosopher Nikolai Berdyaev wrote: "War is possible only in a certain psychological atmosphere and this psychological atmosphere is created in a variety of ways, sometimes in unnoticed ways. Even an atmosphere of fear of war can be favourable to war. Fear never leads to any good." See, Slavery and Freedom (NewYork: Charles Scribner's Sons, 1944), 156.

12. Douglas Sloan, "Toward an Education for a Living World," Teachers College Record 84, No. 1 (Fall 1982), 1-14; Erick Markusen, "Education about Nuclear War," Educational Perspectives XXI (Fall 1982), 32-36; "Artists Protest Nuclear Threat," New York Times (December 11, 1983), 40.

13. Ground Zero was formed by two brothers, Roger and Earl Molander. The group, based in Washington, D.C., had a staff of 12 and a budget of about $290,000.

14. Cooney & Michalowski, eds., The Power of the People, 233-35.

15. New York Times, April 19, 1982, 16; John Lofland, Polite Protestors: the American Peace Movement of the 1980s (Syracuse: Syracuse University Press, 1993), 37-52.

16. Fox Butterfield, "Anatomy of the Nuclear Protest," New York Times Magazine (July 11, 1982), 14-17, 32-34, 38-39. A very fine analysis was recently written by Chatfield. See, Charles Chatfield, "American Insecurity: Dissent from the 'Long War'" in Andrew Bacevich, ed., The Long War: A New History of U.S. National Security Policy Since World War II (New York: Columbia University Press, 2007), 485-488.

17. Newsday, July 31, August 1 & 2, 1983; Also consult, Chatfield, The American Peace Movement, 146-65; Kleidman, Organizing for Peace, 138-44.

18. New York Times, August 28, 1983,1, 30; Newsday, August 26,1983, 6& 19, August 27, 4, 9, August 28, 4-5; Kleidman, Organizing for Peace, 135-182.

19. Patterson, Meeting the Communist Threat, 265-272.

20. New York Times, October 23, 1983, 1, 16; October 26-27, 1-2, 27; November 13,17; Newsday, October 26-7, 1 & ff, November 13, 4; New York Daily News, October 27, p.23.

21. Christian Smith, Resisting Reagan: The U.S. Central America Peace Movement (Chicago: University of Chicago Press, 1996), 376-77; Van Gosse, Where the Boys Are: Cuba, Cold War America and the Making of the New Left (New York: Verso, 1993), passim.

22. Sharon Erickson Nepstad, "Sanctuary Movement" in Roger S. Powers & William B. Vogele, eds., Protest, Power, and Change: An Encyclopedia of Non-violent Action from ACT-UP to Women's Suffrage (New York: Garland Publishers, 1997), 457; Ann Crittenden, Sanctuary: A Story of American Conscience and Law (New York: Weidenfeld & Nicholson, 1988), passim.; David Cortright, Peace Works: The Citizen's Role in Ending the Cold War (Boulder, CO: Westview Press, 1993), 220-230.

23. Nepstad, "Sanctuary Movement," 457; Chatfield, "American Insecurity," 488-91; Cortright, Peace Works, 224-26.

24. Nepstad., "Sanctuary Movement," 457; Smith, Resisting Reagan, 278-90.

25. Nepstad, "Sanctuary Movement," 458; Cortright, Peace Works, 218-220.

26. Nepstad, "Sanctuary Movement,' 458; Chatfield, "American Insecurity," 488-490; Paterson, Meeting the Communist Threat, 267-78.

27. Ed Griffin Nolan, "Witness for Peace" in Protest, Power, and Change, p. 568; Virginia Williams, "Grassroots Movements and Witness for Peace: Challenging U.S. Policies in Latin America in the Post-Cold War Era," Peace & Change 29 (July 2004), 419-430.

28. Ibid., p. 568; Cortright, Peace Works, 225-26; Williams, "Grassroots Movements," 423-429. See also, Jackie Smith and Hank Johnson, eds., Globalization and Resistance: Transnational Dimensions of Social Movements (New York: Rowman & Littlefield, 2002), 10-24, 209-235.

29. Sharon Erickson Nepstad, "Nicaragua, Non-violence and Revolution," in Protest, Power, and Change, p. 353; Michael Sullivan, American Adventurism Abroad (Boston: Wiley-Blackwell, 2007), passim.

30. "Lessons from the Struggle against the Gulf War (1991)," http://www.uhc-collective.org.uk/knowledge/toolbox (cited May 11, 2006). Some of the more reliable sources worth consulting are the following: Noam Chomsky, Hegemony or Survival: America's Quest for Global Dominance (New York: Metropolitan Books, 2003); Chalmers Johnson, The Sorrows of Empire: Militarism, Secrecy, and the End of the Republic (New York: Metropolitan Books, 2004); and Claes G. Ryan, America the Virtuous: The Crisis of Democracy and the Quest for Empire (New Brunswick, NJ.: Transaction Books, 2003). For a useful discussion on the First Gulf War involving matters of collective security see, Metta Spencer, "Anti-war Hawks and Prowar Doves in the Gulf War: Common Security versus Collective Security" Peace & Change 17 (April 1992), 172-197.

31. Barbara Epstein, "Notes on the Anti-war Movement," Monthly Review 55 No. 3 (July-August 2003), pp. 1-2. See also, Robert W. Tucker and David C. Hendrickson, The Imperial Temptation (New York: Council on Foreign Relations Press, 1992), passim.

32. Andrea Lamberti, "Students respond to Gulf War." http://www.tech.mit.edu (cited May 11, 2006).

33. "The War Within," Newsweek (February 4, 1991), 58.

34. New York Times, October 3, 2002, A13.

35. Brent Scowcroft, "Don't Attack Saddam," The Wall Street Journal (August 15, 2002), editorial commentary; no author, "Nelson Mandela: The U.S.A. Is a Threat to World Peace," Newsweek (August 28, 2002), 6-7; David Cortright, "The Movement and the 2003 War in Iraq," in Randy Scherer, ed., The Movement (Farmington Hill, MI.: Greenhaven Press, 2004), 146-152; New York Times (February 16, 2003), 20-21. For a thorough discussion on Bush's assertion to initiate a preemptory unilateral strike consult, Ivo H. Daalader and James M. Lindsay, America Unbound: The Bush Revolution in Foreign Policy (Washington, D.C.: Brookings Institution, 2003), 125-128.

36. "Thousands at Central Park Rally Oppose an Iraq War," New York Times (October 7, 2002), B3.

37. "LIers to Join March on D.C.," Newsday (October 24, 2002), A 23.

38. "99 Protesters Arrested," Newsday (December 11, 2002), A39.

39. Michael Walzer, "Is There an American Empire," Dissent 50 (2003), 14-17; Jerry Goldberg, "The Unknown," New Yorker (February 10, 2003), 2-5; no author, "War in Iraq," Iraqjournal .org (March 25, 2003), 1; "Student Groups Plan Walkout to Protest War," New York Times (March 1, 2003), A10; Cortright, "The Movement," 148-151. Additional commentary on the Iraq War can be found in the following works: Chalmers Johnson, Nemesis: The Last Days of the American Republic (New York: Henry Holt, 2007); Joseph Margulies, Guantanamo and the Abuse of Presidential Power (New York: Simon & Schuster, 2007); Christian T. Miller, Blood Money: Wasted Billions, Lost Lives, and Corporate Greed in Iraq (New York: Little, Brown, 2006); Bob Woodward, State of Denial (New York: Simon & Schuster, 2006); George Packer, The Assassins' Gate: America in Iraq (New York: Farrar, Straus, & Giroux, 2005); and Thomas Ricks, Fiasco: The American Military Adventure in Iraq (New York: Penguin Books, 2006).

40. "Rally Invokes King's Spirit," Newsday (January 20, 2003), A2; "Mass Appeal: Millions Around the World Rally Against War in Iraq," Newsday (February 16, 2003), A4-5; New York Times (February 16, 2003), 1, 20-21; "Student Groups Plan Walkout to Protest War," New York Times (March 1, 2003), A10; "Protest Puts Pink Blush around the White House," Newsday (March 9, 2003), A4; "Tens of Thousands March against Iraq War," New York Times (March 16, 2003), 15; Chatfield, "American Insecurity," 495-498.

41. "Nationwide, Peace Rallies continue, non-violently," New York Times (March 22, 2003), B9; March 23, 2003, B11; "Taking It to the Streets," Newsday (March 28, 2003), A4-5; "Demonstrators Demand U.S. Withdraw Troops from Iraq," New York Times (October 26, 2003), 18; "FBI Scrutinizes Anti-war Rallies," http://aolsvc.news.aol.com (cited November 23, 2003); Jerry Lembecke, The Spitting Image, Myth, Memory

and the Legacy of Vietnam (New York: New York University Press, 1998); Ron Briley, "The Vietnam War and Modern Memory," http://htm.us/articles (cited August 21, 2007).

42. Newsday, January 22, 2004, A7; March 17, 2004, A48; "From Midtown to Madrid, Tens of Thousands Peacefully Protest War in Iraq," New York Times (March 21, 2004), 27; "Nice and Easy," Newsday (August 30, 2004), W3-W-4; "Anti-war Group's Tactics: Stealth and Pink Lingerie," New York Times (September 4, 2004), p. 2; "Anti-war Rallies Staged in Washington and other Cities," New York Times (September 25, 2005), 26; David Johnson, "Dozens Are Arrested in Anti-war Protest Near the Capitol," New York Times (September 16, 2007), 21; Matthew Chayes, "Rain can't stop anti-war march," Newsday (October 28, 2007), A32; John Mueller, "the Iraq Syndrome," Foreign Affairs 84 (November/December, 2005), 44-54.

43. "A Court date for grannies," Newsday (November 16, 2005), A34; "Demonstrations Mark Third Anniversary of Iraq Invasion," New York Times (March 19, 2006), 31; Stephen Biddle, "Seeing Baghdad, thinking Saigon," Foreign Affairs 85 (March/April 2006), 2-14; Johnson, The Sorrows of Empire, 45-68.

44. "Bush Begins Day-to-Day Push to Defend Iraq War," http://aolsvc.news.aol.com (cited August 20, 2005); "Sheehan Arrested during Protest," http://cnn.netscape.cnn.com/news (cited September 26, 2005); "Peace Mom's Still Campaigning Against War," http://aolsvc.news.aol.com/news (cited March 6, 2006); "Mom's rally raises tensions," Newsday (August 17, 2005), . A26; "A Mom's protest spreads," Newsday (August 18, 2005), A22; "Sheehan arrested during war protest," Newsday (September 27, 2005), A22. See also, Ibrahim M. Oweiss, "Why did the United States Fail in its War on Iraq?," Washington Report on Middle East Affairs 26 (May/June 2007), 34-35; Chatfield, "American Insecurity," 496-499.

45. Peace Action was an activist group born in 1987 out of a merger of two noted organizations, SANE and the Nuclear Weapons Freeze Campaign, which mobilized peace and justice groups behind a program promoting human rights and closer cooperation with the world community to reduce the threat of wars and weapons of mass destruction. Polling Report.Com, http://www.pollingreport.com/Iraq.htm (August 21, 2007); National Priorities Project, http://nationalpriorities.org (August 21, 2007); Tina Marie Macias, "Dems: Hidden costs of wars to balloon," Newsday (November 14, 2007), A26; Dean Baker, "The cost of the war is hurting our economy," Newsday (February 10, 2008), A43.

46. Consult Erik Saar and Viveca Novak, Inside the Wire: A Military Soldier's Eyewitness Account of Life at Guantanamo (New York: Penguin Books, 2005), 15-25, passim; Alfred W. McCoy, A Question of Torture: CIA Interrogation from the Cold War to the War on Terror (New York: Metropolitan Books, 2006), passim; and Clive Stafford Smith, Eight O'Clock Ferry to the Windward Side: Seeking Justice in Guantanamo Bay (New York: Nation Books, 2007), 67-89 and passim.

47. Victoria Carty & Jake Onyett, "Protest, Cyberactivism, and New Social Movements: The Reemergence of the Peace Movement Post 9/11," unpublished paper, Peace History Conference, November 4, 2005, Winthrop University, 23; Jennifer Lee, "How Protestors Mobilized so Many and so Nimbly," New York Times (2003), photocopy in author's possession.

48. Carty & Onyett, "Protest, Cyberactivism and New Social movements," 24-25.

49. Ibid., p. 27; Chatfield, "American Insecurity," 497-500.

50. Ibid., p. 33; Lee, "How Protestors Mobilized," copy in author's possession.

51. Epstein, "Notes on the Anti-war Movement," p. 1. On August 21, 2007 the Pentagon announced that it was destroying a database, TALENT, which for the years 2003 to 2006 collected private information on protestors and peace groups. This secret program was widely criticized after it became public knowledge and was reminiscent of the covert programs the government conducted during the Vietnam War.

52. Ibid., 8-9.

53. Ibid., 9.

CONCLUSION

1. Some years ago the noted sociologist Quincy Wright, when discussing the concept of peace, observed: "The negative idea has... often frustrated realization of...a positive peace. Peace propaganda has frequently in timeof crisis urged particular groups to isolate themselves from areas of contention in order to avoid war and has thereby disintegrated the international community and assured the initiation and subsequent spread of war. In an interdependent world, propagandas of isolationism, neutrality, and absolute pacifism, however honestly pursued in the name of peace, have been causes of war." See, A Study of War (Chicago: University of Chicago Press, 1964), 266.

2. Sharon Wigutoff & Sergui Herscovici, "The Treatment of Militarism in History Textbooks," Interracial Books for Children XIII (nos. 6 & 7), 15-17; Nigel Young, "Why Peace Movements Fail: An Historical and Social Overview," Social Alternatives 4 No. 1 (1984), 11-14. Young argues that peace movements are reactionary in nature because they are always preparing for the next war. His analysis only deals with war and militarism, not other aspects that our book takes into account. He points out that there are six characteristics involved in describing peace movements: (1) ambiguity; (2) a cyclical nature; (3) diffuse general programs successful in mobilizing the mass but having little political impact; (4) group incorporation that leads to a ritualistic protest; (5) harassment and repression of peace activism by entrenched institutions such as the government in power; and (6) a feeling of impotence or paralysis. Relying on a reactionary thesis Young can be challenged based on the historical record in the United States. There are numerous examples where the peace movement has taken the initiative such as halting territorial ambitions for annexing parts of Canada during the War of 1812, condemning slavery and the lynching of blacks, employing nonviolent strategies in the modern civil rights movement in order to turn the tide of segregation, successfully organizing grassroots campaigns to quickly assist refugees fleeing death squads and paramilitary forces in authoritarian countries like El Salvador, and sponsoring divestment campaigns on college campuses to help bring down the pernicious policy of apartheid in South Africa.

3. DeBenedetti, The Peace Reform, 199-200; Merle Curti to Charles F. Howlett, April 8, 1982. In this letter to the author, Curti stated in part: "To neglect American glorification of war heroes and generally enthusiastic

acceptance of wars once we were engaged in them, poses a problem which I [did not] meet clearly and cogently. In other words, my own sympathy with pacifism made me insufficiently critical of its limitation in [the] face [of] probably much stronger emotional thrusts and the existing realities in the power structure. This doesn't mean at all that I think it wasn't important for historians to work on the peace movement, only that it should be set more in the context of what opposed it, with more emphasis on that, than I managed to do. Still, someone had to make a beginning. . . ." ; Carlton J.H. Hayes, Nationalism: A Religion (New York: Macmillan Co., 1960), 172-3; David Potter, "The Historian's Use of Nationalism and Vice Versa," in Don E. Fehrenbacher, ed., History and American Society: Essays of David M. Potter (New York: Oxford University Press, 1973), 61-108; Boyd Shafer, The Faces of Nationalism (New York: Harcourt, Brace & Jovanovich, 1972), passim; Merle Curti, The Roots of American Loyalty (New York: Athenaeum, 1968), passim.. A recently declassified document, moreover, revealed that FBI director J. Edgar Hoover had a plan to suspend habeas corpus and imprison over 12,000 American citizens suspected of disloyalty only 12 days after the Korean War started. The need to promote patriotic loyalty led Hoover to request President Truman to permit the mass arrests "to protect the country against treason, espionage and sabotage." The proposal was rejected despite Hoover's plea to "apprehend all individuals potentially dangerous" to the national security of the United States. See Tim Weiner, "A 1950 Plan: Arrest 12,000 And Suspend Due Process," New York Times (December 23, 2007), 40.

4. David S. Patterson, " A Historical View of American Security," Peace & Change VII, No. 4 (Fall 1981), 7-14.

5. Chatfield, The American Peace Movement, . 180-82. For a brief analysis on the historic composition and makeup of the American peace movement consult, Howlett and Zeitzer, The American Peace Movement, 39-41.

6. David Callahan, "Marching Forward," New York Times (March 23, 2003), A11.

ADDENDUM

THE DISCIPLINE AND THE PEACE HISTORY SOCIETY

DISCIPLINE OF PEACE HISTORY

What is peace history? It is defined as the historical study of non-violence efforts for peace and justice. Peace history has become widely recognized and accepted as a subfield of the discipline of history, and as part of a larger multidisciplinary approach known as Peace Studies. Peace historians generally see themselves as engaged scholars, involved in the study of peace and war and in efforts to eliminate or at least restrict armaments, conscription, nuclear proliferation, colonialism, racism, sexism, and, of course, war. The work of peace historians presents alternatives to the policies they oppose.

The discipline's basic focus has been historical analysis of peace and anti-war movements and individuals, international relations, and the causes of war and peace. The origins of the study of modern peace history were the result of two important developments in professional scholarship. One was the rapid expansion toward increased specialization overtaking the historical professional associated with significant social forces like the civil rights and feminist movements that impacted American life and the country's historical receptiveness. The other was the mid-1950s peace research movement that applied social scientific techniques in an effort to resolve the problem of global warfare.

Although Cold War consensus mitigated the professional historians' reception to peace history during its initial stages things picked up quickly in the early 1960s. After 1965, in particular, inspired by peace consciousness on campus, the efforts of reputable historians within professional organizations, a growing number of mature historians disillusioned with the war in Vietnam, and newer scholars receiving their doctorates and influenced by New Left ideas began legitimizing the field of peace history as a professional endeavor. Peace history proliferated rapidly from the Vietnam War to the 1980s. Along with this development was the creation of an organization composed of historians interested in the study of peace.

PEACE HISTORY SOCIETY

The predecessor to the Peace History Society (PHS) – Committee on Peace Research in History – was established in 1964 to coordinate national and international scholarly work related to matters involving the conditions and causes of war and peace. PHS has since emerged as one of the foremost professional groups devoted to examining and understanding peace movements and peace cultures. Membership is drawn from around the world. Composed of practicing historians and independent scholars, PHS is an organization designed to make peace research relevant to the scholarly disciplines, nongovernmental organizations, government policymakers, and the global society at large.

In December 1963, at the annual meeting of the American Historical Association (AHA) in Philadelphia, Pulitzer Prize-winning historian and author of the first scholarly history of the American peace movement, *Peace or War: The American Struggle, 1636-1936*, Merle Curti of the University of Wisconsin joined forces with Edwin Bronner of Haverford College to post a call for an ad hoc meeting of historians interested in peace research and peace scholarship. According to Curti, many members at the AHA meeting were moved by the noted University of Michigan economist and peace researcher Kenneth Boulding's challenging statement that historians had been more interested in glorifying war than in exploring the problems of how to prevent it. Some forty people turned up at the gathering at the Race Street Meeting House in Philadelphia interested in how scholarly studies might help promote a greater understanding of the problems of war and peace.

Reeling from the aftermath of the assassination of President John F. Kennedy, the near nuclear collision with the Soviet Union over missile placements in Cuba, and the impending military conflict in Vietnam, the historians who gathered for this meeting quickly realized that little disciplinary efforts had been made to examine the role of peace movements in the past. A committee was established consisting of the following historians: Charles Barker of Johns Hopkins University, Edwin Bronner, Hilary Conroy of the University of Pennsylvania, Merle Curti (who later would become president of the group), Roderick Davison of George Washington University, Staughton Lynd of Spellman (who by this time was known for his civil rights activism), Arthur A. Ekirch of American University (a Conscientious Objector during World War II and author of the popular work, *Decline of American Liberalism*), William Neumann of Goucher College (also a World War II Conscientious Objector), Bradford Perkins of the University of Michigan, Theodore Roszak of California State University at Hayward, Quaker historian Frederick Tolles of Swarthmore College, and the chairman, former Curti doctoral student Arthur I. Waskow of the Institute for Policy Studies.

The group members adopted the name of the Committee on Peace Research in History, with the objective of educating the public about the importance of peace scholarship. In June 1964, the Committee issued a call to other historians to join its efforts to encourage research on the history of war, peace, violence and conflict in order to clarify and examine the causes of international peace and difficulties encountered when trying to create it.

In 1966, the Committee officially became affiliated with the AHA and adopted the name of Conference on Peace Research in History (CPRH). CPRH's establishment encouraged historians to undertake a systematic and collaborative study of America's historic alternations between violence and reconciliation and explore movements concerned with the cause of peace and its connection to social justice. Although its initial focus was on American issues, the organization's bylaws were much broader in scope and encouraged historians in all fields to participate: "The Conference seeks to communicate its findings to the public at large in the hope of broadening the understanding and possibilities of world peace." In 1986, as the organization grew in numbers and importance, its name was changed to the Council on Peace Research in History. In 1994, members voted to adopt its present name to reflect its current composition: the Peace History Society.

Organizationally, PHS has executive officers consisting of the President, Vice President, Executive Secretary and Treasurer. There are two separate boards: the North American Board comprised of some thirteen members from the United States, Canada, and Mexico; and the International Board, with eleven members who hail mostly from Europe (this board also has two American representatives). At present, there are approximately four hundred members. Most members are from the United States and almost all are scholars and teachers of history; a considerable number teach American history, but there are many who also teach outside of the U.S. field. The organization is an affiliated society of the AHA and has joined the National Coordinating Committee for the Promotion of History, the International Peace Research Association, and the International Congress of Historical Sciences. PHS is also recognized as a significant nongovernmental organization by the United Nations. Some members of the organization, in particular Larry Wittner, have testified before U.S. Congressional Committees on matters of disarmament, peace, and social justice.

Peace history can be properly classified into three categories. The first is *conflict management*, which involves efforts to achieve peace through negotiation, mediation, arbitration, international law, and arms control and disarmament. The second is *social reform*, which involves movements that sought to change political and economic structures and traditional ways of thinking. The third is a *world order transformation*, which incorporates attempts to create world federation, better economic and environmental relationships, and a common feeling of security. The latter two also take into account peace/anti-war campaigns. A considerable portion of the scholarly work has been devoted to a historical analysis of peace and anti-war movements and individuals, international relations, including diplomatic studies, and causes of war and solutions for peace.

Since its inception PHS has organized peace research panels for scholarly bodies such as the AHA, Organization of American Historians, Society for Historians of American Foreign Relations, the International Peace Research Association, and the Berkshire Conference of Women Historians. In addition, as part of its educational mission, PHS has distributed papers on special topics to libraries and governmental agencies, compiled lists of relevant research in progress, and published important works documenting international activism for world peace. Some of its most impressive publication endeavors are the "Garland Library of War and Peace," edited by Charles Chatfield, Blanche W. Cook, and Sandi Cooper; the *Biographical Dictionary of Modern Peace Leaders* (1985), under the general editorship of Harold Josephson; *Peace Heroes in Twentieth Century America* (1986), edited by the late Charles DeBenedetti; the *Syracuse Studies on Peace and Conflict Resolution* edited by Harriet Hyman Alonso, Charles Chatfield, and Louis Kriesberg, and *Give Peace a Chance: Exploring the Vietnam Anti-war Movement* (1992), which grew out of a memorial conference in honor of DeBenedetti and was edited by Melvin Small and William D. Hoover.

One of the Society's most important contributions to peace education and peace research in history has been the sponsorship of major conferences of its own and in collaboration with other organizations. In recent years, PHS has been responsible for conferences such as "Peace and War Issues: Gender, Race, Identity, and Citizenship" (1997), "Politics of Peace Movements: From Non-violence to Social Justice" (2000), "Peace Work: The Labor of Peace Activism Past, Present, and Future" (2003), "Peace Activism and Scholarship: Historical Perspectives on Social, Economic and Political Change" (2005), and "Historical Perspectives on Engendering War, Peace, and Justice" (2007). The Society has also been instrumental in organizing panels for international conferences like the

Hague Appeal for Peace in 1999 and the International Congress of Historical Sciences in Oslo in 2000. PHS scholars, moreover, have presented their research at the International Peace Research Association meetings in Malta (1994), Brisbane, Australia (1996), Durban, South Africa (1998), and Tampere, Finland (2000). More conference information is located at the PHS website noted below.

PHS continues to educate the public regarding the latest trends in peace history scholarship through its own journal, which first appeared in 1972. *Peace & Change: A Journal of Peace Research*, published quarterly, is a refereed periodical offering scholarly and interpretative articles on topics related to peace movements, conflict resolution, peace education, non-violence and pacifism, internationalism, and race and gender issues. The periodical's title reflects the organization's belief that peace is more than the absence of war. Carrying on the tradition established by the emergence of the "modern" peace movement after World War I, peace historians are convinced that the process of peace must be built upon a just and equal society. Efforts at building a safer world through the eradication of racism, gender inequality, economic oppression, and environmental hazards have become part of the journal's blueprint.

Throughout its existence the journal has been served by some of the leading historians in the field of peace research. The journal's first coeditor was Bernice Carroll. She was followed by others who included prize-winning historians like Charles Chatfield, the late Charles DeBenedetti, and Lawrence Wittner as well as Robert Schulzinger, a recognized diplomatic historian, the late Scott Bills, Don Birn, Linda Forcey, Mitchell K. Hall, and Kathleen Kennedy. The current editor and co-author of this volume is Robbie Lieberman of Southern Illinois University.

The journal continues to publish articles on peacemaking, cross-cultural studies, economic development, the deleterious impact of imperialism on developing states, post-Cold War upheaval, and the crisis in the Middle East. In recent years special issues, based on conference proceedings, have featured forums on the field of peace history, the trajectory of the Vietnam War, peace discourse, dilemmas of industrial development, internment of Japanese Americans during World War II, and the debate over world federalism. The tremendous body of published works since the Vietnam War is indicative of the influence the field of peace history and its representative organization, PHS, has had within the profession. The Society's web site is: www.peacehistorysociety.org.

BIBLIOGRAPHIC ESSAY

For quite some time the vicissitudes of peace history writing followed the general currents of American historiography. Much like the early participants in the American experience lived the history about which they wrote, so pacifists themselves did the lion's share of early peace writing. John Woolman's Journal, Elihu Burritt's "Letters," William Ladd's "Essay on a Congress of Nations," and Benjamin Trueblood's The Federation of the World, for instance, described their times and their hopes for a warless world and just society.

Attempts at scholarly peace history writing were undertaken after World War I, and were largely the result of the efforts of Merle Curti. Between 1929 and 1937, influenced by progressive historical scholarship and Columbia University historian James Harvey Robinson's "New History," Curti produced an impressive set of books on American peace work. He published The American Peace Crusade, 1815-1860 in 1929, which was a revised version of his Harvard University dissertation in history. This was followed two years later by Bryan and World Peace, part of the Smith College Studies Series where he was then teaching. His major work in the field, a book receiving high praise from Charles Beard, appeared in 1936 as Peace or War: The American Struggle, 1636-1936. This work carefully detailed the heroic struggle for peace on the part of numerous individuals and organizations while criticizing the peace movement's persistent conservative, middle class orientation. The significance of this work was how Curti interwove the theme of peace as social progress and how peace ideas are not only influenced by the environment but are also capable of encouraging social reform. With this work he became America's pioneer peace historian.

The experiences of two world wars proved sobering to reformers seeking to abolish wars through treaties or isolation. Curti's individual efforts were silenced for awhile as peace history writing lost its momentum. Despite the euphoria surrounding the international spirit of post-World War II with the creation of the United Nations, the realities of power politics, cold war, atomic weapons, and superpower mentalities dampened the spirits of historians attempting to follow in Curti's footsteps. One such historian a student of Curti's at Columbia University, Arthur A. Ekirch, Jr., did produce his own important work in 1956 entitled, The Civilian and the Military: A History of American Antimilitarist Thought.

Following on the heels of mainstream historiography, however, peace history writing was rejuvenated by the ideology of the 1960s. Although peace history writing was scarcely touched by the new methodologies of cliometrics, econometrics, and psychohistory – except for some efforts in the area of conflict resolution – the field was greatly influenced by the movement demanding a more representative history that included women, people of color, the poor, and the less articulate members of American society.

The effort to make peace history writing and scholarship a permanent feature of American historiography started in the 1960s. The Vietnam War proved significant in that opposition to the conflict demanded that pacifism and peace work became as much a part of the scholarship and the college curriculum as had the civil rights movement. Peace activists were now joined by the general public in working to understand better the roots of social justice and a warless world. The result of this dual desire to consider the philosophical foundations of non-violence and its practical political applications for change produced an outpouring of scholarly work and curriculum development.

From the 1960s to the present the discipline of peace history has grown by leaps and bounds. Peace historians seeking to understand and legitimate past movements for peace and social justice, produced numerous monographs about peace movements and biographies of pacifists and other social activists. This effort was accompanied by a spate of monographs surveying the secular and religious peace movements in the United States in the decades between the 1880s and 1960s. The outpouring of scholarly monographs continued throughout the 1970s and 1980s as numerous books studied the anti-Vietnam War movement and efforts for internationalism. By the 1990s new subspecialties were on the horizon as peace historians focused on the role of women in the peace and justice movements, looking for connections between peace and civil rights activism, and exploring the expanding definition of Conscientious Objection. At the same time, historians began opening new frontiers in the field with examinations of Non-governmental organizations, the relationship between political culture and peace movements, and ambitious studies of transnational movements to end the threat of nuclear war.

In today's nuclear world, peace is a far more desirable national policy to adopt. The search for peace and justice has become a necessary reform upon which human existence depends. Based on the outpouring of peace history scholarship readers are being provided not only with the essential tools to understand more clearly the past and to explain the present, but also the necessary ingredients from which citizens can begin the process of using non-violent methods to achieve justice and guarantee the existence of the human race.

The search for peace history, therefore, begins with some outstanding finding aids and broad surveys. Blanche W. Cook's Bibliography on Peace Research in History (Santa Barbara, CA: American Bibliographical Center, 1969) needs updating and in some instances revising, but nevertheless is an excellent starting point. It represents a pioneering effort. In a broader context is the superb compilation of Bernice Carroll. Jane E. Mohraz, and Clinton Fink Peace and War: Guide to Bibliographies (Santa Barbara, CA: ABC-CLIO, 1982). In a more specialized vein, with respect to the American scene, is the craftsman-like unpublished paper by Charles DeBenedetti, "Peace History: In the American Manner," delivered as The Stuart Bernath Memorial Lecture, Washington, D.C., August 1983, and later published in The History Teacher 18 (November 1984), 75-110. An excellent analysis with a foreign policy perspective is Lawrence S. Wittner, "Peace Movements and Foreign Policy: The Challenge to Diplomatic Historians," Diplomatic History XI (Fall 1987), 355-70. Perhaps the most comprehensive analysis of the literature for American peace history is Charles F. Howlett, "Studying America's Struggle Against War: An Historical Perspective," The History Teacher 36 (May 2003), 297-330. The most complete annotated reference work on the American peace movement is Charles F. Howlett, The American Peace Movement: References and Resources (Boston: G.K. Hall & Co., 1991). Scholars can now rely on the commendable "Garland Library of War and Peace" (New York: Garland Publishing, 1971-1976) edited by Blanche Weisen Cook, Charles Chatfield, and Sandi Cooper. It contains over three hundred titles; many of these reprints are cited in this bibliographic essay, along with illuminating introductions that trace the development of peace and war literature from Dante's De Monarchia (1312) to the 1970's. Researchers can also draw upon the Library of World Peace Studies, which was organized and directed by the late Warren F. Kuehl. This library has now reproduced over six hundred volumes of peace and internationalist journals; also the library includes the card catalogue of the Library of Peace Palace at The Hague. A model of its genre that touches many peace related issues is Justus D. Doenecke's pamphlet, The Literature of Isolationism: A Guide to Non-Interventionist Scholarship, 1930-1972 ,(Colorado Springs, CO: Ralph Myles, 1972). Worthy of note also is Richard D. Burns, editor, Guide to American Foreign Relations since 1700 (Santa Barbara: ABC-CLIO, 1983). Chapter 1 on "Reference Aids" is particularly helpful to peace researchers; Chapter 16 treats "Peace, Arbitration, and Internationalist Movements to 1914"; and Chapter 38 deals with "International Organization, Law, and Peace Movements since 1941." All introductions to each chapter comment on past trends as revealed by the literature and offer many useful suggestions for future research. Peace & Change, published by the Peace History Society, is devoted to peace history. Articles on related subjects also appear in American Historical Review, Journal of American History, American Quarterly, Journal of American Studies, Historian, Mid-America, Journal of Conflict

Resolution, World Affairs, Diplomatic History, and Journal of Contemporary History, as well as many political science and religious history journals. These journals, however, are limited in scope and sequence; rarely will one find an article dealing specifically with peace history scholarship.

Because war affects every aspect of social and intellectual life a number of approaches have been developed in recent decades. One such approach is Keith L. Nelson, editor, The Impact of War on American Life: The Twentieth-Century Experience (New York: Holt, Rinehart & Winston, Inc., 1971). Examining the economic, political, social, intellectual and cultural effects of war on American life, Nelson has drawn upon the findings of noted scholars and social critics where analyses merit careful consideration. Two small but nonetheless informative pamphlets are: Peter Brock, The Roots of War Resistance: From the Early Church to Tolstoy (Nyack, NY: F.O.R. Publications, 1981) and Larry Gara, War Resistance in Historical Perspective (New York: War Resisters league, 1980). See also, Charles F. Howlett & Glen Zeitzer, The American Peace Movement: History and Historiography (Washington, D.C.: American Historical Association, 1985). This is a pamphlet published by the AHA for teachers. High School teachers can consult, Charles F. Howlett, "Peace History: The Field and Sources," OAH Magazine of History 8 (Spring 1994), 26-32 and Gerloff Homan, "Peace History: A Bibliographic Overview," Choice (May 1995), 1408-1419. For a very persuasive and scholarly analysis of the role of dissent and organized protest from the Cold War to the present readers are encouraged to read Charles Chatfield, "American Insecurity: Dissent from the 'Long War'" in Andrew Bacevich, ed., The Long War: A New History of U.S. National Security Policy Since World War II (New York: Columbia University Press, 2007), 456-516. In his analysis Chatfield looks at common patterns, motifs of protest, and to what extent were dissent and protest a function of past American traditions.

An annotated bibliography of this nature would not be complete without some mention of the teaching and curriculum guides currently available. Although lacking in scholarly analysis to a certain degree, they are nevertheless helpful in the realm of consciousness raising. One such reference aid is Robert Pickus & Robert Woito, To End War: An Introduction – Ideas, Books, Organizations. Work That Can Help (New York: Harper & Row Publishers, 1970). Burns H. Weston, Sherle R. Schwenninger, & Diane E. Shamis, editors, Peace and World Order Studies: A Curriculum Guide (New York: Institute for World Order, 1978) is an invaluable compilation of teaching strategies geared to political science methodology. Moreover, researchers interested in audio-visual and discography aspects of peace history should consult John Dowling's War/ Peace: Film Guide (Chicago: World Without War Publications, 1980) and R. Serge Densioff's Songs of Protest, War and Peace: A Bibliography and Discography (Santa Barbara: ABC-CLIO, 1973) and Great Day Coming: Folk Music and the American Left (Urbana: University of Illinois Press, 1971). The fall 1982 edition of Teachers College Record, with the theme of "Education for Peace and Disarmament: Toward a Living World," is a collection of essays on peace and disarmament. It is a valuable resource for educators concerned about the future of the earth. More recent works in this vein include the following: David P. Barash, Introduction to Peace Studies (Belmont, CA: Wadsworth Publishing Co., 1991), and his edited collection, Approaches to Peace Studies (New York: Oxford University Press, 1999); Francesca M. Cancian & James William Gibson, eds., Making War/Making Peace: the Social Foundations of Violent Conflict (Belmont, CA: Wadsworth Publishing Co., 1990); Ian M. Harris & Mary Lee Morrison, Peace Education (Jefferson, N.C.: McFarland & Co. Inc., 2nd ed. 2003); George A. Lopez, ed., "Peace Studies: Past and Future," The Annals of the American Academy of Political and Social Science 504 (July 1989); Mike Forrest Keen, ed., "The Pedagogy of Peace," Peace & Change 15 (July 1990); Linda Forcey and Ian Harris, eds., Peacebuilding for Adolescents: Strategies for Educators and Community Leaders (New York: Peter Lang Publishers, 1999); and Aline M. Stomfay-Stitz, Peace Education in America, 1828-1990: Sourcebook for Education and Research (Metuchen, NJ: Scarecrow Press, 1993).

Peace researchers rely on the extraordinary primary and secondary collections gathered at the Swarthmore College Peace Collection (SCPC). Founded in 1930 with the acquisition of a substantial cache from Nobel Prize winner Jane Addams, the SCPC now contains well over 200 Document Groups, 3,000 smaller collections, a large World War I poster collection, a fine array of secondary material, and numerous peace related memorabilia. Included are the papers of such leading pacifists and peace organizations as: Emily Greene Balch, AJ. Muste, Frederick J. Libby, the Fellowship of Reconciliation, the National Council for Prevention of War, the National Service Board for Religious Objectors, the Women's International League for Peace and Freedom, the Friends Committee on National Legislation, War Resisters League, and the National Committee for a Sane Nuclear policy. An out-of-date Guide to the SCPC published in 1947 had made access to the Collection difficult, but another Guide to the Swarthmore College Peace Collection (Swarthmore, PA: Swarthmore College Press, 1981) was completed under the sponsorship of the National Endowment for the Humanities. Other archives, although not devoted entirely to pacifism, contain much relevant material. For example: the Columbia Oral History Collection, the Hoover Library of War and Peace, the Wisconsin Historical Library, the New York Public Library, the Library of Congress, the American Friends Service Committee Archives, the Friends Historical Library at Swarthmore College, Haverford College Quaker Collection, Jane Addams' Hull House, various Presidential Libraries, and special collections in labor and women's history. These archives reveal that pacifism and peace activism are much more than a negative response to war; they are positive efforts to address inequality, environmental issues, the role of science in society, racism, militarism, cooperative group living, and, of course, foreign policy.

The early studies of Merle Curti serve as a valuable passageway to the secondary literature. His American Peace Crusade (Durham, NC: Duke University Press, 1929); Bryan and World Peace (New York: Octagon Books, 1969) (reprint of 1931 edition); and Peace or War: The American Struggle 1636-1936 (New York: W.W. Norton, 1936) has inspired much of recent works. One of

Curti's books, The Learned Blacksmith: The Letters and Journals of Elihu Burritt (New York: J.S. Ozer, 1972) (reprint of the 1937 edition) encouraged Peter Tolis' Elihu Burritt: Crusader for Brotherhood (Hamden, CT: Shoestring Books, 1968). Together, Curti and Tolis have done justice to this important 19th century pacifist. Another early book, A.F.C. Beales' The History of Peace (New York: Dial Press, 1931), is helpful on contemporary issues to that time.

The richness of the new secondary sources is well illustrated by Peter Brock's encyclopedic Pacifism in the United States: From the Colonial Era to the First World War (Princeton, NJ: Princeton University Press, 1968) and his Twentieth Century Pacifism (New York: Van Nostrand, Reinhold, 1970). Charles Chatfield's For Peace and Justice: Pacifism in America, 1914-1941 (Knoxville, TN: University of Tennessee Press, 1971), analyzes pacifism within the context of the two world wars and argues that pacifists were political realists. Lawrence S. Wittner picks up the chronological thread from Chatfield in his Rebels Against War: The American Peace Movement, 1941-1960 (New York: Columbia University Press, 1969). Wittner's study was updated to the year 1983 and republished by Temple University Press, in 1984. Although less comprehensive than Brock (Pacifism in the United States) or Chatfield, Wittner's topical approach touches the most seminal and controversial issues. These books represent an outstanding chronicle of American peace movements from the colonial period to the marches of the 1960's. Charles Chatfield, with Robert Kleidman, The American Peace Movement: Ideals and Activism (New York: Twayne Publishers, 1992) is important for its application of social movement theory to the American peacemaking. A more religious, pacifist survey is the recent overview by James C. Juhnke & Carol M. Hunter, The Missing Peace: The Search for Non-violent Alternatives in United States History (Kitchner, Ontario: Pandora Press, 2001). Arthur A. Ekirch, Jr., Civilian and the Military (New York: Oxford University Press, 1956) remains the standard account of civilian-military relations from the pacifist perspective.

A spate of noted monographs command attention because they expand, complement, or challenge many of the assumptions made in broader surveys. Two especially good studies are: David S. Patterson's Toward a Warless World: The Travail of the American Peace Movement, 1887-1914 (Bloomington, IN: Indiana University Press, 1976); and C. Roland Marchand's The American Peace Movement and Social Reform, 1898-1918 (Princeton: Princeton University Press, 1972). Invaluable for its comprehensive coverage of the Great War is H.C. Peterson and Gilbert File's Opponents of War, 1917-18 (Madison, WI: University of Wisconsin Press, 1957). Radical opposition to World War I can be found in Frederick C. Giffin, Six Who Protested: Radical Opposition to World War I (Port Washington, NY: Kennikat Press, 1977). A more general analysis of war opposition is supplied by Samuel Eliot Morrison, Frederick Merk and Frank Freidel's Dissent in Three American Wars (Cambridge, MA: Harvard University Press, 1970). Reginald C. Stuart's War and American Thought (Kent, OH: Kent State University Press, 1982) traces the founding fathers' view of war as policy and practice, and how they changed as the nation grew. For the Catholic peace movement, see Patricia McNeal's American Catholic Peace Movements, 1928-1972 (New York: Arno, 1978) and Harder than War: Catholic Peacemaking in Twentieth Century America (New Brunswick, NJ: Rutgers University Press, 1992). Ronald G. Musto's The Catholic Peace Tradition (Maryknoll, NY: Orbis Books, 1986) is also worth consulting. Charles DeBenedetti searches for the roots of modern American pacifism and social change in his Origins of the Modern American Peace Movement, 1915-1929 (Millwood, NY: KTO Press, 1978) and his broader approach The Peace Reform in American History (Bloomington: Indiana University Press, 1980). Charles F. Howlett, Brookwood Labor College and the Struggle for Peace and Justice in America (Lewiston, NY: Edwin Mellen Press, 1993) is the only study examining the efforts of interwar pacifists to connect with the labor movement in the campaign for social change and economic justice. A rather bizarre episode which constituted two giant steps backwards for pacifism is explored by Barbara S. Kraft's The Peace Ship: Henry Ford's Pacifist

Adventure in the First World War (New York: Macmillan, 1978). Paul A. Carter's The Decline and Revival of the Social Gospel (Ithaca, NY: Cornell University Press, 1954) is a crucial link because of the significant influence of social gospel thought on many of the American churches that were important to 20th century American peace movements. The numerous legislative attempts between the wars to have the question of war or peace decided by a direct vote of the American people is the subject of Ernest C. Bolt's Ballots Before Bullets: The War Referendum Approach to Peace in America, 1914-1941 (Charlottesville, VA: University of Virginia Press, 1977). Another valuable work addressing the issue of intervention is Justus Doenecke, The Battle Against Intervention, 1939-1941 (Malabar, FL: Krieger Publishing Co., 1997).

Works discussing the issue of Conscientious Objection to war are plentiful. The standard work on the state of Conscientious Objectors during World War II is Mulford Q. Sibley & Philip E. Jacob, Conscription of Conscience: the American State and the Conscientious Objector, 1940-1947 (Ithaca, NY: Cornell University Press, 1952). One of the earliest historical studies on COs and war is Edward Needles Wright, Conscientious Objectors in the Civil War (Philadelphia: University of Pennsylvania Press, 1931). Two other works should be consulted regarding Conscientious Objection: Heather T. Frazer & John O'Sullivan, "We Have Just Begun Not to Fight": An Oral History of Conscientious Objectors in Civilian Public Service During World War II (New York: Twayne Publishers, 1996) and Rachael Waltner Goosen, Women Against the Good War: Conscientious Objection and Gender on the American Home Front, 1941-1947 (Chapel Hill: University of North Carolina Press, 1997). Mennonite opposition to warfare between 1935 and 1975 is the subject of Perry Bush's Two Kingdoms, Two Loyalties: Mennonite Pacifism in Modern America (Baltimore, MD: The Johns Hopkins University Press, 1998).

The best study on the history of the War Resisters League is Scott H. Bennett, Radical Pacifism: The War Resisters League and Gandhian Non-violence in America, 1915-1963 (Syracuse: Syracuse University Press, 2003). His scholarship has also enriched the field with his edited work, Army GI, Pacifist CO:

The World War II Letters of Frank and Albert Dietrich (New York: Fordham University Press, 2005) containing a fifty page archival-based introduction offering a neglected perspective on conscription, pacifism, conscientious objection, and dissent during the "good war" and "'Free American Political Prisoners': Pacifist Activism and Civil Liberties, 1945-1948," Journal of Peace Research 40 (July 2003), 413-433, detailing the three-year campaign by the Committee for Amnesty to obtain amnesty for the 6,000 American COs sentenced to prison for their refusal to participate in World War II as well as win the release of those still imprisoned long after the war ended. An important sociological analysis of neutrality and nuclear disarmament is Robert Kleidman, Organizing for Peace: Neutrality, the Test Ban, and the Freeze (Syracuse: Syracuse University Press, 1993). Scholars interested in issues involving Latin America and the peace movement should refer to Ann Crittenden, Sanctuary: a Story of American Conscience and Law (New York: Weidenfeld & Nicholson, 1988), Van Gosse, Where the Boys Are: Cuba, Cold War America and the Making of the New Left (New York: Verso, 1993) and Christian Smith, Resisting Reagan: The U.S. Central American Peace Movement (Chicago: University of Chicago Press, 1996). An excellent analysis of the interwar debates in Congress regarding isolationism is Robert David Johnson, The Peace Progressives and American Foreign Relations (Cambridge, MA: Harvard University Press, 1995). A very valuable study on free speech and war is Geoffrey R. Stone, Perilous Times: Free Speech in Wartime from the Sedition Act of 1798 to the War on Terrorism (Chicago: University of Chicago Press, 2004). Stone's legal analysis raises many interesting questions. Since little has been done to examine the legal perspectives of opposition to war and the constitutionality of the draft, students are encouraged to consult, Charles F. Howlett, "Case Law Historiography in American Peace History," Peace & Change 22 (January 1997), 49-75. Two useful legal studies of men who were imprisoned because of conscience is that of Stephen M. Kohn, Jailed for Peace: The History of American Draft Law Violators, 1658-1985 (Westport, CT: Praeger, 1986) and American Political Prisoners: Prosecutions under the Espionage and Seditions Acts (Westport, CT, Praeger, 1994).

There are also additional specialized monographs indicating how the field has flourished since the Vietnam War. Three important works covering the antebellum and post-civil War period are Valerie H. Zeigler, The Advocates of Peace in Antebellum America (Bloomington, IN: University of Indiana Press, 1992); Thomas F. Curran, Soldiers of Peace: Civil War Pacifism and the Postwar Radical Peace Movement (New York: Fordham University Press, 2003); and Dan McKanan, Identifying the Image of God: Radical Christians and Non-violent Power in the Antebellum United States (New York: Oxford University Press, 2002). An important study examining the role communists played in the peace movement and how they were excluded other organizations is Robbie Lieberman, The Strangest Dream: Communism, Anticommunism, and the U.S. Peace Movement, 1945-1963 (Syracuse: Syracuse University Press, 2000). A very interesting take on culture and peace, one involving the role of the media, is Matthew Lasar, Pacifica Radio: the Rise of an Alternative Network (Philadelphia: Temple University Press, 2000). The issue of civil defense is the subject of Dee Garrison's Bracing for Armageddon: Why Civil Defense Never Worked (New York: Oxford University Press, 2006). On the matter of social injustice and lynching one should read Jacqueline Goldsby's A Spectacular Secret: Lynching in American Life and Literature (Chicago, IL: University of Chicago Press, 2006). One of the more recent, challenging works describing how women worked within traditionally male-dominated peace organizations in an effort to construct a new paradigm of political and social change is Marian Mollin, Radical Pacifism in Modern America (Philadelphia: University of Pennsylvania Press, 2006). A new look, though at the role of civil-military relations, though less satisfactory, is Thomas S. Langston, Uneasy Balance: Civil-Military Relations in Peacetime America Since 1783 (Baltimore, MD: The Johns Hopkins University Press, 2003). There are several solid studies on peace and civil rights which should be consulted: Gerald Horne, Communist Front? The Civil Rights Congress, 1946-1956 (Rutherford, N.J.: Farleigh Dickinson University Press, 1987), Penny von Eschen, Race against Empire: Black Americans and Anticolonialism, 1937-1957 (Ithaca, NY: Cornell University Press, 1997), Michael B. Friedland, Lift

Up Your Voice Like a Trumpet: White Clergy and the Civil Rights and Anti-war Movements, 1954-1973 (Chapel Hill: University of North Carolina Press, 1998), and Simon Hall, Peace and Freedom: The Civil Rights and Anti-War Movements in the 1960s (Philadelphia: University of Pennsylvania Press, 2006). A very sound and well-written work describing the evolution of non-violent direct action is James Tracy, Direct Action: Radical Pacifism from the Union Eight to the Chicago Seven (Chicago: University of Chicago Press, 1996). For a thorough analysis of the crisis at Kent State readers should consult, Scott Bills, Kent State/May 4: Echoes Through a Decade (Kent, OH: Kent State University Press, 1988). The role of liberal internationalists and pacifists in dealing with containment in the early Cold War years is the subject of E. Timothy Smith, Opposition beyond the Water's Edge: Liberal Internationalists, Pacifists, and Containment, 1945-1953 (Westport, CT.: Greenwood Press, 1999). The role of American internationalists with respect to the League of Nations is discussed in Warren F. Kuehl and Lynne K. Dunn, Keeping the Covenant: American Internationalists and the League of Nations (Kent, OH: Kent State University Press, 1997). For examinations on the role of African Americans and foreign policy concerns consult Brenda Gayle Plummer, Rising Wind: Black Americans and U.S. Foreign Affairs, 1935-1960 (Chapel Hill: University of North Carolina Press, 1996) and Carol Anderson, Eyes off the Prize: The UN and the African Americans Struggle for Human Rights, 1944-1955 (New York: Cambridge University Press, 2003). In the field of war literature Philip Metres' Behind the Lines: War Resistance Poetry on the American Homefront since 1941 (Iowa City: University of Iowa Press, 2007) is a valuable work. The author's unique thesis is that war resistance poetry represents a largely unexamined body of literature that stands at the epicenter of numerous dissident political movements. What the author has done is place the literature within the context of historical examination and how poems serve as a passageway to uncovering political dissent during war time. Another valuable study is Michael True, An Energy Field More Intense than War: The Nonviolent Tradition and American Literature (Syracuse: Syracuse University Press, 1995).

The anti-Vietnam War period has seen its share of scholarly productivity. Robert Cooney & Helen Michalowski, eds., The Power of the People: Active Nonviolence in the United States (Culver City, CA: People Press, 1977) contains good information on social protest movements and the role of peacemaking in American history with an emphasis on the post World War II and Vietnam periods. One of the best studies regarding the role of protest during the war is Terry H. Anderson, The Movement and the Sixties: Protest in America from Greensboro to Wounded Knee (New York: Oxford University Press, 1995). Scholars should also consult James J. Farrell, The Spirit of the Sixties: The Making of Postwar Radicalism (New York: Routledge, 1997). One of the most popular works on the war is George C. Herring's America's Longest War: The United States and Vietnam, 1950-1975 (New York: McGraw-Hill, 3rd ed., 1996). Perhaps the authoritative work on the coalitions of anti-war groups is Charles DeBenedetti, with the assistance of Charles Chatfield, An American Ordeal: the Anti-war Movement of the Vietnam Era (Syracuse: Syracuse University Press, 1990). For a comprehensive look at the draft and its impact see Michael S. Foley, Confronting the War Machine: Draft Resistance during the Vietnam War (Chapel Hill: University of North Carolina Press, 2003). Some of the popular works covering the war and opposition to it are the following: Tom Wells, The War Within: America's Battle over Vietnam (Berkeley: University of California Press, 1994); Nancy Zaroulis & Gerald Sullivan, Who Spoke Up? American Protest Against the War in Vietnam, 1963-1975 (New York: Holt, Rinehart & Winston, 1984); Melvin Small, Antiwarriors: the Vietnam War and the Battle for America's Hearts and Minds (Wilmington, DE.: Scholarly Resources, 2002); Melvin Small & William D. Hoover, eds., Give Peace a Chance: Exploring the Vietnam Antiwar Movement (Syracuse: Syracuse University Press, 1992); Andrew E. Hunt, The Turning: A History of Vietnam Veterans Against the War (New York: New York University Press, 1999); Richard Moser, The New Winter Soldiers: GI and Veteran Dissent During the Vietnam Era (New Brunswick, NJ: Rutgers University Press, 1996). Two works critical of the peace movement because of its radical posture are: Guenter Lewy, Peace and Revolution: the Moral Crisis of American Pacifism

(Grand Rapids, MI: William B. Erdmann Publishing Co., 1998) and Adam Garfinkle, Telltale Hearts: the Origins and Impact of the Vietnam Anti-war Movement (New York: St. Martin's Press, 1995). For the religious opposition to the war consult Mitchell K. Hall, Because of their Faith: CALCAV and Religious Opposition to the War in Vietnam (New York: Columbia University Press, 2005). The Latino/a perspective on the Vietnam War are the subject of Lorena Oropeza's Raze Si! Guerra No! Chicano Protest and Patriotism During the Viet Nam War Era (Berkeley:University of California Press, 2005). For insiders' accounts consult Fred Halstead, Out Now!: A Participant's Account of the American Movement Against the Vietnam War (New York: Monad Press, 1978) and Bradford Lyttle, The Chicago Anti-Vietnam War Movement (Chicago: Midwest Pacifist Center, 1988). See also, Penelope Moon, "'We Have Got to Lead Them in the Ways of Peace': The Catholic Peace Fellowship in the Vietnam Era" (Ph.D. diss., Arizona State, 2001).

Works examining the sixties radicalism include Todd Gitlin, The Sixties: Years of Hope, Days of Rage (New York: Bantam Books, 1987), Lyman T. Sargent, New Left Thought: An Introduction (Homewood, IL.: Dorsey Press, 1972) Wini Breines, Community and Organization in the New Left, 1962-1968 (New Brunswick, N.J.: Rutgers University Press, 1989), Maurice Isserman, If I had a Hammer: the Death of the Old Left and the Birth of the New Left (New York: Basic Books, 1987); Robbie Lieberman, "Prairie Power": Voices of the 1960s Midwestern Student Protest (Columbia: University of Missouri Press, 2004); Kenneth J. Heineman, Put Your Bodies upon the Wheels: Student Revolt in the 1960s (Chicago, IL: Ivan Dee, 2001); Gael Graham, Young Activists: American High School Students in the Age of Protest (DeKalb, IL.: Northern Illinois University Press, 2006); Doug Rossinow, The Politics of Authenticity: Liberalism, Christianity and the New Left in America (New York: Columbia University Press, 1999); and Jeremy Varon, Bringing the War Home: The Weather Underground, the Red Army Faction and Revolutionary Violence in the Sixties and Seventies (Berkeley: University of California Press, 2004). An important work dealing with the poor is

Jennifer Frost, "An Interracial Movement of the Poor": Community Organizing and the New Left in the 1960s (New York: New York University Press, 2001).

One of the more important developments in the field of peace history literature has been that of describing the contributions of female peace activists. A very important survey is Harriet H. Alonso's Peace as a Women's Issue: A History of the U.S. Movement for World Peace and Women's Rights (Syracuse: Syracuse University Press, 1993). The 1960's Women Strike for Peace organization is the subject of Amy Swerdlow's, Women Strike for Peace: Traditional Motherhood and Radical Politics in the 1960s (Chicago: University of Chicago Press, 1993). It remains the only study of WSP and helped pave the way for other works on women and peace reform. There are a number of sound works on the Women's International League for Peace and Freedom: Linda Schott, Reconstructing Women's Thoughts: The Women's International League for Peace and Freedom Before World War II (Stanford, CA: Stanford University Press, 1997) takes an in-depth look at the ideological premise behind feminist peace work; Carrie A. Foster, The Women and the Warriors: the U.S. Section of the Women's International League for Peace and Freedom, 1915-1946 (Syracuse: Syracuse University Press, 1995); Joyce Blackwell's No Peace without Freedom: Race and the Women's International League for Peace and Freedom, 1915-1975 (Carbondale: Southern Illinois University Press, 2004); and Gertrude Bussey and Margaret Tims, Women's International League for Peace and Freedom, 1915-1965: A Record of fifty Years' Work (London: Allen & Unwin, 1965). Examining the historical roots and later contributions of WILPF, including many of its notable figures, is the subject of Patricia Ward D'Itri's Cross Currents in the International Women's Movement, 1848-1948 (Bowling Green, OH: Bowling Green State University Popular Press, 1999). Three very exciting studies involving the role of women during and after World War I are: Frances H. Early, A World Without War: How U.S. Feminists and Pacifists Resister World War I (Syracuse: Syracuse University Press, 1997); Kathleen Kennedy, Disloyal Mothers and Scurrilous Citizens: Women and Subversion During World War I (Bloomington, IN: Indiana University Press, 1999);

and Harriet Alonso, The Women's Peace Union and the Outlawry of War (Knoxville: University of Tennessee Press, 1989).

Since pacifists are usually internationalists and not isolationists, the theme of world cooperation permeates peace history. The emergence of the United States as a world power following the Spanish-American War is the period covered by Sondra R. Herman's extremely well- done and scholarly book Eleven Against War: Studies in American Internationalist Thought, 1898-1921 (Stanford, CA: Hoover Institution Press, 1969). Robert Beisner's Twelve Against Empire: The Anti-Imperialists, 1898-1900 (New York: McGraw-Hill, 1968) is also somewhat helpful. Another essential study is Warren F. Kuehl's Seeking World Order: The United States and International Organization to 1920 (Nashville TN: Vanderbilt University Press, 1969). Two international conferences to end war are well chronicled in Calvin C. Davis' The United States and the First Hague Conference of 1899 (Ithaca: Cornell University Press, 1962), and his follow-up study The United States and the Second Hague Conference: American Diplomacy and International Organization. 1899-1914 (Durham, NC: Duke University Press, 1976). A nice historical overview of the period is John Whiteclay Chambers II, The Eagle and the Dove: The American Peace Movement and United States Foreign Policy, 1900-1922 (Syracuse: Syracuse University Press, 1991). Robert H. Ferrell describes the euphoria surrounding the international agreement to outlaw war that gave pacifism a black eye in his Peace in Their Time: The Origins of the Kellogg-Briand Pact (New Haven, CT: Yale University Press, 1952). John F. Greco "A Foundation for Internationalism: The Carnegie Endowment for International Peace, 1931-1941" (Unpublished diss., Syracuse University, 1971), and Michael A. Lutzker "The Formation of the Carnegie Endowment for International Peace: A Study of the Establishment -Centered Peace Movement, 1910-1914" in Jerry Israel, editor, Building the Organizational Society (New York: Free Press, 1972) provide solid accounts of the peace organization. Additional studies on internationalism are found in Joseph Preston Baratta's two volume work, The Politics of World Federation (Westport, CT: Praeger 2004).

The isolationist perspective and the role of peace organizations is the subject of Justus D. Doenecke's informative "Non-Intervention of the Left: 'The Keep America Out of the War Congress', 1938-41," Journal of Contemporary History, 12, no. 2 (April 1977), 221-31. Another important publication by Doenecke is Storm on the Horizon: the Challenge to American Intervention, 1939-1941(New York: Rowan & Littlefield, 2000). The definitive study of the World War II period is Robert Devine's Second Chance: The Triumph of Internationalism in America During World War II (New York: Athenaeum, 1967). It should be noted, however, that most pacifists opposed or at least very reluctantly supported the United Nations because they saw such features as the Security Council Veto power as being the introduction of power politics into international organization.

Researchers have begun to turn their attention to leading pacifists. Jane Addams, of course, has received prominent attention. Her pacifism is still best described by an early biography written by her nephew James Weber Linn, Jane Addams: A Biography (New York: D. Appleton Century, 1937). A renaissance of interest in Addams was spurred by Jill Conway's fine article "Jane Addams: An American Heroine," in The Woman in America edited by Robert Jay Lifton (Boston: Beacon Press, 1964). This was followed by: John C. Farrell's Beloved Lady: A History of Jane Addams' Ideas on Reform and Peace (Baltimore: The John Hopkins University Press, 1967); Daniel Levine's Jane Addams and the Liberal Tradition (Madison: Wisconsin Historical Society Press, 1971); and Allen F. Davis's popular American Heroine: The Life and Legend of Jane Addams (New York: Oxford University Press, 1974). The most recent scholarly book is that by Louise W. Knight, Citizen: Jane Addams and the Struggle for Democracy (Chicago: University of Chicago Press, 2005). The development of her personality has been perceptively analyzed in Dominick Cavallo's "The Sexual Politics of Social Reform: Jane Addams from Childhood to Hull House" in New Directions in Psychohistory edited by Mel Albin (Lexington, MA: D.C. Heath, 1980). For the influential pacifist leader of the Women's International League for Peace and Freedom, Emily Greene Balch, we have only a starting point in Mercedes M. Randall's Improper Bostonian: Emily Greene Balch (New York: Twayne, 1964). Margaret Hope Beacon's One Woman's Passion for Peace and Freedom: the Life of Mildred Scott Olmstead (Syracuse: Syracuse University Press, 2003), is a thorough discussion of one of WILPF's most influential leaders; Pacifist-socialist Norman Thomas has been the subject of several studies. The most rewarding biography is Bernard Johnpoll's Pacifist Progress: Norman Thomas and the Decline of American Socialism (Chicago: Quadrangle, 1970). The Journal of Presbyterian History (52. 1, Spring 1974) contains James C. Duram's informative article "In Defense of Conscience: Norman Thomas as an Exponent of Christian Pacifism During World War I." Two leading exponents of the de-legalization of the war system in the 1920's, William E. Borah and Salmon O. Levinson, are the subject of two authoritative biographical sketches: John E. Stoner's S. O. Levinson and the Pact of Paris (Chicago: University of Chicago Press, 1943) and John C. Vinson's William E. Borah and the Outlawry of War (Athens, GA: University of Georgia Press, 1957). For John Dewey's significant role, see Charles F. Howlett's Troubled Philosopher: John Dewey and the Struggle for World Peace (Port Washington, NY: Kennikat Press, 1977). Although not a pacifist, James T. Shotwell was very influential in the internationalist movement for many years. Interested readers should consult the following: Charles DeBenedetti "American Internationalism in the 1920's: Shotwell and the Outlawrists" (Unpublished diss., University of Illinois, 1969); Harold Josephson's comprehensive work, James T. Shotwell and the Rise of Internationalism in America (Rutherford, NJ: Fairleigh Dickinson University Press, 1975); Albert Marrin's Nicholas Murray Butler (Boston: Twayne Publishers, 1976); and the more critical examination by Michael Rosenthal, Nicholas Miraculous: the Amazing Career of the Redoubtable Dr. Nicholas Murray Butler (New York: Farrar, Straus & Giroux, 2005). The recent work of Robert I. Rotberg, A Leadership for Peace: How Edwin Ginn Tried to Change the World (Stanford, CA.: Stanford University Press, 2006) represents a conventional biography of one dedicated peace organization leader. America's most influential 20th Century pacifist, A.J. Muste, has been the subject of a dissertation, William G. Batz's "Revolution and Peace: The Christian Pacifism of A.J. Muste (1885-1967)" (Unpublished diss., University of Minnesota, 1974) and a superb book, Jo Ann O. Robinson's Abraham Went Out: A Biography of A.J. Muste (Philadelphia: Temple University Press, 1982) that have added substantially to Nat Hentoff's Peace Agitator: The Story of A. J. Muste (New York: Macmillan, 1963). Robert Moats Miller's article, "The Attitudes of the Major

Protestant Churches in America Toward War and Peace, 1919-1929," The Historian (19, November 1956) is extremely important. So, too, is his How Shall They Hear Without a Preacher? The Life of Ernest Tittle (Chapel Hill: University of North Carolina Press, 1977). It is a model of biographical history. In the same vein it is worthwhile to read Warren Goldstein's William Sloane Coffin, J.: A Holy Impatience (New Haven, CT.: Yale University Press, 2004). It highlights the changing times of mainline Protestantism and his leading role in religious dissent. Andrew Hunt's biography of David Dellinger, Yale graduate and Gandhian disciple, David Dellinger: The Life and Times of a Non-violent Revolutionary (New York: New York University Press, 2006) is a must read. Dorothy Day and the Catholic Worker Movement have been the subject of scholarly examination: Nancy Roberts, Dorothy Day and the Catholic Worker (Albany: State University of New York Press, 1984); Anne & Alice Klejment, Dorothy Day and the Catholic Worker: A Bibliography and Index (New York: Garland Publishers, 1986); and Paul Elie, The Life You Save May Be Your Own: An American Pilgrimage (New York: Farrar, Straus & Giroux, 2003). For a look at the role of the Catholic priests Philip and Daniel Berrigan, consult Anne Klejment, The Berrigans: A Bibliography of Published Works by Daniel, Philip, and Elizabeth McAlister Berrigan (New York: Garland Publishers, 1979). For fine studies of the African-American pacifist, Bayard Rustin, refer to Daniel Levine, Bayard Rustin and the Civil rights Movement (New Brunswick, NJ: Rutgers University Press, 2000) and John D'Emilio, Lost Prophet: The Life and Times of Bayard Rustin (New York: Free Press, 2003). A fine account of DuBois' views on the Cold War is Gerald Horne, Black and Red: W.E.B. DuBois and the Afro-American Response to the Cold War, 1944-1963 (Albany: State University of New York Press, 1986). Robert F. Martin's Howard Kester and the Struggle for Social Justice in the South, 1904-1977 (Charlottesville: University of Virginia Press, 1991) ably captures the spirit of one religious pacifist from the Fellowship of Reconciliation who devoted his entire life's work to improving race relations in America. There are some notable biographies and historical accounts on Martin Luther King, Jr., his pacifism, and his leadership in the Civil Rights Movement worth examining: Taylor Branch, Parting the Waters: America in the King Years, 1954-63 (New York: Simon & Schuster, 1988); James A. Colaiaco, Martin Luther King, Jr.: Apostle of Militant Non-violence (Basingstoke: Macmillan, 1993); Adam Fairclough's To Redeem the Soul of America: The Southern Christian Leadership Conference and Martin Luther King, Jr. (Athens: University of

Georgia Press, 2001) and Martin Luther King, Jr (Athens: University of Georgia Press, 1995); David J. Garrow, Bearing the Cross: Martin Luther King Jr., and the Southern Christian Leadership Conference (New York: Vintage, 1993); and Thomas F. Jackson, From Civil rights to Human Rights: Martin Luther King, Jr. and the Struggle for Economic Justice (Philadelphia: University of Pennsylvania Press, 2006). The most recent publication by Gregory A. Barnes, A Biography of Lillian and George Willoughby: Twentieth Century Quaker Peace Activists (Lewiston, NY: Edwin Mellen Press, 2007) represents the traditional approach to non-violent peacemaking with the attempt to create an alternative living community known as the New Movement Society that was born during the tumultuous Vietnam War period. The standard biographical reference work in the field is Harold Josephson, ed., Biographical Dictionary of Modern Peace Leaders (Westport, CT: Greenwood Press, 1985).

Unfortunately, some pacifist leaders and their organizations have received scant notice. One such omission is Frederick J. Libby, founder and guiding spirit of the Washington, D.C. based National Council for Prevention of War (NCPW). Although Libby exerted an enormous influence on behalf of noninterventionism, only a limited amount of work has been done with the NCPW papers deposited at the SCPC. Scholars have Libby's recollections in To End War: The Story of the National Council for Prevention of War (Nyack: Fellowship Publications, 1969) and George P. Mirabel's "Frederick Libby and the American Peace Movement, 1921-1941" (Unpublished diss., Michigan State University, 1975). Neither of these works compensates for Libby's almost complete absence from political studies, histories of American reform, and, even, specific studies of the Congressional battles in the 1930's and 1940's in which he played a pivotal role. Justus D. Doenecke's, Not to the Swift: The Old Isolationists in the Cold War Era (Lewisburg,PA: Bucknell University Press, 1979) has taken the first step toward including Libby in historical scholarship. Regarding pacifist organizations, the Fellowship of Reconciliation has been the focus of two dissertations: Betty L. Barton, "The Fellowship of Reconciliation: Pacifism, Labor and Social Welfare, 1915-1960" (Unpublished diss., Florida State University, 1974); and Glen Zeitzer, "The American Peace Movement During the Second World War" (Unpublished diss., Bryn Mawr College, 1978), but a lot of work remains to be done in terms of producing a scholarly analysis of this important religious pacifist group.

Student pacifists have been the subject of two books: Eileen Eagan's Class, Culture and Classrooms: The Student Peace Movement of the 1930's (Philadelphia: Temple University Press, 1981) and Ralph S. Brax, The First Student Movement: Student Activism in the United States During the 1930's (Port Washington: Kennikat Press, 1981). A superb study of student radicalism is Robert Cohen, When the Old Left was Young: Student Radicals and America's First Mass Student Movement, 1929-1941 (New York: Oxford University Press, 1993). With respect to the Vietnam War and student activism works to consult are: Kenneth J. Heineman, Campus Wars: The Peace Movement at American State Universities in the Vietnam Era (New York: New York University Press, 1993) and Marc Jason Gilbert, ed., The Vietnam War on Campus: Other Voices, More distant Drums (Westport, CT: Praeger, 2001).

The growing importance of direct action opposing nuclear weapons and nuclear power plants and the call for social justice is the subject of numerous works. Michael Bess, Realism, Utopia, and the Mushroom Cloud: Four Activist Intellectuals and the Strategies for Peace, 1945-1989 (Chicago: University of Chicago Press, 1993) is an important study worthy of consultation. So, too, is Barbara Epstein's Non-violent Direct Action in the 1970s and 1980s (Berkeley: University of California Press, 1991). Epstein, a participant in the protests against nuclear power plants, provides details and analysis in her study. Looking at the power of individuals and community-based action is Robert D. Holsworth, Let Your Life Speak: a Study of Politics, Religion, and Antinuclear Weapons Activism (Madison: University of Wisconsin Press, 1989). An organizational study of SANE is Milton Katz's Ban the Bomb: a History of SANE, the Committee for a Sane Nuclear Policy (Westport, CT: Praeger, 1986). Another interesting study from a "personalist" perspective is John Lofland, Polite Protestors: the American Peace Movement of the 1980s (Syracuse: Syracuse University Press, 1993). Clearly, one of the most impressive historical studies on the transnational antinuclear movement is Lawrence S. Wittner's triology, The Struggle Against the Bomb: A History of the World Nuclear Disarmament Movement (Stanford, CA: Stanford University Press, 1993-2003). Scholarly challenges to the decisions to drop the Atomic Bomb are the subject of David Holloway, Stalin and the Bomb (Stanford, CA.: Stanford University Press, 1994), Barton J. Bernstein, ed., The Politics and Policies of the Truman Administration (New York: Quadrangle Books, 1968), Barton J.

Bernstein, "The Atomic Bomb and American Foreign Policy, 1941-1945: An Historiographical Controversy," Peace & Change 2 (Spring 1974): 1-16, and Gar Alperovitz's Atomic Diplomacy (New York: Simon & Schuster, 1985), and The Decision to Use the Bomb (New York: Alfred A. Knopf, 1995). Peace researchers are just beginning to break new ground with examinations into the divestment movement.

Disarmament and divestment are also topics of interest to peace historians. Works to consult on disarmament include the following: Charles A. Barker, ed., Problems of World Disarmament: A Series of Lectures Delivered at the Johns Hopkins University (Boston: Houghton Mifflin, 1963); Emile Benoit and Kenneth E. Boulding, eds., Disarmament and the Economy (New York: Harper & Row, 1963); Richard I. Barnet, Who Wants Disarmament? (Boston: Beacon Press, 1960); Richard Barnet and Richard Falk, eds., Security in Disarmament (Princeton: Princeton University Press, 1965); and Richard Barnet, The Economy of Death (New York: Athenaeum, 1969). The divestment effort on campus in the 1980s is the subject of Bradford Martin's engaging essay, "'Unsightly Huts': Shanties and the Divestment Movement of the 1980s," Peace & Change 32 (July 2007): 329-360. A thorough historical examination of the historical roots of opposition to apartheid in American can be found in David L. Hostetter's Movement Matters: American Antiapartheid Activism and the Rise of Multicultural Politics (New York: Routledge, 2006). Readers should also refer to Paul Rogat Loeb, Generation at the Crossroads: Apathy and Action on the American Campus (New Brunswick, NJ: Rutgers University Press, 1994) and Neta C. Crawford and Audie Klotz, eds., How Sanctions Work: Lessons from South Africa (New York: St. Martin's Press, 1999). For a look at the negative aspects of American intervention in third world countries consult, Richard Barnet, Intervention and Revolution: The United States in the Third World (New York: World Publishing, 1968).

Dissertations often fill some of the gaps left by surveys and blaze fresh bibliographical trails. Veteran scholars, graduate students, and activists do well when they test the waters of peace history by first perusing dissertations. Some recent examples are Nancy Hornick, "Anthony Benezet: Eighteenth Century Social Critic, Educator, and Abolitionist" (Unpublished diss, University of Maryland -College park, 1974); David C. Lawson, "Swords into Plowshares, Spears into Pruninghooks: The Intellectual Foundations of the First American Peace Movement, 1815-1865" (Unpublished diss.,

University of New Mexico, 1975); Michael A. Lutzker, "The 'Practical' Peace Advocates: An Interpretation of the American Peace Movement, 1898-1917" (Unpublished diss., Rutgers University, 1969); James Parker Martin, "The American Peace Movement and the Progressive Era, 1910-17" (Unpublished diss., Rice University, 1978); Blanche W. Cook, "Woodrow Wilson and the Antimilitarists, 1914-1917" (Unpublished diss., The Johns Hopkins University, 1970); David Katz, "Carrie Chapman Catt and the Struggle for Peace" (Unpublished diss., Syracuse University, 1973); Daniel W. Barthall. "The Committee on Militarism in Education, 1925-1940" (Unpublished diss., University of Illinois-Urbana, 1972); John L. LeBrun, "The Role of the Catholic Worker Movement in American Pacifism, 1933-1972" (Unpublished diss., Case Western University, 1973); Theodore R. Wachs, "Conscription, Conscientious Objection and the Context of American pacifism, 1940-1945" (unpublished diss., University of Illinois, 1976); Zelle A. Larson, "An Unbroken Witness: Conscientious Objection to War, 1948-1953" (Unpublished diss., University of Hawaii, 1975); Neil H. Katz, "Radical Pacifism and the Contemporary American Peace Movement: The Committee for Non-violent Action, 1957-1967" (Unpublished diss., University of Maryland, 1974); Ted Galen Carpenter, "The Dissenters: American Isolationists and Foreign Policy, 1945-1954" (Ph.D. diss., University of Texas, 1980); Joseph L. Jaffe, "Isolationism and Neutrality on Academe, 1938-1941" (Ph.D. diss., Case Western Reserve University, 1979); Marc Hirsch Ellis, "Peter Maurin: Prophet in the Twentieth Century" (Ph.D. diss., Marquette University, 1980); Kenneth Jackson Smith, "John Haynes Holmes: Opponent of War" (B.D. diss, University of Chicago, 1949); Luther William Spoehr, "Progress' Pilgrim: David Starr Jordan and the Circle of Reform, 1891-1931" (Ph.D. diss., Stanford University, 1975); Carrie Foster-Hays, "the Women and the Warriors: Dorothy Detzer and WILPF" (Ph.D. diss., University of Denver, 1984); Lois Diane Wasserman, "Martin Luther King, Jr.: the Molding of Non-violence as a Philosophy and Strategy" (Ph.D. diss., Boston University, 1972); Helen L.W. Bonner, "The Jeanette Rankin Story" (Ph.D. diss., Ohio University, 1982); Wynn M. Goering, "Pacifism and Heroism in American Fiction, 1770-1860" (Ph.D. diss., University of Chicago, 1984); Roger W. Pettenger, "The Peace Movement of the Augustana Lutheran Church as a Catalyst in the Americanization Process" (Ph.D. diss., Washington State University, 1987); Ellen Margaret

Thompson, "Episcopalians against War: Individual Conscience and Institutional Reform" (Ph.D. diss., University of Texas, 1988); William E. Hensley, "The Vietnam Movement: History and Criticism" (Ph.D. diss., University of Oregon, 1979); Clyde Winfield MacDonald, "The Massachusetts Peace Society, 1815-1828: A Study in Evangelical Reform" (Ph.D. diss., University of Maine, 1973); James Parker Martin, "The American Peace Movement and the Progressive Era, 1919-1917" (Ph.D. diss., Rice University, 1975); Marjorie Mae Norris, "Non-violent Reform in the United States, 1860-1886" (Ph.D. diss., University of Maryland, 1970); Francis J. Sicius, "The Chicago Catholic Worker Movement 1936 to the Present" (Ph.D. diss., Loyola University of Chicago, 1979); Paul Allen Heffron, "The Antimilitarist Tradition of the Founding Fathers and its Continuation in the Writings of Carl Schurz, Charles A. Beard, and Walter Millis" (Ph.D. diss., University of Minnesota, 1977); Matthew Edwin Mantell, "Opposition to the Korean War: A Study in American Dissent" (Ph.D. diss., New York University, 1973); Richard W. Fanning, "The Geneva Naval Conference of 1927: Disarmament in the 1920s and 1930s" (Ph.D. diss., Indiana University, 1988); Rosemary Rainbolt, "Arms Reduction versus Arms Modernization: U.S. Non-governmental Organizations and Arms Conferences, 1920-1935" (Ph.D. diss., Carnegie-Mellon University, 1988); Lawrence Flynt Leverett, "Solving the Deterrence Problem: Western Antinuclearism, Strategic Revisionism, and U.S. Arms Control Policy, 1979-1991" (Ph.D. diss., Princeton University, 1992); Kristin Lee Hoganson, "The 'Manly' Ideal of Politics and the Imperialist Impulse: Gender, U.S. Political Culture, and the Spanish-American and Philippine-American Wars" (Ph.D. diss., Yale University, 1995); Richard Charles Ciotti, "Internationalism and the Quest for Peace: the United States and Collective Security in the Twentieth Century" (Ph.D. diss., St. John's University, 1997); Julie Taker Weber, "The Reign of Peace We Hoped For: A History of the American School Peace League (Ph.D. diss., Penn State University, 1997); Patricia Natalie Atkin, "Protest and Liberation: War, Peace, and Women's Empowerment, 1967-1981" (Ph.D. diss., Wayne State University, 1999); Arielo De, "International Understanding an World Peace: The American Council of Learned Societies, 1919-1957" (Ph.D. diss., City University of New York, 2004); Christopher Carl Mirra, "US Foreign Policy since 1945 and the Prospects for Peace Education" (Ph.D. diss., Columbia University, 2004); Joseph W. Winn, "The Carnegie

Endowment for International Peace: Missionaries for Cultural Internationalism, 1911-1939" (Ph.D. diss., University of Kentucky, 2004); Joseph Kip Kosek, "Spectacle of Conscience: Christian Non-violence and the Transformation of American Democracy" (Unpublished diss., Yale University, 2004) ; James Eichsteadt, " 'Shut It Down!': The May 1970 National Student Strike at the University of California at Berkeley, Syracuse, and the University of Wisconsin-Madison" (Ph.D. diss., Syracuse University, 2007).

Anthologies often include useful historical introductions whether they are collections of essays or passages to primary sources. The development of mass protest movements in the civil rights and anti-war struggles of the 1960's and 1970's created a renewed concern for the ideological foundations of American civil disobedience. Responding to this need, scholars published such documentary collections as: Mulford Q. Sibley, ed., The Quiet Battle: Writings on the Theory and Practice of Non-Violent Resistance (Boston: Beacon, 1963); Arthur & Lila Weinberg, editors, Instead of Violence (Boston: Beacon Press, 1963), an anthology covering the writings of the great advocates of peace and non-violence from ancient through modern times. An excellent anthology about twentieth century peace activists is Charles DeBenedetti, ed., Peace Heroes in Twentieth Century America (Bloomington, IN: Indiana University Press, 1986). Staughton Lynd, ed., Non-violence in America: A Documentary History (Indianapolis: Bobbs-Merrill, 1966), which has been updated with Alice Lynd as co-editor, still remains an indispensable source on the underpinnings of non-violence in American society; Lillian Schissel, ed., Conscience in America: A Documentary History of Conscientious Objection in America, 1957-1967 (New York: Dutton, 1968); David R. Weber, ed., Civil Disobedience in America: A Documentary History (Ithaca: Cornell University Press, 1978); James Finn, ed., Protest. Pacifism and Politics (New York: Random House, 1967), Journalist Nat Hentoff, ed., The Essays of A.J. Muste (New York: Clarion, 1970), introduces some of the pacifist writings of the twentieth century's most influential theoretician-activist. Two additional excellent anthologies on Conscientious Objection are: Peter Brock, ed., Liberty and Conscience: A Documentary History of the Experiences of Conscientious Objectors in American through the Civil War (New York: Oxford University Press, 2002) and Charles Moskos & John W.Chambers, eds., The New Conscientious Objection: From Sacred to Secular Resistance (New York: Oxford University Press, 1993). Religious pacifism is found in Theron F. Schlabach and Richard T. Hughes, eds., Proclaim Peace: Christian Pacifism from Unexpected Quarters (Urbana: University of Illinois Press, 1997). Charles F. Howlett, ed., looks at the role of the 20th century movement in History of the American Peace Movement, 1890-2000: The Emergence of a New Scholarly Discipline (Lewiston, NY: Edwin Mellen Press, 2005). Charles Chatfield, ed., Peace Movements in America, (New York: Schocken, 1973), takes a collection of essays first published in American Studies (12, 1, Spring 1972) and gives them a paperback audience larger than the readership of a scholarly journal. He also edited three other valuable collections: with Ruzanna Ilukhina, Peace/Mir: an Anthology of Historical Alternative to War (Syracuse: Syracuse University Press, 1993); with Peter van den Dungen, Peace Movement and Political Cultures (Knoxville: University of Tennessee Press, 1987); and with Jackie Smith and Ron Pagnucco Transnational Social Movements and Global Politics: Solidarity beyond the State (Syracuse: Syracuse University Press, 1997). Joseph. R. Conlin, editor, American Anti-War Movements (Beverly Hills, CA: Glencoe press, 1968) is a useful anthology for delineating the larger themes of political opposition to war. The view that peaceful ties among nations has as much to do with the help of private citizens as with the actions of ambassadors and campaigns of military leaders is the subject of Joan R. Challinor and Roberts L. Beisner, eds., Arms at Rest: Peacemaking and Peacekeeping in American History New York: Greenwood Press, 1987). Other appropriate collections of essays are Solomon Wank, ed., Doves and Diplomats: Foreign Offices and Peace Movements in Europe and America in the Twentieth Century (Westport, CT: Greenwood, 1978); and Ken Booth and Moorhead Wright, eds., American Thinking About Peace and War (New York: Barnes and Noble, 1978). An indispensable work is Roger S. Powers & William B. Vogele, eds., Protest, Power, and Change: An Encyclopedia of Non-violent Action from ACT-UP top Women's Suffrage (New York: Garland Publishers, 1997). Peace Action: Past, Present, and Future (Boulder, CO.: Paradigm Publishers, 2007), edited by Glen Harold Stassen and Lawrence S. Wittner offers insider accounts into the actions of politicians and activists opposed to human rights and the reduction of weapons of mass destruction. Students interested in examining the writings of America's native radical tradition should look at Timothy Patrick McCarthy & John McMillian, eds., The Radical Reader: A Documentary History of the American Radical Tradition (New York: The New Press, 2003). The Sixties radicalism is covered in Alexander Bloom and Wini Breines, eds., Takin' It to the Streets: A Sixties Reader (New York: Oxford University Press, 1995). Scholars interested in examining the evolution of ideas, policies, and institutions affecting U.S. foreign policy since the United States assumed the role of global superpower are encouraged to consult Andrew Bacevich, ed. The Long War: A New History of U.S. National Security Policy since World War II (New York: Columbia University Press, 2007). The contributors include economists, national security analysts, and peace historians, among others. Another important collection of essays examining economic globalization and its consequences is Jackie Smith and Hank Johnson, eds., Globalization and Resistance: Transnational Dimensions of Social Movements (New York: Rowman & Littlefield, 2002). An important anthology on female spirituality and communitarianism is Wendy Chmielewski, Louis Kern, and Marlyn Klee-Hartzell, eds., Women in Spiritual and Communitarian Societies in the U.S. (Syracuse: Syracuse University Press, 1993)._Judith Porter Adams', ed., Peacework: Oral Histories of Women Peace Activists (Boston: G.K. Hall, 1992), contains lively accounts well worth consulting.

Activist-scholars have a long tradition in contributing to the writing of peace history. Such insider accounts are furnished by Jane Addams, Peace and Bread in Time of War (New York: Kings Crown, 1945) (reprint of 1922 edition) and her Second Twenty Years at Hull House (New York: Macmillan, 1930); see also, The Newer Ideals of Peace (New York: Macmillan & Co., 1907); Adin Ballou, Christian Non-Resistance in All Its Important Bearings, Illustrated and Defended (New York: Garland Publishers, reprint, 1972); George C. Beckwith, The Peace Manual; or War and Its Remedies (Boston: American Peace Society, 1897); Daniel Berrigan, To Dwell in Peace: An Autobiography (San Francisco: Harper & Row, 1987); Philip Berrigan, No More Strangers (New York: Macmillan & Co., 1965); Norman Cousins, Who Speaks for Man (New York: Macmillan & Co., 1953); Dorothy Day, Loaves and Fishes (New York: Harper & Row, 1963) and The Long Loneliness (New York: Harper & Row, 1981); Eugene Debs, Walls and Bars (Chicago: Charles H. Kerr Co., 1927);

Richard B. Gregg, *Power of Nonviolence* (Nyack, NY: FOR Press, 1959); David Starr Jordan, *The Days of Man* (New York: World Book, 1922); William Ladd, *The Essays of Philanthropos on Peace and War* (New York: Garland Publishers, 1971); David Low Dodge, *War Inconsistent with the Religion of Jesus Christ* (New York: Garland Publishers, 1971); Noah Worcester, *A Solemn Review of the Custom of War: Showing that War is the Effect of a Popular Delusion and Proposing a Remedy* (New York: Garland Publishers, 1971); Louis Lochner, *Always the Unexpected: A Book of Reminiscences* (New York: Macmillan & Co., 1956); Frederick H. Lynch, *The Christian in Wartime* (New York: Garland Publishers, 1971); Abraham J. Muste, *Not By Might* (New York: Harper Bros., 1947) and *Nonviolence in an Aggressive World* (New York: Harper Bros., 1940); James Peck, *We Who Would Not Kill* (New York: Lyle Stuart, 1958); Clarence E. Pickett, *For More than Bread* (Boston: Little, Brown & Co., 1953); Vida Scudder, *On Journey* (New York: E.P. Dutton & Co., 1937); Scott Nearing, *War: Organized Destruction and Mass Murder by Civilized Nations* (New York: Garland Publishers, 1971); Benjamin Spock, *Decent and Indecent: Our Personal and Political Behavior* (New York: Fawcett, Crest, 1971); Charles Sumner, *Addresses on War* (New York: Garland Publishers, 1971); Benjamin F. Trueblood, *The Development of the Peace Idea and Other Essays* (Boston: Plimpton Press, 1932) and *The Federation of the World* (New York: Garland Publishers, 1971); Norman Thomas, *A Socialist's Faith* (Port Washington, NY: Kennikat Press, 1971); Lillian D. Wald, *Windows on Henry Street* (Boston: Little, Brown & Co., 1934); Mary Hoxie Jones, *Swords Into Ploughshares: An Account of the American Friends Service Committee. 1917-1937* (New York: Macmillan, 1937); Dorothy Detzer, *Appointment on the Hill* (New York: Holt, 1948); Sidney L. Gulick, *The Christian Crusade for a Warless World* (New York: Macmillan, 1922); Clarence E. Pickett, *For More than Bread* (Boston: Little, Brown, 1953) Sherwood Eddy, *A Pilgrimage of Ideas, or the Re-education of Sherwood Eddy* (New York: Farrar and Reinhart, 1934); and his *Eighty Adventurous Years: An Autobiography* (New York: Harper, 1955); *Kirby Page. Social Evangelist: The Autobiography of a 20th Century Prophet for Peace,* edited by Harold E. Fey (Nyack: Fellowship Press, 1975); *Oswald Garrison Villard: The Dilemmas of the Absolute Pacifist in Two World Wars,* edited by Anthony Gronowicz (New York: Garland, 1983); Jessie Wallace Hughan, *Three Decades of War Resistance* (New York: The War Resisters

League, 1942); Harry Emerson Fosdick, The Living of These Days (New York: Harper, 1956); Raymond P. Fosdick, Chronicle of a Generation: An Autobiography (New York: Harper, 1958); John Haynes Homes, I Speak for Myself (New York: Harper, 1959); Little by Little; The Selected Writings of Dorothy Day, edited by Robert Ellsberg (New York: Knopf, 1983); Lucia Ames Mead, Swords into Ploughshares (New York: G.P. Putnam's Sons 1912); Betty Reardon, Sexism and the War System (New York: Teachers College Press, 1985); Emma Goldman, Living My Life (New York: Alfred A. Knopf, 1931); Nicholas Murray Butler, Across the Busy Years (New York: Scribner, 1939). Contemporary accounts come from: James P. Shotwell, The Autobiography of James T. Shotwell (Indianapolis: Bobbs-Merrill, 1961); E. Raymond Wilson, Uphill for Peace: Quaker Impact on Congress (Richmond, IN: Friends United Press, 1976); Clark M. Eichelberger, Organizing for Peace: A Personal History of the Founding of the United Nations (New York: Harper, 1977); and Gordon C. Zahn's book about his Civilian Public Service camp experience during the Second World War, Another Part of the War: The Camp Simon Story (Amherst, MA: University of Massachusetts Pres, 1979). Also, Sidney Lens' Unrepentant Radical: An American Activist's Account of the Turbulent Decades (Boston: Beacon, 1980) recounts one labor activist's struggle against war. Insiders bring a sensitivity and commitment that makes history both meaningful and alive. Bayard Rustin's Down the Line: The Collected Writings of Bayard Rustin (Chicago: Quadrangle Books, 1971) offers valuable insights into his non-violent acts of civil disobedience. Three works by Martin Luther King, Jr. deserve attention: Stride Toward Freedom (New York: Harper & Row, 1961) and Where Do We Go From Here: Chaos or Community (New York: Harper & Row, 1967); and Carson Clayborne et al., editors, The Autobiography of Martin Luther King, Jr. (New York: Warner Books, 1998). David Dellinger recounts his own radical pacifism in Yale to Jail: Life of a Moral Dissenter (New York: Pantheon, 1993). Historian and political activist, Howard Zinn has carved his own niche in American history, primarily through his writings. One should consult his book, Passionate Declarations: Essays on War and Justice (New York: Perennial, 2003). Harriet H. Alonso, ed., Women at the Hague: The International Congress of Women and Its Results (Urbana: University of Illinois Press) represents an important collection of writings by Jane Addams, Emily Greene Balch, and Alice Hamilton during World War I; see also her Growing Up Abolitionist: The Story of the Garrison Children (Amherst: University of

Massachusetts Press, 2002). There are two useful collections compiling the writings of the female non-violent abolitionists Sarah and Angelina Grimke` worthy of consultation: Kathryn Kish Sklar, ed., Women's Rights Emerges within the Antislavery Movement, 1830-1870 (Boston: Bedford/St. Martins, 2000) and Larry Ceplair, The Public Years of Sarah and Angelina Grimke`: Selected Writings, 1835-1839 (New York: Columbia University Press, 1989). The most authoritative study of Nobel Peace Prize recipients remains Irwin Abrams, The Nobel Peace Prize and the Laureates: An Illustrated History (Boston: G.K. Hall & Co., 2001).

The haunting specter of nuclear war, especially during the Freeze Campaign, produced a spate of interesting, informative, and useful works. A particularly telling work is Hiroshima and Nagasaki (New York: Basic Books, 1981), a 706 page compendium of the physical, medical, and social effects of the atomic bombings in August, 1945; this book, translated by Eisei Ishikawa and David L. Swain, offers the reader the definitive account of the horrible effects of atomic bombing. Though not the definitive book on the effects of atomic testing on American military personnel in the 1950s, Thomas H. Saffer and Orville E. Kelly's Countdown Zero (New York: Putnam's Sons, 1982) offers some insights into the medical and psychological impact of atmospheric testing. Between 1945 and October 1958, an estimated 250,000 servicemen were exposed to the awesome force of the blast, heat, the turbulence and the metallic smell and taste of the elements of the fallout. Nuclear Hostages (Boston: Houghton-Mifflin, 1983) by Bernard J. O'Keefe is a firsthand account of the destructive power of the forces that hold together the subatomic particles of matter. As a scientist he helped redesign the firing mechanisms of atomic bombs; now some twenty years later, he wishes to free humankind from the possible fate of extermination. In terms of developing strategies to cope with the arms race, E.P. Thompson, the popular British labor and social historian, provides a stunning glimpse of the new peace movement, which he refers to as "militantly neutralist," in Beyond the Cold War (New York: Pantheon, 1982); the highlight of Thompson's polemic is the challenge he raises about the Atlantic Alliance, for 38 years the centerpiece of American global security policy. On a much less alarmist note are Leon Wieseltier, Nuclear War, Nuclear Peace (New York: Holt, Rinehart, & Winton, 1983), and Paul Bracken, The Command and Control of

Nuclear Forces (New Haven: Yale University Press, 1983). Though not directly connected to peace history writing per se, these works offer trenchant analyses and accurate assessments of the dangers of nuclear conflict; both works are valuable in emphasizing the importance of more work and thought on the question of ending a nuclear war.

At the time of submission to the publisher David S. Patterson's The Search for Negotiated Peace: Women's Activism and Citizen Diplomacy in World War I (New York: Routledge, 2007) just appeared. Patterson, following peace history's developing transnational approach in the discipline, discusses the events surrounding a number of European and American women in their attempts to discredit the art of secret diplomacy, militarism, and the narrowness of patriotism in order to create a new type of diplomacy based on internationalism.

A study of the original sources, books, articles, and dissertations described in this work reveals both the richness and diversity of materials available to potential researchers and students of American peace movements. These new studies not only added volumes to library shelves, but also have gone a long way in helping to establish peace history as a legitimate intellectual and scholarly pursuit. The task remains for historians to integrate peace history into the mainstream of American history writing. While writing a pamphlet for the American Historical Association many years ago one of the co-authors of the present work observed that readers looking into the nation's past need to be aware that good history records the deeds of winners and losers, minorities and majorities, and insiders and outsiders. Only when this is done, do we accurately mirror the past and have hope of learning from it. The continued cooperation between activist scholars and professional historians reduces the fragmentary tendencies of American history writing, while it helps us steer a middle course between the Scylla of historical detachment and the Charybdis of unrestrained partiality.

INDEX